ECONOMICS
Theory & Practice

Second Edition

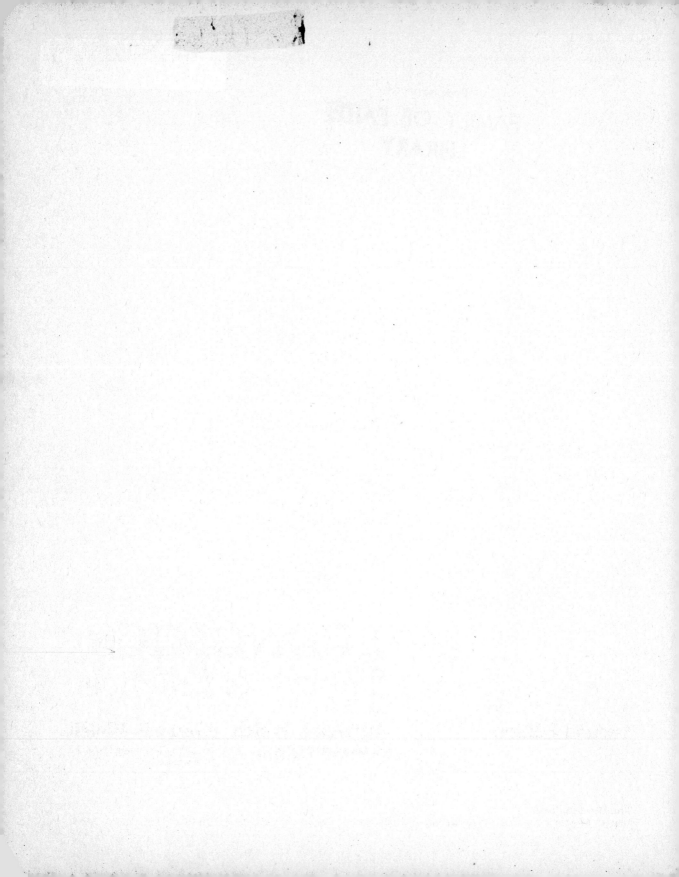

ECONOMICS
Theory & Practice

Second Edition

Patrick J. Welch
St. Louis University

Gerry F. Welch
St. Louis Community College
at Meramec

The Dryden Press
Chicago New York Philadelphia San Francisco Montreal Toronto London Sydney Tokyo Mexico City Rio de Janeiro Madrid

Acquisitions Editor: Elizabeth Widdicombe
Developmental Editor: Judy Sarwark
Project Editor: Anne Knowles/Becky Ryan
Managing Editor: Jane Perkins
Design Director: Alan Wendt
Production Manager: Claire Roth/Diane Tenzi
Permissions Editor: Doris Milligan

Text and Cover Designer: C. J. Petlick, Hunter Graphics
Copy Editor: Maggie Jarpey
Indexer: Ann Tomchek
Compositor: University Graphics, Inc.
Text Type: 10/12 Palatino

Library of Congress Cataloging-in-Publication Data

Welch, Patrick J.
Economics, theory & practice.

Includes bibliographies and index.
1. Economics. I. Welch, Gerry F. II. Title.
III. Title: Economics, theory & practice.
HB171.5.W3935 1986 330 85-15966
ISBN 0-03-004879-6

Printed in the United States of America
678-016-98765432

Address orders:
383 Madison Avenue
New York, NY 10017

Address editorial correspondence:
One Salt Creek Lane
Hinsdale, IL 60521

CBS COLLEGE PUBLISHING
The Dryden Press
Holt, Rinehart and Winston
Saunders College Publishing

CONTENTS

PREFACE xi

ALTERNATE COURSE OUTLINE xvii

Part I **INTRODUCTION TO ECONOMICS** 1

Chapter 1 **INTRODUCTION TO ECONOMICS** 2

What Is Economics 2
Application 1.1 The Opportunity Cost of Success 4
Factors of Production 6
Application 1.2 Taking the Scare Out of Scarcity 8
Economic Theory and Policy 10
Tools of the Economist 13
Application 1.3 Interpreting a Graph 15
Scarcity, Model Building, and Graphs 16
Appendix to Chapter 1 Graphing 24

Chapter 2 **ECONOMIC DECISION MAKING AND ECONOMIC SYSTEMS** 28

Scarcity and Society's Basic Economic Decisions 28
Economic Systems 30
Application 2.1 Life in a Planned Economy: The Russians 34
The U.S. Economic System 45
Application 2.2 The Factory Girl's Last Day 48
Application 2.3 Cartoon of 1882 Illustrates the Fear That Technology and Machinery Will Destroy Workers 50

Chapter 3 **DEMAND, SUPPLY, AND THE DETERMINATION OF PRICE** 58

Demand and Supply 59
Market Demand, Market Supply, Equilibrium Price, and Equilibrium Quantity 63
Changes in Demand and Supply 67
Changes in Equilibrium Price and Equilibrium Quantity 73
Application 3.1 Test Yourself: Changes in Supply and Demand 74

	Limiting the Movement of Prices	77
	Application 3.2 Market Could Meet Demand for Organs	82
	Price Elasticity of Demand and Supply	83
	Macroeconomics and Microeconomics	85
	Application 3.3 Supply and Demand in Practice	86
Part II	**THE MACROECONOMY**	93
Chapter 4	**GOALS AND PROBLEMS OF THE MACROECONOMY: EMPLOYMENT, PRICES, AND PRODUCTION**	94
	Unemployment and Full Employment	95
	Application 4.1 The Hidden Psychological Costs of Unemployment	98
	Application 4.2 Determining the Unemployment Rate	104
	Inflation and Stable Prices	107
	Production	117
	A Policy Problem	124
Chapter 5	**FOUNDATIONS OF THE MACROECONOMY**	128
	Changes in the Level of Economic Activity	129
	Total Spending and the Level of Economic Activity	134
	Application 5.1 Interest Rates and Investment Spending	142
	Application 5.2 Pittsburgh's Recession Shows How Layoffs Ripple through Economy	156
	Application 5.3 Test Yourself: Leakages, Injections, and Economic Activity	158
	Application 5.4 The First Fireside Chat	159
	Total Spending and Macroeconomic Policy	160
	Appendix to Chapter 5 Equilibrium in the Macroeconomy	165
Chapter 6	**THE ROLE OF GOVERNMENT IN THE MACROECONOMY**	170
	Government Revenues and Expenditures	171
	Application 6.1 Back Off a Little, Kiddies	176
	Fiscal Policy	181
	Government Budgets	184
	The National Debt	189
	Application 6.2 Do We Need a Budget Amendment?	190

Application 6.3 Climbing Federal Debt Is Inexorably Raising U.S. Interest Burden 194

Chapter 7 **MONEY, FINANCIAL INSTITUTIONS, AND THE FEDERAL RESERVE** 200

Money 201

Application 7.1 Fixed Assets, or: Why a Loan in Yap Is Hard to Roll Over 204

Financial Institutions 209

Application 7.2 Gold! Gold! Gold! 210

The Federal Reserve System 213

Application 7.3 Treasury Officials Have Money to Burn but Generally Don't 216

Chapter 8 **MONEY CREATION, MONETARY THEORY, AND MONETARY POLICY** 224

The Money Supply and the Level of Economic Activity 225

Money Creation 227

Application 8.1 Questions and Answers about Reserves and Loans 230

Excess Reserves, Interest Rates, and the Level of Spending 233

Application 8.2 The Effects of Interest Rates on Spending Decisions 234

The Federal Reserve and Monetary Policy 238

Application 8.3 More Concerns Hire Fed Watchers to Interpret Central Bank's Policies 244

Chapter 9 **QUESTIONS AND ISSUES IN THE MACROECONOMY: ASSESSING GOALS AND TOOLS** 252

Goals of the Macroeconomy: A Restatement 253

Controlling the Effects of Inflation 258

Alternative Macroeconomic Viewpoints and Policies 264

Application 9.1 John Maynard Keynes 266

Application 9.2 Milton Friedman 268

A Final Word on Macroeconomic Thinking 270

Part III **THE MICROECONOMY** 275

Chapter 10 **HOUSEHOLDS AND BUSINESSES: AN OVERVIEW** 276

Overview of Households 277

Application 10.1 The Saga of Bill and Sarah 284

Overview of Business 285

Application 10.2 The Supply, Demand, and Price of Stock Shares 288
Application 10.3 Deft Defenses 296

Chapter 11 **BENEFITS, COSTS, AND MAXIMIZATION** 300
Balancing Benefits and Costs: The Individual 301
Application 11.1 Anything Worth Doing Is Not Necessarily Worth Doing Well 308
Balancing Benefits and Costs: The Business 311
Private vs. Social Benefits and Costs 317
Application 11.2 Test Yourself: Maximizing Profit 318
Application 11.3 Forests Declining throughout Eastern United States 320
Public Choice 322

Chapter 12 **PRODUCTION AND THE COSTS OF PRODUCTION** 328
Overview of Production in the U.S. Economy 329
Methods of Production 332
Application 12.1 Technology and the Steam Locomotive 336
Economic Time, Production, and the Cost of Production 336
Application 12.2 Test Yourself: Calculating Costs and Averages 344

Chapter 13 **COMPETITION AND MARKET STRUCTURES** 356
Markets vs. Industries 357
Application 13.1 Defining the Boundaries of a Market: *United States* v. *Du Pont* 358
The Market Structures 359
Pure Competition 360
Monopolistic Competition 368
Application 13.2 The Public Doesn't Get a Better Potato Chip without a Bit of Pain 372
Oligopoly 374
Application 13.3 Airlines Play Games for Customers 378
Monopoly 379
Market Structures and the Consumer 382
Appendix to Chapter 13 Determining the Profit-Maximizing Price and Output for a Firm 387

Chapter 14 **LABOR MARKETS, UNIONS, AND THE DISTRIBUTION OF INCOME** 394
Labor Markets 395
Application 14.1 Computer Games 400
Application 14.2 Working 404
Unions 408
The Distribution of Income 413
Application 14.3 New Data Change Image of Poverty 418

Chapter 15 **QUESTIONS AND ISSUES IN THE MICROECONOMY: GOVERNMENT AND THE MARKETS** 426
Antitrust 428
Application 15.1 Defining the Relevant Market 432
Government Regulation 437
Application 15.2 Mending the Rules 446

Part IV **THE INTERNATIONAL ECONOMY** 451

Chapter 16 **THE INTERNATIONAL ECONOMY: TRADE** 452
An Overview of U.S. International Trade 453
Comparative Advantage and International Trade 456
Free Trade vs. Protectionism 460
Application 16.1 Saving the World Economy 460
Application 16.2 National Security and Shoes 466
Application 16.3 Is World on Brink of Trade War? 468

Chapter 17 **THE INTERNATIONAL ECONOMY: FINANCE** 472
International Transactions and Balances 473
Exchange Rates 478
Application 17.1 What the I.M.F. Does 478
Application 17.2 Postponement of Third World Debts Threatens Upheaval, Financial Collapse 480

GLOSSARY 489

INDEX 500

The Dryden Press Series in Economics

Asch and Seneca
Government and the Marketplace

Breit and Elzinga
The Antitrust Casebook

Breit and Ransom
The Academic Scribblers, ***Revised Edition***

Campbell and Campbell
An Introduction to Money and Banking, ***Fifth Edition***

Dolan
Economics, ***Fourth Edition***

Dolan
Macroeconomics, ***Fourth Edition***

Dolan
Microeconomics, ***Fourth Edition***

Heertje, Rushing, and Skidmore
Economics

Hyman
Public Finance

Johnson and Roberts
Money and Banking: A Market-Oriented Approach, ***Second Edition***

Kaufman
The Economics of Labor Markets and Labor Relations

Kidwell and Peterson
Financial Institutions, Markets, and Money, ***Second Edition***

Leftwich and Eckert
The Price System and Resource Allocation, ***Ninth Edition***

Lindsay
Applied Price Theory

Link, Miller, and Dolan
EconoGraph: Interactive Software for Principles of Economics

Morley
Inflation and Unemployment, ***Second Edition***

Morley
Macroeconomics

Nicholson
Intermediate Microeconomics and Its Application, ***Third Edition***

Nicholson
Microeconomic Theory: Basic Principles and Extensions, ***Third Edition***

Pappas and Hirschey
Fundamentals of Managerial Economics, ***Second Edition***

Pappas, Brigham, and Hirschey
Managerial Economics, ***Fourth Edition***

Poindexter
Macroeconomics, ***Second Edition***

Puth
American Economic History

Richardson
Urban Economics

Rukstad
Macroeconomic Decision Making in the World Economy: Text and Cases

Welch and Welch
Economics: Theory & Practice, ***Second Edition***

PREFACE

Developments in the international, national, and local economies, and the decisions of economic policy makers in businesses, governments, and other organizations affect our lives daily. For example, a strong dollar in the international economy makes travel abroad less expensive for U.S. citizens and causes U.S. farmers to have greater difficulty in selling their grain overseas. Changes in government fiscal policies may lead to lower taxes for some people and to the cancellation of programs on which others depend. Technology and changes in consumer demand create new jobs and destroy existing jobs.

Because of the importance of these and other economic events, many students whose primary interests are in other areas want to learn something about fundamental economic relationships and institutions. It is for these students that *Economics: Theory & Practice,* second edition, is written. The book, designed as a primary text for a one-semester introduction to economics or survey of economics course, offers a balanced presentation of macroeconomics and microeconomics, and of concepts and institutions.

OBJECTIVE OF THE BOOK

The overall objective of the book is to introduce and survey basic economic concepts and institutions in a way that will give the student a foundation to apply economic reasoning to his or her major field of interest, and to evaluate news reports, opinions, and other sources of economic information with some understanding of key relationships and terms. We also hope that the student will enjoy economics enough to become interested in further reading or other pursuits in the field.

Economic Concepts

In introducing and surveying economic concepts, *Economics: Theory & Practice,* second edition, includes a broad and selective overview of what economists generally label the "principles of macroeconomics and microeconomics." In covering these areas, basic concepts are presented, including (but not limited to) supply and demand, spending and business fluctuations, money creation, alternative viewpoints on macroeconomic policy, cost-benefit analysis, and the behavior of the firm in different market settings. These concepts are explained and applied in a manner that aims at the understanding of key relationships rather than at in-depth analysis for its own sake. While a detailed explanation of theoretical tools is essential for the student who continues in economics, the same may not be true for the nonmajor whose potential application of economics will rest on a simpler conceptual and institutional foundation. We also understand that instructors of introductory economics courses typically establish that foundation by basic understanding and breadth, rather than with an in-depth analysis.

Economic Institutions

In addition to surveying basic economic concepts, the text introduces those key institutions with which the student should be familiar if he or she is to understand the operation of the economy. These institutions range from the Federal Reserve System, to the method for gathering unemployment statistics, to the antitrust laws, and others. Including institutional considerations in an introductory economics text is important for two reasons. First, institutions link the real world to the conceptual world of basic economic principles, and provide a vehicle through which the student can relate to those concepts. Second, institutional considerations that have economic, social, political, and other dimensions allow economics to be viewed in a broader perspective, thereby permitting the student to better tie economics to his or her primary field of interest.

FEATURES OF THE BOOK

There are several important features of *Economics: Theory & Practice* that contribute to the successful teaching and learning of introductory economics. These include the balance and flexibility of the text; the range of topics covered; the applications, learning aids, and organizers in each chapter, and ancillary materials for both instructor and student.

Balance and Flexibility of the Text

Economics: Theory & Practice offers a balanced presentation of macroeconomic and microeconomic topics. The book is divided into four parts: a three-chapter introduction covering basic concepts and definitions, economic systems, and supply and demand; six chapters on macroeconomics; six chapters on microeconomics; and a fourth part containing two chapters on international economics. Thus, there is a roughly equal distribution between macroeconomic and microeconomic coverage.

Economics: Theory & Practice is also written and arranged in a way that permits flexibility. The text is easily adapted to an instructor's preference for the sequencing of topics, the breadth of coverage, and the inclusion of outside assignments.

First, the topics are arranged so that the book can be used in a *macroeconomic-microeconomic* sequence, by going directly through the text, or in a *microeconomic-macroeconomic* sequence, by simply reversing the order of Parts II and III. Because the basic tools and definitions, such as opportunity cost, graphing, and supply and demand, are presented in the introductory part of the text, the macroeconomic and microeconomic parts are independent of each other.

Second, a course could be shortened by eliminating various chapters. These include Chapter 9, "Questions and Issues in the Macroeconomy: Assessing Goals and Tools," and/or Chapter 15, "Questions and Issues in the Microeconomy: Government and the Markets," and/or, perhaps, Chapters 16 and 17, on international trade and international finance. Coverage could also be reduced by eliminating various chapter subtopics. For example, unionism and collective bargaining could be omitted from the treatment of labor in Chapter 14.

Third, those wishing to add to the content of a course could do so by including the various chapter appendixes. These include the appendix to Chapter 1 on graphing, to Chapter 5 on the determination of aggregate equilibrium, and to Chapter 13 on profit maximizing behavior. A course could also be expanded by assigning annotated suggested readings at the end of each chapter. These readings span from Adam Smith to current economists, and from science fiction on scarcity to a short story on inflation in Germany by Thomas Mann. Finally, computational exercises from the text's *Study Guide* could be assigned.

Range of Topics

A broad and up-to-date range of topics is presented throughout the book. For example, in addition to the traditional core topics, Part II (on the macroeconomy) includes material on rational expectations, productivity, indexation, the relationship between the federal budget and monetary policy, and changes in the financial depository institutions system. On the microeconomic side, in addition to the traditional basic subject matter, are such topics as cost-benefit analysis, public choice, externalities, mergers and acquisitions, production and technological change, and antitrust, regulation, and deregulation.

Applications

The range of the text is further broadened by the applications in each chapter. These applications add to the concepts covered in the basic text by highlighting examples, giving background information, and introducing problems. Many are readings from nontraditional sources of economic literature such as the books *Working,* by Studs Terkel, *The Russians,* by Hedrick Smith, and *The Twilight of Steam Locomotives,* by Ron Ziel, while others are from more conventional sources such as *The Wall Street Journal* and *The New York Times.* The applications add to the real world focus of the text and are quite popular with students. Topics covered in applications include pollution and the decline of forests, the social security controversy, "Fed watching," and the balanced budget amendment.

Chapter Learning Aids and Organizers

There are several learning aids and organizers in every chapter. Every chapter begins with a listing of *chapter objectives,* identifying the major topics and concepts that will be covered. Important terms and concepts are highlighted in the text and defined in the margin. This *running glossary* is an excellent aid for student review. An alphabetical *cumulative glossary* follows at the back of the text. Each figure and table includes a full *legend* that describes or adds to the information presented. Selected chapters also include *self-tests* so students can check their progress. Finally, each chapter ends with a *summary,* a list of that chapter's *key terms and concepts, discussion and review questions,* and *annotated suggested readings.*

ANCILLARY MATERIALS

Three separate ancillary volumes supplement *Economics: Theory & Practice.* For the student, there is the *Study Guide* that includes, for each chapter, the listing of chapter objectives from the text, a study organizer indicating important terms and concepts, a chapter review self-test, computational exercises, and sample examination questions.

The *Instructor's Manual* includes, for each chapter, a restatement of chapter objectives, teaching suggestions, recommendations on incorporating the discussion and review questions and suggested readings into a course, and the study organizer and solved exercises from the *Study Guide. Transparency Masters* for many of the illustrations in the text are also included with the *Instructor's Manual.*

A separate *Test Bank* contains over 1,100 multiple-choice and true/false questions, many of which require the student to make computations. Several hundred new multiple-choice questions have been added to the second edition *Test Bank,* and most multiple-choice questions carried over from the first edition *Test Bank* either have been modified or the order of the answer choices has been altered.

NEW TO THE SECOND EDITION

The second edition of *Economics: Theory & Practice* retains the essential features of the first edition, such as the balance between macroeconomics and microeconomics and the flexibility of topic coverage, and is updated in terms of data, applications, and state-of-the-art concepts and topics.

All data in figures, tables, and the text reflect the latest available at time of publication. Applications have been updated to introduce more recent real-world problems (such as pollution and the decline of forests in the United States, and the international debt crisis) and to explore popular policy areas such as deregulation and a balanced federal budget. New applications that test student understanding of concepts and computations have been added.

Most changes in this edition result from the inclusion of new terms, concepts, and topics in order to keep current in the field. Some highlights of these changes are:

- Coverage of market failure (Chapter 2), crowding-out (Chapters 6 and 8), public choice (Chapter 11), and deregulation (Chapter 15).
- Greater emphasis on economic growth as a macroeconomic goal (Chapter 4).
- Incorporation of the foreign sector in the determination of macroeconomic activity (Chapter 5).
- An appendix demonstrating the relationship between spending and macroequilibrium via a tabular and graphic approach (Chapter 5).
- Update of the money supply definition as well as institutional changes brought about by the Monetary Control Act (Chapter 7).
- A new chapter section on the relationship between federal government deficits and monetary policy (Chapter 8).
- Expanded and updated treatment of alternative macroeconomic viewpoints, including monetarism, Keynesian economics, supply-side economics, and rational expectations (Chapter 9).
- Inclusion of the international debt crisis (Chapter 17).

In addition, all ancillaries have been revised by the authors to coincide with the text's revisions, and many new test questions have been added to the expanded *Test Bank.*

ACKNOWLEDGMENTS

There are many people who have contributed to this project and to whom we owe our gratitude. We were fortunate in both editions to receive valuable, constructive reviewers' comments from: Frederick Arnold, *Madison Area Technical College;* Mark Berger, *University of Kentucky;* Ronald Brandolini, *Valencia Community College;* G. E. Breger, *University of South Carolina;* William Brown, *California State University, Northridge;* Gerald Carlino, *The Federal Reserve Bank of Philadelphia;* Ronald Dulaney, *University of Montana;* Donald Fell, *Ohio State University;* Arthur Friedberg, *Mohawk Valley Community College;* David Green, *Tidewater Community College;* Roberta Greene, *Central Piedmont Community College;* Stephen King, *Midstate Technical Institute;* John Lafky, *California State University, Fullerton;* Charles Lave, *University of California, Irvine;* Carole Lundeberg, *Hartford State Technical College;* Beth Matta, *New Mexico State University;* Bernard McCarney, *Illinois State*

University; Kenneth McKnight, *Spokane Community College;* Terry Riddle, *Central Virginia Community College;* Hushang Shahidi, *Wright State University;* and Sidney Wilson, *Rockland Community College.*

Students, colleagues, family, and friends have provided suggestions and support. Among these are: Dusty Welch, Cel Nasiatka, Sharon Callaghan, Mariellen Barker, Dan Cobb, Gladys Gruenberg, and countless students who have taken the one-semester introductory economics course at Meramec and at St. Louis University.

Our typists, Audrey Reilly and Patricia Feldmann, deserve very special thanks. At times they performed the impossible—with a short deadline, converting unreadable manuscript into a finished product.

Finally, there is the staff at The Dryden Press with whom we have had the good fortune of working: Liz Widdicombe, Judy Sarwark, Alan Wendt, Jane Perkins, Anne Knowles, Becky Ryan, and Doris Milligan. Also, thanks to Maggie Jarpey. We are grateful to have worked with this talented group.

Patrick J. Welch
Gerry F. Welch
October 1985

ALTERNATIVE COURSE OUTLINE

Economics: Theory & Practice is written to permit an instructor to teach in either a macro-micro sequence of topics or a micro-macro sequence. Since Parts II and III are independent of each other, either can follow Part I, the introductory section. Instructors who choose the micro-macro sequence should consider the following.

Part I	**Introduction to Economics**
Chapter 1	Introduction to Economics
Chapter 2	Economic Decision Making and Economic Systems
Chapter 3	Demand, Supply, and the Determination of Price
Part III	**The Microeconomy**
Chapter 10	Households and Businesses: An Overview
Chapter 11	Benefits, Costs, and Maximization
Chapter 12	Production and the Costs of Production
Chapter 13	Competition and Market Structures
Chapter 14	Labor Markets, Unions, and the Distribution of Income
Chapter 15	Questions and Issues in the Microeconomy: Government and the Markets
Part II	**The Macroeconomy**
Chapter 4	Goals and Problems of the Macroeconomy: Employment, Prices, and Production
Chapter 5	Foundations of the Macroeconomy
Chapter 6	The Role of Government in the Macroeconomy
Chapter 7	Money, Financial Institutions, and the Federal Reserve
Chapter 8	Money Creation, Monetary Theory, and Monetary Policy
Chapter 9	Questions and Issues in the Macroeconomy: Assessing Goals and Tools
Part IV	**The International Economy**
Chapter 16	The International Economy: Trade
Chapter 17	The International Economy: Finance

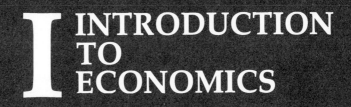

I INTRODUCTION TO ECONOMICS

1 INTRODUCTION TO ECONOMICS

Chapter Objectives

1. To define economics and introduce the scarcity problem, which underlies economics.
2. To understand the relationship between scarcity, tradeoffs, and opportunity costs.
3. To identify the four factors of production and the income return to each type of factor.
4. To differentiate between economic theory and economic policy.
5. To introduce the tools economists use to express theories and policies.
6. To show through a production possibilities example how the tools of economics can be used to illustrate and explain the basic problem of scarcity.

WHAT IS ECONOMICS?

Economics
The study of how scarce, or limited, resources are used to satisfy unlimited material wants and needs.

Economics is the study of how scarce, or limited, resources are used to satisfy people's unlimited material wants and needs. Broadly, economics is concerned with material things and how people make decisions about these things. It is concerned with having and not having, with shoes, food, stereos, hamburgers, bridges, bombers, medical services, entertainment, and the like. Happiness, sorrow, beauty, virtue, and sin are not direct concerns of the discipline of economics (although they have been known to be of concern to some economists). Rather, the focus is on the standard of living of individuals and societies as defined in terms of material goods and services.

The field of economics is extensive and it is always growing. Economists are willing to examine almost anything that affects the material aspects of life. Most often economists voice concern over unemployment, inflation, interest rates, labor problems, government regulation, energy, and international trade. But this just scratches the surface. The list of what interests economists goes on and on. This text will introduce you to some of the major areas of study in economics, some key institutions and relationships, and some controversial policy issues. A quick glance through the table of contents will give you an idea of the breadth of topics included in the discipline of economics.

Economics and Scarcity

Scarcity
The condition of not having enough material goods and services to satisfy the wants and needs of all individuals, households, and societies.

Scarcity is the framework within which economics exists. Put another way, without scarcity there would be no reason to study economics. This scarcity framework means that there are not enough, nor can there ever be enough, material goods and services to satisfy the wants and needs of all individuals, families, and societies. An examination of your own situation makes this obvious. Do you own the car you would most enjoy? Do you have enough financial resources for the stereo, tapes, dates, concerts, textbooks, and boots you want? Does your family ever remark that the recent automobile repair bill means hamburgers, beans, and franks this month? Societies face the same scarcity problem on a larger scale. Money spent for roads is money not available for hospitals. Resources devoted to defense are not available for schools or welfare. Gasoline and oil used now for automobiles will not be available in the future.

If scarcity exists, then choices must be made by individuals and societies. These choices involve "tradeoffs" and necessitate an awareness of the consequences of those tradeoffs. For example, suppose that you have $25 to spend and have narrowed your alternatives to a textbook or a date. Scarcity prohibits the purchase of both and imposes a tradeoff—a book or a date. Each choice has a consequence. The textbook might enable you to attain a good grade (and increase your knowledge), and the date might mean an evening of merriment.

Value judgment
The relative values one assigns to alternatives in making a decision or analyzing a situation.

In arriving at a decision your value judgment plays a key role. A **value judgment** is what you hold to be important in your estimation of a situation. If you value good grades more than a good time, you may choose the book; if you value a good time more than good grades, you will probably choose the date.

If someone in your family were to win $1,000 in a lottery, the same problem of choice would arise. The $1,000 is a limited sum; it buys only so much. Your family would have to consider alternatives, or tradeoffs, for spending the $1,000. Ultimately, the decision as to how the money would be used would be based on a value judgment of some member of the family.

Society faces the same scarcity-related tradeoff problem. In some communities, the public school conditions, both physical and intellectual, are appalling. This may be a reflection of the value judgments of the community. Individuals face on the ballot the choice of increasing or not increasing tax dollars for their schools. The tradeoff is whether to use household income for schools or for additional shoes, food, furniture, or other preferences of the family. On the national level, if a society chooses to go to war, it must give up some consumer goods (like jeans and pickup trucks) for defense goods (like uniforms and tanks). If society chooses to increase its population, there will be less space and fewer resources for each person. Each of these tradeoffs is necessary because we cannot have everything. And each tradeoff reflects the value judgment of the decision makers.

In making decisions, individuals and societies evaluate both the benefits and the costs of their choices. Because of scarcity, every decision to acquire a particular good or service or to spend time or money in a certain way has a cost attached to it. Economists call these costs **opportunity costs.** An opportunity cost is the cost of a purchase or a decision measured in terms of a forgone alternative; that is, what was given up to attain the purchase or make the decision. Once time or money is devoted to one thing, the opportunity to use that time or money for other things is lost. If you spend $25 to acquire a textbook, the opportunity cost of that text is what was given up to obtain it—perhaps a date.

Opportunity cost
The cost of a purchase or decision measured in terms of a forgone alternative (what was given up to attain the purchase or make the decision).

The opportunity cost to parents of choosing to acquire more shoes or food, rather than supporting an increase in a school tax, might be an inferior education for their children. The opportunity cost of going to war would include the jeans and pickup trucks that were not produced in order to obtain more uniforms and tanks. Because of scarcity, individuals, families, and societies must make tradeoffs—choices based on both the benefits and the opportunity costs of their decisions. In fact, as Application 1.1, "The Opportunity Cost of Success," shows, even "having it all" often requires giving up something valuable.[1]

Why Scarcity?

The root of the scarcity problem lies in the definition of economics—that people have limited resources to satisfy their unlimited material wants and needs.

[1]Opportunity costs are discussed more fully in Chapter Eleven.

Application 1.1
THE OPPORTUNITY COST OF SUCCESS

Getting to run the corporation may be a dream come true, but the personal cost of reaching that goal can be tremendous.

Because chief executives typically work 60 to 70 hours a week, travel six to 10 days a month and give up many of their weekends, family relationships and physical health suffer. . . .

The Wall Street Journal and the Gallup Organization jointly surveyed 780 chief executives about their work attitudes, the kinds of personal sacrifices they have made to advance, and the ways they cope with job pressures. . . .

The respondents were candid about the personal toll that the stress of their jobs has taken. Six in every 10 said they believe a business executive must make personal sacrifices to succeed, and 80 percent of those who professed that belief acknowledged that their family lives have suffered because of their careers.

The regret mentioned most frequently: too lit-

Material needs are the goods and services we must have to maintain our existence, such as food, shelter, and medical care. Material wants are those items we would like to have, such as videotaping equipment, stereophonic sound systems, or a third pair of shoes. Whether a good or service is a need or want is sometimes hard to determine. Medical care, for example, might be needed by one person but only wanted by another. What is more, we often confuse our own wants and needs. You may think you need a new sports car while, in fact, you may only have an intense want for it.

For either wants or needs, however, people appear to possess the psychological ability to continually require more goods and services and to become dissatisfied with what they currently possess. This drive for more, when considered for all members in society, causes wants and needs to be so great in number that they can be thought of as virtually unlimited. For example, you could devote one class period to listing everything everyone in the class desired, completely exhausting all wishes. By the next class period, and for all others, the list would increase as students added goods and services originally forgotten or goods and services introduced to them throughout the semester. The list would never be completed! One might recall that ten years ago the average American did not "need" a speedy hot dog cooker, microwave oven, personal computer, frozen waffles, or stereo headphones for jogging.

Resources (factors of production)
Persons and things used to produce goods and services; limited in nature; categorized as land, labor, capital, and entrepreneurship.

People's unlimited wants and needs are satisfied by goods and services which are produced by **resources,** or **factors of production.** These resources are all of the people, materials, and machinery that contribute to the production of a good or service. For example, in creating a Big Mac, McDonald's uses beef, special sauce and other food products, cooks, order takers, electricity, water, ovens, refrigerators, trucks, managers, paper, engineers, warming lights, and so on.

Each of these resources, or in fact any resource that any business uses, is limited. Ovens and managers are not available to McDonald's or to any

---

tle time spent with family. Some spoke of failing to provide enough parental guidance and feeling guilty about neglect. Others said they missed getting to see their children grow up. A few said they feel they hardly know their children. More than one in 10 said serious family problems had resulted from their work situations. . . .

Now that they've succeeded, two of every three chief executives believe the pressures are greater at the top than when they were middle-level executives. A significant number of chiefs acknowledge that job pressures have affected their physical health. Among large-company bosses, 17 percent said they had experienced physical problems as a consequence of their jobs. In smaller companies, the percentage was somewhat higher. . . .

Source: Frank Allen, "Chief Executives Say Job Requires Many Family and Personal Sacrifices," *The Wall Street Journal,* August 20, 1980, pp. 21, 33. Reprinted by permission of *The Wall Street Journal,* other business in infinite amounts; there is only so much beef; and "help wanted" signs for cooks and other types of labor sometimes appear. Nothing that McDonald's or any other business uses is unlimited in its supply.

FACTORS OF PRODUCTION

Thousands upon thousands of different types of resources can be used in the production of goods and services. To bring some order and manageability to our thinking about these resources, economists have found it helpful to classify them into four groups: labor, capital, land, and entrepreneurship.

Labor
All physical and mental human effort used to produce goods and services.

Capital
All man-made items such as machinery and equipment used in the production of goods and services.

Land
All productive inputs that originate in nature, such as coal and fertile soil.

Entrepreneurship
The function of organizing resources for production and taking the risk of success or failure in a productive enterprise.

Labor includes all human effort, both physical and mental, going into the production of goods and services. It encompasses the efforts of everyone from physicians to drill press operators to lifeguards—all who work to produce goods and services.

Capital includes warehouses, machines and equipment, computers, paper clips, and all other goods that are used in the production of other goods and services and that are not used for final consumption.

Land includes all inputs into production that originate in nature and are not man-made—for example, oil reserves, iron ore, and fertile soil.

There is no resource that could not be classified into one of these three groups. To say that something is direct human effort, is man-made, or originates in nature covers all possibilities. Yet economists speak of the four, not three, factors of production. The final factor of production, **entrepreneurship,** is the performance of a number of critical tasks that must be carried out in all productive processes. Without the performance of these tasks, no economic activity would occur. First, entrepreneurship involves the organization, or the bringing together, of labor, land, and capital to produce a good or service. A small business owner may do this alone, while large corporations hire managers and engineers to perform this function. Second, entrepreneurship involves bearing risk. If a business is successful, someone makes a profit; if it is a failure or does poorly, someone takes a loss. In a small business the risk taker is the proprietor; in a large corporation risk is taken by the stockholders. The proprietor or stockholder receives the residual, or what is left over, after all contractual obligations have been met. Thus, the proprietor or stockholder does very well if a great deal of money is left after expenses or very poorly if little is left. Entrepreneurship, in essence, is the function of organizing and risk taking.

The relationship between productive resources and society's material wants and needs is summarized in Figure 1.1.

Factors and Income

Obviously no resource will be contributed to the production of a good or service unless the owner of the resource expects some personal gain from the effort. The gain may take the form of simple personal satisfaction, or the feeling of belonging to a group such as a family, sorority, or lodge. But most

Figure 1.1
Relationship between Resources and Material Wants and Needs

Producers transform factors of production into goods and services to satisfy society's material wants and needs.

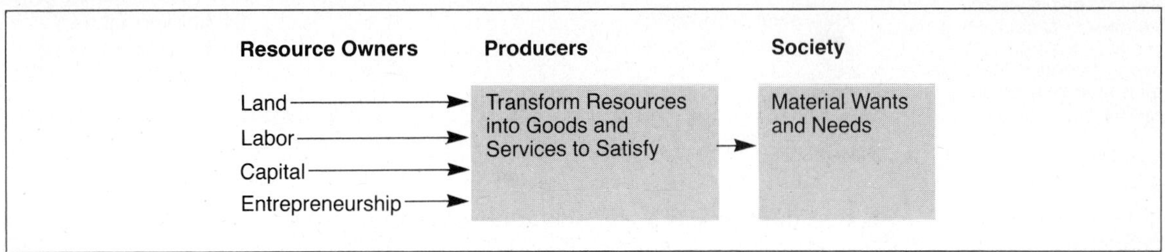

often, the personal gain takes the form of money income. Although money is money, and $100 received by a worker is no different from $100 received by the owner of a machine, it is helpful to give different names to the income received by the different types of resources. Thus, we have:

Wages
Income return to labor.

Interest
Income return to owners of capital.

Rent
Income return to owners of land resources.

Profit
Income return to those performing the entrepreneurial function.

- **wages,** the income received by the suppliers of labor;
- **interest,** the income received by owners of capital;
- **rent,** the income received by owners of land resources; and
- **profit,** the income received by those who carry out the entrepreneurial function.

It might appear trivial to give a separate name to the income received by each of the different groups of resources. Yet the distinction can be significant. The classification of people into different earning groups is important for social as well as for economic reasons. As the economist Robert Heilbroner put it, "It is not just Labor on the one hand and Land or Capital on the other; it is the Bronx on the one hand and Park Avenue on the other."[2] Also, the Marxian critique of capitalism, which is the most persistent and powerful critique of capitalism, dwells on what it means to be a worker as opposed to being an owner of land or capital. Finally, at different points in the history of the United States, the government has tried to deal with inflation by using policies known as "wage-price controls." Notice these are called "wage" rather than "income" price controls. Under policies such as these, some types of incomes are frozen while others are allowed to continue to rise.[3]

Scarce Resources

Part of the economic problem is that resources, or factors of production, are scarce, or limited. How scarce are resources? A look at Table 1.1 suggests that there is an abundance of people and things with which to produce

[2]R. L. Heilbroner, *The Limits of American Capitalism.* Harper Torchbook ed., Harper and Row, 1967, p. 71.

[3]Wage-price controls are explained more fully in Chapter Nine.

Table 1.1
Availabilities of Selected Resources in the U.S. Economy

While there is a large number of resources in the U.S. economy, there are not enough to satisfy all material wants and needs.

Resource	Amount in 1983
Total labor force	113.2 million people
Total area of national forest lands	230.0 million acres
Domestic crude petroleum production	3.171 billion barrels
Raw steel production	84.6 million net tons
Shipments of aluminum mill products	10.624 billion pounds[a]

[a]Preliminary figure.

Source: U.S. Bureau of the Census, *Statistical Abstract of the United States: 1985* (105th ed.), Washington, D.C., 1984, pp. 390, 673, 709, 771.

goods and services. Over one hundred million people are working or looking for work in the U.S. economy alone. Billions of barrels of crude oil and millions of tons of steel are produced in the economy each year. The list of available resources goes on and on. Yet, we say resources are scarce. The problem is that while large numbers of resources may be available in an *absolute* sense, they are still limited. Furthermore, resources are scarce compared to the goods and services they would have to produce in order to satisfy our unlimited material wants and needs. That is, they are scarce *relative* to the wants and needs their production attempts to satisfy. Even if there were no oil embargoes, no crop-destroying floods or droughts, no production-stopping strikes, and no wars, people's wants would continue to outrun the economy's ability to satisfy them.

Application 1.2
TAKING THE SCARE OUT OF SCARCITY

We have become experts in the art of producing what can only be called nightmare economics. . . .

There are at least two kinds of nightmares. The first conjures up dreadful pictures of shortages, particularly of energy and of water: visions of stranded automobiles, parched gardens, empty water tanks, and frozen pipes. The other conjures up even more dreadful "scenarios" of action to be taken in order to avoid such shortages: the abandonment of most of the hardly won safeguards against pollution and environmental degradation; the turning of thousands of square miles into moonscapes because coal, shale, and uranium have been ripped from the earth; littering with highly radioactive materials. . . .

The art of life is to focus on difficulties and deal with them as best one can, without making psychological problems out of them that then lead to nightmares. We could also say that the art is to maintain a sense of proportion in our lives.

But we can keep a sense of proportion only when dealing with sensible proportions. If things become so vast that the mind cannot any more "encompass" them, a sense of proportion becomes an impossibility. When we are told that there are, say, 8 million unemployed in the United States, the size of the problem paralyzes our imagination and all we can have is nightmares. It would be different if we were told that there are, for example, 90 unemployed in our neighborhood. We could then focus on the prob-

If we cannot solve the scarcity problem, can we at least ease it? Over the years we seem to have accomplished some goals: life expectancies have increased because of the availability of improved medical techniques, technological changes in transportation allow us to rapidly get from one place to another, fashionable clothing is available to buyers of all income levels, and we can prepare food faster than ever before.

But there is evidence to suggest that, in some respects, the scarcity problem may have worsened. At one time economics students learned about gifts of nature, or free goods, such as air and water, available for everyone's use at no cost. Since then we have discovered that although air and water are free, clean air and plentiful water are not free. The opportunity cost of freely using these resources has been a general decline in air and water quality and specific problems such as acid rain and a slow deterioration of our forests.Thus, while we have come a long way in satisfying people's desires for material goods and services, we have not broken free from the spectre of scarcity. Indeed, some people might argue that we are more acutely aware of the limits of our productive capability than ever before.

An interesting approach to alleviating the problem of scarcity is given in Application 1.2, "Taking the Scare Out of Scarcity." Do you agree with E. F. Schumacher that our hope in dealing with scarcity is found in "voluntary simplicity"?

lem, find out who they are, what they could do, what they would want to do. Local action would then become at least conceivable: it is not even conceivable as long as our minds are fixed on large *national totals*. . . .

People ask the strangest questions. For instance: How will the people of the United States, with their history of limitless expansion and boundless expectations, adjust to the coming of scarcity? Such questions are quite unanswerable, because the concepts are much too big. "The people of the United States"—whom are we talking about? Rockefeller or sharecroppers, labor union chiefs or bank clerks, people in high-rise apartments or people in suburbia, in rural areas or in city slums? Their histories are as different as their expectations, and so are the difficulties they will have to meet. Above all, the spirit of self-reliance differs from person to person. Traveling across the United States quite recently, I met many people with a splendid spirit of self-reliance. Many of them had a better time than they ever had in their lives because they were discovering a *new freedom*—the less you need, the freer you become. The idea of possible scarcity did not give them nightmares; on the contrary, it stimulated and exhilarated them. "Let's discover whether we really *need* all that." . . .

America's hope, in my view, is this movement for voluntary simplicity. Need less and live better—and no more nightmares about incomprehensible totals.

Source: E. F. Schumacher, "Taking the Scare Out of Scarcity," *Psychology Today*, September 1977, p. 16. From *Psychology Today Magazine*,

ECONOMIC THEORY AND POLICY

Since scarcity keeps people from having all that they want, households, businesses, and governments are forced to make millions of choices as they conduct their economic activities. From the complex environment in which these decisions are made emerges some combination of goods and services (a product mix) to satisfy wants and needs. In order to intelligently make the choices that will maximize our satisfaction, we need to know about production, or how to get the most from our resources; about employment, or how to put all available resources to work; about consumer behavior; about a money system; about government in the market; and so on. In short, we need to bring order to the complexity in which the decisions are made and to gain a clear concept of some of the basic relationships in the economy. This is the task of economic theory.

In any economic situation there are several different courses of action which could be followed, each leading to a different result. For example, a city budget could be analyzed and the decision reached to build hospitals rather than prisons, or parking lots instead of playgrounds. When a decision maker follows a specific course of action, he or she is said to be following a policy. Thus, when people speak of different policies for dealing with rising prices or unemployment, they are referring to different ways of dealing with these problems. Ideally, theories and policies are related. Before becoming committed to a particular course of action, a person should make an effort to order and understand the basic relationships with which he or she is dealing.

Economic Theory

Economic theory
A formal explanation of the relationship between economic variables.

An **economic theory** is a formal explanation of the relationship between economic conditions, or variables.[4] Very simply, a theory gives a reason why something happens, or offers a cause-and-effect interpretation for a set of events. There are economic theories to explain unemployment, inflation, price increases in the hog market, teenage wage rates, urban decay, and almost any other economic condition. For example, one simple economic theory deals with the relationship between the price of an item, say coffee, and the quantity of that item demanded by a consumer. According to this theory, if other circumstances do not change (for example, if there is no newly published health report extolling the virtues of coffee drinking or no shift in people's taste toward tea), as the price rises, consumers will decrease

[4]A dictionary definition of a theory is: "Systematically organized knowledge applicable in a relatively wide variety of circumstances; especially, a system of assumptions, accepted principles, and rules of procedure devised to analyze, predict, or otherwise explain the nature or behavior of a specified set of phenomena." From *The American Heritage Dictionary of the English Language,* ed. William Morris (New York: American Heritage Publishing Co., Inc., 1973), p. 1335.

the amount of coffee they demand. This theory then offers one explanation for a drop in coffee sales.

The economist defends economic theories by showing that the relationships under consideration are mathematically or logically valid, or by using statistics to show that the real world behaves as the theory says it should. The federal government and private sources of information provide valuable and extensive data on many facets of economic life, and the computer has made possible speedier and more sophisticated testing of ideas. As a result, **econometrics,** which is the use of statistical techniques to describe the relationship between economic variables, has become an important part of economic analysis.

Econometrics
The use of statistical techniques to describe the relationship between economic variables.

In economics, as in the other social sciences, theories are much more open to dispute than they are in the natural sciences. One reason for this is that the variables in the social sciences are not identical in each instance. In chemistry, for example, one learns that two molecules of hydrogen and one of oxygen form H_2O, or water. This is always true because molecules of hydrogen and oxygen are all the same. In applying an economic theory to coffee consumption, however, the economist must consider that buyers of coffee have different tastes, incomes, and so on. By controlling for these differences in tastes and such, the economist can statistically and mathematically show that consumers will decrease the quantity of coffee demanded as the price rises. But this conclusion is a generalization. There are always buyers who do not fit the economist's pattern. For example, some few individuals may still buy the same amount of an item regardless of the price.

A second reason that theoretical disputes are likely in economics is that a variety of factors can be considered in analyzing an economic problem. In constructing a theory an economist may choose to explore the relationship between an event and only one or a few of the many variables affecting that event. For example, if an unusually large number of students were to receive high grades on the first exam in this course, one could theorize as to why this happened by considering any of several factors: the caliber of the instruction, the excellence of the textbook, the students' IQs, hours studied, suggested readings completed, amount of sleep before the exam, food intake, and so on. Suppose your instructor statistically examined the relationship between hours studied, suggested readings completed, and the test scores. At the same time one of the students explored the relationship between sleep and food intake and the grades. Assume your instructor found that the class studied and read for many long hours, hence the high grades. The student discovered that each classmate took the exam thoroughly rested and after a nutritious breakfast, hence the high grades. In reading the results the department chairperson claimed that both studies were unreliable because neither considered IQ or quality of instruction. Enter controversy! Who is correct? In each of these instances, a clear relationship was established: several reasons for the high grades were identified.

There has always been serious controversy among economists concerning their theories. Scholarly publications sometimes devote many pages to running disputes between practitioners in the field. Much of this is similar to the dispute that could result from the high grades example. Questions arise as to the significance and appropriateness of the variables studied, the importance of the overall problem, the narrowness of the study, and the possibility that a more influential factor has not yet been tested. This questioning, of course, gives rise to the continuing development of economics.

Economic Policy

Economic policy
An action taken to change an economic condition.

An **economic policy** is an action taken to change an economic condition. A tax decrease to speed up the economy, mandatory energy conservation measures, and quotas on foreign-produced items are all examples of economic policies.

Economic policy is the result of a decision by a policy maker such as a business manager, state or local legislature, the Congress, voters, the president, or the Federal Reserve.[5] In most instances of economic policy creation, several courses of action are available. For example, a state governing body could choose to either increase, decrease, or leave unchanged its sales tax on luxury items; there are several alternative methods for fighting inflation; and there are many options for easing an energy crisis.

It is important when selecting a policy to remember that each alternative carries consequences which may be further reaching than the problem itself. Take the problem of job loss in the auto industry due to imports of foreign-produced cars. A policy could be designed to discourage Americans from buying foreign cars by increasing the tax (tariff) imposed on vehicles as they enter the United States (thereby increasing their price), or by putting quotas, or limits, on the number of imported autos that may enter the United States. The result of this policy to slow down sales of foreign cars could be an improvement in American car sales and in employment for auto workers. But what about the other consequences? Foreign nations could retaliate by taxing products the United States exports, thus decreasing employment in a different industry; or price increases on foreign cars could worsen an inflation problem as the consumer is forced to pay more. The policy maker must select a course of action not only on the basis of the problem to be solved, but also on the basis of the consequences resulting from the chosen policy.

An actual policy decision is based on the value judgment of the policy maker. In the case of foreign-produced automobiles, if the policy maker values jobs in the domestic auto industry as the most important consideration, an effort will be made to enact job-saving legislation. If the main concern is with inflation and the consumer, the policy maker will not favor tariffs and quotas. The question of granting tax credits for college tuition is another example of policy making and value judgments. Families facing financial dif-

---

[5]The Federal Reserve System is the central banking system in the United States and oversees the money supply. The Federal Reserve System and its operations are explained in Chapter Seven.

ficulties in sending their children to college may favor this type of tax break. People who think that existing programs for granting aid to college students are sufficient may find this policy unimportant and oppose it.

Since economic theory explains how economic variables interact, and since economic policy involves the manipulation of those economic variables, it is crucial that policy makers have some knowledge of these theories and their complexities. If policy makers do not understand basic economic principles, the consequences of their policy decisions could be disastrous. One benefit of a course in economics is that it enables you to better evaluate the consequences of policies and to judge how well or how poorly policy makers are informed.

TOOLS OF THE ECONOMIST

Words, Graphs, and Mathematical Equations

There are several ways that economic theories and policies can be expressed. The first and most basic method used by the economist is a verbal presentation, or descriptive statement. Earlier we noted that the quantity of coffee demanded will fall as its price increases. This is a simple verbal statement about buyer demand. The advantage of using this method to express a theory is the ease with which concepts can be conveyed.

But the advantage hides a weakness. One reason verbal descriptions are easy to convey is that they tend to be imprecise. In the above example, we have merely stated that a relationship exists between coffee prices and the quantity of coffee demanded, without saying anything about the strength of that relationship. We do not know if consumers will be prepared to buy 10 percent less coffee when the price increases from, say, \$2 to \$4 a pound, or 75 percent less coffee when the price increases from \$2 to \$4 a pound, or just what numbers are involved. Unfortunately, when one tries to be numerically precise, verbal explanations become very clumsy. (To prove this to yourself, try explaining the meaning of $2 + 2 = 4$ using only words with no mathematical symbols.)

The second method for expressing theories and policies, graphs, allows a more precise statement about the relationships between economic variables. A **graph** is a picture illustrating the relationship between two variables, one shown on the horizontal axis and the other on the vertical axis. For instance, returning to our coffee example, the graph in Figure 1.2 shows a relationship between the price of a pound of coffee and the number of pounds of coffee demanded by consumers over a certain period of time.

Graph
An illustration showing the relationship between two variables which are measured on the vertical and horizontal axes.

There are several advantages to using graphs. Numbers can easily be incorporated into graphs while the same is not true for verbal descriptions. The verbal description given in our example merely states that less coffee would be demanded at higher prices. With a graph we can be much more specific. For example, the graph in Figure 1.2 tells us that at a price of \$4 per

Figure 1.2
Relationship between Coffee Prices and the Amount of Coffee Demanded

The downward sloping line in this graph illustrates the various amounts of coffee demanded at several different coffee prices.

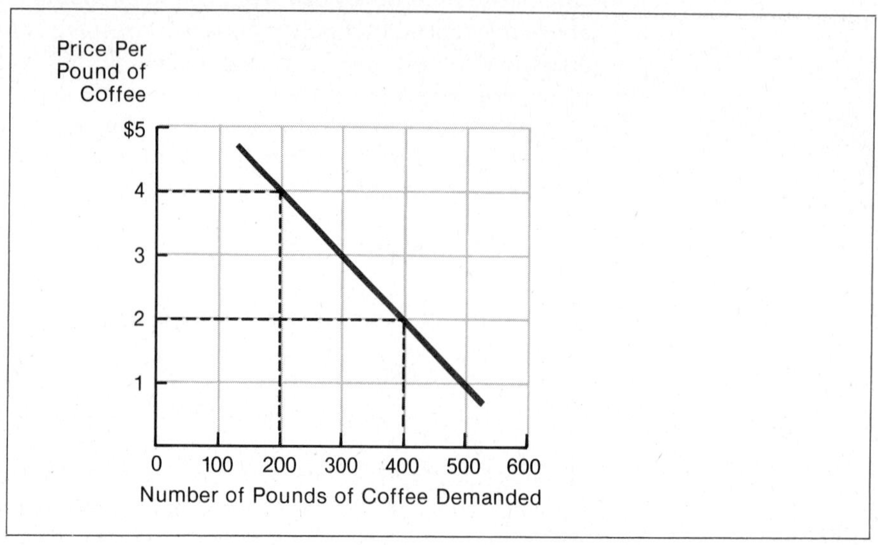

pound 200 pounds of coffee are demanded, and at a price of $2 the quantity demanded increases to 400. Or, if the price is $4 and you lower it by 50 percent, you will increase the quantity of coffee demanded by 100 percent. Or, if you are interested in selling 300 pounds of coffee, the price will need to be $3 per pound. Also, once you have had some practice in reading graphs, you will discover that a line or curve illustrates at a glance whether the relationship between the variables graphed is direct or inverse (see Application 1.3), as well as the strength of the relationship. Additional information on reading and interpreting a graph can be found in the appendix to this chapter.

The third method used by economists to express theories and policies is mathematical equations. The main drawback in using equations is that many people lack confidence in using mathematics. But equations have an important advantage: they are very specific about how economic variables are related. Let us return to our coffee example.

Suppose we found that the relationship between the price of coffee and the amount demanded is shown by the equation

$$Qc = 600 - 100\ Pc.$$

Here Qc represents the quantity of coffee demanded and Pc represents the price of coffee. By putting different prices in place of the Pc term you can see how much coffee buyers would want. For example, if the price were $4 per

Application 1.3
INTERPRETING A GRAPH

The two basic relationships between the variables in a graph are "direct" and "inverse."

A **direct** relationship exists when both variables move in the same direction; that is, as one gets larger or smaller, so does the other. For example, if you observed how many hot fudge sundaes an ice cream store would like to sell at different prices you would probably find a direct relationship. Graphically, this is illustrated by a line that slopes upward to the right like that in Figure 1.3. At a price of $2.25, hot fudge sundae sellers would like to sell 2,000 a day; when the price falls to $0.75 they would like to sell only 500 (preferring instead to devote their attention to more profitable items).

An **inverse** relationship exists when the variables move in opposite directions; that is, as one becomes larger, the other becomes smaller, and vice versa. For example, when sugar prices increase, the amount demanded for purchase falls. Graphically, this is illustrated by a line that slopes downward to the right such as that in Figure 1.4. Note in Figure 1.4 that when the price per pound of sugar is $0.20, consumers would like to purchase 5 tons per day, and when the price drops to $0.15 per pound, tons demanded per day increase to 6. (It is conventional in economics to insert price on the vertical axis in a graph.)

Can you illustrate the following relationships?

1. Inches of rain and sales of umbrellas
2. Tuition and students demanding to enroll in a university
3. Price of gasoline and consumers purchasing the same amount regardless of price
4. Years of education and salaries

Direct relationship One that occurs when two variables move in the same direction: when one increases, so does the other; graphs as an upward sloping line.

Inverse relationship Occurs when two variables move in opposite directions: when one increases, the other decreases; graphs as a downward sloping line.

Figure 1.3
A Direct Relationship

The number of sundaes supplied is directly related to the price per sundae: more are supplied at higher prices than at lower prices. A direct relationship is illustrated by an upward sloping line in a graph.

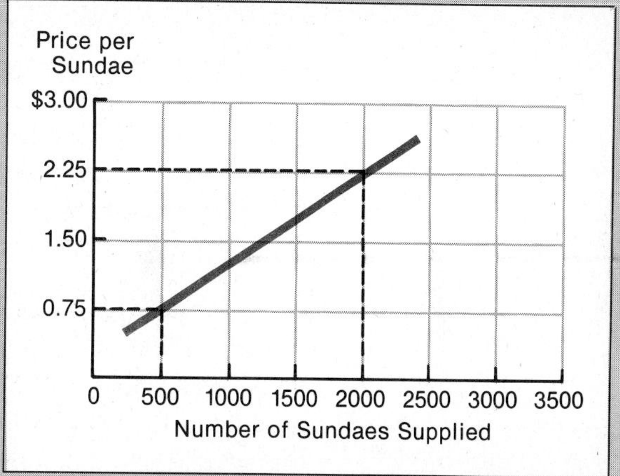

Figure 1.4
An Inverse Relationship

Tons of sugar demanded are inversely related to the price of sugar: as the price increases, the amount demanded decreases. An inverse relationship is illustrated by a downward sloping line in a graph.

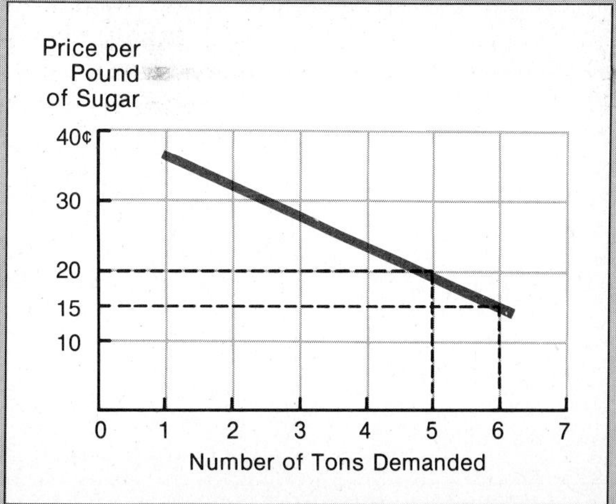

pound, buyers would want 200 pounds of coffee [200 = 600 − 100(4)]. If the price fell to $2, they would want 400 pounds [400 = 600 − 100(2)]. If coffee were given away, people would want 600 pounds; and if coffee were $6 per pound, people would stop buying it.

SCARCITY, MODEL BUILDING, AND GRAPHS

The purpose of this section is to review the basic scarcity principle, to introduce economic model building, and to demonstrate how graphs are used to illustrate basic economic concepts.

Modeling Scarcity

Model
The setting within which an economic theory is presented.

Economists often build a formal model to illustrate an economic theory. A **model** is the setting within which a relationship is explained or a problem is analyzed. For example, a model railroader usually constructs a setting, or display, in which to operate a train. An architect creates a scale model, or replica, of a building before it is constructed. Students, perhaps subconsciously, establish a mental model of their lifestyle (work schedule, sleep habits, car pooling arrangements, and so on) before selecting a semester's class schedule.

In developing a model, both facts and assumptions need to be defined. Facts serve as boundaries to set some limits on the model. For example, a common boundary-setting fact in economic model building is a time period. In the coffee example, the time period tells us whether we are looking at coffee demand for a day, a week, or a year. It would be difficult to determine how much of a product was demanded without knowing what time period to consider.

Assumption
A condition held to be true, usually in a model.

Assumptions are conditions held to be true and assigned to a model. Most often assumptions are held to be constant; that is, they do not change through the course of the example unless the reader is warned. For instance, in an economic model we could assume population growth at a particular rate, income at a certain level, or taxes as fixed. In building a model to plan study time during a semester, a student could assume that a certain number of hours per week would be devoted to a part-time job and that classes would be regularly held as scheduled. Whether or not an assumption is true does not matter within the context of the model. For purposes of the model, it is assumed to be true. However, if the conclusions drawn from the model are to be relevant, the assumptions selected for the model must be reasonably true in the "real world." For example, in building a model to plan a semester, a student probably should not assume that he or she can successfully complete twenty credit hours while working forty hours a week.

In the example that follows, a model is developed for a hypothetical economy operating in the framework of a short period of time, under the following assumptions.

1. All resources, or factors of production, are held constant. This means that there are no increases or decreases in the available amounts of the economy's labor, machinery, trucks, and so on.
2. All resources are fully employed. Everyone who wants a job has one, and all other resources (such as factories and tractors) available for use are being used. There is no involuntary unemployment of resources.
3. The existing technology is held fixed; no new inventions or innovations will occur.

Although this model economy, like any economy, has the potential for producing a large assortment of goods and services, we will divert all of its resources to the production of only two items: pizzas and bicycles. Table 1.2 lists some possible combinations of pizzas and bicycles that could be produced in our model economy given our assumptions. Notice from this table that if all resources are fully employed in the creation of pizzas, then 25 million pizzas can be made, but no bicycles. If some bicycles are manufactured (for example, 200,000), then some resources employed in the production of pizzas must be diverted to the construction of bicycles, and fewer pizzas will be produced. If all factors are used in the manufacture of bicycles, no pizzas can be made.

Production possibilities table (or graph)
An illustration of the various amounts of two goods that an economy can produce with full employment and fixed resources and technology.

The **production possibilities table** in Table 1.2 can be graphed to illustrate the same relationship. In Figure 1.5 the different combinations of bicycle and pizza production possibilities are plotted on a graph and the points connected with a smooth line.

Interpretation of the Model

The basic conclusion of the production possibilities model is a restatement of the scarcity problem: even with full employment, limited resources allow limited production of goods and services. In our hypothetical economy it would be impossible to produce 35 million pizzas in the time allowed, even if desired, because there are not enough factors of production to do so. In a sense, scarcity imposes a boundary on an economy. The curve in Figure 1.5 illustrates this boundary, or limit. Our hypothetical economy cannot produce beyond (to the right of) this curve.

The model also emphasizes the tradeoff concept. When an economy oper-

Table 1.2
Possible Combinations of Pizzas and Bicycles

This production possibilities table illustrates various combinations of pizzas and bicycles that a hypothetical economy could produce with full employment and fixed resources and technology.

Pizzas (Millions)	Bicycles (Hundreds of Thousands)
25	0
24	2
20	4
15	6
9	8
0	10

ates at full employment, more of one good can be produced only by giving up some amount of another good. If our economy were producing 20 million pizzas and 400,000 bicycles, and households demanded 600,000 bicycles, then households could have the additional bicycles only by giving up some pizzas. This tradeoff concept is a restatement of the principle of opportunity cost, which was introduced earlier: the cost of additional bicycles can be measured by the number of pizzas given up, and vice versa. The opportunity cost of going from 400,000 to 600,000 bicycles is 5 million pizzas.

Figure 1.5
Possible Combinations of Pizzas and Bicycles

The production possibilities curve illustrates the various combinations of two goods that an economy could produce at full employment with fixed resources and technology. Under these conditions, more of one good can be produced only by producing less of the other.

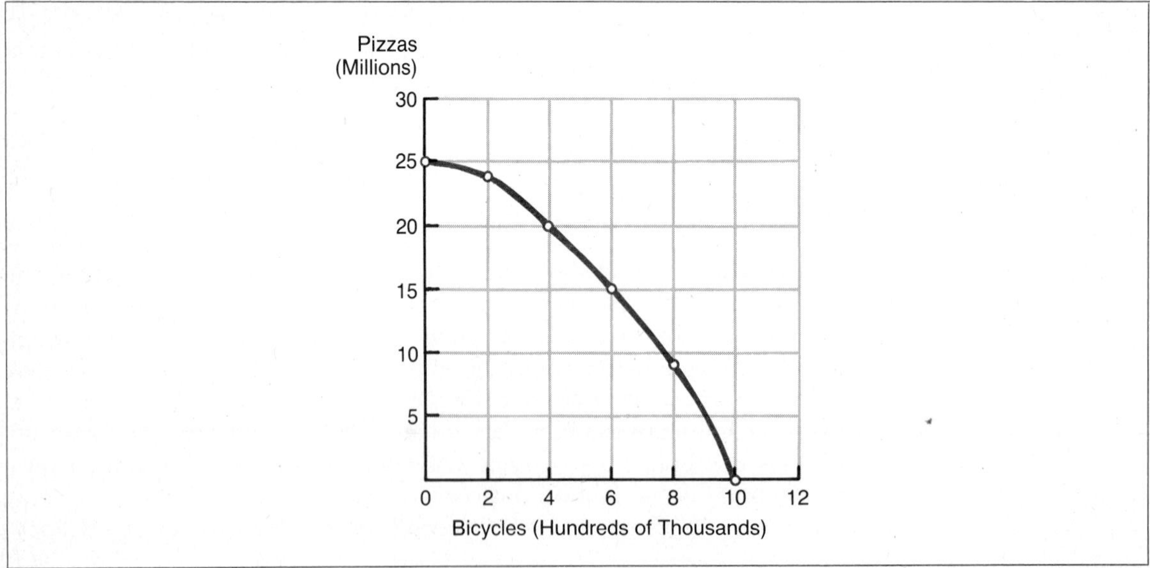

Several other economic concepts can be illustrated with the production possibilities model by altering the model's assumptions. If the assumption of full employment is dropped and some resources are assumed unemployed, then the economy cannot produce as much as it did under the condition of full employment. With full employment, one production combination was that of 15 million pizzas and 600,000 bicycles. If some labor, machinery, or other resource is idle, then less will be produced—perhaps only 10 million pizzas and 400,000 bicycles. This condition resulting from unemployment is illustrated graphically by a point inside, or to the left of, the production possibilities curve, such as point A in Figure 1.6. It can be concluded, then, that with unemployment, less goods and services are produced than with full employment.

If the assumptions of fixed resources and fixed technology are dropped, the growth of a nation's economy can be explained. With more labor, machinery, and/or better methods of production (technology), the economy would effectively have more resources with which to produce goods and services. For example, more labor would provide more workers in pizza and bicycle production, who could increase total output. The same effect could be accomplished with a newly automated process for the production of either good. This economic growth can be illustrated graphically by a point

Figure 1.6
Unemployment in a Production Possibilities Model

With unemployment, an economy is unable to reach the combinations of goods and services that it could produce if resources were fully employed. Point A represents production with unemployment.

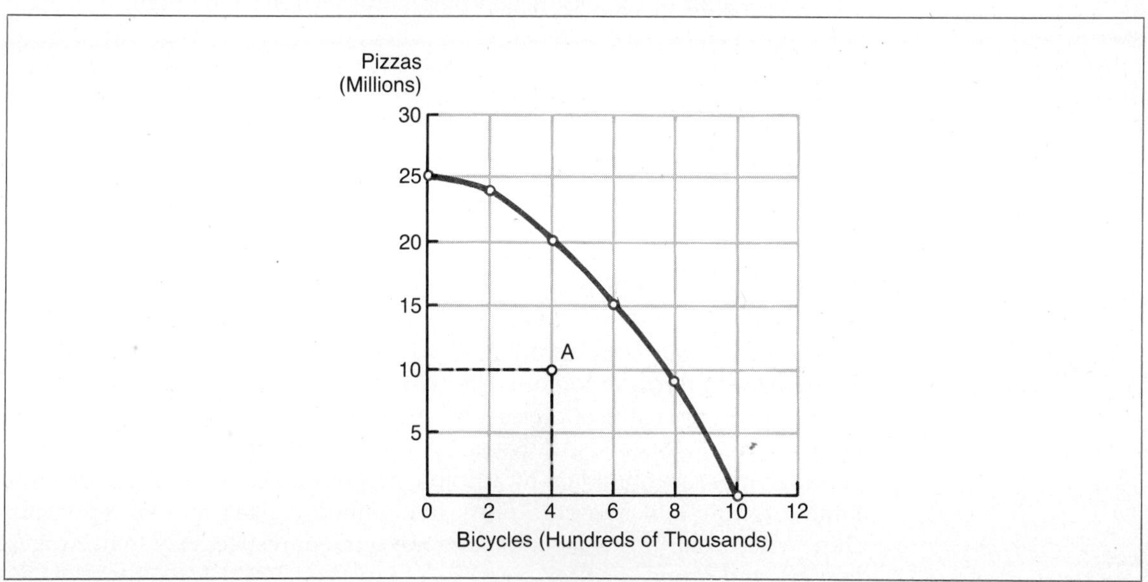

Figure 1.7
Economic Growth in a Production Possibilities Model

An increase in the number of available resources or an improvement in technology allows the production of goods and services to increase, and the economy's production possibilities curve shifts to the right.

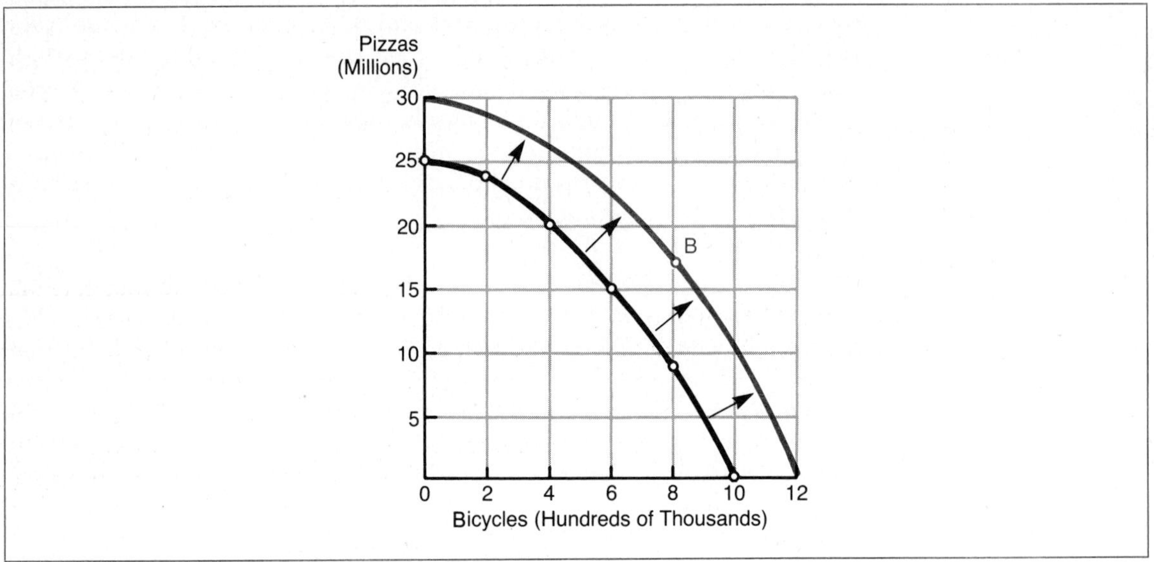

outside the production possibilities curve, or a shift of the curve to the right as shown in Figure 1.7. Point B, which was unattainable under the old condition, is now within reach of the economy. Thus, economic growth is illustrated by a shift of the production possibilities curve to the right.

SUMMARY

Economics is the study of how limited resources are used to satisfy unlimited material wants and needs. The basis of economics is a scarcity of goods and services caused by people's insatiable desire for material things coupled with a limited amount of resources to produce them. Since individuals and societies cannot have everything they desire, they must make choices, or tradeoffs. These tradeoffs are influenced by the decision maker's value judgments. Tradeoffs carry an opportunity cost, which measures the cost of a decision or purchase in terms of forgone alternatives.

Resources, or factors of production are those items used in the production of goods and services. All resources are scarce, or limited, in amount, although most are abundant by absolute measures. Economists classify these limited factors into four categories: land, labor, capital, and entrepreneurship. When sold, these generate incomes termed, respectively: rent, wages, interest, and profit.

In studying economics it is necessary to know the distinction between economic theory and policy. Economic theory explains why an event occurs, or gives a generalized interpretation of the relationship between economic variables. Economic policy is an action taken to change an economic condition. Value judgments are important in the selection of economic policies. In expressing theories and policies the economist uses the tools of verbal statements, graphs, and mathematical equations, with each tool having some advantages and disadvantages. An upward sloping line in a graph illustrates a direct relationship between variables, and a downward sloping line indicates an inverse relationship.

Economists build models to illustrate economic concepts. Assumptions, which are conditions held to be true, are important in the development of these models.

A production possibilities table and graph can be used to illustrate scarcity. These show that with assumptions of full employment and constant resources and technology, more of one good can be obtained only by giving up some of another good, making tradeoffs necessary. Unemployment, which means an economy produces fewer goods and services than with full employment, is shown by a point inside, or to the left of, the production possibilities curve. Increases in technology and/or resources allow for economic growth, enabling an economy to reach points outside the original curve, or permitting a shift of the curve to the right.

Key Terms and Concepts

Economics
Scarcity
Value judgment
Opportunity cost
Resources (factors of production)
Land
Labor
Capital
Entrepreneurship
Wages
Rent
Interest
Profit
Economic theory
Econometrics
Economic policy
Graph
Direct relationship
Inverse relationship
Model
Assumption
Production possibilities table and curve

Discussion and Review Questions

1. If resources are scarce and if people are always wanting more than the economy can provide, how is it possible that we would ever have unemployment?

2. Suppose that you are an advisor to a health team working in a less developed country. In that country, 20 percent of the children die of a particular disease. If the health team were to inoculate the population, the disease would cease to be a problem. However, with more people surviving, the country's food supply would become grossly inadequate, and it is estimated that about 20 percent of the children would die of starvation. Which policy would you follow: inoculation or no inoculation? Why would you follow this policy, and how are your values important in reaching a decision?
3. Why do economists devote so much time to the concepts of tradeoffs, choices, and opportunity costs? With this in mind, is there anything in this world that is free?
4. Do you agree or disagree with E. F. Schumacher ("Taking the Scare Out of Scarcity") that we are caught up with producing economic nightmares? What are your predictions for the world's resources over the next 100 years?
5. What is meant by a direct and an inverse relationship between economic variables? Illustrate each of these relationships graphically.
6. Distinguish between economic theory and economic policy. Discuss some of the reasons for economic theory controversies and economic policy controversies. Give some recent examples of economic policy actions.
7. What conclusions can be drawn from a production possibilities example? Illustrate a production possibilities curve graphically and indicate how unemployment and economic growth can be shown on this graph.
8. The following production possibilities table gives the various combinations of hours which can be worked and grade-point-averages which can be earned by a college student who holds a job and takes 12 credit-hours of courses a semester. Plot this table on a graph and answer the following questions.
   a. What is the opportunity cost for this student if he or she increases the hours worked per week from 10 to 20?
   b. What factors could cause this curve to shift to the right?
   c. What factors could cause this student to operate inside, or to the left, of this production possibilities curve?

Hours Worked per Week	GPA
50	0.00
40	1.00
30	1.90
20	2.60
10	3.25
0	3.75

Suggested Readings

H. S. D. Cole, C. Freeman, M. Jahoda, and K. L. R. Paviet, *Models of Doom* (New York: Universe Books, 1975). Critique of *The Limits to Growth* (see below).

Robert Frost, "The Road Not Taken," *Robert Frost Poetry and Prose,* eds. E. C. Lathem and L. Thompson (New York: Holt, Rinehart and Winston, 1972), p. 51. A poem about opportunity cost by the well-known poet.

John Kenneth Galbraith, "Corporate Man," *The New York Times Magazine,* January 22, 1984, p. 39. An essay on the opportunity cost of success in the corporate world.

D. H. Meadows, D. L. Meadows, J. Randers, and W. W. Behrens III, *The Limits to Growth* (New York: Universe Books, 1974). A pessimistic view of the future of humanity.

I. Papps and W. Henderson, *Models and Economic Theory* (Philadelphia: W. B. Saunders Co., 1977). An introduction to modeling and problems of modeling in economics.

F. Pohl, "The Midas Plague," *Spectrum: A Science Fiction Anthology,* eds. K. Amis and R. Conquest (New York: Harcourt, Brace and World, Inc., 1962), pp. 13–67. Science fiction about life in a world without scarcity.

Henry C. Wallich, "'The Limits to Growth' Revisited," *Challenge* (September–October, 1982), pp. 36–42. An evaluation of the pressures created by economic growth and our ability to control those pressures, as seen ten years after the publication of *The Limits to Growth.*

Appendix to Chapter One
GRAPHING

A graph is a picture illustrating the relationship between two variables. These variables are given on the vertical and horizontal axes of the graph. For example, the relationship between the price of tennis racquets and the number of tennis racquets demanded is given in Figure 1A.1.

The numbers along the axes of a graph are important for proper interpretation of the graph. In assigning numbers to a graph, several rules need to be remembered: (1) always use zero at the origin (the point where the horizontal and vertical axes meet); (2) work up the number scale as you go out on each axis;[1] and (3) when moving along an axis, use equal spaces for equal amounts. Notice the application of these rules in Figure 1A.1. Zero is used at the origin, numbers along each axis move up the number scale, the vertical axis is labeled in equal series of $10, and the horizontal axis is labeled in equal series of 25 units.

A point on a graph indicates a specific combination of the two variables compared in the graph. For example, point A in Figure 1A.1 indicates that

[1]For those students who are familiar with graphing techniques, we might point out that only the first, or northeast, quadrant of a graph is used in most examples in this text.

Figure 1A.1
A Relationship between the Price of Tennis Racquets and Number Demanded

Points A, B, and C match different prices of tennis racquets with the number of racquets demanded at each price.

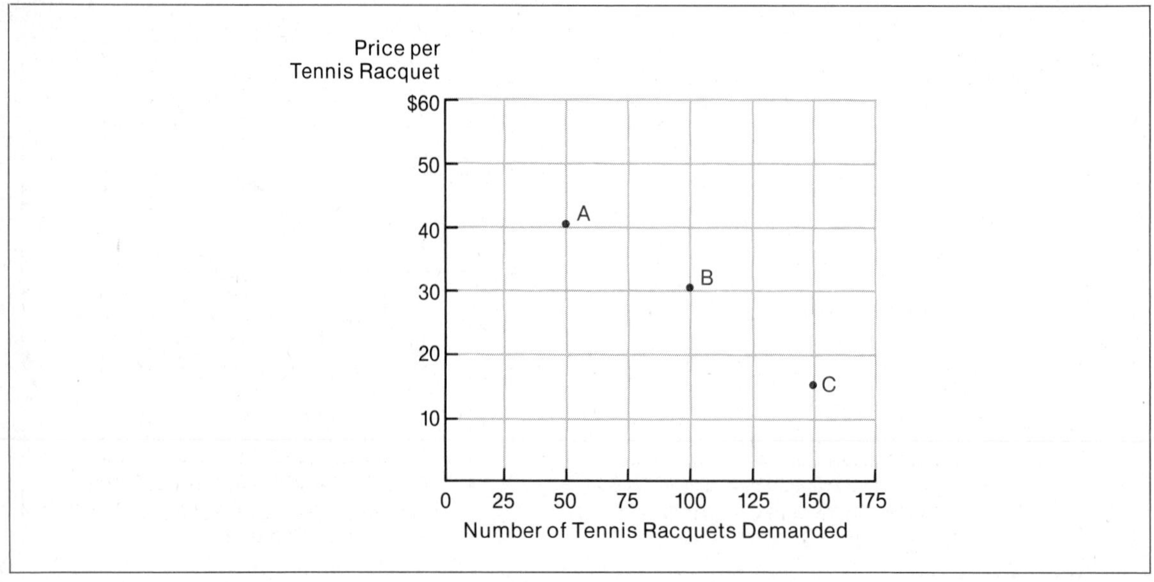

at a price of $40, 50 tennis racquets are demanded. This can be read by putting a real or imaginary line from point A to the vertical axis, and from point A to the horizontal axis. Point B says that at a price of $30, 100 racquets are demanded. What does point C designate? Where would point D be located if it indicates that at $50 per tennis racquet, no racquets are demanded?

A line on a graph is nothing more than a series of connected points. For example, Table 1A.1 lists the numbers of teenagers applying for a position at various hourly wage rates. Each of these wage rate-application combinations from this table is plotted as a point on Figure 1A.2a. These points are

Table 1A.1
Hourly Wage Rates and Numbers of Applications for a Position

This table illustrates a relationship between hourly wage rates and the numbers of teenagers applying for a position.

Hourly Wage Rate	Number of Teenagers Applying for a Position
$1.00	50
1.50	100
2.00	150
2.50	200
3.00	250
3.50	300
4.00	350

Figure 1A.2
Hourly Wage Rates and Numbers of Applications for a Position

A line in a graph is a series of connected points, each point representing a particular combination of two variables.

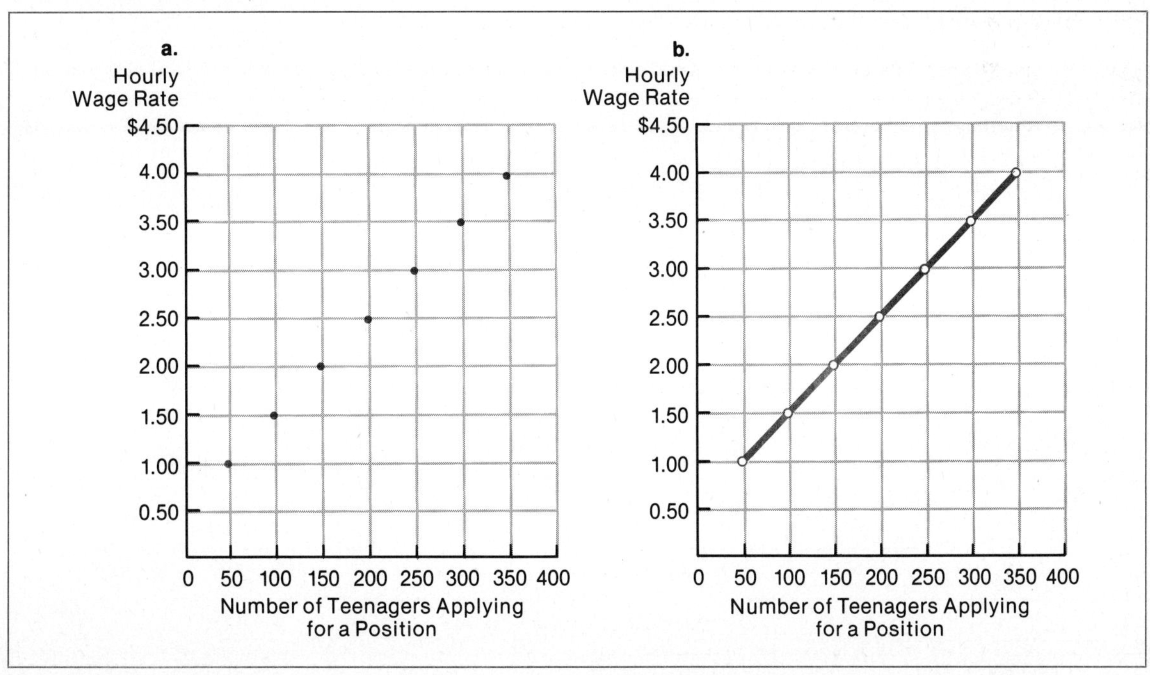

Figure 1A.3
Examples of Direct and Inverse Relationships

What type of relationship (direct or inverse) is illustrated in each of these graphs?

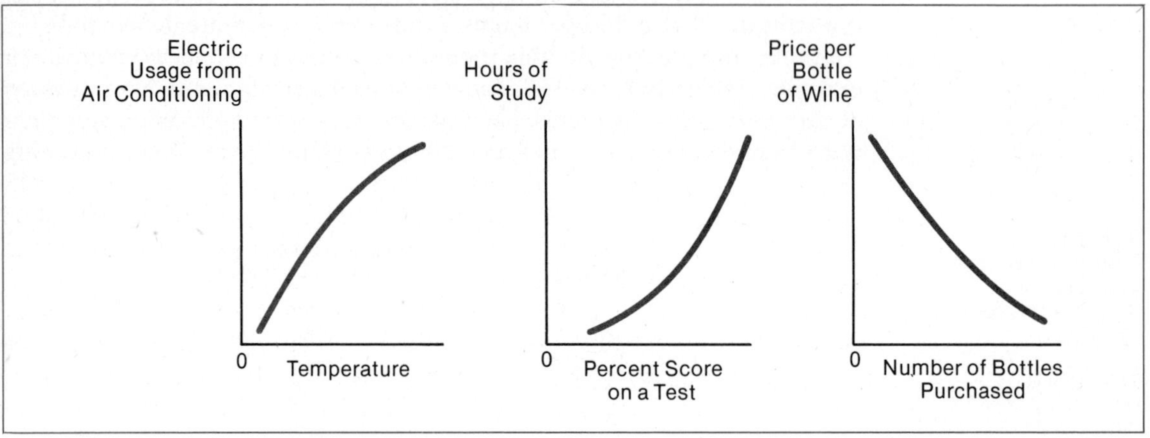

Figure 1A.4
Numbers of Homes with Dishwashers[a]

The appearance of data in a graph and the impression created for the reader can be affected by the spacing of numbers on the axes of the graph.

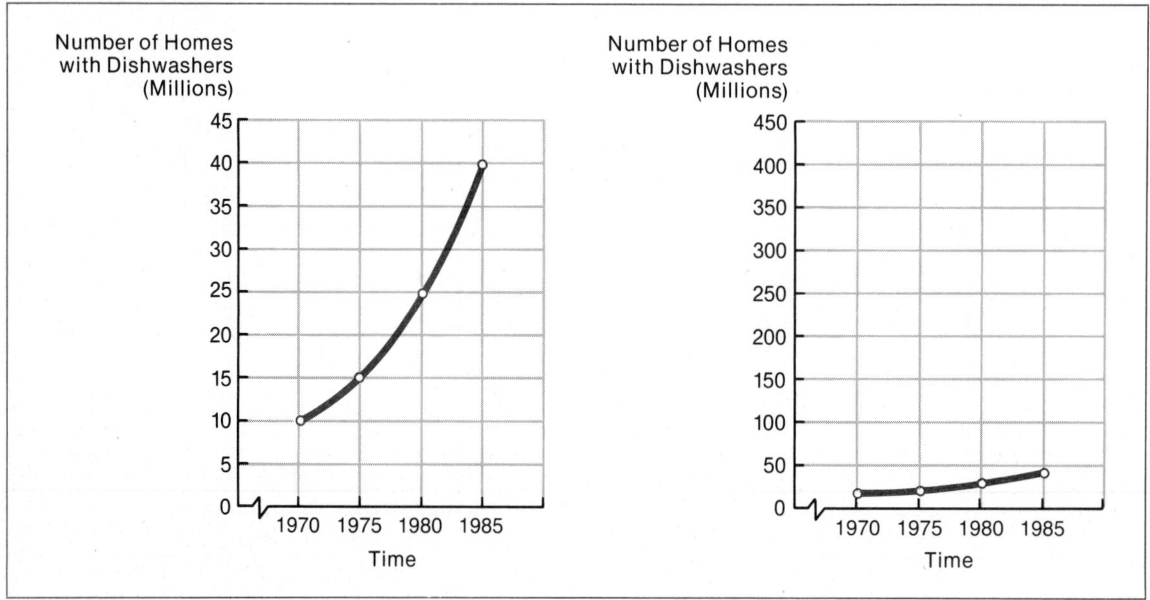

[a] Hypothetical data.

then connected to form the line given in Figure 1A.2b. (Notice that in Figure 1A.2, 50¢ is included on the vertical axis of both graphs although this was not given as a wage rate in the table. Why is this done?)

Earlier in the chapter, in Application 1.3, "Interpreting a Graph," it was pointed out that the slope of a line in a graph indicates whether there is a direct or an inverse relationship between the variables. An upward sloping line results from a direct relationship between the variables, and a downward sloping line results from an inverse relationship between the variables. Obviously, Figure 1A.2b indicates a direct relationship between hourly wage rates and the numbers of teenagers applying for a job. Using the information from Application 1.3, explain what is meant by a direct or inverse relationship. What do the lines in Figure 1A.3 say about the relationships in those graphs? Be specific in your answers.

It should be noted at this point that students often have trouble reading a graph when there are no numbers given on the axes. If this is the case with you, just put a few hypothetical numbers along each axis and try reading it again. (Remember the rules for numbering when you do this.) After you have some practice in reading graphs, this problem should disappear.

In interpreting information given in graphs, one should be aware that graphs can be used to present a point of view in a way that is often not apparent to the reader. For example, the two graphs in Figure 1A.4 give exactly the same information, yet they do not look the same. What is the difference between them? Why would someone choose to use a figure such as the one to the left rather than the one to the right?[2]

[2]The difference between the two graphs in Figure 1A.4 is the spacing used for the numbers on the vertical axis. The graph to the left uses each vertical mark to represent 5 million dishwashers, and the graph to the right uses each vertical mark to represent 50 million dishwashers. When the unit of measure of the variable on the vertical axis is given a wider space, it results in a line that appears to be more steeply sloped than the line that would result if a narrower space were given to the unit of measure. If one wanted to create the impression of a dramatic increase or decrease in the variable measured on the vertical axis, then one would use more exaggerated spacing. To create the impression of a relatively small increase or decrease, narrower spacing would be used.

2 ECONOMIC DECISION MAKING AND ECONOMIC SYSTEMS

Chapter Objectives

1. To introduce the basic economic choices that must be made in every society because of scarcity.
2. To introduce the manner in which different economic systems make the basic economic decisions.
3. To differentiate between a planned and market economy, and to explain the structure and operation of a market economy.
4. To illustrate where and how government can intervene in decision making in a mixed economy.
5. To distinguish among capitalism, mixed capitalism, and socialism.
6. To explore the British foundations of U.S. capitalism and the historical highlights in the development of U.S. capitalism.

Chapter One makes clear that the study of economics is based on the scarcity of material things. No economy can provide enough automobiles, magazines, welding machines, parks, fire engines, and other goods and services to satisfy everyone. Because of this, people in every economy must make decisions about what goods and services will be produced and who will receive them. In this chapter we focus on those decisions and how they are made in different societies or economies.

SCARCITY AND SOCIETY'S BASIC ECONOMIC DECISIONS

Each year every economy produces some combination of goods and services. In a recent year approximately $3.1 trillion worth of goods and services, including 711 billion cigarettes, 131.8 million pairs of women's shoes, and over 18 million hairdryers were made in the United States.[1] Unfortunately, this voluminous amount of "stuff" served only to satisfy some of the wants and needs of some of the people; the economy was incapable of satisfying all the wants and needs of all of its citizens.

How do we decide which wants and needs to satisfy for which people? How does an economy arrive at its particular product mix? Why do some people acquire a new Corvette while others do not, and why do some households eat steak while others eat hamburger? The economic predicament is similar to that faced by Santa Claus—millions of cherubic boys and girls dreaming of endless toys but only one workshop, a few elves, and just one sleigh to carry the goodies. What does Santa put in the bag on Christmas Eve?

Every economy, regardless of its wealth and power, has to make certain choices concerning production and distribution. Specifically, decision makers in every economy must choose: (1) what goods and services are to be produced and in what quantities; (2) how these goods and services are to be produced; and (3) how these goods and services are to be distributed.

The first economic question, what is to be produced, refers to the fact that every society must decide on the types and quantities of goods and services it will produce. In the case of motor vehicles, as an example, it must first be decided that motor vehicles are one of the goods that will be produced. Next the decision must be made as to what types of motor vehicles to produce (passenger cars, buses, pickup trucks, recreational vehicles, and so forth). Finally, how many of each type of vehicle to produce must be determined.

The second economic question, how goods and services are to be produced, refers to the ways in which scarce resources can be combined to make those items. For example, a pair of tennis shoes can be constructed by machinery or by hand, and the material can be vinyl, cotton, or another appropriate fabric. Electricity can be produced by firing generators with water, coal, oil, or nuclear power. Somehow the decision must be made as to which resources and processes to use in production.

The third question, to whom do the produced goods and services go, refers to distribution. It must be decided which members of society will receive what share of the limited goods and services that have been produced. To whom will the running shoes, medical services, homes, and frozen dinners go?

---

[1]U.S. Bureau of the Census, *Statistical Abstract of the United States: 1985* (105th ed.), Washington, D.C., 1984, pp. 431, 766, 768, 777.

ECONOMIC SYSTEMS

The Basic Economic Choices and Economic Systems

Economic system
The way in which an economy is organized; defined by the method chosen to make the basic economic choices.

The manner in which a society makes the three critical economic choices depends upon its **economic system.** An economic system is a particular way of organizing the relationships among businesses, households, and the government to make basic choices about what goods and services to produce, how to produce them, and to whom they will go. For purposes of classification, it is helpful to define three basic types of economic systems: a planned economy, a market economy, and a mixed economy.

In a planned economy, the basic economic decisions are made by planners who are either associated with the government or are in some other way representative of the members of the society. In a market economy, the decisions are made through the interactions of individual buyers and sellers in the marketplace. A mixed economy is one which combines elements of planning and individual decision making. It may range from a basic market economy with some degree of government intervention, to a basic planned economy with some dependence on individual decisions made in markets. The relationship between scarcity, the basic economic choices, and economic systems is summarized in Figure 2.1.

Figure 2.1
Scarcity, Basic Economic Choices, and Economic Systems

Scarcity imposes three basic economic choices on a society. The manner in which these choices are made depends upon a society's economic system.

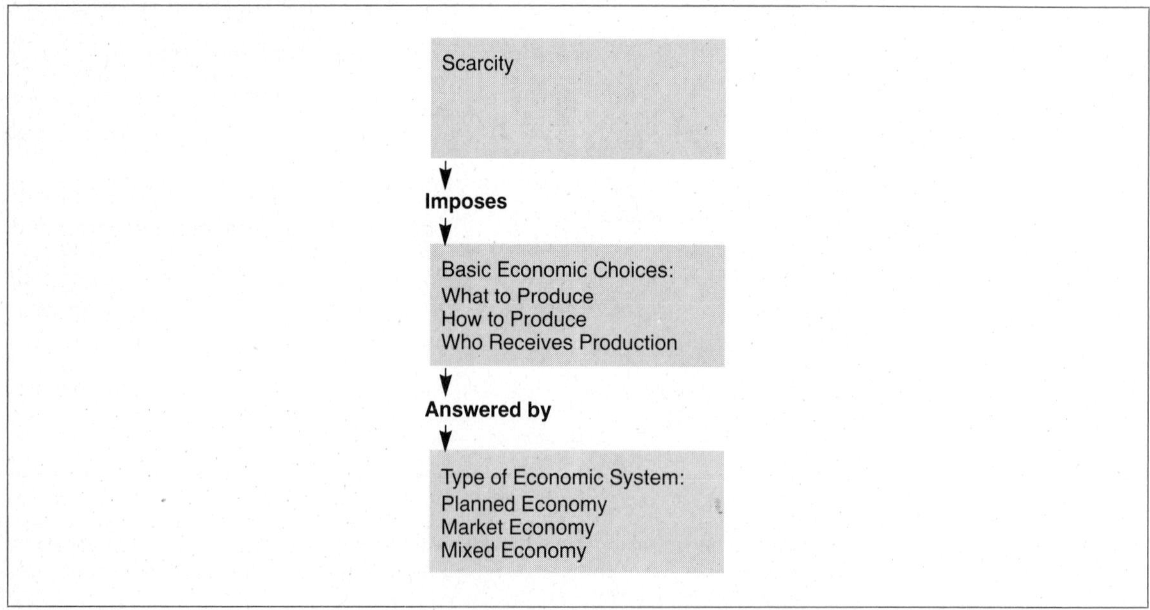

A Planned Economy

Planned economy (command economy)
An economy in which the basic economic decisions are made by planners rather than by private individuals and businesses.

A **planned economy,** also termed **command economy,** is one where the basic economic choices are made by a planning authority, which may be a government agency, bureau, commission, or the like. If the economy is purely planned, allowing no market activity, an extensive bureaucracy may be necessary to make millions of detailed economic decisions and to deal with the vast numbers of problems that invariably arise. A planned economy usually operates according to a blueprint (termed a "plan") that establishes stated general objectives to be accomplished in some specified period of time. There may be an overall long-range plan (perhaps for ten or twenty years) with several short-range plans (perhaps for two or five years) and some yearly or quarterly plans. For example, the Soviet Union, which is considered to be a planned economy although there is some market activity, has operated under a series of five-year plans.

Although the objectives of most plans are primarily economic, noneconomic considerations such as political, social, and military goals can be important as well. For example, a plan may call for the development of a steel industry, the building up of a powerful navy, the elimination of unemployment, or any other objective.

In a planned economy, the first economic question, what should be produced, is decided by the planning authority. The types, as well as the amounts, of goods and services to be produced are decided by administrative command in order to accomplish the stated objectives of the plan. That is, the planners, through their value judgments, determine which goods and services will be made and the amounts of each. Planners determine whether and how many cars, buses, appliances, submarines, dry-cleaning plants, shoes, and other items are to be produced. For example, if the planning authority feels that resources that could be used for assembling television sets are needed for computers, then fewer television sets are produced, regardless of how much they are in demand. If the planners determine that every household should have a television set, then forces will be set into motion to accomplish that objective.

In other words, the desired point at which an economy should operate on its production possibilities curve is decided by administrative command. This is illustrated in Figure 2.2. Whether the economy given in this figure should operate at point A, producing six million television sets and 100,000 computers, or at point B, producing two million television sets and 300,000 computers, or at any other point, is decided by the planners.[2]

The second economic question, how goods and services are to be produced, is again decided by the planning authority, although the authority's

[2]Be careful to note the difference between a plan and an accomplished objective. A planner's determination of where an economy should operate can be vastly different from where it actually does operate. Many events beyond a planner's control may occur to alter a plan: poor weather conditions for crops, international crises, political unrest, and unforeseen bottlenecks in production, to name a few.

Figure 2.2
Production Possibilities in a Planned Economy

In a planned economy, the policy makers decide at which point on the production possibilities curve the economy should operate.

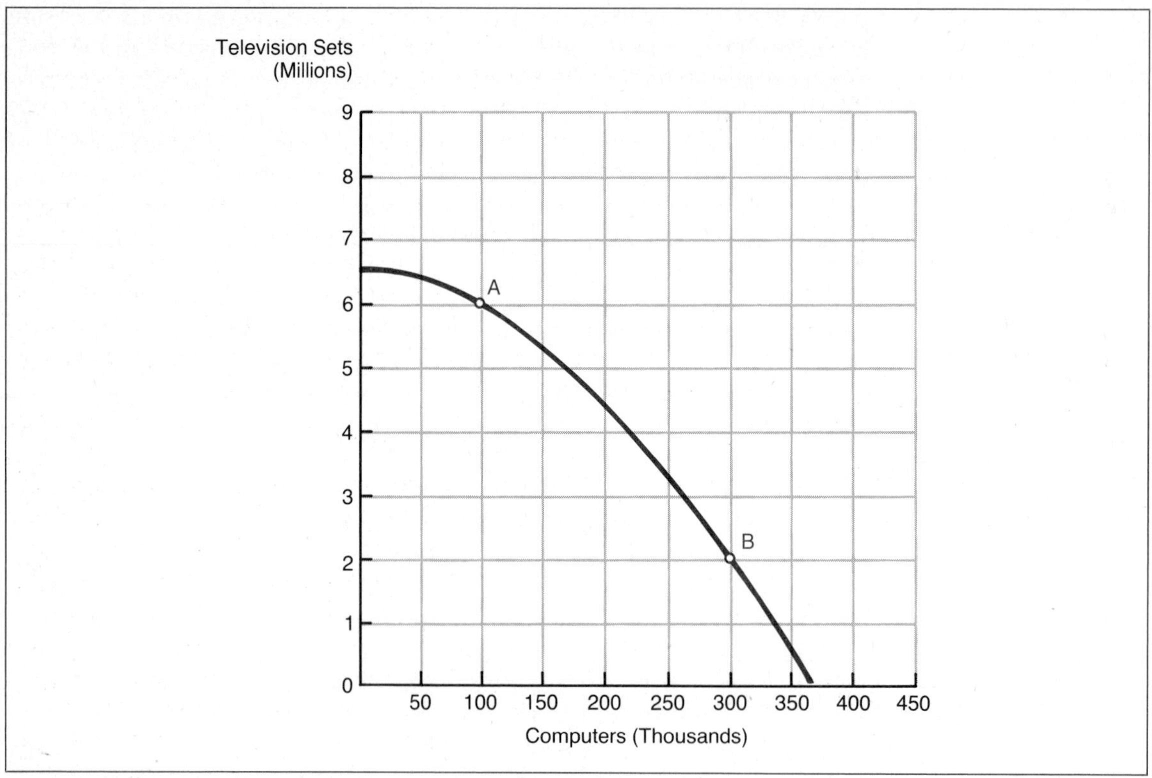

influence is more indirect than it is for the first question. Imagine the difficulty in instructing every business on how to produce its particular type of good or service! Because of this complexity, pure planning to resolve this economic question becomes cumbersome and may force the planning authority to depend on incentives, bonuses, and other nonplanned activities to accomplish its objectives.

The main influence planners have over how goods and services will be produced comes through determining the types of resources, or factors of production, and processes to be made available to producers. For example, in printing, type can be set by a staff of keyboard operators or automatically by sophisticated electronic equipment. If planners wish to keep keyboard typesetters employed, they will simply not permit or "plan for" the production of electronic typesetting machinery. Businesses will then use what is available—the keyboard typesetter. In a purely planned economy a producer cannot order a machine, part, or piece of equipment if the authority has not permitted it to be produced.

To whom do the produced goods and services go, the third economic question, is again decided by the planners. A rationing system for the distribution of goods and services could be instituted where households are allotted specific items (for example, two pairs of shoes per year or one coat). An alternative distribution method would be to permit households to freely purchase what has been produced through the plan. If households are allowed to choose goods and services for themselves, then planners face the additional problem of income determination. That is, they must decide how much the various factors of production should be paid for their services.

Application 2.1 contains excerpts from Hedrick Smith's book, *The Russians,* which focuses on the life of the average Soviet citizen and is based on the experiences of Smith and his family during his three years as *New York Times* Bureau Chief in Moscow. Each of these passages relates to some facet of life in a planned economy. Some passages point out the weaknesses of planning, and some deal with problems that have arisen because Soviet planners have focused on the production of capital and military goods rather than the production of consumer goods in recent decades.

In general, several problems can emerge in a planned economy. First, the goods and services considered to be valuable by the planners may not be important to the consumers for whom they are intended. This could result in the overproduction of some items and the underproduction of others. Second, the complexity of planning the resources and processes used in production may create bottlenecks and stoppages in the production process. And, third, because of a lack of incentives, the quality of goods and services produced may be inferior.

What advantages of the planning mechanism offset these weaknesses? It may be easier in a planned economy than in a less formally organized economy to achieve certain goals set by a society. For example, the build-up of a military establishment, the elimination of poverty, or the construction of heavy industrial plants might be accomplished faster in a planned economy. It is also easier to eliminate unemployment by ordering the use of more labor in production processes.

A Market Economy

A **market economy** is one in which the basic economic choices are made by buyers and sellers interacting in a marketplace.[3] A market system is also termed a **price system** because price is the language through which buyers and sellers communicate their intentions. For example, McDonald's expresses its intention to sell Big Macs by making them available at a particular price, and a student tells McDonald's that he or she wants a Big Mac by

Market economy
An economy in which the basic economic decisions are made through the interaction of buyers and sellers in a market using the language of price.

Price system
A market system; one in which buyers and sellers communicate their intentions through prices in a market.

[3]A market is defined as a place or situation in which the buyers and sellers of a product interact for the purpose of exchange.

paying the price asked. The exchange of the burger is made because the price is suitable to both buyer and seller.

A totally pure market system is virtually nonexistent in the world today, although it is the philosophical basis for economies such as that of the United States. Historically, the U.S. economy has been closer to a pure market system than it is now. Over the years, while still keeping the market tradition, the United States has become more of a mixed economy as government influence and regulation have increased.

It is noteworthy that markets have existed in different types of economies throughout the history of the world. In some instances markets have served simply as allocation mechanisms to aid in answering one of the economic questions. Recall from Application 2.1 that buyers and sellers in the Soviet Union, a basically planned economy, frequently interact in markets. What we are concerned with at this point, however, is not the operation of a market as an allocation mechanism, but rather with the study of an entire economic system in which all decisions are made solely through the interaction of buyers and sellers in markets.

Application 2.1
LIFE IN A PLANNED ECONOMY: *THE RUSSIANS*

In spite of the various tinkering reforms, the Soviet economy still operates by Plan from above rather than in response to consumer demand from below and this produces a lopsided assortment of goods. Goods are produced to fill the Plan, not to sell. Sometimes the anomalies are baffling. Leningrad can be overstocked with cross-country skis and yet go several months without soap for washing dishes. In the Armenian capital of Yerevan, I found an ample supply of accordions but local people complained they had gone for weeks without ordinary kitchen spoons or tea samovars. I knew a Moscow family that spent a frantic month hunting for a child's potty while radios were a glut on the market. . . .

[A] cardinal rule of Russian consumer life is shopping for others. It is an unforgivable sin, for example, to run across something as rare as pineapples, Polish-made bras, East German wall-lamps or Yugoslav toothpaste without buying some extras for your best friend at work, your mother, sister, daughter, husband, brother-in-law, or some other kin or neighbor. As a result, I was amazed to discover, people know by heart the shoe, bra, pant and dress sizes, waist and length measurements, color preferences and other vital particulars for a whole stable of their nearest and dearest to be ready for that moment when lightning strikes a store they happen to be in. Then they spend until the money runs out. . . .

The only real taste of stoical shopping vigils in recent American history were the pre-dawn lines at service stations during the gasoline crisis in the winter of 1973–74. That produced a wave of national self-pity in America. But it was temporary and only for one item. Imagine it across the board, all the time, and you realize that Soviet shopping is like a year-round Christmas rush. The accepted norm is that the Soviet woman daily spends two hours in line, seven days a week, daily going through double the gauntlet

Circular flow model A diagram showing the real and money flows between households and businesses and the relationships between households and businesses in output, or product, markets and input, or resource, markets.

Output markets (product markets) Those markets in which businesses are sellers and households are buyers; consumer goods and services are exchanged.

The Operation of a Market Economy The operation of a market economy can be illustrated by a **circular flow model,** which shows how businesses and households relate to one another as buyers and sellers. In one part of this relationship, businesses are the sellers of goods and services and households are the buyers. Shown in Figure 2.3, this part of the relationship involves a "real flow" of goods and services from businesses to households, and a "money flow" of dollars from households to businesses. For example, autos, t-shirts, records, tacos, and furniture flow to households, which give businesses dollars for these items. Transactions of this type, where businesses are the sellers of goods and services and households are the buyers, occur in **output,** or **product, markets.** In these markets a buyer and seller may deal with one another face to face as in an automobile showroom or restaurant, or their dealings might be more impersonal as in the case of a buyer ordering from a catalogue or using a vending machine.

In the second part of the market household-business relationship, businesses are the buyers and households are the sellers. In order for businesses to produce goods and services they need resources, or factors of production,

that the American housewife undergoes at her supermarket once, maybe twice a week. I noted in the Soviet press that Russians spend 30 billion man-hours in line annually just to make purchases. That does not count several billion more man-hours expended waiting in tailor shops, barbershops, post offices, savings banks, dry cleaners and various receiving points, for turning in empty bottles and so on. But 30 billion man-hours alone is enough to keep 15 million workers busy year-round on a 40-hour week. . . .

One positive result of the consumer's eternal gauntlet, however, is that any unusual purchase is a possession to be prized and cherished. Russians are less materialistic than Americans and yet they have a warm sense of extra pleasure and achievement over relatively simple things, much more than do Westerners for whom the buying is easier. "In America, if your wife has bought a nice new dress and I notice it, I will say, 'Oh, yes, that's nice,' and that's all," suggested a woman journalist who had seen America and mixed with Americans. "But in Moscow, when I get my hands on a pair of shoes that I like, it is an achievement, a feat, an exploit. It means that I have managed to work it out in some complicated way through a friend or perhaps I have found a sales clerk to bribe or I have gone from store to store and I have stood in line for hours. Notice how I put it, not simply 'bought some shoes' but 'got my hands on a pair of shoes.' So when I get the shoes I like, I am *very* proud of them. And friends say to me, 'Oho, you have new shoes! Tell me, where did you get them?' And it is not just an idle, polite question, it is a real question. Because they are thinking, 'Maybe she can help me get a pair. Maybe I can get a pair of nice shoes like that for myself.' Americans simply cannot grasp that, can they?" She was right for I have seen that look of triumphant excitement in the eyes of women who have stood in line for an eon and just come away with a nice chignon or a Yugoslav sweater. It is a heartwarming sight.

Figure 2.3
Exchange in Output Markets

Businesses sell goods and services to households for money in output, or product, markets.

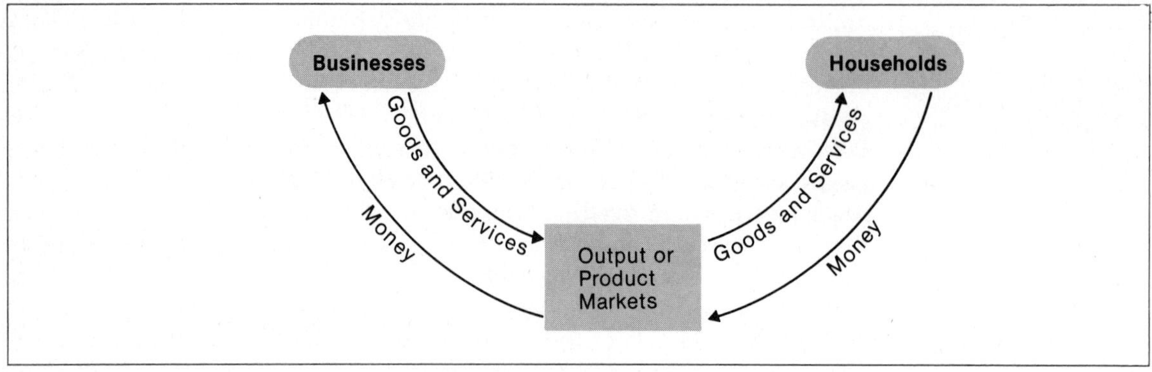

which belong to households. In Figure 2.4, we see a real flow of land, labor, capital, and entrepreneurship going from households (the sellers) to businesses (the buyers). In return for these resources businesses send a money flow of wages, rents, interest, and profits to households. For example, in order to produce a car, auto workers are needed. They sell their services to the car manufacturers for an income. These transactions involving the exchange of factors of production occur in **input,** or **resource, markets.**

Input markets (resource markets)
Those markets in which the factors of production are bought and sold; households are sellers and businesses are buyers.

The structure of a market economy can be fully explained by putting the two buyer-seller relationships of businesses and households together as shown in Figure 2.5. Businesses and households relate to one another through input markets and output markets. Households sell land, labor, capital, and entrepreneurship to businesses in return for income in input mar-

Figure 2.4
Exchange in Input Markets

Households sell factors of production to businesses for an income in input, or resource, markets.

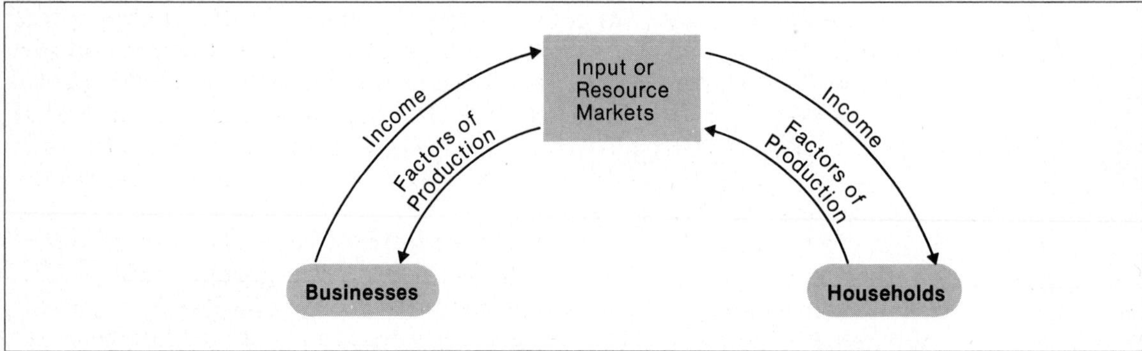

Figure 2.5
Circular Flow of Economic Activity

Households sell factors of production to businesses in input markets, and businesses sell goods and services to households in output markets.

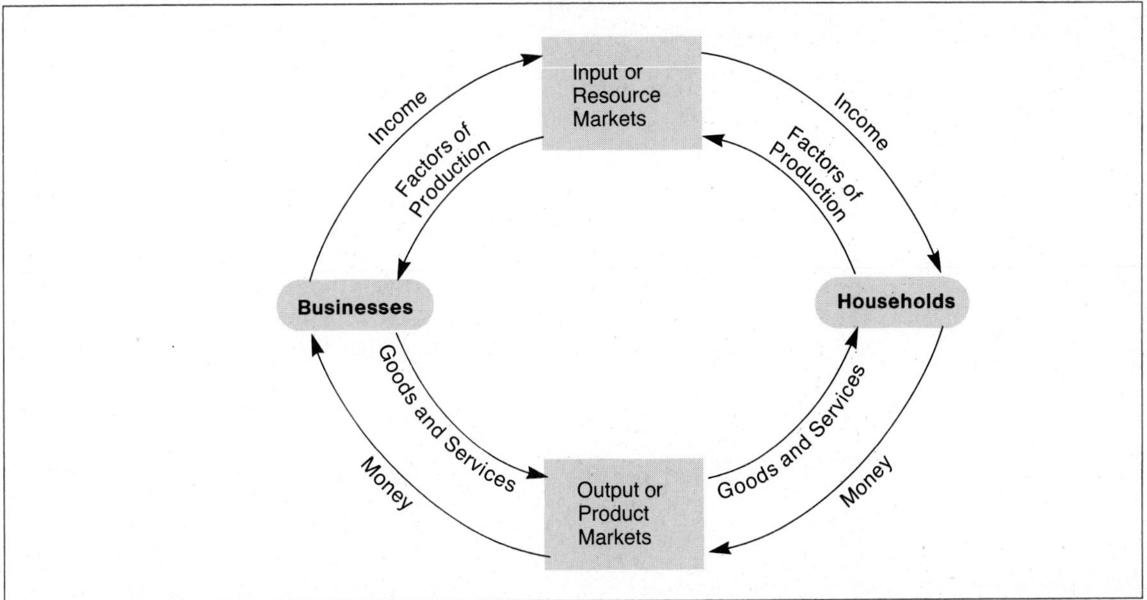

kets. That income is then used to buy goods and services from businesses in output markets.

Economic Decisions in a Market Economy How are the critical economic choices of what, how, and to whom made in a market system? What is produced, as well as how much is produced, is the result of millions of independent decisions by individual households and businesses in the marketplace. An item will be made if a business perceives that enough households will purchase the item at a price that will make its production profitable. If a business determines that individuals do not want a good or service, or will not pay a profitable price, the business will eventually stop producing that item. This type of decision making accounts for the continued appearance of pocket calculators and the Ford Mustang, and the disappearance of particular clothing styles and the slide rule from the market. Also, the emergence of such items as the personal computer and portable television resulted from household demand for these products and the ability of businesses to produce and sell them at a profit.

Is it believable that individual buyers can force large sellers like auto manufacturers or apartment-complex developers to change their products? The power balance between a single person and a single business is obviously weighted in favor of the business. Yet individuals do influence businesses.

Table 2.1
Costs of Stereo Receiver Assembly Using Different Production Methods

Method 2 illustrates the least-cost method of producing stereo receivers.

Methods of Assembly	Cost to Company per Unit
1. All machine-assembled	$150.00
2. Hand-and-machine-assembled	130.00
3. All hand-assembled	160.00

While one buyer acting alone may be virtually powerless against a business, the situation changes when many buyers share the same opinion. Without talking to one another, individual buyers decide for or against a product by the way they spend their money. The dollars consumers spend for businesses' products are tallied in the same way that electoral votes are tallied for a political candidate. Those businesses which do not get enough dollar votes may be forced to change their products or leave the market completely.[4]

The manner in which the second critical question, how goods and services will be produced, is answered in a market economy can be shown by a simple example. Suppose that a company decides that it wants to market a stereo receiver, and its production engineers identify three possible methods for assembling the product: by hand, by machine, or by a combination of the two. The cost associated with each method is given in Table 2.1. Suppose also that there is no difference between a hand-assembled, machine-assembled, or hand-and-machine-assembled receiver.

Efficient method of production
The least-cost method of production.

Which method of production will the company choose? It would be reasonable to expect that it will choose the second method—the **least-cost method of production,** or what economists call the most **efficient** method. This is because it is in the best interest of the individuals owning the business to operate at the lowest cost of production. Owners receive a profit from producing a good or service which is equal to what is left from the income of the business after all accounting costs have been met. The more that is left over, the greater is the owners' profit. For example, if the stereo manufacturer can sell each receiver for $160, its owners will receive a profit of $10 per unit using the first method or no profit per unit using the third method. But if they choose the second method, which is the least-cost method, their profit will be $30 per unit.

What is true for this company selling in a market economy is also true for other sellers in a market economy: that is, in the interest of profit, businesses

[4]An important question must be raised: to what extent are individuals' decisions influenced by businesses' advertising and other promotional activities? If businesses exert a strong influence on people's attitudes and tastes, do the dollars consumers spend reflect their independent choices, or do they represent something else? Put differently, do businesses respond to consumers' preferences, do they shape those preferences, or is there some mixture of the two? The independence of consumers' economic decision making is a very controversial issue. What is your position on this question?

seek the lowest cost of production in providing goods and services. Thus, the second basic economic question of how goods and services will be produced is answered in a market economy by businesses through their choices of the least-cost method of production.

Which method of production is cheapest depends on the prices a business must pay for its factors of production and how those factors are used. In the United States, for example, agriculture has become highly mechanized with a dependence on sophisticated pieces of machinery for planting and harvesting. In many other countries crops are grown by persons using only shovels and hoes. Given the cost of farm machinery and labor and the way each is used, it is cheaper for U.S. farmers to mechanize than to try to grow and harvest the same output using mainly labor. The same is not true for producers in other parts of the world where abundant labor and cheaper labor costs (relative to machinery costs) result in a greater dependence on human effort.

How the third economic question, who receives the produced goods and services, is answered in a market economy can be illustrated through a circular flow model such as that in Figure 2.5. In the output markets, a flow of goods and services going to households from businesses is matched by a flow of dollars going the other way. In a market economy a person will receive an item only if he or she can pay for it. In other words, in a market economy goods and services are distributed to those who can afford them.

A household's ability to afford goods and services depends on the value of the factors of production it has to sell in the resource markets. People lacking marketable skills are not paid well in the resource market, causing them to fare poorly in acquiring goods and services. People commanding many resources, or resources that are highly valued, may enjoy a substantial income from the input markets, enabling them to buy the items they want in the output markets. In other words, if you own a successful corporation (capital and entrepreneurship), a few oil wells (land), and are the president of a bank (labor), you may well afford a Rolls Royce, a country home, an original Matisse, and steak dinners.

In summary, in a market economy the basic economic choices are made by individual buyers and sellers. Businesses produce the goods and services that buyers indicate they want by their spending patterns in the markets. These goods and services are produced using the least-cost method of production, since this method allows the owners of businesses to maximize their profits. Finally, it is the individual household's ability to sell its own resources in the input markets that determines its ability to acquire the goods and services of its choice.

A market economy, like a planned economy, has both strengths and weaknesses. On the plus side, market economies are efficient because of the operation of incentives. The profit incentive causes businesses to produce in an efficient manner, and income rewards provide an incentive for households to use their resources effectively or to improve them. Many students, for example, invest in an education to become more productive in input markets and obtain a higher salary. Market systems are also efficient in that the information required for decisions on production and distribution passes directly between buyers and sellers rather than through a central clearing house as in a planned economy. The market, rather than a planner, coordinates business and household actions. An additional strength of a market economy is that production and distribution decisions reflect the value judgments of buyers and sellers in the market rather than the value judgments of planners.

One of the weaknesses of a market system is that it offers no protection for people lacking adequate knowledge to make informed market decisions. For example, the effects of chemicals used in certain foods and medications or the inner workings of an automobile or appliance may not be fully understood by the average consumer. In a market system, there is no organized effort to ensure that products will be safe for use by the uninformed consumer. There is also nothing in the market mechanism to ensure that households lacking adequate resources will be able to acquire enough goods and services to maintain themselves. Put another way, a market does not have a morality of its own.

A Mixed Economy

Mixed economy
An economy in which the basic economic decisions are made through a combination of market and centralized decision making.

The third type of economic system is a **mixed economy.** In this system the three basic questions are answered by some combination of market and centralized decision making. Technically, all economies are mixed. Pure market and pure planned economies are polar cases that help us order our thinking but have no real world counterparts. Thus, an important factor giving different economies their unique styles is the manner and degree to which individual and planned decision making are combined.

While all economies are mixed, the term "mixed economy" has come to be most closely associated with those systems that depend primarily on markets but also include some government intervention in decision making. The relationship between the government, households, and businesses in a mixed economy can be both extensive and complicated. In understanding that relationship, a useful starting point is to examine where and how government can intervene in economic affairs.

As shown in the circular flow model in Figure 2.6, despite the apparent complexity of a mixed economy, government intervention can occur in only four places: (1) the business sector, (2) the household sector, (3) output markets, and (4) input markets. Since the circular flow of activity in a market system centers around these four components, government intervention is automatically limited to these areas if the basic market system is to be preserved.

Answering the question of how government intervenes in economic affairs is more complicated than the question of where intervention occurs. We can identify several general ways in which government influences decision making: establishing the rules of the game, regulating specific indus-

Figure 2.6
Government Intervention in a Market Economy

Government can intervene in four basic areas of a market economy in specific ways, as the examples illustrate.

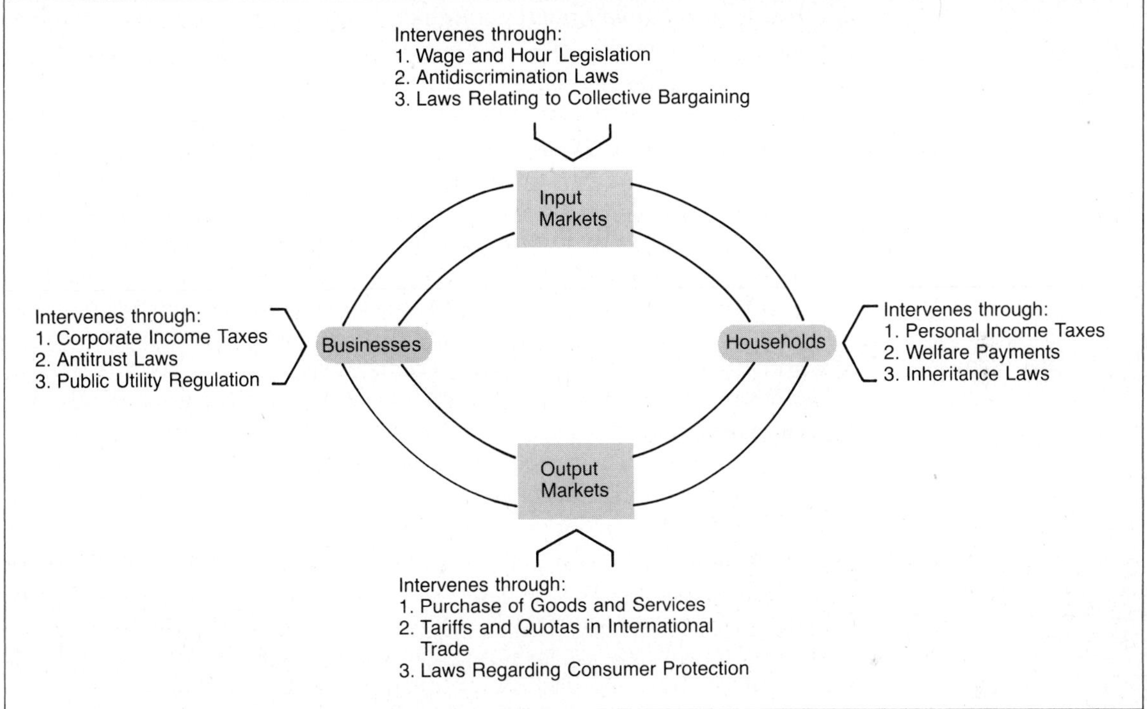

tries, regulating certain aspects of business or production, protecting workers and wages, taxing and spending, and maintaining income support programs. Within these and other broad categories,[5] any number or type of laws can be enacted, their specifics differing from economy to economy. Since the United States is considered to be a mixed economy, we can further understand government's impact on basic market decision making by examining the experience of the United States in each of the above areas.

Establishing the rules of the game refers to the government's role in setting the legal framework within which businesses and households must operate when dealing with one another. This framework extends to all four areas of the circular flow and involves such items as the definition of property rights, contracts, and court procedures. Also included in this category in the United States are the antitrust laws. These were passed in order to preserve and maintain competition and prohibit certain business practices that

[5]Government intervention in a market economy is not limited to the categories identified here.

could ruin competition. For example, the Celler-Kefauver Act of 1950 forbids anticompetitive mergers,[6] and the Sherman Act of 1890 forbids sellers from coming together to fix prices among themselves.

With regulation of specific industries, business ownership remains in private hands but a government commission oversees and becomes involved in many managerial decisions. These decisions range from considerations about pricing and profit to the availability of service. In the United States, the communications, natural gas, water, and electric utility industries are subject to widespread regulation. Each state, for example, has a public utilities commission that basically (although this varies some from state to state) has the ability to allow or disallow price increases and determines the rate of profit to be earned by the utilities. Until recent years the airline industry was subject to extensive regulation. The Civil Aeronautics Board (CAB), for example, had to approve the routes airlines could fly, and an airline could not, without permission, cancel a flight because there were too few passengers nor add a flight because there were too many.

Government regulation of certain aspects of business or production focuses on the business sector and output markets. This type of regulation is directed toward specific problems or activities and may have an impact on many different kinds of businesses. For example, the Environmental Protection Agency (EPA) was set up to deal with various types of pollution problems. The Food and Drug Administration (FDA) is responsible for determining the purity and safety of most foods, medicines, cosmetics, and medical devices. It also tests chemical and color additives and is empowered to ban their use. The U.S. government has also become involved in the regulation of auto safety, general consumer product safety, false and deceptive advertising, weights and measures, and countless other areas.[7]

Worker and wage protection is an example of government intervention into production as well as into input, or resource, markets. In the United States most industries are required to pay workers a minimum wage. The government has also passed many laws relating to collective bargaining and other union activities. For example, the Wagner Act in 1935 set up the National Labor Relations Board (NLRB) to supervise union elections and prohibit unfair labor practices by management. More recently, the Occupational Safety and Health Administration (OSHA) was created to ensure safe and healthy working conditions for the laborer.

Government taxing and spending policies can influence economic activity in two ways. First, as government becomes a large spending unit it can influence certain industries or markets because of the sheer size of its buying ability. Government purchases range from aircraft and ocean-going ships to paper and cement. Second, government can tax and spend in a manner that

---

[6]A merger occurs when one company acquires another. This may be done through the outright purchase of a company's assets or through the acquisition of the controlling shares of stock in a corporation.

[7]See Table 15.4 for further examples of special purpose regulation.

can improve or worsen the employment or inflation conditions in an economy. That is, government taxing and spending policies can expand or contract the economy. For example, Congress has several times cut the personal income tax to stimulate a sluggish economy.

The final type of government intervention is through income support programs. These can take the form of outright grants of money or goods and services to individuals to provide for their maintenance, or they can involve special programs to improve a person's earning potential. Examples of direct government aid include welfare checks, unemployment compensation, social security payments, farm subsidies, and food stamps. Special programs in the area of job training have been created to enable a person to learn marketable skills.

Why does government intervene in the operation of a market economy in areas such as those just described? Basically, government is called upon to interrupt the decision making of households and businesses when society identifies a **market failure.** Market failure occurs when a goal set by society cannot be achieved within the basic framework of a market economy, or when society identifies a problem that arises due to the functioning of a market system. For example, in the United States, government enacted legislation to preserve competition because society identified competition as a goal, and because a market system left unregulated may tend toward monopoly. In a market system, a business may seek to eliminate its competition. Other market failures that have been identified include the failure to provide income for nonproductive members of society, and the failure of market prices to cover the cost of protecting the environment.

Market Failure
Occurs when a market system generates a problem or cannot achieve a goal set by society.

Capitalism vs. Socialism

Up to now we have been classifying economies on the basis of whether the fundamental economic choices are made in markets by households and businesses or according to a plan or command. A second, perhaps more popular, way of classifying economies groups them into capitalism, mixed capitalism, and socialism.

Capitalism describes an economic system in which the factors of production are privately owned and business is operated on a free enterprise basis. **Free enterprise** refers to the ability of businesses to function with a profit motive and to make their own decisions about price, quality, and other product related matters. In pure capitalism there is little room for government interference in economic decision making. Because of its characteristics, a capitalist system is associated with economic decision making in a market environment.

Mixed capitalism is a system which retains the essential features of capitalism, including a dependence on the market for decision making, but incorporates some degree of government intervention in decisions and markets.

Capitalism
An economic system with private property and free enterprise; economic decision making occurs in a market environment.

Free Enterprise
The right of a business to make its own decisions and to operate with a profit motive.

Mixed capitalism
An economic system with the basic features of capitalism but with some degree of government intervention in economic decision making.

Socialism
An economic system in which many of the factors of production are collectively owned and there is an attempt to equalize the distribution of income.

A **socialist** system is one in which many of the factors of production are owned by the society itself and where there is an attempt to make the distribution of income more equal. A socialist system may depend heavily on planning, or may, as in the case of market socialism,[8] employ some planning but also rely heavily on markets.

Why classify economies as market or planned systems when the ideas of capitalism and socialism are available? There are several advantages to the market-planning approach. First, this approach is purely economic. It highlights how societies deal with scarcity and the critical economic decisions caused by scarcity. It also helps to define the roles of households and businesses and points out whether they solve the scarcity problem by acting independently using individual value judgments in markets or through group planning.

A second reason for using this approach is that the notions of markets and planning are more ideologically neutral than those of capitalism and socialism. For many people, "capitalism" and "socialism" have taken on important political and philosophical meanings beyond their simple economic definitions. For example, some people believe that capitalism represents an economic system which allows freedom, independence, and an opportunity to accumulate and control property. Others feel that it is a system where certain members of society are exploited by other members. To some, socialism represents a system where people share wealth and income, while to others it represents the suppression of individualism and self-initiative. As a result of these ideological overtones, this classification system may lead people to view economies as either capitalistic or socialistic, with nothing in between.

A third advantage in classifying economies as market or planned is that this approach allows us to sort economies (as well as changes within economies) according to the degree to which they depend on individual or collective decision making in answering the basic economic questions. For example, we might view different economies as falling along a continuum, such as that in Figure 2.7. At one end are the pure market economies (of which there are none in the real world), and at the other end are the pure planned economies (of which there are also none in the real world). In between are the world's economies, which differ from one another in the degree to which they employ markets or planning to answer the basic economic questions. The United States, which depends heavily on the market system, tends toward the pure market side, and the USSR, which depends primarily on planning, tends toward the other end. An economy such as England's might fall somewhere in the middle. This continuum is also help-

---

[8]In market socialism some goods and services (such as those used by households) are allocated through markets while others (such as machinery and equipment used by businesses) are allocated by the planners. See Oskar Lange, "On the Economic Theory of Socialism," *Comparative Economic Systems: Models and Cases,* ed. Morris Bornstein, (Homewood, Ill.: R. D. Irwin, Inc., 1979), pp. 117–125.

Figure 2.7
Continuum of Economic Decision Making

Economies can be classified according to their dependence on planned versus market decision making.

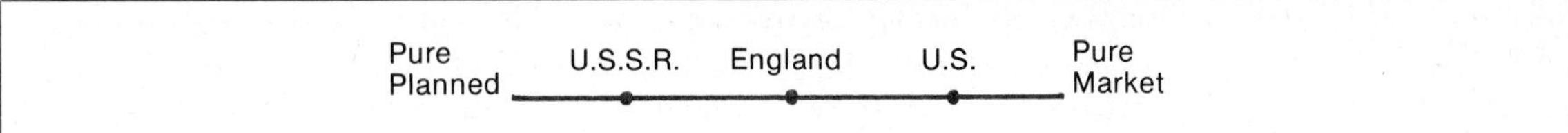

ful in classifying closely related economic and philosophical ideas. For example, the statement is often heard that the USSR is becoming more capitalistic and the United States more socialistic. Technically, this is incorrect because the USSR has not moved toward private ownership and the United States has not moved toward social ownership or nationalization. Rather, the USSR has moved to the right on the planning-market continuum, allowing more market activity, and the United States has moved toward the left on the continuum, relying more upon planning-type activities.

THE U.S. ECONOMIC SYSTEM

The U.S. economy has been described as a mixed economic system, basically dependent on markets and individual decision making with a lesser but important role played by government. The evolution of the U.S. economy into its present form can be understood by focusing on two important sets of developments: the first occurred in England and Scotland in the eighteenth and nineteenth centuries, and the second involved major historical events in the United States.

The British Foundations of U.S. Capitalism

Three factors helped to transform England into an industrial, market economy that served as a model, in both practical and philosophical terms, for United States capitalism. These factors were: the decline of mercantilism, the rise of an intellectual justification for a system of economic individualism, and the British Industrial Revolution.

Mercantilism
An economic system or a philosophy in which the interests of the nation are of the greatest importance; individual interests are subservient to those of the nation.

The Decline of Mercantilism An economic system in which the interests of the national state are of overriding importance is referred to as **mercantilism.** Fundamental to mercantilism is the idea that the state, rather than the individual, is the best judge of what is good for the economy. Historically, the system coincided with the rise of strong national states in England and France during the seventeenth and eighteenth centuries. Under mercantilism the purpose of economic activity was to increase the power of one's own nation relative to that of other nations. For example, a country could achieve this end by exporting goods and services in return for gold and silver, which would then be available for building the king's war chest; or a nation could increase its economic power by colonizing another country or newly discovered territory. Much of the early colonization of North America coincided with the mercantilist period.

By the end of the eighteenth century, mercantilism was challenged by a rising spirit of individualism among the people of Britain. Wesley C. Mitchell, a noted economist, observed that some of this rising spirit was expressed in business ventures spontaneously organized without the aid of government. Along with a growth in new businesses was the development of individual initiative in the arts, exploration, religion, and other areas.[9] In short, the directing role of government was being challenged and the foundations of mercantilism as an economic philosophy were crumbling in the face of growing individual achievement.

The Rise of an Intellectual Justification for a System of Economic Individualism In 1776 a Scottish philosophy professor named Adam Smith (1723–1790) published a book entitled *The Wealth of Nations* that was to have a major impact on economic thinking not only in his generation but in future generations as well. Smith's main contribution was not so much the novelty of his ideas as it was the forcefulness and systematic nature of his argument in favor of free enterprise. His thesis, put simply, was that the best way of increasing the wealth of a nation is through individual decision making with minimal government interference, a system which has come to be called **laissez-faire capitalism.** Smith, incidentally, is still regarded today as a champion of capitalist economies and is often quoted in that regard.

Laissez-faire capitalism
Capitalism with little or no government interference.

Invisible hand doctrine
Adam Smith's concept that producers acting in their own self-interest will provide buyers with what they want and thus advance the interests of society.

Central to Smith's argument for an economic system based on individual decision making was the **invisible hand doctrine.** According to this doctrine, Smith thought it foolish to expect that people would base their business dealings with others on benevolence, or the best interests of the other person. Rather, people carry on their business in a way that serves their own best interests. In a system of free and open competition, it is in the producer's or seller's best interest to try to give the buyer what he or she wants on terms that are acceptable to both of them. In this way, Smith believed, by pursuing one's own best interest, one is guided "as if by an invisible hand" to advance the interests of all society. There is no need for government to oversee the operation of the economy, since people working for their personal gain will achieve the most desired results. Thus, Smith's arguments and concepts provided an intellectual justification for an economic system based on individualism.

---

[9]W. C. Mitchell, *Types of Economic Theory*, vol. I, J. Dorfman, ed. (New York: Augustus M. Kelley, 1967), pp. 67–76.

Industrial Revolution A time period during which an economy becomes industrialized; characterized by social and technical changes such as the growth and development of factories.

The British Industrial Revolution From roughly 1750 to 1850, at the same time as the decline of mercantilism and the rise of the free enterprise philosophy, significant technological and social changes were occurring that would ultimately transform England into a modern industrial economy. These changes come to us today under the general heading of the British **Industrial Revolution.** The British experience with industrialization served as a model for other countries that had their own industrial revolutions at later dates, and it is important for understanding the development of the U.S. economy.

Prior to the mid-1700s, the British economy was primarily agricultural, with manufacturing carried on in simple cottage or home industries. Then a series of inventions and innovations began in the weaving of textiles and spread to other industries, changing the economy from one of agriculture and home production to a system fostering the growth of factories.

With industrialization came increased production as well as the introduction of many new kinds of goods. It was a time in which the economy made great strides in providing goods and services for its members.

Industrialization, however, had its darker side. People who worked in the factories experienced poor working conditions, low pay, and long hours. A reliance grew upon the labor of women and children, who were easier to control than men and would work for less. In fact, the impact of the factory system and industrialization on the people of Britain was staggering. As E. P. Cheyney put it:

> The introduction of the factory system involved many changes: the adoption of machinery and artificial power, the use of a vastly greater amount of capital, and the collection of scattered laborers into great strictly regulated establishments. It was, comparatively speaking, sudden, all its main features having been developed within the period between 1760 and 1800; and it resulted in the raising of many new and difficult social problems. For these reasons the term "Industrial Revolution," so generally applied to it, is not an exaggerated nor an unsuitable term.[10]

It may be no coincidence that in 1818 Mary W. Shelley wrote about the relationship between man and science in a work entitled *Frankenstein,* or that the poem excerpted in Application 2.2 made such a strong statement about factory working conditions.

In summary, the British contribution to U.S. capitalism was twofold. First, a philosophical and intellectual defense of individualism and free enterprise was introduced and adopted. Second, the British economy underwent significant changes that illustrated both the benefits of capitalism and the problems that this system could create.

---

[10]Edward P. Cheyney, *An Introduction to the Industrial and Social History of England* (New York: The Macmillan Co., 1915), p. 213.

Historical Highlights in the Development of U.S. Capitalism

In the early history of the United States, the economy was closer to a pure market system than it is today. It was considered to be laissez-faire capitalism, the system advocated by Adam Smith. Over the years, however, the U.S. economy has developed into one that, although still essentially market in nature, has extensive amounts of government regulation, control, and influence. Several key historical periods and events can be viewed as significant turning points in the movement of the U.S. economy from laissez-faire to increased government activity. These include: the U.S. industrial "boom," the New Deal, the World War II era, and the regulatory wave of the 1960s and 1970s.

The Industrial "Boom" Prior to the Civil War the U.S. economy was primarily agricultural, with production taking place in homes or small workshops and with trade carried on in local markets. In this environment laissez-faire was the prevailing system. But after the Civil War, through the late 1800s and into the early 1900s, substantial and significant changes occurred in American economic and social life. These changes were similar to those the British had undergone a century before in their industrial revolution. Growth in transportation and communication, primarily the railroads and telephone, opened new marketplaces, and the exploitation of energy sources such as oil and electricity permitted mass production and the growth of a factory system. Great numbers of inventions introduced many new goods

Application 2.2
THE FACTORY GIRL'S LAST DAY

The art and poetry of a particular time period often reflect some of the social attitudes of the day. Several poems were written during the British Industrial Revolution to make strong statements about the poor working conditions in factories. Given below is an excerpt from "The Factory Girl's Last Day," written in the early 1800s and attributed to various authors.

"'Twas on a winter morning,
The weather wet and mild,
Two hours before the dawning
The father roused his child:
Her daily morsel bringing,
The darksome room he paced,
And cried: 'The bell is ringing;
My hapless darling, haste!'

"'Dear father, I'm so weary!
I scarce can reach the door;
And long the way and dreary:
O, carry me once more!'
Her wasted form seems nothing;
The load is on his heart:
He soothes the little sufferer,
Till at the mill they part.

"The overlooker met her
As to her frame she crept;
And with his thong he beat her,
And cursed her when she wept.

such as typewriters, light bulbs, automobiles, bicycles, and more efficient farm machinery. At the same time people began to move from the farm to the city seeking work and greater opportunities.

In the midst of this industrial "boom," two changes were occurring which would bring about government intervention. First, some businesses were becoming large and powerful corporations capable of monopolizing an entire industry (as Standard Oil did) and others were joining together with competitors to form trusts (as in the sugar and tobacco industries). Second, the lifestyles of some American workers were becoming inordinately harsh. Many labored long hours for low wages in often intolerable and dangerous conditions; child labor was permitted; city slums flourished; and attempts to form unions were often met with violence. (The concern that these changes generated is suggested by the cartoon from 1882 in Application 2.3.) These two situations were severe enough to cause the introduction of some significant legislation that altered the laissez-faire tradition.

With regard to the monopoly problem, in 1890 Congress made its first attempt to preserve a competitive landscape in America by passing the Sherman Antitrust Act. This act essentially prohibits businesses from acting together to restrain trade and from monopolizing or attempting to monopolize a market. The Sherman Act was followed, in 1914, by the Clayton Act, which prohibits certain other business practices that have anticompetitive effects. Also in 1914 the Federal Trade Commission (FTC) was established, with the charge, among other things, of prohibiting unfair methods of competition.

It seemed, as she grew weaker,
The threads the oftener broke;
The rapid wheels ran quicker,
And heavier fell the stroke.

"She thought how her dead mother
Blessed her with latest breath,
And of her little brother,
Worked down, like her, to death:
Then told a tiny neighbor
A half-penny she'd pay
To take her last hour's labor,
While by her frame she lay.

"The sun had long descended
Ere she sought that repose:
Her day began and ended
As cruel tyrants chose.

Then home! but oft she tarried;
She fell and rose no more;
By pitying comrades carried,
She reached her father's door.

"At night, with tortured feeling,
He watched his sleepless child:
Though close beside her kneeling,
She knew him not, nor smiled.
Again the factory's ringing
Her last perceptions tried:
Up from her straw bed springing,
'It's time!' she shrieked, and died!"

Source: Robert Dale Owen, *Threading My Way* (New York: Augustus M. Kelley, 1967), pp. 129–130. Original publication, 1874.

Application 2.3

Cartoon of 1882 Illustrates the Fear that Technology and Machinery Will Destroy Workers

THE DEMON WHICH IS DESTROYING THE PEOPLE

Source: Otto L. Bettmann, *The Good Old Days—They Were Terrible!* (New York: Random House, 1974), p. 85. This paperback contains some text and is richly endowed with photographs, cartoons, and other illustrations concerned with crime, work, food, housing, travel, and other subjects dealing with life for the average American between the Civil War and the early 1900s. Bettmann is founder of the Bettmann Archive in New York, a library of pictures, books, and other literary artifacts.

The dismal lifestyles and working conditions experienced by many American laborers were not changed by a single sweeping law; rather, improvement resulted from bits and pieces of federal and state legislation that began in the early 1900s. Some of this legislation resulted from action by muckrakers, a group of authors, journalists, photographers, and others who stirred the nation through their exposés of the seamy and unsanitary side of life. For example, Jacob Riis, in *How the Other Half Lives,*[11] wrote about and photographed working conditions and tenement poverty in New York. Upton Sinclair, probably the best-known muckraker, wrote of conditions in the meat packing industry in *The Jungle.* The following excerpt shows the sensationalist manner in which Sinclair and other muckrakers wrote. It is no wonder that one response to this book was the Meat Inspection Act of 1907.

> . . . This is no fairy story and no joke; the meat would be shovelled into carts, and the man who did the shoveling would not trouble to lift out a rat even when he saw one—there were things that went into the sausage in comparison with which a poisoned rat was a tidbit. There was no place for the men to wash their hands before they ate their dinner, and so they made a practice of washing them in the water that was to be ladled into the sausage. There were the butt-ends of smoked meat, and the scraps of corned beef, and all the odds and ends of the waste of the plants, that would be dumped into old barrels in the cellar and left there. Under the system of rigid economy which the packers enforced, there were some jobs that it only paid to do once in a long time, and among these was the cleaning out of the waste barrels. Every spring they did it; and in the barrels would be dirt and rust and old nails and stale water—and cart load after cart load of it would be taken up and dumped into the hoppers with fresh meat, and sent out to the public's breakfast. Some of it they would make into "smoked" sausage—but as the smoking took time, and was therefore expensive, they would call upon their chemistry department, and preserve it with borax and color it with gelatine to make it brown. . . . [12]

Other legislation of this period included a Food and Drug Act in 1906 that has since been amended several times; state legislation limiting the hours and/or ages of child labor; laws setting maximum hours and minimum wages for women; state workmen's compensation insurance for injury on the job; and many other laws affecting matters that ranged from fire regulations to mandatory schooling.

Because of the antitrust legislation and some consumer and worker regulations, by 1920 the government had established precedence for interven-

---

[11]See the suggested readings at the end of this chapter.

[12]Upton Sinclair, *The Jungle* (New York: Signet Classics, The New American Library), pp. 136–137. Original publication, 1906.

ing in economic activity, and the U.S. economy had moved away from laissez-faire capitalism.

The New Deal A second and massive wave of government intervention came in the 1930s. The stock market crash of 1929 and the following Great Depression were met with a series of programs and legislative reforms instituted during the presidential administration of Franklin D. Roosevelt and termed the **New Deal.**

New Deal
A series of programs and legislative reforms instituted during the administration of Franklin D. Roosevelt in the Great Depression of the 1930s.

These programs had various objectives. Some were designed to give government aid in amounts heretofore unheard of to specific sectors of the economy. For example, in an attempt to raise some agricultural prices, farmers for the first time were paid not to grow crops. Farmers could also look to the government for help in refinancing when they could not meet farm mortgage payments. To ease the hardships of the unemployed, agencies such as the Works Progress Administration (WPA) and the Civilian Conservation Corps (CCC) were organized to provide jobs building bridges, roads, schools, and the like, as well as some forestry and park work. Also, the Social Security Act was passed in 1935 to provide income for the aged, blind, and others.

Other programs were designed to regulate or bolster business activity. The Securities and Exchange Commission was created to prevent fraudulent practices in the sale of securities and to establish some safeguards in these markets. Banking was affected by several programs, such as the creation of the Federal Deposit Insurance Corporation, and agencies such as the Federal Communications Commission and Civil Aeronautics Board were established. Also, in 1935 the National Labor Relations Act gave workers the right to bargain collectively.

One other economic event from this period that should be noted is that the government began to run deficit budgets on a regular basis; that is, it typically spent more than it received from taxes and other revenues. This practice was a break from the past and began an era of a type of government budget policy previously not considered.

By the end of the 1930s, government intervention in economic activity was part of U.S. capitalism, and many programs begun in that era are firmly entrenched in the economy today.

The World War II Era Because of the extent and magnitude of World War II, many government agencies were instituted during the war to control production, manpower, wages, prices, and such. Although most of these agencies were dismantled after the war, they did create a precedent for future reestablishment. For example, wage-price controls were instituted again in 1951 and in the early 1970s.

Following World War II, one of the most significant steps toward more government involvement in economic activity occurred with the passage of

Employment Act of 1946
Legislation giving the federal government the right and responsibility to provide an environment for the achievement of full employment, full production, and stable prices.

the **Employment Act of 1946.** This act gave the federal government the right and responsibility to provide an environment in which full employment, full production, and stable prices could be achieved. Under this act Congress could now manipulate taxes and government spending and run deficit budgets in an effort to bring the economy to a desired level of activity. This meant that rather than influencing some specific part of the circular flow model (such as the input or output markets), government could influence the entire model by blowing it up or deflating it like a balloon. Such a powerful influence had never been legislated before this period.

Regulatory Wave of the 1960s and 1970s Another area of increasing government activity was the creation of numerous federal regulatory agencies in the 1960s and 1970s. Between 1963 and 1979, 27 such agencies were established, compared to only 10 during the 1930s.[13] These agencies include those established for protection of the environment (the Environmental Protection Agency), prevention of discrimination (the Equal Employment Opportunity Commission), consumer product safety (the Consumer Product Safety Commission), and worker health and safety (the Occupational Safety and Health Administration).

It can thus be concluded that the U.S. capitalism of today has significantly departed from the laissez-faire capitalism of 100 years ago.

SUMMARY

Scarcity is a problem common to all economies in the world; no economy can completely satisfy all of its members' wants and needs for goods and services. For this reason, every society must answer three basic economic questions: what goods and services will be produced and in what quantities; how will those goods and services be produced; and who will receive those goods and services.

The way in which a society answers these three basic economic questions depends on its economic system. Economic systems can be classified as planned, market, or mixed.

In a planned economy the three basic economic decisions are made by planners associated with the government or otherwise representative of the members of a society. In a market economy the basic decisions are made by individual buyers and sellers communicating through prices. Goods and services are produced in a market economy if buyers demand them and sellers can produce them at a profit. In this type of economy, production is carried out by the least-cost method so that businesses can reap greater profits from what is sold in the market, and goods and services go to those who can pay

[13]See Table 15.3 for a full chronological listing of federal government regulatory agencies.

for them. How much an individual can afford to buy depends largely on the value of his or her resources sold in the input markets. In a mixed economic system the basic economic questions are answered by a combination of market and centralized decision making.

The basic structure of a market economy can be illustrated by a circular flow model. This model shows how businesses and households relate to one another as buyers and sellers in output and input markets. The circular flow model also identifies where government can intervene in the market mechanism in mixed economic systems.

A second method for classifying economies is according to whether they are capitalistic, mixed capitalistic, or socialistic. In capitalism the means of production are privately owned, and businesses operate on a free enterprise basis. In socialism some of the means of production are collectively owned by the members of society. In mixed capitalism resource ownership is basically private, but the government has important decision-making power over how the privately owned resources will be used.

The evolution of the U.S. economy into what it is today can be better understood by examining key developments in eighteenth- and nineteenth-century British history and nineteenth- and twentieth-century U.S. history. The British developments include the decline of mercantilism, the rise of a philosophy of individualism, and the Industrial Revolution. It was in this time period that Adam Smith wrote *The Wealth of Nations,* which was to become a cornerstone in the philosophy of U.S. capitalism. The important events in U.S. history that helped to shape the U.S. economy into what it is today include the industrial boom following the Civil War, the Great Depression and New Deal of the 1930s, the World War II era, and the regulatory wave of the 1960s and 1970s.

Key Terms and Concepts

Basic economic choices
Economic system
Planned economy
Market
Market economy
Price system
Mixed economy
Market failure
Circular flow model
Output, or product, markets
Input, or resource, markets
Efficient method of production
Capitalism
Free enterprise
Mixed capitalism
Socialism
Market socialism
Mercantilism
Laissez-faire capitalism
Invisible hand doctrine
Industrial Revolution
New Deal
Employment Act of 1946

Discussion and Review Questions

1. Suppose that you have been chosen to be on a blue-ribbon panel of experts to determine how well or poorly each of the economies of the world is operating. Your task is to come up with a checklist of five factors by which the different economies of the world could be judged. Which five factors would you pick to judge these different economies, and why?

2. What factors might cause one nation to choose to operate as a market economy and another to choose to operate as a planned economy?

3. Name three strengths and three weaknesses each for a market, planned, and mixed economy. Would the strengths and weaknesses of the different systems be the same regardless of where in the world they operated, or would they differ from country to country?

4. Below are listed six activities. Indicate for each whether it is (a) a real flow through a product market; (b) a money flow through a product market; (c) a real flow through a resource market; or (d) a money flow through a resource market.
   - **a.** Receiving a paycheck at the end of each month
   - **b.** Delivering a specially ordered automobile to a buyer
   - **c.** A physician caring for patients
   - **d.** Using a credit card to buy a meal in a restaurant
   - **e.** Two college students earning profit from their own ice cream stand over the summer
   - **f.** Obtaining college credits

5. In recent years corporations such as Chrysler have requested loans from the U.S. government. Do you regard this type of request for government intervention as appropriate or inappropriate in a capitalist economy? Should government grant these loans? In formulating your opinion, consider, among other factors, the importance of adhering to the principle of free enterprise and the importance of maintaining competition in markets.

6. Identify some of the historical turning points in the United States as it moved from a system of laissez-faire capitalism toward a mixed system. Based on your general knowledge of U.S. history, in your opinion what event was most significant in ensuring that the United States would not return to laissez-faire capitalism?

7. Explain how the three basic economic questions are answered in a planned, a market, and a mixed economy. Use a circular flow diagram to illustrate how these questions are answered in a market economy and where and how government intervenes in a mixed economy.

8. Identify some examples of market failure in the U.S. economy.

Suggested Readings

Friedrich Engels, "Working-Class Manchester," ***The Marx-Engels Reader,*** **ed. Robert C. Tucker (New York: W. W. Norton & Co., Inc., 1972), pp. 429–435.** A description of living conditions in the worker district of an English city during the Industrial Revolution, extracted from Engels's *The Condition of the Working Class in England in 1844.*

Milton Friedman and Rose Friedman, ***Free to Choose*** **(New York: Harcourt Brace Jovanovich, 1980).** A critical view of the proper role of government in the economic process.

Friedrich A. Hayek, "The Price System as a Mechanism for Using Knowledge," ***Comparative Economic Systems: Models and Cases,*** **ed. Morris Bornstein (Homewood, Ill.: R. D. Irwin, Inc., 1979), pp. 49–60.** An argument for the superiority of market forces over central planning in using knowledge to make economic decisions.

Interview with Robert L. Heilbroner on "The Future of Capitalism," ***Challenge*** **(November–December, 1982), pp. 32–39.** Heilbroner answers a series of questions on his views of the nature and future of capitalism.

F. D. Klingender, ***Art and the Industrial Revolution,*** **ed. and rev. Arthur Elton (New York: Schocken Books, 1970).** Text and art on the Industrial Revolution in Britain.

Leonard Silk, "Andropov's Economic Dilemma," ***The New York Times Magazine,*** **October 9, 1983, pp. 51, 86, 92, 93, 98, 100, 101.** Report on Soviet economic inefficiencies, as seen by Silk during a recent visit.

Two muckraker classics include:
Jacob A. Riis, ***How the Other Half Lives,*** **Dover ed. (New York: Dover Publications, 1971).** The unabridged republication of Riis's 1901 edition, with added photographs. Portrays life in the tenements of New York and evoked enough controversy to lead to some tenement reforms.

Upton Sinclair, ***The Jungle*** **(New York: Signet Classics, The New American Library).** Original publication, 1906. Depicts the life of a working class family in Chicago in the early twentieth century. Focuses on the meat-packing industry.

3 DEMAND, SUPPLY, AND THE DETERMINATION OF PRICE

Chapter Objectives

1. To define demand, Law of Demand, supply, and Law of Supply.
2. To explain demand and supply through schedules and graphs.
3. To show how price is determined in a market through the interaction of demand and supply.
4. To define and illustrate equilibrium price, equilibrium quantity, and shortages and surpluses in a market.
5. To explain the reasons for a change in demand or a change in supply and how these changes affect equilibrium price and quantity in a market.
6. To illustrate how government imposed price ceilings and price floors influence market conditions.
7. To introduce the concept of price elasticity which measures buyers' and sellers' sensitivities to price changes.
8. To define macroeconomics and microeconomics.

Chapter Two explained that one way a society can answer the basic economic questions is through individuals coming together as buyers and sellers in markets. This market decision making is a cornerstone in the operation of many economies, especially economies such as that of the United States. For this reason, two basic tools of economics, "demand" and "supply," are designed to study the market behavior of buyers and sellers. Demand is concerned with buyers, and supply with sellers. Together, these tools help us understand the forces at work in a market economy. In this chapter demand and supply will be explored in detail, along with the manner in which they interact to determine the prices of goods and services.

DEMAND AND SUPPLY

Demand

Demand
A buyer's plan for the amounts of a product that would be purchased at different prices in a defined time period.

Demand refers to the buyer's side of the marketplace, or to a buyer's plans concerning the purchase of a good or service. For example, you might have a demand for an airplane ticket to Hawaii, a taco for lunch, or a chemistry lab book. A business might have a demand for workers, raw materials, machinery, or any other factor of production. In formal terms, a buyer's **demand** for a good or service is defined as the different amounts of the good or service that he or she would purchase at different prices in a given time period. Therefore, when we speak of a buyer's demand for coffee, gasoline, or whatever, we are speaking of the different amounts of these items that the buyer would purchase at different prices over some period of time such as a day, a week, or a year.

Demand schedule
A list of the amounts of a product that a buyer would purchase at different prices in a defined time period.

The relationship between the amount of a product that a consumer would buy and the product's price can be illustrated through the use of a **demand schedule.** In drawing up a demand schedule we allow only the product's price to change and "freeze" all of the other factors that influence a buyer's behavior. That is, nonprice factors such as a buyer's income and taste, and prices of other products are held constant. This highlights the relationship between the product's price and the amount of the product a person would buy. Table 3.1, showing John's weekly demand for 16-ounce bottles of root beer, illustrates such a demand schedule.[1]

In this schedule, note the relationship between the price per bottle and the number of bottles of root beer demanded by John. As the price per bottle goes up from 10¢ to 20¢, the number of bottles John would buy falls from 20 to 17; as the price increases from 20¢ to 30¢, the amount demanded falls from 17 to 14; and each additional 10¢ increment further reduces the number of bottles John would buy. In other words, as the price increases, John

[1]All of the examples used in this chapter are hypothetical.

Table 3.1
John's Weekly Demand for 16-Ounce Bottles of Root Beer

This demand schedule lists different amounts of root beer that would be demanded per week at various prices, and illustrates the Law of Demand: there is an inverse relationship between price and quantity demanded.

Price per Bottle	Number of Bottles Demanded Weekly
10¢	20
20	17
30	14
40	12
50	10
60	8
70	6
80	4
90	3

would buy fewer bottles of root beer. Steaks, television sets, clothes, or just about any other good or service, and any other consumer, could have been used for the example in Table 3.1 with the same result: the quantity demanded would have fallen as the price rose, and the quantity demanded would have risen as the price fell.

Thus, the behavior illustrated in Table 3.1 is typical of any buyer's plan to purchase a good or service, and it shows a relationship between price and quantity demanded that we know to be generally true. This relationship is called the **Law of Demand.** It states that as a product's price increases, the quantity of the product demanded decreases, and as a product's price decreases, the quantity demanded increases. In other words, the Law of Demand says that there is an inverse relationship between a product's price and the quantity of that product demanded.

Law of Demand
There is an inverse relationship between the price of a product and the quantity demanded.

Why do consumers react this way to changes in price? The reason for the Law of Demand goes back to the fundamental problem of economics: scarcity and choice. A consumer purchasing goods and services faces a scarcity problem in the form of a limited income. The consumer can buy only so much. This means that as the price of an item goes up, he or she may not be able to afford as much as was afforded at the lower price. On the other hand, when the price of a good or service falls, the consumer typically will want to purchase more. At the lower price more of the good or service is obtained for the money, which presents an opportunity to increase material possessions.

Likewise, choice influences demand because alternative, or substitute, products can be purchased. As the price of root beer increases, John can choose to drink other beverages—coffee, cola, or water, to name a few—in place of root beer. As the price of root beer decreases, he may choose to drink more root beer and, perhaps, less of other beverages.

Typically in economics, demand is displayed in graphs rather than in schedules. Figure 3.1 illustrates John's demand for root beer as shown in the demand schedule in Table 3.1. On this graph, price is measured on the vertical axis and the quantity demanded on the horizontal axis. Observe that when each price-quantity combination in the demand schedule in Table 3.1 is plotted and connected by a line, the line—called a **demand curve**—slopes downward to the right. As indicated in Chapter One, downward sloping lines such as that in Figure 3.1 represent inverse relationships. Because the Law of Demand states that an inverse relationship exists between price and quantity demanded, we can generalize that demand curves slope downward to the right to show that more is demanded at lower prices and less is demanded at higher prices.

Demand curve
A line on a graph that illustrates a demand schedule; it slopes downward because of the inverse relationship between price and quantity demanded.

Supply

Supply
A seller's plan for the amounts of a product that would be offered for sale at different prices in a defined time period.

A seller's plan to make a good or service available in the market is referred to as supply. **Supply** is defined as the different amounts of a product that a seller would make available for sale at different prices in some time period.

Figure 3.1
John's Weekly Demand for 16-Ounce Bottles of Root Beer

The downward sloping demand curve illustrates the Law of Demand by showing that less is demanded at higher prices and more is demanded at lower prices.

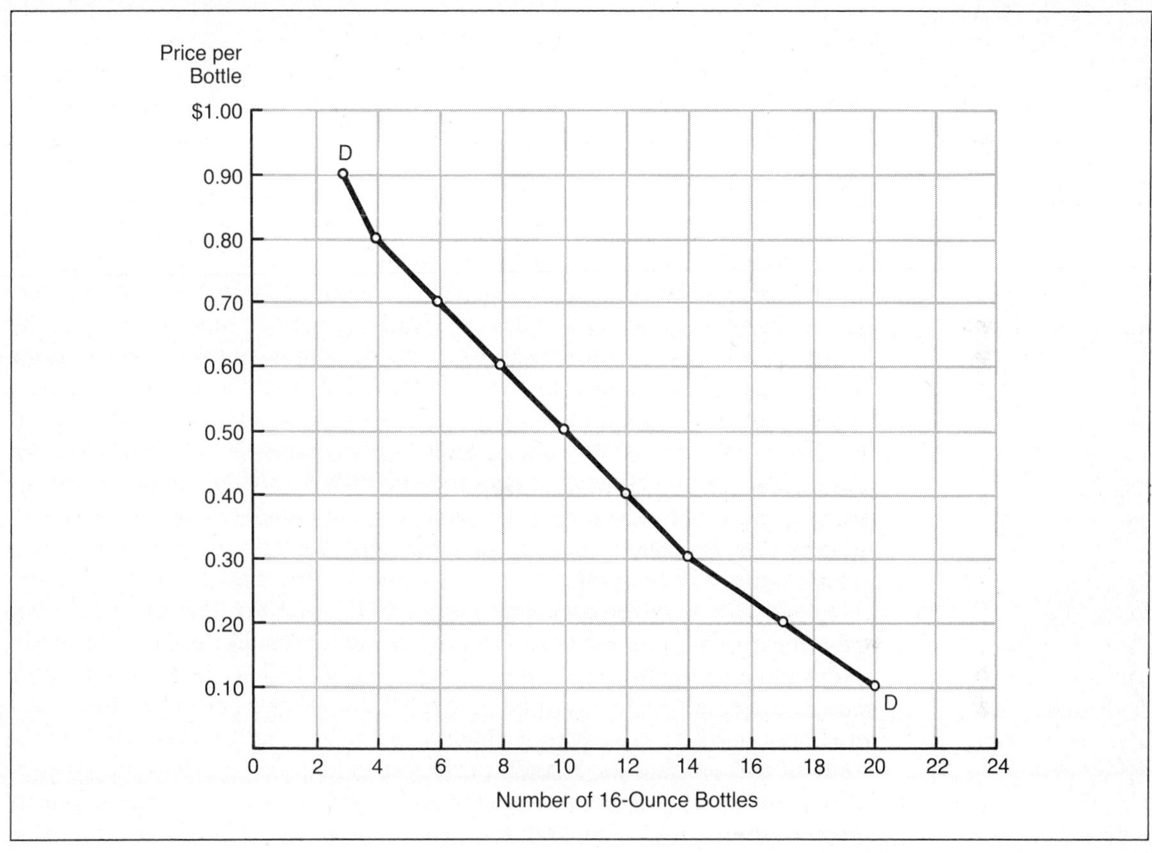

In other words, supply indicates how many hot fudge sundaes, haircuts, tires, or any other product a supplier would be willing to sell at different prices during, say, a week, month, or year.

Supply schedule
A list of the amounts of a product that a seller would offer for sale at different prices in a defined time period.

Like demand, supply can be illustrated in a schedule. In a **supply schedule,** as in a demand schedule, all factors that influence supply, except price, must be held constant. That is, nonprice considerations such as the cost of production must not change. This highlights the relationship between a product's price and the quantity of the product supplied. Table 3.2 is an example of a supply schedule. It shows the various amounts of chocolate donuts that the City Bakery is willing to provide for sale at different prices on a daily basis. Because all factors except price are held constant, the donuts must be of a uniform size and quality throughout the schedule; they must not become better or worse, or larger or smaller at various prices.

Table 3.2
City Bakery's Daily Supply of Chocolate Donuts

The Law of Supply is illustrated in this supply schedule, which shows that more donuts are supplied at higher prices.

Price per Donut	Quantity Supplied per Day
5¢	0
10	0
15	25
20	150
25	250
30	325
35	375
40	400

Observe the direct relationship between price and the quantity supplied in Table 3.2. At a low price the bakery would offer no or few donuts for sale. But as the price increases the bakery is willing to offer more for sale. If the supply of any other good or service were chosen as an example, the same relationship would appear: the quantity supplied would increase as the price increased, and the quantity supplied would decrease as the price decreased. This relationship illustrates the **Law of Supply,** which states that there is a direct relationship between price and quantity supplied. In other words, more is supplied as the price rises, and less is supplied as the price falls.

Law of Supply
There is a direct relationship between the price of a product and the quantity supplied.

Why does the bakery react in this manner? The basic reason for the bakery's or any other supplier's behavior, and for the Law of Supply, is the seller's ability to cover costs and earn a profit. At very low prices a seller may not be able to cover costs. Hence, the seller would not be particularly interested in supplying the product. But at higher prices, costs could be covered and a small profit could be earned. If the seller were producing many products, as is the case with a bakery, the seller might choose to produce some of the product for a small profit, but might also concentrate on producing other items with a more favorable return. At even higher prices, greater profits could be made, or any additional costs from producing more could be covered while still allowing a profit, and the quantity supplied would be further increased. The bakery, for example, might be willing to decrease the production of birthday cakes, danish, eclairs, and other products in order to increase the production of donuts if the price and profit on donuts were extremely high.[2]

Supply curve
A line on a graph that illustrates a supply schedule; slopes upward because of the direct relationship between price and quantity supplied.

Supply, like demand, is typically illustrated graphically. Price is shown on the vertical axis and the quantity supplied on the horizontal axis. Each of the price-quantity combinations from the supply schedule in Table 3.2 is plotted in Figure 3.2, and a **supply curve** is drawn by connecting each of the points. Note that the supply curve slopes upward to the right, showing

[2]Is it valid to assume that the cost per donut might increase as the bakery produces more donuts? Yes. For example, the owner might incur extra expenses from additional repairs on equipment because it is used more often, or producing more donuts might require that the bakery's employees work overtime at a higher wage rate. See Chapter Twelve for details on rising costs associated with increased production.

Figure 3.2
City Bakery's Daily Supply of Chocolate Donuts

The upward sloping supply curve illustrates the Law of Supply by showing that more is supplied at higher prices and less is supplied at lower prices.

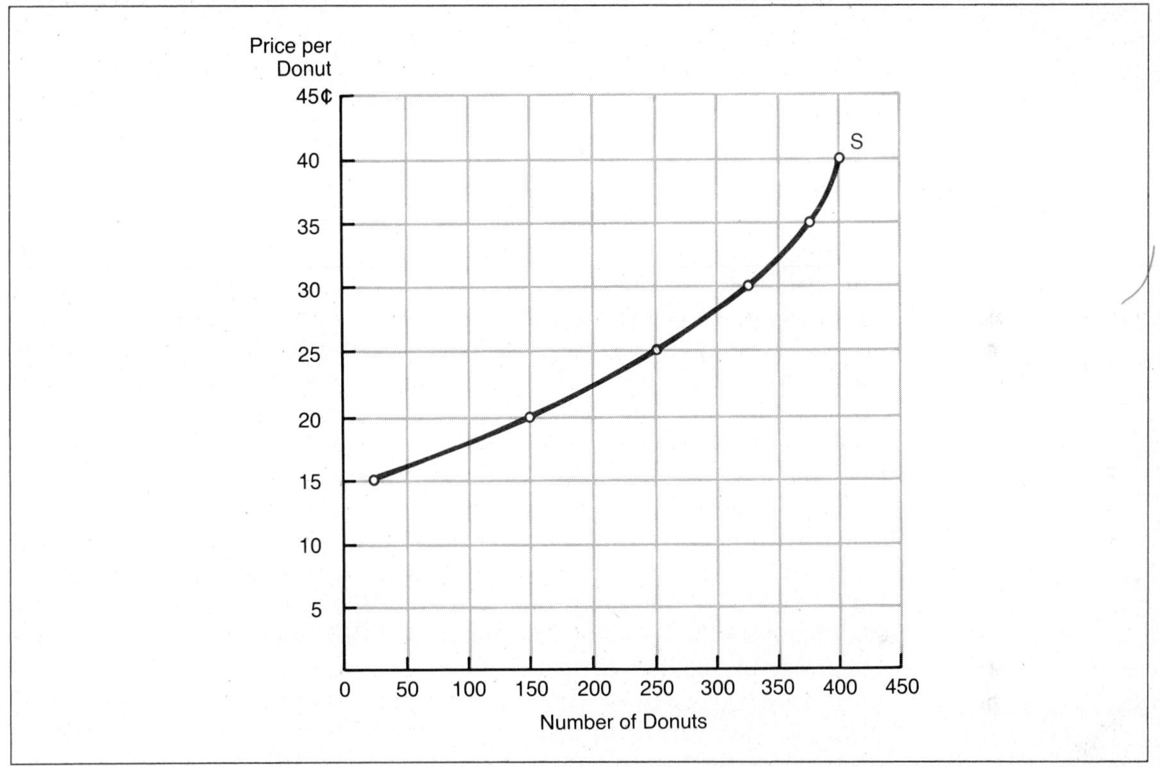

that higher prices are associated with larger quantities supplied. Because the Law of Supply states that there is a direct relationship between price and quantity supplied, and because direct relationships are graphed as upward sloping lines, it can be generalized that supply curves slope upward to the right.

MARKET DEMAND, MARKET SUPPLY, EQUILIBRIUM PRICE, AND EQUILIBRIUM QUANTITY

Market Demand and Market Supply

Market
A place or situation in which the buyers and sellers of a product interact for the purpose of exchange.

When buyers and sellers come together for the purpose of exchanging a good or service, a **market** is formed. This can take place anywhere—at a store, showroom, used car lot, stock exchange, or vending machine, for

Market demand and market supply
The demand or supply in a market for a particular good or service; is found by adding together all individual demand or supply curves or schedules.

example. **Market demand** and **market supply** are, respectively, the sum of all the individual quantities demanded and supplied of a product at each price in a market. For example, the market demand for an Academy Award-winning motion picture is made up of all of the individual demands to see the film. In a market, it is the demand and supply of all buyers and sellers, rather than individual demand and supply, which is important.

Markets and the Setting of Prices

Markets perform a critical function when economic decisions are made by businesses and households, because it is in markets that the prices for goods and services are determined through the interaction of buyers and sellers. In order to understand the operation of a market, particularly with regard to the determination of prices, consider a hypothetical market for the buying and selling of 1-pound bags of popcorn. Table 3.3 shows the market demand and market supply schedules for this commodity. In the analysis of this market and those that follow in this chapter it is assumed that a high degree of competition exists among buyers and sellers. No buyer or seller exerts any unusual or undue influence, and no price-controlling government regulation occurs.

In the market in Table 3.3 the price for a 1-pound bag of popcorn ranges from 10¢ through 50¢. What would happen in this market if the price were 10¢ per bag? At 10¢, buyers would demand 10,000 bags, and sellers would offer only 2,000 for sale. Thus, at a price of 10¢ the quantity supplied would fall short of the quantity demanded by 8,000 bags, or there would be a **shortage** on the market of 8,000 bags. The reaction to this shortage would be a price rise by sellers who would observe the number of buyers left unsatisfied in the market. In response to this price rise, the quantity supplied would increase (because of the Law of Supply), and the quantity demanded would fall (because of the Law of Demand). These responses would reduce the shortage.

Shortage
Occurs in a market when the quantity demanded is greater than the quantity supplied, or the product's price is below the equilibrium price.

What would happen if the price were 20¢ per bag of popcorn? At 20¢, the quantity demanded would be 8,000 bags, and the quantity supplied would be 4,000 bags. The market would again develop a shortage, but of only 4,000

Table 3.3
Weekly Market Demand and Supply of 1-Pound Bags of Popcorn

Market demand and market supply illustrate the different amounts of a product that all buyers in a market would demand and all sellers in a market would supply at various prices.

Price per Bag	Quantity Demanded	Quantity Supplied
10¢	10,000	2,000
20	8,000	4,000
30	6,000	6,000
40	4,000	8,000
50	2,000	10,000

bags of popcorn (8,000 quantity demanded minus 4,000 quantity supplied). Again, the market reaction would be a price rise as sellers observe this shortage. As the price would rise above 20¢, the quantity demanded by buyers would decrease, and the quantity supplied by sellers would increase, causing the shortage to shrink.

What would happen if the sellers charged 50¢ per bag? At 50¢, consumers would want to buy only 2,000 bags, but sellers would offer 10,000 bags for sale. As a result, the quantity demanded would fall short of the quantity supplied by 8,000 bags. In other words, there would be a **surplus** of 8,000 bags of popcorn on the market. Sellers of popcorn would react like any other seller with excess merchandise at a price consumers will not pay: they would lower their price. As the price fell, the Law of Demand would go into operation, and some buyers who would not purchase popcorn at 50¢ per bag would do so at a lower price. At the same time, because of the Law of Supply, the lower price would lead to a reduction in quantity supplied, and the surplus would diminish. If the price charged were 40¢, a surplus of 4,000 bags would develop, sellers would again lower their price, and the surplus would again shrink.

Surplus
Occurs in a market when the quantity demanded is less than the quantity supplied, or when the product's price is above the equilibrium price.

Equilibrium Price and Equilibrium Quantity

The market in Table 3.3 appears to be moving automatically toward a price of 30¢ per bag, where the quantity demanded and quantity supplied are both 6,000 bags of popcorn. If sellers charge 30¢ per bag, there will be no surpluses or shortages and no tendency to raise or lower price. The price which sets buyers' plans equal to sellers' plans, 30¢, is termed the **equilibrium price.** The quantity at which those plans are equal, 6,000 units, is termed the **equilibrium quantity.** Thus, equilibrium price and equilibrium quantity are the price and quantity toward which a market will automatically move. At this price, quantity demanded equals quantity supplied, and there is no tendency to change the price.[3]

Equilibrium price and equilibrium quantity
The price and quantity at which demand equals supply; the price and quantity toward which the free market automatically moves.

If the price of a good or service is below its equilibrium level, a shortage will develop, causing the price to automatically increase toward equilibrium. If price is above equilibrium, a surplus will develop, causing the price to decrease toward equilibrium.

The popcorn market shown in Table 3.3 is graphed in Figure 3.3. The demand curve is derived from the "Price per Bag" and "Quantity Demanded" columns, and the supply curve is drawn from the "Price per Bag" and "Quantity Supplied" columns. From the graph it is easy to see that the equilibrium price and quantity occur at the intersection of the supply and demand curves, in this case at a price of 30¢ per bag and a quantity of 6,000 bags.

[3]The equilibrium price is sometimes referred to as the "market clearing price," since at this price the amount demanded by buyers is equal to the amount supplied by sellers, thereby "clearing" the market of the good or service.

Figure 3.3
Weekly Market Demand and Supply of 1-Pound Bags of Popcorn

The equilibrium price and quantity in a market occur at the intersection of the market demand and supply curves. At equilibrium, the quantity demanded in a market equals the quantity supplied.

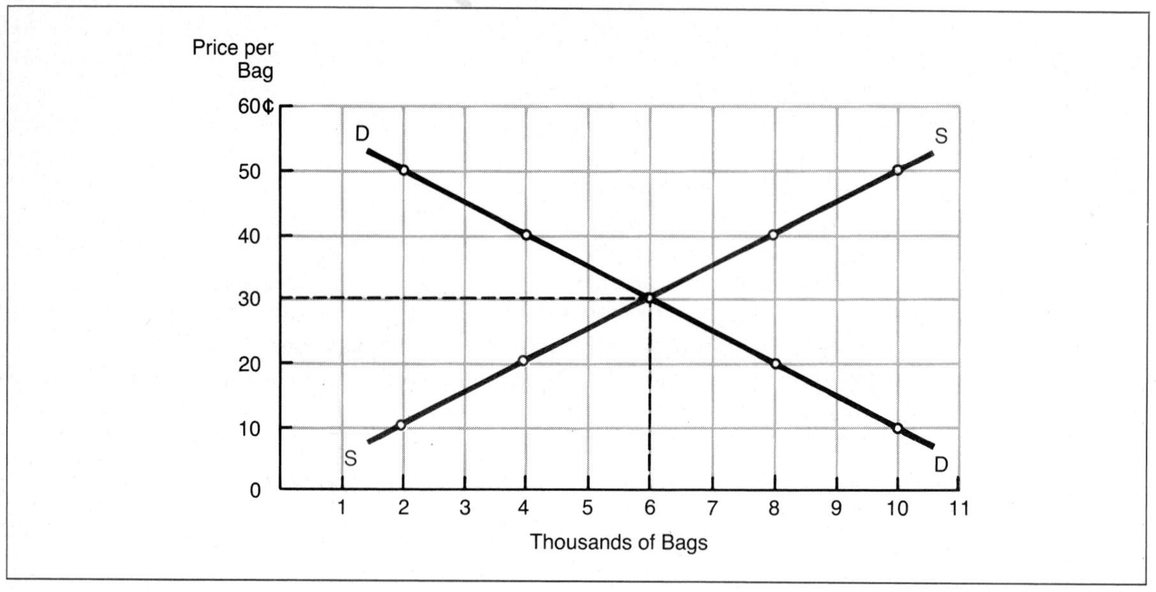

It is also possible to illustrate shortages and surpluses graphically. Figure 3.4a shows that at a price of 50¢ the quantity demanded is 2,000 bags and the quantity supplied is 10,000 bags: there is a surplus of 8,000 bags. The difference between the demand and supply curves at 50¢ is equal to the amount of the surplus. Notice that as the price comes closer to the equilibrium level, the distance between the demand and supply curves narrows, and the surplus becomes smaller. Figure 3.4b measures the 4,000 bag shortage that would occur at a price of 20¢ per bag. Can you determine the shortage at a price of 15¢ per bag?

Changes in Quantity Demanded and Quantity Supplied

Change in quantity demanded and quantity supplied
A change in the amount of a product demanded or supplied that is caused by a change in its price; represented by a movement along a demand or supply curve from one price-quantity point to another.

When the price of popcorn changed in Table 3.3 and Figure 3.3, the amount that buyers would have purchased also changed. For example, as the price rose from 10¢ to 20¢ per bag, the amount buyers demanded fell from 10,000 to 8,000 bags. When a change in a product's price causes a change in the amount that would be purchased, a **change in quantity demanded** occurs. A change in quantity demanded is shown by a movement *along* a demand curve from one price-quantity point to another, such as from the point representing 10¢ and 10,000 bags to the point representing 20¢ and 8,000 bags on the demand curve in Figure 3.3.

Figure 3.4
Measuring Shortages and Surpluses on Demand and Supply Curves

The surplus or shortage at a particular price is equal to the difference between the quantity demanded and the quantity supplied at that price.

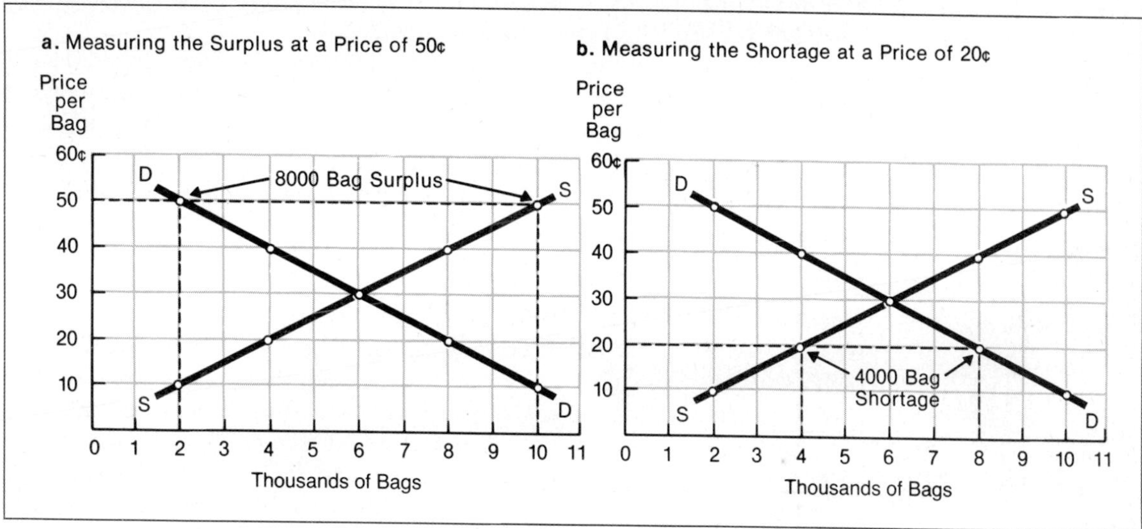

Likewise, the amount of popcorn that the sellers in Table 3.3 and Figure 3.3 were prepared to sell changed as the price changed. As the price fell from 50¢ to 40¢ per bag, the amount supplied fell from 10,000 to 8,000 bags. When a change in a product's price causes a change in the amount of a product that a seller would supply, a **change in quantity supplied** occurs. A change in quantity supplied is illustrated graphically by a movement *along* a supply curve from one price-quantity point to another, such as from the point representing 50¢ and 10,000 bags to the point representing 40¢ and 8,000 bags on the supply curve in Figure 3.3.

CHANGES IN DEMAND AND SUPPLY

Many factors in addition to the product's price help create a demand for a particular good or service. For example, if you have a demand for imported French champagne, this demand may be affected by your taste for champagne, social pressures to drink champagne, your income, the degree of substitutability between French and domestic champagne or between champagne and other spirits, and so on. Each of these nonprice factors influences your demand for the product. Some major **nonprice factors influencing demand** are (1) income; (2) expectations concerning future income, prices, or availabilities; (3) taste, fashion, and popularity; (4) the prices of related goods; and, when considering market demand, (5) the number of buyers.

Nonprice factors influencing demand
Factors such as income, taste, and expectations that help to formulate the demand for a product.

Nonprice factors influencing supply
Factors such as the cost of production and the number of sellers that help to formulate the supply of a product.

On the other side of the market, a seller in determining a supply schedule is also influenced by factors other than the price received for the product. Some major **nonprice factors influencing supply** are: (1) the cost of producing the item;[4] (2) expectations of future market conditions; (3) the prices of other items that the seller produces or could produce; and, when dealing with market supply, (4) the number of sellers.

Earlier in this chapter, in examples of demand and supply schedules, all nonprice considerations were "frozen," or held constant. The reason they were held constant is that *changes in the nonprice factors that influence demand and supply cause demand and supply schedules to change.* These changes are referred to as "changes in demand" and "changes in supply."

Changes in Demand

Change in demand
A change in the demand schedule for a product caused by a change in one or more nonprice factors influencing the product's demand; the demand curve shifts to the right or left.

The expression **change in demand** refers to a change in a consumer's demand schedule that is caused by a change in one or more nonprice factors influencing the demand. The old schedule no longer holds as the consumer develops a new set of plans. Using the schedule from Table 3.1 as an example, John's weekly demand for root beer could change because of a change in a nonprice factor that influences his demand for root beer. For instance, an increase in his income could change his demand by permitting him to buy more root beer than he had previously been able to afford. This change is shown in Table 3.4 as a larger amount of root beer demanded at each price.

Increase in demand
A change in one or more nonprice influences on demand causes more to be demanded at each price; the demand curve shifts to the right.

A change in demand may be designated as either an increase in demand or a decrease in demand. An **increase in demand** means that a change in one or more nonprice factors has caused the buyer to want to purchase more of a product at every price. Some factors that could bring about an increase in the demand for a product are an increase in buyers' incomes, an increase in the popularity of the good or service, an increase in the price of a substitute good or service, expectations of a price increase or of nonavailability of the item in the future, and an increase in the number of buyers in the market.

Graphically, an increase in demand causes the demand curve for a good or service to *shift* to the right. This shift is shown in Figure 3.5, which is a graph of John's demand schedules for root beer in Table 3.4. John's original demand for root beer before he receives an income change is shown by D1 in Figure 3.5. When John's income increases, and he wants to purchase more root beer, his demand schedule changes. When this new schedule is graphed in Figure 3.5, the demand curve shifts to the right, to D2. Observe on the graph that at 20¢ he is now willing to buy 23 rather than 17 bottles, and at 50¢ he is now willing to buy 16 rather than 10 bottles. Clearly, he demands more at each price, or has experienced an increase in demand.

---

[4]Care must be taken to distinguish between the terms *price* and *cost.* Price is the amount for which an item can be sold. Cost is the expenditure required to produce the item.

Table 3.4
John's Weekly Demand Schedule for Root Beer Before and After an Increase in His Income

A change in a nonprice factor causes a change in the amount of an item demanded at each price. After an increase in income, the number of bottles of root beer demanded by John each week increases at every price.

Before		After	
Price per Bottle	Number of Bottles Demanded Weekly	Price per Bottle	Number of Bottles Demanded Weekly
10¢	20	10¢	26
20	17	20	23
30	14	30	20
40	12	40	18
50	10	50	16
60	8	60	14
70	6	70	12
80	4	80	10
90	3	90	9

Figure 3.5
Increase in John's Weekly Demand for 16-Ounce Bottles of Root Beer

An increase in John's demand for root beer causes the demand curve to shift to the right from D1 to D2, indicating that a larger quantity is now demanded at each price.

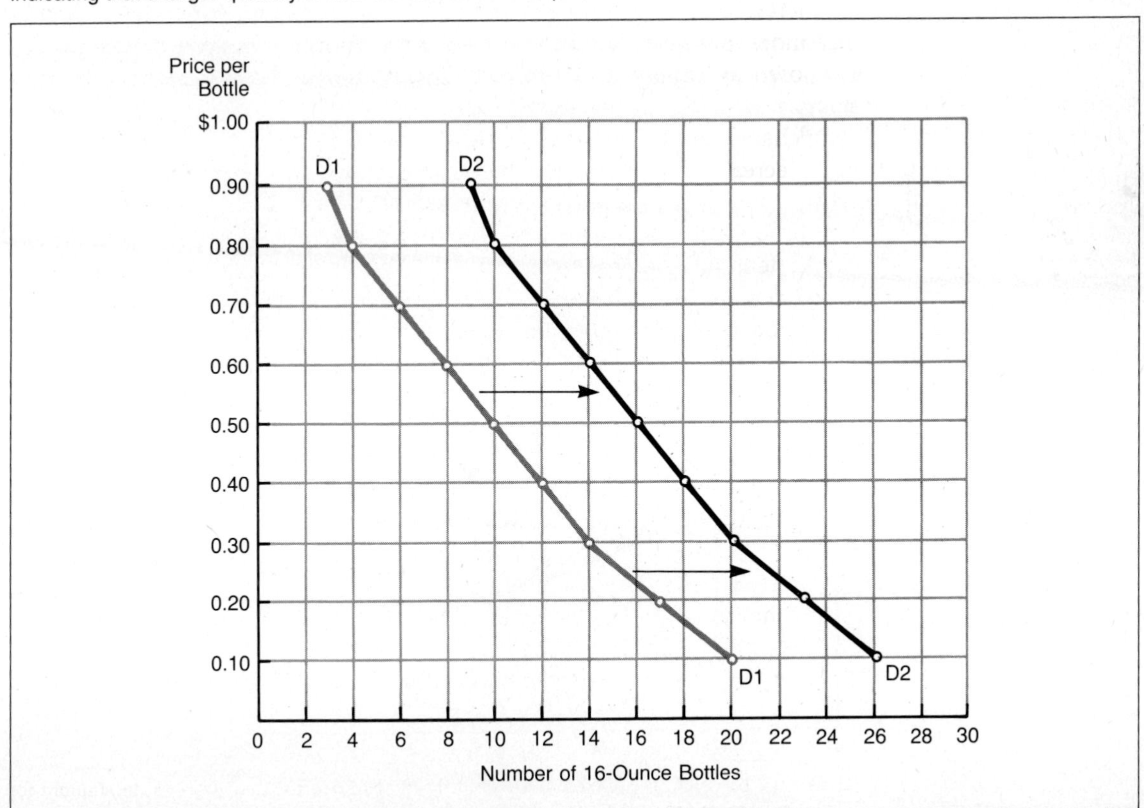

Decrease in demand
A change in one or more nonprice influences on demand causes less to be demanded at each price; the demand curve shifts to the left.

A **decrease in demand** means that a change in one or more nonprice factors has caused the buyer to want to purchase less of a product at every price. Graphically, a decrease in demand causes the demand curve to *shift* to the left. For example, a homeowner who experiences a decrease in income may be willing to buy fewer storm windows at each possible price. This is illustrated in Figure 3.6, where D1 is the homeowner's original demand curve for storm windows. Before the drop in income the homeowner was willing to purchase nine windows at $50 each, or six windows at $75 each. The new demand curve, D2, illustrates the demand after a decrease in income. The homeowner is now willing to buy only six windows at $50 each, or three at $75 each. A decrease in demand has clearly occurred.

Other factors that could cause a decrease in the demand for a good or service are a decrease in the number of buyers in the market, a decrease in the popularity of the item, expectations of future price or income decreases, and a decrease in the price of a substitute good or service.

In summary, an increase in demand means that more is demanded at each price and the demand curve shifts to the right. A decrease in demand means that less is demanded at each price and the demand curve shifts to the left.

Change in supply
A change in the supply schedule for a product caused by a change in one or more nonprice factors influencing the product's supply; the supply curve shifts to the right or left.

Changes in Supply

A **change in supply** results from a change in one or more nonprice factors affecting the supply of a product. The nonprice changes cause either an increase or a decrease in supply.

Figure 3.6
Decrease in a Homeowner's Demand for Storm Windows

A decrease in a homeowner's demand for storm windows causes the demand curve to shift to the left from D1 to D2, indicating that a smaller quantity is now demanded at each price.

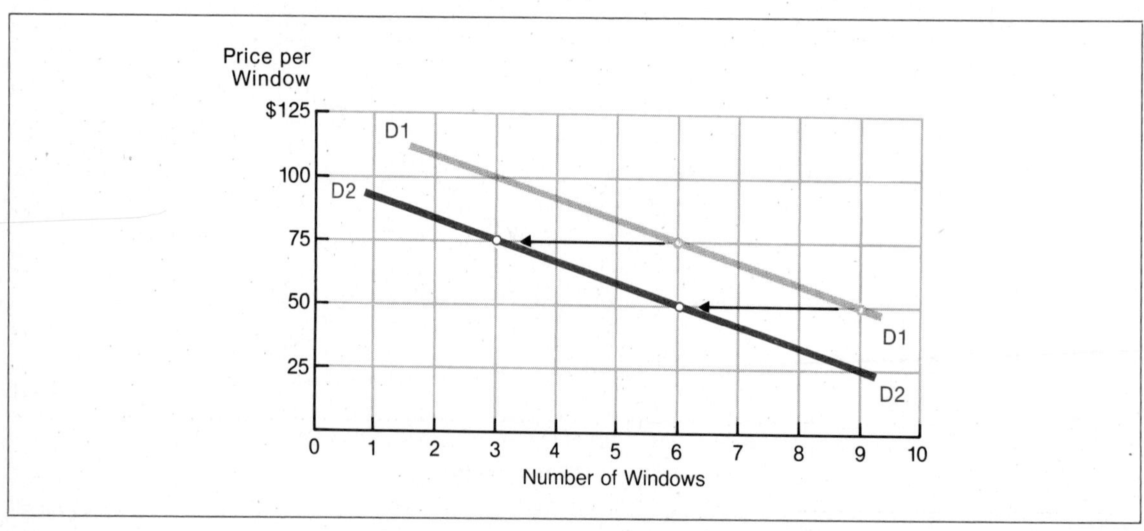

Increase in supply
A change in one or more nonprice influences on supply causes more to be supplied at each price; the supply curve shifts to the right.

An **increase in supply** means that a seller is willing to offer more of a good or service for sale at each price, and that the supply curve for the good or service *shifts* to the right. In Figure 3.7, assume that S1 is the original supply curve indicating that a seller of puzzles is willing to sell 10,000 puzzles at $2 each or 13,000 at $3 each. After an increase in supply, which causes the supply curve to shift to S2, the seller is willing to offer more puzzles at each price: for example, 13,000 at $2 and 16,000 at $3.

What could cause an increase in supply? A seller could experience a decrease in the cost of production which would allow the seller to make more of the product available at the same dollar outlay. Perhaps the raw materials used in producing the item are available at a lower cost, or perhaps the seller can adopt some new technology for producing the item for less. An increase in supply could also come because a seller fears a weakening market for the product in the future, or finds it advantageous to drop the production of a less profitable item and increase the production of another. Finally, in dealing with market supply, new sellers could enter the market, thus shifting the supply curve to the right.

Decrease in supply
A change in one or more nonprice influences on supply causes less to be supplied at each price; the supply curve shifts to the left.

A **decrease in supply** means that a change in one or more nonprice factors has caused a seller to be willing to offer less of a product for sale at each price, causing the supply curve to *shift* to the left. In Figure 3.8, a dairy's

Figure 3.7
Increase in the Supply of Puzzles

An increase in the supply of puzzles causes the supply curve to shift to the right from S1 to S2, indicating that a larger quantity is supplied at each price.

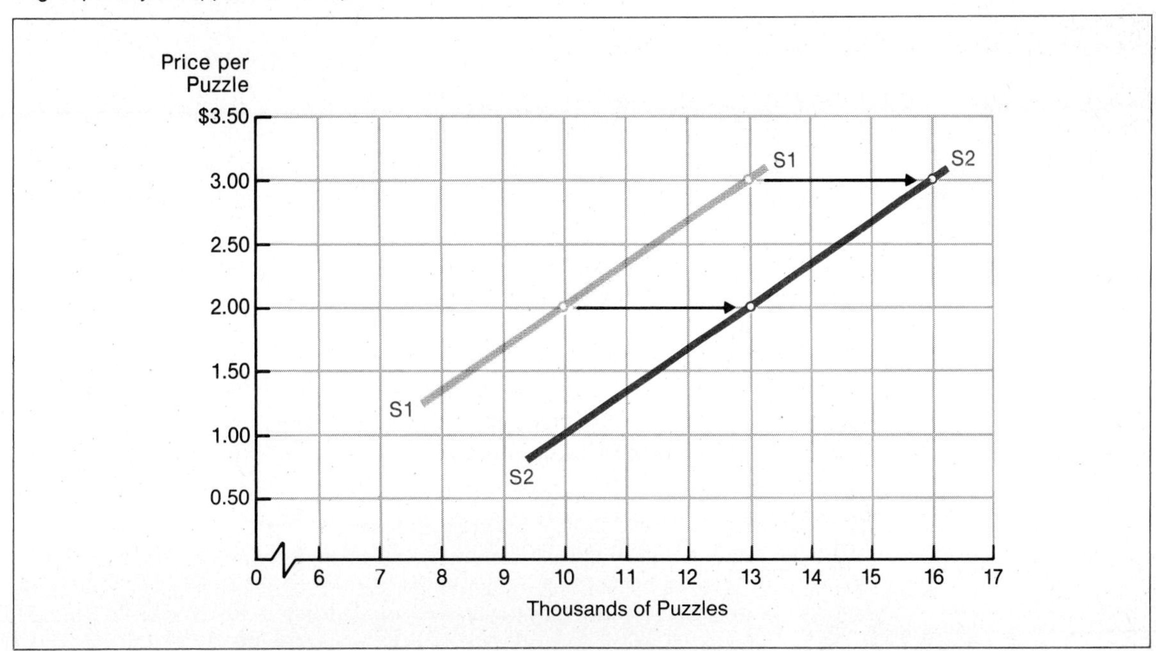

Figure 3.8
Decrease in the Supply of Cheese

A decrease in the supply of cheese causes the supply curve to shift to the left from S1 to S2, indicating that a smaller quantity is supplied at each price.

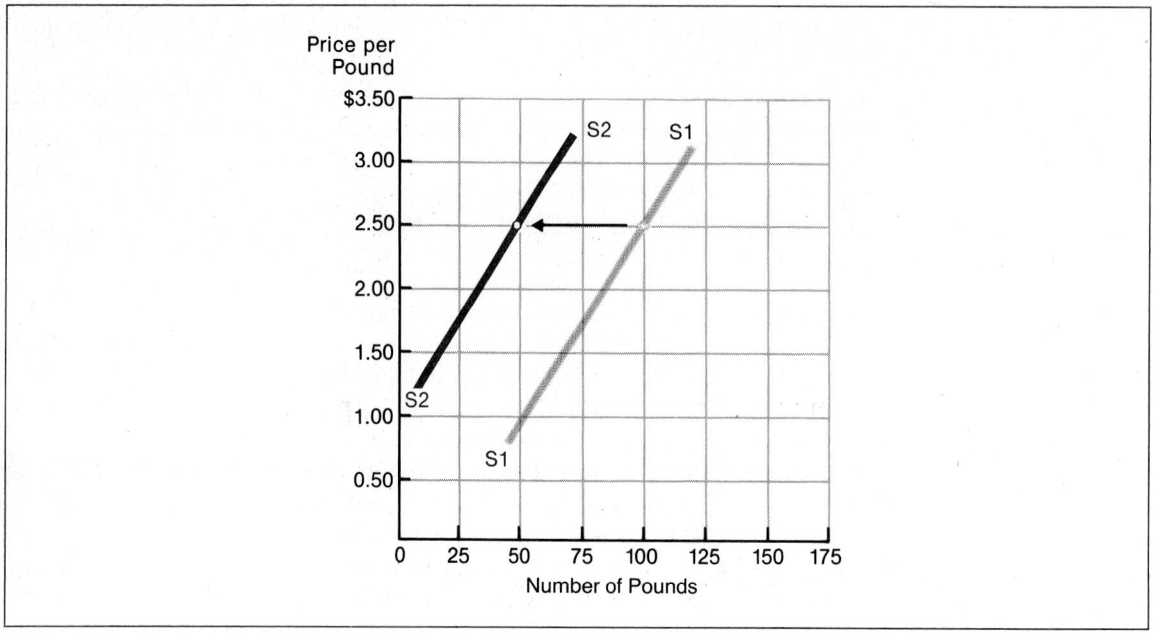

original supply curve for cheese, S1, indicates that it is willing to sell 100 pounds of cheese at a price of $2.50 per pound. A decrease in supply, which is represented by a shift of the supply curve to S2, reveals that the seller is now willing to sell less at each price—for example, only 50 pounds of cheese at $2.50 per pound.

A decrease in the supply of a product can result from increased costs of production due to such factors as higher wages, raw material costs, or costs of borrowing money. Other possible causes of a decrease in supply include a switch in production to another item that is more profitable; an expectation that conditions will improve for sellers at a future date; and, in the case of market supply, the exit of some sellers from the market.

In summary, an increase in supply means that a larger quantity is made available for sale at each price, causing the supply curve to shift to the right. A decrease in supply means that a smaller quantity is made available for sale at each price, causing the supply curve to shift to the left.

Changes in Demand and Supply Versus Changes in Quantity Demanded and Quantity Supplied

It is important to differentiate between price and nonprice changes. A change in price does *not* change demand or supply, or shift these curves. Rather, price changes cause movements *along* a curve. Or, as stated earlier, a change in price causes a change in quantity demanded and quantity supplied. Nonprice changes cause changes in demand or supply and cause these curves to shift. For example, an increase in the price of coffee would cause a decrease in the quantity demanded and an increase in the quantity supplied (no shift in the curves), but an increase in the popularity of coffee would cause an increase in the demand for coffee, and the demand curve would shift to the right. Test your understanding of changes in demand and supply by answering the questions in Application 3.1.

CHANGES IN EQUILIBRIUM PRICE AND EQUILIBRIUM QUANTITY

Thus far it has been shown that (1) a change in a nonprice factor affecting demand or supply will cause a change in demand or supply, and (2) a change in demand or supply causes a shift in a demand or supply curve. Since the equilibrium price and equilibrium quantity of a good or service are shown by the intersection of its demand and supply curves, whenever there is a shift in a product's demand or supply curve, its equilibrium price and quantity will change as well.

It is useful to be able to predict and analyze how changes in buyer and seller behavior can alter both the equilibrium price of a product and the quantity bought and sold. To order our thinking about these changes in market conditions, we will consider separately the effects on equilibrium price and quantity of an increase in demand, a decrease in demand, an increase in supply, and a decrease in supply.

Effect of an Increase in Demand

What effect does an increase in demand have on the equilibrium price and quantity of a product? Consider an item that becomes the vogue. Suppose that volleyball is the "in" sport, and that all over the country people are searching for volleyball nets to put in their yards and to take to parks. Common-sense analysis of the volleyball net market suggests that such an increase in demand would push the price of nets up, and that even at this increased price more nets would be sold. Let us examine the graphic analysis in Figure 3.9 on page 75 to determine whether our common-sense analysis is correct.

S is the monthly market supply curve for volleyball nets, and D1 shows the monthly demand for volleyball nets before the sport becomes a fad. With

Application 3.1
TEST YOURSELF: CHANGES IN SUPPLY AND DEMAND[a]

Determine whether each of the following examples would cause:

a. An increase in demand
b. A decrease in demand
c. An increase in supply
d. A decrease in supply
e. No change in either demand or supply

Example	Result	Graphic Change
1. Some sellers drop out of the carwash business.	d.	supply curve shifts to left
2. A peanut butter producer increases the effectiveness of its advertising campaign without increasing its costs.		
3. A local water company finds its costs increasing because of drilling expenses.		
4. The price of autos goes up.		
5. Potential buyers of sailboats experience a decline in their incomes.		
6. Fans become more supportive of a football team because it has a winning season.		
7. A technological advance makes it cheaper to produce typewriters.		
8. The government requires that the price of gas be lowered.		
9. Buyers expect that laundry detergent will be unavailable or in short supply in the future.		
10. Sellers of exercise classes lower their prices.		
11. Producers of snow blowers expect the next five winters to be mild.		

[a]Answers can be found on page 92.

Figure 3.9
Effect of an Increase in the Demand for Volleyball Nets

An increase in the demand for a product such as volleyball nets causes an increase in the product's equilibrium price and equilibrium quantity.

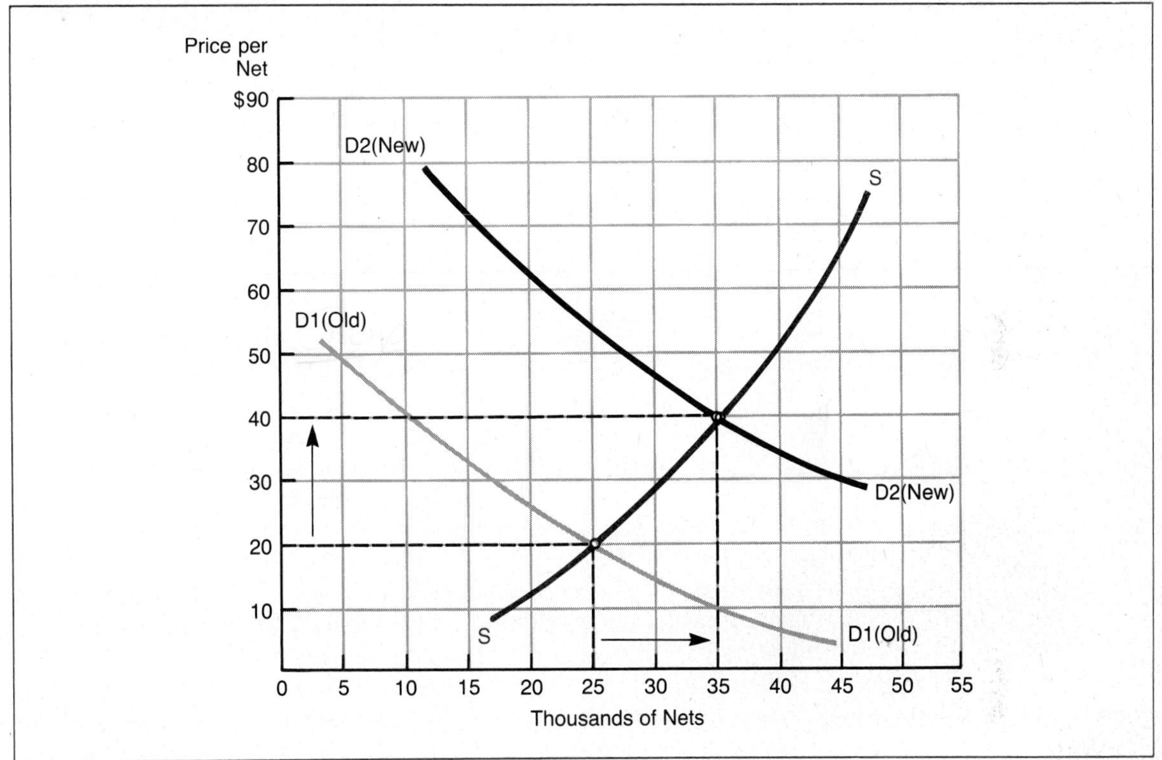

supply curve S and demand curve D1, the equilibrium price is $20 per net, and the equilibrium quantity is 25,000 nets. As the game becomes fashionable, the demand for volleyball nets increases, and the demand curve shifts to the right to D2. At the new equilibrium of S and D2, 35,000 nets are sold to buyers at a price of $40 each. Thus, an increase in the demand for a product causes both its equilibrium price and equilibrium quantity to increase.

Effect of a Decrease in Demand

What effect does a decrease in demand have on the equilibrium price and quantity of a product? Consider the market for black-and-white television sets. Assume that there is no change in supply, but that the demand falls as people switch to color sets. The market situation is shown in Figure 3.10. Here, S is the monthly supply curve for black-and-white television sets, and D1 shows the monthly demand before people start shifting to color sets. With S and D1, the equilibrium price is $200 a unit, and the equilibrium quantity is 800,000 units. But after people become interested in color sets, the demand for black-and-white models falls, and the demand curve shifts to the left to D2. As a result of the decrease in demand, the equilibrium price falls to $100 a unit, and the equilibrium quantity falls to 300,000 sets. Thus, a decrease in the demand for a product causes both its equilibrium price and equilibrium quantity to fall. Consider the passing of any recent fad. Is that not what happened to the price and the quantity sold as the product became unpopular?

Effect of an Increase in Supply

What effect does an increase in supply have on the equilibrium price and quantity of a product? An immediate response to this question might be that an increased supply of a product means that the price will fall and the amount sold will increase. Let us test this response. Over the years several products, such as pocket calculators, have increased significantly in supply because technology has made production cheaper, and because new companies have entered the market. In Figure 3.11, S1 and D are the original supply and demand curves, respectively, for pocket calculators. With this supply and demand, the equilibrium price is $50 a unit, and the equilibrium quantity is 200,000 units. Later, as new technologies and new manufacturers make their impacts on the market, the supply curve shifts to S2. Following this increase in supply, the new equilibrium price is $15 per unit, and the equilibrium quantity is 800,000 units. Thus, with an increase in supply, the equilibrium quantity increases, but the equilibrium price falls.

Effect of a Decrease in Supply

What effect does a decrease in supply have on the equilibrium price and quantity of a product? Assume that the supply of gasoline decreases, but not the demand. D and S1 in Figure 3.12 are the demand and supply curves, respectively, for gasoline before the available amounts are reduced. With D and S1 the equilibrium price is $1.50 per gallon, and the equilibrium quantity is 8 million gallons. Suppose now that there is a sharp cutback in the amount of gasoline brought to the market, causing the supply curve to shift to the left to S2. With this decrease in supply, the new equilibrium price is $2 per gallon, and the equilibrium quantity is 7 million gallons. Thus, a decrease in supply leads to an increase in the equilibrium price and a decrease in the equilibrium quantity.

Figure 3.10
Effect of a Decrease in the Demand for Black-and-White Television Sets

A decrease in the demand for a product such as black-and-white television sets causes a decrease in the product's equilibrium price and equilibrium quantity.

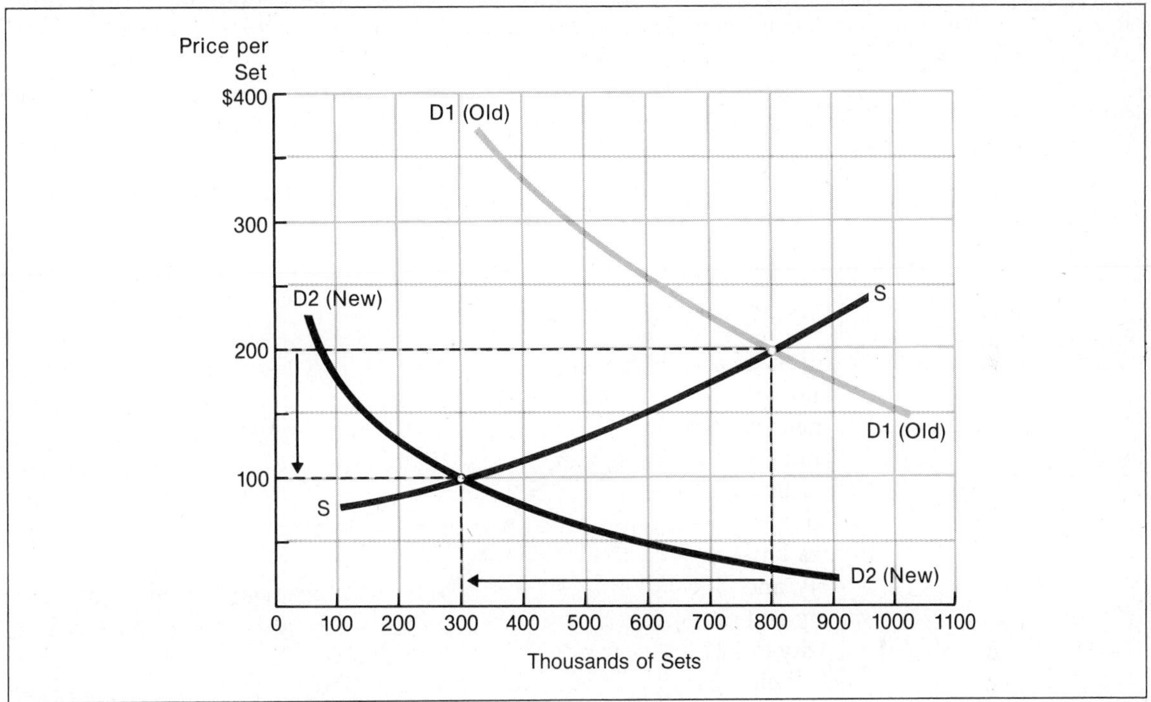

Effect of Changes in Both Demand and Supply

In each of the preceding examples of how equilibrium price and quantity are affected by changes in demand or supply, only one side of the market is changed, while the other side is held constant. In reality, simultaneous changes might occur. For example, both demand and supply might increase at the same time. Although such simultaneous changes are not illustrated here, your graphing skills should enable you to arrive at some conclusions about them.

LIMITING THE MOVEMENT OF PRICES

Up to this point we have dealt with free market conditions, where buyers and sellers interact independent of any other force, such as the government, in determining prices. Government, however, has on occasion stepped into

Figure 3.11
Effect of an Increase in the Supply of Pocket Calculators

An increase in the supply of a product, such as a pocket calculator, causes a decrease in the product's equilibrium price and an increase in its equilibrium quantity.

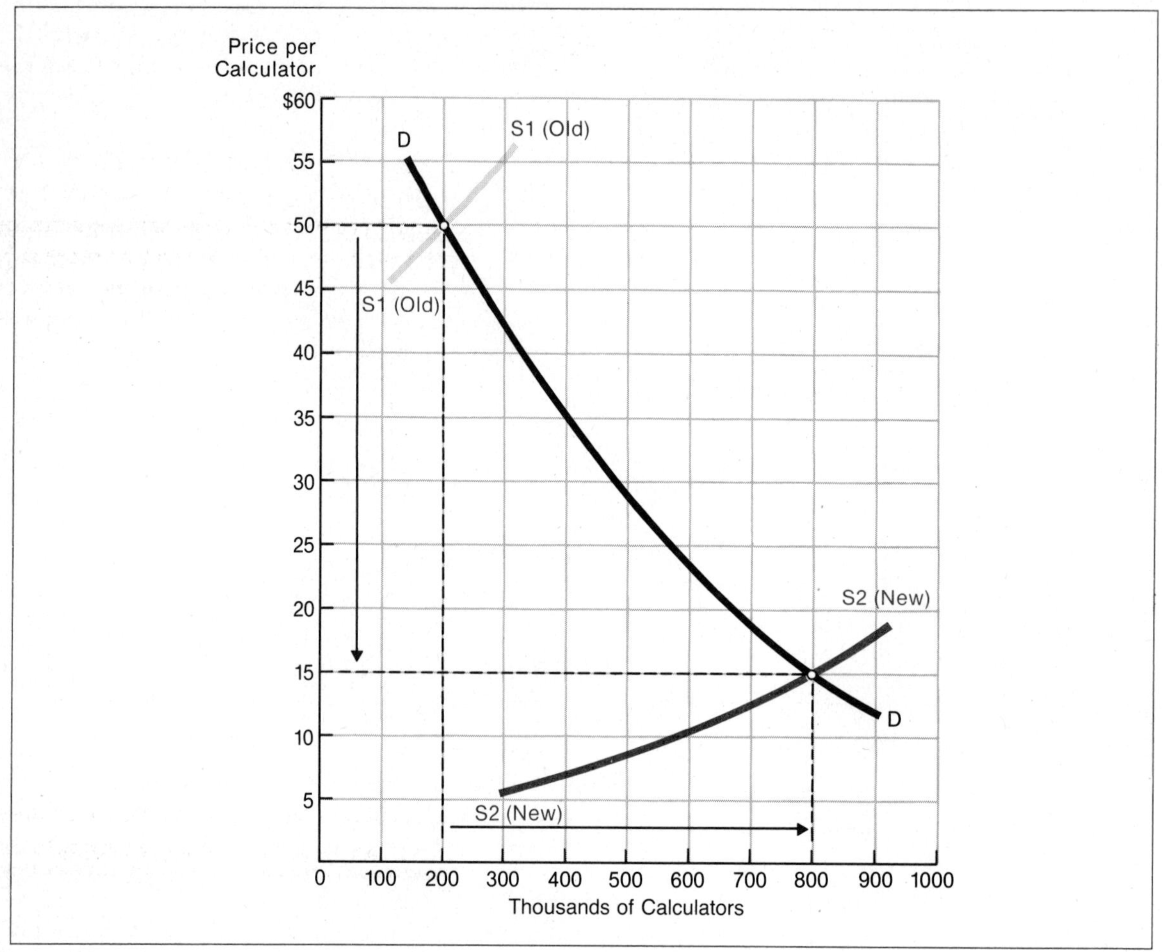

certain markets and interfered with free pricing by setting upper or lower limits beyond which a price cannot go. Several types of goods and services, including some farm products, utilities such as electricity and long-distance phone service, and some types of labor, have had their prices limited in this way to prevent them from becoming too high or too low. Supply and demand analysis can be used to explain how government intervention affects market conditions.

Figure 3.12
Effect of a Decrease in the Supply of Gasoline

A decrease in the supply of a product such as gasoline causes an increase in the product's equilibrium price and a decrease in its equilibrium quantity.

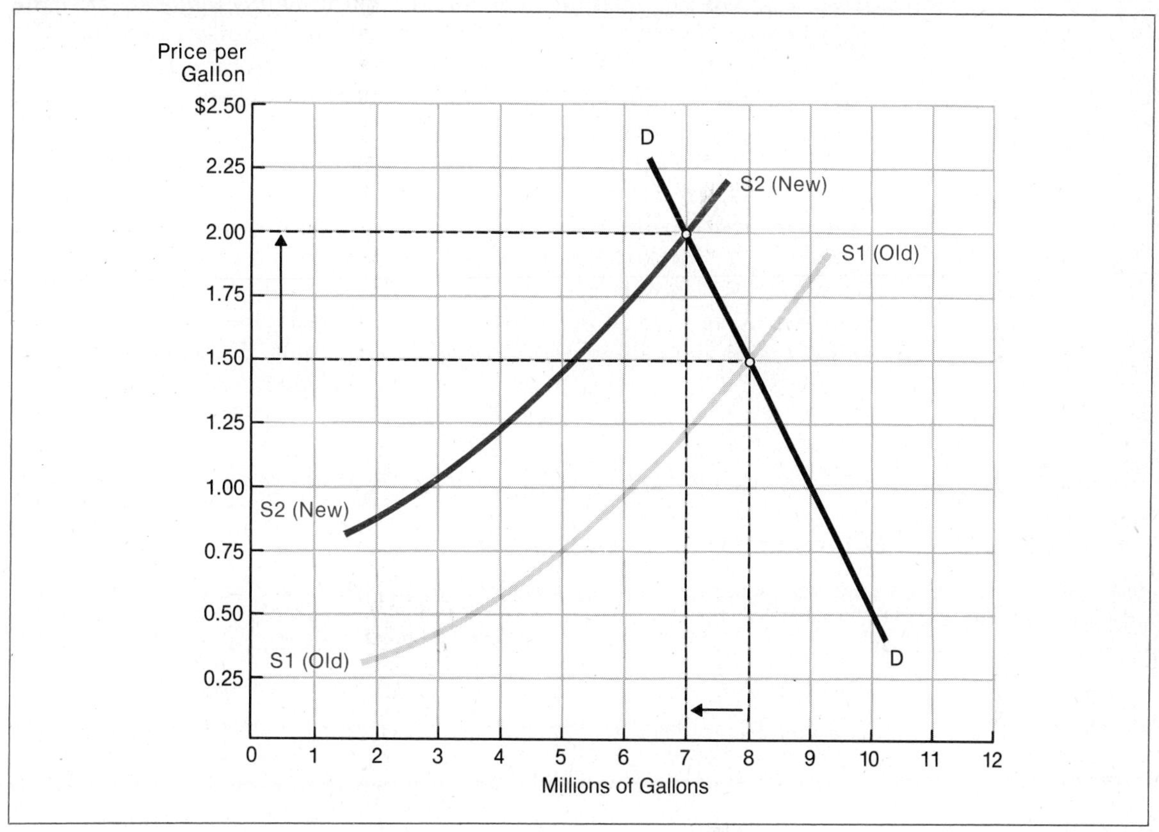

Upper Price Limits

Price ceiling (upper price limit) A government set maximum price that can be charged for a particular good or service; if the equilibrium price is above the price ceiling, a shortage will develop.

Legally imposed upper price limits, called **price ceilings,** keep prices from rising above certain levels. They have at times been placed on such items as natural gas shipped in interstate commerce and on the interest people pay for borrowed money. If the equilibrium price for a good or service is below its government established upper legal limit, or ceiling, the limit will have no noticeable impact on buyers and sellers. But if the equilibrium price for a good or service is above its upper legal limit, there will be two effects: the good or service's price will be kept below its equilibrium level, and shortages will occur.

For example, suppose that a law sets the maximum interest rate to be charged on some types of loans at 12 percent. Such maximum interest rate laws are called "usury laws" and have been adopted in the past by several state governments to apply to some loans, such as those for home mortgages. Figure 3.13a gives the demand for and the supply of loans where the legal limit on interest rates has no impact. Here borrowers' and lenders' wishes are equalized at an interest rate of 10 percent and $10 million is loaned each week. The government imposed ceiling on interest rates has not been reached in the market.

Suppose, however, that an increase in the demand for borrowed money occurs, causing the demand curve to shift to the right. This new situation is shown in Figure 3.13b. If the market were free to go to equilibrium after this increase in demand, the new interest rate would be 14 percent. However, the upper legal limit is 12 percent, so lenders may charge no more. Rather than increasing from 10 percent to 14 percent, the interest rate can rise only to the legal limit of 12 percent. At the 12 percent rate, borrowers would like to have $16 million in loans, but lenders would provide only $12 million in

Figure 3.13
Effect of a Legal Upper Price Limit (Price Ceiling) on the Market for Loans

When the equilibrium price for a product is below its legal upper limit, the price ceiling has no effect on the market; but when the equilibrium price is above its legal upper limit, the price ceiling takes effect and a shortage develops.

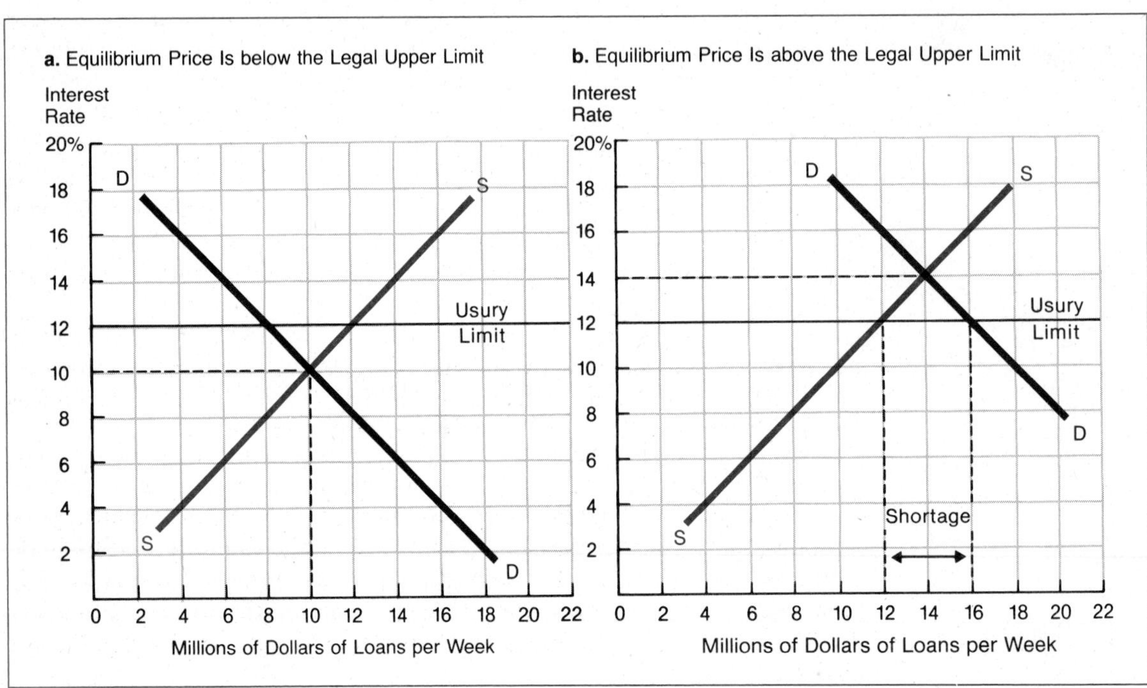

funds. At the 12 percent usury limit, there would be a $4 million shortage of funds for borrowing. Thus, when the free market equilibrium price rises above the government imposed upper limit, or ceiling, a shortage develops.

Lower Price Limits

Price floor (lower price limit)
A government set minimum price that can be charged for a particular good or service; if the equilibrium price is below the price floor, a surplus will develop.

Legally imposed lower price limits, called **price floors,** prevent prices from falling below certain levels. Examples of lower price limits include the minimum wage law, which sets the minimum hourly payment that many workers can earn, and government guaranteed farm prices, which ensure farmers of a minimum price on particular crops. As long as the equilibrium price of a good or service is above its lower legal limit, or price floor, the free market will not be affected by the limit. However, if the equilibrium price of a good or service falls below the lower legal limit, the government set price will be charged. Since this legally imposed price is higher than the price the free market would have permitted, surpluses begin to appear.

Consider the effect of the minimum wage law as an example. Suppose that the minimum wage is set at $4 per hour. If the supply and demand for a certain type of labor are as shown in Figure 3.14a, the minimum wage will have no noticeable impact on the market. The equilibrium wage of $4.50 per hour is greater than the minimum wage, and the number of available workers equals the number demanded.

Now suppose that the government raises the minimum wage from $4 to $5 per hour and that there is no change in supply or demand in this labor market. Since the equilibrium wage rate is $4.50, or less than the minimum wage, the $5 minimum wage will take effect. That is, businesses buying this type of labor must pay $5 per hour rather than $4.50. Figure 3.14b shows the market condition with the new minimum wage rate. At $5 per hour the number of workers demanded falls to 1,000, and the number of willing and able workers rises to 1,200. The price floor has caused a surplus of 200 people unable to obtain a job in this market. Thus, when the free market equilibrium price falls below the government imposed lower limit, or floor, a surplus develops.

In summary, legal upper limits, or price ceilings, when their effects are felt, keep prices lower than they would otherwise be and result in shortages. Legal lower limits, or price floors, when their effects are felt, keep prices higher than what they would otherwise be and result in surpluses.

Other Government Intervention In addition to laws establishing price ceilings and floors, there are laws prohibiting the purchase and sale of certain goods and services. One such good is human organs. Application 3.2, "Market Could Meet Demand for Organs," deals with a proposal to allow the formation of markets for human organs. What is your opinion on this question?

Figure 3.14
Effect of a Legal Lower Price Limit (Price Floor) on the Market for Workers

When the equilibrium price for a product is above its legal lower limit, the price floor has no effect on the market; but when the equilibrium price is below its floor, the floor takes effect and a surplus develops.

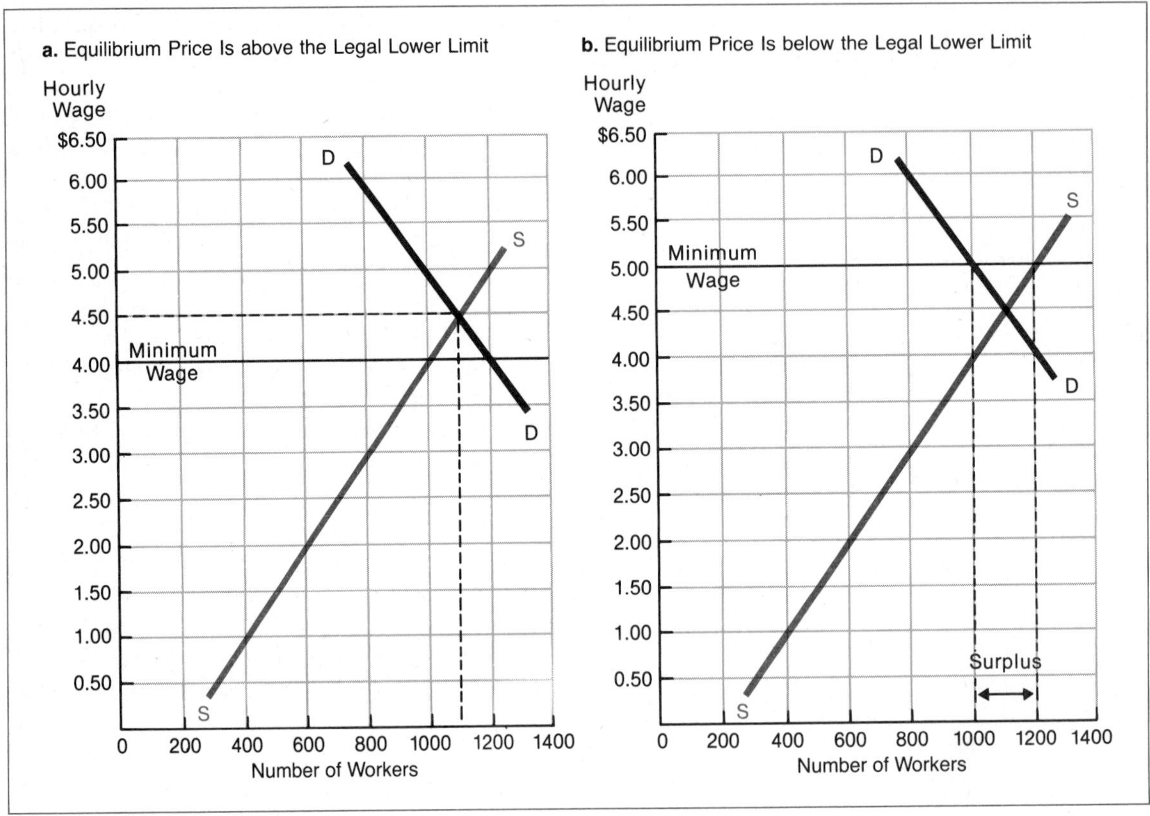

Application 3.2
MARKET COULD MEET DEMAND FOR ORGANS

Anyone who has seen distraught parents on TV, pleading for someone to donate a liver to a dying child, has felt sympathy for their plight. But hardly anyone understands why the potential beneficiaries of organ transplants have to undergo such indignities. There is a simple reason and a simple solution.

The immediate problem is a shortage of human organs for transplant. It arose only recently, thanks in part to a new drug, cyclosporin, which safely suppresses the human body's impulse to reject alien organs. This medical revolution has stimulated a huge increase in the number of people who want transplants. But the supply of organs hasn't kept pace. . . .

What can be done? Despite well-publicized campaigns to persuade Americans to sign "living wills," few bother. But there is a way to right this

PRICE ELASTICITY OF DEMAND AND SUPPLY

It is obvious by now that the quantity demanded of a good or service is inversely related to price and that the quantity supplied is directly related to price. But one more important question has yet to be answered for both buyers and sellers—how much will the quantity demanded and the quantity supplied change as the price changes? In other words, when the price of an item increases, the consumer will demand less, but will the consumer respond weakly, demanding just a little less of the item, or strongly, demanding much less? When the price of an item falls, will the consumer respond by demanding a little more or by demanding much more? Will a seller respond weakly or strongly to a change in the price of the good or service being sold? **Price elasticity** refers to the strength of the response to a price change and applies to both buyers and sellers. Price changes on some items, such as public utilities and prescription drugs, typically bring about weak responses in consumers. Price changes on other items, such as vacation tours and works of art, typically bring about strong responses.

Price elasticity
A measurement of the strength of a buyer's or seller's response to a price change.

Understanding elasticity can be very important to a business. Suppose that you own an ice cream shop in which you sell an average of 100 milkshakes per week at a price of $1.50 each. As a result, your total weekly sales of milkshakes average $150 (100 × $1.50). Now suppose that you decide to increase sales by cutting the price of your milkshakes from $1.50 to $1.25. At the new lower price consumers will want to buy more milkshakes, but how many more? Suppose the consumer response to your price cut is an increase in the sale of shakes to 110 per week. With this new price and quantity combination, your average weekly revenue from the sale of milkshakes falls to $137.50 (110 × $1.25). In other words, although the quantity of milkshakes demanded goes up after your price cut, the increase is not enough to make the price cut worthwhile; the response is so weak that your revenue falls from $150 to $137.50. You might have decided against the pol-

deadly imbalance: legalize the buying and selling of human organs. Well-functioning commercial markets already exist for human blood . . . , providing donors a financial reward for their trouble and recipients with access to what they lack. Why not allow a market in organs, too?

Donors would contract with a firm to sell their usable body parts upon their death, with a fee to be paid to their estates. The more daring, or more altruistic, would also be free to sell any organs whose loss wouldn't be fatal—for instance, a single kidney, since the remaining kidney is ordinarily adequate.

Right now, state laws throughout the U.S. are generally interpreted to forbid the sale and purchase of organs. Rep. Albert Gore, D-Tenn., wants an explicit federal ban, carrying criminal penalties of $50,000 in fines and five years in jail. . . .

Source: Stephen Chapman, "Market Could Meet Demand for Organs," *St. Louis Post-Dispatch*, June 9, 1984, p. 11A. Reprinted by permission: Tribune Media Services.

icy if you knew how little the quantity demanded was going to increase after you lowered your price. If the response to your price decrease is strong—for example, if consumers buy 150 milkshakes at $1.25 each, your weekly revenue will increase from $150.00 to $187.50 (150 × $1.25). With a strong response, the increase in quantity demanded is large enough to raise revenue. In other words, elasticity of demand, or the consumer's responsiveness to a price change, influences a business's revenue from sales.

If buyers or sellers are sensitive to a price change—that is, if their response is strong—their demand or supply is said to be **price elastic.** If buyers or sellers are not sensitive to a price change—that is, if their response is weak—their demand or supply is said to be **price inelastic.** The following rule of thumb is used to determine this sensitivity.

Price elastic
A strong response to a price change; occurs when the percentage change in the quantity demanded or supplied is greater than the percentage change in price.

Price inelastic
A weak response to a price change; occurs when the percentage change in the quantity demanded or supplied is less than the percentage change in price.

Demand or supply is price elastic if a certain percentage change in price leads to a *greater* percentage change in quantity demanded or quantity supplied (the quantity response is strong).

Demand or supply is price inelastic if a certain percentage change in price leads to a *smaller* percentage change in quantity demanded or quantity supplied (the quantity response is weak).

For example, if the price of a particular style of shoe goes up by 10 percent, and the quantity demanded falls by more than 10 percent, say 20 percent, the demand for this shoe is price elastic. Consumers have responded strongly to the price change. If the price goes up by 10 percent, and the quantity demanded falls by less than 10 percent, say 5 percent, the demand is price inelastic. Consumers have reacted weakly to the price change. In other words, price elasticity of demand depends on whether the percentage change in quantity demanded is greater or less than the percentage change in price.

Applying the concept of price elasticity to supply, it can be said that supply is price elastic if, for example, a 10 percent decrease in price leads to a greater than 10 percent decrease in quantity supplied. Supply is price inelastic if a 10 percent decrease in price results in a less than 10 percent decrease in quantity supplied.

Causes of Price Elasticity

Price Elasticity of Demand What causes the demand for a good or service to be relatively price elastic or inelastic? The first consideration is the type of good or service demanded; that is, whether it is a luxury or a necessity. Generally, the demand for luxuries is more sensitive to price changes (more price elastic) than the demand for necessities. It would be difficult for a person to cut back on life-saving treatments or medication because the price rose too much. On the other hand, people have been known to cut back substantially on vacation plans when travel prices have increased.

A second factor influencing the price elasticity of demand for a good or service is its degree of substitutability, or the ability of consumers to switch to other goods or services as its price goes up. If the price of travel increases, people can switch to a vacation spot closer to home or even spend their money on something completely different, such as a new stereo or television set. But if the price of life-saving medication goes up, users have limited alternatives. Consumers react more strongly (demand is more price elastic) to a price change for a good or service with many substitutes, and they react more weakly (demand is more price inelastic) to a price change for a good or service with few substitutes.

A third factor influencing the price elasticity of demand for a good or service is the portion of one's income that the purchase of the item requires. If you are making $16,000 a year, and the price of birthday candles doubles, it will probably have little effect on your demand for birthday candles. If, however, college tuition were to double, you might find yourself looking for an alternative to a college education. The greater the portion of income devoted to a good or service, the stronger the reaction will be to price changes for that good or service.

Price Elasticity of Supply A seller's degree of responsiveness to a price change is determined primarily by time. The more time a seller has to adjust production and react to a price change, the greater will be the seller's sensitivity to price, or the more price elastic will be the response. For example, suppose that a particular style of winter coat becomes very popular and buyers bid its price up. The manufacturers who make that coat are at first able to supply only as many coats as the inventory they have on hand allows. Thus, their immediate response to this increase in price is a very limited change in quantity: supply is price inelastic. Given a little more time, the manufacturers can produce more coats and further increase the quantity supplied. Given even more time, other sellers may see the popularity of the coat and move into the market, with the result that many more coats are supplied in response to the higher price.

How good are you at recognizing buyers' and sellers' sensitivities to price changes, nonprice factors influencing demand and supply, and other concepts discussed in this chapter? Test your skill by analyzing the articles excerpted in Application 3.3.

MACROECONOMICS AND MICROECONOMICS

This chapter completes Part One of this textbook. Part Two is titled "The Macroeconomy" and Part Three "The Microeconomy." Macroeconomics and microeconomics are the two basic approaches for analyzing economic activity. The difference between the two approaches can be illustrated with a circular flow model.

Macroeconomics
The study of the operation of the economy as a whole.

Macroeconomics concerns the operation of the economy as a whole and the major sectors of the economy. It includes such topics as inflation, unemployment, taxes and government spending, and money. In terms of the circular flow diagram in Figure 3.15 on page 88, macroeconomics concerns the interactions among the business sector, the household sector, the government sector, and the foreign sector[5], as well as the functioning of output and input markets taken as a whole. That is, instead of studying prices and production in a specific market such as the market for automobiles, macroeconomics studies all markets together, examining topics such as the general level of prices, total production, and total employment.

[5]The government sector and the foreign sector will be added to the circular flow model in Chapter Five.

Application 3.3
SUPPLY AND DEMAND IN PRACTICE

Much of the information on demand, supply, and prices comes from newspaper articles. And very often, buried in those articles, are concepts which you have studied in this chapter. How many of the concepts from this chapter can you find in the articles excerpted below? We found: changes in sellers' costs, changes in the numbers of buyers and sellers, the Law of Supply, price elasticity of supply, availability of substitute products, and changes in buyers' tastes.

U.S. Sardine Industry Falls on Hard Times, A Victim of Imports and Changing Tastes

Lubec, Maine—The U.S. sardine industry, already hurt by imports and consumers' waning appetite for the little fish, is winding up what may be its most devastating season. Some smaller companies may even be forced to fold. . . .

The sardine industry got its start in the mid-1870s when a cannery opened in Eastport—a thumb of rocky land and the easternmost city in the country. Soon after, dozens of canneries opened along the coast of rural Washington County. By 1952, the first year in which the Maine Sardine Council began keeping records, there were 46 plants packing a total of 3.2 million cases of sardines. But this year, the 14 remaining plants are expected to pack only 600,000 cases—the lowest yearly output on record.

Indeed, Americans' appetite for sardines has plunged. Only 2 million cases including imports, were sold in 1980, compared with 3 million in 1960.

Industry surveys have identified some of the reasons: Many consumers think the canned fish is raw; men like them but their wives don't buy them, and few people know what to do with them except to gobble them from the can. The Maine Sardine Council, a state agency supported by the industry, has tried to promote sardines through advertising, handing out recipes and even offering free comic books to school children, but nothing has helped sales. The future looks even bleaker. Surveys find sardine eaters are an aging group; younger people, increasingly accustomed to fast-food meals, avoid the tinned fish. . . .

Decade's Boom in Prime-Age Consumers Will Offer Vast Opportunities for Business

Before the decade is over, U.S. demographic patterns will be greatly altered. The crop of post

Microeconomics
The study of individual decision-making units and markets within the economy.

Microeconomics focuses on the behavior of individual operating units within each sector of the economy and on the operation of individual output and input markets. It includes such topics as consumer behavior, cost-benefit analysis, the determination of business profits, and the determination of prices in specific markets. In terms of the circular flow model, microeconomics examines the operation of individual business units within the business sector and individual households within the household sector, as well as the operation of specific markets. It is not directly concerned with relationships among sectors and markets.

World War II babies is arriving at the age when consumers do most of their spending. . . .

. . . Almost 60 million Americans were born from 1947 to 1961 and now account for about 40% of the adult population. Members of the group are 19 to 33 years old; by the end of the decade they will be 29 to 43. As a result, middle-aged Americans—those 35 to 54—will increase in number faster than any other age group. By 1990, the ranks of the middle-aged will grow by 13.5 million, or 28% [compared to 1980]. . . .

And there will be far fewer teen-agers. By 1990, their numbers will decline about 17%, or 4.6 million [compared to 1980]. . . .

Companies have long been aware of these trends, and most tied to consumer markets are already adjusting. With fewer teen-agers in sight, Blue Bell Inc. is putting more emphasis on jeans that are "cut for the more mature figure." Levi Strauss & Co., another jeans maker, formed its Levi's for Men division in 1976 for the "over-25 consumer" and is looking toward the 50s and over market. . . .

Revlon Inc. is pitching its formerly teen-age–oriented Natural Wonder cosmetics line to a broader "13-to-40" audience and using older models to promote it. . . .

Bad Weather, Disease Force Egg Prices Up Dramatically

Bad weather and disease have combined to cut the nation's supply of eggs and sent the average retail price rising 16 cents a dozen since October.

Heat and drought last summer reduced harvests and pushed up feed costs. Avian flu then struck poultry flocks in the late fall, mainly in Pennsylvania, prompting the killing of some 10.2 million chickens to prevent the spread of disease. And the winter cold has meant hens are laying fewer eggs. . . .

The higher egg prices may encourage producers to expand their flocks. But that would take time . . . since it takes five or six months to grow a chick into a productive egg layer, while it takes only seven to nine weeks to get a broiler ready for market.

Sources: Stephen P. Morin, "U.S. Sardine Industry Falls on Hard Times, A Victim of Imports and Changing Tastes," *The Wall Street Journal*, October 13, 1982, p. 29; "Decade's Boom in Prime-Age Consumers Will Offer Vast Opportunities for Business," *The Wall Street Journal*, June 26, 1980, p. 23; both reprinted by permission of *The Wall Street Journal*, © Dow Jones and Company, Inc. (1982 and 1980). All Rights Reserved. "Bad Weather, Disease Force Egg Prices Up Dramatically," *St. Louis Post–Dispatch*, February 2, 1984, Section X, page 1. Reprinted by permission.

Figure 3.15
Circular Flow of Economic Activity

Macroeconomics is concerned with the operation of the economy as a whole. Microeconomics is concerned with the behavior of individual decision-making units and markets within the economy.

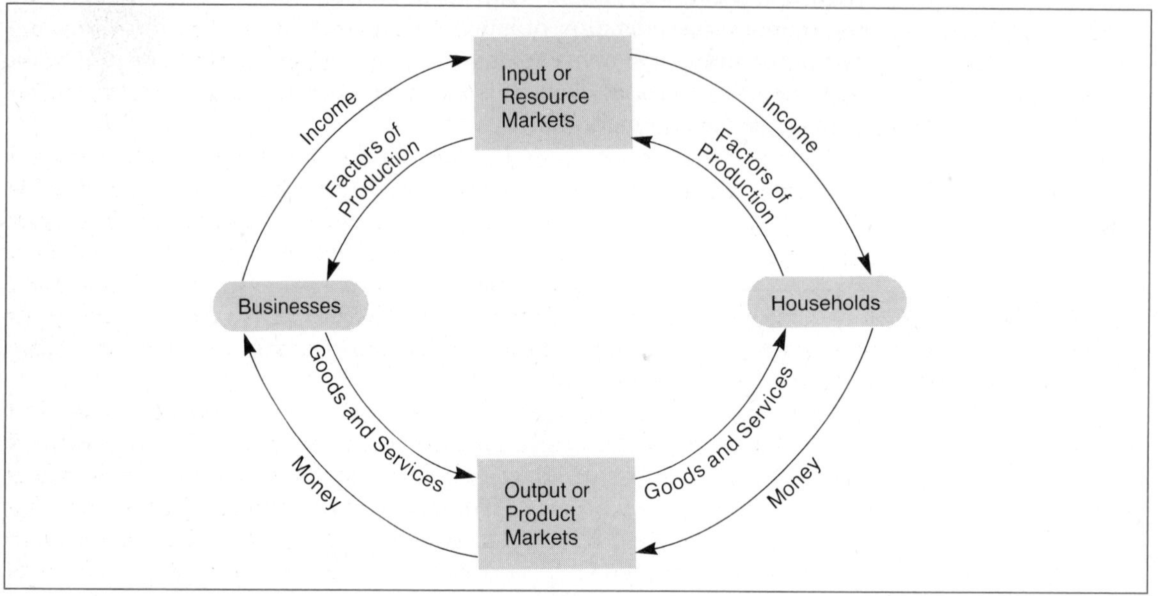

SUMMARY

A knowledge of the concepts of demand and supply is important to an understanding of the operation of a market economy. Demand refers to a buyer's plans to purchase different amounts of a product at different prices in a given period of time. The relationship between a product's prices and the different amounts of the product that a buyer plans to purchase at each of those prices is shown in a demand schedule. Prices and quantities in a demand schedule are graphically illustrated by a demand curve that slopes downward to the right. In both demand schedules and demand curves, higher prices are associated with smaller quantities demanded and lower prices with larger quantities demanded. This inverse relationship between price and quantity demanded is called the Law of Demand. The reasons for the Law of Demand are limited incomes and substitutability. The movement along a demand curve from one price-quantity point to another as a result of a change in a product's price is referred to as a change in quantity demanded.

A supply schedule shows the different amounts of a product that a seller would offer in the market at different prices in a given time period. Graphically, a supply schedule is represented by a supply curve that slopes upward to the right. The supply schedule and supply curve behave as they do because of the Law of Supply, which states that there is a direct relationship between price and quantity supplied. The reasons for the Law of Supply are cost and profitability. The movement along a supply curve from one price-quantity point to another caused by a change in the product's price is called a change in quantity supplied.

The price that equalizes buyers' and sellers' plans, and toward which a market automatically moves, is called the equilibrium price. This price is shown by the intersection of a product's market demand and supply curves. If the actual price of a product is above its equilibrium price, there will be a surplus of the product on the market, and forces will go into motion to bring the price down to its equilibrium level. If the price of a product is below its equilibrium level, there will be a shortage, and forces will go to work to bring the price up to its equilibrium level.

In addition to a product's price, nonprice factors also influence buyers and sellers. Changes in these nonprice factors lead to shifts in buyers' demand curves and sellers' supply curves. An increase in demand or supply means that buyers are demanding or sellers are supplying more of a product than before at each price, and the demand or supply curve shifts to the right. When less of a product than before is demanded or supplied at each price, there is a decrease in demand or supply, and the demand or supply curve shifts to the left. Since the equilibrium price and quantity of a product are shown by the intersection of its demand and supply curves, increases or decreases in demand or supply cause the product's equilibrium price and quantity to change.

If the government sets a price ceiling for a good or service, and the free market equilibrium price is above the government set price, a shortage will develop. If the government sets a price floor for a good or service, and the free market equilibrium price is below the government set price, a surplus will develop.

Economists use the concept of price elasticity to measure the sensitivities of buyers and sellers to changes in the price of a product. Demand or supply is price elastic if the response to a price change is strong, or if the quantity demanded or supplied changes by a greater percentage than the price changes. Demand or supply is price inelastic if the response to a price change is weak, or if the quantity demanded or supplied changes by a smaller percentage than the price changes. Elasticity of demand is affected by whether the product is a luxury or a necessity, by the availability of substitutes, and by the price of the product relative to a buyer's income. Time is the major determinant of a product's price elasticity of supply.

Macroeconomics is concerned with the operation of the economy as a whole and with the interaction of its major sectors. Microeconomics deals with individual operating units and markets within the economy.

Key Terms and Concepts

Demand
Demand schedule
Law of Demand
Demand curve
Supply
Supply schedule
Law of Supply
Supply curve
Market
Market demand and supply
Shortage
Surplus
Equilibrium price and equilibrium quantity
Change in quantity demanded
Change in quantity supplied
Nonprice influences on demand
Nonprice influences on supply
Change in demand
Change in supply
Increase (decrease) in demand
Increase (decrease) in supply
Price ceiling (upper price limit)
Price floor (lower price limit)
Price elastic
Price inelastic
Macroeconomics
Microeconomics

Discussion and Review Questions

1. Minimum wage laws keep many workers' hourly wages above what they would be if there were no such laws. Do minimum wage laws help or hurt college students looking for summer work?
2. What do you think happens or has happened in the markets for high school buildings, houses and apartments, rock music records and tapes, and formal and bridal wear as the people known as the "post–World War II baby boom" keep getting older?
3. What is your position on the question raised in Application 3.2 about a market for human organs? Can you think of any other situations where people could argue over whether a good or service should be prevented from being bought or sold in an open market?
4. Explain how you think each of the following would cause demand or supply to shift and how the equilibrium price and quantity for the good or service in question would change.
   a. An increase in the number of suppliers in the home insulation market
   b. Expectations by automobile buyers that prices on next year's models will increase substantially
   c. An increase in the popularity of a certain clothing maker's product
   d. A wage increase for hospital employees
   e. A cost-reducing invention that is adopted by the producers of a high-technology product

5. Differentiate between an elastic and inelastic response to a price change. Give some examples of goods and services where a consumer's response to a price change might typically be elastic, and examples of goods and services where a consumer's response to a price change might typically be inelastic.

6. Answer questions a through d on the basis of the following demand and supply schedules.

Price per Item	Quantity Demanded	Quantity Supplied
$ 1.25	150	0
2.50	140	50
3.75	125	60
5.00	105	70
6.25	80	80
7.50	50	90
8.75	10	100
10.00	0	110

   a. What is the equilibrium price and equilibrium quantity?

   b. How much of a shortage or surplus would occur at $2.50?

   c. How much of a shortage or surplus would occur at $7.50?

   d. What would happen if the government established a price floor of $8.75 on this item?

7. Is a change in the price of corn a macroeconomic or a microeconomic issue? What about the effect of a change in tax policy on the business sector of the economy, or a change in the amount of spending on goods and services by all households taken as a group?

Suggested Readings

J. Richard Aronson, *The Scorecard: A Guide to the Real World of Economics and Business* (Philadelphia: W. B. Saunders Co., 1979). An introduction to some supply and demand relationships concerning commodities and financial instruments. Gives sources of information on prices and other economic variables and provides a chartbook for recording price movements in various commodity and credit markets.

Douglas R. Bohi and Michael A. Toman, "Understanding Nonrenewable Resource Supply Behavior," *Science* (February 25, 1983), pp. 927–932. Discusses problems in applying economic models of supply to nonrenewable resources such as oil and natural gas.

R. Lee Harris, "How to Measure Market Demand," *Journal of Property Management* (March–April 1977), pp. 81–84. Application of the principles of demand and supply to the multifamily rental housing market.

Ralph Turvey, *Demand and Supply* (London: George Allen and Unwin, Ltd., 1971). A practical approach to supply and demand using examples from the British economy.

J. Karl Wise, "Elasticity of Demand for Veterinary Services," *Journal of the American Veterinary Medical Association* (August 15, 1980), p, 363. Application of the principle of price elasticity of demand to the pricing of veterinary services.

Test Yourself Answers (Application 3.1)

1. D; supply curve shifts to left.
2. A; demand curve shifts to right.
3. D; supply curve shifts to left.
4. E; no shift, movement along the curves.
5. B; demand curve shifts to left.
6. A; demand curve shifts to right.
7. C; supply curve shifts to right.
8. E; no shift, movement along the curves.
9. A; demand curve shifts to right.
10. E; no shift, movement along the curves.
11. D; supply curve shifts to left.

II The Macroeconomy

4 GOALS AND PROBLEMS OF THE MACROECONOMY: EMPLOYMENT, PRICES, AND PRODUCTION

Chapter Objectives

1. To introduce the three fundamental areas on which macroeconomics focuses: employment, prices, and production.
2. To define unemployment and explain its consequences.
3. To identify the different types of unemployment and to introduce measures and statistics on employment and unemployment.
4. To define full employment.
5. To define inflation and explain its consequences.
6. To identify the causes of inflationary pressure and to introduce measures and statistics on inflation.
7. To define full production and economic growth and to introduce GNP, the primary measure of production.
8. To define productivity and discuss changes in U.S. productivity over the years.
9. To highlight the policy problem that occurs in pursuing the goals of full employment, full production, and price stability simultaneously.

This chapter begins the section of the text devoted to macroeconomics, which is the study of the economy as a whole and involves such topics as aggregate (total) employment and production, unemployment, inflation, economic growth, money, and government stabilization policies. The study of macroeconomics will give you an understanding of how the various sectors of the economy interrelate with one another and how that interrelationship causes the system to operate, creates problems, and helps in the solving of those problems. However, before beginning the analysis, it is important to become familiar with some basic concepts involving employment, production, and prices, the three areas around which macroeconomics revolves. These three areas can be viewed as either the major problems of the macroeconomy when considered as unemployment, falling production, and inflation, or as the major goals of the macroeconomy when considered as full employment, full production and economic growth, and stable prices. These problems and goals will be explored in this chapter.

In the United States, full employment, full production and economic growth, and stable prices have been regarded as such important economic goals that, as noted in Chapter Two, Congress enacted Public Law 304 in 1946 to permit the government to have a hand in creating an economic environment that would lead to the achievement of these goals. This legislation, titled the Employment Act of 1946, states that:

> The Congress hereby declares that it is the continuing policy and responsibility of the Federal Government to use all practicable means consistent with its needs and obligations and other essential considerations of national policy, with the assistance and cooperation of industry, agriculture, labor, and State and local governments, to coordinate and utilize all its plans, functions, and resources for the purpose of creating and maintaining, in a manner calculated to foster and promote free competitive enterprise and the general welfare, conditions under which there will be afforded useful employment opportunities, including self-employment, for those able, willing, and seeking to work, *and to promote maximum employment, production, and purchasing power.* (emphasis added)[1]

Through this Act the government is not ensuring that these goals will be achieved, but rather that the government will aid in providing an environment which will lead to their achievement. This is a good example of the distinction between a planned economy and mixed capitalism.

UNEMPLOYMENT AND FULL EMPLOYMENT

Unemployment
A resource available for production is not being used.

A primary objective of almost all economies on the macroeconomic level is employment for all available factors of production. Stated another way, the intention is to minimize unemployment. **Unemployment** means that a resource available for production is not being used. Machines, raw materials, warehouses, trucks, and so forth can all be unemployed. Most often, however, the concern over unemployment focuses on people who would like to be working but are not. This concern results from the more obvious consequences of unemployment among people.

---

[1]*United States Statutes at Large, 1946,* Vol. 60, Pt. 1, *Public Laws and Reorganization Plans* (Washington, D.C.: United States Government Printing Office, 1947), p. 23.

The most dramatic siege of unemployment the United States has ever witnessed occurred in the Great Depression of the 1930s. From 1932 through 1935 the unemployment rate stayed at 20 percent or more, and in 1933 it reached almost 25 percent of the civilian labor force: roughly one out of every four people who wanted to work could not.[2]

Consequences of Unemployment

Why is there so much concern about unemployment, especially among workers? Unemployment has several undesirable consequences, including an economic loss for all of society, and individual hardship for the unemployed.

Economic Loss for Society Recall that economics is the study of how people use scarce resources to satisfy unlimited material wants and needs. If more resources are available and put into use, a greater number of wants and needs can be satisfied. If some resources are unemployed, some wants and needs that might have been satisfied will go unsatisfied. Thus, unemployment intensifies the scarcity problem, and the loss to society is the goods and services it might have enjoyed.

How serious is the loss in goods and services resulting from unemployment? One way of answering this question is to compare what was actually produced with what the economy could have produced if all willing and available resources were used. This is shown for the years 1978 through 1984 in Table 4.1. The column titled "Potential Output" indicates the value of the goods and services that could have been produced with resources fully employed. The column titled "Actual Output" shows the total value of the goods and services that were actually produced. The difference between what might have been produced and what actually was produced is shown in the column titled "Lost Output."[3] For example, in 1984, $118.2 billion more goods and services could have been produced if the economy's resources had been fully employed. Put another way, if the unemployment problem had been eliminated in 1984, the economy would have come $118.2 billion closer that year to lessening the scarcity problem.

Individual Hardships In addition to its effects on society, unemployment can cause private hardships for people who would like to be working but are not. Unemployment intensifies an individual's personal struggle with scarcity. As a period of unemployment lengthens, people might be forced to alter spending habits and thus their lifestyles. And if the loss of income due to unemployment reaches the point where finances are exhausted, dramatic

---

[2]U.S. Bureau of the Census, *Historical Statistics of the United States, Colonial Times to 1957* (Washington, D.C.: United States Government Printing Office, 1960), Series D 46–47, p. 73.

[3]The difference between potential output and actual output is generally referred to as the GNP gap. The expression GNP (gross national product) is introduced later in this chapter.

Table 4.1
Potential Output, Actual Output, and Lost Output from Unemployment (Billions of 1972 Dollars)

Because of unemployment, goods and services that might have been produced are lost to society, and the scarcity problem is intensified.

Year	Potential Output	Actual Output	Lost Output
1978	$1,487.4	$1,438.6	$ 48.8
1979	1,526.6	1,479.4	47.2
1980	1,558.5	1,475.0	83.5
1981	1,607.2	1,512.2	95.0
1982	1,653.6	1,480.0	173.6
1983	1,702.4	1,534.7	167.7
1984	1,757.2	1,639.0[a]	118.2

Real GNP

[a]Preliminary figure.

Source: Potential Output is from the Federal Reserve Bank of St. Louis. Based on R. H. Rasche and J. A. Tatom, "Energy Resources and Potential GNP," Federal Reserve Bank of St. Louis *Review* (June 1977), pp. 10–24; and J. A. Tatom, "Potential Output and the Recent Productivity Decline," Federal Reserve Bank of St. Louis *Review* (January 1982), pp. 3–16. Actual Output is from U.S., *Economic Report of the President* (Washington, D.C.: U.S. Government Printing Office, 1985), p. 234.

changes such as moving to cheaper housing or liquidating some assets might be necessary.

In addition to the financial dimension, a person's self-esteem and relationships with others may suffer from unemployment. How many times can a person be told that his or her services are not needed before frustration and self-doubt begin to set in? Do families who face the prospect of having to leave their friends and relocate, or of going without things they need, really grow closer in dealing with their problems, or is this often a romantic vision? The reading in Application 4.1 suggests that there is adequate evidence that unemployment has hidden psychological, and sometimes physiological, costs. The problems of depression, suicide, mental hospitalization, ulcers, and even the common cold can be aggravated by unemployment.

How serious could the hardships of unemployment become? William Manchester, in *The Glory and the Dream,* gives the following description of what unemployment was like for some in the Great Depression.

> The smartly dressed young lawyer who always left home at the same time each morning may have been off to sell cheap neckties, magazines, vacuum cleaners, pressure cookers, or Two-in-One shoe polish door-to-door in a remote neighborhood. He may have changed his clothes and gone to another part of the city to beg. Or he may have been one of the millions who looked for work day after day, year after year, watching his children grow thinner and fighting despair in the night. There were certain skills developed by men who spent their days in the streets. You learned to pay for a nickel cup of coffee, to ask for another cup of hot water free, and, by mixing the hot water with the ketchup on the counter, to make a kind of tomato soup. In winter you stuffed newspapers under your shirt to ward off the cold; if you knew you would be standing for hours outside an employment office, you wrapped burlap bags around your legs and tied them in place. Shoes were a special problem. Pasteboard could

> be used for inner soles, and some favored cotton in the heels to absorb the pounding of the concrete. But if a shoe was really gone, nothing worked. The pavement destroyed the cardboard and then the patch of sock next to it, snow leaked in and accumulated around your toes, and shoe nails stabbed your heels until you learned to walk with a particular gait.[4]

Fortunately, the effects of unemployment are less severe today than during the Great Depression. Since the 1930s the government has instituted some forms of income supplements for those without a job. While the payments do not completely replace lost income, they do soften the impact of unemployment. Unemployment compensation and food stamps are two examples of this government aid.

---

[4]*The Glory and the Dream: A Narrative History of America 1932–1972,* by William Manchester. Copyright © 1973, 1974 by William Manchester. Pages 34–35. By permission of Little, Brown and Company.

Application 4.1
THE HIDDEN PSYCHOLOGICAL COSTS OF UNEMPLOYMENT

. . . [Unemployment] figures, cold and devoid of emotion, fail to reflect the personal and social costs of such a widespread economic problem. To be unemployed in America is to be subjected to great psychological pain. . . .

A central theme involved in the reaction to being unemployed is loss. However, the loss is much more than simply the loss of income derived from one's work—it also involves the loss of crucial aspects of a person's psychological well-being. Being laid off is not only commonly interpreted as an indictment of one's personal competence and economic value to society, but additionally disrupts the sense of continuity and stability of an individual's life. . . .

Psychologists have long held that a common reaction to the experience of personal loss is depression, often mixed with anger. . . . Clinical impressions of the reactions of workers affected by the closing of their factory are replete with references to the depression common among the unemployed workers. More indirectly, depression is a cardinal characteristic of the suicidal person. Historically, the suicide rate has increased during periods of rising unemployment—a fact that strongly suggests widespread depressive reactions among the unemployed. More specifically, examination of worker reactions to plant closings reveals a sharp jump in both suicide attempts and successful suicides[1]. . . .

In a classic research project, Harvey Brenner of Johns Hopkins University documented the positive relationship between economic downturns and rates of hospitalization for mental illnesses. Brenner found that fluctuations in the national economy were the single most important determinant of mental hospitalization rates. Furthermore, this relationship has held up since the middle of the 19th century[2]. . . .

The hidden costs of unemployment are more than only psychological—they appear to be physiological as well. The stresses of being without a job in America frequently result in either the onset of new psychosomatic disorders or the flare-up of old and formerly controlled ailments,

Types of Unemployment

With unemployment leading to losses for society and hardships for those out of work, it is obvious why such a high priority is given to alleviating it. But before a problem can be alleviated, its cause must be known. Unfortunately, there is no single cause of unemployment. Three main sources of the problem are (1) friction in the labor market, (2) cyclical or periodic changes in the demand for goods and services, and (3) changes in the structure of the economy. These three sources form a framework for defining different types of unemployment. Thus, economists speak of frictional unemployment, cyclical unemployment, and structural unemployment.

Frictional Unemployment Some people looking for employment have voluntarily quit a job to search for another one. Some others are entering the job market for the first time or after a period of not looking for work. Will these people obtain a new job in a matter of moments by making one telephone call? The answer is probably not. There will likely be a period of

---

such as peptic ulcers. Cobb and Kasl studied the reactions of workers and their families to a plant closing and found that the symptoms of peptic ulcers were "unduly common" at the time of worker termination. They also uncovered an "extraordinarily high" incidence of ulcers among the wives of laid-off workers, which would suggest an increase in family stress which was related to being out of work[3]. . . . Other studies of worker reactions to job loss have found that such physiological reactions as the incidence of common colds and intestinal flu and increases in blood pressure (both systolic and diastolic), uric acid, serum cholesterol, and norepinephrine excretion frequently occur as a result of job loss. Significantly, many of these physiological measures returned to normal levels when the men were reemployed.[4]

In addition to the psychological and physiological costs of unemployment, there are more socially broad costs that transcend the individual and involve the concerns of society-at-large. Brenner's massive study not only found that mental hospitalization rates increased systematically with economic downturns, but also revealed that economic downturns were associated with increases in the rates of alcoholism and criminal imprisonment.[5] Others claim that divorce rates and child abuse rates increase markedly during periods of rising unemployment. Clearly, the hidden costs of tolerating a high level of unemployment are more than merely an individual concern. All of us—employed and unemployed alike—pay part of the cost. . . .

[1] Sidney Cobb and Stanislav V. Kasl, *Some Medical Aspects of Unemployment* (Ann Arbor: Institute for Social Research, University of Michigan, May, 1971), p. 4.

[2] Harvey Brenner, *Mental Illness and the Economy* (Cambridge, Mass.: Harvard University Press, 1973).

[3] Cobb and Kasl, *op. cit.*, p. 5.

[4] Sidney Cobb, "Physiologic Changes in Men Whose Jobs Were Abolished," *Journal of Psychosomatic Research*, 1974, vol. 18, pp. 245–258.

[5] Brenner, *op. cit.*, p. 224.

Source: John E. Hesson, "The Hidden Psychological Costs of Unemployment," *Intellect* (April 1978), pp. 389–90.

unemployment between leaving an old job and beginning a new one, or between entering the labor market and finding work. During this time the job seeker will be collecting references and credentials, following up leads, and interviewing prospective employers.

This failure to make a quick and smooth transition from an old to a new job, or from entering the labor market to employment, can be thought of as "friction" in the labor market. Thus, the **frictionally unemployed** are those who are voluntarily out of work and are searching for a job.

Frictional unemployment
Occurs when people are voluntarily out of work and in the process of obtaining a new job.

In a mobile economy such as that of the United States, there are always people voluntarily unemployed. They may have quit a job because they were disgruntled with it, or they may want to relocate to a different part of the country, or they may want to change their occupation, or they may have some other reason for being voluntarily unemployed. Thus, there are always workers voluntarily in the process of seeking employment, and there is always some frictional unemployment. Because of this, when we say that the economy is at full employment we do *not* mean that 100 percent of the labor force is working. Rather, **full employment** means that everyone in the labor force, except the frictionally unemployed, is working.

Full employment
Occurs when only those voluntarily out of work are unemployed, or the unemployment rate includes only frictional unemployment.

Cyclical Unemployment Market economies such as that of the United States do not produce goods and services at a constant rate over time. Rather, the economy goes through wavelike movements, or upswings and downswings in production, called business cycles. Periodically the economy falls into a downswing, or a recession, during which decreases in production and employment occur. When the demand for a good or service decreases in a recession, the workers producing that good or service may be involuntarily laid off. This type of unemployment is termed **cyclical unemployment** because it is the result of a recession, or a downswing in the business cycle.

Cyclical unemployment
Involuntary unemployment that results from a downswing in a business cycle, or a recession.

Cyclical unemployment is a matter of serious concern because, unlike frictional unemployment, it is involuntary and continues until the economy breaks out of the recession. This could be a matter of a few months and involve a small number of workers, or it could be a period of several years and extend to millions of families. In 1958 recessionary pressures led to a short period of cyclical unemployment, whereas during the early 1980s a lengthier period of cyclical unemployment occurred.

Some industries are more sensitive than others to changes in general economic conditions, and workers in these industries are particularly vulnerable to cyclical unemployment. When a recession is impending, the purchase of consumer durable goods, such as automobiles, and business capital goods, such as heavy machinery, may be postponed, causing sales to decline. Workers producing these types of products may then be laid off. Auto workers, steel workers, and construction workers, among others, are especially susceptible to cyclical unemployment.

Workers who are young and lacking in seniority are also vulnerable to cyclical unemployment. When a downswing occurs, the young are usually among the first workers to be laid off; and when the economy improves, they are usually among the last to be rehired.

Structural unemployment
Involuntary unemployment that results when a worker's job is no longer part of the production structure of the economy.

Structural Unemployment Like cyclical unemployment, **structural unemployment** is involuntary. It occurs when a worker loses a job because that occupation is no longer a part of the structure of the economy. The good or service the worker produced is either no longer demanded or is now made in a manner that has eliminated that particular job. Unlike cyclical unemployment, structural unemployment offers no prospect for rehire in the future.

Structural unemployment results mainly from technological changes in the economy, such as automation, and changes in the goods and services people demand. For example, the smooth operation of an office used to depend on large numbers of workers to type, file, keep books, and such. Today, office work has become highly mechanized; with the word processor and other computer systems, fewer workers are needed to accomplish these tasks. As a result, the services of many typists, bookkeepers, and file clerks are no longer needed. Other examples of structural unemployment include the coal miner and the switchboard operator who are being replaced by sophisticated equipment, and the keyboard typesetter whose occupation is being eliminated by electronic wizardry.

The structurally unemployed face the choice of finding new occupations or of going without work. Locating new work or learning a new skill is not always a simple matter. It imposes a particular hardship on the older worker. The structurally unemployed coal miner who may possess no other salable skill might find it difficult to learn a different trade. Schooling might present a financial burden, or the miner may be too close to retirement to want to retrain. Or, finding work might mean relocating in a new community away from family and friends. For these and other reasons, structural unemployment can bring about serious personal difficulties for the worker and the worker's family.

In recent years technological advancements in production processes have caused structural changes in the U.S. economy and have eliminated many types of blue-collar, assembly-line jobs. The era of "high tech" and robotics is changing the nature of job requirements in U.S. industry. Retraining workers may become increasingly important to reduce structural unemployment.

Measures and Statistics on Employment and Unemployment

Labor force
All persons 16 years of age and older who are working or actively seeking work.

When we speak of the labor force, the employed, and the unemployed, whom do we include and how do we arrive at the numbers we use? The **labor force** is defined as all persons 16 years of age and older who are working or actively seeking work. Thus, if an individual is capable of performing innumerable jobs, but is not working nor interested in seeking a job, then that individual is not included in the labor force. It is the desire for employment, not the capability, that determines whether a person is or is not in the labor force.

Table 4.2 presents some frequently used statistics on the labor force. Columns 2 and 3 of Table 4.2 give, respectively, the number of people in the noninstitutional civilian population who are eligible for the labor force, and the number actually in the labor force for selected years. It is important to appreciate how many millions of people are employed or actively seeking work each year. For example, in 1984 over 113 million people were in the labor force.

Participation rate
The percentage of some specified group that is in the labor force.

Participation rates for the noninstitutional civilian labor force are shown in column 4 of Table 4.2. The term **participation rate** refers to the percentage of some group that is in the labor force. The group being studied may be the entire noninstitutional civilian population, women, persons in different age groups or of different ethnic backgrounds, and so on. For example, according to Table 4.2, in 1984, 64.4 percent of the noninstitutional civilian population 16 years of age and older was in the civilian labor force. That is, approximately 113.5 million people out of a population group of approximately 176.4 million were employed or seeking work.

Table 4.2
The Labor Force, the Partipation Rate, and Unemployment

There are many statistics collected on labor in the United States. Some of the most important relate to the population eligible for the labor force, the labor force, the participation rate, and the unemployment rate.

1 Year	2 Noninstitutional Civilian Population Eligible for the Labor Force[a]	3 Civilian Labor Force	4 Participation Rate	5 Unemployment	6 Unemployment Rate
1929	—	49,180,000	—	1,550,000	3.2%
1933	—	51,590,000	—	12,830,000	24.9
1940	99,840,000	55,640,000	55.7%	8,120,000	14.6
1945	94,090,000	53,860,000	57.2	1,040,000	1.9
1950	104,995,000	62,208,000	59.2	3,288,000	5.3
1955	109,683,000	65,023,000	59.3	2,852,000	4.4
1960	117,245,000	69,628,000	59.4	3,852,000	5.5
1965	126,513,000	74,455,000	58.9	3,366,000	4.5
1970	137,085,000	82,771,000	60.4	4,093,000	4.9
1975	153,153,000	93,775,000	61.2	7,929,000	8.5
1976	156,150,000	96,158,000	61.6	7,406,000	7.7
1977	159,033,000	99,009,000	62.3	6,991,000	7.1
1978	161,910,000	102,251,000	63.2	6,202,000	6.1
1979	164,863,000	104,962,000	63.7	6,137,000	5.8
1980	167,745,000	106,940,000	63.8	7,637,000	7.1
1981	170,130,000	108,670,000	63.9	8,273,000	7.6
1982	172,271,000	110,204,000	64.0	10,678,000	9.7
1983	174,215,000	111,550,000	64.0	10,717,000	9.6
1984	176,383,000	113,544,000	64.4	8,539,000	7.5

[a]For years prior to 1947, the noninstitutional civilian population eligible for the labor force, and the civilian labor force included persons 14 years of age and older. Since 1947, the measures include persons 16 years of age and older.

Source: U.S., *Economic Report of the President* (Washington, D.C.: U.S. Government Printing Office, 1985), p. 266.

Feb. 88 121.3 6.9 5.7%

Table 4.3 lists the participation rates for various subgroups within the labor force. It shows, for instance, that in 1983, 50.8 percent of all women 16 through 19 years old were working or actively seeking work. Participation rates are important because, when examined over time, they aid in determining changes in the composition of the labor force. For example, Table 4.3 shows that much of the recent growth in the labor force may be due to the increased participation of women and teenagers. At the same time it shows that there has been a drop in the participation rate for men. What do you think are some of the reasons for these changes? Why are a larger percentage of women and teenagers and a smaller percentage of men employed or actively seeking work?

Unemployment rate
The percentage of the labor force that is unemployed.

Returning to Table 4.2, columns 5 and 6 give some statistics on the unemployed in the labor force. Column 5 shows the number of unemployed persons in the labor force, and column 6 gives the **unemployment rate,** which is the percentage of the civilian labor force that is unemployed and actively seeking work. For example, the unemployment rate of 7.5 percent in 1984 reflects the fact that 8,539,000 persons in a labor force of 113,544,000 were unemployed and actively seeking work. Since the current labor force is approximately 114 million persons, a 1 percent rate of unemployment translates into approximately 1.1 million persons out of work. A 7 percent rate of unemployment represents over 7.7 million persons unemployed.

The unemployment rate is calculated on a monthly and an annual basis by the U.S. Department of Labor, Bureau of Labor Statistics, and is publicly announced through the media. Many people have a misconception about the method used to calculate this rate. They do not realize that the government uses a random-survey technique, not information from state employment offices, to determine the number of workers unemployed. A discussion of this data collection method is found in Application 4.2, "Determining the Unemployment Rate."

Along with the overall rate of unemployment, rates are also calculated for various subgroups within the labor force. Table 4.4 lists unemployment rates for selected labor market subgroups during several different years. Some interesting observations can be made from this table. For one, in any given year there is a disparity in the unemployment rates of the various subgroups.

Table 4.3
Participation Rates for Selected Labor Market Subgroups for Different Years

Participation rates differ for subgroups in the labor force, and changes in participation rates affect the composition of the labor force over time.

Group	1965	1970	1975	1980	1983
Male[a]	80.7%	79.7%	77.9%	77.4%	76.4%
Female[a]	39.3	43.3	46.3	51.5	52.9
Male, 16–19 years old	53.8	56.1	59.1	60.5	56.2
Female, 16–19 years old	38.0	44.0	49.1	52.9	50.8

[a]Includes persons 16 years of age and older.

Source: U.S. Bureau of the Census, *Statistical Abstract of the United States: 1985* (105th ed.), Washington, D.C., 1984, p. 392. Figures for 1965 are from the *Statistical Abstract of the United States: 1982–83* (103d ed.), 1982, p. 377.

Table 4.4
Unemployment Rates for All Workers and Selected Labor Market Subgroups for Different Years

Over the years, some subgroups in the labor force, such as teenagers, have faced more severe unemployment problems than other subgroups.

Group	1960	1965	1970	1975	1980	1984
All civilian workers	5.5%	4.5%	4.9%	8.5%	7.1%	7.5%
White	5.0	4.1	4.5	7.8	6.3	6.5
Male	4.8	3.6	4.0	7.2	6.1	6.4
Female	5.3	5.0	5.4	8.6	6.5	6.5
Black and other	10.2	8.1	8.2	13.8	13.1	14.4
Male	10.7	7.4	7.3	13.6	13.2	—
Female	9.4	9.2	9.3	13.9	13.1	—
Married men, spouse present	3.7	2.4	2.6	5.1	4.2	4.6
Women who maintain families	—	—	5.4	10.0	9.2	10.3
Men 20 years old and over	4.7	3.2	3.5	6.8	5.9	6.6
Women 20 years old and over	5.1	4.5	4.8	8.0	6.4	6.8
Teenagers (16–19 years old)	14.7	14.8	15.3	19.9	17.8	18.9

Source: U.S., *Economic Report of the President* (Washington, D.C.: U.S. Government Printing Office, 1985), pp. 271, 273. Data for Black and Other Males and Females are from the 1984 *Economic Report of the President*, p. 261.

Application 4.2
DETERMINING THE UNEMPLOYMENT RATE

The monthly Current Population Survey (CPS) of the U.S. Bureau of the Census uses a stratified probability sample of living quarters representative of the civilian noninstitutional population of the United States. About 60,000 households are interviewed each month. . . . The first interview for each household is carried out in person when possible, while a greater proportion of later interviews are by telephone. The respondent in the household is asked questions about all members of the household.

Among other questions (concerning age, education, marital and veterans status, and so forth), the respondent is asked a series of questions concerning the major activities of each person in the household who was 16 years of age or older during the previous week. . . . The respondent's answers are used to place the individuals in one of three mutually exclusive and exhaustive categories: employed, unemployed, or out of the labor force. The respondents are not asked directly to place the respective household members in these categories, however. Rather, specific questions are asked about labor force activ-

For example, in 1984 the unemployment rate for married men was 4.6 percent, compared to 18.9 percent for teenagers and 6.8 percent for women 20 years of age and older. Next, notice that some groups within the labor force have traditionally experienced unemployment rates that are higher than the overall unemployment rate for all workers, and other groups have experienced unemployment rates lower than the overall rate for all workers. This can be seen in Table 4.4 by comparing the unemployment rates for any labor market subgroup with the rates for all workers over several years. For example, the data show a better employment experience for married men in the labor market than for all workers taken as a group, but not for women who maintain families. Women 20 years of age and older have fared slightly better than all workers, while teenagers have fared poorly. Statistics such as these have led some policy makers to question whether government programs to alleviate unemployment should be directed toward the unemployed generally or toward specific groups within the labor force such as teenagers.

The Goal of Full Employment

As stated earlier, full employment is a major macroeconomic goal. However, full employment does *not* mean that 100 percent of the labor force is working. It means that only those who are voluntarily out of work are unemployed.

How do we determine when full employment occurs? How much unemployment can the economy have and still be at full employment? What is the unemployment rate beyond which genuine concern is warranted? There

---

ities during recent weeks and the reasons for them. . . .

The answers to these questions determine each eligible household member's labor force status: people are counted as *employed* if during the past week they worked at least 1 hour as paid employees or in their own business, profession or farm, or for at least 15 hours as unpaid workers in a family-operated enterprise, or if they had jobs or businesses from which they were temporarily absent because of illness, bad weather, vacation, labor-management dispute, or various personal reasons. Each employed person is counted only once, no matter how many jobs they might have worked at during the week. Individuals are classified as *unemployed* only if they meet *all* the following conditions: they did not work at all during the survey week, and were looking for work (had made specific efforts to find work within the preceding 4-week period) or were on layoff, and were available for work during the reference period (except for temporary illness). All civilians 16 years of age and older who are not classified as employed or unemployed are defined as being *not in the labor force.*

Source: Richard J. McDonald, "The 'Underground Economy' and BLS Statistical Data," *Monthly Labor Review* (January 1984), p. 8.

are no absolute answers to these questions. Economists, statisticians, and government policy makers have not been able to agree about the percentage of the labor force that is frictionally unemployed. In practice it is difficult to draw the line between those who are voluntarily and involuntarily without work, or between those who are and are not looking in earnest for a new position. Moreover, the percentage that is generally considered to represent full employment appears to change with time. In the 1950s, a 3 percent rate of unemployment was generally considered to represent full employment. During the 1960s we began to associate full employment with a 4 percent rate, and by the 1970s many believed it was 5 percent. At present some still concur with the 3 to 4 percent rate, and others have extended the rate to close to 6 percent. In determining the potential output for the economy from 1975 through 1979, the Council of Economic Advisors benchmarked the unemployment rate at 5.1 percent.[5]

The unemployment rate that represents full employment has been disputed and pushed up over the years for several reasons. First, the increased rate may be caused in part by changes in the composition of the labor force. As shown in Table 4.3, the participation rates for women and teenagers have increased over the last few decades, while that for men has fallen. And as shown in Table 4.4, women and teenagers typically experience higher unemployment rates than do men. Thus, the increased labor force attachment of women and teenagers, with their traditionally higher rates of unemployment, may be contributing to an increase in the unemployment rate associated with full employment.

A second reason for increasing the unemployment rate that represents full employment may be the availability of unemployment compensation from the government to those who have lost their jobs. Some studies have indicated that higher amounts of payments and longer periods of eligibility for payment increase a tendency to remain out of work. Thus, although a person may be technically unemployed, that person's situation might be more voluntary than it would have been if there were no unemployment compensation payments.

Because of the disagreement as to the unemployment rate that represents full employment, it is difficult to make policy recommendations or to assess the seriousness of the unemployment problem. If the full employment rate is, say, 5 percent, and the actual rate of unemployment is 6 percent, then approximately 1.1 million workers are involuntarily without a job. If the full employment rate is 6 percent and the actual rate is also 6 percent, then those unemployed are voluntarily so, and no serious problem exists.

Humphrey-Hawkins Full Employment and Balanced Growth Act
Passed by Congress in 1978, it requires that the government set annual numerical goals for such things as unemployment over a five-year period.

In 1978 Congress passed the **Humphrey-Hawkins Full Employment and Balanced Growth Act,** which strengthens the Employment Act of 1946. This new act requires that the government set annual numerical goals for

[5]U.S., *Economic Report of the President* (Washington, D.C.: U.S. Government Printing Office, 1980), p. 90.

such things as unemployment over a five-year period. The first set of goals established target rates to be reached in 1983 of 4 percent unemployment for workers aged 16 through 19, and 3 percent for workers aged 20 and older.[6] Some economists were skeptical about the possibility of attaining goal rates that low. The 1983 unemployment figures given in Table 4.4 for these groups indicate that the first set of goals was not attained.

INFLATION AND STABLE PRICES

Inflation
An increase in the general level of prices.

Another primary macroeconomic concern of most market economies is the maintenance of stable prices, or the control of inflation. Like unemployment, inflation can have severe consequences. **Inflation** is an increase in the general level of prices. It does not mean that prices are high, but rather that they are increasing. For example, assume that over the past two years the price of a particular combination of consumer goods in Country A has been stable at $100. Assume that in Country B the price of that same combination of consumer goods has gone up over the last two years from $10 to $30. Country B, not Country A, faces a problem with inflation. Inflation refers to price movements, not price levels.

With inflation, the price of every good and service does not need to increase because inflation refers to an increase in the *general level* of prices. An inflation rate of 7 percent does not mean that all prices are increasing by 7 percent; it means that, on the average, prices are going up by that amount. Also, the mere existence of an increase in the general level of prices is not necessarily a matter of concern in an economy. An inflation rate of 2 to 3 percent per year would not present a major policy problem. However, when prices increase by a larger percentage, such as 8 to 10 percent or more per year, inflation is a serious issue.

How serious can inflation become? In January 1922, nearly 290,000 Russian rubles were necessary to buy what one ruble would have purchased in 1913. Also in January 1922, 48 German paper marks were worth one German gold mark. By July of that year the ratio was 160 paper marks to one gold mark, and by November 1923 it took over one trillion paper marks to equal one gold mark.[7] More recently, in Chile, by 1977 the general level of consumer prices had increased to about 1,662 times the level in 1970. Over that same period wholesale prices were more seriously affected. What cost one escudo wholesale in 1970 cost 4,813 escudos in 1977.[8]

---

[6]U.S., *Economic Report of the President* (Washington, D.C.: U.S. Government Printing Office, 1979), pp. 107–108.

[7]Shephard B. Clough, Thomas Moodie, and Carol Moodie, eds., *Economic History of Europe: Twentieth Century* (New York: Harper and Row, Publishers, Inc., 1968), pp. 111, 124.

[8]U.S. Bureau of the Census, *Statistical Abstract of the United States: 1979* (100th ed.), Washington, D.C., 1979, p. 899.

Consequences of Inflation

When the general level of prices in an economy increases, especially at an unacceptable rate, several problems emerge. Inflation intensifies the scarcity problem when income does not rise as quickly as prices; it penalizes some groups such as savers receiving low interest rates; it changes the value of assets; and inflation can be politically and socially destabilizing.

Inflation and Income As noted earlier, unemployment intensifies the scarcity problem by reducing or even terminating the income of some people. Inflation also reduces income, not in the same way as unemployment, but by reducing the purchasing power of money. When inflation sets in, prices increase, so the same amount of money income buys fewer goods and services. Expressed differently, **real income** falls. Consequently, the scarcity problem for households and individuals is aggravated when incomes do not rise as rapidly as prices.

Real Income
The amount of goods and services that can be purchased with a particular amount of money income.

How much must income increase in the face of inflation to sustain the same purchasing power from year to year? The answer is suggested in Application 4.3, "The Purchasing Power of Income." Notice from this application that to maintain the same purchasing power, or real income, with inflation, money income must rise to compensate for both price increases and increases in taxes. The structure of the federal personal income tax in the United States is such that rising money income places individuals in progressively higher tax brackets. For example, according to Application 4.3, a person earning $25,000 in 1970 would have been able to purchase $20,639 worth of goods and services after taxes. In order to buy the same amount of goods and services in 1984, this person would have needed $64,197! Part of this increase was due to the extra $29,369 necessary to keep up with the rising prices on goods and services, and part was due to this individual's tax bill of $14,189 resulting from the larger money income.

The impact of inflation on households and businesses depends in part on which prices are moving up rapidly and which are not. If the prices of luxuries or products with many substitutes are increasing rapidly, the impact of inflation can be reduced by altering or curtailing purchases. For example, if the prices of new automobiles are increasing rapidly, consumers could purchase used cars, maintain and repair their currently owned cars, or use public transportation. If prices of necessities or goods and services with few substitutes are increasing quickly, the effects of inflation on a household or business might be more pronounced. For example, if increases in the prices of food and heating fuels were particularly acute, consumers would be limited in their abilities to adjust their spending patterns by reducing their food intake and warmth. They would have to absorb most of the impact of these price increases and, as more of their income would go to food and heat, either reduce their level of savings or reduce their consumption of other goods and services.

Application 4.3
The Purchasing Power of Income

With inflation, incomes must grow to compensate for higher prices. But larger incomes mean more taxes paid to the government because of the progressive nature of the U.S. tax system. Thus, with inflation, to maintain the same purchasing power, incomes must increase by enough to cover both price increases and increased taxes.

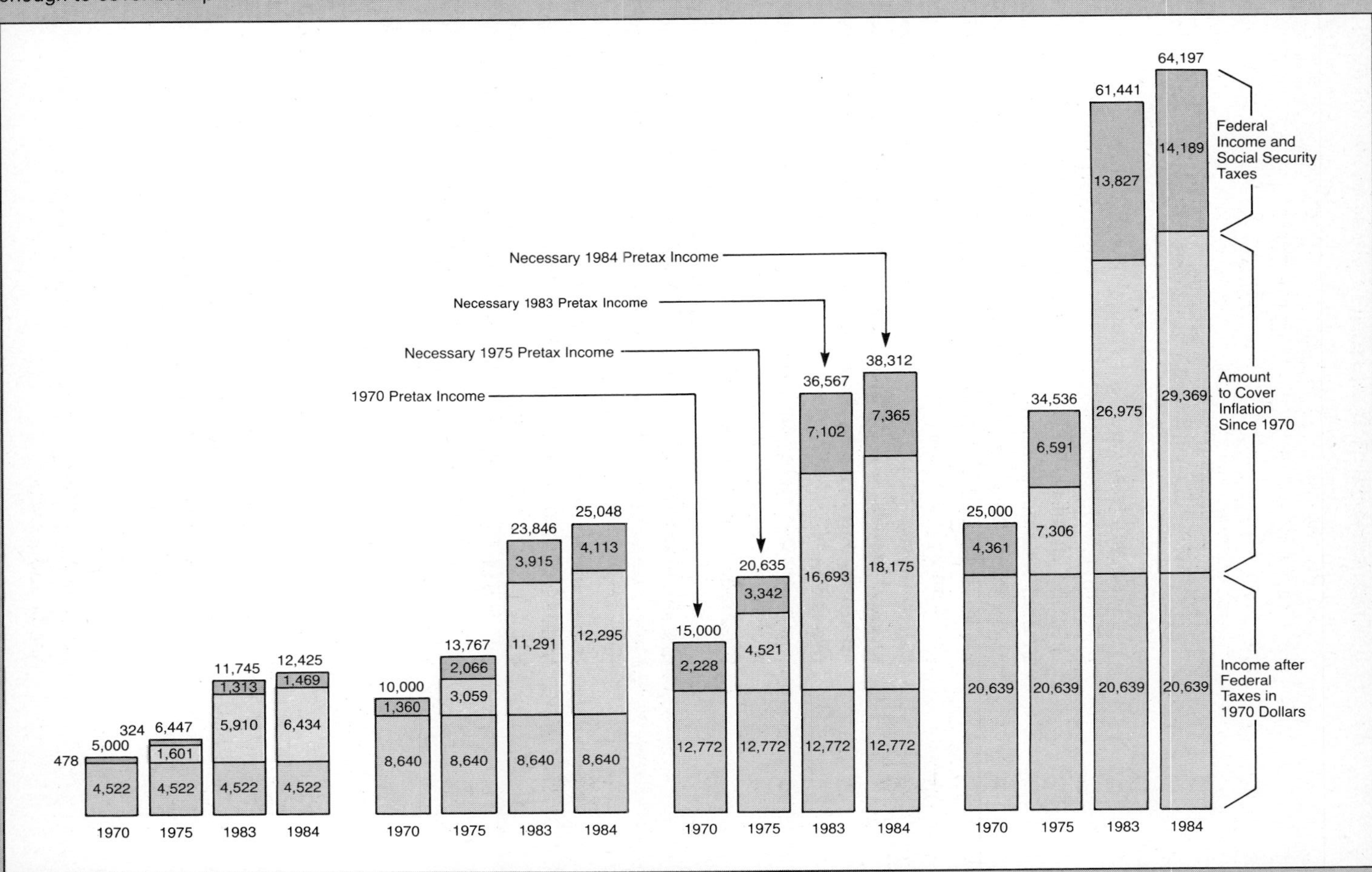

Source: The Conference Board, "The Two-Way Squeeze, 1984," *Economic Road Maps*, No. 1970, April 1984. Reprinted by permission.

There are some groups in society whose incomes typically do not keep up with inflation. People living on a fixed income, such as pensioners, are one such group. If the size of a person's pension check remains unchanged and prices keep rising, the purchasing power of that check keeps getting smaller. Over time, with a severe bout of inflation, a pensioner's standard of living may decline significantly.

Those who work under contract may also be hurt by inflation if their contracted wage increases are less than the inflation rate. For example, a union might negotiate a 7 percent annual wage increase for three years, and then encounter an inflation rate that ranges from 9 percent to 13 percent annually over the life of the contract. These workers will clearly experience a decline in their real standard of living. To avoid this situation, many contracts provide for a **cost of living adjustment (COLA),** which is an automatic wage increase when prices go up.

Cost of living adjustment (COLA)
An arrangement whereby an individual's wages automatically increase with inflation.

Inflation and the Interest Rate An interest rate is a price for borrowed money. Interest is the return received by savers of money and individuals and institutions that make loans, and the cost to borrowers of money for the use of funds.

Those who save may be penalized by inflation if the interest rate they receive is less than the rate of inflation. Take the case of a woman who planned to retire in early 1985 and put $10,000 in the bank in 1967, where it earned 5 percent annual interest. By the time she retired and withdrew her money, that $10,000 had grown to $24,066.18. Was this a good investment? How much better off was she in 1985 with her additional $14,066.18? Between the time when she put her money in the bank and the time of her retirement, prices had been going up. What could be purchased for $10,000 in 1967 cost $31,100.00 at the beginning of 1985.[9] The original $10,000 plus $14,066.18 in interest that our retiree had in 1985 bought less than the original $10,000 would have bought in 1967. Plus, the retiree's purchasing power was further reduced because she had to pay income tax on the interest! Thus, those who save their money can be hurt by inflation if the after-tax interest they earn on their savings does not keep up with the inflation rate.

Those who make loans may also be hurt by inflation if the interest rate they charge is less than the rate of inflation, and if the terms of the loans are fixed and cannot be altered to allow interest rate increases. This type of problem often emerges when a lender makes a long-term loan commitment. In the 1970s and early 1980s, many banks and savings and loan associations were caught with long-term, fixed-rate home mortgages[10] carrying interest

[9]See Table 4.6.

[10]A fixed rate means that the interest rate does not change during the loan repayment period. A long-term loan means that the borrower has a considerable period of time for repayment, perhaps as much as 30 years.

rates as low as 6 to 8 percent. These low interest rates were far below annual inflation rates and the rates charged for new loans. Both the low interest rates and the long terms of the loans were costly to these financial institutions. As a result of this experience, many home mortgages are currently made with variable rates and flexible terms.

Wealth
A measure of the value of economic assets; includes items such as real estate and corporate securities.

Inflation and Wealth Income and wealth are two different measures of economic well-being. Income represents a flow of funds, or earnings, from selling factors of production; **wealth** is a measure of the stock, or value, of one's economic assets, or a measure of what one owns. It includes items such as stocks, bonds, real estate, precious metals and stones, and fine art. A person could have a substantial income and little wealth, or great wealth (a large number of valuable assets) and a small income.

During inflation, the value of many assets tends to increase as prices rise. Thus, the wealthy become wealthier. Consider real estate. A home purchased in 1970 for $30,000 might have well been worth $100,000 by the early 1980s largely as a result of inflation over the decade of the 1970s.

While inflation benefits the holders of wealth, it penalizes those wishing to acquire assets in the future. Again, consider real estate. As prices rapidly increase, those desirous of purchasing a residence find it more and more difficult to do so. In this sense, younger people pay a higher penalty than others for inflation as it becomes more difficult for them to accumulate assets.

Social and Political Consequences of Inflation Finally, in addition to its economic consequences, inflation may have social and political implications as well. Inflation-related issues often form planks in election campaign platforms: incumbents may argue for a return to office to continue their successful fight against increasing prices, and the opposition may argue that it is time for new solutions to old problems.

If prolonged or severe enough, inflation might lead not only to changes in leadership, but to changes in social and political institutions as well. The eminent British economist John Maynard Keynes wrote, "There is no subtler, no surer means of overturning the existing basis of society than to debauch the currency."[11] The rise in the popularity of Hitler and Nazism can be traced in part to the discontent and social disruption caused by the German hyperinflation of the early 1920s.

Causes of Inflationary Pressure

Since inflation means an upward movement in the general level of prices, and since prices result from the interaction of buyers' demand and sellers' supply decisions, a logical way of classifying the causes of inflation is to

---

[11]John M. Keynes, *The Economic Consequences of the Peace* (New York: Harcourt, Brace and Howe, 1920), p. 236.

determine whether they come from the buyers' or the sellers' side of the market. Inflation caused by upward pressure on prices coming from the buyers' side of the market is termed demand-pull inflation. Inflation caused by upward pressure coming from the sellers' side of the market is called cost-push inflation.

Demand-pull inflation
Caused by pressure on prices from the buyers' side of the market; tends to occur when buyers' demands (or spending) are greater than the abilities of sellers to supply goods and services.

Demand-pull inflation occurs when buyers' demands to purchase goods and services outstrip sellers' abilities to supply them. When sellers are unable to respond sufficiently to meet buyers' demands, prices are forced up on what is available. If demand subsides, so will the pressure on prices.

Demand-pull inflation has a tendency to occur when the economy is close to or at full employment. At full employment the economy is operating at full capacity and producing the maximum amount of goods and services possible. Production cannot be readily expanded. At the same time, with all but the frictionally unemployed working and earning income, consumer demand for goods and services is high. Also, because consumer demand is high, businesses may find it profitable to expand and invest in new buildings and machinery. This demand, or spending pressure, by both households and businesses, coupled with peak production, sets off demand-pull inflation.

Demand-pull inflation is also related to the amount of money in the economy. The ability of households and businesses to spend depends in part on the amount of money available for spending. If the supply of money in the economy increases at a faster rate than the increase in production, there may be upward pressure on prices. Also, if the economy is at full employment, and more money is put into the hands of businesses and consumers, the result will be inflationary. Thus, too much money in the economy and in the hands of businesses and consumers can contribute to demand-pull inflation. On the other hand, controlling the money supply places curbs on the ability to spend, and thus on demand-pull inflation.

Cost-push inflation
Caused by pressure on prices from the sellers' side of the market, particularly from increases in costs.

Cost-push inflation occurs when price increases are caused by pressures from the sellers' side of the market. With this type of inflation, increases in sellers' costs are translated into higher prices for goods and services. That is, when sellers pay higher prices to get an input into a production process, the increased costs to the sellers may be wholly or partially passed on to buyers in the form of higher prices. Anything that represents a cost to a business is a potential source of price increases, and thus of cost-push inflation. This means that upward pressure on prices could come from increased costs of labor, raw materials, fuels, machinery, borrowing, and so on.[12] Certainly the increased cost of energy contributed to cost-push inflation in the 1970s and early 1980s. For example, a barrel of crude oil that sold for $3.18 in 1970 increased to $31.77 by 1981.[13]

---

[12]The attempt to increase profit by raising prices can also be a source of cost-push inflation.

[13]U.S. Bureau of the Census, *Statistical Abstract of the United States: 1985* (105th ed.), Washington, D.C., 1984, p. 705.

Cost-push inflation can be the result of bargaining power by resource owners, poor productivity, limited availability of resources, or chance events that reduce the supply of an important factor of production. For example, a severe drought or too much rain could reduce the harvest of a crop, or political and social unrest overseas could lead to a reduction in the availability of a resource important to production in the United States. In both of these cases the supply of the resource decreases, causing its price to go up, thereby contributing to inflationary pressure.

Cost-push inflation would more likely affect the economy when cost increases push up the prices of large firms which play an important role in the economy, such as automobiles or oil producers, or push up the prices of a significant number of smaller firms, such as cattle producers.

Inflation need not come solely from the buyers' side or solely from the sellers' side of the market; it could come simultaneously from both sides. Consider the potential effect of a recently negotiated wage contract for a large union. On the one hand, these workers are consumers, so the contract puts more spending power in the hands of buyers, making it a potential source of demand-pull inflation. On the other hand, the contracted wages will increase labor costs, creating the potential for cost-push inflation. It is easy to see from this example how inflation has a tendency to spiral.

It should be noted that wage increases (or any other increases in costs) may be as much a response to inflation as they are a cause. That is, an increase might be designed to cover costs that have resulted from earlier inflation or to compensate for expected higher costs of living.

The influence of expectations of future economic conditions on both demand-pull and cost-push inflation is important. On the demand-pull side, buyers' fear of higher prices in the future may lead them to increase their current purchases as they attempt to obtain desired goods and services before the expected higher prices become reality. At full employment, this increased demand will put additional pressure on an economy already operating at its productive capacity and will result in a rise in prices. On the sellers' side, firms' expectations of increasing costs for their inputs might cause them to raise prices in anticipation of those higher costs. Thus, a curious situation results in which the expectation of rising prices could aggravate inflation.

Measures of Inflation

Consumer price index (CPI)
Measures changes in the prices of goods and services that consumers typically purchase, such as food, shelter, clothing, and medical care.

The three most widely used measures of price changes, or indicators of inflation, are the consumer price index (CPI), the producer price index (PPI),[14] and the GNP deflator. The **consumer price index** measures changes in the prices of goods and services that households typically purchase: shelter, util-

[14]The producer price index was previously termed the wholesale price index.

Producer price index (PPI)
Measures changes in the prices of goods that businesses buy either for further processing or for sale to a consumer.

GNP deflator
A composite price index that measures price changes for the entire economy, regardless of whether the goods and services measured go to households, businesses, or the government.

Price index
Measures changes in the price of an item or a group of items using a percentage scale.

ities, food, clothing, and so forth. The **producer price index** measures changes in the prices of goods that businesses buy, either for further processing or for sale to a consumer. This includes, for example, grain, wool products, iron, steel, and chemicals. The **GNP deflator** is a composite index that refers to price changes for the entire economy, regardless of whether the goods and services measured go to businesses, households, or the government. Before these indexes are examined further, it is helpful to understand what a price index is and how it is calculated and interpreted.

A **price index** is a measure of price changes using a percentage scale. It is generally based on the prices of a selected group of goods and services (a market basket) that does not change in its composition from year to year. For example, approximately 400 items such as rent, electricity, and automobiles are included in the market basket for the consumer price index. This market basket allows those who calculate the index to determine what it would cost to purchase these same items year after year.

Table 4.5 shows how a price index is calculated. The column headed "Dollar Outlay for Market Basket" gives the expenditure required to purchase the same items in years 1 through 5. Notice that this expenditure increases with each year: the same goods and services that cost $475 in year 1 cost $600 in year 4.

Base year
The year against which prices in other years are compared in a price index.

Actual dollar outlays for the market basket are converted to a percentage scale, the price index, which is shown in the right-hand column of Table 4.5. Because it uses percentages, the index provides an easy method for comparing and evaluating price changes. To create an index, a **base year** is selected to serve as the year against which all other years' prices are compared. The base year is given the number 100.0, or 100 percent, in the index. In Table 4.5, year 2 is the base year.

The index numbers for the other years represent, in percentages, how many more or fewer dollars than base year dollars are needed to buy the same items. For example, in year 3, $550 are needed to buy what $500 bought in the base year. Put differently, one needs the base $500 plus $50, or 10 percent more dollars, to buy the same goods and services. The index number of 110.0 for year 3 reflects that prices have gone up by 10 percent from year 2 to year 3. In year 4, an additional $100, or 20 percent more dollars than in the base year, are needed to buy the market basket; hence, the index reads 120.0, or 120 percent. Prices have gone up by 20 percent between year 2 and year 4.

Table 4.5
A Price Index

The annual dollar outlays over time for a market basket of goods and services are converted to a percentage scale called a price index. Year 2 is the base year in this index.

Year	Dollar Outlay for Market Basket	Price Index
1	$475	95.0
2	500	100.0
3	550	110.0
4	600	120.0
5	625	125.0

In year 1 the same goods and services were $25 less than in the base year. Since $25 is 5 percent of the base year's outlay, this represents a 5 percent reduction in price. The index number for year 1 is 95.0, meaning that only 95 percent of the dollars used in the base year were needed in year 1. In summary, indexes permit us to measure changes in prices between a base year and various other years.

The Consumer Price Index Table 4.6 presents the overall consumer price index and the indexes for various categories of goods and services in the consumer price index, such as rent, medical care, and fuel oil, coal and bottled gas for selected years. In this table 1967 is the base year.

Some interesting observations can be made from this table. Under the column headed "All Items," notice the changes in the overall consumer price index for the 15-year intervals between 1952 and 1967, and between 1967 and 1982. What cost $100 in 1967 cost $79.50, or $20.50 less, in 1952. However, those same items that cost $100 in 1967 cost $289.10 in 1982—$189.10 more than 15 years earlier! Also, notice that as of 1984 it took more than three times as many dollars to buy what could have been purchased in 1967. These figures indicate that the 1970s and early 1980s clearly were inflation-plagued.

You might also observe in Table 4.6 that some goods and services have increased in price by less than the overall increase in the consumer price index. Rent and apparel, for example, might be considered "bargains" in the market basket. Other products have increased by much more than the over-

Table 4.6
Consumer Price Index and Various Categories within the Index for Selected Years (1967 = 100.0)

The consumer price index measures changes in the prices of goods and services that consumers typically purchase. Increases in prices for some components within the index, such as fuel and medical care, have been greater than the increase in the overall index.

Year	All Items	Food	Rent, Residential	Fuel Oil, Coal, and Bottled Gas	Apparel and Upkeep	Medical Care
1952	79.5	84.3	76.2	78.0	85.3	59.3
1957	84.3	84.9	87.5	90.3	87.3	69.9
1962	90.6	89.9	94.0	91.5	90.9	83.5
1967	100.0	100.0	100.0	100.0	100.0	100.0
1972	125.3	123.5	119.2	118.5	122.3	132.5
1973	133.1	141.4	124.3	136.0	126.8	137.7
1974	147.7	161.7	130.6	214.6	136.2	150.5
1975	161.2	175.4	137.3	235.3	142.3	168.6
1976	170.5	180.8	144.7	250.8	147.6	184.7
1977	181.5	192.5	153.5	283.4	154.2	202.4
1978	195.4	211.4	164.0	298.3	159.6	219.4
1979	217.4	234.5	176.0	403.1	166.6	239.7
1980	246.8	254.6	191.6	556.0	178.4	265.9
1981	272.4	274.6	208.2	675.9	186.9	294.5
1982	289.1	285.7	224.0	667.9	191.8	328.7
1983	298.4	291.7	236.9	628.0	196.5	357.3
1984	311.1	302.9	249.3	641.8	200.2	379.5

Source: U.S., *Economic Report of the President* (Washington, D.C.: U.S. Government Printing Office, 1985), pp. 291, 292.

all price index. Items such as medical care and fuel oil, coal, and bottled gas have helped to raise the overall index. In fact, the fuel oil, coal, and bottled gas figures offer some evidence of cost-push inflation in the 1970s and 1980s due to rapidly rising energy prices.

Changes in the consumer price index are calculated monthly and announced to the public. Because they show monthly changes, the numbers are usually small. These monthly changes must be "compounded" to arrive at an annual figure for comparison. That is, if a 1.1 percent monthly change in the prices of all items were to persist throughout the year, it would lead to an annual inflation rate of 14.0 percent.[15]

The Producer Price Index The producer price index (PPI), which measures changes in the prices that businesses pay for materials they consume and for goods they buy for further sale, is illustrated in Table 4.7. Observe that the base year is 1967. The overall producer price index is shown in the column headed "All Commodities," and the remaining columns give the price changes for some categories within the producer price index. Notice again the substantial increases in energy prices.

Just as with the consumer price index, the producer price index is calculated monthly and announced publicly. The producer price index has an important connection to the consumer price index and is therefore watched carefully. Changes in the prices that businesses pay later contribute to changes in the prices that consumers pay. Consequently, changes in the producer price index may lead to changes in the consumer price index a few months later.

GNP Deflator The GNP deflator, the economy's composite index, is calculated and interpreted similarly to the consumer and producer price indexes. The use of this index is discussed later in this chapter.

Importance of Indexes The consumer price index, the producer price index, and other measures are not studied by academics and government officials out of idle curiosity. Rather, the indexes have an important impact on policy makers' decisions and on the operation of the economy. They directly affect the determination of wages to union workers who receive cost-of-living adjustments based on the consumer price index, and they indirectly influence the size of nonunion income payments. Some government programs, such as social security, base changes in monthly checks on a vari-

---

[15]You can arrive at the annual rate of inflation of 14 percent by compounding in the following way. For each month, 1.1 percent is added to the price level. This means that at the end of each month the price level would be 1.011 times the price level at the end of the preceding month (100 percent, or 1.00, for prices at the beginning of the month, plus 1.1 percent, or 0.011, for the addition to the price level during the month). To determine the annual rate of inflation multiply 1.011×1.011, find your answer, and multiply this by 1.011. Continue multiplying by 1.011 for a total of eleven times, and it will give you the annual rate. A shorter method is to plug $(1.011)^{12}$ into your calculator and wait for the answer.

Table 4.7
Producer Price Index: All Commodities and Major Groups for Selected Years (1967 = 100.0)

The producer price index measures changes in the prices of goods that businesses purchase. As was the case with consumer goods, energy prices have risen faster than prices for producers' goods in general.

Year	All Commodities	Farm Products	Processed Foods and Feeds	Industrial Commodities	
				Total	Energy
1952	88.6	117.2	91.6	84.1	90.1
1957	93.3	99.5	87.4	93.3	99.1
1962	94.8	98.0	91.9	94.8	96.7
1967	100.0	100.0	100.0	100.0	100.0
1972	119.1	125.0	120.8	117.9	118.6
1977	194.2	192.5	186.1	195.1	302.2
1978	209.3	212.5	202.6	209.4	322.5
1979	235.6	241.4	222.5	236.5	408.1
1980	268.8	249.4	241.2	274.8	574.0
1981	293.4	254.9	248.7	304.1	694.5
1982	299.3	242.4	251.5	312.3	693.2
1983	303.1	248.2	255.9	315.7	664.7

Source: U.S. Bureau of the Census, *Statistical Abstract of the United States: 1985* (105th ed.), Washington, D.C., 1984, p. 469.

ation of one of these indexes. Private business contracts may include price adjustments based on the producer price index and, in some instances, other payments such as alimony and rent have been tied to one of these indexes.

Stop

PRODUCTION

Production
The creation of goods and services that satisfy wants and needs.

Production refers to the creation of goods and services. The construction of a piano, the filling of a cavity, the shipping of goods from factories to buyers, and the service provided in a grocery store are all productive activities.

Full Production and Economic Growth

Full production
Occurs when an economy is producing at its maximum capacity, or when it is experiencing full employment.

The macroeconomic goal of **full production** is achieved when an economy is producing as much as it possibly can with its available resources, or producing at its maximum capacity. Although the problem of scarcity always exists, full production permits an economy to minimize its impact. The further an economy moves away from full production, the greater the scarcity problem becomes.

Factors of production are required to produce goods and services. Production, therefore, is closely interwoven with employment. When an economy reaches full production, it also reaches full employment; when it moves away from full production and is operating below its peak capacity, it is also experiencing unemployment. This relationship was illustrated earlier in the chapter in Table 4.1, which compared the U.S. economy's actual and potential output from 1978 through 1984. With unemployment, an economy's actual output is below its potential, and goods and services that might have been produced are not.

Economic growth
An increase in an economy's full production output level over time.

In addition to full production, the third macroeconomic goal includes **economic growth,** which is an increase in the economy's full production level of output over time. That is, not only is it necessary that the economy's maximum capacity be met, but also that the maximum capacity grows. Referring to the production possibilities curves for pizzas and bicycles in Figure 4.1, full production would be reached in the first year by producing at any point, such as A, on the production possibilities curve for year 1. Economic growth would occur when the production possibilities curve shifts to the right, as is done for the second and third years in Figure 4.1. This economy would achieve the third macroeconomic goal of full production and economic growth if it were to produce at a point such as B in year 2 and C in year 3.

Measures of Production

Gross national product (GNP)
A dollar figure that measures the value of all finished goods and services produced in an economy in one year.

Because production is essential to the material well-being of an economy, the United States, as well as most other countries, calculates on a regular basis how much its economy has produced. **Gross national product,** or **GNP,** is the dollar figure that measures the value of all the finished goods and services produced in an economy in one year. Only finished goods and services, which are goods and services ready for sale to their final users, are counted. Products in a stage of production or not yet completed are not measured in GNP. To include an item that is in the process of production and then to again include the item when it is completed would cause a double count, and production would be overstated. Also, GNP is a measure of goods and services produced, not of goods and services sold. Thus, goods

Figure 4.1
Growth of an Economy's Productive Potential over Time

An economy must produce up to its potential each year, and that potential must grow over the years if the scarcity problem is to be minimized and material well-being is to increase over time.

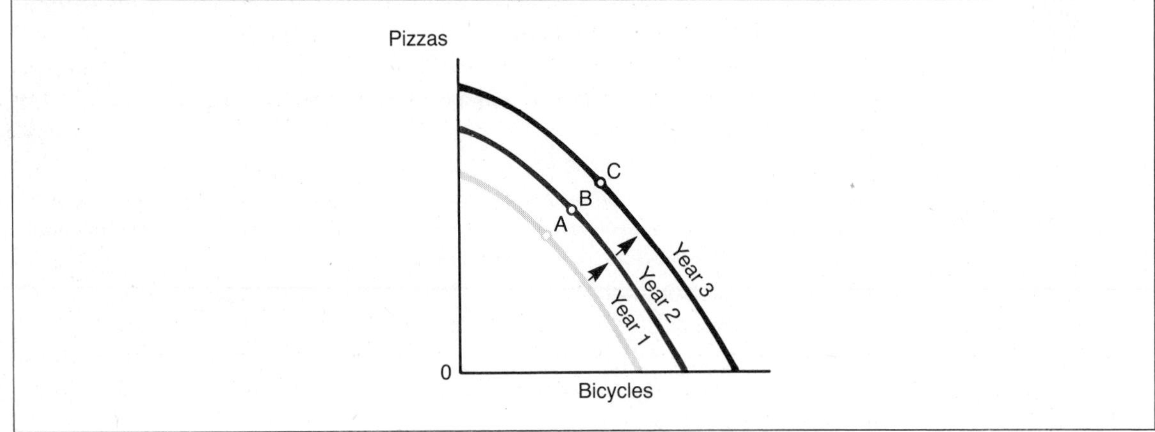

involved in second-hand sales are eliminated since these goods were previously counted in GNP when originally produced.

Money GNP (current GNP) Measures the value of production in terms of prices at the time of production.

Real GNP (constant GNP) GNP with the effects of inflation erased from the figures; measures real production.

GNP figures are usually given in two forms: money GNP and real GNP. **Money,** or **current, GNP** is GNP measured according to prices during the year in which the goods and services are produced. It measures the value of current production in terms of current prices. Money GNP is influenced by both changes in production and changes in the prices of what is produced. **Real,** or **constant, GNP** is GNP with the effects of inflation erased. It measures actual (real) production and shows how actual production, not the prices of what is produced, has changed. Real GNP is preferable to money GNP for gauging the state of the economy and for analyzing production conditions. Table 4.8 illustrates why this is so.

In Table 4.8, a hypothetical economy is producing only automobiles. In each of the three years given, the economy produces 60 cars. Production is stagnant and there is no real growth. The economy's output, shown in the column titled "Actual Output of Autos," does not change.

The economy, however, is experiencing inflation, and the price of autos increases year after year as shown in the column headed "Price per Auto." When the current dollar value of production, or money GNP, is measured, these prices are attached to the actual output. Thus, in the first year, when the 60 cars were $5,000 each, money GNP was $300,000; in the second year, when they were $6,000 each, money GNP was $360,000; and by the third year, money GNP was $420,000. Price increases alone caused money GNP to climb.

If the true productivity of the economy in Table 4.8 is to be assessed, real levels of production, or real GNP, rather than money GNP should be examined. To evaluate the economy using the money GNP figures from Table 4.8 would be misleading. These figures would have us believe that GNP increased significantly from year to year when, in fact, it did not change. Inflation, not actual growth, has occurred. In analyzing an economy, real GNP figures must be examined if changes in production are to be properly assessed.

In order to calculate real GNP, it is necessary to have some measure of price changes over the years. In Table 4.8 the prices of the autos over the three years are translated into a price index using year 1 as the base year. This information is given in the column titled "Auto Price Index." This price index provides the mechanism for converting money GNP to real GNP. Real

Table 4.8
Actual Output, Money GNP, and Real GNP

Money GNP gives a misleading impression of the output performance of an economy over time when the level of prices is changing.

Year	Actual Output of Autos	Price per Auto	Production in Dollar Terms (Money GNP)	Auto Price Index	Production in Real Terms (Real GNP)
1	60	$5,000	$300,000	100.0	$300,000
2	60	6,000	360,000	120.0	300,000
3	60	7,000	420,000	140.0	300,000

GNP is found by moving the decimal point two places to the left on the price index, and then dividing money GNP for a given year by the altered index number for that year. For example, the real GNP for year 2 in Table 4.8 is calculated by dividing the money GNP of $360,000 by 1.20, the altered price index number for year 2. Notice in Table 4.8 that real GNP does not change from year to year, reflecting the fact that the actual annual output of autos has not changed.

Table 4.9 gives money GNP and real GNP figures for the U.S. economy in selected years. The first noticeable feature of Table 4.9 is the sheer magnitude of the numbers. Money GNP was more than $1 trillion in 1971, and by 1982 it exceeded $3 trillion. In 1982, the average daily output of the U.S. economy was over $9 billion!

Table 4.9 includes the GNP price deflator, the composite price index for the entire economy, which was mentioned earlier in this chapter. The GNP deflator is included in Table 4.9 because it is the price index used for converting money GNP to real GNP. This conversion is made in the same manner as that for the figures in Table 4.8.[16] Money GNP equals real GNP in the deflator's base year because the index value for that year is 100.0, or 100 percent. Thus, in 1972, the base year in Table 4.9, the money GNP of $1.1859 trillion is equal to the real GNP of $1.1859 trillion. In years when a dollar buys more than in the base year, the deflator is less than 100.0, and real GNP is greater than money GNP. In Table 4.9, 1950's real GNP of $534.8 billion is greater than its money GNP of $286.5 billion because the dollar bought more in 1950 than it did in the base year. In 1983, because the dollar bought less than in the base year (the deflator is greater than 100.0), the real GNP of $1.5347 trillion is less than the money GNP of $3.3048 trillion.

Table 4.9 also illustrates the value of using real GNP rather than money GNP to evaluate economic conditions. This is evident in examining the figures for 1972 through 1975. In these years, the economy experienced significant inflation as indicated by the GNP deflator. Overall, prices were 25.79 percent higher in 1975 than they were three years earlier in 1972. If one examines money GNP from 1972 through 1975 there is a substantial increase—in fact, more than a third of a trillion dollar increase. These figures could give a false impression of the economy to someone who is not aware of inflation or the meaning of money GNP. The behavior of real GNP from 1972 through 1975 indicates that the economy experienced an increase in production from 1972 to 1973 but a decline in the output of goods and services in 1974 and 1975. In 1975 the U.S. economy was worse in real terms than it was in 1973. An increase in money GNP accompanied by a decrease in real GNP also occurred from 1979 to 1980 and from 1981 to 1982.

The government calculates and publicly announces GNP figures on both

[16]For example, 1983 money GNP was $3,304.8 billion and the GNP deflator was 215.34. Moving the decimal two places to the left on the deflator gives 2.1534. This number is then divided into money GNP for 1983 to arrive at real GNP ($3,304.8 billion/2.1534 = $1,534.7 billion).

Table 4.9
Money GNP, Real GNP, and the GNP Deflator for Selected Years

Real GNP for a particular year is calculated by dividing that year's money GNP by the GNP deflator, after the decimal has been moved two places to the left on the deflator.

Year	Money GNP (Billions)	Real GNP (Billions of 1972 Dollars)	GNP Deflator (1972 = 100)
1950	$ 286.5	$ 534.8	53.56
1955	400.0	657.5	60.84
1960	506.5	737.2	68.70
1965	691.1	929.3	74.36
1970	992.7	1,085.6	91.45
1971	1,077.6	1,122.4	96.01
1972	1,185.9	1,185.9	100.00
1973	1,326.4	1,254.3	105.75
1974	1,434.2	1,246.3	115.08
1975	1,549.2	1,231.6	125.79
1976	1,718.0	1,298.2	132.34
1977	1,918.3	1,369.7	140.05
1978	2,163.9	1,438.6	150.42
1979	2,417.8	1,479.4	163.42
1980	2,631.7	1,475.0	178.42
1981	2,957.8	1,512.2	195.60
1982	3,069.3	1,480.0	207.38
1983	3,304.8	1,534.7	215.34
1984[a]	3,661.3	1,639.0	223.38

[a] Preliminary figures.

Source: U.S., *Economic Report of the President* (Washington, D.C.: U.S. Government Printing Office, 1985), pp. 232, 234, 236.

a quarterly and an annual basis. Quarterly figures are used to gauge the "healthiness" of the economy. Concern tends to be generated if little or no growth occurs in GNP from quarter to quarter.

Does GNP Tell the Whole Story?

GNP may not represent a true measure of production in the U.S. economy. Studies have suggested that GNP understates actual output, because many goods and services that are produced are never included in the calculation. For example, many goods and services are not accounted for in GNP because they are not bought and sold in a marketplace. Such nonmarket and unmeasured production includes people repairing their own automobiles, painting their own homes, or sewing their own clothes. Actions such as these involve the actual production of goods or services and improve the economy's material well-being, but they are not included in GNP because no pay is involved. If someone were paid to perform the same tasks, the dollar value of those tasks would be included in the accounts. For example, if you change a tire on your own car, it is not included in GNP; but if you pay someone else to change the tire, the value of the tire change is included in GNP.

The classic example of work performed but not paid for or included in GNP is the typical range of chores completed by a homemaker—cooking, cleaning, shopping, child care, and so forth. Studies estimating the dollar value of these chores suggest that the expenditure required to hire a person to perform such tasks could be substantial. Imagine how GNP would soar if this work were included.

Another type of unmeasured production is work performed for cash payments and not reported. Small jobs such as grass cutting and snow removal are included in this category, as well as major productive activities such as moonlighting by plumbers, painters, and housekeepers. Also, services are sometimes swapped, so that production is exchanged for production rather than cash. For example, a dentist might maintain the teeth of a lawyer in return for legal advice. Still another type of unmeasured production involves illegal goods or services such as illegal drugs, prostitution, and much underworld activity.

Underground economy
Productive activities that are not reported for tax purposes and are not included in GNP.

In recent years, the term **underground economy** has been used to refer to productive activities that are not reported for tax purposes and are not included in GNP. While there is concern that these goods and services are not included in GNP, the primary concern about the underground economy is the lost tax revenue.

Productivity

In addition to measuring annual changes in real production, or real GNP, it is also important to the well-being of an economy to periodically evaluate how productively its resources are being used. The basic scarcity problem is affected by the ways in which resources are combined, the efficiency of factor usage, and the types of technology used in production. The concept of assessing the amount of output produced by an economy's resources is called **productivity.**

Productivity
Concept of assessing the amount of output produced by an economy's resources; often measured specifically by output per worker.

A basic measure of productivity is output per worker. This measure takes labor plus the other factors of production into consideration. It does not measure how hard a person works, but rather how much production results from labor and other inputs combined. For example, the output of a laborer on an assembly line at an auto plant is the result of the work performed by that person with the aid of machinery, energy, a factory, and other resources. As equipment becomes more technologically advanced and efficient, a worker becomes more productive. The output of an office clerk using a computer is far greater than that of a clerk performing the same tasks by hand.

Table 4.10 gives the average annual percentage change in labor productivity in the United States for groups of years from 1950 through 1984. The most important observation from these numbers is that increases in productivity have been declining over the years. For example, the average annual rate of growth in labor productivity in the business sector from 1960 through 1964 was 3.32 percent, but since the middle 1960s this rate has fallen, with average productivity increases of less than 2 percent in the 1970s and early 1980s. This decline in productivity has also been experienced by other

Table 4.10
Labor Productivity Growth, 1950–1984 (Average Annual Percentage Change)

The growth in productivity, measured by average output per worker, has declined since the middle 1960s.

Years	Business Sector	Nonfarm Business Sector
1950–54	3.74%	2.62%
1955–59	2.76	2.34
1960–64	3.32	2.88
1965–69	2.48	2.10
1970–74	1.62	1.44
1975–79	1.44	1.30
1980–84[a]	1.58	1.52

[a] Preliminary figures.

Source: U.S., *Economic Report of the President* (Washington, D.C.: U.S. Government Printing Office, 1985), p. 279.

industrialized nations over the years and has become a matter of utmost concern to policymakers.[17]

The causes of this decline in productivity are not easily identified. It has been suggested that the problem may be due to a decline in the amount of capital used per worker, the diversion of resources to fulfill government regulations, and changes in spending for research and development. Other factors such as inflation and energy prices may affect productivity,[18] and some economists have noted that in certain industries the capital equipment and technological processes are outmoded and aging and may contribute to a decline in productivity.

Concern about the poor performance of the economy in terms of productivity gains in recent years has led to widespread interest in proposals known as **supply-side economics,** which center on the use of tax policy and regulatory reform to induce investment activity by businesses and stimulate productivity. These proposals will be presented in greater detail in Chapter Nine.

Supply-side economics
Proposals centering on the use of tax policy and regulatory reform to stimulate business investment activity and productivity.

What are the benefits of increased productivity? The most fundamental benefit comes from improved efficiency in the use of the economy's scarce resources. When productivity per worker is below what it could be, there is an opportunity cost imposed on society in the form of goods and services that could have been provided but are lost because resources were not employed in the most efficient manner. When productivity per worker increases, this opportunity cost diminishes.

More immediate to the goals of economic policy, improved productivity could ease inflationary pressure by allowing firms to meet rising costs through increased output rather than higher prices. Also, if policies to stimulate productivity lead to a general expansion of business activity, another benefit could be improved employment opportunities.

[17]U.S., *Economic Report of the President* (Washington, D.C.: U.S. Government Printing Office, 1980), p. 84.

[18]Ibid., pp. 86–87.

A POLICY PROBLEM

In the Employment Act of 1946 the federal government officially committed itself to help create an environment conducive to the attainment of full employment, full production, and price stability. These goals were restated in the Humphrey-Hawkins Full Employment and Balanced Growth Act of 1978. Each of these goals is desirable, but it may be impossible to attain all of them simultaneously.

When the economy reaches full production and full employment, pressures from increased spending power on the buyers' side of the market combine with the inability of the economy to expand its output to cause demand-pull inflation. However, removing upward pressure on prices by curbing buyers' demands could lead to unemployment and less than full production. Policy makers are thus faced with a tradeoff: do they seek full employment and full production accompanied by inflation, or stable prices accompanied by unemployment and less than full production? There are no clear solutions to this tradeoff question. Some prefer full employment and production at the expense of price stability, and others would be willing to endure some unemployment for the sake of controlling inflation. The tradeoff decision is difficult because either way some groups in the economy will be hurt.

SUMMARY

The three fundamental problems of the macroeconomy are unemployment, inflation, and falling production. The three fundamental objectives are full employment, stable prices, and full production and economic growth. To help create an environment in which these objectives can be reached, Congress enacted the Employment Act of 1946, which was strengthened by the Humphrey-Hawkins Act of 1978.

Unemployment is a matter of concern because it leads to an economic loss to society by intensifying the scarcity problem. It also leads to personal hardships for individuals who are out of work. Unemployment can be frictional, cyclical, or structural in nature. Frictional unemployment is voluntary and is primarily due to the time required to locate work. Cyclical and structural unemployment are involuntary. Cyclical unemployment is caused by downswings in the general level of economic activity, and structural unemployment occurs when a particular occupation is no longer in demand.

The labor force includes all persons 16 years of age and older who are employed or actively seeking work. The overall participation rate is the percentage of the civilian noninstitutional population 16 years of age and older that is in the labor force. The overall unemployment rate is the percentage of the labor force that is unemployed and actively seeking work. Unemployment rates and participation rates can also be calculated for subgroups within the labor force and differ from group to group.

Full employment occurs when everyone in the labor force except the frictionally unemployed is working. The unemployment rate associated with full employment is not universally agreed upon and has changed over time.

Inflation refers to an increase in the general level of prices. While a small amount of inflation is not a serious problem in an economy, rapid inflation can intensify the scarcity problem for households and businesses. Inflation reduces the purchasing power of money, it hurts some groups in society more than others, and it may lead to social and political instability. Inflation can be caused by upward pressure on prices coming from the buyers' side of the market, upward pressure on prices coming from the sellers' side of the market, or upward pressure coming from both sides of the market. When it originates on the buyers' side of the market, it is termed demand-pull inflation; and when it originates on the sellers' side of the market, it is termed cost-push inflation. Households' and businesses' expectations of future economic conditions can influence demand-pull and cost-push inflation.

Three widely used indicators of inflation are the consumer price index, producer price index, and the GNP deflator. Each index expresses the prices for a collection of goods and services in different years as a percentage of the prices for those same goods and services in a base year. A price index of 120.0 means that prices in a certain year are 20 percent higher than prices for the same items in the base year.

An economy's level of production is closely related to its level of employment. Full production is reached when an economy is operating at maximum capacity, or at full employment. Since a nation's level of material well-being is related to its production, it experiences economic growth when it increases its full production level of output over time.

The basic measure of production is gross national product (GNP), which is a dollar figure for all of the finished goods and services produced in an economy in one year. Money GNP is GNP in prices at the time production occurs and is affected by changes in both output and price levels. Real GNP is GNP with the effects of inflation erased and changes only as the level of output changes. Real GNP is a better measure of production in an economy than money GNP. Evidence exists that GNP understates actual output, since some production is never included in the calculation.

It is also important to measure the productivity of an economy's resources. This is calculated by determining output per worker, which combines the results of production from labor and other inputs. In the United States, increases in productivity have been declining over the past few decades.

It may be impossible to attain full employment, full production, and price stability at the same time. As the economy approaches full employment, increased spending causes demand-pull inflation. The reduction of spending to dampen demand-pull inflationary pressures can cause employment and production to fall.

Key Terms and Concepts

Employment Act of 1946
Unemployment
Frictional unemployment
Cyclical unemployment
Structural unemployment
Full employment
Labor force
Participation rate
Unemployment rate
Inflation
Real income
Demand-pull inflation
Cost-push inflation
Price index
Consumer price index
Producer price index
GNP deflator
Full production
Economic growth
Gross national product
Money (current) GNP
Real (constant) GNP
Underground economy
Productivity
Supply-side economics

Discussion and Review Questions

1. Full employment occurs when everyone in the labor force except the frictionally unemployed is working. What would happen if 100 percent of the labor force were working and virtually no one were seeking employment? What good effects could this have on the economy? What bad effects could it have?
2. How would you go about reducing frictional unemployment, cyclical unemployment, and structural unemployment? What would be the greatest obstacle to success in each case? Do you think these types of unemployment can be completely cured, or can they only be controlled?
3. Suppose that you are retained by a candidate for president of the United States to serve as an advisor on economic affairs. The candidate wants recommendations on how to control demand-pull and cost-push inflation. What policies would you recommend to control each type of inflation? Why would you recommend these particular policies? How would these policies affect the economy's ability to operate at full employment?
4. It may be impossible to have the economy operate at full employment and full production without experiencing inflation. This means that a choice must be made: seek full employment and full production combined with inflation, or seek price stability combined with unemployment and less than full production. Regardless of which choice you make, some people are going to be adversely affected. What questions would you raise and what information would you want before deciding to seek full employment and full production or to seek price stability?
5. Estimate the addition to GNP that might be made if all of the goods and services you produce that are never counted in GNP are included.

6. Several definitions and statistical measurements pertain to employment and unemployment. Define labor force, unemployment rate, participation rate, and full employment, and explain the value of measuring each of these.
7. Explain some of the changes in the labor force statistics given in Table 4.2 for the years 1929, 1933, 1945, and 1965.
8. Several different price indexes have been developed, notably the consumer price index, producer price index, and GNP deflator.
   a. What are some possible reasons for developing separate indexes for consumers, businesses, and the entire economy?
   b. How do increases or decreases in a price index translate into changes in purchasing power?
   c. What is the relationship between real GNP and money GNP when the GNP deflator is greater than, equal to, or less than 100.0?
9. Why is there so much concern about declining productivity in the United States? Give some reasons for this decline.

Suggested Readings

David C. Colander, ed., *Solutions to Inflation* (New York: Harcourt Brace Jovanovich, Inc., 1979). A collection of 29 readings on inflation theory and solutions, wage-price controls, and incomes policies. Includes articles by Solow, Friedman, Galbraith, Fellner, Hayek, Okun, and others.

John A. Ganaty, "To Be Jobless in America," *American Heritage* (December 1978), pp. 64–69. A discussion of how attitudes toward unemployment and the unemployed have changed over time.

Robert D. Hershey, Jr., "Inflation Hurts, But Deflation Could Be Worse," *The New York Times*, April 18, 1982, p. 8F. Presents problems that would arise if prices fell in an economy accustomed to prices rising.

Thomas Mann, "Disorder and Early Sorrow," *Stories of Three Decades*, translated by H. T. Lowe-Porter (New York: Alfred A. Knopf, 1955), pp. 500–528. Fiction about life in Germany during the hyperinflation of the 1920s.

Joseph J. Minarik, "Who Wins, Who Loses from Inflation?" *Challenge* (January–February 1979), pp. 26–31. An analysis of the effects of inflation on different groups of income earners in the economy.

W. W. Rostow, "Technology and Unemployment in the Western World," *Challenge* (March–April 1983), pp. 6–17. Takes a long-term look at the world economy and identifies a Fourth Industrial Revolution; discusses prospects for change and policy implications.

"Special Report: America's Productivity Crisis," *Newsweek*, September 8, 1980, pp. 50–69. An extensive report on the decline in U.S. productivity.

"The New Economy," *Time*, May 30, 1983, pp. 62–70. Surveys changing trends and problems in U.S. production and jobs caused by technology and foreign competition.

"The Underground Economy's Hidden Force," *Business Week*, April 5, 1982, pp. 64–70. Discusses sources of underground income and estimates of its size; assesses macroeconomic problems associated with the underground economy and its effect on GNP.

5 FOUNDATIONS OF THE MACROECONOMY

Chapter Objectives

1. To identify reasons for changes in the level of macroeconomic activity.
2. To define and explain business cycles.
3. To understand the relationship between total spending and the levels of aggregate employment and production, and total spending and the level of prices.
4. To examine the spending behavior of households, businesses, government units, and the foreign sector.
5. To establish how the relationship between leakages from the spending stream and injections into the spending stream affects the level of economic activity.
6. To introduce the multiplier effect.
7. To introduce the importance of expectations in maintaining a healthy economy.
8. To identify the role of total spending in the formation of macroeconomic policies.
9. To provide, in an appendix, an explanation of equilibrium in the macroeconomy.

A market economy continually changes in its level of economic activity; it goes through upswings and downswings, or periods of expansion and contraction, without ever staying at a particular level of activity. These fluctuations are obvious from newspapers, magazines, and news broadcasts which regularly carry stories of the changing pulse of the economy and of impending recessions or recoveries. People are forever forecasting when a downturn or upturn will occur, resulting in a continual flow of predictions of good or bad times ahead.

Two indicators of this constant economic change were discussed in the last chapter. First, in surveying unemployment it was noted that the unemployment rate tends to increase or decrease from year to year. Much of this change comes from cyclical unemployment, which is a response to changes in the general level of economic activity. Second, in the discussion of real

GNP, it was shown that production figures tend to change from year to year; in some years growth occurs and in others the economy backslides.

This chapter deals with fluctuations in the level of activity in the macroeconomy. It identifies the pattern of these changes and explains why they occur.

CHANGES IN THE LEVEL OF ECONOMIC ACTIVITY

When speaking of changes in the level of macroeconomic activity—upswings and downswings, expansions and contractions—we are generally referring to changes in real GNP. The movement of real GNP from 1973 through 1984 is plotted in Figure 5.1. This figure indicates that in the 1970s and early 1980s, the economy experienced both increases and decreases in its activity level. For example, from the first quarter of 1976 through the first quarter of 1979, real output grew at an annual rate of 4.8 percent. Then the expansion weakened, and the economy experienced a brief downswing in 1980. Following this contraction, production grew until mid-1981, when the economy slipped into a longer downswing, which continued until late 1982. Then a strong recovery began, and real GNP grew at an annual rate of 7.1 percent.

One of the primary reasons for concern over changes in real GNP is that changes in the level of real output cause changes in the level of employment. When production increases, more labor is needed and unemployment falls; when production decreases, less labor is needed and unemployment rises. This is shown in Figure 5.2, which plots real GNP and unemployment rates for 1973 through 1984. Note the inverse relationship between output and unemployment. Observe, for example, that in late 1982, when real GNP was at a low point, the unemployment rate was at its peak. Thus, when a downswing appears imminent, the primary concern is that the macroeconomic problem of unemployment will be aggravated.

Changes in the level of real GNP may also influence the inflation problem. Demand-pull inflation has a tendency to occur when real GNP expands to the full-production, full-employment level. However, when real GNP increases, but is well below the full-production level, or when real GNP decreases, price levels may not be affected by the output change. Therefore, while we are cognizant of the full-production, demand-pull inflation problem, we tend to relate the expression "changes in economic activity" to changes in production and employment rather than to changes in prices.

Business Cycles

While fluctuations in the level of output can adversely affect employment, and perhaps prices, the output changes themselves are somewhat predictable, so their impact can be controlled or at least anticipated. That is, changes

Figure 5.1
Real Gross National Product in 1972 Dollars (1973–1984)

A market economy such as that of the United States constantly goes through upswings and downswings in its level of production.

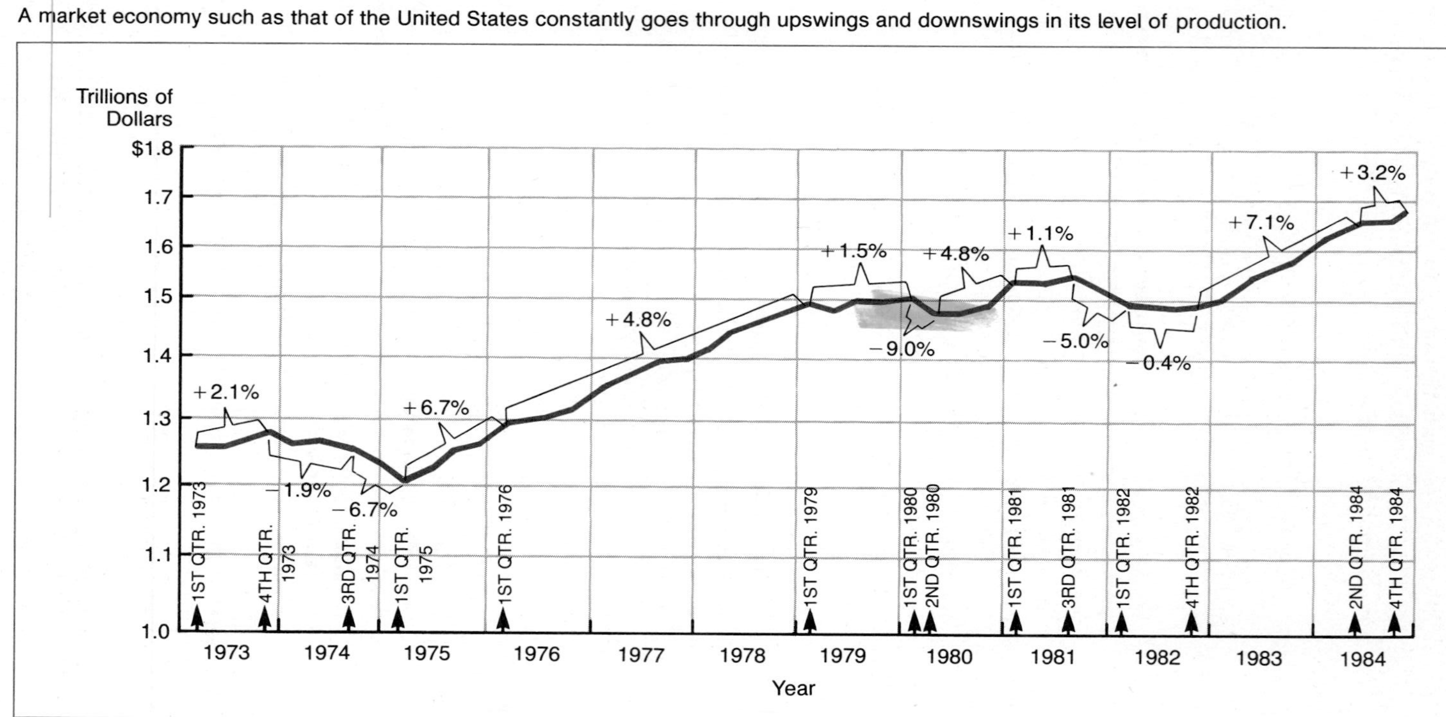

Source: *National Economic Trends,* prepared by the Federal Reserve Bank of St. Louis. Data for 1973–1979 are from the February 27, 1981 release, p. 13. 1980–1984 data are from the February 1985 release, p. 13.

Figure 5.2
Real Gross National Product in 1972 Dollars and the Unemployment Rate (1973–1984)

There is an inverse relationship between the rate of unemployment and the level of output: the unemployment rate tends to rise or fall as the level of output decreases or increases.

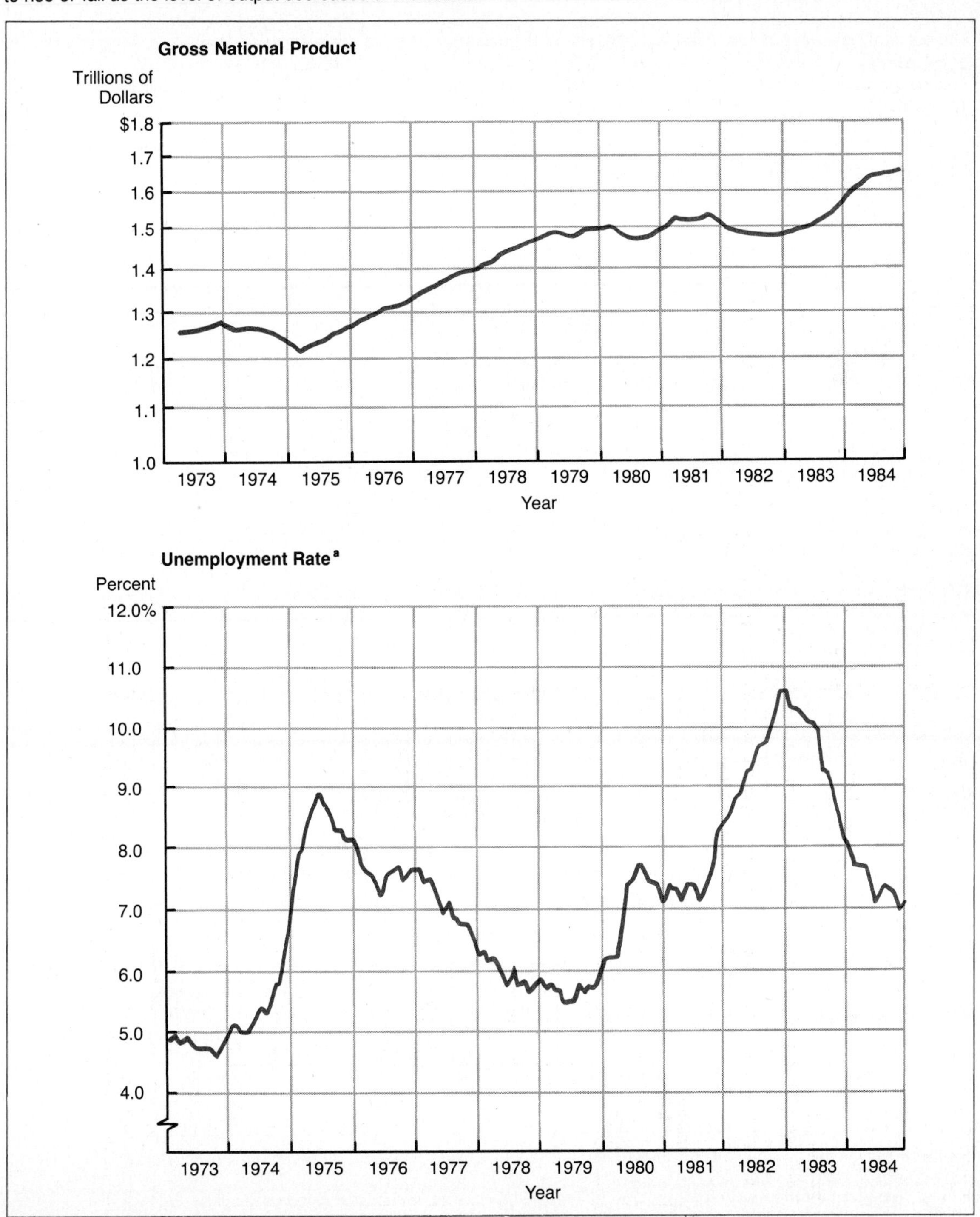

[a]Seasonally adjusted.

Source: *National Economic Trends,* prepared by the Federal Reserve Bank of St. Louis. Data for 1973–1979 are from the February 27, 1981 release, pp. 3, 13. 1980–1984 data are from the February 1985 release, pp. 3, 13.

Figure 5.3
Phases of the Business Cycle

The economy is always in one of the four phases of the business cycle. Activity is either at a peak, receding, at a trough, or recovering.

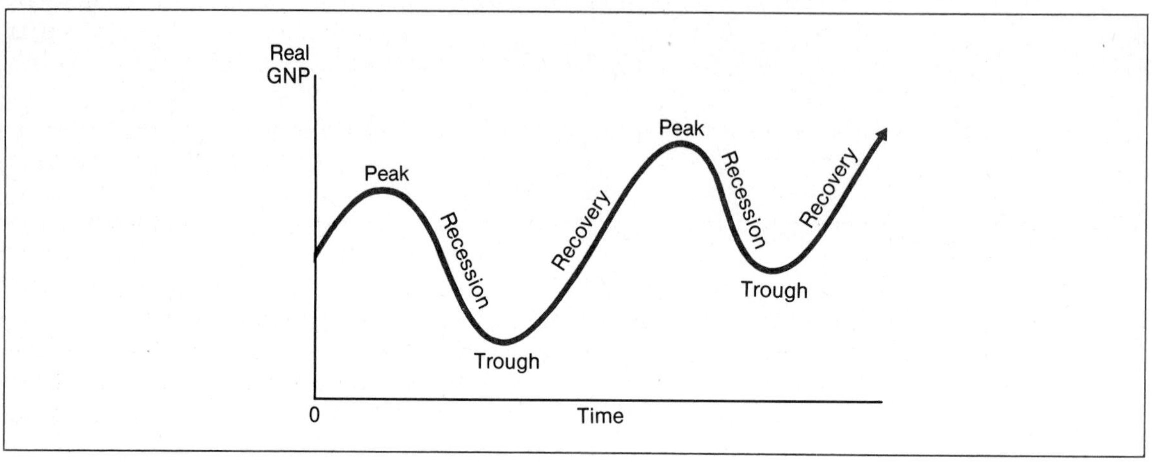

Figure 5.4
Economic Activity 1900–1983

The length of each phase and the intensity of the change in output differ from cycle to cycle.

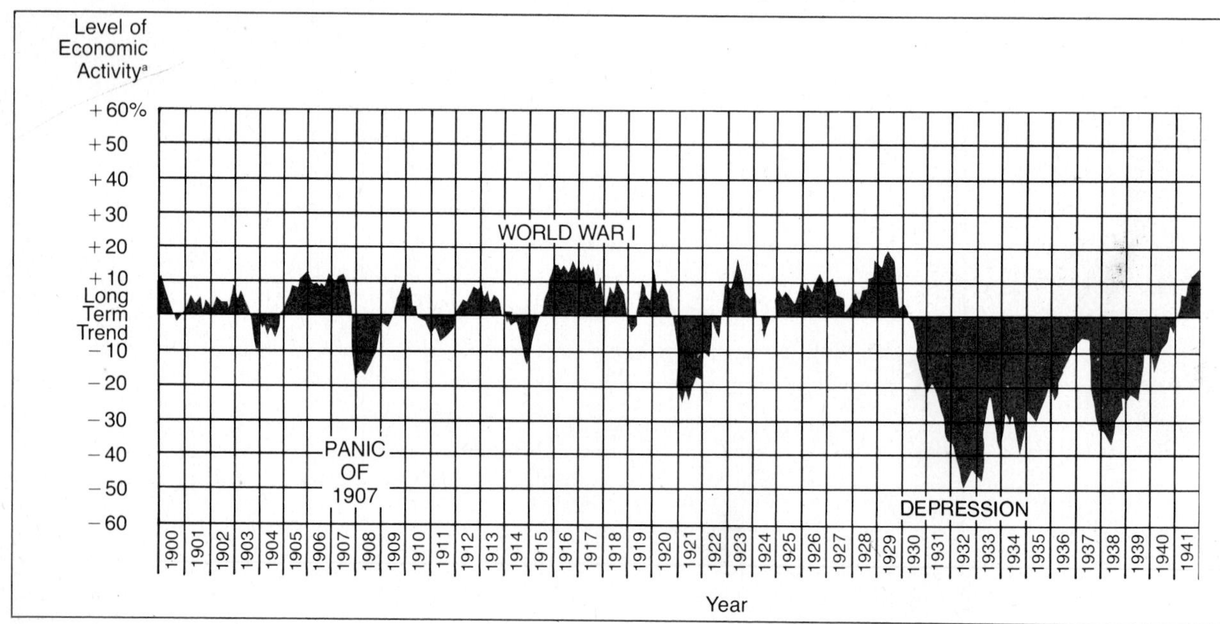

[a]Figure shows the deviation of actual economic activity above or below its long-term trend or average value.

Source: "American Business Activity from 1790 to Today." (Cleveland: AmeriTrust Corporation, June 1984).

in the level of economic activity do not occur randomly or haphazardly. Rather, they occur in wavelike patterns called business cycles.

Business cycles
Recurring periods of growth and decline (or expansion and contraction) in an economy's real output, or real GNP.

Business cycles are recurring periods of growth and decline in the real output, or real GNP, of an economy. In a business cycle the level of output increases to a peak from which it ultimately falls. Output then continues to drop to a minimum, where it turns around, rises, and the whole process is repeated again. Figure 5.3 illustrates the wavelike movement of business cycles.

Phases of a business cycle
The four stages through which every business cycle goes: recovery, peak, recession, and trough.

Recovery, peak, recession, trough
The phases of the business cycle during which real GNP, or output, increases, reaches its maximum, falls, and reaches its minimum, respectively.

Each cycle is divided into four stages called **phases.** The expansionary phase during which real GNP increases is called the **recovery,** maximum output occurs at the **peak** of the cycle, real GNP falls in the **recession** and reaches its minimum in the **trough.** The economy is always in some phase of a business cycle. It does not remain stationary at a particular level of output until some force causes it to increase or decrease. Instead, the economy is always expanding, contracting, or at a turning point in activity.

The cyclical behavior of real GNP in the U.S. economy can be seen by referring back to Figure 5.1, which traces the movement of real output from 1973 through 1984. Notice the wavelike pattern of recovery, peak, recession, and trough in this figure.

Figure 5.4 presents a longer view of business cycles in the United States by illustrating output movements from the early 1900s through 1983. This longer period of time shown in Figure 5.4 more easily illustrates some of the properties of cycles. First, notice that the phases of the business cycles are

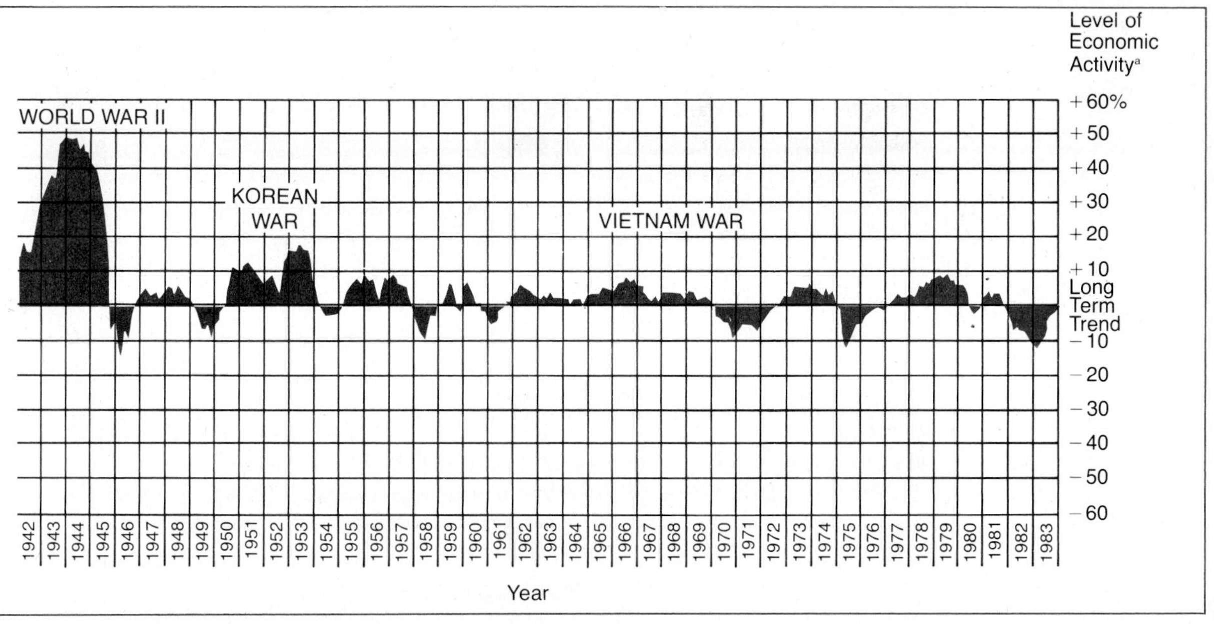

not of equal length. The recovery of 1959 lasted just a few months, whereas the recovery that began in 1975 lasted until 1979. Notice also that since the 1940s, periods of expansion have far outweighed periods of recession. This might be due in part to the passage of the Employment Act of 1946 and to the government's commitment to providing an environment conducive to full production, full employment, and stable prices. A second important property of business cycles is that cyclical expansions and contractions are not of equal intensity. For example, the declines in output from 1929 to 1932 and in 1945 are dramatic, whereas the decline in 1970 is not. Every business cycle is unique in the lengths of its phases and the intensity with which output increases or decreases. There is no exact rule for determining the duration and magnitude of any given cyclical change.

Perhaps the single most important question to ask about business cycles is what is their cause: what makes the level of economic activity alternately expand and contract? The answer to this question is important since it helps us understand the nature of cyclical movements, and such understanding is necessary for their control.

The cause of economic fluctuations has been pondered for centuries. Over the years some theories have emerged and then disappeared while others have been accepted and refined. In the following section the cause of economic fluctuations is explained in terms of the most popular and generally accepted theory of the day.

TOTAL SPENDING AND THE LEVEL OF ECONOMIC ACTIVITY

Total, or aggregate, spending
The total combined spending of all units in the economy (households plus businesses plus government plus foreign) for new goods and services.

The most generally accepted theory today is that changes in the level of total spending are the basic cause of expansions and contractions in economic activity. That is, real output responds to changes in total spending. **Total, or aggregate, spending** refers to the total of all spending for all new goods and services by households, businesses, government units, and foreign buyers.

Why do changes in spending cause the level of economic activity to change? In a market economy, when buyers choose goods and services through their spending, those goods and services are produced by suppliers. If buyers do not spend their money on products, those products will not stay on the market. Thus, if total spending were to increase, output would increase; if total spending were to decrease, output would decrease; and if total spending remained unchanged, output would not change.

When the level of spending goes up and sellers increase production, more land, labor, capital, and entrepreneurship are required. This means that there will be an increase in the employment of resources which will in turn enlarge incomes. Thus, increased spending leads to economic expansion, or recovery, since it stimulates a growth in output, employment, and income.

When spending falls and sellers reduce their outputs, a cutback occurs in the employment of resources. This cutback in turn leads to a decrease in

Figure 5.5
Spending and the Level of Economic Activity

Changes in total, or aggregate, spending lead to changes in output, employment, and income.

Recovery or Expansion	Recession or Contraction
Increased Spending	Decreased Spending
↓	↓
Causes	Causes
↓	↓
Larger Output	Smaller Output
↓	↓
Causes	Causes
↓	↓
Increased Employment	Decreased Employment
↓	↓
Causes	Causes
↓	↓
More Income	Less Income

resource owners' incomes. Thus, a reduction in spending leads to a recession, or contraction, in economic activity because of its dampening effect on output, employment, and income. The relationship between spending, output, employment, and income is summarized in Figure 5.5.

Since aggregate spending is composed of expenditures by households, businesses, the government, and foreign buyers, the spending behavior of each of these sectors will be examined, along with how that behavior affects the level of economic activity.

The Household Sector

In the aggregate, the largest spending group in the economy is households. Households buy far more goods and services than do businesses, government units, and foreign purchasers combined. For example, of the approximately \$3.7 trillion output produced in 1984, households purchased about \$2.3 trillion, and businesses and governments purchased about \$637 billion and \$748 billion, respectively.[1] Also, over time, household spending increases at a relatively stable pace. Because individuals do not radically alter their expenditure patterns from year to year, aggregate household spending on new goods and services, which is technically termed **personal consumption expenditures,** tends to fluctuate very little as it grows over time. This is indicated in Figure 5.6, which plots real personal consumption expenditures in 1972 dollars for 1960 through 1984.

Personal consumption expenditures
Household spending on new goods and services.

The Household Sector and the Circular Flow of Economic Activity The circular flow model, which was introduced in the discussion of a market economy in Chapter Two, illustrates how household spending affects production, employment, and income. On the diagram in Figure 5.7, the bottom

[1]U.S., *Economic Report of the President* (Washington, D.C.: U.S. Government Printing Office, 1985), pp. 232, 233. The 1984 figures are preliminary.

Figure 5.6
Real Personal Consumption Expenditures for 1960–1984 (1972 Dollars)

The behavior of total spending by households does not widely fluctuate, and the growth of personal consumption expenditures is relatively stable over time.

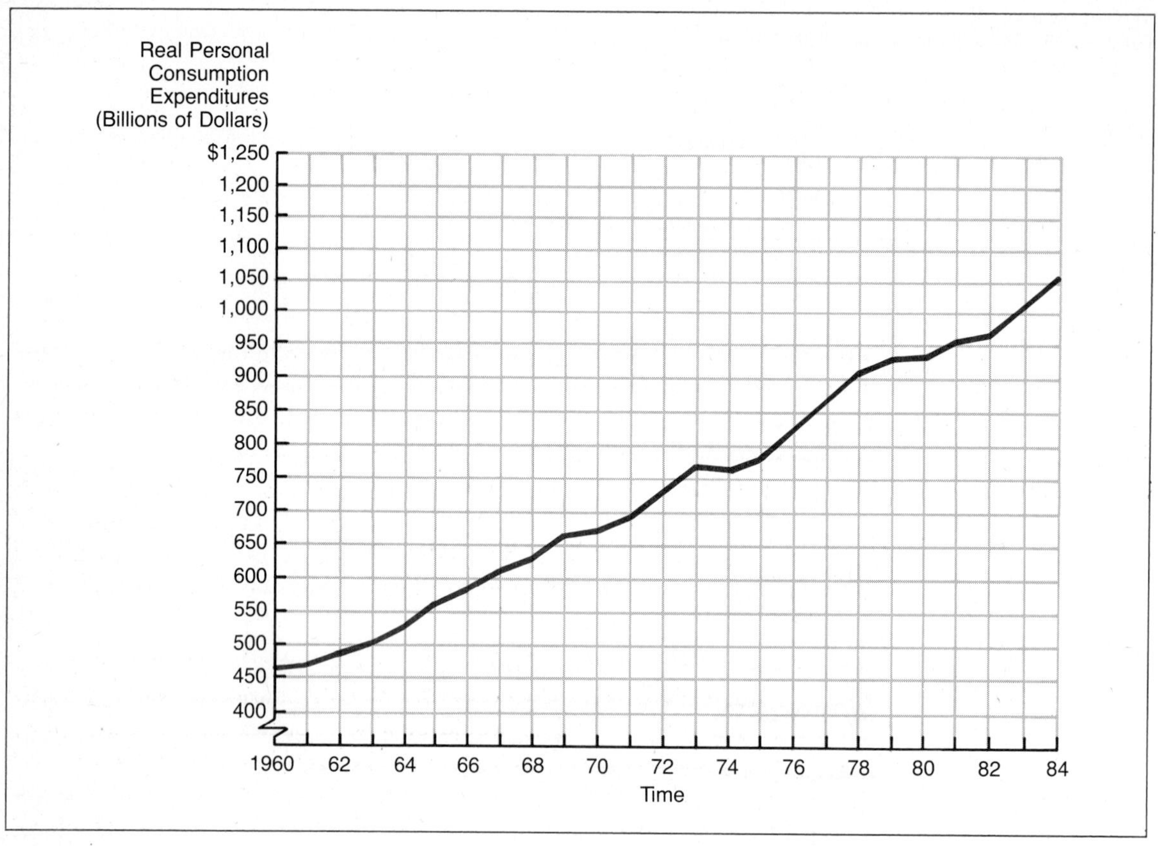

Source: U.S., *Economic Report of the President* (Washington, D.C.: U.S. Government Printing Office, 1985), p. 234. 1984 figure is preliminary.

line, labeled (1), represents the flow of household spending (personal consumption expenditures) for the purchase of goods and services. Line (2) indicates that businesses respond to this spending by providing the goods and services households demand. Line (3) shows businesses employing the resources needed to produce those goods and services, and line (4) illustrates the flow of income to those resource owners. Thus, a flow of output, employment, and income results from household spending.

If household spending stayed the same, say, at $6 billion every day, there would be no tendency to produce more or less output, hire more or less resources, or pay more or less income. The same level of output that was demanded and produced yesterday would be demanded and produced today, tomorrow, and so on. In short, the level of economic activity would

Figure 5.7
Household Spending and the Circular Flow

The circular flow model illustrates how spending by households influences the levels of output, employment, and income.

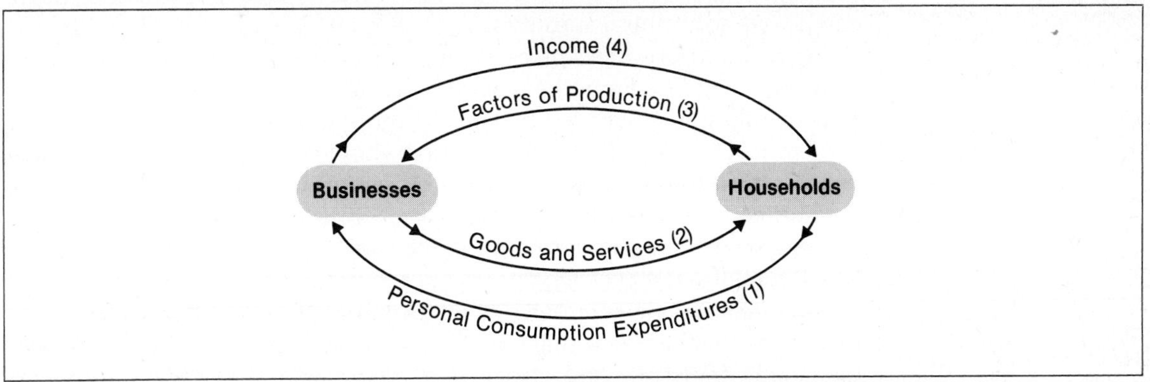

remain unchanged. However, if daily spending increased, say, to $6.1 billion, businesses would respond by producing more goods and services, with the result that employment and income would also expand. If household spending fell, say, to $5.9 billion a day, businesses would respond by cutting back production, which would in turn lead to a drop in employment and income.

The amount households actually spend on goods and services depends primarily upon the size of their earned incomes. If all households together earned $3 trillion a year, they would be able to spend far more than they could if they earned just $2 trillion. However, the amount of household spending is also influenced by other factors: notably, the alternative uses to which household income can be put, and additional money received from sources other than earned income.

Financial institutions
Organizations such as banks, savings and loan associations, and insurance companies, which provide a means for channeling saving into borrowing.

Saving, Taxes, Borrowing, and Transfers Purchasing goods and services is only one method of disposing of households' incomes. One alternative to consuming is to save income for the future by placing it in a **financial institution.** Financial institutions are organizations such as banks, savings and loan associations, insurance companies, brokerage houses, and the like, which perform services for buyers, sellers, and holders of money, stocks, bonds, and other financial instruments. Another alternative is to use income to pay personal taxes. Both saving and taxation reduce households' personal consumption expenditures: the greater the saving or tax payments by households, the less the income that remains for the purchase of goods and services.

On the other hand, household spending is increased when earned income is supplemented through borrowing and/or government transfer payments.

Transfer payment
Money from the government for which no work is performed in return.

Borrowing may be done in several different ways, ranging from seeking a loan from a bank to extending payments on a credit card purchase. A **transfer payment** is a check from the government for which no work is performed in return. Examples include social security, unemployment compensation, and agricultural subsidies.

Figure 5.8 incorporates taxes, saving, borrowing, and transfers into a circular flow diagram. From the diagram it is easy to see that aggregate household spending is influenced by each of these factors. A change in any one of them will cause a change in total household spending. For example, fear of a recession could cause households to increase their saving, with a resulting decline in spending; or a decrease in interest rates could lead to an increase in spending by encouraging households to borrow for such items as automobiles and vacations.

Leakages from the spending stream
Uses other than spending for earned income, such as taxes and saving.

Injections into the spending stream
Spending that comes from a source other than household earned income.

Taxes and saving represent **leakages from the spending stream:** they are income that has been channeled to uses other than consumption. Spending from transfers and borrowing represents **injections into the spending stream:** they permit households to purchase more than their earned incomes alone would allow. Since the size of the spending stream is reduced by leakages and increased by injections, leakages and injections ultimately shrink and expand the levels of output, employment, and income in the economy.

While all of these influences affect household spending and economic activity, the impact of a change in the household sector could be negated by spending changes in the business, government, or foreign sectors. Therefore, before drawing any conclusions about the effect on the economy of changes in household spending behavior, one should examine the other sectors.

Figure 5.8
Household Spending, Taxes, Saving, Borrowing, and Transfers

Spending from transfers and borrowing are injections into the spending stream; saving and taxes are leakages from the spending stream.

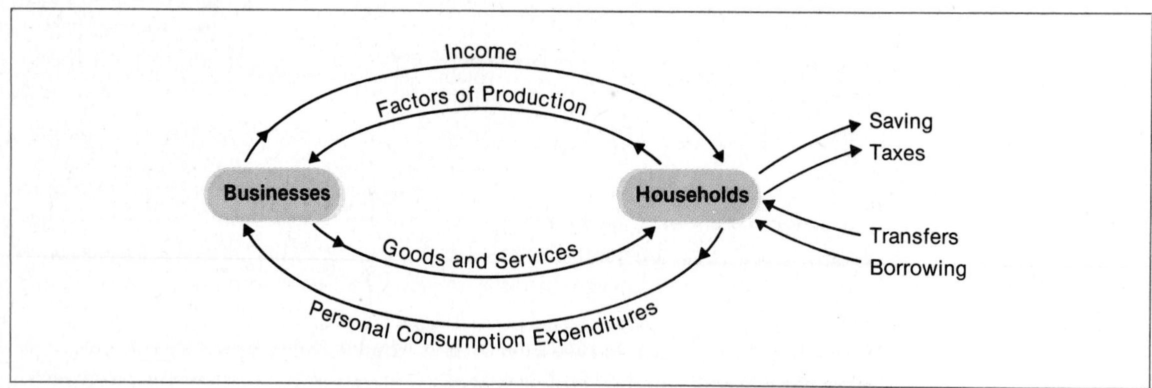

The Business Sector

Investment spending Business spending on new goods such as new machinery, equipment, buildings, inventories, and such.

Businesses are major purchasers of goods and services. Each year they buy billions of dollars worth of machinery, equipment, replacement parts, new buildings, inventories, and the like. Business spending on these types of new goods is called **investment spending.** Like household spending, business investment spending influences output, income, and employment. However, unlike household personal consumption expenditures, investment spending tends to fluctuate widely from year to year. Figure 5.9, which plots real gross investment[2] in 1972 dollars for 1960 through 1984, illustrates the fluctuating pattern characteristic of investment spending. Because of these fluctuations, investment spending is a primary cause of changes in economic activity. When business spending declines, it can bring about a slowdown or recession; when it increases, it can help pull the economy into a recovery. For example, Figure 5.9 shows a dramatic decline in investment spending for 1974 and 1975 and lesser declines in 1980 and 1982. During these years the United States experienced recessions and high unemployment rates.

Why does business spending fluctuate from year to year? Why does it not exhibit the stability associated with household spending? Primarily, business spending fluctuates because it is influenced by profit expectations. A business will invest in new equipment, a new building, or whatever, because it expects that this investment will increase its profit level. For example, the owners of a record shop will build a second location if they expect that two stores will be more profitable than one. If conditions suggest that a proposed investment expenditure will not be sufficiently profitable, the investment may be postponed or eliminated. Because many investment goods are bought for expansion or replacement purposes, postponement is feasible. It would be easier for a food chain to postpone the replacement of an old but operating refrigerator, or for an amusement park to eliminate the construction of a new roller coaster, than it would be for a family to postpone its expenditures on food and utilities.

Profit expectations, and thus investment spending, are related to expectations of future overall levels of economic activity. The fear that a recession is about to occur may encourage a reduction in investment spending, as businesses speculate that falling demand and growing inventories of unsold goods might make it unprofitable to expand or replace old equipment. Likewise, expectations of healthy sales and a surge in economic activity can bring about an increase in business spending.

The interest rate that businesses must pay for borrowed funds greatly influences the level of investment spending. If the interest rate is high, businesses may decide that it is to their best advantage to postpone spending because the high cost of borrowing reduces the profitability of the investment. If the interest rate is low, businesses may take advantage of the

---

[2]Gross investment is outright purchases of investment goods plus a depreciation allowance for capital that was used up during the current year.

Figure 5.9
Real Gross Investment for 1960–1984 (1972 Dollars)

Investment spending can fluctuate widely from year to year and is a primary cause of changes in economic activity.

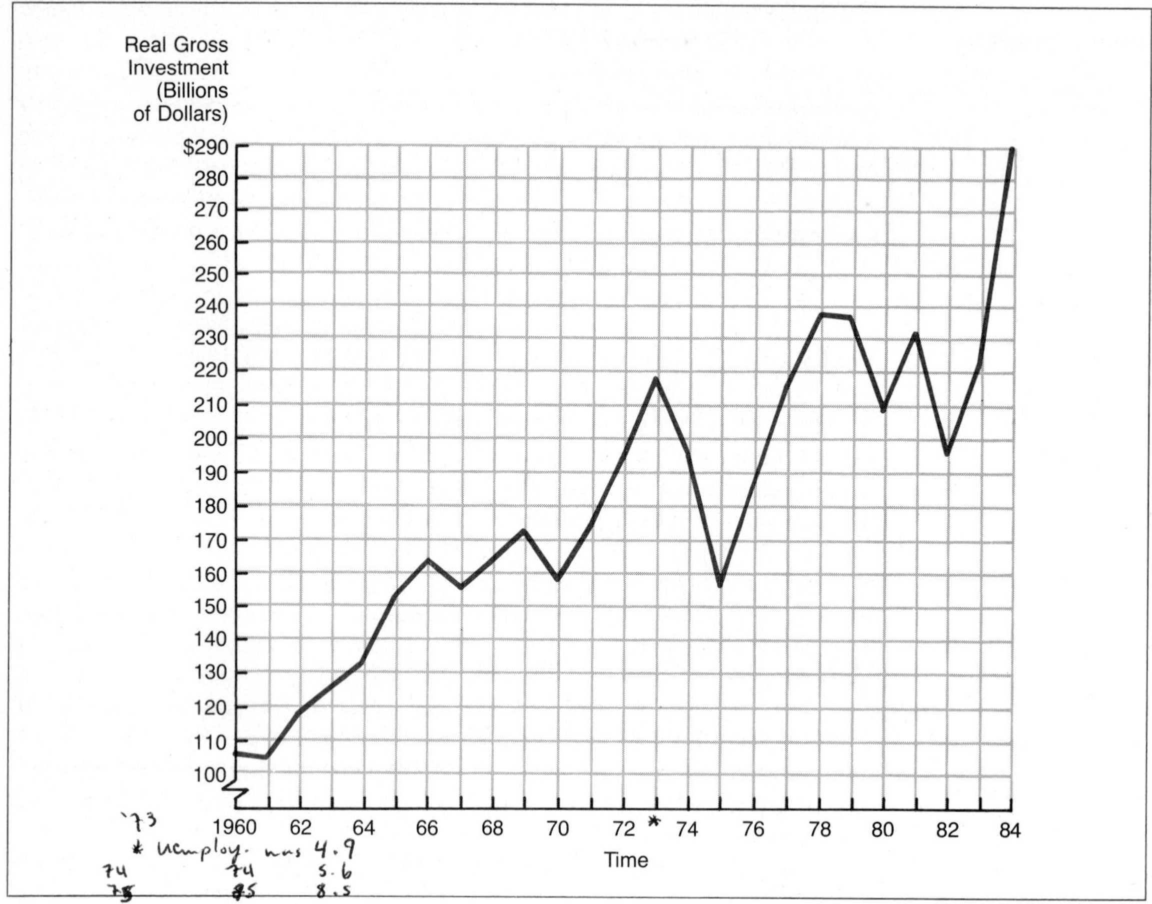

Source: U. S., *Economic Report of the President* (Washington, D.C.: U.S. Government Printing Office, 1985), p. 234. 1984 figure is preliminary.

reduced cost of funds and increase their borrowing for investment purposes. Application 5.1 on pages 142–143 provides an example of how an investment decision is affected by the interest rate. The importance of the effect of changes in the interest rate on economic activity will be discussed further in Chapter Eight.

When a business invests in such things as machinery, equipment, or a building, the expense can be staggering. Imagine the price tag on the construction of a large shopping mall or a multi-storied building such as the Sears Tower in Chicago. From where do the funds for these types of expenditures come? A business is like an individual who buys a house, a car, or another expensive item that is not a part of the normal everyday budget. The individual can make his or her purchase either with money that has been saved or with money that is borrowed. Businesses face a similar choice—they can use earnings saved from their past operations, which are called **retained earnings,** or they can borrow from outside sources.

Retained earnings
The portion of a business's accumulated profits that has been retained for investment or other purposes.

The Business Sector and the Circular Flow of Economic Activity Business saving and investment spending are incorporated into the circular flow model in Figure 5.10. Line (1) represents business saving. Like household saving, business saving is a leakage from the spending stream. Line (2) represents business investment spending, which is an injection into the spending stream. Because they are leakages and injections, any changes in the levels of business saving or investment spending will cause changes in output, employment, and income.

Figure 5.10 emphasizes that business saving and investment spending are channeled through financial institutions. When a business saves, the company does not keep the savings in a lock box or buried on its premises. Rather, it puts its savings into a financial institution such as a bank, or into stocks, bonds, or some other security which allows the savings to earn interest until the funds are needed. Investment spending also involves financial institutions because investments are financed from retained earnings or from borrowing. If financed through retained earnings, a business would make its investment by cashing in its savings. If the investments were financed through borrowing, the company would also go to a financial institution, but this time to make a loan.

Saving, Investment, and the Level of Economic Activity Figure 5.11 extends the circular flow diagram of Figure 5.10 by adding household saving and borrowing. This added dimension points out a critical relationship in the operation of the economy: the saving-borrowing and investment relationship, or, as it is more commonly called, the **saving-investment relationship.** Figure 5.11 illustrates that dollars saved by households and businesses—dollars that are leakages from the spending stream—can be borrowed and spent by other households and businesses and thereby returned to the spending stream. In other words, financial institutions provide vehicles for changing leakages from the spending stream into injections.

Saving-investment relationship
The relationship between the amount saved by households and businesses and the amount returned to the spending stream through investment and household borrowing.

But is every dollar saved put back into the spending stream through investment and household borrowing? Does the amount of saving always equal the amount that businesses would like to invest and households borrow? Because savers have entirely different motives for their actions than do investors and borrowers, it is likely that saving will not equal investment and borrowing.[3] Rather, in this relationship, there are three possible situations: (1) saving equals investment and household borrowing; (2) saving is greater than investment and household borrowing; or (3) saving is less than

---

[3]Savers are motivated by a desire to have funds available in the future for specific purchases, or as a precaution against unknown adversity, or for opportunities that may present themselves. Investors and borrowers are motivated by a desire for profit, as in the case of business, or for personal satisfaction, as in the case of an individual borrowing to purchase an automobile or vacation.

Figure 5.10
Business Saving, Investment, and the Circular Flow

Business saving and investment spending are leakages from and injections into the spending stream that are typically channeled through financial institutions.

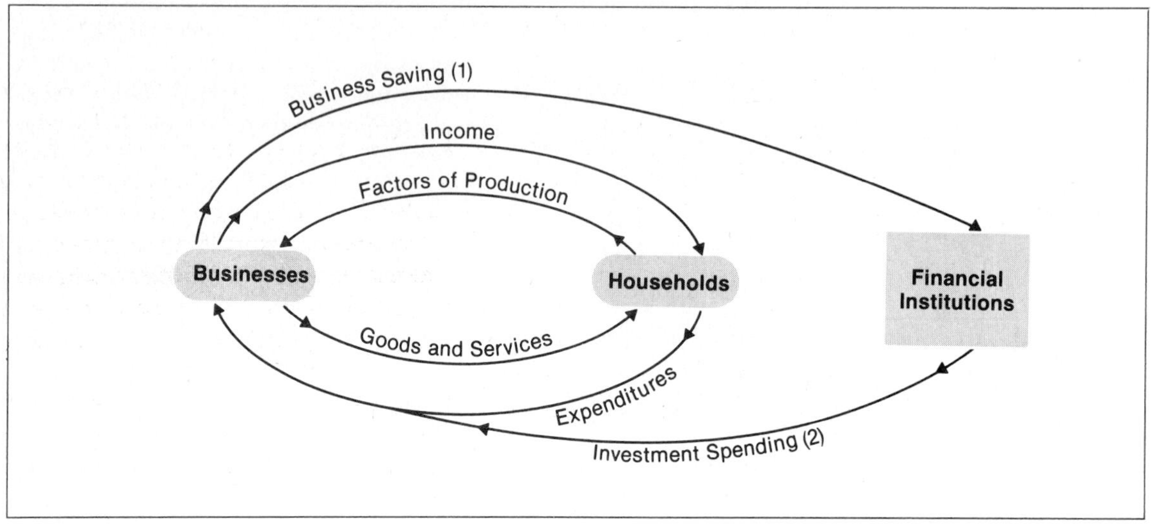

Application 5.1
INTEREST RATES AND INVESTMENT SPENDING

Suppose that your favorite pizza spot has become so popular that customers must often wait for an hour or longer for a table. The owners, because of this demand, are contemplating refurbishing currently unused space in their facility. They have determined that $100,000 will be needed for this investment and are analyzing the cost of borrowing the money. How will the interest rate that they must pay for these borrowed funds affect their decision to refurbish?

With an annual interest rate of 6 percent, the interest for borrowing $100,000 for one year is $6,000 (6% × $100,000 = $6,000); at 12 percent the interest for borrowing $100,000 for one year is $12,000 (12% × $100,000); and at 18 percent the interest is $18,000. This means that the annual interest *alone* will change by $1,000 when the annual interest rate changes by 1 percent. If the restaurant borrows $100,000 for a year at 18 percent rather than at 6 percent, it will cost an additional $12,000! If lenders are charging high interest rates, the owners must decide whether they want to pay those rates: it will mean a substantial reduction in profit, or perhaps no profit at all.

Assume further that the owners would like to borrow the necessary $100,000 and pay it off in equal monthly installments for five years. Also

Figure 5.11
Saving, Investing, and Borrowing by Households and Businesses

The relationship between saving and investment spending and household borrowing can cause the economy's levels of output, employment, and income to increase, decrease, or remain unchanged.

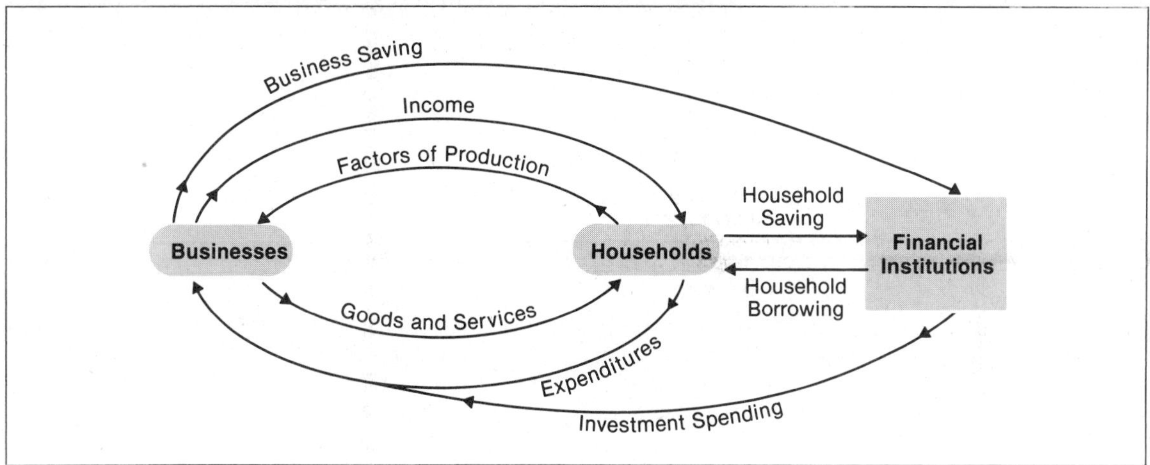

assume that the interest would be recalculated each month to account for the declining balance of the loan as it is paid off.

The following table summarizes the monthly payment necessary and the total interest paid for a loan of $100,000 over five years at various interest rates. Notice that the monthly payment for borrowing $100,000 at 18 percent is $2,539.30, and that the monthly payment at 6 percent is $1,933.30—a difference of $606 *per month.* Notice also the total interest paid over five years. At 6 percent it is $15,998 and at 18 percent it is $52,358. A loan made at 18 percent rather than 6 percent would mean additional foregone profit of $36,360!

Monthly Payments and Total Interest Paid for Retiring a $100,000 Loan Over Five Years at Various Interest Rates[a]

Interest Rate	6%	12%	18%
Monthly Payment	$ 1,933.30	$ 2,224.40	$ 2,539.30
Total Interest Paid	$15,998.00	$33,464.00	$52,358.00

[a]Payments are calculated from amortization tables in Steven C. Lawlor, *Business Mathematics* (San Francisco: Canfield Press, 1976), pp. 216–217.

investment and household borrowing.[4] Let us examine each situation. To keep matters simple, assume that there are no government taxes or transfers. These will be analyzed later.

If $5 billion is saved, and the entire $5 billion is borrowed and spent, the levels of output, employment, and income will not change. All of the dollars leaked from the spending stream are returned, and no change occurs in the level of aggregate spending. Thus, if saving equals investment and household borrowing, there is no change in output, income, and employment.

If $5 billion is saved, and only $4 billion is borrowed and spent, the economy will contract. This means $1 billion has been removed from the spending stream that is not being returned. The level of aggregate spending falls by $1 billion, causing a decline in output, employment, and income. Thus, when saving is greater than investment and household borrowing, the economy contracts.

If $5 billion is saved, and $6 billion is spent through investment and household borrowing, the economy will expand. An additional $1 billion of spending is injected into the economy that was not there before. This increase in spending causes an increase in output, employment, and income. Thus, when investment and household borrowing are greater than saving, the economy expands.

Business Taxes Another leakage from the circular flow is business taxes. Businesses must pay several types of taxes to government: corporate income tax, sales tax, license fees, and so on. Each of these taxes represents business income that is not spent and is therefore a leakage. Figure 5.12 summarizes the business sector's saving and tax leakages and investment injections into the spending stream.

The Government Sector

The third major group that influences economic activity with its spending patterns is the government sector. Government outlays occur at the federal, state, and local levels and can be classified into two categories: purchases of goods and services, and transfer payments.

Government purchases of goods and services
Government spending on new goods and services.

Government purchases of goods and services refers to spending on such items as new fire trucks, bombers, cement, paper, postal equipment, services of government employees, and the like. Because these purchases represent outright spending, they have the same impact on the economy as do household and investment spending. That is, increases in government purchases can increase output, employment, and income; and decreases in government purchases can decrease output, employment, and income. In 1984 government units in the United States purchased about $748 billion worth of goods

---

[4]We will discuss later how some financial institutions can lend more than they have taken in.

Figure 5.12
Business Saving, Taxes, and Investment

In addition to business saving, business taxes are also a leakage from the spending stream.

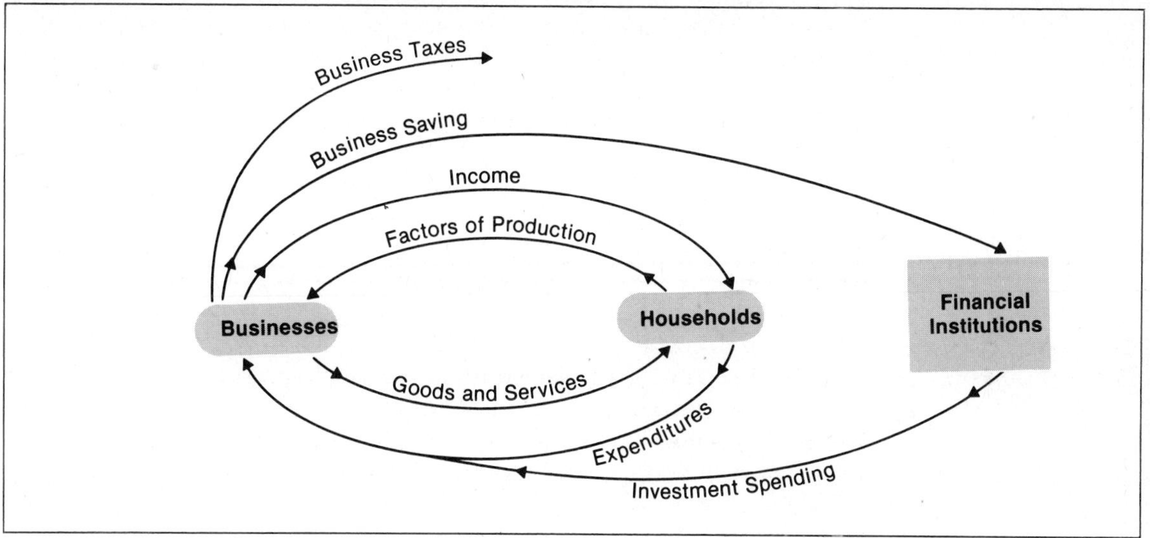

and services. Of this total, the federal government acquired $295.5 billion, and state and local governments bought $452.4 billion.[5]

Since government spending for goods and services is the second largest component of total spending, it is important to observe the pattern of these purchases over time. Figure 5.13 plots real government purchases of goods and services in 1972 dollars for 1960 through 1984. Like household spending and unlike business spending, government purchases tend to be stable and increasing over time. However, some occurrences, such as war, can cause deviations from this pattern. Note the Vietnam War years in Figure 5.13.

Government transfer payments are government payments or checks to individuals or households who have performed no direct work in return. For example, social security and welfare checks are transfers, whereas the payroll check of a civil service employee is not. As was pointed out earlier, households can use all or part of their transfer payments for the purchase of goods and services. While changing the amount of government transfer payments does not affect what is termed government purchases, it does affect the level of economic activity by changing the amount that households have available to spend. In 1984, $407 billion went from government units to

[5] *Economic Report of the President,* 1985, p. 233. Figures are preliminary.

Figure 5.13
Real Government Purchases of Goods and Services for 1960–1984 (1972 Dollars)

Except in war years, the growth in government purchases of goods and services has been relatively stable.

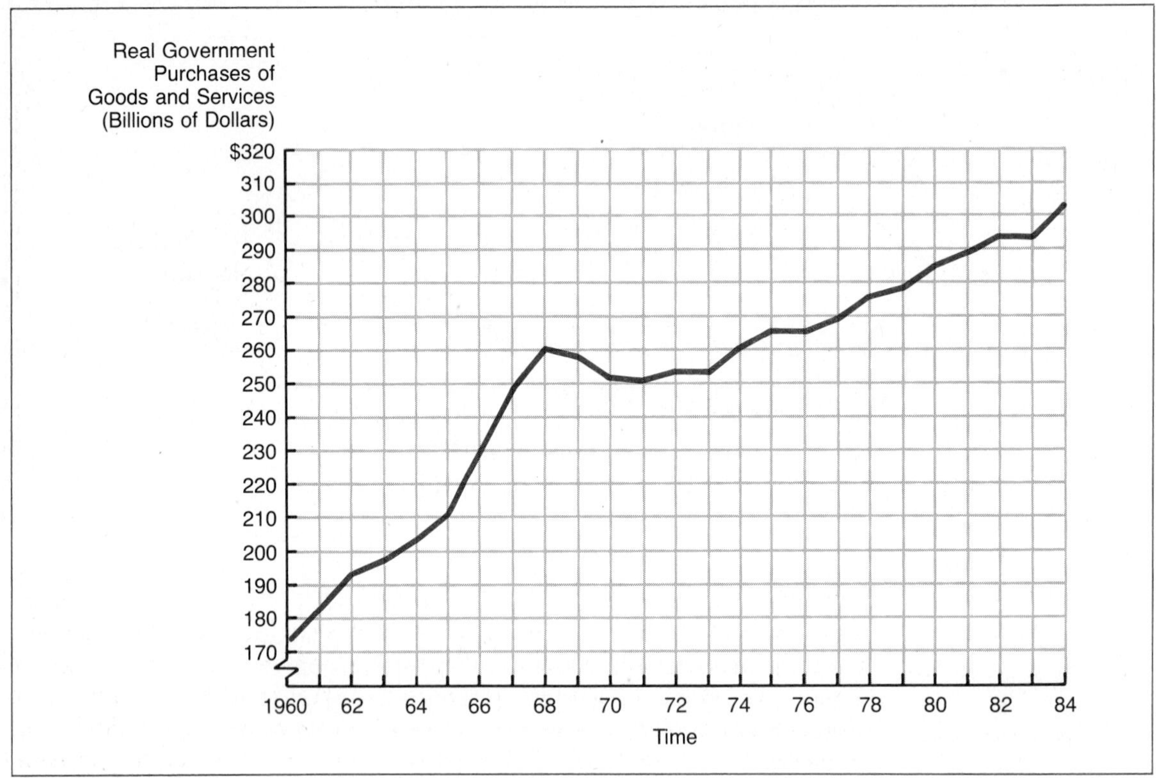

Source: U.S., *Economic Report of the President* (Washington D.C.: U.S. Government Printing Office, 1985), p. 235. 1984 figure is preliminary.

households in the form of transfer payments.[6] It will be shown in the next chapter how Congress can, and has, deliberately altered the amount of federal government purchases and transfers to change economic conditions.

The Government Sector and the Circular Flow of Economic Activity
The government sector is added to the circular flow model in Figure 5.14. In this figure, line (1) shows the flow to households of transfer payments, which can be used for consumption spending. Line (2) represents government purchases of goods and services, and lines (3) and (4) illustrate the flow of taxes from households and businesses to government. The circular flow diagram shows clearly that government purchases are a direct injection into

[6]*Economic Report of the President*, 1985, p. 321. Figure is preliminary.

Figure 5.14
The Government Sector and the Circular Flow

Government purchases of goods and services and spending from transfer payments are injections into the spending stream, and taxes paid to government by businesses and households are leakages from the spending stream.

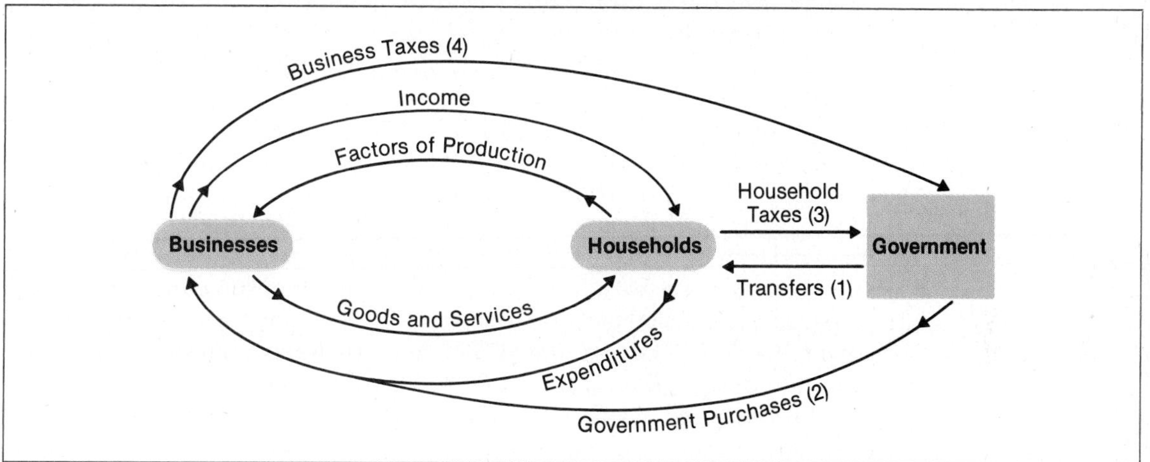

the spending stream, transfers provide an injection, and taxes are a leakage.

Just as with the saving-investment and household borrowing relationship, it is not necessary that the tax-government expenditure relationship be equal. Sometimes (1) the amount put into the spending stream through government purchases and transfers is equal to the amount taken from the spending stream in taxes; (2) the amount put into the spending stream through purchases and transfers is less than the amount withdrawn as taxes; or (3) the amount returned through purchases and transfers is greater than the amount taken from the spending stream as taxes.[7]

---

[7]We are being careful to compare the amount returned to the *spending stream* through government purchases and transfers with the amount taken from the *spending stream* through taxes. This is because not all transfer payments are used to purchase goods and services, and not all taxes are paid with money that would have been spent. When households receive transfer payments, a portion of what they receive from the government may be saved. When households pay taxes, part of that payment comes from money that would have been used for personal consumption expenditures, and part comes from money that would have been saved. For this reason, assessing the impact of government expenditures and taxes becomes somewhat complex. Let us illustrate with the following example.

Suppose that the government taxes households by $100 billion and uses that money to purchase $100 billion of goods and services. Suppose also that $70 billion of that tax is paid with dollars that households would have used for personal consumption expenditures, and $30 billion is paid with dollars they would have saved. Because of this, the tax of $100 billion reduces household spending by only $70 billion. Thus, the tax of $100 billion and expenditure program of $100 billion enlarges the spending stream by $30 billion and the economy grows. This is because $30 billion that would have been saved by households is now being spent by the gov-

If the government, through taxes, reduces household and business spending by, say, $2 billion, and if all of this $2 billion is used by the government to purchase goods and services or is transferred to households who spend all of their portion, then the flow of leakages and injections will not be altered. All that is taken from the spending stream through taxes will be respent through government purchases or transfers. Because aggregate spending does not change, the levels of output, employment, and income do not change either.

If government withdraws $2 billion from the spending stream through taxes and expends only $1.5 billion on purchases and transfer payments, the leakages from spending will be greater than the injections, causing the economy to contract. Because aggregate spending falls, the levels of output, employment, and income also fall.

If government withdraws $2 billion from the spending stream and expends $2.5 billion on purchases and on transfer payments that are all spent, then it will be injecting $0.5 billion into the spending stream that was not there before. Because aggregate spending increases, the levels of output, employment, and income also increase.

In short, if all tax dollars which have been withdrawn from the spending stream are spent by the government or by households, economic activity will stay the same. If these tax dollars are not all spent, output, employment, and income will fall; and if more is spent than collected, the economy will expand.

The Foreign Sector

Transactions between U.S. and foreign buyers and sellers take place in the foreign sector. The sale overseas of corn raised in Illinois, the purchase of a Japanese television set by a family in Texas, and the sale of U.S.-built airplanes to a European government all occur in the foreign sector. As with the other sectors, changes in spending on goods and services in the foreign sector affect the levels of output, employment, and income in the U.S. economy.

Export
A good or service that is sold abroad.

Import
A good or service purchased from abroad.

The real values in 1972 dollars of **exports,** or U.S.-produced goods and services sold abroad, and **imports,** or foreign-produced goods and services sold to U.S. buyers, are plotted in Figure 5.15. The figure illustrates that both exports and imports of goods and services have generally grown over the years. However, the growth, especially in exports, has not been steady. For

---

ernment. In this example, if the government wanted the effect of its spending and taxes to be neutral, it would spend $70 billion and tax $100 billion.

This example could be further complicated by assuming that out of the $100 billion in government expenditures, only $50 billion is spent for the purchase of goods and services and that the other $50 billion goes for transfer payments. The $50 billion spent on goods and services goes directly into the spending stream, but part of the $50 billion in transfers could go into savings. If households saved $15 billion and spent $35 billion, then only $85 billion of the government's total expenditures would go into the spending stream.

Figure 5.15
Real U.S. Exports and Imports of Goods and Services for 1960–1984 (1972 Dollars)

Real U.S. exports and imports of goods and services have generally increased from 1960 through the early 1980s.

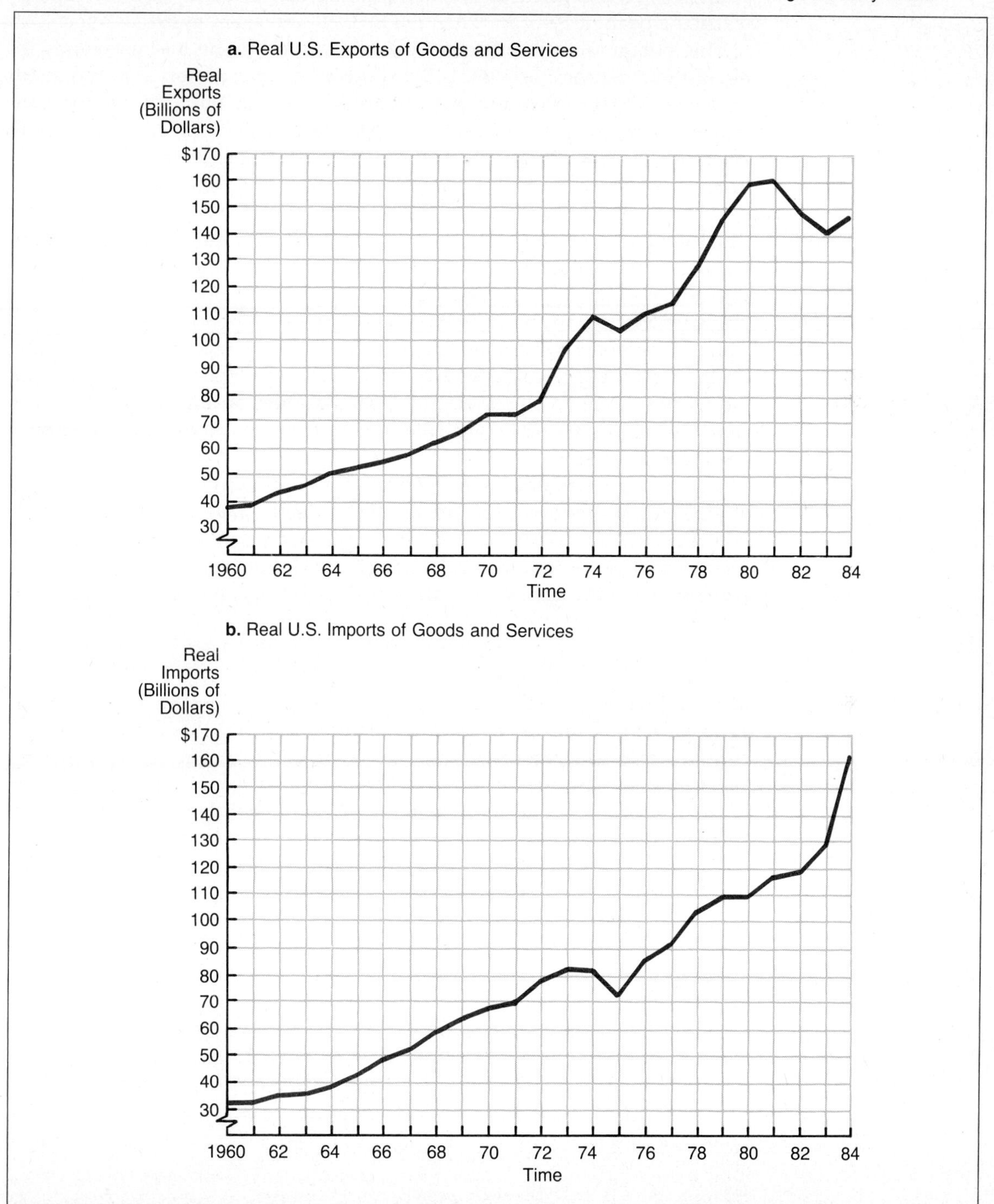

Source: U.S., *Economic Report of the President* (Washington, D.C.: U.S. Government Printing Office, 1985), p. 235. Figure for 1984 is preliminary.

example, graph a (the upper graph), shows that the real value of exports reached a peak in 1981 and then fell in 1982 and again in 1983.

The foreign sector has become more important to the macroeconomy in the last few decades. In 1960 U.S. exports of goods and services amounted to 5.7 percent of GNP and imports to 4.6 percent. By 1984 exports and imports had grown to 9.9 and 11.7 percent of GNP, respectively.[8] Trade between the United States and other nations, and international finance are examined in greater detail in Chapters Sixteen and Seventeen.

The Foreign Sector and the Circular Flow of Economic Activity When buyers in the United States purchase foreign goods and services, their expenditures cause income, output, and employment to increase in foreign countries, but not in the United States. Similarly, when foreign businesses, households, and governments purchase goods and services produced in the United States, their expenditures cause output, employment, and income in the United States to increase. Thus, income spent on imports is a leakage from the spending stream, and sales of U.S. exports produce injections into the spending stream.

Figure 5.16 illustrates the effect of exports and imports on the U.S. economy using a variation of the circular flow model. Line (1) represents injections into the U.S. economy resulting from expenditures by foreign buyers for exported goods and services. Line (2) illustrates leakages from the U.S. economy resulting from expenditures by U.S. buyers on imported goods and services.

As with the other sectors, in the foreign sector leakages and injections are not necessarily equal. If the value of exports is greater than the value of imports, then the injections into the spending stream from the foreign sector exceed leakages, causing aggregate spending, and thus the levels of output, employment, and income in the United States to grow. If the value of exports equals the value of imports, then injections equal leakages, and the movement of goods and services in the foreign sector does not change total spending or, consequently, the levels of output, employment, and income in the United States. If the value of exports is less than the value of imports, then leakages exceed injections from the foreign sector into the spending stream, causing economic activity in the United States to decrease.

Net exports
Exports minus imports; is positive when exports exceed imports and negative when imports exceed exports.

The difference between the value of exports and the value of imports (exports minus imports) is termed **net exports.** If the value of exports is greater than the value of imports, net exports is greater than zero; if imports are greater than exports, net exports is negative. The behavior of U.S. net exports of goods and services from 1960 through 1984 is plotted in Figure 5.17 on page 152. Net exports has been positive throughout that period except for 1984, indicating that the value of exports has been generally

[8]U.S., *Economic Report of the President* (Washington, D.C.: U.S. Government Printing Office, 1985), pp. 232, 233. 1984 figures are preliminary.

Figure 5.16
The Foreign Sector and the Circular Flow

Exports of goods and services generate injections into the U.S. economy's spending stream, and imports cause leakages from the U.S. economy's spending stream.

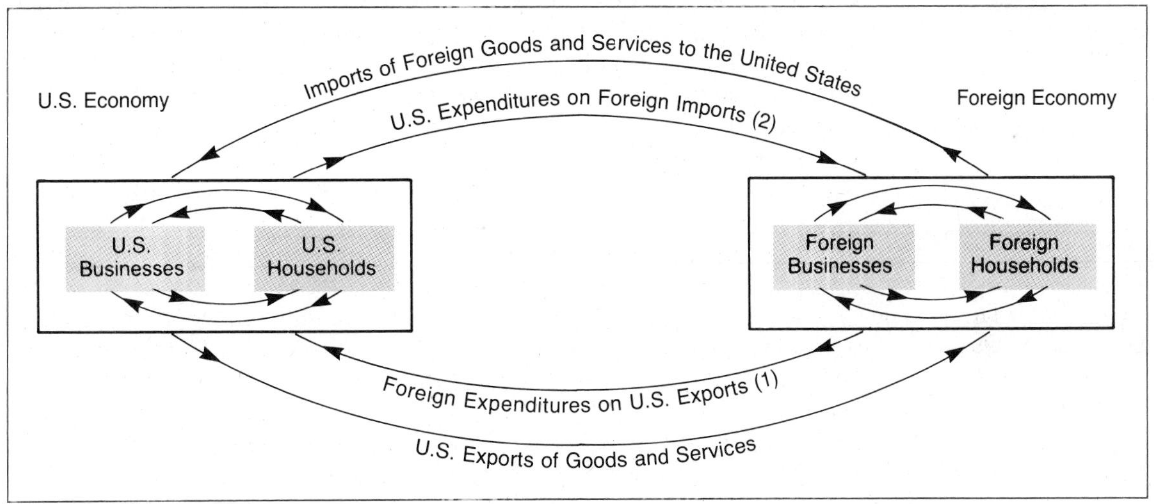

greater than the value of imports, or the injections into the spending stream from the international sale of goods and services have exceeded the leakages. This was especially true for much of the 1970s and early 1980s.

Summary of Aggregate Spending, Leakages, and Injections

By now it should be clear that the level of aggregate spending determines the levels of output, employment, and income in the economy. If aggregate spending increases, the economy expands as output, employment, and income increase; if aggregate spending decreases, the economy contracts as output, employment, and income fall. Aggregate spending is determined by adding together the spending of households, businesses, government units, and foreign buyers. Of these four groups, business investment spending, because of its size and instability, is a primary cause of changes in output, employment, and income.

Certain actions can be taken in each of the four spending sectors to cause leakages from the spending stream. These actions include saving by households and businesses, paying taxes by households and businesses, and importing foreign goods and services. Actions can also be taken in the four sectors to cause injections into the spending stream. These actions include household spending of borrowed dollars and government transfer payments, business investment spending, government purchases of goods and services, and foreign purchases of exported goods and services.

Figure 5.17
Real U.S. Net Exports of Goods and Services for 1960–1984 (1972 Dollars)

Since 1960 net exports has been positive in every year except 1984, indicating that the movement of goods and services in the foreign sector has generally generated more injections into the spending stream than leakages from it.

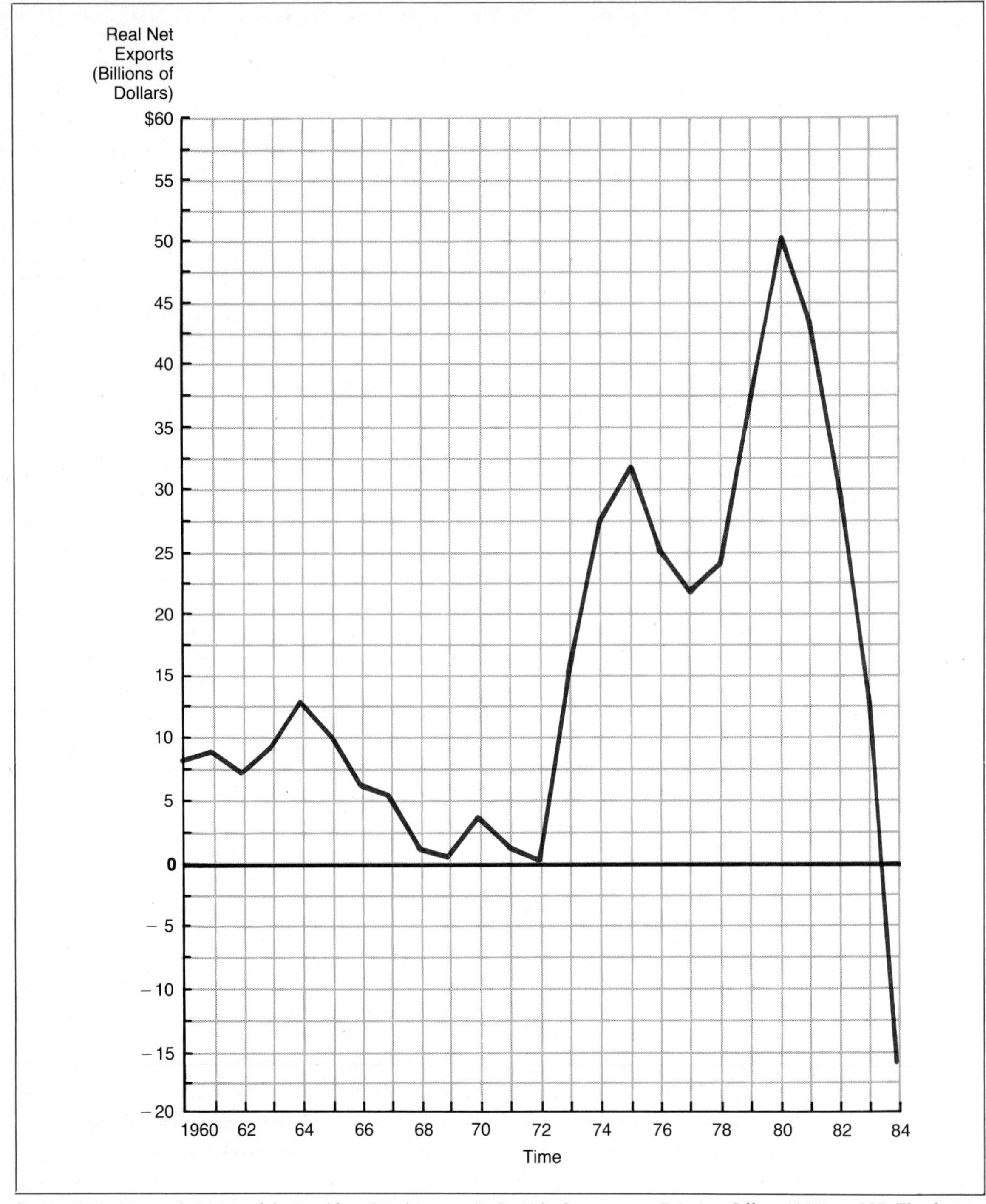

Source: U.S., *Economic Report of the President* (Washington, D.C.: U.S. Government Printing Office, 1985), p. 235. The figure for 1984 is preliminary.

Expansions and contractions in the economy result from the relationship between leakages and injections in total spending. Up to this point in our discussion, we have isolated the expansionary and contractionary impacts of the saving-investment and household borrowing relationship, the tax-government expenditures relationship, and the import-export relationship. To assess the operation of the economy, these relationships must be considered together. For example, while saving could exceed borrowing, causing a contraction, government expenditures could exceed taxes, or exports of goods and services could exceed imports, causing an expansion. Ultimately, what happens to output, employment, and income depends upon the impact of all leakages and injections taken together. If all leakages from the spending stream are equal to all injections, the economy will not change. If leakages are greater than injections, the economy will contract, or fall into a recession. If injections are greater than leakages, the economy will expand into a recovery. These cause-and-effect relationships are summarized in Table 5.1.

The Multiplier Effect

Because the economy operates in a circular flow pattern, changes in spending lead to changes in production, employment, and income. Most of the spending that occurs in the economy comes from the income earned by households. Any time that there is a change in households' earned income, there is a change in the spending originating from this income. Other spending in the economy, such as investment spending, government and net foreign purchases of goods and services, and the household spending that results from transfers and borrowing, is not related to nor determined by household earned income. When there is a change in this type of spending, it is not because of a change in earned income. Let us label the spending that is *not* generated from household earned income as **nonincome-determined spending.**

Nonincome-determined spending
Spending that is *not* generated from household earned income.

Changes in nonincome-determined spending lead to even larger changes in the level of economic activity. For example, an addition of $100 million

Table 5.1
Leakages from and Injections into the Spending Stream

The economy's levels of output, employment, and income depend on the combined impact of all leakages from and all injections into the spending stream.

Leakages	Injections
Household saving	Household spending from borrowing
Business saving	Household spending from transfer payments
Household taxes	Business investment spending
Business taxes	Government purchases of goods and services
Import expenditures	Export expenditures

The Level of Economic Activity Will:

Remain unchanged	if	all leakages equal all injections
Contract	if	all leakages exceed all injections
Expand	if	all injections exceed all leakages

in nonincome-determined expenditures to the economy would cause the value of production to go up by more than $100 million, and a withdrawal of $100 million in nonincome-determined expenditures would cause the value of production to decrease by more than $100 million. Thus, changes in nonincome-determined spending are subject to a **multiplier effect,** meaning that their effect on the level of economic activity is magnified, or multiplied.

Multiplier effect
The change in total output and income generated by a change in nonincome-determined spending is larger than, or a multiple of, the spending change itself.

The reason for the multiplier effect is that new dollars introduced into the circular flow through nonincome-determined spending are spent over and over again. When nonincome-determined expenditures are made, these expenditures become income to the individuals who own the resources that produce the goods and services purchased. These individuals then use part of that income to buy goods and services from others, who in turn spend part of the income they receive, and so on.

A hypothetical example will illustrate how the multiplier principle works. Suppose a company borrows $100,000 from the local bank to build a garage to house some equipment. When the $100,000 is spent and the garage is built, factors of production are used and are paid $100,000 in income. Thus, this new injection of nonincome-determined investment spending creates $100,000 worth of output, employment, and income that were not in the economy before. Households that receive this newly created $100,000 of income from the building of the garage will now use part of it, say, $80,000, for personal consumption expenditures. (The rest will be saved or used for taxes.) When this $80,000 is spent, new output, employment, and income of $80,000 is created. Thus, so far, the initial investment spending injection of $100,000 has caused an increase in the economy's output and income of $180,000.

The process does not stop here. The households that receive the $80,000 of income will take part of that money, say, $64,000, and spend it on new goods and services. That $64,000 will in turn create an output and income of $64,000, part of which will be spent, and on and on. Thus, the initial injection of $100,000 of new spending continues through the economy in a circular pattern, multiplying output and income along the way. Table 5.2 carries this example of the multiplier process through several rounds. When this example is carried through enough successive rounds to approach a zero increase in the last round, and the output and income created in each round are summed, $500,000 in total output and income results. This means that the initial injection of $100,000 has been multiplied, or magnified, into $500,000 of output and income; there has been a multiplier effect of five.

The multiplier effect that results from a change in nonincome-determined spending depends upon how much is spent and not spent from each successive round of income and output that is created. The more that is spent, the greater the multiplier effect will be. The more that is not spent, the less the multiplier effect will be. Imagine how much less output and income

Table 5.2
Effect on Output and Income from a Nonincome-Determined Spending Injection of $100,000

Because of the multiplier effect, an injection of nonincome-determined spending into the spending stream causes output and employment to increase by more than the amount of the nonincome-determined spending itself.

	Output	Income	New Personal Consumption Expenditures
Round 1	$100,000.00	$100,000.00	$80,000.00
Round 2	80,000.00	80,000.00	64,000.00
Round 3	64,000.00	64,000.00	51,200.00
Round 4	51,200.00	51,200.00	40,960.00
Round 5	40,960.00	40,960.00	32,768.00
Round 6	32,768.00	32,768.00	26,214.40
Round 7	26,214.40	26,214.40	20,971.52
Round 8	20,971.52	20,971.52	16,777.22
Round 9	16,777.22	16,777.22	13,421.77
Round 10, 11, 12 . . .	|	|	
Total	$500,000.00	$500,000.00	

would have grown in the example above if households had spent only 50 percent from each successive round of income created.[9]

The mechanism also works in reverse when nonincome-determined expenditures are cut back. A decrease in investment spending of $100,000, by the time it works its way through the economy, will cause the level of economic activity to decline by far more than the initial $100,000 decrease.

In summary, changes in nonincome-determined spending such as investment spending, government and net foreign purchases, or household expenditures from transfer payments or borrowing will cause changes in the level of economic activity that are a multiple of the initial change in spending. A good example of the multiplier effect is presented in Application 5.2, "Pittsburgh's Recession Shows How Layoffs Ripple Through Economy."

A Word about Inflation

When the economy expands or is in the recovery phase of the business cycle, the full production–full employment level of output sets a limit on how far spending can cause production and employment to increase. But what happens when aggregate spending continues to grow after the full production–full employment level is reached? If spending continues to increase when the economy is at or close to full employment, demand-pull inflation will result.

[9]There is an easier way to calculate the multiplier effect than to go through each round of spending. Divide the change in nonincome-determined spending by the percent of the additional income received in each round that is *not spent.* For instance, in the preceding example, $100,000 can be divided by .20 (the percent not spent in each round) to result in an answer of $500,000 ($100,000/.2 = $500,000). Using this approach, what would have been the multiplier effect if 25 percent of additional income were not spent, or if 50 percent of additional income were not spent?

This means that it is possible for inflation to occur when injections into the spending stream are greater than leakages. If the economy is at or near full employment, and investment spending and household borrowing are greater than saving, and/or government expenditures are greater than taxes, and/or exports are greater than imports, then the size of the spending stream could be causing inflation. Either there is too much spending through investment, household borrowing, exporting, and/or government expenditures, or too little saving, importing, and/or taxing. We must be careful to understand that it is not always to the benefit of the economy to encourage more spending.

Test your understanding of the role of spending, leakages, injections, and full employment by completing the exercise in Application 5.3.

A Word about Expectations

Earlier it was noted that the expectation of a recession might induce households to increase their saving as they fear possible job losses, and that it might bring about cutbacks in investment spending as businesses anticipate a decline in sales. Such actions prompted by the fear of a recession can actually cause a recession to occur. Fear-induced increases in saving bring

Application 5.2
PITTSBURGH'S RECESSION SHOWS HOW LAYOFFS RIPPLE THROUGH ECONOMY

PITTSBURGH—It's called the ripple-effect theory, and in simple form, it goes like this: A basic industry falters and lays off workers. Suppliers soon succumb and lay off workers too. Next come service firms and more layoffs. Presto, a recession.

The theory works, judging by a visit to the state unemployment claims office in a blue-collar area on this city's South Side. Hundreds of steelworkers who in better times clocked in at Jones & Laughlin Steel Corp.'s big mill just a few blocks away now line up to file for unemployment benefits. . . .

And as the slump in steel continues, out-of-work steelworkers are being joined by thousands of other people formerly employed in steel equipment and repair shops, as well as in restaurants, stores and offices that depend on the steel business. "We're seeing unemployment ripple right through the job market," says John Lester, manager of the South Side unemployment claims office. "With so many steelworkers trying to get by on unemployment checks, local merchants aren't selling and have had to lay off people too." . . .

. . . [A] steelworker at the J&L mill who has worked on and off for about five months during the last 12 months, reports here on Friday to sign for his unemployment check. . . .

. . . .His unemployment benefits, he notes, total just $183 a week, less than half the $500 a week he averaged in wages at J&L. . . .

Getting by on $183 a week has been "very tight," he says. After he pays for rent ($220 a about a greater leakage from the spending stream, and a reduction in investment lessens this injection into the spending stream. As saving is increased and investment reduced, the resulting decrease in spending causes output, employment, and income to fall, and the economy slips into a recession.

As also noted, expectations can cause or worsen inflation. If households and businesses expect prices to be higher, they may try to "beat" the price increases by buying now what they want and need in the future. The surge in spending may serve only to cause or worsen the inflation that is feared.

Expectations of good economic conditions are important to maintaining a healthy economy. Recovery from a recession is more difficult when households and businesses are unwilling to spend because they are pessimistic about the prospects of recovery. Controlling inflation is more difficult if businesses and households believe that prices will continue to go up in the future and that they will be penalized for postponing their expenditures.

An example of the recognized importance of expectations is found in Application 5.4, "The First Fireside Chat." This reading is an excerpt from the first of several informal and famous radio messages President Franklin D. Roosevelt delivered to the public during the course of his administrations. At the time of this speech, March 12, 1933, the economy was deep in the Depression, and the banking system had virtually collapsed.

month), heat (as much as $250 a month) and food for his family of six, "there isn't anything left," he says. . . .

Along with steelworkers, [the steelworker] has the company of numerous blue-collar workers from plants that supply the mills. Behind him in line one recent morning were a production worker from a chemical company that manufactures a chemical coating used in steelmaking, several workers from local steel equipment plants and several truck drivers who haul steel.

Most are very aware of the ripple pattern of recession layoffs. "Once the mills shut, the equipment plants shut too, the haulers stop hauling and it's that way down the line," says . . . an [unemployed machinist] . . . .

Farther along the line at the South Side office are several white-collar and service employes [sic] who also have suffered recession layoffs or been forced to accept reduced work weeks. For . . . a photography printer at [a photo shop] which is near the South Side, it is the first time she has been in an unemployment line in her 21 years of working.

"The last thing people on layoffs are going to spend money on is photos," says [the printer]. Since January she has been working just two days a week, instead of full time.

The same sort of work reduction has hit . . . a waitress [at a downtown] department store restaurant. [She] began noticing the effects of the recession at the restaurant in January: Instead of her usual 80 to 90 customers a day, she suddenly found that she was serving only 35 to 40. In February she was told to report to work just one day a week instead of her customary four days. . . .

Source: Carol Hymowitz, "Pittsburgh's Recession Shows How Layoffs Ripple Through Economy," *The Wall Street Journal*, March 16, 1982, p. 31. Reprinted by permission of *The Wall Street Journal*,

Application 5.3
TEST YOURSELF: LEAKAGES, INJECTIONS, AND ECONOMIC ACTIVITY[a]

In the following examples explain the effect on output and employment that would result from each action taken alone.

1. Businesses in general install new electronic mail systems.
2. Congress increases the personal income tax rates by 1 percent.
3. A decrease in mortgage loan rates and a continued strong demand for houses cause a boom in the home construction business.
4. An overseas buyer purchases a large amount of personal computers manufactured by a U.S. firm.
5. Because the economy is at full employment, several companies that issue major credit cards establish successful campaigns to increase the number of cardholders and to encourage more charges by current cardholders.
6. Social security payments are no longer made to college students.
7. The interest rates for borrowing money increase.
8. Net exports of goods and services changes from a positive to a negative number.
9. Unemployment compensation payments are increased by $15 a week.
10. Businesses increase their retained earnings and postpone their expansion plans while they wait for better economic times.
11. Political pressure prompts Congress to cut its spending on federal highway projects.
12. Each U.S. taxpayer receives a tax rebate check when the economy is at full employment.
13. A law is passed limiting the number of new foreign automobiles that can enter the country each year.
14. U.S. citizens in general begin to change their attitudes toward thrift and start to increase their levels of saving.

---

[a]Answers can be found on page 164.

Application 5.4
THE FIRST FIRESIDE CHAT

I want to talk for a few minutes with the people of the United States about banking—with the comparatively few who understand the mechanics of banking but more particularly with the overwhelming majority who use banks for the making of deposits and the drawing of checks. I want to tell you what has been done in the last few days, why it was done, and what the next steps are going to be. . . .

What, then, happened during the last few days of February and the first few days of March? Because of undermined confidence on the part of the public, there was a general rush by a large portion of our population to turn bank deposits into currency or gold—a rush so great that the soundest banks could not get enough currency to meet the demand. The reason for this was that on the spur of the moment it was, of course, impossible to sell perfectly sound assets of a bank and convert them into cash except at panic prices far below their real value.

By the afternoon of March 3d scarcely a bank in the country was open to do business. Proclamations temporarily closing them in whole or in part had been issued by the Governors in almost all the States.

It was then that I issued the proclamation providing for the nationwide bank holiday, and this was the first step in the Government's reconstruction of our financial and economic fabric. . . .

It is possible that when the banks resume a very few people who have not recovered from their fear may again begin withdrawals. Let me make it clear that the banks will take care of all needs—and it is my belief that hoarding during the past week has become an exceedingly unfashionable pastime. . . . I can assure you that it is safer to keep your money in a reopened bank than under the mattress. . . .

We had a bad banking situation. Some of our bankers had shown themselves either incompetent or dishonest in their handling of the people's funds. They had used the money entrusted to them in speculations and unwise loans. This was, of course, not true in the vast majority of our banks, but it was true in enough of them to shock the people for a time into a sense of insecurity and to put them into a frame of mind where they did not differentiate, but seemed to assume that the acts of a comparative few had tainted them all. It was the Government's job to straighten out this situation and do it as quickly as possible. And the job is being performed. . . .

. . . [T]here is an element in the readjustment of our financial system more important than currency, more important than gold, and that is the confidence of the people. Confidence and courage are the essentials of success in carrying out our plan. You people must have faith; you must not be stampeded by rumors or guesses. Let us unite in banishing fear. We have provided the machinery to restore our financial system; it is up to you to support and make it work.

It is your problem no less than it is mine. Together we cannot fail.

Source: S. I. Rosenman, ed., *The Public Papers and Addresses of Franklin D. Roosevelt,* vol. II (New York: Random House, Inc., 1938), pp. 61–66.

Notice two points in this excerpt: the effort to restore faith in the banking system; and the problem caused by people who withdrew their funds from financial institutions. In terms of the circular flow, faith was lost in the institutions that could turn leakages into borrowing and investment.

TOTAL SPENDING AND MACROECONOMIC POLICY

It was noted in Chapter Four that the major objectives of the macroeconomy are full employment, price stability, and full production and economic growth. Chapter Five has shown how changes in the level of spending lead to changes in production, employment, and, through demand-pull inflation, the level of prices. Thus, policies to attain the objectives of the macroeconomy must be based on an understanding of the role of total spending in the economy and on how output, employment, and prices can be affected by actions designed to change the level of spending.

There are two major policies for influencing the level of spending to accomplish the objectives of the macroeconomy. In terms of the circular flow model, these policies are designed to regulate the leakages and injections that travel through the government sector and through financial institutions. The first policy focuses on increasing or decreasing the size of the spending stream by changing government taxes and/or expenditures. To increase the level of economic activity, spending is enlarged by lowering taxes and/or increasing government expenditures. The economy is slowed (to counteract demand-pull inflation) by withdrawing spending through increasing taxes and/or reducing government expenditures. This strategy for influencing the economy through government-induced spending changes is called **fiscal policy.** Fiscal policy will be discussed in Chapter Six.

Fiscal policy
Influencing the levels of aggregate output and employment or prices through changes in federal government spending, transfer payments, and/or taxes.

The second policy approach focuses on changing the levels of saving and, especially, borrowing through the economy's financial institutions. The amount of loans that financial institutions can make and the interest rate that is charged on these loans are influenced by actions of the Federal Reserve. The Federal Reserve has the ability to set conditions conducive to borrowing and spending by households and businesses, or to tighten credit conditions and discourage borrowing and spending. These changes in borrowing are related to changes in the money supply. Changing the level of spending by influencing borrowing and the supply of money in the economy is called **monetary policy.** The Federal Reserve, loan making, interest rates, and monetary policy are covered in Chapters Seven and Eight.

Monetary policy
Influencing the levels of aggregate output and employment or prices through changes in the money supply.

There are strong opinions and disagreements about the desirability of using fiscal rather than monetary policy, and vice-versa. Other policy approaches also exist, such as supply-side economics and wage-price controls, for dealing with problems in the macroeconomy. The various points of view on the proper method for reaching objectives or dealing with problems in the macroeconomy, and some alternatives to fiscal policy and monetary policy, are introduced in Chapter Nine.

In closing this chapter, it should be noted that macroeconomics, with its emphasis on spending and its policy prescription of using spending to change the economy, owes an intellectual debt to the British economist John Maynard Keynes (1883–1946). It was Keynes who focused attention on the role of spending in the economy and, in so doing, revolutionized the discipline. While there are debates over the desirability of depending on taxes and government spending or on changing the supply of money to control the economy, the generally agreed starting point for these diverse views is the work of Keynes.

SUMMARY

Market economies such as that of the United States are constantly experiencing expansions and contractions in their levels of real GNP. These recurring upswings and downswings in production are called business cycles. Business cycles are a matter of concern because they affect not only output, but employment, and income. Cyclical fluctuations are divided into four phases: recovery, peak, recession, and trough. The length of time in each phase and the intensity of the expansion or contraction differ from cycle to cycle.

Business cycles occur because of changes in total, or aggregate, spending on new goods and services. As a result of an increase in total spending, output, employment, and income increase and the economy grows. If total spending decreases, output, employment, and income fall and the economy contracts. The effect of total spending on the level of economic activity can be shown with a circular flow diagram.

Household spending on new goods and services is called personal consumption expenditures. These expenditures are fairly stable as they increase from year to year, and they exceed the combined purchases of businesses, government units, and the net foreign sector. The amount of household spending depends on the size of households' incomes, as well as on other uses of those incomes and additional money for spending received from sources other than income. The other uses of income are saving and taxes, and the other sources of money for spending are household borrowing and government transfer payments. Household expenditures will increase if income increases, or if the borrowing and transfer payment injections increase, or if the saving and tax leakages decrease.

Business purchases of new goods such as machinery and equipment are called investment spending. Of the major components of total spending, investment is the most unstable and is a major source of fluctuations in the levels of output, employment, and income. Investment spending is influenced by business profit expectations, which can be affected by such factors as the expected overall level of economic activity and the interest rate on funds borrowed for investment purposes. When a business invests in new goods and services, it can finance its expenditures from its own savings, called retained earnings, or from borrowed funds. Investment spending is an injection into the spending stream; increases in investment stimulate the level of economic activity, and reductions in investment lead to reductions in output, employment, and income. Business saving and taxes are leakages from the spending stream.

Government, another major spending group in the macroeconomy, can influence the spending stream in three ways: through the purchase of goods and services, through transfer payments, and through taxes on households and businesses. Government purchases of goods and services are direct injections into the spending stream, transfer payments provide injections, and taxes are a leakage.

Transactions between U.S. and foreign buyers and sellers which occur in the foreign sector also cause leakages from and injections into the spending stream. Expenditures by U.S. buyers on imported goods and services are leakages, and purchases of exported U.S. goods and services by foreign buyers are injections. In recent years both exports and imports have grown as a percentage of GNP.

If the leakages from the spending stream equal the injections, the level of economic activity will continue unchanged. If leakages exceed injections, spending decreases, and the level of economic activity falls. If injections are greater than leakages, the spending stream expands, and the level of economic activity grows.

An increase or decrease in nonincome-determined household expenditures, investment spending, government purchases, or net foreign spending leads to a multiple increase or decrease in the levels of output, employment, and income. This multiplier effect occurs because dollars introduced into the circular flow are spent over and over again. New spending to buy goods and services becomes income to the owners of the resources used in production, who in turn use it to buy goods and services, and so on.

If the economy is operating at or near full employment, increases in spending may lead to demand-pull inflation rather than to increases in output and employment. For this reason, additional total spending is not always desirable and does not always cause the economy to expand.

Expectations can influence total spending and therefore complicate the job of stabilizing the economy. Because of the effect of expectations on spending, fears can cause self-fulfilling prophecies: the fear of a recession can lead to a recession, and the fear of inflation can lead to inflation.

One important avenue for accomplishing the objectives of full production and economic growth, full employment, and stable prices is through increasing or decreasing the level of total spending. Two tools for changing the size of the spending stream to attain these objectives are fiscal policy and monetary policy. Fiscal policy influences total spending through changes in government expenditures and taxation, and monetary policy influences spending through changes in the money supply or borrowing.

Key Terms and Concepts

Business cycle
Phases of the business cycle
Total, or aggregate, spending
Personal consumption expenditures
Transfer payment
Leakages from the spending stream
Injections into the spending stream
Investment spending
Retained earnings
Financial institutions
Saving-investment relationship
Government purchases of goods and services
Exports
Imports
Net exports
Nonincome-determined spending
Multiplier effect
Expectations
Fiscal policy
Monetary policy

Discussion and Review Questions

1. Figure 5.1 shows that since the early 1970s business cycles in the U.S. economy have had long recovery. and relatively short recession phases. Why do you think this has happened? Do you think this pattern is typical of what we can expect from the economy in the future?
2. Suppose the economy were in a recession and someone said to you: "If we only had more production, everything would take care of itself." How would you evaluate this statement? Would the act of producing more goods and services by itself be enough to cause the economy to recover?
3. Expectations play an important role in determining the level of economic activity and how the level of activity will change. What sorts of events might cause people to expect a recession? What sorts of events might cause people to expect inflation? What could be done to make the economy more predictable and help stabilize expectations?
4. Changes in the level of economic activity are related to changes in the spending of households, businesses, government units, and buyers in the foreign sector.
   a. How do personal consumption expenditures, investment spending, government purchases, and net exports compare in terms of their relative sizes and stability?
   b. How are personal consumption expenditures and investment spending affected by taxes, transfer payments, saving, and borrowing?
   c. What effects do transactions in the foreign sector have on the domestic levels of output, employment, and income?

d. Under what circumstances would an increase in total spending lead primarily to an increase in output, and under what circumstances would it lead primarily to an increase in prices?

5. How does the relationship between leakages from and injections into the spending stream cause the level of economic activity to expand, contract, or remain unchanged? Why are financial institutions important for the relationship between leakages and injections?
6. What is a multiplier effect, and how is it related to nonincome-determined spending and the circular flow of economic activity?
7. Fiscal and monetary policies are designed to affect the level of economic activity through their impacts on total spending. Using the circular flow model, explain on which leakages and injections each of these policies is focused.

Suggested Readings

Milton Friedman and Anna J. Schwartz, *The Great Contraction* (Princeton: Princeton University Press, 1965). A view of the Great Depression that stresses the role of money-related factors.

John Kenneth Galbraith, *The Great Crash, 1929* (Boston: Houghton, Mifflin Co., 1961). An alternative view of the Great Depression and its causes.

Gottfried Haberler, "Preliminary Remarks," *Prosperity and Depression* (New York: Atheneum, 1963), pp. 5–13. An introduction to business cycle theories. The author identifies the existence of different explanations of the business cycle and introduces several methods for classifying the causes of cycles.

Robert L. Heilbroner, "The Heresies of John Maynard Keynes," *The Worldly Philosophers* (New York: Simon and Schuster, 1967), pp. 225–261. A summary of John Maynard Keynes's life, work, and contribution to our understanding of the relationship between saving and investment, and the operation of the macroeconomy.

Hyman P. Minsky, "Can 'It' Happen Again? A Reprise," *Challenge* (July–August 1982), pp. 5–13. Addresses the question of whether another Great Depression could happen in the 1980s economy.

Richard D. C. Trainer, *The Arithmetic of Interest Rates* (New York: Federal Reserve Bank of New York, 1982). A short pamphlet on the basics of calculating various types of interest rates.

Test Yourself Answers (Application 5.3)

From each action taken alone, output and employment would:

1. increase;
2. decrease;
3. increase;
4. increase;
5. not change (demand-pull inflation would result);
6. decrease;
7. decrease;
8. decrease;
9. increase;
10. decrease;
11. decrease;
12. not change (demand-pull inflation would result);
13. increase;
14. decrease.

Appendix to Chapter Five
EQUILIBRIUM IN THE MACROECONOMY

Equilibrium (in the macroeconomy)
Occurs when the amount of total planned spending on new goods and services equals total output in the economy.

When the amount that all households, businesses, government units, and foreign buyers plan to spend on new goods and services is just equal to the total amount of output the economy is producing, the economy is said to be in **equilibrium.** At equilibrium there is no tendency for change in the level of economic activity, since the planned spending of all buyers is just sufficient to purchase all of the goods and services that are being produced. However, when the amount that households, businesses, government units, and foreign buyers plan to spend on new goods and services differs from the total output being produced, the economy is not in equilibrium, and output, employment, and income will change. If the total spending plans of all buyers are greater than total output, then output, employment, and income will increase, assuming that full employment has not been reached. If total spending plans are less than total output, then output, employment, and income will fall.

The key to understanding how spending can be more or less than production is the role played by inventories. Most businesses maintain an inventory of their products. When total spending in the economy is greater than current production, inventories begin to fall, signaling a need to increase output levels. When total spending is less than current production, inventories begin to accumulate, causing businesses to cut back on production.

Equilibrium, Leakages, and Injections

The most important factor in determining whether the economy is at equilibrium, or expanding, or contracting is the relationship between leakages from and injections into the spending stream.

When leakages equal injections, the economy is at equilibrium. For example, if an economy produces $2 trillion of goods and services, $2 trillion in income is created. Assume that from this $2 trillion income, households spend $1.5 trillion and the rest, $0.5 trillion, is leaked from the spending stream through saving, taxes, and the purchase of imports. In order to keep the production level unchanged, or to maintain equilibrium in the economy, the $0.5 trillion that was leaked must be replaced by an injection back into the spending stream of an equal amount. Business investment spending, government purchases of goods and services, household spending from transfer payments and borrowing, and expenditures on exports must equal $0.5 trillion.

What if the $0.5 trillion that was leaked from the spending stream is not matched by an equal injection back into the stream? What happens if injections amount to only $0.4 trillion, for example? If injections are less than leakages, economic activity will contract. The size of the spending stream will be reduced to a level below output, and businesses will respond by cutting back on output and employment.

On the other hand, if injections are greater than leakages, the size of the spending stream will increase to a level greater than output. If $0.5 trillion is leaked, and $0.6 trillion is injected, the economy will expand, assuming that full employment has not yet been reached.

Illustrating the Equilibrium Level of Output

A popular method for illustrating equilibrium in the macroeconomy is presented in Table 5A.1 and Figure 5A.1. Both the table and the figure show the amount of planned total spending and the relationship between leakages and injections that would occur at each level of output produced by a hypothetical economy.

The column in Table 5A.1 titled "Total Spending" represents the total planned expenditures of households, businesses, government units, and foreign buyers at each level of output. For example, all buyers would purchase $2.5 trillion worth of goods and services at an output level of $2.0 trillion, or $3.5 trillion worth of goods and services at an output of $4.0 trillion. Notice that total spending is greater at higher levels of output than at lower levels. This is primarily because personal consumption expenditures, the largest component of total spending, depend mainly on earned income. When output is high, earned income and personal consumption expenditures are high as well, causing more total spending than at lower levels of output.[1]

The columns titled "Spending Minus Output" and "Injections Minus Leakages" show, respectively, the difference between planned spending and output, and between injections into and leakages from the spending stream at each level of output. The values in each of these columns are identical since the difference between total spending and total output is equal to the difference between injections into and leakages from the spending stream at each level of output.

Notice in Table 5A.1 that there is one level of output, $3.0 trillion, where planned spending equals total output. Here the economy is in equilibrium. Equilibrium occurs at this output level of $3.0 trillion because leakages and injections are equal. Notice also that at output levels less than $3.0 trillion, planned spending is greater than output, and injections into the spending

---

[1]Notice that planned spending is $1.5 trillion when the level of output in the economy is zero. But since there is no output, there is no earned income, and no personal consumption expenditures based on earned income. From where does the total spending of $1.5 trillion come? Remember that household spending from transfers and borrowing, investment spending, government purchases, and exports are all nonincome-determined expenditures, which are expenditures *not* generated from income earned producing goods and services. The entire amount of $1.5 trillion in total spending is due to injections such as these into the spending stream. Can you explain why there would be no leakages from the spending stream when output is zero?

Table 5A.1
Total Spending and Total Output (Trillions of Dollars)

This macroeconomy is in equilibrium at $3.0 trillion, where the injections into the spending stream are equal to the leakages, and planned total spending is equal to total output.

Total Output	Total Spending	Spending Minus Output	Injections Minus Leakages	Economic Condition
$0.00	$1.50	$1.50	$1.50	expansion
0.50	1.75	1.25	1.25	expansion
1.00	2.00	1.00	1.00	expansion
1.50	2.25	0.75	0.75	expansion
2.00	2.50	0.50	0.50	expansion
2.50	2.75	0.25	0.25	expansion
3.00	3.00	0.00	0.00	equilibrium
3.50	3.25	−0.25	−0.25	contraction
4.00	3.50	−0.50	−0.50	contraction
4.50	3.75	−0.75	−0.75	contraction
5.00	4.00	−1.00	−1.00	contraction

Figure 5A.1
Equilibrium in the Macroeconomy

The macroeconomy is in equilibrium at the output level where the Total Spending line crosses the Spending Equals Output line.

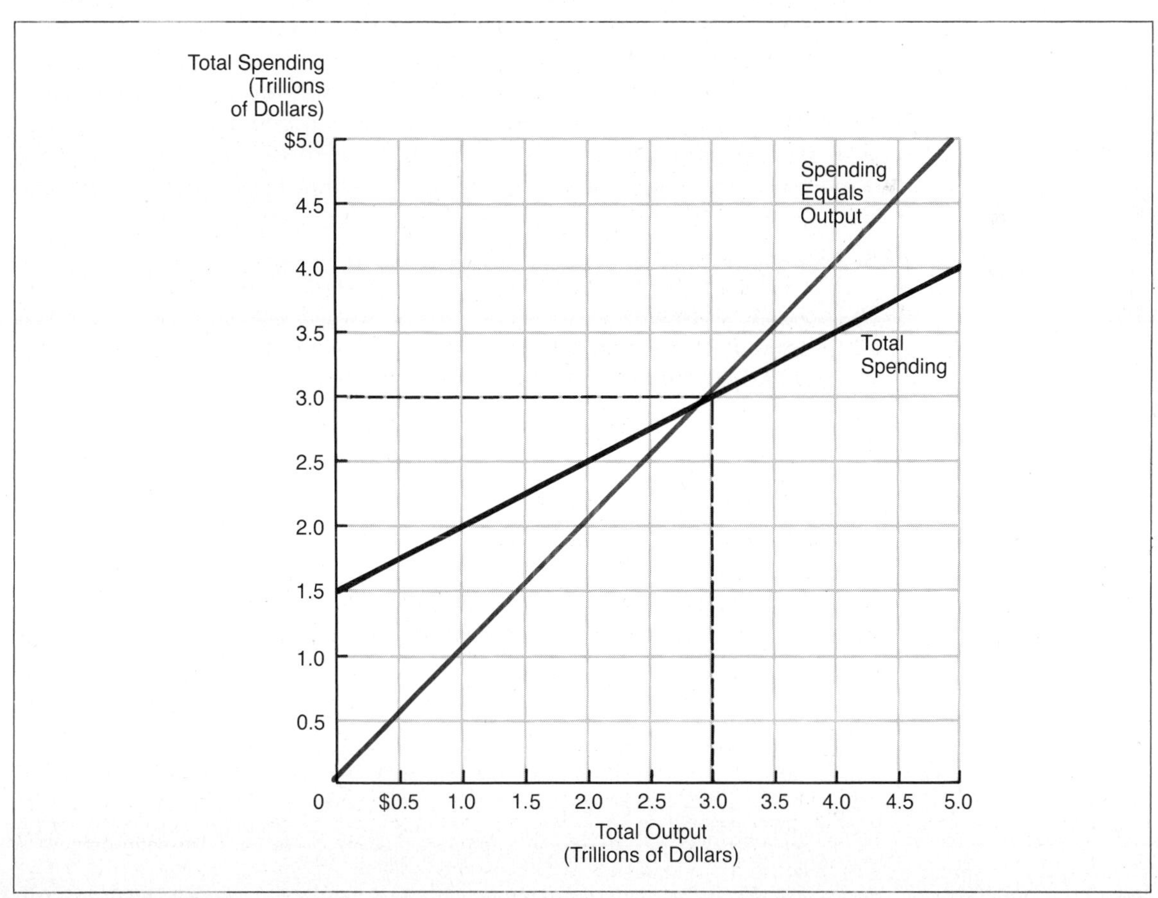

stream are greater than leakages. Because of these relationships, the economy will expand toward the equilibrium output level of $3.0 trillion, causing production, employment, and income to grow. This expansion is indicated in the column titled "Economic Condition." For output levels greater than $3.0 trillion, total planned spending is less than output, and injections into the spending stream are less than leakages. Because of these relationships, output, employment, and income will shrink toward the equilibrium level of $3.0 trillion.

In short, given these spending plans, there is one output level (the equilibrium level) toward which the economy is moving and from which, if reached, economic activity will not change.[2] This equilibrium level occurs where planned total spending equals total output, and leakages equal injections.

Figure 5A.1 illustrates the same relationships as in Table 5A.1. Total output is measured along the horizontal axis and total spending along the vertical axis. A 45° line is also plotted on this graph. Every point on this line matches a level of output with exactly the same level of spending. For this reason, the line is named the "Spending Equals Output" line.

The numbers from Table 5A.1 showing total spending at each level of output are illustrated by the "Total Spending" line in Figure 5A.1. Notice that the "Total Spending" line crosses the "Spending Equals Output" line at exactly $3.0 trillion of output, which is the equilibrium level in Table 5A.1. At output levels less than equilibrium, the "Total Spending" line is above the "Spending Equals Output" line. Because spending is greater than output, output will increase toward equilibrium. At output levels greater than $3.0 trillion, the "Total Spending" line is below the "Spending Equals Output" line, and output will fall toward equilibrium.

The difference between the 45° line and the "Total Spending" line is equal to the difference between injections and leakages. When the "Total Spending" line is above the 45° line, injections are greater than leakages; and when it is below, leakages are greater than injections.

[2]Because of changes in nonincome-determined spending, the equilibrium itself may change, causing the level of economic activity to change as well.

6 THE ROLE OF GOVERNMENT IN THE MACROECONOMY

Chapter Objectives

1. To identify the major sources of revenues and the major types of expenditures of federal, state, and local governments.
2. To distinguish among progressive, proportional, and regressive taxes.
3. To introduce fiscal policy, explain its mechanics, and differentiate between discretionary and automatic fiscal policy.
4. To define a surplus, a balanced, and a deficit budget, and identify the economic impact of each.
5. To explain the relationship between the federal budget and fiscal policy.
6. To introduce some realities of fiscal policy and the budgetary process that can hamper the attainment of fiscal policy objectives.
7. To define national debt and explain its financing, size, and burden on taxpayers.

This chapter focuses on the government sector of the economy and on taxes and public expenditures in particular. It is important to understand the operation of the government sector for several reasons. First, the sheer magnitude of taxes and expenditures makes government units extremely important in the functioning of the economy. Not surprisingly, the largest single purchaser of goods and services in the United States is the federal government. A decision made at the federal level to initiate or cancel an irrigation project, defense system, housing or some other program, or to increase or decrease taxes, can have a far-reaching effect on the economy. Similar, if somewhat weaker, effects are felt when state and local governments change their tax and expenditure patterns.

A second reason for understanding the operation of the government sector is that the overall level of economic activity can be influenced through changes in taxes and spending. As shown in the previous chapter, leakages from and injections into the spending stream affect the levels of output, employment, income, and, sometimes, prices in the economy. Taxes paid to the government are leakages, while government spending on goods and services and spending from transfer payments are injections. Thus, by adjusting the balance between taxes and purchases and transfers, government can influence the size of the spending stream and, through that, the levels of output, employment, income, and prices. As noted at the end of the previous chapter, this strategy for modifying the operation of the economy is called fiscal policy.

A third reason for examining the government sector is to gain a foundation for critical evaluation of policies affecting taxes and government spending. These policies have received increasing attention by the public in recent years. The appropriateness of persistent federal deficit spending, the enactment of a constitutional amendment requiring a balanced budget, tax reform legislation, and the restructuring of some transfer payment programs such as social security are areas of serious debate. In addition, government taxing and spending issues have played an increasingly important role in political platforms and elections.

An overview of government expenditures and taxes begins this chapter. Fiscal policy is then examined to illustrate how taxes and government expenditures can be manipulated in an effort to make the economy expand or contract. Next, the federal government's budget and its relationship to fiscal policy and the overall level of economic activity are explored. And finally, the chapter deals with the national debt and some problems surrounding the debt.

GOVERNMENT REVENUES AND EXPENDITURES

Government Revenues

Government units can divide their sources of revenue into two broad categories: taxes and other sources. If all of the taxes paid in 1982 were divided equally among all of the individuals in the United States, every man, woman, and child would have forwarded $2,845.38 to the federal, state, and local governments combined.[1] People pay federal income tax, state income tax, and, in some instances, a local wage tax on earnings. They may also pay sales tax on many of the items purchased on a day-to-day basis, property tax on a residence, and personal property tax on some belongings. If they sell some assets, they may pay a capital gains tax. If they receive an inheritance or certain gifts, or buy liquor or imported items, they may pay a tax

[1]U.S. Bureau of the Census, *Governmental Finances in 1982–83*, series GF84, No. 5, U.S. Government Printing Office, Washington, D.C., 1984, p. 1. Figure is for fiscal year 1982–83.

on those items as well. In addition, people in business pay certain business taxes and, if the firm is incorporated, corporate income tax.

As just noted, in addition to taxes governments receive revenue from other sources. One major source is contributions to social insurance programs—the most familiar being the federal government's social security program. Although payment is required from those individuals who participate in the program, the payment is considered to be a contribution to a retirement and welfare fund rather than a tax. At the state and local levels, an important source of nontax revenues is intergovernmental grants: grants of money from one government unit to another. Typically, these grants are from the federal to state and local governments.

Government revenues have increased substantially over the last few decades. Figure 6.1 gives the annual dollar amount of total government revenues from 1960 through 1984, as well as revenues of the federal government and state and local governments over these years. Observe from this figure that in 1960 all government units combined received $139.5 billion in revenue from taxes and other sources, and that by 1983 this amount had increased to over $1 trillion.[2] Notice also that federal revenues are greater than state and local revenues combined: generally, over 60 percent of the annual total is received by the federal government.

Which taxes go to which government units? What proportion of revenue comes from taxes and what proportion from other sources? Table 6.1 gives the major sources of federal government revenue, in percentages, for selected years from 1960 through 1983. This table indicates that the principal taxes received by the federal government include personal and corporate income taxes, excise taxes on certain types of goods, estate and gift taxes, and customs duties on foreign goods entering the country. Notice from the table that the single most important source of revenue is individual income taxes and that this household contribution to federal revenue has fluctuated relatively little over the years; it has ranged from roughly 42 to 48 percent of total revenue. Over these same years, however, the portion of federal revenue accounted for by corporate income taxes and excise taxes has fallen. Observe also in Table 6.1 that contributions for social insurance have increased substantially: from 15.9 percent in 1960 to 34.8 percent in 1983. The growing reliance over the last two decades of the federal government on household income as a source of revenue, particularly through increasing contributions to social insurance, has helped stir public agitation about the size of the tax burden imposed directly on individual households.

State and local government revenues come from a greater variety of sources than do federal revenues. Taxes, which account for the majority of state and local government revenues, include sales taxes, property taxes, and income taxes. Revenue is also generated from grants from the federal gov-

---

[2]The dollar figures given are in current dollars, not real or constant dollars. Consequently we must remember that much of the increase in revenues is not a real increase but the result of inflation.

Figure 6.1
Government Revenues: Total Government, Federal Government, and State and Local Government for 1960–1984[a]

Total government revenues have increased more than eightfold from 1960 through 1984.

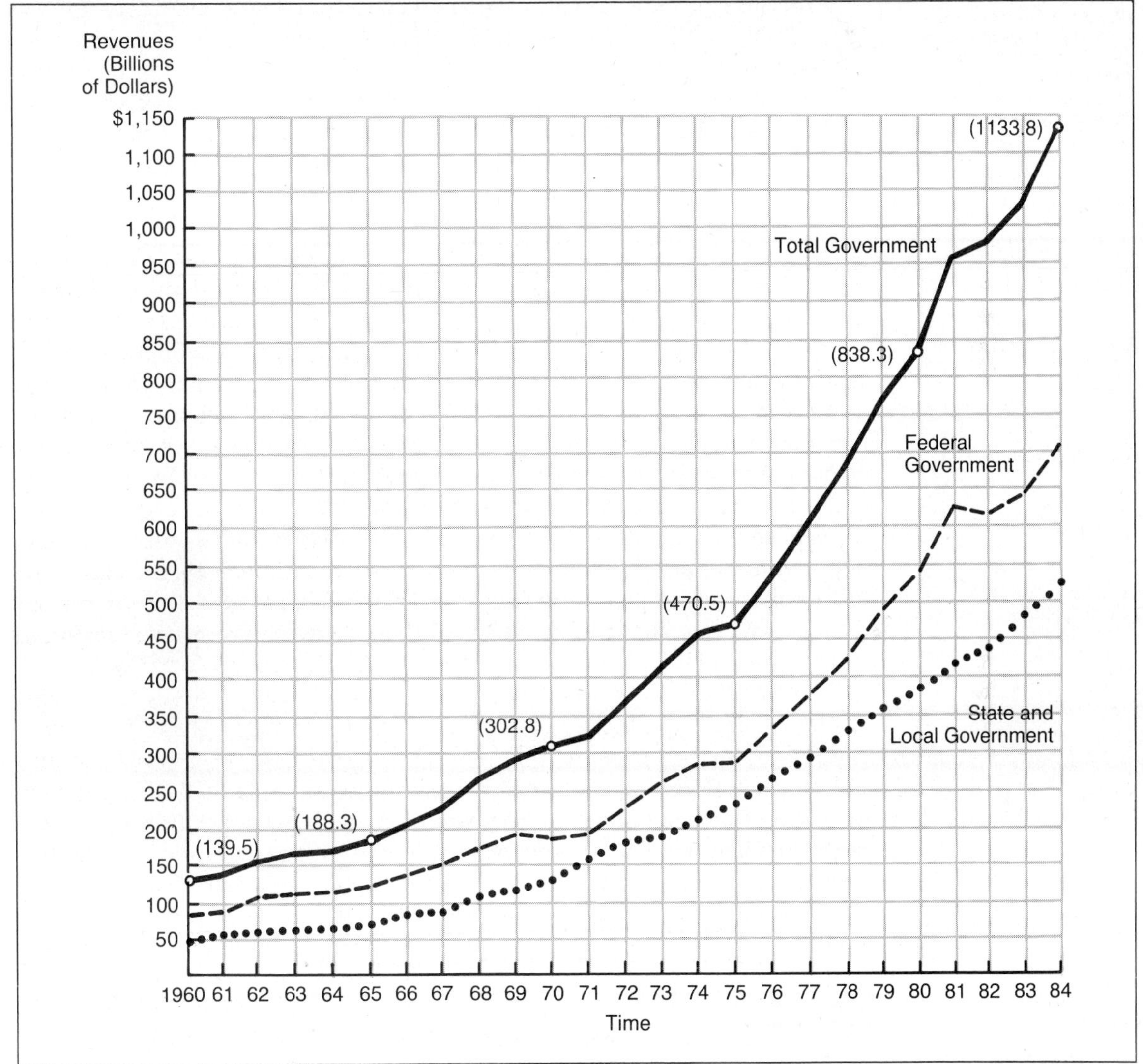

[a]1984 figures are preliminary.

Source: U.S., *Economic Report of the President* (Washington, D.C.: U.S. Government Printing Office, 1985), p. 320.

Table 6.1
Sources of Federal Government Revenue[a]

Corporate income taxes and excise taxes have decreased in relative importance over the years as sources of federal government revenue. Social insurance payments have increased in relative importance. By 1983 approximately 83 percent of federal revenue came from individual income taxes and social insurance payments.

Source	Percent of Total Revenue Per Year[c]					
	1960	1965	1970	1975	1980	1983
Individual income taxes	44.0%	41.8%	46.9%	43.9%	47.2%	48.1%
Social insurance[b]	15.9	19.1	23.0	30.3	30.5	34.8
Corporation income taxes	23.2	21.8	17.0	14.6	12.5	6.2
Excise taxes	12.6	12.5	8.1	5.9	4.7	5.9
Customs, estate, and gift taxes	2.9	3.6	3.2	3.0	2.6	2.4
Miscellaneous receipts	1.3	1.4	1.8	2.4	2.5	2.6
Total	100.0%	100.0%	100.0%	100.0%	100.0%	100.0%

[a]Fiscal years.
[b]Includes social insurance contributions and taxes.
[c]Percentage may not add to 100% due to rounding.

Source: U.S. Bureau of the Census, *Statistical Abstract of the United States: 1985* (105th ed.), Washington, D.C., 1984, p. 307.

ernment, license fees, charges from operations such as public hospitals and public colleges, and even recreation fees. Some states have or have had unusual revenue sources: for example, a tax on income earned by "persons expounding religious doctrines" in Hawaii, a tax on raw fish in Alaska, and a fee for each parachute jump in New Hampshire.[3]

Table 6.2 gives, in percentages, the major sources of state and local government revenue for selected years from 1960 through 1982. Notice the increasing dependence upon funds from the federal government and on charges and miscellaneous receipts, and the decreasing proportion collected from taxes.

Progressive, Proportional, and Regressive Taxes

The burden of paying taxes is not the same for all individuals. The proportion of one's income that goes to taxes differs with each specific tax paid and with the changing level of one's income. For this reason, taxes can be classified according to whether they are progressive, proportional, or regressive.

Progressive tax
A tax reflecting a direct relationship between the percentage of income taxed and the size of the income.

With a **progressive tax** the percentage of income taxed increases as income increases, or decreases as income decreases. In other words, there is a direct relationship between the percentage of income taxed and the size of the income. A classic example of a progressive tax is the federal personal income tax. The progressive nature of the federal income tax is illustrated in Table 6.3, which reprints the tax rate schedule for a single taxpayer. Notice that as an individual moves into higher income categories, the base amount and percent of income taxed increase. For example, for an income over \$2,300 the tax is 11 percent of any income between \$2,300 and \$3,400; for an income over \$3,400 the tax is \$121 plus 12 percent of any income

[3]"Your Tax Bite is Even Bigger Than You Think," *U.S. News & World Report*, September 11, 1978, p. 78.

Table 6.2
Sources of State and Local Government Revenue

Taxes, the main source of state and local government revenue, have decreased in relative importance over the years. Federal government funds and charges and miscellaneous receipts have grown in relative importance.

	Percent of Total Revenue Per Year[b]					
Source	**1960**	**1965**	**1970**	**1975**	**1980**	**1982**
Taxes	71.5%	69.2%	66.4%	62.0%	58.4%	58.4%
Property	32.5	30.5	26.0	22.6	17.9	18.0
Sales[a]	23.5	23.1	23.2	21.8	20.9	20.5
Individual income	4.9	5.5	8.3	9.4	11.3	11.1
Other	10.7	10.1	8.9	8.2	8.3	8.8
Charges and miscellaneous receipts	14.7	15.9	16.9	17.4	19.8	22.6
Federal government funds	13.8	14.9	16.7	20.6	21.7	19.1
Total	100.0%	100.0%	100.0%	100.0%	100.0%	100.0%

[a]Includes sales and gross receipts taxes.
[b]Percentages may not add to 100% due to rounding.

Source: Figures for 1960 and 1965 are from U.S. Bureau of the Census, *Statistical Abstracct of the United States: 1982–83* (103d ed.), Washington, D.C., 1982, p. 282; Figures for 1970–1982 are from *Statistical Abstract of the United States: 1985* (105th ed.), 1984, p. 270.

Table 6.3
Federal Personal Income Tax Rate Schedule for a Single Taxpayer

The federal personal income tax is a progressive tax: the percentage of income taxed increases as income becomes larger.

If Your Taxable Income Is Over	Through	Your Federal Income Tax is
$2,300	$3,400	11% of the amount over $2,300
$3,400	$4,400	$121 + 12 of the amount over $3,400
$4,400	$6,500	$241 + 14 of the amount over $4,400
$6,500	$8,500	$535 + 15 of the amount over $6,500
$8,500	$10,800	$835 + 16 of the amount over $8,500
$10,800	$12,900	$1,203 + 18 of the amount over $10,800
$12,900	$15,000	$1,581 + 20 of the amount over $12,900
$15,000	$18,200	$2,001 + 23 of the amount over $15,000
$18,200	$23,500	$2,737 + 26 of the amount over $18,200
$23,500	$28,800	$4,115 + 30 of the amount over $23,500
$28,800	$34,100	$5,705 + 34 of the amount over $28,800
$34,100	$41,500	$7,507 + 38 of the amount over $34,100
$41,500	$55,300	$10,319 + 42 of the amount over $41,500
$55,300	$81,800	$16,115 + 48 of the amount over $55,300
$81,800	—	$28,835 + 50 of the amount over $81,800

Source: U.S. Department of the Treasury, Internal Revenue Service, *1984 1040 Federal Income Tax Forms and Instructions* (Washington, D.C., 1984), p. 39.

between $3,400 and $4,400; and so on. For incomes over $81,800 the tax is $28,835 plus 50 percent of every dollar over $81,800.

Proportional tax
A tax equal to the same percentage of income regardless of the size of the income.

With a **proportional tax** the percentage of income taxed is the same for any income, large or small. An example of such a tax would be a city wage tax of, say, 1 percent. An individual earning $10,000 per year would pay 1 percent, or $100, to the city and another individual earning $100,000 would also pay 1 percent, or $1,000. In each case, the same percentage of income is taken as tax.

Regressive tax
A tax reflecting an inverse relationship between the percentage of income taxed and the size of the income.

With a **regressive tax** the percentage of income taxed increases as income decreases, and decreases as income increases. In other words, a regressive tax hits those with lower incomes the hardest. Sales taxes are regressive. With a sales tax of 5 percent on food, an annual grocery bill of $3,000 means that a tax of $150 must be paid. For a family earning a low income, say, $9,000 a year, that $150 tax poses a greater burden than for a family earning a higher income, say, $30,000 a year. The lower income family feels the "pinch" of the tax more because $150 is a greater percentage of their income than it is of the other family's income.

Tax Issues

Since the early 1980s several proposals for tax reform have received serious consideration, and some have become law. In 1981 Congress passed the Economic Recovery Tax Act, which caused a number of changes in the U.S. tax structure, including a reduction in personal income tax rates and indexation of the federal personal income tax brackets. Since January 1985, personal income tax brackets, such as those in Table 6.3, have been annually indexed to inflation. That is, the brackets are adjusted each year to reflect

Application 6.1
BACK OFF A LITTLE, KIDDIES

Speaking as one who looks forward to many years of happiness on Social Security, I want to urge the increasingly surly youth of America to stop whining about their obligation to finance me through old age and start thinking about what they must do to make their own future happy.

A young whippersnapper writing in The Washington Monthly complains that we senior citizens, having squandered the nation's prodigious wealth in our salad days, now want to force his generation to submit to soul-crushing taxation so that we may continue our profligate ways. Rot and balderdash. . . .

. . . The reason we are in the present pickle is that science, never willing to let well enough alone, wrecked the actuarial tables on which the Social Security system was built.

In the 1930's when it was set up, both penicillin and the birth-control pill were undreamed of. If science hadn't dreamed them up years later, the robust death and birth rates on which the system was based would still be holding down the number of people eligible for Social Security while grinding out the multitudes of young taxpayers needed to finance the program at very low tax rates.

Is it our fault that science plunged on to penicillin and birth-control pills without consulting the manager of the Social Security program? . . .

It isn't hard to see what has to be done. First, the law has to be revised to say that every young person entering the work force is entitled to Social Security when he reaches 65, but only if he promises never to use penicillin—or any of its that year's inflation rate. As a result, increases in income that match increases in prices do not push taxpayers into a higher tax bracket.

Another proposal for reform of the federal personal income tax that has gained some popularity is the flat tax proposal. A flat tax is a proportional tax. Although there are variations on the proposal, generally this tax plan would eliminate the current system of exemptions, deductions, and progressive rate structures and replace it with a simple tax percentage applicable to all incomes regardless of size.

In recent years, federal, state, and local governments have faced difficulties in generating sufficient revenues to carry out their functions. For example, many of the larger cities in the United States have experienced declines in population and the departure of businesses to other locations, causing local officials to become concerned about their eroding ability to raise adequate revenues through taxes levied on fewer businesses and smaller, generally poorer, populations. Perhaps the most publicized problem of raising sufficient revenue is the federal government's difficulty in funding social security. In Application 6.1, "Back Off A Little, Kiddies," Russell Baker proposes that technological changes beyond the control of government have been the basis of problems for the social security system. Can you suggest solutions for reform that are perhaps more likely to be adopted than Mr. Baker's tongue-in-cheek recommendations?

---

newer antibiotic cousins—to get there.

If he weakens along the way and gasps, "Give me the penicillin, doc," very well, he can have penicillin. The law must not be Draconian. When he takes it, though, his name will be instantly stricken from the rolls of those eligible for Social Security at 65.

Instead he will be entitled to receive a form letter saying, "Sorry, old-timer, but you settled for penicillin security years ago."

If he has the strength of character to abstain from antibiotics throughout his lifetime, thus preserving the actuarial probabilities on which the system was built in 1935, there is a lively chance that he will not need Social Security at 65, nor security of any other kind. Thus the program's cost will be reduced by reducing the number of elderly recipients. . . .

The second legal revision must deal with the birth-control pill. This economic monstrosity created by science has severely reduced the production of new taxpayers required to keep the Social Security tax within reasonable bounds. . . .

Thus, new people entering the Social Security system should be notified that use of the pill or intimate relations with any user thereof will mean forfeiting entitlement to benefits at 65. Alternatively, people who chose to use the pill might still collect benefits if they agreed to pay a Social Security tax 10 times the rate levied on nonusers. This would make up for the revenue they deny the program by their failure to create five new taxpayers. . . .

Source: Russell Baker, "Back Off A Little, Kiddies," *The New York Times*, December 11, 1982, p. 31.

Government Expenditures

Government expenditures
All dollar outlays by all government units.

Public good
A good (or service) provided for all of society; no one is excluded from use of a public good.

Government expenditures are all dollar outlays by all government units. Of these, the most important are purchases of goods and services and transfer payments. As noted in Chapter Five, purchases of goods and services include government expenditures on the services of individuals and on goods ranging from straight pins, shoelaces, and flowerpots to highway networks, schools, medical facilities, and missiles for national defense. Many of these purchases, such as defense systems, are **public goods,** which are goods provided for all of society, with no one excluded from their use.

Transfer payments are direct government outlays of money, for which nothing is received in return. Some major transfer programs include social security, veterans' benefits, unemployment compensation, and public assistance programs such as Aid to Families with Dependent Children (AFDC).

In addition to purchases of goods and services and transfer payments, other major categories of government expenditures exist. At times, government units need to finance some of their activities through borrowing. This borrowing can be accomplished by using various U.S. Treasury securities at the federal level or with municipal bonds or other instruments at the state or local levels. The interest on these borrowed funds is an expense that the government unit must meet. Governments may also incur expenses in running or contributing to the operation of various public enterprises such as toll roads, airports, hospitals, and sewage plants. Another category of expenditures is intergovernmental grants. These expenditures occur primarily at the federal level, where general revenue sharing and grants-in-aid for projects such as community development and law enforcement assistance are given to state and local governments.

How much does government spend each year? Table 6.4 lists expenditures for all government units combined, as well as for the federal and for state and local governments for the years 1960 through 1984. Notice from this table that in 1984 government expenditures totaled approximately $1.26 trillion: over nine times the amount government spent in 1960.[4] Notice also that federal expenditures in any year have exceeded state and local spending by a wide margin.

There has been growing concern in the United States over the increase in government spending and the size of the government sector. Is this concern justified? The last column of Table 6.4 gives total government expenditures as a percentage of GNP. This column indicates that over the years government spending has increased in relation to GNP from approximately 27 percent in 1960 to over 34 percent in 1984. In 1950 government spending as a percentage of GNP was 21.3 percent and in 1940 it was 18.4 percent.[5]

[4]Care must be taken in evaluating expenditures over time since current rather than constant dollar figures are shown in Table 6.4.

[5]U.S., *Economic Report of the President* (Washington, D.C.: U.S. Government Printing Office, 1985), pp. 232, 320.

Table 6.4
Expenditures by All Government Units, the Federal Government, and State and Local Governments; Total Government Expenditures as a Percentage of GNP, 1960–1984 (Billions of Dollars)

Over the years, government expenditures have increased both in absolute terms and as a percentage of GNP.

Year	Expenditures: Total Government[a]	Expenditures: Federal Government	Expenditures: State and Local Government	Total Government Expenditures as a Percentage of GNP
1960	$ 136.4	$ 93.1	$ 49.8	26.9%
1961	149.1	101.9	54.4	28.4
1962	160.5	110.4	58.0	28.4
1963	167.8	114.2	62.8	28.1
1964	176.3	118.2	68.5	27.6
1965	187.8	123.8	75.1	27.2
1966	213.6	143.6	84.3	28.3
1967	242.4	163.7	94.7	30.3
1968	269.1	180.5	107.2	30.8
1969	286.8	188.4	118.7	30.4
1970	313.4	204.3	133.5	31.6
1971	342.0	220.6	150.4	31.7
1972	371.6	244.3	164.8	31.3
1973	405.3	264.2	181.6	30.6
1974	460.0	299.3	204.6	32.1
1975	534.3	356.6	232.2	34.5
1976	574.9	384.8	251.2	33.5
1977	623.3	421.1	269.7	32.5
1978	681.1	461.0	297.3	31.5
1979	750.8	509.7	321.5	31.1
1980	869.0	602.1	355.5	33.0
1981	983.6	689.1	382.4	33.3
1982	1,090.1	764.9	409.0	35.5
1983	1,167.5	819.7	434.1	35.3
1984[b]	1,258.1	879.9	471.1	34.4

[a]Total government expenditures have been adjusted to eliminate the duplication of spending from federal grants-in-aid to state and local governments.

[b]Preliminary figures.

Source: U.S., *Economic Report of the President* (Washington, D.C.: U.S. Government Printing Office, 1985), pp. 232, 320.

Clearly, government expenditures have increased both in absolute terms and relative to GNP.

Significant changes in the way the federal government spends its money have occurred over the last two decades. Table 6.5 shows, for selected years from 1960 through 1984, the percentage of federal spending allocated to the various spending categories identified earlier. For 1970 and prior years, the largest single category of federal expenditures was purchases of goods and services, but by 1975 the amount spent on purchases was surpassed by the amount going to transfer payments. Currently, transfer payments are the largest federal government expenditure category. Notice also that grants-in-aid to state and local governments increased as a percentage of federal expenditures until the early 1980s, when they fell. Finally, observe the changes in net interest paid. Increases in federal government borrowing to

Table 6.5
Federal Government Expenditure Categories[a]

The composition of federal spending has changed over the years. Transfer payments is currently the largest expenditure category, replacing the previously largest category of purchases of goods and services.

	Percentage of Total Expenditure[b]					
Expenditure Category	**1960**	**1965**	**1970**	**1975**	**1980**	**1984**
Purchases of goods and services	57.9%	54.5%	49.7%	35.9%	32.8%	33.2%
Transfer payments	24.5	25.8	29.2	40.9	41.5	40.6
Grants-in-aid to state and local governments	7.6	9.2	11.6	14.7	15.0	10.6
Net interest paid	7.4	6.9	6.9	6.6	8.8	12.8
Cost of government enterprises	2.6	3.6	2.8	1.8	1.8	2.8
Total	100.0%	100.0%	100.0%	100.0%	100.0%	100.0%

[a]Fiscal years.
[b]Percentages will not add exactly to 100 percent due to rounding.

Source: U.S., *Economic Report of the President* (Washington, D.C.: U.S. Government Printing Office, 1985), p. 322.

finance large amounts of deficit spending in the early 1980s clearly imposed increased interest costs on the government. In 1984, 12.8¢ of every dollar the federal government spent went to interest on its debt.

The way state and local governments allocate their spending has not changed over the last few decades. Approximately 10 percent of state and local expenditures goes for transfer payments, and about 90 percent goes for purchases of goods and services.[6] The largest expenditure is for the services of government employees; about 50¢ of every dollar spent is for salaries of police, fire, hospital, school, and other state and local government employees. Table 6.6 gives the percentage distribution of state and local funds for several areas of activity for 1982.

Table 6.6
State and Local Government Expenditures in Selected Areas, 1982[a]

Education is the most important expenditure category of state and local governments.

Expenditure	**Percent of Total Expenditure**
Education	29.7%
Public welfare	10.8
Health and hospitals	7.8
Highways	6.6
Police and fire protection	4.5
Interest on general debt	3.8
Sanitation and sewerage	2.9
Housing and urban renewal	1.6
Parks and recreation	1.4

[a]Includes only examples of direct general expenditures and not items such as employee retirement.

Source: U.S. Bureau of the Census, *Statistical Abstract of the United States: 1985* (105th ed.), Washington, D.C., 1984, p. 269.

[6]In most years, state and local government financing and public enterprises have earned their government units money. For this reason they have been excluded here.

FISCAL POLICY

Fiscal policy
Influencing the levels of aggregate output and employment or prices through changes in federal government spending, transfer payments, and/or taxes.

The economy's levels of output, employment, and income are influenced by the relationship between the amount that government levies in taxes and the amount that it spends. A change in either taxes or spending may induce an expansion or contraction in the economy. Such changes in government inflows and outflows initiated to accomplish the particular objectives of controlling unemployment or demand-pull inflation are termed **fiscal policy**.[7] Such governmental action was warranted by the Employment Act of 1946.

Fiscal policy has evolved largely from the theories of John Maynard Keynes, who focused on the relationship between aggregate spending and the level of economic activity, and suggested that the government could fill in a spending gap created by a lack of private spending. His most famous work, *The General Theory of Employment Interest and Money*,[8] published during the Great Depression, laid a foundation for fiscal policy.

The Mechanics of Fiscal Policy

If you recall the role of aggregate spending in determining the level of economic activity, the circular flow diagram, and the relationship between leakages and injections covered in the previous chapter, the mechanics of fiscal policy should be obvious. Very simply, the manipulation of total spending through taxes and/or government expenditures can expand and contract economic activity.

If the economy is experiencing an undesirably high rate of unemployment due to inadequate demand for goods and services, policy makers can alleviate this condition by actions to increase the level of aggregate spending in the economy. This increased spending could come from (1) increased government purchases of goods and services, and/or (2) increased transfer payments, and/or (3) decreased taxes. Each of these three actions taken separately, or in combination, would raise spending and, consequently, increase the level of economic activity and lower the level of unemployment.

While each of these actions can cause economic activity to advance, the expansionary impact of increasing government purchases by a particular amount is greater than the expansionary impact of increasing transfers or decreasing taxes by the same amount. All of the dollars spent on government purchases are injected directly into the spending stream, whereas increased transfers and decreased taxes provide additional income, part of which will be spent but part of which will be saved.

If the economy is experiencing demand-pull inflation, the correct fiscal policy prescription for lowering the inflation rate is to decrease aggregate spending. Policy makers could seek to remove excess spending from the

[7]The control of cost-push inflation by the government is discussed in Chapter Nine.

[8]John Maynard Keynes, *The General Theory of Employment Interest and Money* (New York: Harcourt, Brace and Co., 1936).

economy by (1) decreasing government purchases of goods and services, and/or (2) decreasing transfer payments, and/or (3) increasing taxes. Again, a more pronounced decrease in spending results from a decrease in government purchases because some of the reduced transfers and increased taxes would affect saving rather than spending.

It should be noted that because government expenditures and tax reductions generate nonincome-determined spending, they are subject to a multiplier effect. This means that, for example, if the government injected $50 billion into the spending stream through increased purchases or transfers, or through decreased taxes, the level of economic activity would increase by more than $50 billion. Alternatively, if the government withdrew $50 billion from the spending stream, output, income, and employment would decrease by more than $50 billion.

Discretionary and Automatic Fiscal Policy

Changes in taxes and government expenditures to control unemployment or demand-pull inflation may be either discretionary or automatic.

Discretionary fiscal policy
Deliberate changes in taxes and/or government expenditures to control unemployment or demand-pull inflation.

Discretionary fiscal policy refers to the deliberate changing of taxes and spending. Congress exercises discretionary fiscal policy when it identifies an unemployment or inflation problem, establishes a policy objective concerning that problem, and then deliberately adjusts taxes and/or spending accordingly.[9] Depending upon the situation, Congress could, for example, institute a tax cut or raise the tax rate, change personal income tax exemptions and/or deductions, grant tax rebates or credits, levy surcharges, initiate or postpone transfer programs, and either initiate or eliminate direct spending projects.

The last few decades have seen several examples of discretionary fiscal policy. Because of the fear of a postwar recession, in 1948 Congress passed a substantial reduction in the personal income tax. The Revenue Act of 1964 lowered both personal and corporate income tax rates. It was passed on the urging of the Kennedy administration, which was concerned with the sluggish state of the economy in the 1950s and sought a more aggressive growth rate in the 1960s. In 1968 a 10 percent surcharge was levied on all individual and corporate income taxes. That is, an additional 10 percent was added to all income tax bills to reduce inflation caused by spending on the Vietnam War. In 1975 a tax cut was passed to counteract the 1974–1975 recession. During the Reagan administration, the Economic Recovery Tax Act of 1981 was passed, which in addition to other provisions, reduced personal income

[9]While Congress actually carries out the changes in taxes and spending, the president or the executive branch of government may have asked for those changes or given some initial impetus to the program.

taxes by 23 percent over a three-year period. In the following year, concern over the extent to which government expenditures were outstripping government income spurred passage of the Tax Equity and Fiscal Responsibility Act, which repealed or changed parts of the 1981 act.[10]

Automatic stabilization
Automatic changes in taxes and/or government expenditures that occur as the level of economic activity changes and that help to control unemployment or demand-pull inflation.

The second type of fiscal policy, **automatic stabilization,** occurs when changing economic conditions cause taxes and government expenditures to automatically change in order to combat unemployment or demand-pull inflation. These alterations in taxing and government expenditures, which occur without any deliberate or additional legislative action, automatically stimulate aggregate spending in a recession and dampen aggregate spending when the economy expands. There are several fiscal policy stabilizers, but of primary importance are the personal income tax and some transfer payments, especially unemployment compensation.

To understand how these automatic stabilizers work, consider a recession. During a downswing, when people lose their jobs and their earned incomes are reduced, two important government responses occur automatically. First, because the federal personal income tax is progressive, the rate, or actual percentage of one's income that is taxed, falls as income declines. Second, unemployed individuals may become eligible for a number of transfer payments, particularly unemployment compensation. Thus, automatically, decreased income taxes and increased transfers provide households with money to spend. Without these built-in stabilizers, personal consumption expenditures would drop more dramatically, and the economy would likely slide into a deeper recession.

When the economy is expanding, unemployment is falling, and incomes are rising, the built-in stabilizers automatically remove spending from the economy to dampen demand-pull inflationary tendencies. This is accomplished through the increasing rate of personal income tax paid on higher incomes, and through the decrease in some government transfer payments that occurs as more people become employed. Without this automatic removal of spending as the economy heats up, particularly toward full employment, inflation could be worse.

Automatic stabilizers soften the impact of cyclical expansions and contractions. Without the help of any deliberate legislative action, they pump spending into the economy during a downswing and decrease aggregate spending during an upswing. However, in the face of a severe recession or inflation, automatic stabilization alone would not be sufficient to correct the problem. The role of fiscal policy in economic stabilization is summarized in Table 6.7.

---

[10]Wallace C. Peterson, *Income, Employment and Economic Growth,* 4th ed. (New York: W. W. Norton & Co., Inc., 1978), pp. 437–453; Henry J. Aaron, "The Choices Ahead," *Setting National Priorities: The 1984 Budget,* Joseph A. Pechman, ed. (Washington, D.C.: The Brookings Institution, 1983), p. 206.

Table 6.7
Fiscal Policy Summary

Discretionary fiscal policy and automatic stabilization can be used to control unemployment or demand-pull inflation by changing the size of the spending stream.

Problem:	Unemployment	Demand-pull inflation
Remedy:	Increase total spending	Decrease total spending
Fiscal Policy Response:		
Discretionary:	Congress can: (a) increase government purchases; (b) increase transfer payments; (c) decrease taxes.	Congress can: (a) decrease government purchases; (b) decrease transfer payments; (c) increase taxes.
Automatic Stabilization:	Automatic increases in some transfer payments (especially unemployment compensation) and decreases in federal personal income taxes.	Automatic decreases in some transfer payments and increases in federal personal income taxes.
Effect:	Puts more dollars into the spending stream.	Withdraws dollars from the spending stream.

GOVERNMENT BUDGETS

Each government unit annually prepares a proposed budget, which is a detailed listing of its intended revenues and expenditures by type and amount for the coming year. At the end of the year, after revenues are collected and expenditures are made, an actual budget is compiled. Although the proposed budget presents the government's intentions, the year-end, actual budget is of greater importance, because it accounts for that government unit's actual leakages from and injections into the spending stream and summarizes how it influenced the level of economic activity over the past year.

The bottom line of every year-end budget is the dollar figure that results when total expenditures are subtracted from total revenues. This figure indicates whether the government has spent an amount equal to, less than, or greater than its revenues. Put another way, it indicates whether the government that year ran a balanced budget, a surplus budget, or a deficit budget.

Types of Budgets

Balanced budget
A government's total expenditures equal its total revenues.

Surplus budget
A government's revenues are greater than its expenditures.

Deficit budget
A government's expenditures are greater than its revenues.

A **balanced budget** occurs when a government's total expenditures equal its total revenues, or when the subtraction of total expenditures from total revenues yields a zero. A **surplus budget** occurs when a government does not spend all of its revenues, or when the subtraction of total expenditures from total revenues yields a positive dollar amount. A **deficit budget** occurs when a government's total expenditures are greater than total revenues, or when the subtraction of total expenditures from total revenues yields a negative dollar amount. As with an individual who spends more than he or she receives, a government with a deficit budget must borrow and go into debt.

While all government units prepare annual budgets, the budget of the federal government is the one most often referred to, analyzed, and evaluated. Let us examine the budget of the U.S. government to assess its experience with surpluses and deficits. Table 6.8 lists federal government receipts, outlays, and resulting surpluses or deficits for the years 1940 through 1984.

It is obvious from the "Surplus or Deficit" columns of Table 6.8 that the federal government typically operates with a deficit budget. In fact, since 1960 a surplus budget has appeared only once: in 1969. Notice also from Table 6.8 that wartime is particularly hard on the federal government budget. World War II and the Vietnam War (especially in 1968) brought high deficits. Finally, observe the deficits of the 1970s and the substantial deficits of the early 1980s. The deficit figure for 1983 was an all-time high. The federal budgets of 1983 and 1984 greatly aroused public concern over deficit spending and its impact on the economy. The effect of federal deficits and the resulting national debt will be discussed shortly in this chapter.

The Budget and Fiscal Policy

Government spending and taxing, the budget, and fiscal policy (both discretionary and automatic) are all interrelated. In the analysis of the tax-government expenditure relationship in Chapter Five, it was concluded that if the

Table 6.8
Federal Budget Receipts, Outlays, and Deficits or Surpluses for Fiscal Years, 1940–1984 (Billions of Dollars)

The federal government has operated with a budget deficit for 37 of the 45 years from 1940 through 1984.

Fiscal Year	Receipts	Outlays	Surplus or Deficit (−)
1940	$ 6.5	$ 9.5	$ −2.9
1941	8.7	13.7	−4.9
1942	14.6	35.1	−20.5
1943	24.0	78.6	−54.6
1944	43.7	91.3	−47.6
1945	45.2	92.7	−47.6
1946	39.3	55.2	−15.9
1947	38.5	34.5	4.0
1948	41.6	29.8	11.8
1949	39.4	38.8	0.6
1950	39.4	42.6	−3.1
1951	51.6	45.5	6.1
1952	66.2	67.7	−1.5
1953	69.6	76.1	−6.5
1954	69.7	70.9	−1.2
1955	65.5	68.4	−3.0
1956	74.6	70.6	3.9
1957	80.0	76.6	3.4
1958	79.6	82.4	−2.8
1959	79.2	92.1	−12.8
1960	92.5	92.2	0.3
1961	94.4	97.7	−3.3
1962	99.7	106.8	−7.1
1963	106.6	111.3	−4.8
1964	112.6	118.5	−5.9
1965	116.8	118.2	−1.4
1966	130.8	134.5	−3.7
1967	148.8	157.5	−8.6
1968	153.0	178.1	−25.2
1969	186.9	183.6	3.2
1970	192.8	195.6	−2.8
1971	187.1	210.2	−23.0
1972	207.3	230.7	−23.4
1973	230.8	245.7	−14.9
1974	263.2	269.4	−6.1
1975	279.1	332.3	−53.2
1976	298.1	371.8	−73.7
1977	355.6	409.2	−53.6
1978	399.7	458.7	−59.0
1979	463.3	503.5	−40.2
1980	517.1	590.9	−73.8
1981	599.3	678.2	−78.9
1982	617.8	745.7	−127.9
1983	600.6	808.3	−207.8
1984	666.5	851.8	−185.3

Source: U.S., *Economic Report of the President* (Washington, D.C.: U.S. Government Printing Office, 1985), p. 318.

amount removed from the spending stream through taxes is greater than the amount returned through government expenditures, all other things being equal, the economy will contract. On the other hand, if the amount returned to the spending stream through government expenditures is greater than the amount removed through taxes, all other things being equal, the economy will expand or, if production is at or near full employment, it will inflate.

Since a surplus budget occurs when revenues are greater than outlays, it can be deduced that, generally, a surplus budget causes economic activity to contract.[11] When all tax leakages are not returned to the spending stream because of a surplus budget, the level of aggregate spending shrinks. Alternatively, if government expenditures are greater than taxes, a deficit budget results. Because it increases the level of aggregate spending by injecting more into the spending stream than it takes out, a deficit budget will expand output, employment, and income or, if the economy is at or near full employment, it will cause demand-pull inflation. A balanced budget, contrary to common belief, does not have a neutral impact on economic activity. In determining the effect of a balanced budget, we must recall that dollars from income that have been taxed by the government would have otherwise been used partly for spending and partly for saving. Thus, when the government spends those tax dollars on goods and services, it is taking some money that would have been saved and is spending it. With this in mind, one can conclude that a balanced budget is slightly expansionary.

How is the budget related to fiscal policy? If the economy has an undesirable level of unemployment, the correct discretionary fiscal policy measure is to increase expenditures and/or decrease taxes. This action will push the budget toward a deficit position or increase an existing deficit. Thus, we can generalize, depending upon the severity of the unemployment problem, that a deficit, or at least a reduction in a surplus, is the correct budget prescription to fight unemployment. When the economy is experiencing demand-pull inflation, Congress can deliberately decrease aggregate spending by decreasing government expenditures and/or increasing taxes. This action should push the government budget toward a surplus position. We might then conclude, based on the severity of the inflationary problem, that the correct policy to curb demand-pull inflation is to have a surplus budget, or at least a reduction in deficit spending.

Automatic fiscal policy also affects the budget. Built-in stabilizers push the government budget toward a deficit in recessionary times as they reduce tax revenues and increase transfers. Automatically, there is a move toward the appropriate budget prescription for correcting a downswing. In periods of expansion, as tax revenues increase and transfers fall, the budget is auto-

---

[11]The expression "generally" is used because the ultimate impact of the budget depends upon the types of taxes collected, the percentage of those taxes that would have been saved, the percentage of expenditures that goes directly into purchases of goods and services, the percentage of transfers that is saved, and so forth.

matically pushed toward a surplus, which is the proper prescription for correcting demand-pull inflation. In Table 6.8, the sizable budget deficits given for fiscal years 1976 and 1983 were in part caused by automatic stabilizers. The unemployment rate for the civilian labor force reached 10.7 percent during the 1983 fiscal year, the highest level since the Great Depression, causing tax collections to fall and transfers to increase.[12]

Fiscal Policy and Budgetary Realities

Does the federal budget always perform according to the proper strategy for fiscal policy control? Is there always an appropriate budget surplus to counteract demand-pull inflation or a budget deficit to reduce unemployment? Are the mechanics of fiscal policy always carried out as smoothly and simply as outlined here? For several reasons, the answer is no.

First, the Employment Act of 1946 does not make the promotion of "maximum employment, production and purchasing power" the sole goal of congressional tax and spending activity. Rather, the act charges " . . . the Federal Government to use all practicable means consistent with its needs and obligations and other essential considerations of national policy, . . . "[13] In short, there may be other objectives that take precedence over the use of taxing and spending to control the level of economic activity. For example, national defense or war priorities may induce inflationary increases in spending, or a scandal-ridden major public employment program may be dropped during a period of unemployment.

Stagflation
Occurs when an economy is experiencing high rates of both inflation and unemployment.

A second consideration in the reality of fiscal policy and the budgetary process is the emergence of simultaneously high rates of inflation and unemployment, termed **stagflation,** and the effect that stagflation has on attempts to control the economy through appropriate adjustments in taxes and government expenditures. For example, in 1975 prices increased by approximately 9.3 percent and the unemployment rate was 8.5 percent.[14] The U.S. economy was faced with two major problems. Fiscal policy action for correcting unemployment could have worsened inflation, and action to curb inflation could have led to higher unemployment. When high rates of unemployment occur along with high rates of inflation, no budgetary policy is clearly appropriate.

[12]U.S., *Economic Report of the President* (Washington, D.C.: U.S. Government Printing Office, 1984), p. 259. The large deficit of 1983 can not be attributed solely to the automatic stabilizers. The first of several tax cuts resulting from the Economic Recovery Tax Act passed in 1981 also went into effect during that period.

[13]*United States Statutes at Large, 1946.* Vol. 60, Pt. 1, *Public Laws and Reorganization Plans* (Washington, D.C.: United States Government Printing Office, 1947), p. 23.

[14]U.S., *Economic Report of the President* (Washington, D.C.: U.S. Government Printing Office, 1985), pp. 237, 266.

A third consideration concerning fiscal policy is the time lag between the occurrence of an economic problem and its identification, and between its identification and the actual implementation of an appropriate response. For example, from the time that unemployment becomes severe, several months may pass before its severity becomes apparent. Then once the problem is recognized and admitted, Congress and the administration may present plans and counter-plans, and debate, discuss, and argue over whether to initiate a tax cut, offer tax rebates, or increase spending. Moreover, the problem of what to do is compounded by the question of how much to do: that is, how large should a tax cut or spending increase be? A significant period of time may elapse before these decisions are made, and then more time may be required for implementation of the chosen program. By the time the unemployment remedy takes effect, the economic environment may even have changed so much that the problem no longer exists.

A fourth consideration regarding the reality of fiscal policy and the government budget is the process by which the budget is formed. Many students, especially after reading this far into the chapter, may think that groups of economists and statisticians simply lay out the budget for the year, adjusting spending and taxing to correct predicted economic conditions. On the contrary, development and passage of the federal government budget is a complicated, political, drawn-out process. First it is formulated by the executive branch of the government and represents the president's financial priorities for the coming year. At this stage of budget development, fiscal policy may not be considered as much as the maintenance and dismantling of various agency operations and programs.

The president's budget is then submitted to Congress, whose members make the final spending decisions through their votes. Congressional review of the president's budget is extensive; it is studied by several committees, and modifications are made by both the House and Senate. As congresspersons consider various aspects of the budget, they may be more responsive to their particular constituencies than to the needs of the macroeconomy. It might be extremely difficult for a representative to place a high priority on controlling demand-pull inflation and thus vote against the funding of a major highway project or hospital in his or her district. In short, the budget, with all of its economic implications, is part of the political process. Consequently, there is growing interest among economists in **public choice,** which is the study of the economic motives and attitudes of voters and public officials, and how those motives and attitudes affect government decision making. Public choice is explained more fully in Chapter Eleven.

Public choice
The study of the economic motives and attitudes of voters and public officials, and their effects on government decision making.

Finally, one other problem associated with fiscal policy and the budgetary process is that careless spending may arise because the government can perpetually borrow to cover budget deficits. From time to time, examples of unproductive programs and studies and extravagant expenditures surface that may not have existed without deficit spending.

Concern over wasteful spending and the frequency and size of deficit budgets has led to support for an amendment to the U.S. Constitution that would require the federal government to balance its budget unless certain conditions prevailed. Application 6.2, "Do We Need a Budget Amendment?", presents arguments on both sides of this important and controversial issue.

THE NATIONAL DEBT

As pointed out in Table 6.8, there has been a persistent tendency in recent decades for the federal government to run deficit budgets. In order to finance this deficit spending, the government must borrow the necessary funds. As more is borrowed each year, the federal government goes deeper and deeper into debt. A surplus budget, which allows some of this debt to be repaid, occurs infrequently. The accumulated total debt of the federal government is called the **national debt.**

National debt
The total accumulated debt of the federal government due to deficit spending.

Financing the National Debt

U.S. Treasury security
A paper instrument issued by the federal government in return for funds lent to it; gives a specified interest rate and repayment date.

U.S. Treasury bill, note, bond
U.S. Treasury securities that mature, respectively, in 13, 26, or 52 weeks; in 2 to 10 years; and in 10 years or longer.

When the federal government needs to raise money to finance its spending, it borrows at the lowest interest rate it can negotiate from anyone who is willing to lend it money. In return for funds, the lender receives a **U.S. Treasury security:** a paper IOU on which the federal government states its promise to make specified interest payments and to repay the loaned funds on a particular date. The time span from issuance to the maturity date determines whether the security is a **U.S. Treasury bill,** which is issued for 13, 26, or 52 weeks; a **U.S. Treasury note,** which matures in 2 to 10 years; or a **U.S. Treasury bond,** a security to be repaid in 10 years or longer.

When it borrows, the government publicly announces the total amount it intends to raise at that time, the repayment date, and the denomination of the security it will be issuing. For example, the Treasury could declare a decision to raise $5 billion over the next week through two-year Treasury notes in minimum or multiple denominations of $5,000. When an announcement such as this is made, potential lenders submit "tenders," which are applications stating both the specific amounts they are willing to lend and the interest rates they will charge the government. Those who submit the tenders charging the lowest interest rates "win" the bid and receive the securities. Small investors, such as a family with a few thousand dollars to lend, can offer funds at the "average rate" that is finally determined and avoid the bidding process. Depending upon the volume of funds it intends to acquire, the government announces plans to borrow weekly as well as at other periods throughout the year. Each Tuesday, for example, the government announces the amount it wishes to borrow that week through 13-week and 26-week Treasury bills. These bills, which are issued in a minimum of $10,000 and multiples of $5,000, are the often referred to "T-bills."[15]

Who loans the federal government money or acquires these Treasury securities? The largest portion of the national debt is held by private domestic investors such as individuals, banks, and corporations. The rest of the debt is owned by foreign investors, the Federal Reserve Banks, and government agencies and trusts. Perhaps the U.S. Treasury is in debt to you or your

[15]Purchasers of Treasury bills do not actually receive a paper certificate. Instead, a receipt is given to the purchaser, and a book-entry is used to record the transaction. Treasury bills are also sold on a discount basis: that is, the bills are sold at a price below their face value, but purchasers are repaid at full face value on the maturity date.

Application 6.2
DO WE NEED A BUDGET AMENDMENT?

YES—"It's clear that Congress won't balance the budget on its own"

Interview With Governor Robert List
Republican, of Nevada

Q. Governor List, why do you favor the proposed constitutional amendment requiring a balanced budget, which has been passed by the U.S. Senate but remains bogged down in the House?

A. Because the economy of this nation has careened out of control. The national debt has more than doubled in the last 10 years. We've had an endless tide of red ink—20 unbalanced budgets in the past 21 years.

So it's clear that Congress won't balance the budget on its own. It lacks the intestinal fortitude to stand up to the special interests. To stop the squandering, we need fundamental reforms.

Q. How would the amendment work?

A. Except in wartime, Congress would need a three-fifths vote to authorize deficit spending, instead of a simple majority as it needs now. That would put Congress and individual lawmakers on the spot and make them accountable for any deficit spending. It would place a heavier burden on those who would spend excessively.

Q. Economic conditions and theories can change rapidly, whereas constitutions are meant to be relatively unchangeable. Does it really make sense to write an economic theory into the Constitution?

A. I think it does. The 16th Amendment authorized the income tax—that was not in the Constitution originally. So the Constitution currently contemplates spending and revenue raising but really doesn't deal with the other side of the issue, which is how much can you spend.

Q. Couldn't the amendment result in sharp cutbacks in federal payments to states for health, welfare and education programs?

A. Conceivably. Congress obviously would have to either raise taxes or cut spending. Which they would do is a matter of conjecture. If it's necessary to cut, where they'll cut, of course, is also a matter of speculation. I have a basic confidence that Congress would not start slashing in areas that the people want to see continued.

But I know that in some states, bureaucrats and public officials are afraid they will lose money because of this. They have a selfish interest in maintaining their enormous federal subsidies.

family. If you own a U.S. Government Savings Bond, you have provided the federal government with borrowed funds.

Size of the National Debt

By the end of 1984, the national debt had grown to over $1.5 trillion ($1,500,000,000,000.00), a sum of money that is incomprehensible to many. Table 6.9 gives, for selected years beginning with 1900, the total amount of the national debt in column 1, and in column 2, the per capita (per person) debt. Because the debt is linked to the federal government budget, those years in which substantial deficit spending occurred were also years during which the national debt increased significantly. Observe the considerable

---

NO—"Flexibility is required when the country is in difficult economic straits"

Interview With Governor William A. O'Neill Democrat, Of Connecticut

Q. Governor O'Neill, why are you opposed to the proposed balanced-budget amendment?

A. I don't think such an amendment—with its requirement for a three-fifths vote to unbalance the budget except during wartime—should be locked into the Constitution of the United States. There are times, other than during a war, where you're in actual conflict with an enemy country and flexibility in spending is needed to prevent the country from perhaps falling apart. Flexibility is also required when the country is in difficult economic straits, as it is at present with unemployment at its highest level in more than 40 years.

Q. How can a balanced federal budget be achieved?

A. There probably are areas in the federal budget that can be cut, and there probably are areas that the states can handle better than the federal government.

The first thing I would *not* have done was to request the massive tax decrease last year, which in theory was to spur the economy and get the country moving again. It didn't work and it's not working.

We have to be honest, lay it out as it really is. You cannot spend it, I agree, if you don't take it in. But you don't make it any easier to balance the budget by cutting the tax revenues of the federal government.

Q. Democrats have taken the lead in opposing this proposed amendment. Will it be an issue in the fall elections?

A. It could be. It would be politically expedient to be for the amendment. It would be very popular to jump up and say, "I'm for the balanced budget." Who isn't for a balanced budget? I am certainly for a balanced budget.

But what would be the consequences of the amendment? That's the other side of the coin. Are we going to increase unemployment across the country? If we attempt to balance the budget now, it is going to result in more millions of unemployed. I'd rather see people working, paying what they can in taxes, even if they have to have public-service-type jobs, than being unemployed and eventually in breadlines and on welfare.

Source: Excerpted from "Do We Need a Budget Amendment?," *U.S. News & World Report* issue of August 30, 1982, pp. 63–64. Copyright, 1982, U.S. News and World Report, Inc.

Table 6.9
The National Debt

Over the years the national debt, the burden of the debt per person, and the interest the government pays to finance the debt have all grown.

Year	Gross Debt		Interest Paid	
	1 Total (Billions of Dollars)	2 Per Capita (Dollars)	3 Total (Billions of Dollars)	4 Percent of Federal Outlays
1900	$ 1.3	$17	$ (Z)	7.7
1905	1.1	14	(Z)	4.3
1910	1.1	12	(Z)	3.1
1915	1.2	12	(Z)	3.0
1920	24.3	228	1.0	15.9
1925	20.5	177	0.9	28.8
1930	16.2	132	0.7	19.2
1935	28.7	226	0.8	12.6
1940	43.0	325	1.0	11.5
1945	258.7	1,849	3.6	3.7
1950	256.1	1,688	5.7	14.5
1955	272.8	1,651	6.4	9.3
1960	284.1	1,572	9.2	10.0
1961	286.4	1,559	9.0	9.2
1962	295.4	1,582	9.1	8.5
1963	302.7	1,598	9.9	8.9
1964	308.1	1,604	10.7	9.0
1965	313.8	1,613	11.3	9.5
1966	316.1	1,605	12.0	8.9
1967	322.9	1,622	13.4	8.5
1968	345.4	1,717	14.6	8.2
1969	352.9	1,737	16.6	9.0
1970	370.1	1,807	19.3	9.8
1971	397.3	1,919	21.0	9.9
1972	426.4	2,042	21.8	9.4
1973	457.3	2,174	24.2	9.8
1974	474.2	2,238	29.3	10.9
1975	533.2	2,496	32.7	10.1
1976	620.4	2,884	37.1	10.1
1977	698.8	3,216	41.9	10.4
1978	771.5	3,463	48.7	10.9
1979	826.5	3,669	59.8	12.1
1980	907.7	3,985	74.9	13.0
1981	997.9	4,338	95.6	14.5
1982	1,142.0	4,913	117.4	16.1
1983	1,377.2	5,870	128.8	16.2
1984	1,576.7	—		

(Z) = Less than $50 million.

Source: 1900–1977 figures from U.S. Bureau of the Census, *Statistical Abstract of the United States: 1979* (100th ed.), Washington, D.C., 1979, p. 273; 1978–1983 figures from U.S. Bureau of the Census, *Statistical Abstract of the United States: 1985* (105th ed.), Washington, D.C., 1984, p. 311; 1984 figure from U.S., *Economic Report of the President* (Washington, D.C.: U.S. Government Printing Office, 1985), p. 318.

increase in the debt from 1915 to 1920 and from 1940 to 1945 caused largely by deficit spending during World War I and World War II. Notice also the substantial increases in the debt during the late 1970s and early 1980s. By 1984 the national debt had grown to almost three times its size in 1975. In comparison, during the 25-year period from 1950 to 1975, the debt only doubled.

Table 6.9 includes some, though not all, of the years in which the debt was reduced. Notice decreases in 1905, 1925, 1930, and 1950. From your study of fiscal policy, budgets, and economic expansions and contractions, can you comment on the appropriateness of a debt reduction in 1930 in light of the depression that had just gripped the country?

The figures in column 2 of Table 6.9, which represent the share of the debt for every man, woman, and child in the United States, are also increasing. To fully pay the debt in 1983, a family of four would have needed to contribute $23,480 as its share, compared to $48 in 1915.[16]

Assessing the Debt

What kinds of burdens does the national debt impose on taxpayers? Is the debt too large? Were the substantial increases in the debt in the early 1980s detrimental to the economy? Should the debt be paid off as soon as possible? These and similar questions typically emerge in discussions—whether academic or political—of the debt. Let us focus on a few critical issues.

One of the most obvious and significant burdens of the national debt is the interest that must be paid to borrow and maintain a debt of this magnitude. Column 3 of Table 6.9 gives the amount of interest paid annually to sustain these obligations. In 1983, for example, the federal government remitted $128.8 billion in interest to its security holders. To put the interest burden into perspective, column 4 presents the percentage of federal outlays for these payments. Since the early 1960s this percentage has edged upward, with dramatic increases since 1978. Notice, for example, that in 1983 approximately 16 percent of all funds spent by the federal government were used to meet interest charges. Many critics of the federal debt point out the alternative uses to which those tax dollars could have been put: the building of schools, hospitals, and highways and the other opportunities that were forgone. Some concerns over the effects of the growing interest burden of the national debt are presented in Application 6.3, "Climbing Federal Debt Is Inexorably Raising U.S. Interest Burden." Do you think it is possible that the interest burden could become severe enough to make the worst fears presented in this application reality?

A second burden of deficit spending and the national debt is the strain that government borrowing puts on funds available for loans. The federal government competes with households and businesses to borrow whatever funds are available for loan making. If government borrowing is sizable, two

[16]A word of caution is in order regarding comparisons of the burden of the debt from year to year. As was the case for the figures in the tables showing government revenues and expenditures, the figures in Table 6.9 are in current, not real, dollars, so part of the increase in the dollar value of the debt is due to inflation. This means that, while the share of the debt for a family of four was $23,480 in 1983 as compared to $48 in 1915, a dollar in 1915 would have purchased more than a dollar in 1983. Thus, while there is a difference in the burden faced by the two families, its actual effect is not as great as the table would suggest.

important effects result in the market for loans. First, because the borrowing and lending of money takes place in a market where the forces of supply and demand determine the interest rate (the price of money), increases in government borrowing increase the demand for loans and cause the interest rate to rise. When the federal government borrows substantial amounts, the impact on interest rates can be significant. A second effect of sizable government borrowing is the **crowding out** of private borrowing. Because households and businesses are interest-rate sensitive, increases in the interest rate cause them to borrow less. The result is that available funds are soaked up by the federal government, which is not interest-rate sensitive in its borrowing, and businesses and households borrow less for capital improvements, plant expansion, homes, automobiles, and such. The major problem that emerges with crowding out is that economic growth may be limited because businesses cannot afford to borrow to buy the machinery and equipment necessary for growth. This was one of the major criticisms of the substantial budget deficits of the early 1980s.

Crowding out
Occurs when borrowing by the federal government reduces borrowing by households and businesses.

The question of whether the national debt has become too large is basically a value judgment. At what point, even in the case of one's own finances, do credit obligations become too high? One way to evaluate the

Application 6.3
CLIMBING FEDERAL DEBT IS INEXORABLY RAISING U.S. INTEREST BURDEN

WASHINGTON—Like any overextended borrower, the U.S. government is scrambling just to keep up with rising finance charges. . . .

As the publicly held national debt . . . balloons ever larger to finance continuing budget deficits, the interest burden grows inexorably. In addition, every rise in interest rates increases the burden as the Treasury Department keeps borrowing to roll over maturing securities and to raise new cash. . . .

And the problem is mind-boggling because in their worst nightmares, economists see the U.S. ultimately facing the same predicament that France did in the 1920s—a debt-service burden so crushing to taxpayers that it forces the government into the inflationary solution: printing money. . . .

The problem boils down to an encumbrance in the living standards of future generations, says Denis Karnosky, a former Reagan administration official. . . . If present budget trends continue, "there's no way the economy can generate the real income required to make the interest payments on the debt," he says. "If you're borrowing that much money, but not creating anything that's going to generate principal and interest payments, it's unsustainable. In that sense, we're no different from Argentina, Peru and Ecuador."

The people who will end up footing the bill "aren't the ones making the decisions," Mr. Karnosky adds. "My kids aren't old enough to vote. But somewhere out in the future, something has to give—either taxes are going to have to be raised . . . or we're going to get inflation." . . .

Even in the absence of apocalyptic disasters, the debt-service issue is troublesome because it significance of the volume of the debt is to examine it as a percentage of GNP. Figure 6.2 gives the debt as a percentage of GNP for the years 1960 through 1984.

Despite the large size of the debt, Figure 6.2 suggests that its growth has not been out of line with the growth in GNP, except perhaps in the most recent years. The debt as a percentage of GNP fell from 1960 to 1974, increased in some years since 1974, and took a larger jump since 1981. It was 34.8 percent of GNP in 1981 and 44.0 percent in 1984. This method of evaluating the size of the debt is analogous to comparing an individual's debt and income. For example, it is obvious that one can comfortably sustain more absolute dollars of debt at an income of $20,000 per year than at an income of $10,000 per year. The problem is whether or not one can sustain a debt that takes a rising percentage of one's income.

Should we pay off the debt and start anew? First of all, it would be a huge, probably impossible, burden, even over several years, to raise through taxes and other revenues the amount needed (more than $1.5 trillion) to pay off the debt. Second, with repayment of the debt, a significant income redistribution would occur as the average taxpayer became poorer due to the increased tax burden and the holders of government securities became richer

---

means that a large and rising portion of federal spending lies beyond congressional control and forces enactment of ever more painful spending cuts or tax increases if the budget is to be balanced. In recent decades, debt service represented a relatively small share of federal outlays, but over the past four years it has grown faster than any other major budget category, including defense. . . .

In testimony before the Senate Budget Committee last February [1984], Budget Director David Stockman stated the problem in dramatic terms. If the interest bill is allowed to balloon to its projected end-of-the-decade level, he said, "I do not think there is anybody on this committee who could think of enough taxes to raise or enough spending to cut to even offset that explosion of debt-service cost. . . ."

Mr. Stockman's warning, like other dire predictions about government debt and interest costs, is based, of course, on a number of "ifs"— the most important being the assumption that the U.S. will fail to deal with deficits projected to exceed $200 billion annually from now until the end of the decade. . . .

Paul Volcker shares the same concern. "I don't know of any other time when one worried in an important way about the compounding effects of interest on deficits," the Fed chairman said at a recent Senate hearing. "These deficits are so big, running in the neighborhood of $200 billion, that the payment of interest on that $200 billion the following year becomes an important factor in the next year's deficit. You go out three or four years, and that becomes a very large factor." . . .

Source: Paul Blustein, "Climbing Federal Debt Is Inexorably Raising U.S. Interest Burden," *The Wall Street Journal*, June 22, 1984, pp. 1, 14. Reprinted by permission of *The Wall Street Journal*,

Figure 6.2
National Debt as a Percentage of GNP[a] (1960–1984)

While the national debt is large in dollar terms, it has fallen as a percentage of GNP through the 1960s and some of the 1970s. The debt has, however, increased significantly as a percentage of GNP in the 1980s.

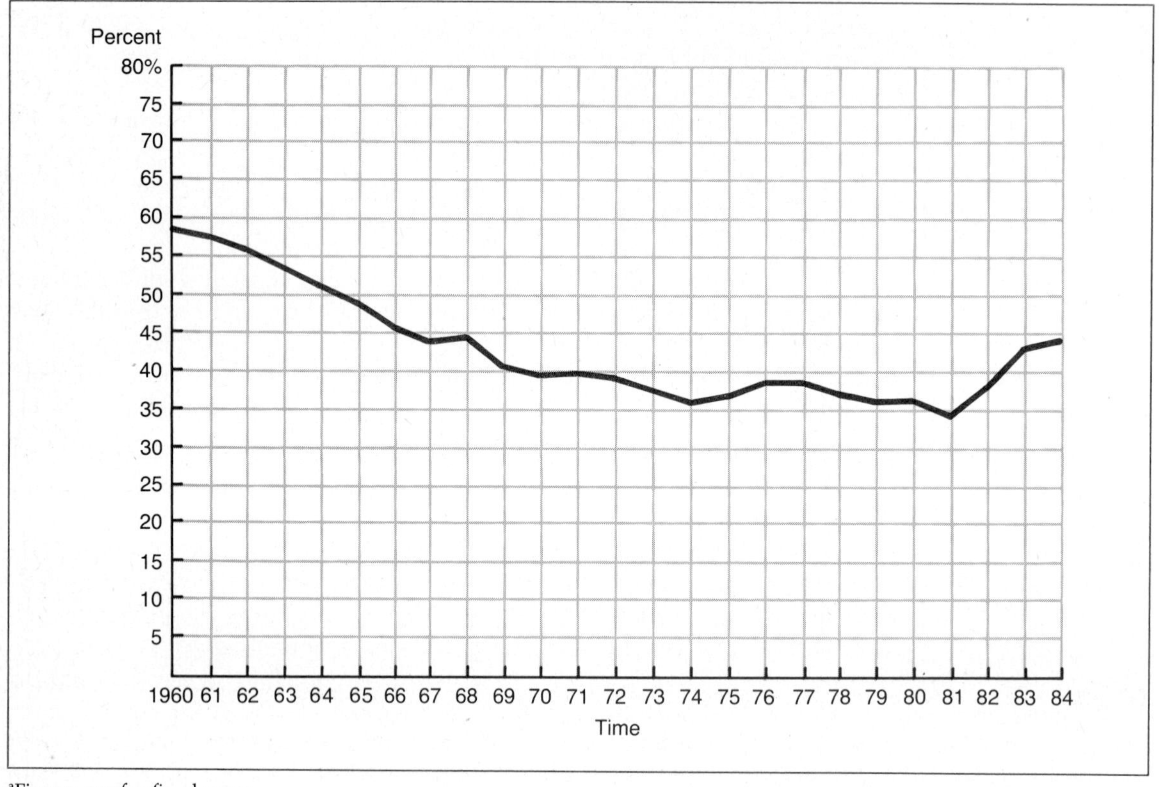

[a]Figures are for fiscal years.

Source: U.S., *Economic Report of the President* (Washington, D.C.: U.S. Government Printing Office, 1985), p. 318.

with their newly redeemed funds. Also, approximately 11 percent of the debt is external, or foreign-owned.[17] While under normal conditions this is not a serious consideration, in a period of accelerated repayment it would mean a notable outflow of dollars from the United States. Finally, in order to pay off the public debt, a series of surplus budgets would be needed. Recall from earlier in the chapter that a surplus budget has a contractionary impact on the economy. Thus, while the debt was being paid off, economic activity would decline.

[17]Figure is for September 1984. From *Monetary Trends,* prepared by the Federal Reserve Bank of St. Louis, released March 1985, p. 13. This percentage fluctuates from year to year.

SUMMARY

Government units receive revenues from taxes and other sources such as contributions for social insurance and, at the state and local levels, federal grants-in-aid. Taxes may be classified as progressive, proportional, or regressive when compared with incomes. The main types of government expenditures are purchases of goods and services and transfer payments.

Fiscal policy refers to changes in government expenditures and/or taxes for the purpose of influencing the levels of output, employment, or prices in the economy. Fiscal policy can be used to reduce unemployment by injecting more spending into the economy through increased government purchases, increased transfer payments, and/or decreased taxes. Demand-pull inflation is reduced through decreased government purchases, decreased transfer payments, and/or increased taxes.

Fiscal policy is either discretionary or automatic. Discretionary fiscal policy is the deliberate adjustment of government purchases, transfers, and/or taxes by Congress to control unemployment or inflation. Automatic stabilization is the automatic change in some taxes (particularly federal personal income taxes) and some transfer payments (particularly unemployment compensation) that occurs as the level of economic activity changes. These changes in taxes and transfers help to soften the impact of unemployment or inflation.

When a government's outlays are less than its revenues, it is operating with a surplus budget. When its outlays exceed revenues, it is operating with a deficit budget. When its outlays and revenues are equal, it is operating with a balanced budget. Surplus budgets generally cause economic activity to contract, since the government is withdrawing more from the spending stream than it is returning. Deficit and balanced budgets are expansionary, since the government is injecting more into the spending stream than is being taken out as taxes. Thus, a surplus budget would be proper policy for fighting demand-pull inflation, while a deficit budget would be appropriate for fighting unemployment.

Fiscal policy considerations compete with other economic and noneconomic objectives in establishing the federal budget, and the budgetary process is largely political. Also, the effectiveness of fiscal policy may be reduced by the combined presence of high rates of inflation and unemployment and by the time lag between the onset and discovery of a problem, and between its discovery and the implementation of a remedy. The government's freedom to persistently run budget deficits sometimes leads to unwise amounts or types of expenditures.

The national debt is the debt owed by the federal government from the financing of its deficit budgets. In raising funds, the government borrows at the lowest interest rates offered from whomever is willing to lend and gives U.S. Treasury securities in return. The size of the public debt has grown substantially over the years, and the interest the government must pay to carry the debt is a significant amount. In addition, as the federal government increases its borrowing, it crowds out private borrowing.

Key Terms and Concepts

Progressive tax
Proportional tax
Regressive tax
Government expenditures
Public good
Fiscal policy
Discretionary fiscal policy
Automatic stabilization
Balanced budget
Surplus budget
Deficit budget
Stagflation
Public choice
National debt
U.S. Treasury security
Crowding out

Discussion and Review Questions

1. Suppose that government policy makers want to increase spending in the economy by $100 million and can follow any one of three policies: $100 million can be put into the spending stream through the purchase of goods and services; transfer payments can be increased to the point where household expenditures would go up by $100 million; or taxes can be reduced to the point where $100 million more would be spent by businesses and households. Does it make any difference whether purchases are increased, transfer payments are increased, or taxes are reduced to expand spending by $100 million? Why might policy makers choose one policy over another?
2. Do you favor a balanced budget amendment to the U.S. Constitution? Why? What are the economic implications of your position?
3. One area of concern regarding the national debt is the burden it might place on future generations. What are some ways in which a national debt could burden future generations?
4. Assume that you are a congressperson whose congressional district may be awarded a multimillion-dollar rapid transit project. The economy, however, is in the throes of one of the more severe inflationary periods of the decade. How would you vote on the passage of funds for the project? What would you tell your colleagues? your constituents?
5. Explain whether the economy will expand, contract, stay the same, or inflate with each of the following fiscal actions.
   a. Congress votes a $35 tax credit to each taxpayer.
   b. Households are taxed an extra 15 percent and the government does not spend all of these additional tax dollars.
   c. Households are taxed an extra 15 percent and the government spends the entire amount on purchases of goods and services.
   d. Congress allows many new income tax deductions when the economy is at full employment.
   e. Although Congress intends to balance the budget, a deficit occurs.
   f. At the end of a war, defense expenditures drop dramatically but

are replaced by domestic spending programs for health and education.

   g. At the end of a war, defense expenditures drop with no increase in other spending programs.

6. What effect would each of the following have on a federal budget that is currently balanced? How might the budgetary changes, where they occur, affect the national debt?

   a. An increase in the percentage of income taxed in each of the federal personal income tax brackets

   b. An increase in government expenditures on pollution control

   c. An equal increase in government expenditures and income tax revenues

   d. An increase in defense expenditures and a decrease in corporate income tax revenues

   e. An increase in social security payments by the government matched by a decrease in a subsidy to a particular group in the economy

7. Suppose that the legislators in a particular state are choosing between three strategies to raise revenue: (1) imposing an income tax that increases with the level of income; (2) imposing a sales tax on food; and (3) imposing a 1 percent tax on all earnings within the state. Would it make any difference to residents of the state in the upper, middle, or lower income groups which tax was imposed? Under what circumstances might an individual in the middle income group favor a tax that increases with income over a sales tax on food? Under what circumstances might the same person prefer the sales tax on food?

8. Give some arguments for and against a federal personal income tax that would be proportional rather than progressive. Who stands to win and who stands to lose from a flat tax?

Suggested Readings

Tom Alexander, "The Grass-Roots Revolt Against Federal Deficits," *Fortune,* November 28, 1983, pp. 51–52, 54, 58. Background on the effort to introduce a balanced budget amendment to the Constitution.

"Do $200 Billion Deficits Really Matter?" *U.S. News & World Report,* October 17, 1983, pp. 33–34. A series of opinions by noted individuals on the large budget deficit of 1983.

***Economic Report of the President* (Washington, D.C.: U.S. Government Printing Office, published annually).** Includes the annual economic report of the president to congress, the report of the Council of Economic Advisors relating to the state of the economy, and extensive data on the past and current performance of the economy.

Abba P. Lerner, "The Burden of the National Debt," *Public Debt and Future Generations,* James M. Ferguson, ed. (Chapel Hill: The University of North Carolina Press, 1964), pp. 16–19. An exploration of some of the ways the national debt is considered to be a burden and whether those burdens are real or imaginary.

***Setting National Priorities* (Washington, D.C.: The Brookings Institution, published annually).** Series which evaluates the federal budget and budget-related matters. Begins with the 1971 federal budget.

7 MONEY, FINANCIAL INSTITUTIONS, AND THE FEDERAL RESERVE

Chapter Objectives

1. To define money and explain the functions of money.
2. To identify the components of the U.S. money supply and different monetary standards.
3. To introduce the financial institutions that are important for the maintenance and control of the U.S. money supply, and to highlight commercial banks and commercial bank regulation.
4. To explain the role of the Federal Reserve System, its organization, and the functions that Federal Reserve Banks perform.
5. To identify the Depository Institutions Deregulation and Monetary Control Act of 1980 and its effects on financial institutions.

Thus far we have explored several topics that in one way or another involve money. For example, recall that the circular flow model is concerned in part with the passing of money between households and businesses. It was also shown that economic activity can be expanded or contracted by increasing or decreasing the size of the spending stream; and that with inflation, the purchasing power of money deteriorates.

Money is the lifeblood of an economy. Without it, modern economies as we know them could not exist. Even though money does not itself produce goods and services as do land, labor, capital, and entrepreneurship, it makes possible the bringing together of resources on a large scale and the sale of what they produce. In fact, the very idea of the circular flow of economic activity is predicated on the movement of dollars from businesses to households in return for resources, and from households to businesses in return for goods and services. If a nation's monetary system becomes unstable, its impact may be felt throughout the entire economy.

This chapter lays the groundwork in money and financial institutions for Chapter Eight, where the creation and management of money and the effects of changes in the money supply on the economy are studied. First, this chapter defines money, explains why it is important in an economy, identifies what constitutes the money supply of the United States, and discusses monetary standards. The remainder of the chapter is devoted to examining the financial institutions central to the operation of the U.S. economy's monetary system, and to studying the Federal Reserve System.

MONEY

The Definition and Functions of Money

Many people believe that money must be made of precious metal or something that can be traded for precious metal at the central banking authority or the government. That is, they believe money must have a high intrinsic value or give claim to something of high intrinsic value, such as gold or silver. This is not necessarily true.

Money
Anything that is generally acceptable as a medium of exchange.

Medium of exchange
Something that is generally acceptable as payment for goods, services, and resources; the primary function of money.

Money is *anything* that is generally acceptable as a medium of exchange. A **medium of exchange** is anything that people are readily willing to accept in payment for purchases of goods, services, and resources because they know it can be easily used for further transactions. For example, in the United States a $10 bill is a medium of exchange; people are willing to take this bill in payment, knowing that they can in turn use it for their own purchases.

A medium of exchange, or money, could be anything: possibilities include precious metals, stones, beads, coins, cigarettes, pieces of paper, and electronically transferred numbers. As long as it is the generally accepted means of payment for purchase in an economy, it makes no difference what physical form money takes. Some types of money that have been used at different times and in different places are listed in Table 7.1.

Value of money
Measured by the goods, services, and resources that money can purchase.

If anything can serve as money, how is the **value of money** determined? The value of any money, a $10 bill for example, is measured by the goods, services, and resources that it can purchase. With inflation the value of money declines, simply because less can be purchased with the same amount of money.

Barter system
A system where goods and services are exchanged for each other rather than for money.

What would happen if there were no money—no generally accepted means of payment? In the absence of a medium of exchange a **barter system** would develop. With barter, a direct exchange of goods and services occurs: for example, I might give you some camping gear in return for your psychology text. It is virtually impossible to operate an economy with any degree of sophistication on a barter system. Not only must individuals decide what to buy or sell, they must also locate people willing to take what they offer in trade for what they wish to have. A medium of exchange, or money, removes the problems of barter. Wants need not coincide, because

Table 7.1
Different Forms of Money

Anything can serve as money in a society, provided it is generally acceptable as payment for goods, services, and resources.

Form	Location
Cowrie shells	Africa, India, South Seas (perhaps the first money in the world)
Snail shells	Queen Charlotte Islands
Porpoise teeth	Malaita (island in the Solomon Group)
Boar tusks	New Guinea
Red woodpecker scalps	Karok Tribe on the west coast of North America
Feathers	South Seas
Beer	English coal mines in the mid-19th century
Bars of crystal salt	Ethiopia
Round stones with centers removed	Yap
Glass	Ancient Egypt
Wampum (polished beads) Animal skins Rice Sugar Rum Molasses Indigo Tobacco	North American settlements and Colonial period
Cowries Tortoise shells Agricultural implements	Ancient China

Source: Norman Angell, *The Story of Money* (Garden City, N.Y.: Garden City Publishing Co., Inc., 1929), pp. 73–76, 78–80, 82, 84, 85, 88–90. Courtesy of Harper & Row.

every person one deals with is willing to accept money in return for resources, goods, or services.

Measure of value
A function of money; the value of every good, service, and resource can be expressed in terms of, or as a multiple of, an economy's basic unit of money.

Method for storing wealth and delaying payments
A function of money; allows for saving, or storing wealth for future use, and permits credit, or delayed payments.

While money serves primarily as a medium of exchange, it also performs two additional functions: it is a **measure of value,** and it provides a **method for storing wealth and delaying payments.** Let us consider money as a measure of value first.

Every nation's money can be expressed in terms of a base unit or in multiples of a base unit. In the United States the base unit is the dollar, in France it is the franc, in Germany the mark, and so on. Because the basic unit of a nation's money is generally understood, it is possible to express the value of every resource, good, and service as a multiple of that unit. When a house is priced at $90,000 and a new automobile at $9,000, it is understood that the house is worth 90,000 times the base unit and that the automobile is worth 9,000 times the base unit, or one-tenth of the value of the house. In the absence of money as a measure of value, simple comparisons such as these would be difficult. The worth of all resources, goods, and services would have to be determined by comparing each item to each other item. Thus, the ability to express the values of all resources, goods, and services according to a common measure greatly reduces the amount of information needed to make economic decisions.

Money also provides a method for storing wealth. That is, it allows persons to accumulate their wealth or income with the intention of using it in the future. In short, money eases the process of saving. Money also permits the delay of payment for a good or service and thus facilitates lending and borrowing. A lender might be hesitant to provide either money or goods if there were some question as to the future acceptability of the means of payment.

In light of this last function of money, it can be understood how a chronic and severe inflation could weaken or even destroy the fabric of an economy. With serious and prolonged periods of price increases, money's ability to serve as a method for accumulating wealth may be impaired. People might become unwilling to save their money if they anticipate that its future purchasing power will be seriously eroded by rising prices. Correspondingly, borrowing for investment or other purposes might be extremely difficult if lenders anticipate that future dollars used for repayment will have a much lower purchasing power. The functions of money as well as some of the types of money described in this section are illustrated in Application 7.1, "Fixed Assets, Or: Why a Loan in Yap Is Hard to Roll Over."

The Money Supply

Every economy has a supply, or quantity, of money that is used to transact exchange. What makes up the money supply of the U.S. economy and how large is this supply? There is disagreement over the answers to these questions, since some define the money supply more broadly than others.

M1
The narrowest definition of the U.S. money supply, which includes coins and paper money in circulation, nonbank-issued traveler's checks, most demand deposits at commercial banks, and other checkable deposits.

Table 7.2 lists the components of the U.S. money supply according to its narrowest and most popular definition, which is termed **M1.** Included in this definition are coins and paper money in circulation, nonbank-issued traveler's checks, almost all demand deposits (checking accounts) at commercial banks, and other accounts offered by both commercial banks and other depository institutions that have become generally acceptable as a medium of exchange in recent years.[1] These other accounts, which are classified as "other checkable deposits," include NOW (negotiable order of withdrawal) and ATS (automatic transfer service) accounts, credit union share draft accounts, and demand deposits at thrift institutions.

Token money
Money with a face value greater than the value of the commodity from which it is made.

Components of the Money Supply Coins are issued by the U.S. Treasury and range from 1¢ pieces to the Susan B. Anthony dollar. In the U.S. economy, coins are **token money:** the value of the metal in the coin is less than the face value of the coin. If this were not the case, coins might disappear

[1]Only coins and paper money *in circulation* are included in the money supply. A large amount of both of these items is "warehoused" in bank and Federal Reserve vaults for future use. Until it is in the hands of the public, it is not spendable or acceptable as a medium of exchange and therefore not counted as money. For an explanation of which demand deposits are excluded from the money supply see note a in Table 7.2.

Table 7.2
The U.S. Money Supply: M1

M1 is the narrowest and most popular definition of the U.S. money supply.

M1
Coins
Paper money
Nonbank-issued traveler's checks
Demand deposits[a]
Other checkable deposits
NOW accounts
ATS accounts
Credit union share draft accounts
Demand deposits at thrift institutions

[a]Includes demand deposits at commercial banks exclusive of deposits due to domestic banks, the U.S. government, and foreign banks and official institutions. For details on further adjustments to this measure, see the source given below.

Source: Notes to Table 1.10, "Reserves, Money Stock, Liquid Assets, and Debt Measures," *Federal Reserve Bulletin* (March 1985), p. A3.

Application 7.1
FIXED ASSETS, OR: WHY A LOAN IN YAP IS HARD TO ROLL OVER

YAP, Micronesia — On this tiny South Pacific island, life is easy and the currency is hard.

Elsewhere, the world's troubled monetary system creaks along. . . . But on Yap the currency is as solid as a rock. In fact, it *is* rock. Limestone to be precise.

For nearly 2,000 years the Yapese have used large stone wheels to pay for major purchases, such as land, canoes and permission to marry. Yap is a U.S. trust territory, and the dollar is used in grocery stores and gas stations. But reliance on stone money . . . continues.

Buying property with stones is "much easier than buying it with U.S. dollars," says John Chodad, who recently purchased a building lot with a 30-inch stone wheel. "We don't know the value of the U.S. dollar." Others on this 37-square-mile island 530 miles southwest of Guam use both dollars and stones. Venito Gurtmag, a builder, recently accepted a four-foot-wide stone disk and $8,700 for a house he built in an outlying village.

Stone wheels don't make good pocket money, so for small transactions, Yapese use other forms of currency, such as beer. Beer is proffered as payment for all sorts of odd jobs, including construction. . . .

Besides stone wheels and beer, the Yapese sometimes spend *gaw*, consisting of necklaces of stone beads strung together around a whale's tooth. They also can buy things with *yar*, a currency made from large sea shells. But these are small change.

The people of Yap have been using stone money ever since a Yapese warrior named Anagumang first brought the huge stones over from limestone caverns on neighboring Palau, some 1,500 to 2,000 years ago. Inspired by the moon, he fashioned the stone into large circles. The rest is history.

from circulation. For example, in the past, when the price of copper increased to a level where a penny contained almost 1¢ worth of copper, pennies became short in supply. Also, in this regard, a "sandwich" was created by inserting cheaper metal in the middle of the dime and quarter in more recent years.

Federal Reserve Notes
Paper money issued by the Federal Reserve Banks; includes almost all paper money in circulation.

Paper money constitutes a larger share of our money supply than coins, but is only a small fraction of the total when compared to demand deposits and other checkable deposits. Almost all U.S. paper money is **Federal Reserve Notes.** Federal Reserve Banks, which will be discussed shortly, issue and back this paper money. Notice on a paper bill the inscription at the top which states "Federal Reserve Note" and the circle identifying the particular Federal Reserve Bank that issued the note. Coins and paper money constitute "currency."

Traveler's checks, the third and smallest component of the money supply, can be purchased from American Express and other companies, and from banking organizations, and are honored both domestically and in foreign countries. However, only traveler's checks from "nonbank issuers" are cat-

---

Yapese lean the stone wheels against their houses or prop up rows of them in village "banks." Most of the stones are 2½ to five feet in diameter, but some are as much as 12 feet across. Each has a hole in the center so it can be slipped onto the trunk of a fallen betel-nut tree and carried. It takes 20 men to lift some wheels.

By custom, the stones are worthless when broken. You never hear people on Yap musing about wanting a piece of the rock. Rather than risk a broken stone—or back—Yapese tend to leave the larger stones where they are and make a mental accounting that the ownership has been transferred. . . .

The worth of stone money doesn't depend on size. Instead, the pieces are valued by how hard it was to get them here. . . .

There are some decided advantages to using massive stones for money. They are immune to black-market trading, for one thing, and they pose formidable obstacles to pickpockets. In addition, there aren't any sterile debates about how to stabilize the Yapese monetary system. With only about 6,600 stone wheels remaining on the island, the money-supply level stays put. "If you have it, you have it," shrugs Andrew Ken, a Yapese monetary thinker.

But stone money has its limits. Linus Ruuamau, the manager of one of the island's few retail stores, won't accept it for general merchandise. And Al Azuma, who manages the local Bank of Hawaii branch, the only conventional financial institution here, isn't interested in limestone deposits or any sort of shell game. So the money, left uninvested, just gathers moss.

But stone money accords well with Yapese traditions. "There are a lot of instances here where you cannot use U.S. money," Mr. Gurtmag says. One is the settling of disputes. Unlike most money, stones sometimes *can* buy happiness, of a sort; if a Yapese wants to settle an argument, he brings his adversary stone money as a token. "The apology is accepted without question," Mr. Chodad says. "If you used dollars, there'd be an argument over whether it was enough."

Source: Art Pine, "Fixed Assets, Or: Why a Loan in Yap Is Hard to Roll Over," *The Wall Street Journal*, March 29, 1984, pp. 1, 23. Reprinted by permission of *The Wall Street Journal*, egorized separately in M1, since bank-issued traveler's checks are included in the demand deposit component. Like paper money, traveler's checks come in denominations such as $20, $50, and $100. Unlike paper money, traveler's checks must be signed by the holder when used to purchase goods and services. Also, the owner of lost or stolen traveler's checks may be able to stop payment on the checks and to replace them, a characteristic shared with the remaining two forms of money included in M1.

Demand deposits
Checking account balances kept primarily at commercial banks.

Demand deposits, the fourth component of the money supply, are checking account balances. These accounts, against which checks can be written, are kept primarily at commercial banks. Demand deposits are merely bookkeeping numbers. When a check is deposited or written, numbers are transferred from one set of books or computer to another. Since demand deposits are a very large portion of our money supply, it can be said that much of our money is simply numbers in accounts! It is important to realize that checks themselves are not money. They are merely sheets of paper giving a bank the instruction and authority to draw out all or part of a demand deposit account so that its owner can use the funds.

Other checkable deposits
Interest-bearing accounts such as NOW, ATS, and credit union share drafts that are similar to demand deposits and are offered by banks, savings and loans, and other financial institutions.

Other checkable deposits such as NOW, ATS, and credit union share draft accounts are similar to demand deposits but offer interest on the funds in these accounts. While some types of these accounts existed in the 1970s, they did not become broadly permitted and accepted until the early 1980s. Banks and other depository institutions such as savings and loans and credit unions provide these accounts. In recent years, interest-bearing checkable deposits have become increasingly popular, and merchants, utility companies, and other payment receivers make little distinction among checks, drafts, withdrawal orders, and such.

For several reasons, demand deposits and other checkable deposits form the largest and most important component of the money supply. First, it is more convenient to transact large or complicated payments by check or draft. Imagine the amount of paper money, even using $100 bills, necessary to purchase an automobile! Second, checks, drafts, and similar instruments serve as records of payment, making it unnecessary to receive and retain a receipt for all transactions. Third, these accounts offer an element of safety. If checks or withdrawal orders are stolen or lost, the institutions against which they are drawn can be instructed not to honor payment on them.

Table 7.3 gives the amount of currency, traveler's checks, demand deposits, and other checkable deposits in circulation each December from 1980 through 1984. Notice that demand deposits are a much larger component of the money supply than are the other components. For example, in December 1984 approximately 45 percent of the money supply was in demand deposits. Also notice the substantial growth in other checkable deposits, especially from December 1980 to December 1981. As a result of the Depository Institutions Deregulation and Monetary Control Act of 1980, all depository institutions were allowed to offer interest-bearing checkable deposits beginning January 1, 1981. Obviously, from Table 7.3, these accounts have been very

Table 7.3
Currency, Traveler's Checks, Demand Deposits, and Other Checkable Deposits in Circulation (Billions of Dollars[a])

Demand deposits make up the largest component of the money supply, but other checkable deposits have grown in importance since 1980.

Year	Currency (Coins and Paper Money)	Traveler's Checks	Demand Deposits	Other Checkable Deposits	Total	Total as a Percentage of GNP
1980	$118.8	$3.9	$274.7	$ 27.4	$424.8	16.1%
1981	126.1	4.1	243.6	78.5	452.3	15.3
1982	136.4	4.1	247.3	104.1	491.9	16.0
1983	150.5	4.6	251.6	131.2	537.9	16.3
1984	160.9	4.9	256.9	145.7	567.9	15.5[b]

[a]Figures are not seasonally adjusted and are given for the month of December.
[b]1984 GNP figure is preliminary.

Source: Table 1.21, "Money Stock, Liquid Assets, and Debt Measures," *Federal Reserve Bulletin* (May 1984) and (March 1985), p. A13. GNP figures for calculation of percentages in last column from: U.S., *Economic Report of the President* (Washington, D.C.: U.S. Government Printing Office, 1985), p. 232.

successful, growing from 6.5 percent of the money supply in 1980 to 25.7 percent in 1984.

The far right-hand column of Table 7.3 shows the total M1 money supply figure for each year as a percentage of that year's GNP. Every year the total amount spent on new goods and services exceeds the amount of money in circulation. For example, the money supply in 1984 was equal to only 15.5 percent of the total expenditures made on new goods and services over that year. Obviously, so much output can be purchased with so few dollars because of the circular flow of economic activity: the same dollars are spent several times over during the course of the year.

As noted earlier, some controversy exists as to what constitutes the nation's money supply. The narrowest and most fundamental definition is M1. Many, however, consider this definition too narrow. For example, suppose a student earns $60 and puts $20 of it in a demand deposit account at a commercial bank, $20 in a savings account at a commercial bank, and $20 in a savings passbook at a savings and loan. According to the definition of M1, only the $20 that went into the checking account at the commercial bank would be considered money. Here is the source of the controversy. One observer might argue that funds placed in a savings account are readily available and just as acceptable as a medium of exchange as are currency or demand deposits, and that they should be considered money. Another observer might argue that the funds in the savings account must be converted to cash, a demand deposit, or a checkable deposit before they can be spent. Hence, they are not money. Arguments such as this have led to other definitions of the money supply, with each additional definition becoming broader. Table 7.4 summarizes the definitions of M2, M3, and L.

Table 7.4
Definitions of M2, M3, and L[a]

There are several definitions of the money supply, each becoming broader by building on the preceding definition.

M2	M3	L
M1	M2	M3
+money market deposit accounts	+time deposits of $100,000 or more	+commercial paper
+savings deposits	+other[b]	+savings bonds
+time deposits of less than $100,000		+liquid Treasury obligations
+money market mutual funds		+other[b]
+other[b]		

[a]For more specific information on these definitions, see the source given below.
[b]"Other" items include such things as Eurodollar deposits and repurchase agreements.

Source: Notes to Table 1.10, "Reserves, Money Stock, Liquid Assets, and Debt Measures," *Federal Reserve Bulletin* (March 1985), p. A3.

Everyone agrees that the money supply includes M1, but there is disagreement over defining it as broadly as M2, or M3, or L. The differences among these definitions are not trivial. For example, in September 1984 M1 was $546.3 billion, M2 was $2.3 trillion, M3 was $2.9 trillion, and L was $3.4 trillion.[2] For the remainder of this chapter and the next, we will focus on M1.

Monetary Standards

There are those who think that if individuals give up their valuable goods and services in return for money, the money itself should represent a claim to something of value. That is, it should be backed by something of value. An economy in which money is backed by something of tangible value is said to be on a **commodity monetary standard.** With this type of standard, the monetary authority has an amount of gold, silver, or other item equal in value to the money. If the money is backed by gold, the economy is on a gold standard; if it is backed by silver, the economy is on a silver standard.

Commodity monetary standard
Exists when an economy's money is backed by something of tangible value such as gold or silver.

For much of its history the U.S. economy was on a commodity standard. Prior to 1933 the United States had a gold-coin standard, where gold not only backed the money supply, but also freely circulated in the hands of the public. The use of gold pieces as money was common. Then, U.S. citizens were asked to turn their gold in to the government, and in 1934 the United States went on a gold-bullion standard. This meant that gold backed the money supply but was no longer available to the general public. Under this gold-bullion standard, however, foreign holders of dollars were paid in gold. In the years after 1950 more and more international debts were paid in gold, and the U.S. gold supply gradually diminished. This brought about a reduc-

[2]Table 1.21, "Money Stock, Liquid Assets, And Debt Measures," *Federal Reserve Bulletin* (March 1985), p. A13. Figures are not seasonally adjusted.

tion in the gold backing of the money supply. By 1971 official U.S. gold reserves had decreased to the point where President Richard Nixon thought it advisable to freeze the gold supply. U.S. gold was to be made available to no one, and the dollar was no longer to be converted to gold, not even to settle international transactions.

Paper monetary standard
Exists when money is not backed by anything of tangible value such as gold or silver.

Since 1971 the U.S. economy has been on a **paper monetary standard.** This means that money itself has little or no intrinsic value and that it does not represent a claim against any commodity such as gold or silver. The backing on a paper money standard is the strength of the economy, the willingness of people to accept the money in exchange for goods and services, and faith and trust in the purchasing power of the money.

Is it better or worse for a nation to be on a paper standard rather than a gold, silver, or other commodity standard? It could be argued that there is more faith in a money supply if it is backed by gold or silver. However, history does not bear this out. In the past, panics and monetary crises have occurred even when money was backed by precious metal. In fact, the knowledge that paper money can be converted into gold or silver could make people willing to act more dramatically on their fears than they would if the monetary authority would only redeem paper money for more paper money. It is also true that the amount of gold or silver a nation possesses may have very little to do with its economic needs and potential. Since a nation's money supply is the lifeblood of its economy, it may not be desirable for the amount of money in an economy to be tied to the availability of a commodity like gold or silver rather than tied to conditions and needs of the economy itself. However, an important potential problem with a paper standard is that the administrators of the money supply may have wide latitude in the decisions they make concerning that supply and may not properly manage and control it.

Application 7.2 gives some information about U.S.–owned gold and the gold held at the Federal Reserve Bank in New York.

FINANCIAL INSTITUTIONS

A number of financial depository institutions are important for maintenance and control of the U.S. money supply. These include commercial banks, savings and loan associations, variations on savings and loans such as mutual savings banks, and credit unions. These institutions are important because they have the ability to create and destroy money. Money is created when loans are made by these institutions and destroyed when loans are repaid. The process through which this is done will be thoroughly explored in the next chapter. For now it is important to know that these institutions, with their special loan-making ability, are an important vehicle for expanding and contracting the money supply.

Commercial Banks

Commercial bank
An institution that holds and maintains checking accounts (demand deposits) for its customers and performs other functions such as making loans.

The expression "banking" refers to the operations of a particular type of financial organization called a commercial bank. A **commercial bank** is an institution that holds and maintains checking accounts, or demand deposits, for its customers and performs a number of other functions such as industrial, commercial, and consumer loan making, the servicing of savings accounts, and the sale of traveler's checks. Other financial institutions, like savings and loan associations, perform functions similar to those of commercial banks such as the granting of mortgages, the rental of safe deposit boxes, and the maintenance of other checkable deposits. Since the Monetary Control Act of 1980 it has become difficult to distinguish between commercial banks and other financial depository institutions. Prior to that time, the ability to offer checkable deposits was held almost exclusively by commercial banks and served as the primary differentiating characteristic.

As noted earlier with regard to Table 7.3, approximately 45 percent of the U.S. money supply (M1) in 1984 was composed of demand deposits, or checking accounts, at commercial banks. Figures also indicate that in 1984 demand deposits at commercial banks amounted to $256.9 billion and other

Application 7.2
GOLD! GOLD! GOLD!

The largest known accumulation of gold in the world—about 319 million troy ounces in early 1981—and about a third of the official monetary gold reserves of the noncommunist nations is stored in the Federal Reserve Bank of New York. . . . Here, in one of the most unusual vaults in the world, about 80 feet below Nassau Street—one of the busiest streets in the Wall Street district—gold belonging to the U.S., foreign nations, central banks and international monetary organizations rests on the bedrock of Manhattan Island. An awesome and impressive chamber nearly half the length of a football field, the gold vault is a popular tourist stop, attracting about 16,000 visitors a year. . . .

Only a very small fraction of the gold in the vault is U.S. owned. More than half of the U.S. gold stock, which totaled $11.2 billion in early 1981, is kept in the Bullion Depository at Fort Knox, Kentucky. Most of the remainder is kept at the Denver and Philadelphia Mints and the New York and San Francisco Assay Offices. . . .

Handling billions of dollars of gold seems like a glamorous job, but it's just plain hard work. Hydraulic lifts and conveyor belts, which can boost bars to ceiling height and bring them down, have partially relieved the physical strain, but lifting, swinging and positioning 27 pounds again and again is arduous. Teams of "gold stackers" work in shifts that allow them frequent rest periods. The job also has its hazards. The stackers wear lightweight, but strong, magnesium shoe covers to protect their feet against accidentally dropped bars. . . .

Storing about $13.5 billion of gold—not to mention billions of dollars in securities, paper currency and coin—makes extreme security measures mandatory. The total weight of the checkable deposits, some of which were held at commercial banks, were $145.7 billion. With these figures it is easy to see that commercial banks are the most important and dominant of all financial institutions.

In the United States there are over 14,000 commercial banks, each organized to be a profit-making corporation. These banks operate by attracting deposits and converting them to loans, securities, and other interest-earning assets for the bank.

Commercial Bank Regulation Although commercial banks are like other businesses in that they are profit-oriented organizations, they are unlike other businesses due to the indispensable roles they play in the proper functioning of the monetary system of the U.S. economy. Because these banks maintain demand deposits, which are the largest portion of the money supply, and because their actions can change the actual quantity of money in the economy, it is necessary to ensure that commercial banks be sound and secure, and not abuse their money-creating abilities. To accomplish this aim, a number of agencies, both governmental and quasi-governmental, set standards and regulations for commercial banks.

---

bullion—about 13,000 tons—makes it virtually impossible to steal, but this is only one deterrent. . . .

The vault's design is a masterpiece of security engineering. The gold vault is actually one floor of a three-story bunker of vaults arranged like strongboxes stacked on top of one another. The massive walls of each vault are made of reinforced structural concrete and are virtually impregnable. . . .

The bank has one of the largest private, uniformed protection forces in the nation. Guards must prove their ability with a revolver each month on the bank's firing range. Although the minimum requirement is a marksman's score, most are qualified as experts. Guards must also be proficient with other "heavier" weapons. The protection force is supplemented by closed-circuit television monitors and by an electronic surveillance system that signals the central guardroom if a vault door is opened or closed. An alarm system alerts guards to seal all security areas and exits from the bank, which can be done very quickly. . . .

A gold bar physically shows its origin and history. Its shape indicates whether it was cast in the U.S. or abroad. U.S. bars are rectangular bricks, 7 inches long, 3⅝ inches wide and between 1⅝ and 1¾ inches thick. It is often possible to tell by its shape where a particular U.S. bar was cast—bars cast at the Denver Mint have rounded corners while those cast at the New York or San Francisco Assay Offices have sharp corners. Most bars cast abroad are trapezoidal.

Occasionally, visitors may see bars that are slimmer than usual. These bars, nicknamed "Hershey bars," result when an amount of gold too small to make a full bar is left in the smelter's crucible at the end of the casting process. Since the purity of the gold varies between different pourings, this leftover metal cannot be added to other pourings and must be cast into a separate bar.

Source: C. J. Parnow, *Key to the Gold Vault* (New York: Federal Reserve Bank of New York, 1981), pp. 2, 4, 6, and 8.

The regulations imposed upon commercial banks are varied; they differ according to the function of the overseeing agency. Included among these regulations are the amount of backing needed for deposits, the degree of risk permitted in a bank's investments, the amount of money capital needed to begin operations, and the ability of a bank to open branch offices.

Dual banking system
The label given to the U.S. banking system because both the federal and the state governments have the right to charter banks.

When a commercial bank is organized, a corporate charter must be obtained before it can function. Because both the federal and state governments have the right to charter banks, the United States has a **dual banking system.** That is, a bank may be chartered by the federal government or by a state government. Thus, the first line of regulation for a commercial bank comes from the government unit from which it obtains its charter. If a bank incorporates under a federal charter, it is subject to regulation by the U.S. Comptroller of the Currency; and if it incorporates as a state bank, a state banking agency has supervisory authority.

National bank
A commercial bank incorporated under a federal rather than a state charter.

The second line of regulation comes from the Federal Reserve, an agency that will be discussed shortly. Banks that incorporate with a federal charter, called **national banks,** must belong to the Federal Reserve System. State chartered banks may choose to belong to the system and, on joining, are termed state member banks. In addition to regulating its members, the Federal Reserve imposes some uniform regulations on all commercial banks regardless of whether they belong to the system or not. Since the Monetary Control Act of 1980, the distinction between Federal Reserve member and nonmember banks has lessened.

Federal Deposit Insurance Corporation (FDIC)
A government agency established in 1933 to insure deposits in commercial banks up to a specified amount; banks belonging to the Federal Reserve System must join the FDIC.

The third line of regulation comes from the **Federal Deposit Insurance Corporation (FDIC).** The Federal Deposit Insurance Corporation, established in 1933, insures deposits in commercial banks up to a specific amount.[3] Banks that belong to the Federal Reserve must join the Federal Deposit Insurance Corporation, so that all national and state member banks are insured. State banks that do not belong to the Federal Reserve may affiliate with the Federal Deposit Insurance Corporation. These are termed nonmember state insured banks and constitute the majority of commercial banks. There are relatively few banks that are nonmember noninsured state banks.

Other Financial Depository Institutions

Other financial depository institutions that play an important role in the maintenance of the money supply are savings and loan associations, mutual savings banks, and credit unions. In 1983 there were 3,513 savings and loan associations, 393 mutual savings banks, and 15,877 credit unions.[4] While the number of these institutions is larger than commercial banks, their total size is considerably smaller. For example, all credit unions together had $82.0

[3]In April 1980 the amount insured was raised from $40,000 to $100,000.

[4]U.S. Bureau of the Census, *Statistical Abstract of the United States:* 1985 (105th ed.), Washington, D.C., 1984, p. 491. Excludes federally chartered mutual savings banks.

billion of assets in 1983, while total commercial bank assets were over $2 trillion.[5]

Prior to the banking legislation of the early 1980s, these institutions primarily offered savings passbook accounts and certificates of deposit. Savings and loan associations and mutual savings banks in turn used their deposited funds mainly for mortgage loans, while credit unions made shorter-term loans for such purposes as home improvements and the purchase of durable consumer goods. Regulation of these institutions was under the jurisdiction of a number of agencies such as the Federal Home Loan Bank.

In more recent years, with changes in banking laws, these institutions have been permitted to offer checkable deposit accounts, which, as noted earlier, are part of the basic M1 money supply measurement. Regulations on the types of loans that these institutions are allowed to make have been loosened: some commercial and agricultural loans are permitted, and credit unions may make mortgage loans. In addition, some aspects of the operation of these institutions have been brought under Federal Reserve control.[6]

THE FEDERAL RESERVE SYSTEM

Federal Reserve System
Coordinates commercial banking operations, regulates some aspects of all depository institutions, and oversees the U.S. money supply.

Established in 1914, the **Federal Reserve** is the system that coordinates commercial banking operations, regulates some aspects of all depository institutions, and oversees the U.S. money supply. Congress created the Federal Reserve System, or the Fed, as it is often called, because money and banking practices had been in disarray. Previous to the creation of the Fed, there had been a lack of central organization, a hodgepodge of state and federal banking legislation, a history of questionable banking practices, and a recurrence of monetary panics.

The authority of the Federal Reserve is considerable. Primary among its responsibilities is the adjustment of the supply of money to meet the needs of the economy. Through its control of the size of the money supply, the Fed has the ability to influence the levels of employment and prices in the economy and to alleviate the problems of unemployment and inflation.

Organization of the Federal Reserve System

The Federal Reserve System is organized on both a functional and a geographic basis. Figure 7.1 outlines the important features in the system's functional structure.

Board of Governors
The seven-member board heading the Federal Reserve System; develops objectives concerning monetary policy and banking and other financial institutional practices; determines appropriate policies to meet those objectives.

At the head of the system is the **Board of Governors,** a group of seven members, each appointed by the president of the United States and confirmed by the Senate for a 14-year term. One member is designated by the

[5]Ibid. Includes only insured commercial banks.

[6]For further details on the information given on these institutions see: Colin D. Campbell and Rosemary G. Campbell, *An Introduction to Money and Banking,* 5th ed. (Hinsdale, Illinois: The Dryden Press, 1984), pp. 175–179.

Figure 7.1
Functional Structure of the Federal Reserve System

The Federal Reserve System is headed by the Board of Governors. Many system activities are carried out through the Federal Reserve Banks and their branches, and the Open Market Committee authorizes the buying and selling of government securities by the Federal Reserve.

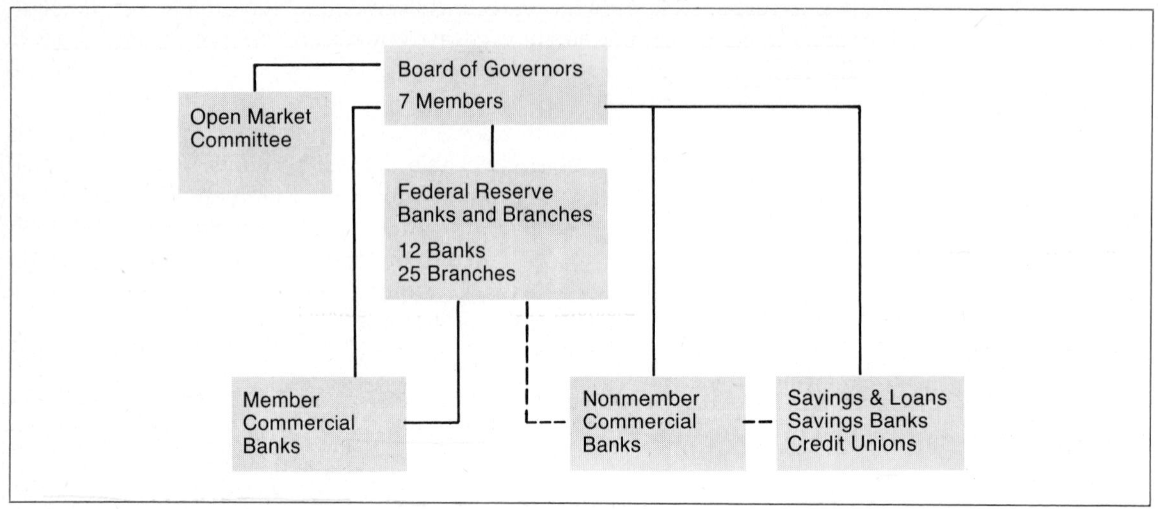

Open Market Committee
Oversees the buying and selling of government securities by the Federal Reserve System.

Federal Reserve Banks
Twelve banks, located in different parts of the country, that deal with commercial banks and other financial institutions.

president as chairman and serves as the spokesperson for Federal Reserve policy. The Board of Governors assumes duties and responsibilities typical of the head of any organization: it develops objectives consistent with its authority over money and banking practices, and it determines appropriate policies to meet those objectives. The **Open Market Committee,** which includes the Board of Governors among its members, carries out the most important procedure for money supply control: it authorizes the buying and selling of government securities by the Federal Reserve.[7]

The middle of the Federal Reserve System structure is made up of the 12 **Federal Reserve Banks** and their 25 branches, which are located throughout the country. These are not commercial banks, but instead deal with commercial banks and other financial institutions and perform a variety of functions that will be covered shortly. Each Federal Reserve Bank is an independent corporation with its own board of directors, and all 12 Federal Reserve Banks execute the same functions. The remainder of the Federal Reserve System is made up of member commercial banks, which have a direct relationship with a Federal Reserve Bank, and nonmember commercial banks,

[7]The operation of the Open Market Committee will be discussed in detail in Chapter Eight.

savings and loan associations, savings banks, and credit unions, which are influenced by some Federal Reserve policies and may depend on the Fed to perform some services for them.

The Fed is also organized geographically. The United States is divided into 12 Federal Reserve districts, each represented by a Federal Reserve Bank that is responsible for its own branch banks and the member commercial banks in its geographic area. Figure 7.2 illustrates the 12 Federal Reserve districts.

Figure 7.2
Federal Reserve Districts

The United States is divided into 12 Federal Reserve Districts, each with its own Federal Reserve Bank.

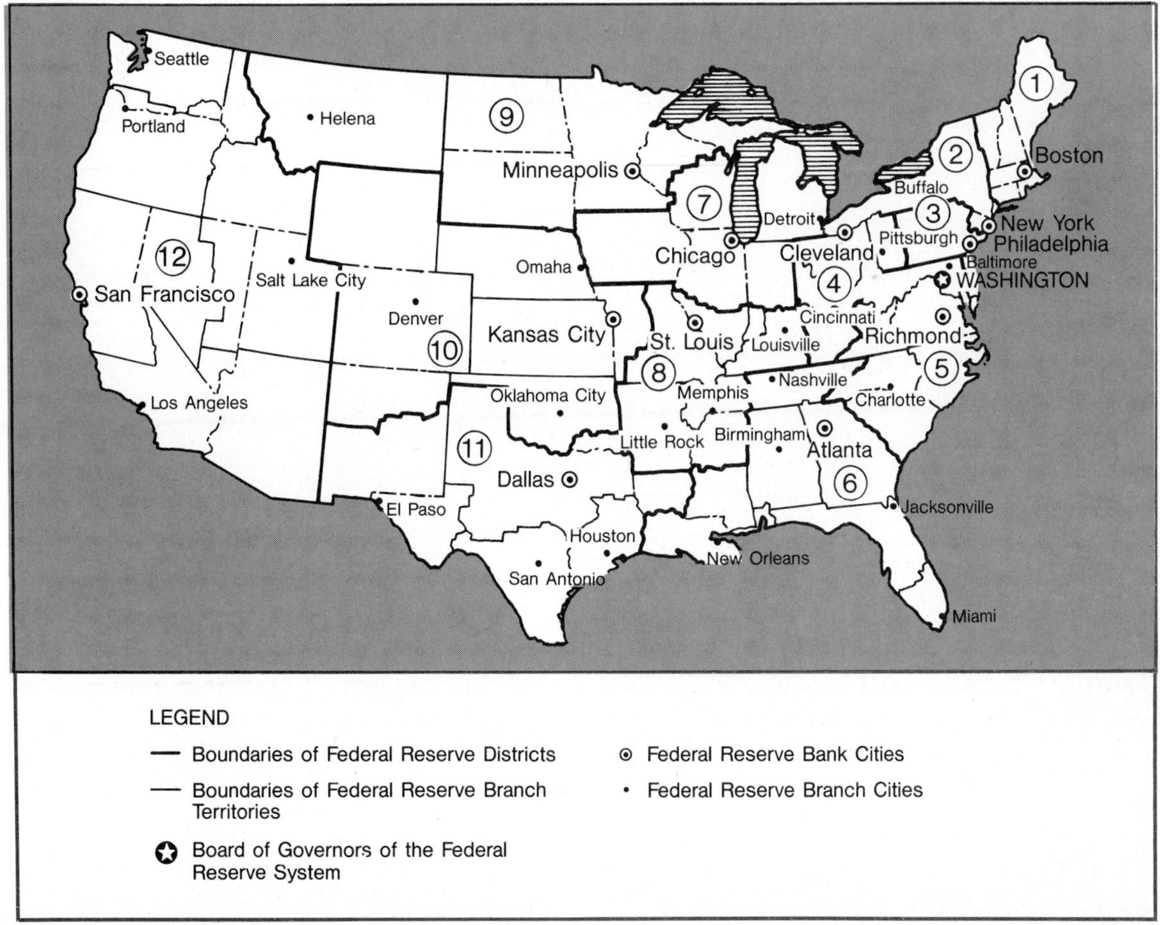

Source: *Federal Reserve Bulletin*, (December 1983), p. A105.

Functions of the Federal Reserve Banks

The Federal Reserve Banks and their branches perform a variety of functions that do not directly involve the typical commercial bank or savings and loan customer. In fact, there is little reason for the average individual or business manager to ever enter a Federal Reserve Bank.

One function of a Federal Reserve Bank is to supervise and examine member banks within its district. For this purpose, each Federal Reserve Bank employs a staff of examiners who periodically check the financial condition and compliance to system regulations of each member bank.

Reserve account
A deposit in the name of a financial institution held at a Federal Reserve Bank or other designated place.

A second function of a Federal Reserve Bank is to maintain reserve accounts for member commercial banks and for nonmember financial institutions that desire to keep their reserves at the Fed. A **reserve account** is a deposit in the name of a financial institution that is held at a Federal Reserve Bank or other designated place. While financial depository institutions must hold a minimum amount on reserve, the actual amount fluctuates daily and may exceed the minimum. Because no interest is earned on these reserves, financial institutions like to keep the balances in their accounts close to the minimum required.

Application 7.3
TREASURY OFFICIALS HAVE MONEY TO BURN BUT GENERALLY DON'T

How do you get rid of $20 billion?

The Federal Reserve System had to scrap that much paper cash last year because of wear and tear.

Naturally, American ingenuity has come up with enterprising ways of disposing of dilapidated dollars. A Salt Lake City man uses them to make artificial logs for fireplaces. A firm in Great Bend, Kans., sells shredded currency for use in oil-drilling lubricants. One entrepreneur has proposed making old money into wallpaper.

The wallpaper idea hasn't gained much currency. And imaginative new uses aren't enough, anyway, to soak up all the old money. To Treasury officials who have the ultimate responsibility, the disposal problem is serious. The average $1 bill wears out in 18 months, while larger bills take longer. Last year the government had to junk three billion bills weighing more than 3,000 tons.

"Burning is the best way to destroy currency because you get a very small amount of ash," says Rudy Villarreal, the Treasury's senior adviser for cash management. "But with antipollution laws, we had to stop."

Although bank tellers routinely pull bills when handling cash, most worn currency is yanked by high-speed electronic money-sorters at certain Federal Reserve banks. As a bill runs through the sorter, it is inspected electronically. When a worn bill is detected, it is usually sent to a shredder, which slices the bill into strips one-eighth of an inch wide. At some of these Fed banks, the old bills are then sent to a pulverizer and pounded into confetti.

Whether sliced or confettied, the money is then baled or bagged and thrown down chutes

Third, Federal Reserve Banks provide the means for putting coins and paper money into or out of circulation. Each bank maintains a warehouse of used and newly minted coins and paper in its vault (with extensive security arrangements). When the public desires to carry more money in the form of coins and paper, as happens, for example, around the Christmas holidays, more checks, drafts, and such are cashed. And as financial institutions require more coins and paper to convert their customers' deposits to currency, they order what they need from the Fed. When the Fed delivers cash to a financial institution, it is paid for out of that institution's reserve account. When less cash is desired by the public, as happens, for example, after the Christmas season, currency begins to build up at banks, savings and loans, and other depository institutions. These institutions may return their cash to the Fed and receive credit in their reserve accounts. Also, when currency is worn-out, it is retired by the Fed and, in the case of paper money, destroyed. Application 7.3 discusses some enterprising uses for worn-out cash.

A fourth function of Federal Reserve Banks is check clearing. Each day millions of checks are sorted through the Fed's machinery as financial institutions send in checks drawn on other institutions that they have received as deposits. These checks are sorted to be returned to the institutions on

---

to large trash containers. From there it is usually hauled off to landfills for burial or, infrequently, is burned by trash collectors with other paper products in special incinerators.

Or some resourceful soul finds a use for it. . . .

. . . [Thomas] Padavona owns Money Promotions Inc., which manufactures novelty and promotional items from shredded currency that is still plainly recognizable as such. Among his products is a framed money tree bearing the caption "Money Is the Root of All Evil."

Mr. Padavona's shredded currency, tons of it, is shipped from the Federal Reserve banks in San Francisco and Jacksonville, Fla., about once every three months. He is required by contract to accept all the dollars that the two banks dump. He pays about $10 a ton for the cache.

The artificial-log maker is David Holdaway of Salt Lake City, who buys his shredded currency from the Salt Lake Federal Reserve bank. Mr. Holdaway, a marble worker, makes the logs by hand, mixing hot wax and the shredded currency and pouring the mixture into a press that molds it into the proper size and shape. . . .

Davis Mud & Chemical Co. of Great Bend, Kans., a supplier of oil- and gas-drilling equipment, sells finely ground currency purchased from the Federal Reserve banks in Dallas and San Antonio for an important oilfield use. When an oil well is being drilled, the shaft and drill head must be lubricated to prevent friction. If the drill hits a geological fracture or a porous area, the lubricant is drained off and drilling must stop. So the confettied cash is mixed with the lubricant to form a thicker substance that is pumped down the drill shaft to fill in the fracture or porous area and allow the drilling to continue. Hence the old phrase "a driller, a dollar."

Source: Peter W. Barnes, "Treasury Officials Have Money to Burn But Generally Don't," *The Wall Street Journal,* August 20, 1980, p. 1. Reprinted by permission of *The Wall Street Journal,* which they were drawn. If a check is drawn on a bank or other financial institution within the same Federal Reserve district, the process is simple. However, if the check is drawn on an institution in another Federal Reserve district, it is forwarded to that district for further processing.

Check clearing causes a financial institution's reserve account to fluctuate. When a check that has been deposited at a financial institution is sent to the Fed for clearing, the full amount of that check is credited (added) to that institution's reserve account. When a check drawn on an institution (written by a customer with an account there) goes through the Fed clearing procedure, the full amount of that check is subtracted from that institution's reserve account. Thus, a financial institution's reserve account fluctuates daily, depending upon the value of checks deposited and written. It is not necessary that all checks go through the Federal Reserve Banks. Other clearing-house arrangements exist, especially where the Federal Reserve Bank is a far distance from financial institutions. Checks that are cleared through other than a Federal Reserve facility still have the same effect on a financial depository institution's reserve account: checks deposited increase reserves, and checks written by a bank's customers decrease reserves.

Finally, the Federal Reserve Banks act as fiscal agents for the U.S. government. In this regard, they perform a variety of chores, such as servicing the checking accounts of the federal government and handling many of the tasks associated with the maintenance of Treasury securities. For example, the Fed conducts the bid auctions for Treasury bills, notes, and bonds, maintains the necessary records for these securities, and prepares the interest payments.

Many of the functions performed by the Federal Reserve Banks are necessary for the smooth operation of the banking system. However, sometimes banks depend upon each other instead of the Fed for these operational tasks. In this case, banks set up a relationship called **correspondent banking.** Typically, in this arrangement a smaller bank keeps some deposits with a larger bank and receives advice and various services in return.

Correspondent banking
An interbank relationship involving deposits and various services.

The Federal Reserve and the Monetary Control Act of 1980

In March 1980 one of the most significant laws pertaining to money and banking in the United States was passed: Public Law 96-221, **The Depository Institutions Deregulation and Monetary Control Act of 1980.** This law substantially altered the traditional roles of many financial institutions and increased the control of the Federal Reserve.

The Depository Institutions Deregulation and Monetary Control Act of 1980
Legislation that altered the traditional roles of many financial institutions and increased the control of the Federal Reserve System.

Prior to this act there was a clear distinction between commercial banks on the one hand, and savings and loans, savings banks, and credit unions on the other. The traditional roles played in the economy by these organizations were changed by this act because it permitted all of these depository institutions to perform some nearly identical functions. One example of the similarity of functions permitted by this act is the ability of all depository institutions to offer interest-bearing checking accounts to individuals and nonprofit organizations. Before this new regulation, commercial banks were the only institutions offering checking accounts. The similarity between these organizations further expanded because, as noted earlier, the act changed the lending abilities of some of these depository institutions; for example, it authorized federal credit unions to make residential real estate loans and permitted savings and loan associations to issue credit cards.[8]

The Monetary Control Act also increased the authority of the Federal Reserve in monetary matters and added a relationship between the Federal Reserve and nonmember depository institutions that had not previously existed. Prior to the act, Federal Reserve activity centered primarily around its member banks. After the act, all depository institutions were able to keep reserves at a Federal Reserve Bank, and Federal Reserve control over these reserves was broadened. Also, the services of Federal Reserve Banks (such as check clearing) are now available to all member and nonmember institutions for a fee. Additionally, the Board of Governors determines the various documents that must be filed by these organizations for monetary reporting and control purposes.[9] Other important changes brought about by the Monetary Control Act will be covered in Chapter Eight.

SUMMARY

Modern economies as we know them could not exist without money. Money is anything generally acceptable as a means of payment for resources, goods, and services. It is an economy's medium of exchange. Without money to facilitate transactions, an economy would need to rely on a barter system. Money also serves as a measure of value and method for storing wealth and delaying payment. Given these functions of money, it is easy to see how severe and prolonged inflation could weaken the fabric of an economy.

There is disagreement as to exactly what constitutes the U.S. money supply. However, the most popular definition of the money supply is one that includes coins, paper money, nonbank-issued traveler's checks, demand deposits (checking accounts) at commercial banks, and other checkable deposits such as NOW and ATS accounts. This definition is referred to as M1. Demand deposits are a much larger component of the money supply than are the other components. Other definitions of the money supply, such as M2 and M3, are broader and include items such as time and savings deposits. For any year, the economy's money supply is smaller than the value of goods and services produced.

When money is backed by a tangible item such as gold or silver, the economy is on a commodity standard. The United States formerly had its money backed by gold but is now on a paper standard, where money is generally

---

[8]"Banking Act Makes Major Changes," *Economic Review,* Federal Reserve Bank of Atlanta (March–April 1980), pp. 4, 5.

[9]Charles R. McNeill (with some discussion by Denise M. Rechter), "The Depository Institutions Deregulation and Monetary Control Act of 1980," *Federal Reserve Bulletin* (June 1980), pp. 445–448.

backed by people's willingness to accept it and the strength of the economy. There are both advantages and disadvantages to a paper standard.

Financial institutions such as commercial banks, savings and loans, and credit unions play a critical role in the economy because they can create and destroy money through their loan-making activities. Commercial banks are the most important of these financial institutions because they keep and maintain the largest component of the money supply. Agencies such as federal and state banking authorities, the Federal Reserve, and the Federal Deposit Insurance Corporation regulate commercial banks.

The Federal Reserve System coordinates commercial banking operations, regulates some other financial institutions, and oversees the U.S. money supply. The system, which is organized geographically into 12 districts, is headed by the Board of Governors and carries out its most important procedures for money supply control through the Open Market Committee, which authorizes the Fed's purchase and sale of government securities. The 12 Federal Reserve Banks and their branches provide services to financial institutions rather than directly to the general public. The functions of the Federal Reserve Banks include supervising and examining the operations of member banks in their district, maintaining reserve accounts, circulating coins and paper money, clearing checks, and acting as fiscal agents for the federal government.

The Depository Institutions Deregulation and Monetary Control Act of 1980 altered the traditional roles of some financial institutions and increased the control of the Fed.

Key Terms and Concepts

Money
Medium of exchange
Barter system
Functions of money
Definitions of the money supply
Token money
Federal Reserve Notes
Demand deposits
Other checkable deposits
Commodity monetary standard
Paper monetary standard
Commercial bank
Dual banking system
National banks
State nonmember insured bank
Federal Deposit Insurance Corporation
Federal Reserve System
Board of Governors
Open Market Committee
Federal Reserve Bank
Organization of the Federal Reserve System
Reserve account
Correspondent banking
Monetary Control Act of 1980

Discussion and Review Questions

1. If demand deposits are a medium of exchange, and if a medium of exchange is generally acceptable as payment for goods and services, why is it sometimes so hard to cash a check?
2. Can you make an argument for returning the U.S. economy to a commodity standard based on gold and/or silver? More generally, under what circumstances might a commodity standard be preferable to a paper standard?
3. What would happen to an economy where: (a) the supply of money never changed over a long period of time; (b) the supply of money grew very rapidly over a period of several years; and (c) the supply of money erratically expanded and contracted?
4. The First National Bank of Anytown had $500,000 in its reserve account at the Fed one morning. Later that morning $250,000 in checks that had been deposited at the Bank of Anytown were processed at the Fed. Anytown also ordered $100,000 in currency to cash checks. Later that day $300,000 worth of checks written by the bank's customers cleared through the Fed. How much did the First National Bank of Anytown have in its reserve account at the Fed at the end of the day?
5. There are several definitions for the supply of money. How do these various definitions differ from one another? With money so important to the economy, why do you think we cannot settle on one definition and use it in all cases?
6. What is the function of the Board of Governors and of the Open Market Committee of the Federal Reserve System? What are the functions of the Federal Reserve Banks? How has the Depository Institutions Deregulation and Monetary Control Act of 1980 affected the span of control of the Federal Reserve System?
7. What are the various classifications of commercial banks and their regulating agencies? Why are commercial banks subject to a large amount of regulation?

Selected Readings

Colin D. Campbell and Rosemary G. Campbell, *An Introduction to Money and Banking* (Hinsdale, Illinois: The Dryden Press, 1984). A basic textbook for a money and banking course. The authors cover such topics as the functions of money, commercial banking, the Federal Reserve System, monetary theory, inflation, and international monetary considerations.

John Kenneth Galbraith, *Money: Whence It Came, Where It Went* (Boston: Houghton Mifflin Co., 1975). A critical look at money, banking, monetary policy, and fiscal policy through the years.

Martin Mayer, "The Banking Story," *American Heritage* (April/May 1984), pp. 26–35. A brief history of banking in the United States.

Charles R. McNeill (with some discussion by Denise M. Rechter), "The Depository Institutions Deregulation and Monetary Control Act of 1980," ***Federal Reserve Bulletin*** **(June 1980), pp. 444–453.** A comprehensive treatment of the significant banking legislation passed in March 1980.

Dale K. Osborne, "Ten Approaches to the Definition of Money," ***Economic Review,*** **Federal Reserve Bank of Dallas (March 1984), pp. 1–23.** A critical evaluation of several approaches to the definition of money.

U.S. Commission on the Role of Gold in the Domestic and International Monetary Systems, "Ch. 2: The Past Role of Gold in the U.S. Monetary System," and "Ch. 3: Types of Monetary Standards," ***Report to the Congress of the Commission on the Role of Gold in the Domestic and International Monetary Systems,*** **Vol. 1 (March 1982), pp. 51–133.** Chapters cover the role of gold in the U.S. economy from 1834 to 1981 and alternative monetary standards.

8 MONEY CREATION, MONETARY THEORY, AND MONETARY POLICY

Chapter Objectives

1. To explain the relationship between the money supply and the level of economic activity.
2. To explain how money is created and destroyed through the loan-making activities of financial depository institutions.
3. To introduce the multiple expansion of money.
4. To explain the role of the interest rate in encouraging or discouraging borrowing from financial depository institutions.
5. To show how interest rates are affected by changes in financial depository institutions' excess reserves.
6. To define monetary policy and explain the operation of the major tools for carrying out monetary policy by the Federal Reserve.
7. To show the relationship between government borrowing to cover deficit spending and monetary policy.
8. To critically evaluate monetary policy.

Chapter Seven presented the institutional groundwork in three important areas in the U.S. economy: money, financial institutions, and the Federal Reserve System. It was pointed out that the United States is on a paper monetary standard and that control over the size of the money supply is of utmost importance when an economy is on such a standard. Control is a concern because there is a significant relationship between an economy's supply of money and its levels of output, income, employment, and prices: a change in the quantity of money in an economy can lead to a change in its overall level of activity. Because of this, altering a nation's money supply is an important method for trying to attain the macroeconomic objectives of full production and economic growth, full employment, and price stability. This method for accomplishing the macroeconomic goals is called monetary policy and is carried out by the Federal Reserve.

This chapter expands on Chapter Seven by studying the effect of the money supply on the macroeconomy, and the operation of monetary policy. First, a general explanation of how the money supply influences output and prices is presented. Next, the process of increasing or decreasing the supply of money by financial institutions is covered. Third, an explanation is developed of how changes in financial institutions' abilities to lend affect interest rates, borrowing, and the level of total spending. And finally, the tools of monetary policy are introduced and their use by the Federal Reserve to alter and control the supply of money to accomplish the macroeconomic objectives is explained.

THE MONEY SUPPLY AND THE LEVEL OF ECONOMIC ACTIVITY

The primary determinant of the overall level of activity in an economy is the level of total spending by businesses, households, government units, and foreign buyers. The importance of total spending, or aggregate demand, was highlighted in Chapter Five. An increase in total spending leads to an increase in output, income, and employment if the economy is at less than full employment. If the economy is at or near full employment, increased spending leads to an increase in the general level of prices. Decreases in spending result in a reduction in output, income, and employment, and if the economy is at or near full employment, in a dampening of inflationary pressure.

The ability of households and businesses to spend is related to the amount of money in the economy. More spending is generated when the money supply is increased, and spending falls when the money supply is decreased. Chapter Seven stated that money is created (the money supply is increased) when financial institutions such as commercial banks make loans. Because loans are taken out by households to finance the purchase of such things as new homes, automobiles, and appliances, and by businesses to invest in machinery, equipment, and the like, increased loan making results in more spending.[1] Thus, increases in loans by commercial banks and other depository institutions mean a larger money supply and more spending. When loan making falls, the money supply is decreased and spending declines.

---

[1]Banks and other financial institutions also make loans to the government when they purchase government securities for their portfolios.

The Equation of Exchange

The importance of money for total spending and the relationship of the supply of money to the overall level of economic activity is summarized in the **equation of exchange:**

Equation of exchange Illustrates how changes in the supply of money (M) influence the level of prices (P) and/or the total output of goods and services (Q).

$$MV = PQ.$$

On the left-hand side of this equation, M represents the supply of money in the economy and V the velocity, which is the number of times each dollar is spent in a year. (Recall from Chapter Seven that the economy's money supply is much less than GNP.) The larger the supply of money in the economy, the greater is the value of M; the more frequently each dollar is spent per year, the higher is the velocity and the greater is the value of V. On the right-hand side of the equation, P represents the level of prices and Q the actual output of goods and services.

MV, the supply of money multiplied by the number of times it is spent each year, can be viewed as total spending in the economy. PQ, the price level multiplied by the actual output of goods and services, can be interpreted as the dollar value of output produced in the economy, or current GNP. Since the circular flow model tells us that a given level of spending brings forth an output of equal value, we know that MV and PQ are equal.[2] Thus, if the supply of money were $600 billion and velocity were 5, MV (or total spending) would equal $3 trillion, as would PQ (the value of the economy's output).

What happens to the level of economic activity when the supply of money changes? The equation of exchange helps answer this question. To keep matters simple and clear, let us assume that the velocity of money does not change. That is, let V be constant in the equation of exchange.[3]

Enlarging the supply of money causes the left-hand side of the equation of exchange (total spending) to increase. Since the two sides must be equal, this means that the right-hand side of the equation (dollar value of output) must also increase by the same amount. If the economy were experiencing unemployment and operating below full production, you would expect the increase in the value of output to come primarily in the form of an expansion

---

[2]Some economists write the equation of exchange as an identity: $MV \equiv PQ$.

[3]In reality, the velocity of money (M1) has been changing, but the change has been gradually upward over the long run. During the last few decades the average annual increase in the M1 velocity has been approximately 3 percent. Thus, in looking at the effect on the economy of increasing or decreasing the money supply *at any particular moment in time,* the assumption that V is fixed is appropriate. It is easy to understand why V is fairly constant over short periods of time when one considers that there is little variation from month to month in the frequency with which a paycheck is received and the time pattern in which major payments are made. For more on the velocity of money, see: Colin D. Campbell and Rosemary G. Campbell, *An Introduction to Money and Banking,* 5th ed. (Hinsdale, Illinois: The Dryden Press, 1984), pp. 297–303.

in production and employment. That is, you would expect the increase in the right-hand side of the equation of exchange to come mainly in the Q term. However, if the economy were at or near full employment, production and employment would be at or near their upper limits. If the money supply were to increase under these circumstances, Q in the equation of exchange could go up very little, if at all. In this case, an increase in the supply of money would lead primarily to an increase in the price level, the P term, or to inflation.

A decrease in the supply of money causes a reduction in total expenditures, the left-hand side of the equation of exchange. This, in turn, causes a decrease in the dollar value of output, the right-hand side of the equation. When a decrease in the money supply causes a reduction in total expenditures, it results in a decrease in Q, or employment and income. P, or the price level, usually does not fall because businesses in general respond to decreases in spending by cutting production, rather than by lowering price. However, if the economy were operating at or near full employment and experiencing inflationary pressure, a decrease in the money supply would dampen some of that pressure by reducing total spending.

In summary, the relationship between total spending and the level of economic activity is influenced by changes in the economy's supply of money. Increasing the money supply facilitates spending and contributes to an expansion of economic activity. Whether this leads to increased production and employment or to inflation depends in large part on how close the economy is to full employment. Decreasing the supply of money inhibits the spending ability of businesses and households and in turn slows the level of economic activity.

MONEY CREATION

Because changes in the supply of money affect the economy's levels of output, employment, and prices, it is important to understand how the money supply is increased and decreased. In Chapter Seven it was noted that some financial institutions play a critical role in the economy because they can create and destroy money through their loan-making activities. Stated simply, money is created when these institutions make loans, and money is destroyed when those loans are repaid. Although these loan-making institutions include savings and loan associations, savings banks, and credit unions, the primary organizations engaged in money creation and destruction are commercial banks.

The Process of Money Creation

Actual legal reserves A financial depository institution's reserve account plus its vault cash.

Every financial depository institution has two assets that it classifies as its **actual legal reserves:** the institution's reserve account (which was introduced in Chapter Seven) and its vault cash.[4] A commercial bank that belongs to the Federal Reserve System must keep its reserve account at its Federal Reserve Bank. A nonmember institution may choose to keep its reserve account at the Fed or at a correspondent institution that will pass it through to the Fed.[5]

Reserve requirement
A specific percentage of deposits that a financial depository institution must keep as actual legal reserves.

These depository institutions also have a reserve requirement that they must honor. This **reserve requirement** is a specific percentage of deposits that must be kept as actual legal reserves. For example, a reserve requirement of 10 percent on demand deposits means that a bank must have an amount on reserve equal to 10 percent of the value of the demand deposits it is holding. If a bank has $8,000,000 in checking accounts and a 10 percent reserve requirement, it must have at least $800,000 (.10 × $8,000,000) in actual legal reserves. The amount of actual legal reserves that a financial depository institution must keep to back its deposits is called its **required reserves.**

Required reserves
The amount of actual legal reserves that a financial depository institution must keep to back its deposits.

Every day each depository institution must make several calculations pertaining to its deposits and reserves. First, it must compute the value of deposits held in the institution that day. Second, it must calculate its required reserves. And, third, it must ascertain how much it has in actual legal reserves. (Remember — Chapter Seven pointed out that reserves fluctuate daily due to check clearing and periodically due to currency orders and returns.) In short, the institution must determine what it needs to have and what it actually does have on reserve.

These calculations permit an institution to determine its excess reserves. **Excess reserves** are the institution's actual legal reserves minus its required reserves, or reserves over and above those that the institution must maintain. Assume that the Hometown Bank, which has a reserve requirement of 10 percent, calculates its demand deposits to be $6,000,000. This means that the bank's required reserves are $600,000 (.10 × $6,000,000). Assume further that Hometown Bank computes its actual legal reserves to be $1,000,000. Since excess reserves are actual legal reserves ($1,000,000) minus required reserves ($600,000), Hometown Bank has excess reserves of $400,000. That is, the bank has $400,000 on reserve that it need not keep there. Table 8.1 summarizes these calculations.

Excess reserves
Reserves of a financial depository institution over and above the amount it is required to maintain in actual legal reserves; actual legal reserves minus required reserves.

Excess reserves are important because they are the foundation for an institution's loan-making abilities. Very simply, *a depository institution can make new loans up to the value of its excess reserves.* Why is this so? When a bank, for example, makes a loan to a business or an individual, it usually arranges to give the borrower those funds in either a cashier's check or through a

---

[4]Vault cash is all of the cash in the institution's vault and cash drawers. It does not include anything customers may have in their safe deposit boxes.

[5]A correspondent institution may be another depository institution holding required reserves at the Fed, a Federal Home Loan Bank, or the National Credit Union Administration Central Liquidity Facility. See: Board of Governors of the Federal Reserve, Press Release, August 15, 1980, taken from Regulation D, p. 5.

Table 8.1
Hometown Bank's Reserve Calculations

A financial depository institution's excess reserves are equal to its actual legal reserves minus its required reserves.

Actual legal reserves =	$1,000,000	
−Required reserves =	$ 600,000	(.10 × $6,000,000)
Excess reserves =	$ 400,000	

direct deposit of the loan into the borrower's checking account. In either case, when the borrower spends these loaned funds and the check for this spending is deposited in another institution and cleared through the check clearing machinery, the lending bank loses reserves. For example, if Hometown Bank loans Joe Smith $20,000 for a delivery van, it will lose $20,000 in reserves when Joe Smith's check for the van is deposited by the seller in another institution and cleared through the check clearing machinery.[6]

Because an institution loses reserves when a loan is spent, it must be careful to make loans only up to the value of its excess reserves in order to meet reserve requirements. Return to the example of Hometown Bank, which had $1,000,000 in actual legal reserves, $600,000 in required reserves, and $400,000 in excess reserves. Given these figures, Hometown Bank could make new loans of up to $400,000. If, however, Hometown Bank made loans of over $400,000, say, $450,000, its $1,000,000 in actual legal reserves would drop to $550,000 when the checks written against the loans were cleared. In this case, Hometown Bank would be short on its required reserves. Clearly, an institution can make new loans only up to the amount of its excess reserves.

In making a loan, an institution does *not* take away one customer's money to give to another. Those who hold money at the institution (in demand deposits, negotiable orders of withdrawal, automatic transfer service accounts, and such) do not have their deposits altered; they retain all of their account balances and are free to spend their money when they so desire. Instead, in making a loan a financial institution creates new deposits or new money; that is, it provides dollars for spending that were not in the economy before the loan was made. If a bank maintains $1 million in demand deposits and makes new loans of $400,000, then the $1 million in demand deposits is still money, but it has been supplemented by the creation of an additional $400,000.

How is money destroyed? When a loan is repaid, money is destroyed. Repayment of a loan withdraws money from the economy by returning it to the lending institution, where it becomes reserves. Until the institution

[6]When a financial institution lends money to the U.S. government by buying a Treasury security, it pays for that security out of its reserve account, causing the reserve account to decrease. Thus, the effect on reserves from lending to households, businesses, or the government is the same.

makes another loan based on these reserves, this money has disappeared from the system. Application 8.1 gives some typical questions and answers about reserves and loans.

It should be clear by now that excess reserves form the basis for loan making and thus for changing the money supply. If the supply of money is to be controlled, it can be done through altering the amount of excess reserves in depository institutions. An increase in excess reserves is appropriate to increase the money supply, and a decrease in excess reserves is appropriate to decrease the money supply.

The Multiple Expansion of Money

Thus far we have dealt with the money-creating ability of a single depository institution. However, to understand the potential impact of changes in reserves on money creation and destruction, all such institutions must be considered together as a system. When the system as a whole is studied, one can observe that changes in excess reserves in the system cause a multiplier effect on the creation and destruction of money. That is, an initial increase in excess reserves in the system will cause the money supply to increase by some multiple of the increase in excess reserves, and an initial decrease in excess reserves in the system will cause the money supply to shrink by some multiple of that decrease. The following example illustrates this principle.

Assume that Hometown Bank experiences a $1,000 increase in excess reserves because of a policy change by the monetary authorities. (Different

Application 8.1
QUESTIONS AND ANSWERS ABOUT RESERVES AND LOANS

Q: Do all financial institutions have the same reserve requirement?

A: There are uniform reserve requirements on all financial depository institutions, although the actual percentage requirements differ by type of account (for example, checkable versus time). These requirements are given in Table 8.4 on page 240.

Q: What happens if an institution does not meet its reserve requirement?

A: First of all, for requirement purposes, depository institutions average their deposits and reserves over a period of time (currently two weeks) rather than every day. This permits an institution with a reserve deficiency on one day to correct it within the next few days and still meet its requirement. If an institution has not met its reserve requirement on the average over its given time period, it can usually borrow the needed reserves.

Q: From whom can banks borrow reserves?

methods for carrying out these policy changes will be discussed shortly.) These new excess reserves permit Hometown Bank to make a new loan of $1,000, which we will assume goes to a borrower named Mary Jones. This transaction is shown in Table 8.2. Suppose Mary Jones uses her $1,000 loan to purchase stereo equipment and writes out a check in that amount to the seller, who deposits it in the seller's account at Bank B. If Bank B, as well as each other bank in this example, has a reserve requirement of 10 percent, then that $1,000 deposit gives Bank B actual legal reserves of $1,000, of which $100 are required reserves and $900 are excess reserves (remember — check deposits, when cleared, increase a bank's reserves). On the basis of this check, Bank B can now make a new loan of $900.

Assume that Sam Stone borrows $900 from Bank B for a used car. The car dealer takes Stone's check for that amount and deposits it in the dealer's account at Bank C, where it brings Bank C $900 in actual legal reserves, of which $90 are required reserves and $810 are excess reserves. On the basis of this $900 deposit, Bank C can now make a new loan of $810. Someone can now borrow $810 from Bank C, and it will be eventually deposited in Bank D, and on and on. Table 8.2 carries this example through several more rounds, showing how each succeeding bank can make new loans. It is extremely important to realize that none of these loans could have been made without the initial increase in excess reserves at Hometown Bank. It is this increase in excess reserves that caused other banks to experience an increase in their excess reserves.[7]

[7]The situation would be the same if any of these banks received multiple deposits: that is, if Hometown Bank or Bank B, C, or so on were repeated on the list in Table 8.2.

A: Banks can borrow reserves from a Federal Reserve Bank or from other banks through the federal funds market. In the federal funds market, banks lend excess reserves to other banks, usually for a period of one day. Banks borrow in the federal funds market to cover reserve deficiencies or to obtain additional reserves with which to make loans.

Q: What is the prime rate, and who determines it?

A: The prime rate is the interest rate a commercial bank charges its "best" customers for short-term commercial and industrial loans; it is the bank's lowest rate on these types of loans. The prime rate is set by each individual bank but is influenced by general credit conditions. The media typically announce changes in the prime rates of major banks or banks of local interest. Smaller banks frequently follow changes in the prime rate made by major banks.

Source: Colin D. Campbell and Rosemary G. Campbell, *An Introduction to Money and Banking*, 5th ed. (Hinsdale, Illinois: The Dryden Press, 1984), pp. 12, 99, 114, 136, 206, 249.

Table 8.2
Multiple Expansion of Money (10% Reserve Requirement)

An increase in excess reserves in the system causes the money supply to increase by a multiple of the initial excess reserve change.

	Demand Deposits	Actual Legal Reserves	Required Reserves	Excess Reserves	Loans
Hometown Bank				$1,000.00	$ 1,000.00
Bank B	$ 1,000.00	$1,000.00	$100.00	900.00	900.00
Bank C	900.00	900.00	90.00	810.00	810.00
Bank D	810.00	810.00	81.00	729.00	729.00
Bank E	729.00	729.00	72.90	656.10	656.10
Bank F	656.10	656.10	65.61	590.49	590.49
Bank G	590.49	590.49	59.05	531.44	531.44
Bank H	531.44	531.44	53.14	478.30	478.30
Bank I	478.30	478.30	47.83	430.47	430.47
Bank J	430.47	430.47	43.05	387.42	387.42
Bank K	387.42	387.42	38.74	348.68	348.68
Bank L	348.68	348.68	34.87	313.81	313.81
Bank M	313.81	313.81	31.38	282.43	282.43
Bank N	282.43	282.43	28.24	254.19	254.19
Bank O	254.19	254.19	25.42	228.77	228.77
Bank P	228.77	228.77	22.88	205.89	205.89
Bank Q	205.89	205.89	20.59	185.30	185.30
Banks R, S, T . . .	. . .	. . .	. . .	. . .	. . .
Total	$10,000.00				$10,000.00

When the full effect of this initial change in excess reserves is carried through the system, all of the new loans can be added together to determine the total amount of money created. It is apparent that the change in the money supply is some multiple of the initial change in excess reserves. In Table 8.2 a $10,000 increase in the money supply has resulted from a $1,000 increase in excess reserves. In this case there has been a **money multiplier** of 10.

Money multiplier
The multiple by which an initial change in excess reserves in the system can change the money supply.

The size of the money multiplier depends upon the reserve requirement. The money multiplier itself is the reciprocal of the reserve requirement.[8] A 10 percent (1/10) reserve requirement means a multiplier of 10/1 or 10; a 25 percent (1/4) requirement means a multiplier of 4; and a 15 percent (3/20) requirement yields a multiplier of 20/3 or 6.67. The multiplier times the initial change in excess reserves gives the resulting total change in the money supply. An initial increase in the banking system of $8 million in excess reserves with a reserve requirement of 20 percent (multiplier of 5) could generate $40 million of new money, and an $8 million decrease in

[8]The reciprocal of a fraction is the fraction "flipped over." The reciprocal of 1/10 is 10/1 or 10; of 1/4 is 4/1 or 4.

excess reserves with a 10 percent reserve requirement could decrease the money supply by $80 million. The multiplier can work in either direction: increases or decreases in excess reserves are subject to its effect.

The examples here are simplistic versions of the outcome of the money multiplier. In reality, the multiple expansion resulting from a change in reserves can be altered or weakened by such actions as converting some portion of the deposits to cash, putting some portion into savings accounts, or having institutions lend less than the maximum amounts available.

EXCESS RESERVES, INTEREST RATES, AND THE LEVEL OF SPENDING

We know that changes in the money supply are executed through changes in loan making by depository financial institutions. We also know that increases in loan making lead to increases in spending and, ultimately, to increases in output and employment, or to increases in prices if the economy is at or near full employment. Decreases in loan making lead to decreases in spending and decreases in the level of economic activity. This relationship between lending, the money supply, spending, and economic activity is summarized in Table 8.3.

When a business or household takes out a loan with a depository institution, it borrows because it chooses to, not because it has been coerced into doing so by the institution. For this reason, simply having excess reserves available in these institutions does not ensure that money will be created through borrowing. This leads to two important questions. If borrowing is voluntary, how can businesses and households be stimulated to take out loans in situations where an increase in the money supply and spending would help reduce unemployment? And, how can businesses and households be encouraged to borrow less when the money supply should be reduced to dampen inflationary pressures?

Table 8.3
Relationship Between Loan Making, the Money Supply, Spending, and the Level of Economic Activity

Changes in loan making lead to changes in spending, which in turn affect the levels of output, employment, and/or prices.

Increases in the Money Supply	Decreases in the Money Supply
Increases in the money supply occur when there are increases in lending by depository financial institutions.	Decreases in the money supply occur when there are reductions in lending by depository financial institutions.
↓	↓
Increased loan making leads to increased spending.	Decreased loan making leads to decreased spending.
↓	↓
Increased spending leads to an increase in output and employment if the economy is at less than full employment and/or an increase in the price level if the economy is near or at full employment.	Decreased spending leads to a decrease in output and employment, and a reduction of inflationary pressure if the economy is near or at full employment.

Interest rate
The price that is paid to borrow money; is a percentage of the amount borrowed.

The answers are found in the role performed by the **interest rate,** the price that must be paid to borrow money. If $1,000 were borrowed for one year at an interest rate of 8 percent, at the end of the year the borrower would have to repay the $1,000 that was loaned plus $80 in interest, or a total of $1,080. If the interest rate were 12 percent, at the end of one year the borrower would have to repay $1,120. Thus, the higher the rate of interest, the greater the price that must be paid to borrow money. Since borrowed money is like any good or service subject to the Law of Demand (discussed in Chapter Three), the quantity of funds demanded for borrowing falls as the interest rate rises and rises as the interest rate falls.

Businesses are particularly sensitive to the interest rate when making their decisions about borrowing for investment spending.[9] The cost of borrowing to finance machinery, equipment, construction, and so forth must be

[9]Recall the discussion of this point in Chapter Five on page 139–140 and in Application 5.1.

Application 8.2
THE EFFECTS OF INTEREST RATES ON SPENDING DECISIONS

Interest rates are normally an arcane subject, thought to be of passionate concern only to bankers and other financiers, and not fully understood even by them. Yet one way or another interest rates are paid by everyone who borrows money, which in the modern credit economy means just about everyone, period. Interest rates help to determine whether a business can hire workers, whether a consumer can afford his or her dream house, whether a farmer can plant seed. If they escaped the front-page headlines and the TV news in the past, that was because rates usually changed only slowly and by small amounts.

No more. In the past three years [before 1982], interest rates have shot up higher than anyone could have imagined earlier, and they have suddenly become Topic A in the beleaguered American economy. . . . Expensive and scarce money has begun driving homebuilders, auto dealers and businessmen from every walk of life out of business, and in such numbers that bankruptcies around the country are beginning to rival those of the Great Depression. The cost of money is crimping the investment that U.S. industry needs to make to become more productive. . . .

[Below are some examples of the impact interest rates can have on the operations of businesses and decisions of managers.]

Autos. Sales of U.S.–made cars plunged to 6.2 million in 1981, the lowest level in 20 years. Signs of a vicious circle are appearing. Interest rates on auto loans, averaging 16%, discourage buyers, and unsold cars start piling up on dealer lots. Meanwhile, the dealers have to borrow at rates generally two or three percentage points above the prime to support the bulging inventory. Not only has that burden alone helped to drive some 3,200 dealers, or roughly one in eight, into bankruptcy in the past 2½ years, but the survivors, in order to trim costs, have now begun ordering fewer and fewer models for their showrooms. That cuts down the volume of walk-in trade and reduces sales still further. . . .

Consumer Buying. In the late 1970s, consumer installment debt outstanding jumped by any-

recovered if the investment is to break even, much less earn a profit. As the interest rate goes up, certain investment projects that would have been profitable at lower rates become unprofitable and are dropped from consideration. This in turn leads to a drop in the amount of funds demanded to finance such projects. The effects of interest rates on decision making are discussed in Application 8.2.

The Determination of Interest Rates on Loans

How is the interest rate determined for loans made by depository financial institutions? What causes it to change? The interest rate is determined in the same way other prices are determined — through the interaction of demand and supply.

The demand for loans by businesses and households from financial institutions is equal to the different amounts that they plan to borrow at different interest rates. A hypothetical demand for loans is given in Figure 8.1 by the

---

where from $35 billion to $43 billion annually, intensifying the decade-long inflation. But last year [1981], debt expanded by only $19.6 billion, a slowdown that is itself proving disruptive. The University of Michigan's most recent quarterly survey of consumer attitudes, conducted late last year, leaves little doubt as to why: exorbitant interest rates.

Though consumers are popularly believed to have only a vague notion of the amount of interest that they pay on credit purchases, Survey Director Richard T. Curtin found them actually to be quite well informed. His researchers asked those who were postponing purchases what interest rate they thought they would pay if they did buy. Their answers averaged 17.5% — which was almost exactly right. How much would they be willing to pay? Average answer: 11.9%.

Retailers glumly affirm that this wariness is holding down sales of all sorts of goods. In Boston, Dennis Gedzuin, manager of The Riverboat, a women's clothing store, estimates that charge-card purchases dropped by a third at his store last year. . . .

Agriculture. Farmers traditionally borrow heavily in order, among other things, to finance planting and machinery purchases, paying off the loans when they sell their crops. For some, the costs are becoming ruinous. In northwest Wisconsin, Walter Betzel grossed $100,000 last year from his 350 acres of corn and oats and his 30 milk cows. Some $19,000 of the amount went right off the top for interest payments. . . .

Interest costs have set off a kind of chain reaction in the farm lands. Food processors rely on short-term financing to stock up on the raw goods that they package, can and otherwise process into food. But to hold down interest costs, the processors are now slashing inventories and buying less from their farmer-suppliers. Those cutbacks are coming precisely when the farmers need every penny to pay their interest charges. The squeeze on the farmers is forcing more and more of them to try to cut back on their interest burdens, and many are doing so by postponing the purchase of tractors, combines and other farm equipment. The retrenching simply passes the interest-rate misery on to the farm-equipment manufacturers, which are starting to buckle under their own swelling inventories. . . .

Source: George J. Church, "Paying More for Money," *Time*, March 8, 1982, pp. 74, 79–81.

Figure 8.1
Determining the Interest Rate for Loans

The interest rate for loans is determined by the demand for and supply of funds for loans.

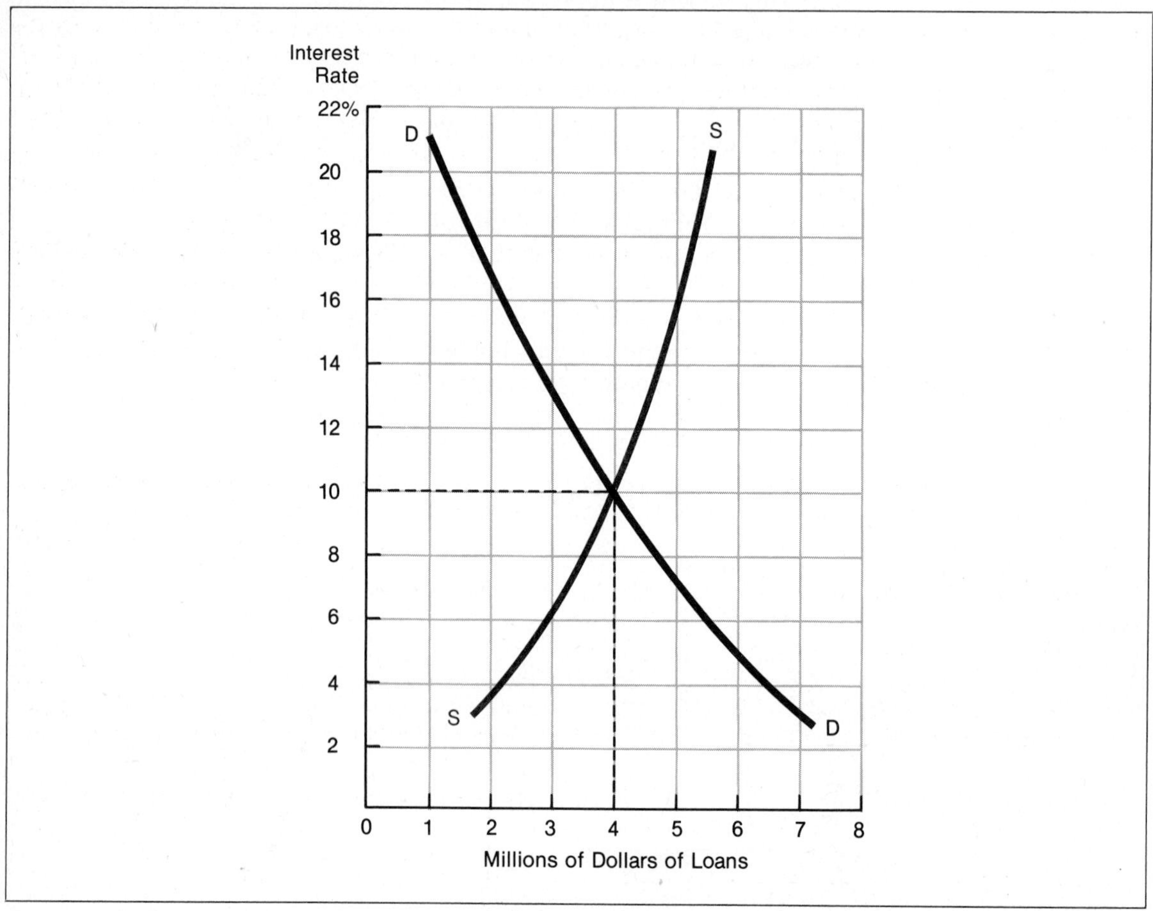

demand curve D. As with other demand curves, D in Figure 8.1 slopes downward to indicate an inverse relationship between the amount of planned borrowing and the interest rate.

On the other side of the transaction, the amount of loans that depository institutions are willing to make varies directly with the interest rate. Because a financial institution earns its profit from loan making and other sources, it is motivated to use excess reserves in the manner that brings the highest return. If the interest rate it can earn on loans is low, a bank or other depository institution will probably prefer converting some of its excess reserves to higher yielding assets. But when the institution can obtain a high interest rate for loaning funds, it will convert more of its excess reserves to loans. S in Figure 8.1 gives a hypothetical supply of loans by financial institutions.

Given D and S in Figure 8.1, the interest rate that emerges would be 10 percent, with $4 million in loans resulting. This equilibrium condition, however, could change. Since the basis for a depository institution's lending ability is excess reserves, a change in excess reserves will shift the supply curve and thereby alter the equilibrium price and quantity. For example, if excess reserves are decreased, institutions can make fewer loans and the supply of loans decreases. This is shown in Figure 8.2a as a shift in the supply curve to the left from S1 to S2. As a result of this decrease in reserves, the interest rate rises to 14 percent in Figure 8.2a, and the quantity of loans made declines to $3 million. In other words, a decrease in excess reserves causes interest rates to rise and the amount of loans made to fall.

An increase in excess reserves causes the supply of loans to increase and the supply curve to shift to the right as shown in Figure 8.2b. When S1 is shifted to S2 in Figure 8.2b, the interest rate falls to 6 percent, and loans

Figure 8.2
Effect of Changes in Excess Reserves on the Interest Rate and the Quantity of Loans

A decrease in excess reserves in the system will cause interest rates to rise and the amount of loans granted to fall. An increase in excess reserves will cause interest rates to fall and the amount of loans granted to rise.

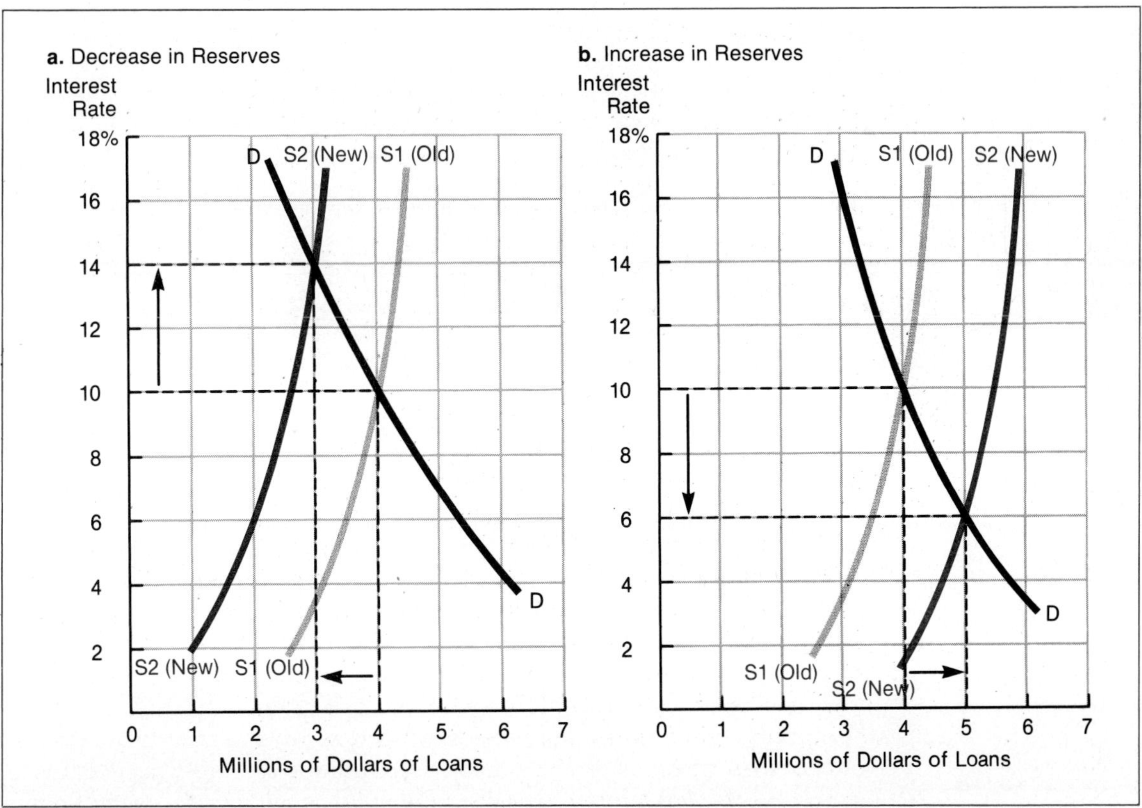

increase to $5 million. Thus, an increase in excess reserves decreases the interest rate and increases the amount of loans made.

Figure 8.3 extends the relationship between loan making, the money supply, spending, and the level of economic activity summarized in Table 8.3, by including excess reserves and the interest rate.

An additional note of clarification about interest rates is in order. Although we frequently use the expression "the interest rate," in reality no singular interest rate exists. Instead, there are many different types of markets in which money is borrowed and lent: markets for home mortgages, secured corporate loans, student loans, and personal auto loans, for example. The interest rates in these markets differ because of dissimilarities in risk, loan size, length of repayment, and other factors. Therefore, when we refer to a rise in the interest rate because of declining excess reserves, we mean that interest rates *in general* are rising. Likewise, a fall in the interest rate due to increasing excess reserves in the system means that interest rates *in general* are falling.

THE FEDERAL RESERVE AND MONETARY POLICY

Since changes in loans result from changes in excess reserves, it is obvious that control over the money supply can be exerted through control over excess reserves. Thus, it should come as no surprise that the Federal Reserve, whose responsibility it is to oversee and change the money supply, carries out this charge by altering excess reserves in the banking and financial institutions system. When the Fed acts to deliberately change excess reserves

Figure 8.3
Relationship between Excess Reserves, the Interest Rate, Loan Making, and the Level of Economic Activity

Changes in the level of excess reserves in the system influence institutions' lending abilities, interest rates, the money supply, total spending, and the economy's levels of output, employment, and prices.

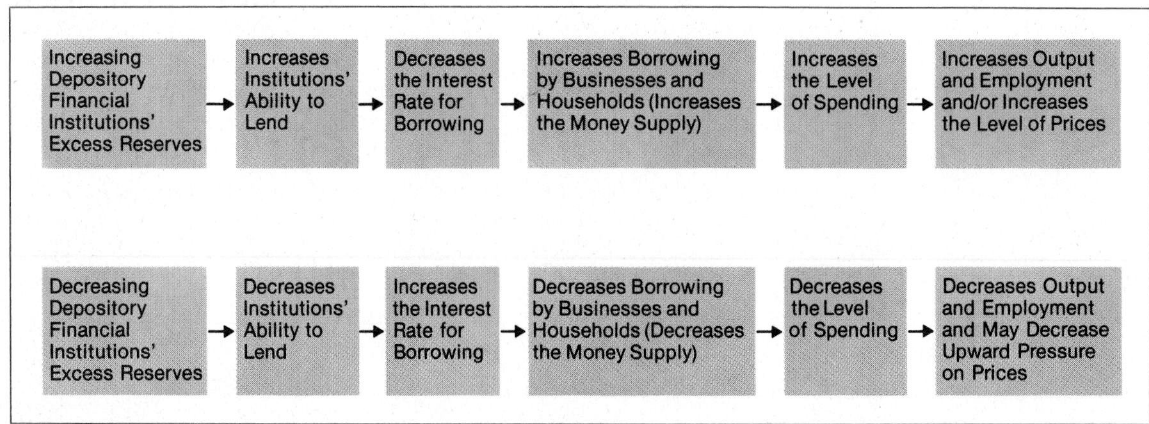

(and, thus, the money supply) to influence the levels of output, employment, and/or prices in the economy, it is engaging in **monetary policy.**

Monetary policy Changing the money supply to influence the levels of output, employment, and/or prices.

If the economy is experiencing a high rate of unemployment, the correct policy action is one to stimulate the level of total spending. To accomplish this goal, the Federal Reserve would act to increase excess reserves in the system, which should in turn decrease the interest rate and encourage borrowing. When the money supply is deliberately expanded and loans are more readily available, the Fed is said to be pursuing a policy of **easy money.**

Easy money policy A policy by the Federal Reserve to increase excess reserves of depository institutions in an effort to increase spending and reduce unemployment.

Tight money policy A policy by the Federal Reserve to reduce excess reserves of depository institutions in an effort to reduce spending and inflationary pressure.

If the economy is encountering a problem with demand-pull inflation, the correct policy prescription is to reduce spending. In this case the Fed would act to decrease the level of excess reserves in the system, thereby causing the interest rate to rise and borrowing to be dampened. When the money supply is deliberately reduced, the Fed is said to be pursuing a policy of **tight money.**

Monetary Policy Tools

The Federal Reserve uses three major tools to alter excess reserves in the financial institutions system: (1) the reserve requirement, (2) the discount rate, and (3) open market operations.

The Reserve Requirement If the Federal Reserve wanted to reduce excess reserves to discourage borrowing, it could do so by increasing the reserve requirement. For example, suppose that Hometown Bank has $5 million in demand deposits with a 10 percent reserve requirement; Hometown must keep $500,000 on reserve. If, however, the reserve requirement were raised to 11 percent, Hometown would need to keep $550,000 on reserve to back the $5 million in demand deposits: it would lose $50,000 of its excess reserves. Because the bank would have less excess reserves, it would have less loan-making ability, and its reduced loan-making ability would increase the interest rate the bank charges and thus dampen borrowing.

On the other hand, a decrease in the reserve requirement would increase excess reserves in the system, giving institutions the ability to make new loans. This decrease in the reserve requirement would be appropriate to stimulate the economy, whereas an increase in the reserve requirement would be appropriate to fight demand-pull inflation.

Prior to the Monetary Control Act of 1980, reserve requirements differed among the various types of financial institutions and were imposed by different regulatory organizations. For example, a Federal Reserve member commercial bank had a different reserve requirement than a savings and loan. Since the act, all depository institutions[10] must meet the same reserve

---

[10]These include commercial banks, mutual savings banks, savings banks, savings and loan associations, and credit unions that are federally insured or eligible for federal insurance. See: Charles R. McNeill (with some discussion by Denise M. Rechter), "The Depository Institutions Deregulation and Monetary Control Act of 1980," *Federal Reserve Bulletin* (June 1980), p. 444.

requirement, although this requirement differs according to the type of deposit. The uniform reserve requirement regulated by the Federal Reserve gives the Federal Reserve greater control over the money supply.

Table 8.4 shows the reserve requirements designated by the Monetary Control Act of 1980 on various types of accounts.[11] Notice in this table that the reserve requirement on checkable accounts (demand and other checkable deposits) totaling more than $25 million is considerably higher than the requirement on total accounts of less than $25 million.[12] In addition to the reserve requirements given in the table, a supplemental reserve requirement of up to 4 percent on total checkable accounts may be imposed if necessary.

The Federal Reserve has not radically changed the reserve requirements in carrying out monetary policy. Either an influx or removal of an extremely large volume of excess reserves would be a shock to the banking system. An increase in the reserve requirement of 1 or 2 percent could cause banks to have to "find" millions of dollars of reserves to meet that requirement. Usually when the reserve requirement has been changed, it has been by only ¼ percent or ½ percent in any one or more of the deposit categories.

The Discount Rate All depository financial institutions may under certain circumstances borrow from a Federal Reserve Bank.[13] Typically, when an institution borrows, its reserve account is increased; and when the institution

Table 8.4
Reserve Requirements

All depository institutions are subject to the same reserve requirements, which vary according to type of deposit.

Type of Account	Reserve Requirement
All checkable accounts including demand deposits, NOW, ATS, credit union share drafts, and others	
$0–$25 million	3%
over $25 million	12% (can vary from 8–14%)
Nonpersonal time deposits and savings accounts[a]	3% (can vary from 0–9%)
Personal time deposits and savings accounts	No reserve requirement

[a]Generally includes nontransaction accounts in which the depositor is not a natural person (for example, a corporation). These requirements may vary by maturity.

Source: The Federal Reserve Bank of Chicago, *Leveling the Playing Field* (December 1983), p. 12; and Board of Governors of the Federal Reserve System, *Federal Reserve Bulletin* (June 1984), p. A7.

[11]In order to avoid severe reserve shocks in adjusting to these new percentages, a period of up to eight years, depending upon the type of institution and account, has been given to institutions to "phase into" these requirements. See: The Federal Reserve Bank of Chicago, *Leveling the Playing Field* (December 1983), p. 9.

[12]The $25 million step is to be adjusted each year. See: The Federal Reserve Bank of Chicago, p. 12.

[13]Prior to the Monetary Control Act of 1980 only member commercial banks could borrow from a Federal Reserve Bank.

repays the Fed, its reserves are decreased. Thus, borrowing increases the loan-making capabilities of financial institutions.

Discount rate
The interest rate that a Federal Reserve Bank charges a financial institution for borrowing reserves.

The interest rate that the Fed charges a financial institution for borrowing is called the **discount rate.**[14] An increase in the discount rate, because it increases the price institutions must pay for reserves, is an attempt by the Federal Reserve to discourage reserve borrowing. A decrease in the discount rate is an attempt to encourage reserve borrowing.

The Federal Reserve does not provide an endless supply of borrowed reserves for financial institutions. It requires the borrowing institution to present a good reason for its loan request, such as an emergency or seasonal problem. Thus, in addition to its control over the actual discount rate, the Federal Reserve can further affect the level of reserves by accepting or refusing institutional loan requests.

Discount rate changes are always announced publicly and serve as an indicator of the intentions of the Fed. For example, an increase in the discount rate signals an attempt to tighten up the money supply, with the probable consequence of an increase in the interest rate that financial institutions charge their loan customers. This would be an appropriate policy to fight demand-pull inflationary pressure. A decrease in the discount rate signals an attempt to loosen the money supply, with the probable consequence of a decrease in the interest rate. This measure might be followed when policy makers are concerned with unemployment. Table 8.5 lists the various discount rates charged between the beginning of 1976 and the end of 1984.

Open market operations
The buying and selling of securities, primarily U.S. government securities, on the open market by the Federal Reserve.

Open Market Committee
The committee that determines the general policy on Federal Reserve open market operations.

Open Market Operations The buying and selling of securities, primarily U.S. government securities,[15] on the open market by the Federal Reserve is referred to as **open market operations.** Of the three tools of monetary policy, open market operations is the one used most often for changing excess reserves in the financial institutions system. Open market operations are housed in the Federal Reserve Bank of New York and are carried on each business day, thus allowing for immediate alteration of reserves. The **Open Market Committee,** consisting of the Board of Governors and five representatives of the Federal Reserve Banks, determines the general direction of open market policy. Let us examine first the process through which the Fed buys securities.

When the Fed buys securities on the open market it can do so from banks or from dealers.[16] If a security is purchased by the Federal Reserve from a

[14]Be careful to distinguish between the discount rate, which is the interest rate paid by banks to the Fed for borrowing reserves, and the prime rate, which is the interest rate banks charge their best short-term commercial and industrial customers.

[15]Recall that U.S. Treasury securities result from federal government borrowing to finance deficit spending.

[16]The Federal Reserve cannot demand that a bank or dealer sell its securities to, or buy them from, the Fed. Rather, if the Fed intends to buy, it must offer a price high enough to induce a bank or dealer to sell. The reverse holds true if the Fed intends to sell. Most of the buying and selling by the Fed is done through dealers. In fact, many banks work through a dealer rather than directly with the Fed.

Table 8.5
Federal Reserve Bank Interest Rates (Percent per Annum)

Changes in the discount rate encourage and discourage the borrowing of reserves by financial depository institutions from the Fed, and serve as an indicator of the money supply intentions of the Federal Reserve.

Effective Date	Range for All Federal Reserve Banks[a]	Effective Date	Range for All Federal Reserve Banks[a]
1976 Jan. 19	5½–6	1980 June 13	11–12
23	5½	16	11
Nov. 22	5¼–5½	July 28	10–11
26	5¼	29	10
1977 Aug. 30	5¼–5¾	Sept. 26	11
Sept. 2	5¾	Nov. 17	12
Oct. 26	6	Dec. 5	12–13
1978 Jan. 9	6–6½	8	13
20	6½	1981 May 5	13–14
May 11	6½–7	8	14
12	7	Nov. 2	13–14
July 3	7–7¼	6	13
10	7¼	Dec. 4	12
Aug. 21	7¾	1982 July 20	11½–12
Sept. 22	8	23	11½
Oct. 16	8–8½	Aug. 2	11–11½
20	8½	3	11
Nov. 1	8½–9½	16	10½
3	9½	27	10–10½
1979 July 20	10	30	10
Aug. 17	10–10½	Oct. 12	9½–10
20	10½	13	9½
Sept. 19	10½–11	Nov. 22	9–9½
21	11	26	9
Oct. 8	11–12	Dec. 14	8½–9
10	12	17	8½
1980 Feb. 15	12–13	1984 Apr. 9	8½–9
19	13	13	9
May 29	12–13	Nov. 21	8½–9
30	12	26	8½
		Dec. 24	8

[a]Each individual Federal Reserve Bank determines the discount rate it charges. Generally, the rate of all 12 banks is the same. However, in the event that it is not, the range is given here.

Source: Table 1.14, "Federal Reserve Bank Interest Rates," *Federal Reserve Bulletin* (March 1985), p. A6.

bank, the Fed takes the security for its own and credits the amount of the security to the selling bank's reserve account. For example, if the Fed wanted to buy government securities and if Hometown Bank were holding $1 million in Treasury notes in its portfolio, Hometown could exchange the securities for a $1 million increase in its reserve account.

When the Fed buys securities from a dealer, it pays for them by issuing the dealer a check. The dealer then deposits the check in a depository institution where, when it is cleared, the reserve account of the institution is increased by the amount of the check. A $1 million purchase of securities by the Fed from a dealer will eventually increase reserves in the dealer's financial institution by $1 million. Thus, whether the Fed buys securities from a bank or a dealer, the effect of its buying is an increase in reserves in the system.

When the Fed sells securities, it again trades with banks or dealers. If it sells to a bank, the bank exchanges its reserves for the securities, thus decreasing reserves. For example, if the Fed wants to sell Treasury notes and Hometown Bank wants to buy $2 million worth, Hometown could trade $2 million in its reserve account for these securities.

If the Fed sells to a dealer, the dealer pays for the securities by giving a check to the Fed. When the dealer's check clears, the dealer's depository institution loses reserves. A $2 million sale to a dealer will decrease the reserve account of the dealer's depository institution by $2 million. Thus, when the Fed sells securities, reserves are removed from the system.

When the Fed increases or decreases reserves either directly or through a dealer's check, it is not transferring reserves from one account to another. Rather, it is either creating new reserves for the system or destroying those that already exist.

Open market operations provide a powerful tool for enacting monetary policy for two reasons. First, changes in reserves can be achieved quickly because operations are carried on every business day. Second, the quantity of reserves can be altered slightly or greatly depending upon whether government securities are bought or sold in small or large quantities.

In summary, the Federal Reserve can increase or decrease depository institutions' excess reserves (and the supply of money) through its open market operations, and/or changes in the reserve requirement, and/or changes in the discount rate. If the Fed were pursuing an expansionary policy to increase excess reserves in the system, it could buy securities from banks and dealers, and/or lower the reserve requirement, and/or lower the discount rate. If the Fed were pursuing a policy to fight demand-pull inflation, it could sell securities, and/or increase the reserve requirement, and/or increase the discount rate to remove excess reserves from the system and shrink the money supply.

The actions of the Federal Reserve are closely watched because of the impact of policy decisions on interest rates and on economic activity. The public in general has become more aware of monetary terms such as M1 and M2 and of actions such as changes in the discount rate because of the way such matters affect jobs, mortgage rates, automobile loans, and other facets of everyday life. Businesses, particularly those in financial areas, have begun to hire experts to anticipate Federal Reserve moves because changes in the interest rate by even a small percentage can cost them millions of dollars. Application 8.3, "More Concerns Hire Fed Watchers To Interpret Central Bank's Policies," deals with a fairly new profession: Fed watching.

Government Deficits and Monetary Policy

The relationship between the money supply and the federal government's borrowing to cover deficit spending is important to understand. Recall that the downward sloping demand curve for loans illustrated earlier in Figures 8.1 and 8.2 came from the demand for loans by households and businesses, which are interest-rate sensitive in their plans to borrow. When the government, which is not interest-rate sensitive, plans to borrow to finance its deficit spending, its demand for borrowing is added to that of households and businesses, thus shifting the demand curve for loanable funds to the right. This is illustrated in Figure 8.4a by a shift in the demand curve for loanable funds from D1 to D2. As a result of an increase in government borrowing, the interest rate rises—in this example, from 12 percent to 18 percent—and the quantity of loans made rises—in this example, from $250 million to $300 million.

This rise in the interest rate could be prevented if the Federal Reserve would increase excess reserves in the system by an amount equal to the increase in the demand for funds by the government. Figure 8.4b illustrates a shift in the supply curve for loanable funds to the right, from S1 to S2, by an amount necessary to compensate for the increase in demand. Notice that the increase in supply to S2 keeps the interest rate at the original level of 12 percent.

Why doesn't the Federal Reserve simply create enough reserves to cover

Application 8.3
MORE CONCERNS HIRE FED WATCHERS TO INTERPRET CENTRAL BANK'S POLICIES

At 8:15 every morning, a dozen senior executives in pin-striped suits gather around a conference table in the trading department at First National Bank of Chicago. Conspicuously out of uniform, in a paisley tie and colored shirt, is David Resler, the only assistant vice president allowed to attend.

But when the brainstorming begins, the 36-year-old Mr. Resler talks first and longest—about Federal Reserve policy, about the U.S. Treasury's current cash horde and about the nation's money-supply outlook. After a brief discussion, the group disbands to begin supervising the day's $8 billion or so in financial-market transactions, while Mr. Resler moves from desk to desk imparting money-market wisdom.

Mr. Resler is a professional Fed watcher, a growing specialty among bank and brokerage-firm economists. His assignment is to divine the policies and activities of the Federal Reserve Board, probably the most powerful but least understood influence in the financial markets. The job involves the usual analysis of numbers that economists do, but also something extra: insight into the secretive and often ambiguous ways of the nation's central bank. . . .

The Fed's moves influence interest rates on everything from overnight loans between banks the government's demand for funds, thereby eliminating the upward pressure that government borrowing puts on interest rates? The Federal Reserve has adhered to a philosophy of controlling the money supply for the benefit of the macroeconomy and has not increased reserves to finance government deficits. If it increased reserves to meet government needs, the money supply could increase too quickly, causing inflation and weakening the value of the dollar. Notice in Figure 8.4b that when the Fed increases excess reserves to meet increased government demand for borrowing, a $150 million increase in loans made results: from the original $250 million when demand and supply were at D1 and S1 to $400 million when demand and supply are at D2 and S2. As illustrated in Figure 8.4a, were the Fed not to increase excess reserves to accommodate government borrowing, the quantity of loans would increase by only $50 million.

Advantages and Disadvantages of Monetary Policy

There are several advantages and disadvantages to using monetary policy as a tool for correcting the problems of inflation and unemployment. A primary advantage is the speed with which changes can be implemented. Unlike fiscal policy, which could take months of deliberation, the first steps toward changing the money supply can be taken the day the decision to do so is made.

A second advantage of using monetary policy is its flexibility with regard

to 30-year mortgages. Correctly anticipating the effects of the intervention thus gives traders a major advantage in playing the bond market and other interest-sensitive markets, including certain commodities and listed options.

Experts on the Fed try to help their trading colleagues use the best timing in these markets by guessing when the Fed will expand or contract reserves. But the Fed never discloses whether it is trying to influence credit and money supply or whether it's merely making a routine technical adjustment in the reserve system. The Fed also withholds the dollar size of certain transactions and for a month, keeps secret the minutes of its Open Market Committee, which sets Fed trading policy. . . .

At First Chicago, Mr. Resler's ruminations help the bank decide how to set its "WAM," or the weighted average maturity of the certificates of deposit and other loans it secures to fund the bank's day-to-day operations. About a month ago, for instance, Frank Byrne, the chief funding officer, questioned Mr. Resler about how the Fed's activities would influence rates on overnight loans between banks. Mr. Resler calculated that these rates would most likely decline. As a result, Mr. Byrne borrowed heavily in the overnight market, and avoided getting stuck with a fixed rate in a declining interest rate trend.

"Resler helps us decide which way to drive the bus," Mr. Byrne says.

Source: Thomas Petzinger, Jr., "More Concerns Hire Fed Watchers To Interpret Central Bank's Policies," *The Wall Street Journal*, October 21, 1983, p. 31.

Figure 8.4
Changes in the Demand for and Supply of Funds for Loans and the Interest Rate

When excess reserves are increased to keep the interest rate from rising due to an increase in demand, a larger quantity of loans is made than would be made if excess reserves were left unchanged.

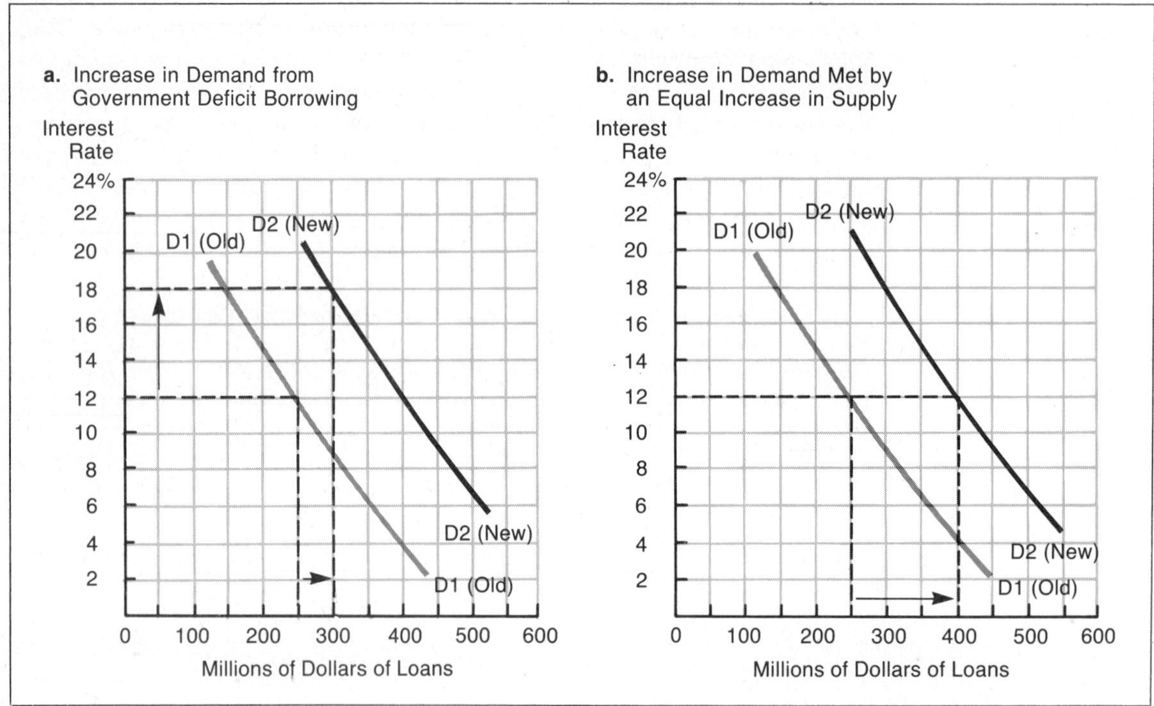

to the size of the change to be implemented. Reserves can be increased or decreased in small or large increments.

A third advantage is that monetary policy is removed from politics. The members of the Board of Governors, although appointed by a president, are not as subject to political pressure as the members of Congress. This may be partially due to the fact that board members are appointed for lengthy (14-year) terms and are not campaigning for reelection. The Board of Governors' motives in expanding and contracting the money supply are usually purely economic.

One of the major disadvantages of monetary policy is the loan-making link through which it is carried out. That is, the Fed can increase reserves to stimulate economic activity as much as it wishes, but the reserves themselves do not alter the money supply. Before the money supply is increased, someone must be willing to borrow and a bank must be willing to lend. Since the Fed cannot force the loan-making process, it has only indirect control over increasing the money supply.

This loan-making link may reduce the effectiveness of monetary policy in fighting unemployment during a deep and serious recession. If economic conditions are severe, no expansion of reserves or lowering of the interest rate may be enough to induce borrowers to take out loans.

A second problem with monetary policy occurs during inflation. As the Federal Reserve tightens up the money supply and forces the interest rate higher, it raises the price for borrowed money. Businesses that borrow at this high rate may in turn raise prices on their products to compensate. Thus, fighting inflation with monetary policy could worsen it.

Finally, there are those who feel that having the Federal Reserve and monetary policy removed from the political process is a disadvantage. Over the years there have been several proposals to place the Federal Reserve under more congressional control. Proponents of this action do not favor the independence of the Fed and presume that with control it would be more sensitive to public reaction in its policy making.

Before ending this chapter, it should be pointed out that there is an economic philosophy called monetarism, and that those who adhere to it are termed monetarists. Generally, monetarists believe that controlling the money supply is the main vehicle for controlling economic activity. Monetarism, Keynesian economics, and other viewpoints are discussed in the next chapter.

SUMMARY

A significant relationship exists between an economy's supply of money and its levels of output, employment, and prices. Because of this relationship, one method for accomplishing the macroeconomic goals is altering the money supply.

The effect of money on the level of economic activity can be illustrated by the equation of exchange. This equation shows that, operating through aggregate spending, changes in the supply of money lead to changes in output, employment, and/or prices, depending on how close the economy is to full employment. Generally, if the economy is at less than full employment, an increase in the money supply expands output and employment. If the economy is at or near full employment, increases in money will cause increases in prices. A decrease in the money supply contracts output and employment and may dampen upward pressure on prices.

Changes in the money supply occur through lending by financial depository institutions: money is created when loans are made and destroyed when they are repaid. The ability of an institution to make loans is limited by the amount of its excess reserves, which is the difference between the institution's actual legal reserves and its required reserves. Required reserves are the amount of deposits that the institution is required to hold on reserve. If loans were made in an amount greater than the institution's excess reserves, the institution would risk dropping its actual reserves below its required reserves. Lending is not accomplished by transferring funds from one account to another. Rather, loans represent newly created money.

Any change in excess reserves permits a single financial institution to change its loans by that amount. However, when this change is carried through the entire system, total lending and the money supply change by a much larger, or a multiple, amount. The money multiplier itself is the reciprocal of the reserve requirement, and the maximum change in the money supply is the multiplier times the initial change in excess reserves.

Because borrowing from financial institutions by businesses and households is voluntary, simply having excess reserves available will not ensure that loans will be taken out. The stimulus for businesses and households to borrow when increased spending is desired, or to reduce borrowing when spending is excessive, is the interest rate, which is a cost of borrowing money. The greater the interest rate, the smaller will be the amount of borrowing by businesses and households and the smaller the amount of total spending based on borrowing. When the interest rate is lowered, the reverse holds true.

The rate of interest on loans made by financial institutions is determined by the demand for loans and by the supply of loans available, which is based on excess reserves. Increasing excess reserves lowers the interest rate and raises the amount of loans made, while decreasing excess reserves increases the interest rate and reduces the amount of loans made.

Adjusting the money supply to accomplish the macroeconomic goals is a major responsibility of the Federal Reserve. This adjustment is performed through the use of three tools of monetary policy: the reserve requirement, the discount rate, and open market operations. The purpose of each tool is to influence the level of borrowing and spending by causing changes in the excess reserves of depository financial institutions. Monetary policy to stimulate spending would call for lowering the reserve requirement, and/or reducing the discount rate, and/or buying securities by the Fed on the open market. Monetary policy to dampen spending would call for raising the reserve requirement, and/or raising the discount rate, and/or selling securities by the Fed on the open market. Of the three policy tools, open market operations is the most important and the most frequently used.

The Federal Reserve could keep the interest rate stable in the face of large government borrowing to finance deficit spending by increasing excess reserves to accommodate the government's demand for funds. However, such action could weaken the value of the dollar, and has not been followed.

The use of monetary policy to correct unemployment or demand-pull inflation has the advantage of flexibility in timing and size. It has the disadvantages, however, of possible ineffectiveness in a severe recession and of the potential to make inflation worse in a tight money situation. Whether the fact that the Federal Reserve is removed from politics is an advantage or disadvantage is a matter of debate.

Key Terms and Concepts

Equation of exchange	**Interest rate**
Velocity of money	**Prime rate**

Actual legal reserves
Reserve requirement
Required reserves
Excess reserves
Creation and destruction of money
Money multiplier
Monetary policy
Easy money policy
Tight money policy
Discount rate
Open market operations
Open Market Committee

Discussion and Review Questions

1. Why are depository institutions required to hold a certain percentage of their deposits as reserves? Is it to provide a source of funds for these institutions in case of emergencies? Is it for some other reason?
2. In a discussion with a friend you are told that it makes no difference whether the Federal Reserve uses open market operations, the reserve requirement, or the discount rate to change the supply of money, because the impact of each of the policies is exactly the same. Do you agree or disagree with your friend's position?
3. Control by the Federal Reserve over the money supply and over total spending is weakened by the fact that borrowing by businesses and households is voluntary. How might the power of the Federal Reserve over borrowing be strengthened? Is this method consistent with the philosophy of capitalism?
4. If you were trying to control inflation, would you depend on fiscal policy or monetary policy? Why? If you were trying to reduce unemployment, would you depend on fiscal or monetary policy? Why?
5. Assume that Hometown Bank has $3,000,000 in demand deposits, a 15 percent reserve requirement, and $520,000 in actual legal reserves. Based on these figures, how much in new loans could Hometown Bank make?
6. How is the level of economic activity affected by changes in the money supply? What would be the effect on the output of goods and services and the level of prices of an increase or decrease in the supply of money?
7. What is the money multiplier, and how is it related to the reserve requirement? If the Federal Reserve increases excess reserves in the system by $18 million with a reserve requirement of 12 percent, what is the maximum amount by which the money supply could increase as a result of the increased excess reserves?
8. Assume that the economy is at full employment and that the federal government needs to borrow $100 million to finance a deficit budget. Should the Federal Reserve put an extra $100 million in reserves into the system to finance this borrowing? If not, what action should the Fed take?

Suggested Readings

Federal Reserve Bank of Kansas City, *Issues in Monetary Policy: II* (March 1982). A collection of articles originally published in various issues of the Kansas City Federal Reserve's *Economic Review* that deal with various aspects of monetary policy, especially in light of recent changes in the financial system.

Milton Friedman, "A Theoretical Framework for Monetary Analysis," *Milton Friedman's Monetary Framework,* R. J. Gordon, ed. (Chicago: The University of Chicago Press, 1974), pp. 1–62, particularly pp. 1–15. A discussion of different methods of representing the equation of exchange and of factors influencing the demand for and supply of money.

Milton Friedman and Walter Heller, *Monetary vs. Fiscal Policy* (New York: W. W. Norton and Co., 1969). A critical discussion by two well-known economists — Milton Friedman representing the monetary policy position, and Walter Heller representing the fiscal policy position — concerning the strengths and weaknesses of the two approaches to accomplishing the macroeconomic goals.

Jonas Prager, "The Fed Wasn't Always Independent," *New York Times,* October 30, 1977, Section 3, p. 16. Traces the changing relationship between the Federal Reserve Board of Governors and the executive branch of the federal government.

Linda Snyder, "How to Forecast the Money Supply," *Fortune,* January 16, 1978, pp. 139, 142. Deals with the relationship between changes in the money supply and stock market activity, and introduces some of the different indicators used to forecast the money supply.

Andrew Tobias, "A Talk with Paul Volker," *The New York Times Magazine,* September 19, 1982, pp. 34 and following. Gives some background on Volker and his thoughts about the economic challenges he has faced as chairman of the Federal Reserve Board of Governors.

9 QUESTIONS AND ISSUES IN THE MACROECONOMY: ASSESSING GOALS AND TOOLS

Chapter Objectives

1. To more fully explore the tradeoff between employment and price stability.
2. To introduce the Phillips curve and recent U.S. experiences with unemployment and inflation.
3. To discuss wage-price controls and highlight recent U.S. experiences with wage-price controls, and discuss indexing.
4. To survey the Keynesian, monetarist, supply-side, and rational expectations viewpoints on macroeconomic policy.
5. To present some final thoughts on evaluating macroeconomic policy proposals.

In Chapters Four through Eight the goals of the macroeconomy (full production and economic growth, full employment, and price stability) and fiscal and monetary policies, the main tools for accomplishing those objectives, were introduced. At this point you should be familiar with the relationships between the goals, the measures of the extent to which they are accomplished, and the mechanics of fiscal and monetary policies.

Some fundamental questions and issues regarding these goals and policy instruments should be highlighted to complete your understanding of macroeconomics. For example, we have learned to think in terms of attaining either full employment or price stability, but not both. Why do we believe that a choice must be made between these two objectives? Is this tradeoff an accurate representation of how the economy actually operates?

A second set of questions and issues surrounds the use of fiscal and monetary policies. How well do these policy instruments perform? Are certain types of macroeconomic problems not readily solved by these policies? Do effective alternatives exist? What are the different schools of thought on how these policy instruments should be used?

Chapter Nine is divided into three sections devoted to these issue areas. The first explores the relationship between the levels of unemployment and prices, and introduces the Phillips curve, a widely recognized device for illustrating that relationship. The second section evaluates the effectiveness of fiscal and monetary policies in the control of cost-push inflation and discusses two additional tools of economic policy: wage-price controls, and indexing. The final section examines some major macroeconomic policy viewpoints, including several recently popular ideas.

GOALS OF THE MACROECONOMY: A RESTATEMENT

Inflation and Unemployment Tradeoff

By now, the relationship between aggregate spending and economic conditions should be clear: changes in the level of total spending cause changes in production, employment, and, under some circumstances, the price level. According to this relationship, increases in aggregate spending cause increases in employment, but only up to a point. At some level of economic activity full employment is reached. As aggregate spending pushes the economy toward full employment, prices begin to rise, and demand-pull inflation occurs. Decreases in aggregate spending, on the other hand, result in decreases in employment. An attempt to alleviate demand-pull inflationary pressure through reduced spending contributes to unemployment.

From this spending, employment, and price scenario, one message is clear: it is virtually impossible for an economy to have both full employment and no inflation. The attainment of one of these goals creates an obstacle to the other. As a result, a choice must be made between which goal to pursue: full employment with strong upward pressure on prices, or price stability with involuntary unemployment. One method for illustrating this tradeoff is a Phillips curve.

The Phillips Curve

Phillips curve
A curve showing the relationship between an economy's unemployment and inflation rates.

A **Phillips curve** shows the relationship between an economy's unemployment and inflation rates. A Phillips curve, using hypothetical data, is illustrated in Figure 9.1. The horizontal axis measures rates of unemployment, and the vertical axis measures rates of price increases, or inflation. The curve itself slopes downward, illustrating the inverse relationship, or tradeoff, between inflation and unemployment: when one increases, the other declines, and vice-versa. For example, for the economy represented in Figure 9.1, a low 3 percent inflation rate is associated with a high 12 percent unem-

Figure 9.1
A Phillips Curve (Hypothetical Figures)

A Phillips curve slopes downward, illustrating the inverse relationship between unemployment and inflation.

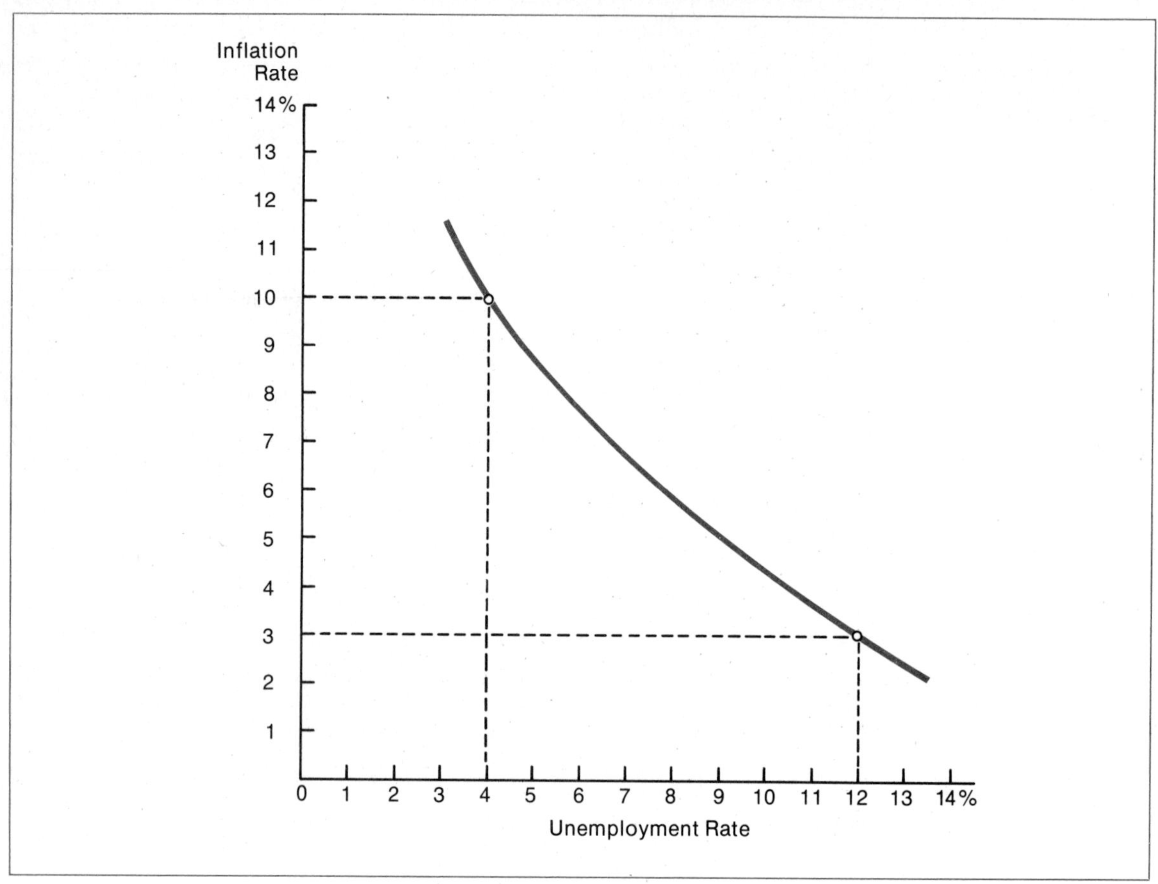

ployment rate. Conversely, a low 4 percent unemployment rate is associated with a high 10 percent inflation rate.

How might a Phillips curve for the U.S. economy appear? Data from the U.S. experience with unemployment and inflation from 1950 through 1984 are presented in Table 9.1. The second column gives the annual rate of unemployment for each year, and the third column gives the annual change in the GNP price deflator. The GNP price deflator is used as a measure of inflation because it is a composite price index, as opposed to the consumer price index, which measures price changes for goods and services purchased by households, or the producer price index, which measures price changes for items that businesses purchase for use in production. Notice in this table that both the inflation and unemployment rates are generally higher in the 1970s and 1980s than in the 1950s and 1960s.

Table 9.1
Annual Rates of Unemployment and Inflation in the U.S.

Both inflation and unemployment rates are generally higher in the 1970s and 1980s than in the 1950s and 1960s.

Year	Unemployment Rate[a]	Inflation Rate[b]
1950	5.3%	2.1%
1951	3.3	6.6
1952	3.0	1.4
1953	2.9	1.6
1954	5.5	1.2
1955	4.4	2.2
1956	4.1	3.2
1957	4.3	3.4
1958	6.8	1.7
1959	5.5	2.4
1960	5.5	1.6
1961	6.7	0.9
1962	5.5	1.8
1963	5.7	1.5
1964	5.2	1.5
1965	4.5	2.2
1966	3.8	3.2
1967	3.8	3.0
1968	3.6	4.4
1969	3.5	5.1
1970	4.9	5.4
1971	5.9	5.0
1972	5.6	4.2
1973	4.9	5.8
1974	5.6	8.8
1975	8.5	9.3
1976	7.7	5.2
1977	7.1	5.8
1978	6.1	7.4
1979	5.8	8.6
1980	7.1	9.2
1981	7.6	9.6
1982	9.7	6.0
1983	9.6	3.8
1984	7.5	3.7[c]

[a]Percentage of civilian labor force unemployed.
[b]Annual percentage change in the GNP implicit price deflator.
[c]Preliminary figure.

Source: U.S., *Economic Report of the President* (Washington, D.C.: U.S. Government Printing Office, 1985), pp. 237, 266.

Data from Table 9.1 are plotted in Figure 9.2. Each year's experience with unemployment and inflation is represented by a point on the graph. For example, a line drawn down from the point for 1980 would hit the horizontal axis at the 7.1 percent mark, 1980's annual rate of unemployment. A line drawn to the vertical axis from the 1980 point would hit at 9.2 percent, that year's inflation rate. Observe that the points representing each year shift to the right for the 1970s and 1980s, and that in several years, particularly 1975

Figure 9.2
Annual Rates of Unemployment and Inflation in the United States and Representative Phillips Curves

The generally higher unemployment and inflation rates in the 1970s and 1980s, as compared to the 1950s and 1960s, have caused the Phillips curve to shift to the right from PC1 to PC2.

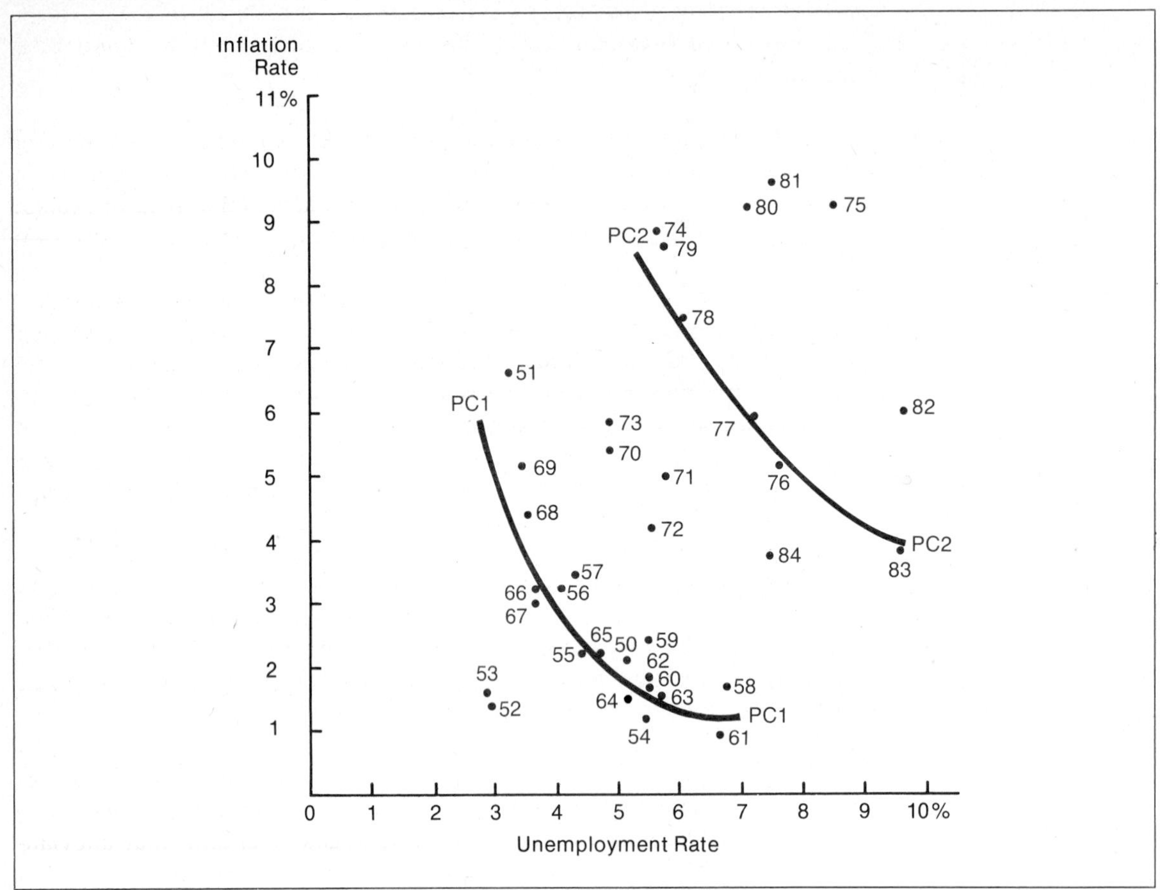

and 1981, the economy was plagued with unusually high rates of both unemployment and inflation.

One can relate these data to the Phillips curve by observing the inflation-unemployment combinations over the years and fitting representative curves through these points. The experience of the 1950s and 1960s provides a fairly clear-cut Phillips curve relationship. This is shown in Figure 9.2 as line PC1. However, with the inflation rate–unemployment rate combinations of the 1970s and 1980s, it is not as easy to derive a Phillips curve. If the assumption about a tradeoff between unemployment and inflation is maintained, one could develop a curve that lies to the right of the 1950s–1960s Phillips curve. This is shown by PC2.

The downward slope of PC2 indicates that a tradeoff between inflation and unemployment is still assumed to exist. The tradeoff, however, now occurs between higher rates of inflation and higher rates of unemployment. For example, in Figure 9.2, PC1 shows that an inflation rate of 4 percent is associated with approximately a 3.5 percent rate of unemployment, whereas PC2 illustrates a 4 percent rate of inflation with unemployment of about 9.5 percent.

Analyzing the Behavior of the Phillips Curve Is it valid to assume that the Phillips curve has shifted to the right? If so, will this shift continue? In answering these questions, let us review several factors that help to explain the movement toward higher rates of unemployment and inflation in recent years.

First, as noted in Chapter Four, the rate of unemployment considered to represent full employment appears to have risen over the years. This may be due in part to the increased participation in the labor force of women and teenagers with their traditionally higher rates of unemployment. Many people today associate full employment with an unemployment rate much higher than the 3 or 4 percent rate formerly accepted. Consequently, a 6 percent rate of unemployment today may have the same economic implications that a 3 percent rate did years ago. With this in mind, the higher rates of unemployment in recent years are not as critical as they appear.

Second, in recent years the United States has been plagued with cost-push inflation — that is, price increases that come from forces on the sellers' rather than the buyers' side of the market.[1] Examples of cost-push inflation would be price increases induced by higher costs of labor, petroleum, or other inputs. Much of the inflationary pressure in the mid-1970s and in 1981 was due to rising energy prices. (See Tables 4.6 and 4.7.)

It is not clear whether cost-push inflation can be controlled by decreases in aggregate spending or whether it is affected by increases in unemployment. In other words, the decreases in aggregate spending that alleviate demand-pull inflation and cause unemployment may have no impact on cost-push inflation. For example, price increases by foreign producers of commodities such as oil may be imposed without regard to the economic conditions in the purchasing countries. Thus, it may be possible to have high rates of inflation and unemployment simultaneously, thereby shifting the Phillips curve to the right, if the inflation is of the cost-push type.

A third reason for higher rates of unemployment and inflation may be that members of the U.S. work force are less sensitive to unemployment than they have been in the past. Prolonged unemployment compensation payments and other government transfers allow the laid-off employee to partially "fill in" the spending gap created by unemployment. With these programs, workers may be less prone to accept available alternative employ-

[1]Cost-push inflation was defined and discussed in Chapter Four.

ment and less vulnerable to price increases than they would otherwise be. In turn, the rate of inflation may not slow as quickly, and the unemployment rate may remain higher than it would be without this extra transfer-based spending.

In summary, it is quite likely that the Phillips curve has shifted to the right. If so, the shift does not refute the major assumption of a tradeoff between inflation and unemployment, but rather, it indicates that the trade-off is becoming more severe. Structural changes such as a rise in the unemployment rate representing full employment, and perhaps even shorter term factors such as changes in people's expectations of economic conditions, may be responsible for this shift. It may also be due in part to cost-push inflationary pressures.

CONTROLLING THE EFFECTS OF INFLATION

As noted earlier, changes in the level of aggregate spending affect unemployment and demand-pull inflation, but may not affect cost-push inflation. Since both monetary and fiscal policy are directed toward changing aggregate spending, these two major types of policies are not very effective in dealing with inflation of the cost-push variety.

Nothing comparable to monetary and fiscal policy exists for controlling cost-push inflation because the causes of price increases of the cost-push type are so varied that they do not lend themselves to correction through any single policy such as reducing spending. Also, cost-push inflation may be the result of long-term forces such as changes in the bargaining power of certain resource suppliers, changes in technology, or scarcities of resources, that cannot be altered by short-term policy. For example, cost-push inflation could result from price increases by a few sellers who control a major market and have no direct competition to stop them, from negotiations by a large, powerful union that result in high wages that are paid through increasing prices, from foreign control of a commodity, or from many other such sources. In none of these cases is there available a fiscal or monetary policy tool that would bring a quick and effective remedy.

One policy instrument that has been used and is often suggested as a remedy for inflation is wage-price controls. These controls provide one possible method for alleviating the symptoms of cost-push inflation.

Wage-Price Controls

Wage-price controls Mandatory government imposed restrictions on increases in prices, and wages and other incomes.

The expression **wage-price controls** refers to government imposition of some type of restriction on wage and price increases. It means that price determination through private decision making in the market is overseen by the government. Controls may prescribe a total freeze, where no wages or prices are permitted to rise during a specified period of time, or they may permit wages and prices to rise by a certain percent or gradually through a series of steps. Wage-price controls may apply to all prices, wages, rents, and such, or to just some of these categories. For example, prices and wages, but not profits, could be subject to control.

Usually the expression wage-price controls refers to mandatory government restrictions that carry the force of law. When they are violated, punishment such as a fine can result. There have, however, been instances when voluntary wage-price controls have been announced. In these cases the controls are more often referred to as **wage-price guideposts** or **guidelines** because they are not legally binding like mandatory controls.

Wage-price guideposts
Voluntary wage-price controls sought by the government.

Wage-price controls have been imposed during periods of substantial inflation or when there has been fear of serious future price increases. In most cases there has been a belief that the usual fiscal and monetary policy tools will not adequately alleviate the expected price increases.

Wage-price controls have not been used solely for combating cost-push inflationary pressures; they have also been imposed during periods of demand-pull inflation. During World War II, for example, controls were enacted because of the inflationary potential of large amounts of aggregate spending.

It is important to realize that wage-price controls are a stopgap measure. They do not cure inflation; they merely provide a temporary salve and reduce the symptoms. Unless steps are taken to attack the root cause of the inflationary problem while controls are imposed, the inflation will still be there when the controls are lifted.

It is possible to aggravate an inflation problem during the imposition of controls, so that prices may be even higher when controls are removed. For example, increasing government spending far beyond what is collected in taxes during controls builds up spending pressures and will, in all likelihood, cause a serious inflation problem after the controls are removed.

The U.S. Experience with Wage-Price Controls

In recent decades the United States has experienced mandatory wage-price controls on three occasions: during World War II, the Korean War, and the early 1970s. Voluntary controls have also been suggested several times, the most notable being the Kennedy guideposts of the early 1960s and the Carter standards of the late 1970s. Some insight into the operation and effect of wage-price controls can be gained from a brief examination of the recent experiences with mandatory controls in the United States.

World War II Controls Wage-price controls were imposed on the U.S. economy in 1942.[2] The primary reason for levying these controls was the pressure from aggregate spending that developed with the World War II

---

[2]Jerry E. Pohlman, *Economics of Wage and Price Controls* (Columbus, Ohio: Grid, Inc., 1972), p. 168.

effort. The federal government, for example, began to run huge budget deficits. For the fiscal year 1940 the budget deficit was $2.9 billion, and for 1941 it was $4.9 billion. But by 1942 this figure had increased to $20.5 billion, and by 1943 to $54.6 billion.[3] There were also substantial wage and price increases prior to 1942 that stirred the need to take some action. Hourly wages in manufacturing rose by 30.7 percent and the wholesale (now called producer) price index increased by 24 percent from January 1941 to October 1942.[4]

Stringent wage-price controls ended with the war in 1945, while some controls remained until late 1946.[5] When controls were lifted, a surge of inflation resulted. In 1946 there was a 15.7 percent increase in the GNP implicit price deflator, and in 1947 a 12.9 percent increase.[6] It is easy to understand why the postwar, postcontrol price surge occurred. During the war U.S. citizens accumulated a large amount of potential spending power due to high levels of employment and scarce consumer goods. At the end of the war, this large amount of individual spending power, coupled with significant increases in business investment spending, brought about demand-pull inflationary pressures.

Korean War Controls The next experience with mandatory controls occurred during the Korean War, when wage-price controls were adopted and a freeze announced in late January 1951.[7] For a few months prior to this announcement, there were accelerated increases in wages and prices. The fear of shortages of goods (induced perhaps by the memory of World War II) and of continually rising prices may have been responsible for the buying spurts that caused the precontrol inflationary pressure.[8]

The Korean War wage-price controls ended in February 1953.[9] Unlike the post-World War II experience, no upward surge of prices occurred when the controls were lifted. The economy had "cooled off" during this period, and there was no pent-up spending pressure.[10]

---

[3]U.S., *Economic Report of the President* (Washington, D.C.: U.S. Government Printing Office, 1985), p. 318.

[4]Pohlman, p. 168.

[5]Pohlman, p. 169.

[6]*Economic Report of the President*, 1985, p. 237.

[7]Arthur M. Ross, "Guideline Policy—Where We Are and How We Got There," in George P. Shultz and Robert Z. Aliber, eds. *Guidelines, Informal Controls, and the Market Place* (Chicago: The University of Chicago Press, 1966), p. 118.

[8]U.S., *The Midyear Economic Report of the President* (Washington, D.C.: U.S. Government Printing Office, 1951), p. 42.

[9]H. Scott Gordon, "The Eisenhower Administration: The Doctrine of Shared Responsibility" in Craufurd D. Goodwin, ed. *Exhortation and Controls: The Search for a Wage-Price Policy 1945–1971* (Washington, D.C.: The Brookings Institution, 1975), p. 110.

[10]Ross, p. 118.

Controls in the Early 1970s The Nixon Administration's wage-price controls (1971–1974) provide a more recent example of mandatory controls. This program consisted of four "phases" that appear to have been created as inflationary conditions changed.

Phase I was a 90-day freeze of wages and prices announced by the president in August 1971.[11] This was followed immediately by Phase II, which involved a structured system for wage and price determination and the creation of a price commission and a pay board. The price commission announced a goal of holding price increases to 2.5 percent per year, and the pay board issued a general standard of 5.5 percent for wage increases.[12]

Because inflation slowed in 1972, the decision was made to drop Phase II mandatory controls in January 1973 and begin Phase III. The basic principle of Phase III was that the controls established in Phase II would become self-administered, or voluntary.[13] The Phase III removal of mandatory controls, however, brought unacceptable increases in inflation. As a result, in June 1973, the president announced a 60-day price freeze.[14]

Phase IV began in August 1973, with programs similar to those of Phase II. However, Phase IV was not effective in moderating price increases and ended in April 1974.[15]

In 1974 the United States experienced one of the largest annual price increases in recent times: the inflationary pressures that emerged in 1973 became even more severe in 1974. In that year the GNP implicit price deflator changed by 8.8 percent, the consumer price index by 11 percent, and the producer price index by 15.3 percent.[16] These price increases in 1973 and 1974 occurred for a variety of reasons, such as world crop failures that pushed up food grain prices, the OPEC cartel's quadrupling of the price of petroleum in 1973, and the expansion of the domestic economy, which led to demand-pull inflationary pressures by the end of 1972.[17] Thus, controls ended at a time when inflationary pressures and price increases were far more serious than they had been when the controls were initiated.

---

[11]U.S., *Economic Report of the President* (Washington, D.C.: U.S. Government Printing Office, 1972), p. 75.

[12]*Economic Report of the President*, 1972, pp. 85, 88, 91.

[13]U.S., *Economic Report of the President* (Washington, D.C.: U.S. Government Printing Office, 1974), pp. 88–90.

[14]*Economic Report of the President*, 1974, p. 96.

[15]Phillip Cagan, *Persistent Inflation: Historical and Policy Essays* (New York: Columbia University Press, 1979), pp. 173–174.

[16]*Economic Report of the President*, 1985, pp. 237, 296, 302.

[17]Cagan, pp. 180, 185.

Advantages and Disadvantages of Controls

The suggestion to use wage-price controls to alleviate the problem of inflation generally stirs public debate. Some people advocate the use of controls, and others adamantly oppose them. Let us examine some of the strengths and weaknesses of controls.

One of the greatest advantages of a wage-price control program is that it provides an opportunity to arrest the symptoms of inflation while attacking the causes of the problem. For example, if the root cause of the price increases is excess spending, controls can keep prices from rising while other measures are applied to reduce demand. Perhaps a tax increase and/or a decrease in the supply of money could be implemented during controls so that once they are lifted, the real inflationary problem would be resolved. As noted earlier with the U.S. experience, however, this has not always been the outcome. After both the World War II and the Nixon controls were removed, inflation surged.

A second advantage of controls is the effect that the anticipation of their enactment may have on aggregate spending, particularly that of households and businesses. If households and businesses believe that prices will not continue to rise due to an imposition of controls, they may hold back some of the dollars that they would have otherwise spent trying to "beat" anticipated price increases. This, in itself, could reduce inflationary pressures.

There are several disadvantages to wage-price controls. First, they inhibit the operation of the market system and may lead to shortages of goods and services. Recall from the basic supply and demand analysis of Chapter Three that when the price of a good or service is below its equilibrium price, the quantity demanded is greater than the quantity supplied, and a shortage results. Figure 9.3 should refresh your memory in this regard. If wage-price controls do not permit the price of a product to rise to its equilibrium level, a shortage will develop in the market for that product.

In cases where shortages occur, illegal markets (black markets) frequently emerge. Many of those fortunate enough to purchase goods at the lower, controlled price may sell them at a higher price in an uncontrolled illegal market to people who could not otherwise obtain the goods. Thus, wage-price controls may lead not only to shortages but also to the creation of black markets.

A second disadvantage of controls is that public anticipation of restrictions on price increases may actually encourage both a precontrol and a postcontrol price surge rather than reduce pressure on prices as was indicated earlier. If sellers expect a freeze, or a limit, on the amount by which prices can be increased, they may raise their prices before controls are imposed. Also, unless demand has cooled off, sellers may raise their prices immediately after controls are lifted in order to "catch up" with what they have lost. And if controls are removed in a period of great uncertainty as to future economic policy, sellers may substantially raise prices out of fear of a reimposition of controls.

Figure 9.3
Supply, Demand, Equilibrium Price, and Controlled Price

A shortage, and perhaps a black market, will develop if wage-price controls keep the price of a product below its equilibrium level.

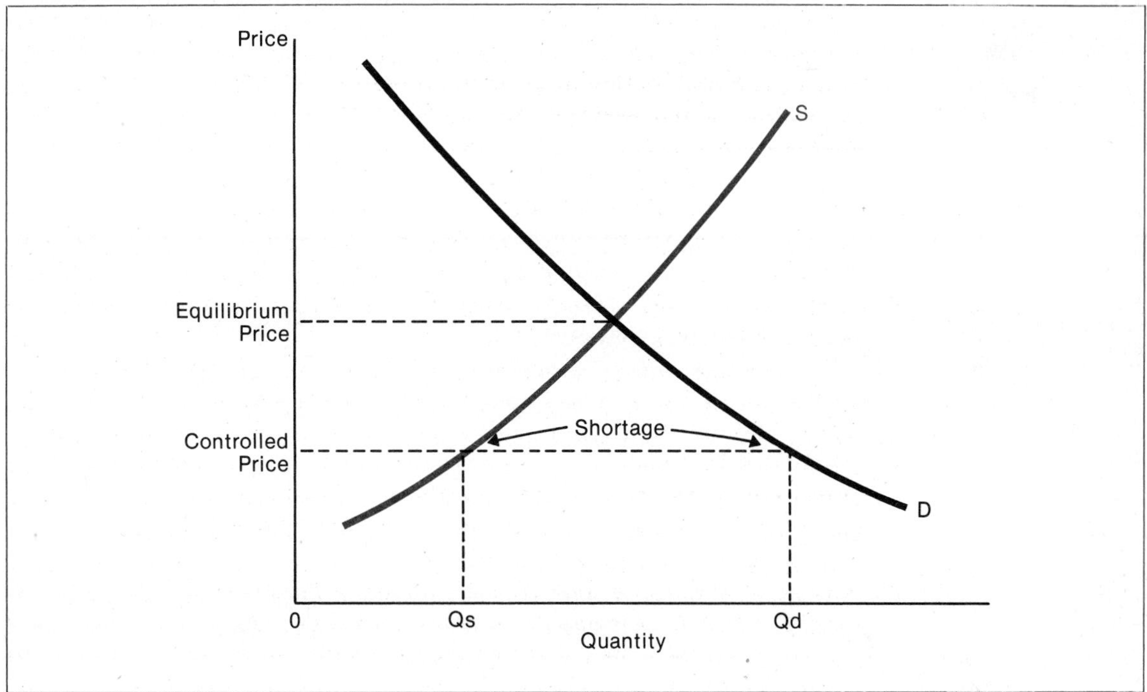

Controls may also affect the distribution of income if they are applied unequally to the various factor payments. For example, if they are imposed on wages and not on rent, interest, and profit, or if they are imposed in another arrangement, some factor suppliers may be injured by controls while others are not, and some income redistribution will result.

Another disadvantage of controls is that they may put the administration implementing them into the embarrassing position of having its authority challenged. This is particularly so with voluntary controls. If, for example, a ceiling of 5 percent on wages is announced, and a major union wins a 10 percent wage increase, an awkward political situation has been created.

Finally, one major disadvantage of wage-price controls is that many policy makers may regard them as a cure for inflation rather than as a method for alleviating its symptoms. The result of this view is that no attempt may be made to correct the root cause of inflation during controls, and their removal may bring serious consequences.

Indexing

Indexing
Factor and/or transfer and/or other payments are automatically increased as prices rise.

A discussion of inflation would not be complete without reference to an increasingly popular response to price pressures called indexing. **Indexing** refers to measures whereby factor, and/or transfer, and/or other payments are automatically raised as prices increase, enabling incomes to keep pace with inflation. Indexing is not a policy tool for curing inflation, but is instead a program to reduce the effects of inflation on the buying power of income recipients. In practice, where indexing is used, a price index such as the consumer price index is adopted as the basis for measuring inflation. Indexed payments are then adjusted periodically, usually monthly or less frequently, to reflect the change in the price index. These upward adjustments may be based on the full percentage change in prices or on some portion of it.

Cost-of-living adjustment (COLA)
An arrangement whereby an individual's wages automatically increase with inflation.

For example, suppose that a union contract contains a **cost-of-living adjustment (COLA)** whereby each worker's pay goes up by an amount equal to the monthly increase in the consumer price index, with the addition to the paycheck beginning one month after the increase. In this case, if the consumer price index were to go up by 1.5 percent in November, an increase by that amount would first be registered in the worker's December check.

As noted in Chapter Four,[18] many income and transfer payments in the United States are adjusted with changes in the various price indexes. These include payments to some union workers as well as Social Security recipients and retired military and federal civil service personnel.

Some advocate indexing because it permits households to keep pace with price increases and lessens the negative effects of inflation. There is, however, much opposition to indexing, including the argument that it tends to worsen inflation.

ALTERNATIVE MACROECONOMIC VIEWPOINTS AND POLICIES

Several policies to achieve the basic goals and alleviate the basic problems of the macroeconomy have been discussed in this and the preceding chapters. Fiscal policy was introduced in Chapter Six, monetary policy was presented in Chapter Eight, and wage-price controls were discussed earlier in this chapter. Is any one of these policy methods more effective than the others? Can monetary policy better solve economic problems than fiscal policy, or is the reverse true? Are there better alternatives to monetary and fiscal policies?

There is no definitive answer to these questions; the choice of a method to stabilize the economy often depends on the preferences of the policy mak-

---

[18]See pages 116–117.

ers. Some people strongly believe that only one policy, such as monetary or fiscal policy, can properly achieve the goals of the macroeconomy, while others believe in some combination of policies.

Over the years, the dispute over preferred macroeconomic policy methods has caused two major camps to emerge: Keynesians and monetarists. In addition to these two major viewpoints, more recent philosophies and theories such as supply-side economics and rational expectations have become popular. Each of these viewpoints merits examination.

Keynesian Economics

Keynesian economics
Based on the work of John Maynard Keynes (1883–1946), who focused on the role of aggregate spending in determining the level of macroeconomic activity.

Classical economic theory
Popularly accepted theory prior to the Great Depression of the 1930s which says that the economy will automatically adjust to full employment.

The ideas of the British economist John Maynard Keynes (1883–1946), whose biographical sketch is given in Application 9.1, form the basis for **Keynesian economics.** Keynes's economics was introduced during the 1930s when the accepted theory of the day, which was called **classical economic theory,** could not explain the cause of, or offer a successful remedy for, the prolonged and severe unemployment that developed during the Great Depression. According to the classical school, which dates back to Adam Smith and the book titled *The Wealth of Nations* in the late 18th century, the use of policy instruments to change economic conditions is unnecessary because a market economy tends to "automatically" operate at full employment. That is, if unemployment were to develop in particular markets where more was produced than demanded, changes would occur in the behavior of businesses and households that would allow the economy to "heal itself" and return to full employment without the aid of any formal policy.[19]

Keynes revolutionized economic thinking by focusing on the role of aggregate, or total, spending in the economy. His major contribution was to link increases and decreases in production and employment with increases and decreases in spending. Keynes refuted the classical notion of an automatic adjustment to full employment, and reasoned that an economy's output and employment position would improve from less than full employment only if aggregate spending increased. Following from this, Keynes pioneered the idea of using government expenditures and taxes to control

[19]The logic behind the automatic adjustment tenet of the classical school rests on the belief that total demand and supply in the economy are equal: there cannot be more produced in the economy than is demanded. According to James Mill (1773–1836), one of the important popularizers of this position, whatever individuals produce over and above their own needs is done to exchange for goods and services produced by others. People produce in order to acquire the things that they desire, so what they supply and what they demand are equal. And if each person's supply and demand are equal, it follows that supply and demand in the entire economy must be equal. Believing that demand and supply are equal for the entire economy, the classical economists saw surpluses in specific markets that would lead to unemployment as being offset by shortages in other markets. The surpluses would be removed by businesses following their own self-interest and guided by the profit motive. See: James Mill, *Elements of Political Economy* (London: Baldwin, Cradock, and Joy, 1826), Chapter IV, Section III, especially pp. 228, 232, 234–235.

the level of economic activity. According to his prescription, the correct policy method for counteracting a depression was to increase aggregate spending, which could be accomplished by increasing government expenditures and/or lowering taxes. Thus, fiscal policy, or the manipulation of government taxes and expenditures to improve overall employment or to dampen demand-pull inflationary pressures, is based on the economic thinking of Keynes. Persons who advocate stabilizing the economy through the use of fiscal policy tend to be referred to as **Keynesians.**

Keynesians
Followers of the ideas of John Maynard Keynes; tend to favor stabilizing the economy through the use of fiscal policy.

Keynesian economics reached its peak of popularity during the 1960s. Since the early 1970s, however, it has become the target for increased attacks. Some have argued that the stagflation of the 1970s could not be explained or remedied in Keynesian terms and that wasteful spending by government and increasing federal government deficits are linked to the Keynesian approach to economic policy. Also, the political mood of the 1980s has called for a movement away from government intervention in the economy, and there has been a surge of interest in other approaches to macroeconomic policy such as monetarism and supply-side economics. As a result, one popular area of debate is whether Keynesian economics still prevails, whether it is dead, or whether it is being revitalized.

Application 9.1
JOHN MAYNARD KEYNES

John Maynard Keynes was born into economics. His father, John Neville Keynes, was a lecturer in economics and logic at Cambridge University. John Maynard began his own studies at Cambridge with an emphasis on mathematics and philosophy. His abilities soon so impressed Alfred Marshall, however, that the distinguished teacher urged him to concentrate on economics. In 1908, after Keynes had finished his studies and done a brief stint in the civil service, Marshall offered him a lectureship in economics at Cambridge, which he accepted.

Keynes is remembered above all for his *General Theory of Employment, Interest, and Money,* published in 1936, although that was by no means his first important work. Keynes's reputation as the outstanding economist of his generation lay in the departure from classical and neoclassical theory he made there. It is hardly necessary to say much about the substance of the *General Theory* in these paragraphs, because they are extensively discussed in every modern textbook on economics. It will be enough to note that its major features are a theory boldly drawn in terms of broad macroeconomic aggregates and a policy position tending toward activism and interventionism.

Keynes was no "narrow" economist. He was an honored member not only of the British academic upper class but also of Britain's highest financial, political, diplomatic, administrative, and even artistic circles. He was intimately involved with the colorful "Bloomsbury set" of London's literary-Bohemian world. He was a friend of Virginia Woolf, E. M. Forster, and Lytton Strachey; and in 1925 he married ballerina Lydia Lopokovia. He was a dazzling success at whatever he turned his hand to, from mountain climbing to financial speculation. As a speculator he made an enormous fortune for himself, and as

Monetarism

Monetarism
The school of thought that favors stabilizing the economy through controlling the money supply.

Monetarists
Persons who favor the economic policies of monetarism.

The school of thought that emphasizes the importance of money in stabilizing the macroeconomy is known as **monetarism.** Those who prefer changing the money supply, rather than fiscal policy, to counteract problems of inflation and unemployment are called **monetarists.**

Monetarism has become an increasingly popular economic viewpoint in recent years. Its most outstanding proponent is Milton Friedman, whose association with the University of Chicago has led some to label followers of his thinking as members of the "Chicago School." Application 9.2 gives some background on Friedman.

One of Friedman's ideas about the proper role of money in the economy is the constant-rate-of-growth rule. This concept challenges traditional thinking on the use of monetary policy by proposing that, rather than increasing or decreasing the supply of money to counteract unemployment or inflation, the money supply should increase by a constant percentage each year. That is, if a 5 percent growth in the money supply is desired, that percentage should be adhered to regardless of economic conditions. It remains to be seen whether the Federal Reserve will continue to adjust the money

John Maynard Keynes

bursar of Kings College he turned an endowment of £30,000 into one of £380,000.

In even the briefest discussion of Keynes, it would be unforgivable not to give his most famous quotation. Writing in the *General Theory,* he pronounced that *the ideas of economists and political philosophers, both when they are right and when they are wrong, are more powerful than is commonly understood. Indeed the world is ruled by little else. Practical men, who believe themselves to be quite exempt from any intellectual influences, are usually the slaves of some defunct economist. Madmen in authority, who hear voices in the air, are distilling their frenzy from some academic scribbler of a few years back. . . . There are not many who are influenced by new theories after they are twenty-five or thirty years of age, so that the ideas which civil servants and politicians and even agitators apply to current events are not likely to be the newest.* Was Keynes issuing a warning here? Whether or not he had any such thing in mind, his words, forty years later, have become one of the great ironies in the history of economic ideas.

---

supply to meet a changing economy or whether it will follow Friedman's prescription.

Monetarism and Milton Friedman are also associated with an emphasis on the free market and limited government intervention in the macroeconomy. Monetarists believe that one of the elements needed to stabilize the economy is free markets.

Supply-Side Economics

Supply-side economics
Policies to stimulate the supply side of the market.

Born in the late 1970s, **supply-side economics** has been popularized by its association with President Ronald Reagan and "Reaganomics." The basic idea behind supply-side economics is to provide an alternative to traditional demand-oriented policies by stimulating the supply, rather than the demand, side of market relationships. Specifically, it proposes the enactment of government policies to stimulate economic activity by creating incentives for individuals and businesses to increase their productive efforts.

The best known supply-side proposal is one to lower taxes for businesses

Application 9.2
MILTON FRIEDMAN

In October 1976 Milton Friedman received the Nobel Memorial Prize in economics, becoming the sixth American to win or share in that prize. Few were surprised. The main surprise was that this most original and influential of economists had had to wait in line so long. The explanation is that Friedman has built his career outside the economics establishment—built it, in fact, by challenging virtually every major establishment doctrine.

Friedman was born in New York in 1912, the son of immigrant garment workers. His hardworking parents sent him across the river to Rutgers University in New Jersey, where Friedman came under the influence of Arthur Burns, then a young assistant professor. From Burns, Friedman learned the importance of empirical work in economics. Statistical testing of all theory and policy prescriptions became a key characteristic of Friedman's later work. From Rutgers, Friedman went to the University of Chicago for an M.A. and then east again to Columbia University, where he got his Ph.D. in 1946. With his degree in hand, he returned to Chicago to teach. There, he became the leading member of the Chicago School, which provides the main intellectual counterweight to the Eastern Establishment in U.S. economics today.

If one were to single out the theme that underlies all of Friedman's work, it would be his conviction that the market economy works—and works best when left alone. This can be seen in his best-known work, *A Monetary History of the United States.* Written with Anna Schwartz, the work challenges two major tenets of orthodox Keynesian economics: first that the market economy is inherently unstable without the guiding hand of government and second that monetary policy had been tried and found useless as a cure for the Great Depression. Friedman and Schwartz found both beliefs to be the opposite of the truth. "The Great Depression," Friedman later wrote, "far from being a sign of the inherent instability of the private enterprise system, is a and individuals. It is argued that lowering the tax burden on businesses will make investments in plants and other productive resources more profitable, thereby stimulating growth in the economy. Also, lowering the tax burden on individuals will lead to greater savings (which can be channeled through financial institutions to businesses for investment purposes) and increase personal incentives to work, both of which should increase productivity. The Economic Recovery Tax Act of 1981 restructured taxes in a direction generally supportive of supply-side ideas.

A second proposal of supply-side economics calls for government regulatory reform to increase productivity. Government regulation is discussed at length in Chapter Fifteen.

Supply-side proposals have a political as well as an economic dimension. Reduced taxes and regulatory requirements lead not only to potentially greater productivity, but also to a lessened presence of government in private economic decision making. Put in terms of economic systems, which were discussed in Chapter Two of the text, supply-side proposals would move the economy more toward individual or market decision making.

Milton Friedman

testament to how much harm can be done by mistakes on the part of a few men when they wield vast power over the monetary system of the country."

Friedman strongly favors a hands-off policy by governments in almost every area, not just in monetary matters. The trouble, in his view, is not that government is evil by nature but rather that so many policies end up having the opposite of their intended effects. "The social reformers who seek through politics to do nothing but serve the public interest invariably end up serving some private interest that was no part of their intention to serve. They are led by an invisible hand to serve a private interest." Transport regulation, public education, agricultural subsidies, and housing programs are among the many policy areas where Friedman believes the government has done more harm than good and where a free competitive market would do better.

Today, Friedman continues to take on new challenges. He promotes his ideas before congressional committees, in professional journals, in his *Newsweek* column, and in face-to-face debate with his colleagues. Economics has never had a more respected heretic.

Rational Expectations

Rational expectations A proposition that the effects of macroeconomic policies might be distorted by the adjustment of business and household behavior in anticipation of policymakers' strategies.

The **rational expectations** theory has developed over the last few years. Its basic proposition is that the effects of macroeconomic policies can be distorted or negated by businesses and households as they anticipate policymakers' strategies and adjust their own behavior accordingly. In its extreme, rational expectations says that government policies to alter the economy may be useless unless they are enacted randomly. The following example illustrates this problem.

Suppose that an instructor has low classroom attendance and decides to improve it by periodic unannounced quizzes. If students have no way of knowing when the quizzes will occur, or if they are given in a truly random fashion, the strategy might be successful and attendance might go up. But suppose that the quizzes are not given randomly and that students notice a pattern: quizzes are given before major campus social or athletic events or holiday breaks. Now, because students can reasonably anticipate when quizzes will be given, they make sure they are present on those days but continue to skip the rest of the classes. In this case, the students' abilities to anticipate the instructor's strategy would significantly reduce or even totally negate its intended effect.

Those favoring the rational expectations approach argue that the same type of problem can occur with economic policy. The results of a policy enacted to stabilize the economy can be distorted by actions taken by households and businesses in anticipation of the policy's enactment. For example, if businesses and households expect the imposition of restrictive fiscal or monetary policy measures to curb inflationary pressure, they might initiate price, wage, and spending adjustments different from those they would have taken had they not anticipated the policy. These adjustments in turn could weaken the effects of the restrictive measures. Can you think of any specific cases where expectations by businesses and households might weaken the effects of stabilization policy?

A FINAL WORD ON MACROECONOMIC THINKING

This completes the section of the book devoted to the goals and instruments of macroeconomic policy. Ideally, a foundation has been established upon which informed judgments can be made about past, present, and future efforts to stabilize the economy.

In assessing various policy proposals it is helpful to keep in mind two facts about economic thinking. First, our understanding of macroeconomic goals and policy instruments must be continually updated and refined as conditions change and knowledge grows. The environment in which goals are pursued and policy tools are employed is continually changing, and new questions and issues are constantly appearing. For example, the age distributions of populations change, international tensions arise and abate, serious worldwide shortages of some resources periodically occur, and new social attitudes evolve over time. These types of developments affect our economic goals and policies. And because of such changes, it is risky to assume that an understanding of the way things operate today will be sufficient to deal with the problems of the future.

Second, in assessing economic policies, keep in mind that the economy is not composed of a set of simple relationships that can be easily manipulated to neatly solve various problems that arise. In learning the role of aggregate spending and the function of fiscal and monetary policies, one can be misled into thinking that economic woes can be easily cured with a simple increase or decrease in the money supply and/or government spending and taxes. In reality, before any macroeconomic policy is initiated, the many ramifications of that policy action must be considered. For example, in decreasing the money supply to fight demand-pull inflation one obvious consequence to consider is the rise in unemployment that occurs as spending declines. But other consequences may also ensue, such as adverse pressures on industries sensitive to the interest rate, like the construction and automobile industries. If one of these industries is already undergoing strain from some other factor, a restrictive monetary policy could cause serious problems.

Economic conditions in late 1980 provided a good example of the complexity of economic problem solving. During this time the Federal Reserve decreased the money supply, causing the prime rate to exceed 20 percent. With high interest rates, automobile purchases fell, which intensified Chrysler Corporation's struggle for survival. In addition, while the Fed was trying to control inflationary pressures, the price of oil increased on world markets, and the effect of the previous summer's poor weather on crops and livestock pushed up food prices. During this time there were constant predictions of an impending recession, and the political mood of the country was to balance the budget. Politicians were also calling for increased defense spending and tax cuts. Clearly, no simple solution existed for all of these economic problems.

Macroeconomics and Microeconomics

In recent years there has been a growing awareness of the impact of microeconomic behavior on the operation of the macroeconomy. That is, more attention has been given to the importance to the macroeconomy of decisions made by individual units within the household and business sectors. The next six chapters are devoted to the operation of individual households and business firms in the microeconomy. The material in these chapters provides an explanation for the behavior of these decision-making units, which is important in its own right, and also sheds additional light on the workings of the macroeconomy.

SUMMARY

A tradeoff exists between full employment and price stability: as the economy approaches full employment, it encounters demand-pull inflationary pressure; and the control of demand-pull inflation is accomplished at the expense of employment. This tradeoff between the rates of unemployment and inflation is illustrated by the downward sloping Phillips curve.

Data from the U.S. economy show that the rates of both unemployment and inflation are generally higher in the 1970s and 1980s than in the 1950s and 1960s. This suggests that in recent years the Phillips curve has shifted to the right, with the tradeoff between unemployment and inflation occurring at higher rates. The shift in the Phillips curve might be explained by an increase in the rate of unemployment that is considered to represent full employment, cost-push inflationary pressure, increased transfer payments to unemployed workers, or other reasons.

Monetary and fiscal policies are not particularly effective for dealing with cost-push inflation. One other policy instrument, wage-price controls, has been resorted to from time to time for dealing with both demand-pull and cost-push inflation. Wage-price controls are restrictions placed by the government on increases in prices and various income payments such as wages. Such restrictions, which may be mandatory or voluntary, are a stopgap measure to alleviate the symptoms but not the causes of inflation. The United States experienced mandatory wage-price controls during World War II, the Korean War, and the early 1970s.

Controls provide an opportunity to curb the symptoms of inflation while attacking its causes with other policies. They may also ease inflationary pressure by improving businesses' and households' expectations about future price increases. At the same time, however, wage-price controls may lead to shortages and black markets, encourage price surges before and after their imposition, redistribute income, and lead to politically embarrassing confrontations and misdirected policy efforts.

Indexing has become a popular response to inflation, although it is not a cure. With indexing, income, transfer, and/or other payments are adjusted as prices change. Both advantages and disadvantages exist for indexing.

There are several points of view on the desirability and effectiveness of different macroeconomic policies. The two major schools of thought are Keynesian economics and monetarism. Keynesians prefer stabilization of the economy through taxes and government spending while monetarists favor adjustments in the money supply. Supple-side economics is a recently popular philosophy that advocates policies such as tax cuts to stimulate productivity in the economy. Rational expectations, another recent approach, is the concept that anticipation of policy decisions distorts their intended impacts.

In evaluating macroeconomic policy proposals, we must continually update our thinking to meet changing conditions. It is also important to realize that the economy is not composed of simple relationships that allow for neat solutions to economic problems. Each policy action has many consequences that must be weighed.

Key Terms and Concepts

Phillips curve
Cost-push inflation
Wage-price controls
Wage-price guideposts
Black markets
Indexing
Cost-of-living adjustment (COLA)
Keynesians
Monetarists
Classical economics
Supply-side economics
Rational expectations

Discussion and Review Questions

1. When the economy is facing high rates of unemployment and inflation, policy makers must decide which of these problems to curb at the expense of the other. What types of information should policy makers possess before deciding to sacrifice employment for price stability, or price stability for employment?
2. What are the unemployment rate and the inflation rate for each year since 1984? Do these numbers generally fall in line with PC2 in Figure 9.2? Comment on your findings.
3. Both demand-pull and cost-push inflation have the same effect on prices. But do these two types of inflation relate in the same way to the level of employment? What policies would you recommend to control inflation if it were of the demand-pull variety? What policy recommendations would you make to limit cost-push inflation?
4. Many people regard wage-price controls as an undesirable policy instrument. Yet, controls are typically given serious consideration in periods of severe inflation. Why do we continue entertaining the use of controls in the absence of their broad support?
5. Would you consider yourself to be Keynesian, classical, monetarist, supply-side, or other in your attitude toward macroeconomic policies? On what reasoning is your preference based?
6. How would you characterize the U.S. trend in unemployment and inflation in recent years? What factors may be contributing to this trend?
7. What is meant by indexing? Give some examples of indexing in the United States. What are some arguments for adopting a national policy of indexing, and what are some problems that could result?
8. What do economists mean by rational expectations? What problems might rational expectations cause for the formulation of economic policy?
9. Macroeconomic policy proposals are frequently tied to politics. In your opinion, which of the policies that you have studied (Keynesian, monetarist, supply-side, rational expectations) is the most politically desirable, and which is the most undesirable? Explain.

Suggested Readings

Phillip Cagan, "Ch. 8: The Reduction of Inflation and the Magnitude of Unemployment," ***Persistent Inflation: Historical and Policy Essays*** **(New York: Columbia University Press, 1979), pp. 203–226.** Discusses changes in the level of full employment, the Phillips curve, and policy implications of the tradeoff between unemployment and inflation.

Thomas J. Hailstones, ***A Guide to Supply-Side Economics*** **(Richmond: Robert F. Dame, Inc., 1982).** An overview of supply-side economics: its background, tenets, and policy implications.

Robert L. Heilbroner, "Modern Economics as a Chapter in the History of Economic Thought," ***Challenge*** **(January–February, 1980), pp. 20–24.** A critical appraisal of modern economic thinking as compared with economic writing from earlier periods.

Thomas R. Swartz, Frank J. Bonello, and Andrew F. Kozak, ***The Supply Side: Debating Current Economic Policies*** **(Guilford, Conn.: Dushkin Publishing Group, Inc., 1983).** Essays and analysis on supply-side economics. Includes writings by President Ronald Reagan, the Council of Economic Advisors, John Kenneth Galbraith, and others.

U.S., "Inflation Control Under the Economic Stabilization Act," ***Economic Report of the President*** **(Washington, D.C.: U.S. Government Printing Office), 1972, pp. 73–100; 1973, pp. 51–70; 1974, pp. 88–109; 1975, pp. 223–229.** A detailed, year-by-year explanation and analysis of wage-price controls during the Nixon administration.

Mark H. Willes, "The Future of Monetary Policy: The Rational Expectations Perspective," ***Federal Reserve Bank of Minneapolis Quarterly Review*** **(Spring 1980), pp. 1–7.** Discusses the importance of expectations in economics, compares rational expectations to the other main approach to economic expectations, and discusses the impact of rational expectations on macroeconomic thinking and policy.

III THE MICROECONOMY

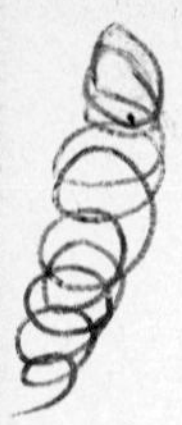

10 HOUSEHOLDS AND BUSINESSES: AN OVERVIEW

Chapter Objectives

1. To provide an overview of some basic characteristics of households and businesses.
2. To introduce the sources and sizes of household income and types of household expenditures.
3. To define the basic objective of economic decision making by individuals.
4. To introduce the balancing process involved in an individual's spending and earning decisions.
5. To identify the legal forms of business.
6. To explain the goal of profit maximization or loss minimization in business decision making and to explore some topics that deal with the goal of profit maximization.

This chapter begins the study of microeconomics. Unlike macroeconomics, which is primarily concerned with businesses and households as groups that influence the operation of the total economy, microeconomics focuses on individual businesses and households as decision-making units and on their relationships to other businesses and households. Because of this focus, a descriptive overview of these two decision-making units and their economic objectives is in order.

This chapter is divided into two sections. The first is devoted to households—their characteristics and the objectives household members seek in making their economic decisions. The second part of the chapter deals with businesses—how they are organized, their overall sizes and structures, and their economic objectives.

OVERVIEW OF HOUSEHOLDS

Characteristics of Households

Before discussing the economic functions and decision making of households in the U.S. economy, let us consider some of their basic characteristics.

By 1983 the population of the United States was about 234 million persons: approximately 114 million males and 120 million females. The median age of this population was 30.9 years, and the great majority lived in urban areas.[1] Almost every one of these persons was part of a household.

Household
A person living alone or a group of related or unrelated persons who occupy a house, apartment, separate group of rooms, or other housing unit.

A **household** is made up of a person living alone or persons, related or unrelated, living in a group, who occupy a "housing unit" such as a house, apartment, or other separate living quarters. Statistics for households are not the same as statistics for families because the definitions of a household and a family are not the same. Only when two or more related individuals are living in a household is it considered to be a family.[2] Thus, for our purposes, household statistics will be used when possible because they are more inclusive than family statistics.

Table 10.1 lists the total number and average size of households in the United States, along with the percentage of single person households for selected years. Although the number of households has been increasing, the average size has been steadily falling, and the percentage of households with one person has been rising. Over the last three decades households with two or more persons living together have come to represent a shrinking portion of the total households in the United States. This is obviously due to an increase in the number of unmarried (single, divorced, and widowed) adults establishing households.

Household Income and Expenditures

In the discussion of a market economy in Chapter Two, the circular flow model illustrated that households perform two basic functions: (1) they sell factors of production to businesses in return for income; and (2) they purchase goods and services from businesses. These two money flows—household income and expenditures—can be examined statistically to obtain a general understanding of the sources and sizes of household income as well as the types of expenditures households make.

Household Income While most household income is from the sale of resources, some income also comes from government transfer payments.[3]

---

[1]U.S. Bureau of the Census, *Statistical Abstract of the United States: 1985* (105th ed.), Washington, D.C., 1984, pp. 22, 26.

[2]*Statistical Abstract: 1985*, p. 4. Households do not include persons living in group quarters such as jails or military barracks.

[3]Recall that government transfers are payments such as unemployment compensation for which no direct work is performed.

Table 10.1
Basic Characteristics of U.S. Households in Selected Years

Over the last several decades the number of households has nearly doubled, but the average number of persons per household has fallen. This decrease in the average size of households can be explained in part by the growing percentage of households made up of one person.

Characteristic	Year				
	1950	1960	1970	1980	1984
Total number of households	43,554,000	52,799,000	63,401,000	80,776,000	85,407,000
Average number of persons per household	3.4	3.3	3.1	2.8	2.7
Percent of households with one person	9.1	13.1	17.1	22.7	23.4

Source: U.S. Bureau of the Census, *Statistical Abstract of the United States: 1985* (105th ed.), Washington, D.C., 1984, p. 40.

Personal income
Household gross, or pretax, income; income households use to pay taxes, spend, and save.

This is shown in Table 10.2, which lists the sources of pretax income, or **personal income,** on a percentage basis for selected years. The figures indicate that income earned from the sale of resources, particularly labor resources, is the primary source of household income. The figures also show that while wages and salaries have remained relatively stable as a percentage of total income through the years, other types of earned income have not. Proprietors' income, dividends, and rent have declined in importance, and interest income has increased.

Table 10.2 also illustrates the growing importance of transfer payments in providing income: up from 6.7 percent of total personal income in 1950 to 14.8 percent in 1983. Recent statistics also indicate that approximately 44 percent of all families received some type of transfer income in 1982.[4] Table 10.3 divides cash transfer payments into various program categories, showing the percentage of total benefits going to each program in 1970 and 1981. The greatest amount of transfer funds in both years went to recipients of social security benefits.

How large is the average household income? How much does income differ from household to household due to the age, sex, or education of the head of the household? Table 10.4 gives the average income of all household heads for 1983, as well as average income according to selected characteristics of the household head. Although this table shows an average income of $20,885 for all households in 1983, there is a significant difference between this average for all households and the average for households in certain subgroups of the population. For example, households headed by a male averaged $25,467 in 1983, while households headed by a female averaged $11,667, or about 46 percent of the average for households headed by

[4] *Statistical Abstract: 1985,* p. 459.

Table 10.2
Sources of Personal Income (Percent Distribution for Selected Years)

Since 1950, the percentage of income attributable to wages and salaries has remained fairly stable, while interest income and transfer payments have grown and rent, dividends, and proprietors' income have fallen in relative importance.

Source of Income	Year 1950	1955	1960	1965	1970	1975	1980	1983
Earned Income								
Wages, salaries, and other labor income	66.6%	70.9%	70.4%	70.2%	71.7%	68.8%	68.6%	66.8%
Proprietors' income	17.0	13.8	11.7	10.5	8.2	7.1	5.4	4.4
Rental income	3.1	3.7	3.5	3.3	2.4	1.8	1.5	2.1
Dividends	3.9	3.3	3.2	3.5	2.7	2.4	2.6	2.6
Interest income	3.9	4.5	6.2	7.4	8.5	9.7	12.3	13.7
Unearned Income								
Transfer payments	6.7	5.7	7.2	7.4	9.9	14.1	13.7	14.8
Personal Contributions for Social Insurance[a]	−1.3	−1.7	−2.2	−2.4	−3.5	−4.0	−4.1	−4.4
Personal Income[b]	100.0	100.0	100.0	100.0	100.0	100.0	100.0	100.0

[a]Contributions for social insurance (social security) are subtracted from earned income in calculating personal income.
[b]Columns may not total 100.0 due to rounding.

Source: 1950–1955 data from U.S. Bureau of the Census, *Statistical Abstract of the United States: 1978* (99th ed.), Washington, D.C., 1978, p. 447; 1960–1965 data from *Statistical Abstract of the United States: 1982–83* (103d ed.), 1982, p. 425; 1970–1984 data from *Statistical Abstract of the United States: 1985* (105th ed.), 1984, p. 438.

Table 10.3
Percentage of Total Cash Benefit Payments to Various Transfer Programs

Over 50 percent of cash transfer payments in 1970 and 1981 went to recipients of social security benefits.

Program	Year 1970	1981
Total[a]	100.0%	100.0%
OASDHI[b]	52.2	53.5
Public employee retirement	15.2	19.2
Railroad retirement	2.9	2.2
Veterans' pensions, compensation	9.1	5.2
Unemployment benefits	7.0	5.7
Temporary disability benefits	1.2	0.7
Workers' compensation	3.3	4.2
Public assistance	8.0	5.5
Supplemental security income	—	3.5

[a]Columns may not total 100.0 due to rounding.
[b]Includes old age, health, and other Social Security programs.

Source: U.S. Bureau of the Census, *Statistical Abstract of the United States: 1985* (105th ed.), Washington, D.C., 1984, p. 358.

Table 10.4
Average Money Income of Households in 1983

The average incomes of households differ according to the age, sex, and education of the household head.

Characteristic	Average Income[a]
All households	$20,885
Households headed by a male	25,467
Households headed by a female	11,667
Households with head aged 25–34 yrs.	21,746
Households with head aged 65 yrs. and over	11,718
Households with head attaining 4 yrs. of high school	20,800
Households with head attaining 4 yrs. of college or more	34,709

[a]The average used is the median.

Source: U.S. Bureau of the Census, *Statistical Abstract of the United States: 1985* (105th ed.), Washington, D.C., 1984, p. 443.

a male. Not surprisingly, the average income of households where the head is from 25 to 34 years old, and probably attached to the labor force, is greater than the average income of households where the head is 65 years of age or older, and perhaps retired from the labor force. Notice also from this table that average incomes correlate positively with education: on the average, households headed by a person with four years of college or more earned over $13,000 a year more in 1983 than households headed by a person with just four years of high school.

Household Expenditures How do households use their incomes? Basically, income is used for three purposes: spending, saving, and paying taxes. In 1983 each person, on the average, spent 81.0 percent of his or her personal income, saved 4.3 percent, and paid 14.7 percent in personal tax and nontax payments.[5] Clearly, the vast majority of income is used to purchase goods and services. These figures, however, can be misleading because they are averages. For incomes higher than the average, a greater percentage is taxed and saved, and for incomes lower than the average, a smaller percentage is taxed and saved.

There are several ways to view how households spend their incomes. One is to categorize expenditures according to whether the items purchased are durable goods, nondurable goods, or services. A **durable good** is one that has a useful lifetime of more than one year—an automobile, musical instrument, or furniture, for example—and a **nondurable good** is one with a short span of use—such as food or gasoline. In recent years, the largest portion of household expenditures has gone for services—medical care, for example—followed by nondurable goods and durable goods. In 1983 the average person used 49.8 percent of total expenditures for services, 37.2 percent for nondurable goods, and 13.0 percent for durable goods.[6] The exact proportions

Durable good
A good that has a useful lifetime of more than one year.

Nondurable good
A good that has a short useful lifetime.

[5]*Statistical Abstract: 1985*, p. 433.

[6]*Statistical Abstract: 1985*, p. 433.

spent on these categories have not stayed constant over time; the proportion spent for services has been increasing.

A second way of examining how households use their money is to observe how much is spent on various types of goods and services such as food, clothing, gasoline, dry-cleaning, and so forth. Table 10.5 illustrates this approach by showing total expenditures for selected items in 1983.

Goals and Decisions of Individuals in Households

Since most household economic activity revolves around earning and spending money, it follows that the main economic decisions of individuals in households relate to how they earn and how they spend their incomes. These decisions range from major considerations such as whether to attend college to possibly improve future earnings and whether to live at home with one's parents or rent an apartment, to minor daily questions such as whether to purchase a soda or pretzels from a vending machine. What objective is being sought in making these earning and spending decisions?

Maximizing economic well-being
Obtaining the greatest possible satisfaction, or return, from an economic decision.

In making economic decisions, individuals are trying to obtain the most satisfaction possible from their decisions. In other words, they are attempting to **maximize their economic well-being.** For example, in choosing how to spend your money this year, you decided upon a course in economics because of the satisfaction, or return, you expected to receive from learning economics and/or completing certain degree requirements.

Maximizing economic well-being is not the same as acquiring all the goods and services that can possibly be acquired, since this course of action would require that an individual spend every waking hour earning income

Table 10.5
Household Purchases of Selected Goods and Services in 1983 (Billions of Dollars)

One method for evaluating the buying behavior of individuals in households is to observe the amounts they spend on different types of goods and services.

Type of Product	Expenditure
Food	$365.1
Alcoholic beverages and tobacco products	79.7
Motor vehicles and parts	129.3
Gasoline and oil	90.0
Clothing and accessories	106.4
Shoes and other footwear	20.5
Jewelry and watches	12.8
Cleaning, storage, and repair of shoes and clothing	7.3
Housing	363.3
Furniture and household equipment	104.1
Household operation	153.8
Transportation	72.5

Source: U.S. Bureau of the Census, *Statistical Abstract of the United States: 1985* (105th ed.), Washington, D.C., 1984, p. 435.

for purchases. After following such a strategy, most people would surely decide that economic satisfaction might be increased with a little more leisure time, even at the expense of some goods and services.

Maximizing economic well-being is a balancing process. It involves weighing the advantages, or benefits, and the disadvantages, or costs, of different courses of action and selecting the one strategy that contributes most to economic satisfaction. This notion of balancing becomes apparent when the maximizing goal is applied to the basic spending and earning decisions.

Maximizing Satisfaction from Consuming Goods and Services Since incomes are limited, individuals are unable to obtain all of the goods and services they would like to have. This reality is the individual's own version of the basic economic problem: limited resources in comparison to the wants and needs to be satisfied. Because of this basic problem, individuals must choose, within the limits of their incomes, which goods and services and how much of each they will acquire.

The actual allocation of dollars for purchases can be done in many different ways. For example, a person might choose dinner in an expensive restaurant instead of enrolling in a recreation program, or might choose many record albums instead of new clothing. The problem in determining how to spend one's money is that each spending arrangement, or each combination of goods and services purchased, leads to a different level of satisfaction. And only one of those combinations of goods and services will give more satisfaction than any other. If an individual is to maximize the satisfaction received from purchasing, or consuming, goods and services, he or she must select that one combination of goods and services that gives more satisfaction than any other combination.

Utility
Satisfaction realized from the consumption of a good or service.

Economists refer to the satisfaction received from consuming a good or service as **utility.** Thus, the goal of the individual in making spending decisions is to pick, within the limits of his or her income, the combination of goods and services that gives maximum total utility. To maximize total utility, an individual must evaluate each good or service that might be purchased by weighing the satisfaction that can be obtained from each unit consumed against the price of the good or service. This decision-making process can be illustrated through some simple examples.

Example 1: Suppose that you are at a movie and have just finished a box of popcorn and a soft drink. You would like more of each; however, a box of popcorn costs 40¢, and a soft drink costs 40¢, and you have only 40¢ left. How should this money be spent?

Obviously, it should be spent on whichever of the two items adds the greatest amount of satisfaction. If the popcorn would satisfy you more than the soft drink, the 40¢ should be spent for the popcorn; if the reverse is true, the 40¢ should be spent for the soda. The point is, to maximize satisfaction, your 40¢ should be spent on the item that adds the most for the money to your total utility.

In this example, the choice is easy because all you have to consider is the added satisfaction provided by a box of popcorn compared to a soft drink. You do not have to consider their prices because they are the same. But what about the situation where a person is choosing between items with different prices? This is taken up in the second example.

Example 2: Suppose that you have $20 to spend over the weekend and would like to see a movie for $5, dine at the local pizzeria for $10, go to a concert where the tickets are $20 each, buy an album for $11, and purchase a $4 paperback book. Obviously you cannot obtain all of these items for $20. How will you allocate your expenditures?

In making your spending decisions, you must consider the satisfaction received from each item in comparison to the dollars spent on that item. If you use your money to purchase a $20 ticket to the concert, the satisfaction that you receive from the concert must be at least twice the satisfaction from the $10 pizza, or four times the satisfaction from the $5 movie to maximize your utility. If the concert would give you the same satisfaction as a movie or a pizza, you would not be allocating your money in the best manner possible by spending it on the concert. If you spend your $20 to purchase a paperback book, an album, and a movie, those items *together* should give you as much satisfaction as the concert. If they do not, you have not maximized your utility with this spending arrangement.

A simple rule emerges here: to maximize satisfaction from purchasing goods and services, expenditures must be allocated in a way that gives the most utility *for the purchaser's money.* In deciding between popcorn and soda, you should have spent your 40¢ on the item that gave the greatest satisfaction for the money. In allocating your $20 among the various alternative goods that it could purchase, you should have weighed the utility received from each item against its price. Maximizing utility is not simply a matter of receiving more satisfaction from one item than another. Rather, it is a matter of receiving more satisfaction for the money. A Porsche or Corvette might give you a great deal of satisfaction—but the price tag is high. You might get more total satisfaction from a less expensive car plus the other goods and services that the lower-priced car allows you to purchase. In making spending decisions, an individual must consider both the utility received from the item and the price of the item.

Can these textbook examples be seen at work in the real world? Do people really use these balancing principles in making purchasing decisions? The answer is yes, they do! The process might not be quite as precise as in the examples presented here, but basically consumers compare the price of an item with the expected addition to satisfaction from acquiring the item. If you have ever walked through a supermarket and noticed a shopper staring intently at a bag of chips, he or she might have been trying to decide if the additional satisfaction from what was in the bag would be worth the price, or whether satisfaction would be increased by taking something else. If you were ever given a free sample of an item, and, on the basis of the sample, decided never to buy it, you applied the additional satisfaction-price test; you thought that, if purchased, what the item would add to your total utility would not be worth its price. If you left a clothing store with, say, a $30 shirt and a $10 belt, and if the shirt did not add three times as much to your enjoyment as did the belt, you could have made more want-satisfying purchases at the clothing store than you actually made. In each of these cases the balancing of satisfactions and prices comes into play. Can you see how this balancing process is at work in Application 10.1, "The Saga of Bill and Sarah"?

Maximizing Satisfaction from Earning Income Why can two people earn the same income on their jobs, and yet one moonlights while the other does not? Obviously, the wants and needs of the two workers must be different. One may contribute to the support of a family while the other may not. One may be saving for a vacation, or paying off a loan, or simply interested in earning a lot of money for the sake of earning a lot of money. More generally, the difference between the two workers is that one is moonlighting because, to that worker, the value of the additional income is greater than the additional effort required to earn it. For the other worker, the extra income is not worth the extra effort.

The moonlighting example illustrates that, as with spending decisions, maximizing satisfaction from earning income is a matter of balancing. On the one hand, there is the additional income from working more hours which can be spent on goods and services. On the other, working extra hours

Application 10.1
THE SAGA OF BILL AND SARAH

Meet Bill and Sarah, both 39. Bill is a vice president at an ad agency and Sarah is a pediatrician. Successful people both. Their estimated 1983 family income is $265,000—an amount that until recently was considered very big money.

. . . I recently accompanied Bill and Sarah on a typical Saturday round of shopping in New York. It began at Bottega Veneta, where Bill purchased a new address book bound in fine leather for $135. Sarah wanted to replace a broken wineglass, so they stopped next at Baccarat, where they spent $209 for the glass and a decanter.

Next? Tiffany's? Saks Fifth? Dunhill's? Nope. They strolled down Fifth Avenue and stopped at a large discount store that sells distressed merchandise—inventories bought from shops and distributors that have gone bankrupt or have overstocked a particular item. There Sarah bought a variety of housewares, dirt cheap. For instance, plastic food storage containers, light bulbs, batteries and gift-wrap paper. Bill bought a new hammer. Total outlay in the store: $21. . . .

It was getting dark, and the two decided to go downtown to Greenwich Village for dinner, dressed casually as they were. Once they got there, they remembered that there was an old Peter Sellers movie they wanted to see on TV at 9 p.m. Dinner would have to be brief.

You have probably already guessed what they did next. They bypassed the fancier places like means less time for other activities. A person who spends the same number of hours on a job week after week may not give a great deal of thought to this balancing until the opportunity to earn more income through longer hours of work presents itself. At some point, as more hours are worked, the extra income and the satisfaction it brings may not be enough to justify the dissatisfaction from forgoing other activities as a result of working, and further overtime is refused.

In summary, both spending and earning decisions involve the goal of maximizing economic well-being. The decision maker must weigh the advantages, or benefits, and disadvantages, or costs, of different strategies to choose the one that will come closest to accomplishing that objective. This weighing, or balancing, which is at the heart of the individual decision-making process, is covered in detail in the next chapter.

OVERVIEW OF BUSINESS

Business
An organization established for the purpose of producing and selling goods and services.

A **business** is an organization established for the purpose of producing and selling goods and services. In the United States there are over 16.4 million legally organized business firms. Many are small operations with annual sales of under $25,000, while others are huge enterprises selling billions of dollars worth of goods and services each year.[7]

[7]See Table 10.7.

the ones where Bill has business lunches four days a week. They had a pizza instead, with mushrooms and green peppers. Then they took a cab back to their Park Avenue co-op. Bill tipped the cabby adequately, but not extravagantly. . . .

If you think of these two as eccentric, you will miss the point entirely. They are anything but. . . .

Although the general public has a picture of the rich as people who merely throw their money away, buying products without even looking at the price tag, I have found the reverse to be true. Wealth and education are correlated; people with high incomes are significantly more likely to be college graduates. Instead of being indifferent or blasé about price, they are usually better comparison shoppers than most.

However, one key aspect of their consumer behavior may at first strike you as paradoxical. For instance, once Bill and Sarah decide to buy a brand-name product, do they head for their favorite department store? No more. They shop at a discount store instead. As long as they know the product is the same, they are not inclined to pay extra for it. But they will go to a prestige store if they want to buy a product bearing a name with which they may not be familiar. In this case, they are depending on the store to act as the guarantor that the product is okay. . . .

To put it another way, the next time you see a Rolls-Royce parked in front of a successful discount store, don't assume it belongs to the store's owner.

Source: Srully Blotnick, "The Saga of Bill and Sarah," *Forbes*, December 19, 1983, p. 236. Reprinted by permission.

Business decisions, especially about output and prices, have a powerful influence on the economy, with the degree of influence depending on the size of the business and the competitive structure of the market in which the business is selling. A very large firm can have a significant impact on employment conditions in the economy in general and in an industry or region specifically. Imagine the consequences of shutting down General Motors or any of the other firms listed in Table 10.6!

The competitive structure of the market in which a business operates influences the prices that it charges for its products. A company producing items with little or no competition can charge higher prices than those charged under more competitive conditions. In fact, a large firm or a few large firms with a substantial share of a market could contribute to cost-push inflationary pressure when they raise prices.

Before the specifics of business decision making are studied, let us examine the legal organizations of business and the current overall structure of American business.

Legal Forms of Business

A business must take on a legal form before it can operate; it may be (1) a proprietorship, (2) a partnership, or (3) a corporation.

Proprietorship
A one-owner business.

Proprietorship A one-owner business that is typically small—for example, a retailing establishment like a drugstore or flower shop, or an independent consultant—is called a **proprietorship.** Usually in a proprietorship the owner is the manager and a jack-of-all-trades, performing functions such as those of a bookkeeper, financial analyst, and marketing specialist. For the owner of the business this legal form has the advantage of independence in decision making; the owner is not responsible or answerable to anyone.

Table 10.6
The Ten Largest U.S. Industrial Corporate Employers in 1984

The employment decisions of very large corporations that employ hundreds of thousands of people can have a major impact on households, other businesses, governments, and the economy in general.

Rank	Corporation	Number of Employees[a]
1	General Motors	748,000
2	International Business Machines	394,930
3	Ford Motor	383,700
4	American Telephone & Telegraph	365,000
5	General Electric	340,000[b]
6	International Telephone & Telegraph	252,000
7	United Technologies	205,500
8	Mobil	178,900
9	Du Pont	157,783
10	Exxon	150,000

[a]Many of these figures are the average for the year.
[b]Figure is for 1983.

Source: "The 500 Largest U.S. Industrial Corporations," *Fortune,* April 29, 1985, pp. 266–267.

A proprietorship, however, poses several problems for its owner: particularly, difficulty in raising money and unlimited liability. The owner of a proprietorship who wants to raise money for expansion, remodeling, or such, can do so only by borrowing from private sources such as family or friends, or from the traditional financial institutions like commercial banks and savings and loan associations, or through certain government programs. Because proprietorships cannot issue stocks and bonds, a large source of money capital cannot be readily tapped by the single-owner business.

Unlimited liability A business owner's personal assets are subject to use as payment for business debts.

A proprietor is also subject to **unlimited liability;** that is, the owner's personal assets are subject to use as payment for business debts. If a creditor cannot be fully paid from the assets of the business, the courts may take the owner's personal property to satisfy such debts.

Partnership The legal organization of a business that is similar to a proprietorship but has two or more owners.

Partnership A business that is similar to a proprietorship but has two or more (perhaps hundreds of) owners is a **partnership.** This arrangement permits the pooling of money, experience, and talent. For example, a person who is skilled in cooking and kitchen administration and a person who is adept at business-related matters such as management and finance might form a successful restaurant operation. Unfortunately, the partnership arrangement often leads to dissension between partners, resulting in dissolution of the business.

General partner An owner of a partnership who is subject to unlimited liability.

In a partnership, unless it is legally specified in writing, all partners become general partners. A **general partner** is one who has the burden of unlimited liability, and each partnership must have at least one general partner. If misunderstood, unlimited liability for a partner can be a potential source of problems. In a partnership each general partner is responsible for 100 percent of the business's debts. In case of default, liability is not necessarily divided in half, or in thirds, or other equal amounts. Instead, the debts beyond those covered by the business's assets will be paid through the personal assets of whichever partners possess the means. If one general partner is penniless and the other wealthy, the partner with the assets will pay the debts.

Corporation A legal entity, owned by stockholders, which can carry on in its own name functions of business normally performed by individuals.

Corporation An entity created by law, a **corporation** is a "legal person" in that it can sue or be sued, make contracts, pay fines, and carry on other aspects of business normally performed by individuals. The one human characteristic that a corporation does not possess is death: a corporation can continue indefinitely.

To form a corporation, a charter must be obtained from one of the states. The choice of the state for incorporation will probably be based on varying regulations, taxes, and the like. This charter, the acquiring of which involves some cost and red tape, usually contains information such as the corporate name, the corporation's purpose, and the number of shares of stock it is authorized to sell.

As a corporation is established, shares of stock are sold (additional shares may be sold later), and the holders of these shares become the owners of the corporation. One major advantage for the owners of a corporation is limited liability; that is, all of their personal assets are *not* subject to payment for business debts. In case of bankruptcy of a corporation, an owner can lose only the money used to purchase the stock. This sum, however, could be considerable.

The owners of a corporation receive profits from the corporation through quarterly dividend checks. The size of the dividend check depends upon the corporation's profitability and the type of stock an owner possesses. Corporations can issue both preferred and common stock. **Preferred stock** remits a stated dividend to its holders. **Common stock** pays a dividend dependent upon the profit position of the firm after creditors and preferred stockholders have been paid. A quarter with healthy sales and sizable profits might yield a high return on common stock, whereas a quarter with no profit will yield no dividend check.[8] Application 10.2 discusses the price of a share of stock and how that price is determined by supply and demand.

Preferred stock
Stock that pays a stated dividend to its holder.

Common stock
Stock that pays a dividend dependent upon the profit position of a firm after all other financial obligations have been met.

Each share of common stock entitles its owner to one vote. These votes

[8]Preferred stock does not guarantee a dividend. If the company has not made enough profit for a return to the preferred stockholders, they will not receive a dividend.

Application 10.2
THE SUPPLY, DEMAND, AND PRICE OF STOCK SHARES

A stock exchange is a facility for trading stock. Only the stocks of corporations listed on a particular exchange may be traded there. The best-known exchanges are the New York Stock Exchange (NYSE) and the American Stock Exchange (AMEX). Most major newspapers carry the daily market data for companies listed on these two exchanges.

The price at which a share of a corporation's common stock is bought and sold may change daily, or hourly, or by the minute. This is due to changes in buyers' and sellers' plans that affect demand and supply. To illustrate, let us assume that a hypothetical company, the Grand Corporation, is listed on the New York Stock Exchange. We will also assume that the demand and supply for Grand common stock as of the opening of the exchange today is given in the figure shown in this application.

The downward sloping demand curve indicates that as the price per share increases, buyers will decrease the quantity of shares demanded. The upward sloping supply curve shows that as the price per share increases, sellers will be willing to sell more. In this market, the equilibrium price is $18.00 per share, and 3,000 shares are bought and sold.

What could cause this equilibrium price to change? Any factor that increases or decreases the supply and/or demand of Grand stock may do so. For example, suppose that the media carry a rumor that Grand is about to sign a lucrative are used to determine some corporate policies and, more importantly, to elect the corporation's board of directors. The board of directors is the governing board of a corporation and makes many major decisions, including the selection of top management of the firm. Top management, in turn, runs the corporation on a day-to-day basis. Figure 10.1 outlines the structure of a corporation.

Because each share of common stock carries a vote, control of a corporation centers around those who hold large numbers of shares. These stockholders have the power to elect themselves or their candidates to the board of directors. The number of shares necessary for control depends upon the number of shares outstanding. A few thousand shares in a small corporation might yield control, but a few thousand shares in a company like General Motors might be negligible.

Bond
A financial instrument through which a corporation can borrow long-term funds.

No discussion of a corporation is complete without some mention of **bonds.** Corporations sell bonds to raise money for building, expansion, and other purposes. Bonds provide a corporation with an avenue other than stocks to tap other corporations, private individuals, and organizations for funds. Corporate bonds are sold in $1,000 denominations and have a specified interest rate and maturity date. A bondholder is a creditor of the company and not an owner.

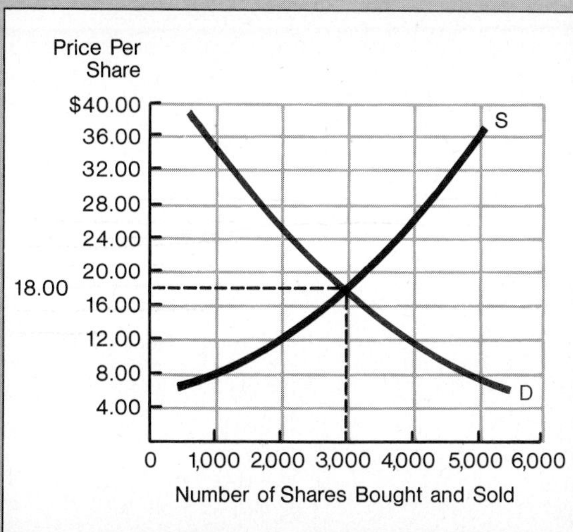

government contract. This rumor may cause investors to want to purchase Grand stock, increasing the demand (shifting the curve to the right) and causing an increase in equilibrium price.

What would be the effect on demand, supply, and equilibrium price of the following?

1. A major pension fund holding a large amount of Grand stock decides to sell its shares.
2. Corporate reports indicate that sales and profits are increasing.
3. Corporate sales and profits are on a slow, constant decline.
4. Returns on alternative investments are increasing.

Figure 10.1
Structure of a Corporation

The stockholders who own a corporation elect a board of directors that makes major decisions for the corporation and appoints top management to run the corporation.

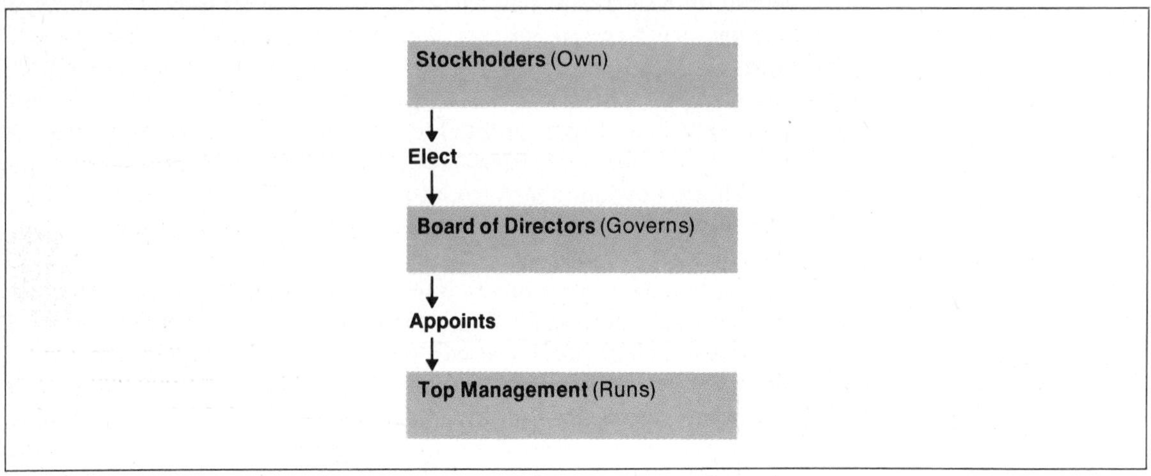

Numbers and Sizes of Businesses

Table 10.7 gives the number of legally organized businesses in the United States and the size of business receipts (sales) in 1981. Statistics are given for all businesses as a group and for each individual legal form. Observe that according to Table 10.7, in 1981 there were 16,458,000 businesses, with the vast majority, 12,185,000 (or 74.0 percent), organized as proprietorships. Only 2,812,000 (or 17.1 percent) were corporations. The table also shows, however, that most of the business receipts went to corporations. Of the approximately $7.8 trillion in total sales, corporations accounted for $7.03 trillion (or 89.9 percent). Proprietorships, on the other hand, received only $0.52 trillion (or 6.6 percent) of the total sales.

This table reveals that the vast majority of businesses are organized as proprietorships, but that these proprietorships are generally small in size and account for a small percentage of the total sales of the economy. While

Table 10.7
Number and Receipts of Proprietorships, Partnerships, and Corporations: 1981

Although the vast majority of U.S. firms are organized as proprietorships, they account for a small percentage of business receipts. Most receipts go to corporations.

Business Firms	Number	Number as a Percentage of the Total	Receipts	Receipts as a Percentage of the Total
Total	16,458,000	100.0%	$7.82 trillion	100.0%
Proprietorships	12,185,000	74.0	0.52 trillion	6.6
Partnerships	1,461,000	8.9	0.27 trillion	3.5
Corporations	2,812,000	17.1	7.03 trillion	89.9

Source: U.S. Bureau of the Census, *Statistical Abstract of the United States: 1985* (105th ed.), Washington, D.C., 1984, p. 516.

corporations are fewer in number than proprietorships, they tend to be larger in size and account for most business sales.

Table 10.8 examines the sizes of businesses by classifying firms according to the amount of their annual receipts or sales. The left-hand column gives various size classes of receipts; for example, if a business sold $125,000 in goods and services, it would be included in the $100,000–$499,999 category. The upper portion of the table gives the number of businesses in each category and the dollar value of all receipts acquired by all businesses in each category during 1981. For example, in 1981 there were 1,474,000 businesses, each of which sold between $25,000 and $49,999 in goods and services and whose sales together amounted to $49.9 billion. The lower portion of the table converts the figures from the upper portion into percentages.

According to the lower portion of Table 10.8, 57.9 percent of all reported businesses sold less than $25,000 in goods and services in 1981. Together these businesses accounted for 0.7 percent of all goods and services sold that year. In other words, most business firms are extremely small in size. On the other hand, only 3.7 percent of all businesses sold over $1,000,000 each in goods and services; but these firms together received 86.9 percent of all receipts in 1981. Thus, a very small percentage of U.S. businesses is providing the vast majority of what is sold. Both Tables 10.7 and 10.8 confirm that there are far more small U.S. businesses than large ones.

Business Ownership of Business

Owners of corporate stock need not be private individuals. Much stock is owned by funds such as pension and endowment funds, and by corporations. In fact, in many instances, the controlling shares of stock in one cor-

Table 10.8
Number of Businesses and Business Receipts Classified by Size of Receipts: 1981

The majority of business receipts goes to a small percentage of firms. For example, in 1981 only 3.7 percent of all reported business firms were in the category of $1 million and over, but together they accounted for 86.9 percent of total receipts.

Size Class of Receipts	Number of Businesses (Thousands)	Receipts (Billions of Dollars)
Under $25,000[a]	8,028	$46.8
$25,000–$49,999	1,474	49.9
$50,000–$99,999	1,352	90.8
$100,000–$499,999	2,068	439.3
$500,000–$999,999	423	282.4
$1,000,000 or more	512	6,023.8
Percent Distribution		
Under $25,000[a]	57.9%	0.7%
$25,000–$49,999	10.6	0.7
$50,000–$99,999	9.8	1.3
$100,000–$499,999	14.9	6.3
$500,000–$999,999	3.1	4.1
$1,000,000 or more	3.7	86.9

[a]Includes firms with no receipts.

Source: U.S. Bureau of the Census, *Statistical Abstract of the United States: 1985* (105th ed.), Washington, D.C., 1984, p. 516.

Figure 10.2
Corporate Ownership of Other Corporations (Hypothetical Examples)

There is no functional relationship between Circle Graphics and T. D. Frozen Pizza, while ABC Real Estate and ABC Building Designs are important to the operation of ABC Homebuilders.

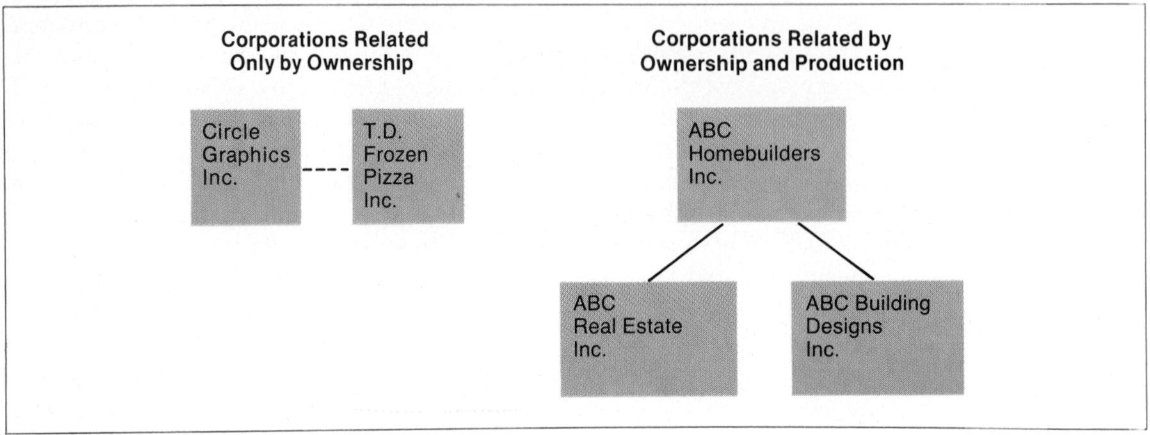

poration are owned by another corporation; in these cases, the corporation that owns the stock is said to own the other corporation.

It is often not readily apparent when one corporation owns another, because both businesses may retain separate identities and operate as distinct entities. For example, the general public may not be aware that the 7-Up Corporation is owned by Philip Morris, or that the publisher of this text, The Dryden Press, is a division of Holt, Rinehart and Winston, which is owned by CBS, Inc.

Sometimes, when corporations own other corporations, there is no relationship between the goods or services that the two corporations produce. A manufacturer of toys could own a carburetor company, or an electronic components producer might own a wallpaper firm. Beatrice Foods, for example, owns the Great Bear Spring Company, Fisher Nut Company, and Samsonite Corporation.[9] In other instances, a corporation may own other corporations that are integral to it and to each other. The U.S. Steel Corporation owns U.S. Steel Mining Company, Duluth, Missabe and Iron Range Railway Company, and U.S.S. Great Lakes Fleet.[10] The distinction between corporations related by ownership, and corporations related by ownership and production is shown in Figure 10.2.

Sometimes a corporation is formed for the purpose of owning or holding

---

[9] Moody's Investors Service, *Moody's Industrial Manual: 1984,* vol. 1 (New York: Moody's Investors Service, Inc., 1984), p. 2605.

[10] *Moody's Industrial Manual: 1984,* vol. 2, p. 6095.

Figure 10.3
The Alltown Bank Holding Company

The purpose of a holding company, such as Alltown Bank Corporation, is to own shares of stock in other companies, such as Hometown Bank and Crosstown Bank.

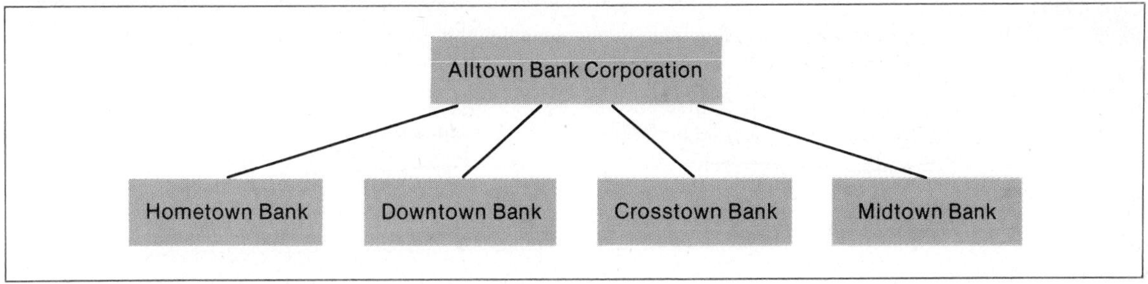

Holding company
A corporation formed for the purpose of owning or holding stock in other corporations.

stock in other corporations. This type of company is termed a **holding company.** A holding company produces nothing itself. Figure 10.3 shows a hypothetical example of a bank holding company, Alltown, which exists only to own controlling shares of stock in Hometown Bank, Downtown Bank, and other banks.

Merger (acquisition)
The acquiring of one company by another company; can be accomplished by buying a controlling amount of stock.

The buying of controlling shares of stock in one corporation by another corporation is referred to as a **merger,** or **acquisition.** Recent years have seen much merger activity, with many of the acquisitions valued in billions of dollars. Table 10.9 lists several large mergers in recent years.

Goals and Decisions of Business Firms

Many decisions must be made over the life of a business firm: whether to organize as a proprietorship, partnership, or corporation; what goods and services to produce, prices to charge, and markets to serve; whether to acquire another firm or to be acquired by another firm; and so on. What is a business firm trying to accomplish? What is the ultimate purpose of its decisions? In the study of economics, it is usually assumed that the fundamental objective of business decision making is to maximize a firm's profit or minimize its loss.

The goal of profit maximization or loss minimization does not mean that a business firm will simply seek to earn a profit and avoid a loss. Rather, the goal says that the firm will operate to earn the largest profit possible or the smallest loss if it cannot earn a profit.

Revenue
Money or income that a company receives from selling its product.

What is profit or loss? When a business sells a product, the money received from its sales is called **revenue.** For example, a firm selling 100,000 units of a product at $10 per unit is earning a revenue of ($10 × 100,000) or $1,000,000. But, in producing its good or service, a firm incurs certain costs such as those for labor, materials, transportation, insurance, and the purchase or rent of a building. These costs must be charged against revenue

Table 10.9
The Largest Mergers: 1981–1984

Corporations spent billions of dollars in the early 1980s to acquire other companies.

Acquiring Company	Acquired/Merged Company	Value (Billions of Dollars)	Year
Socal	Gulf	$13.3	1984
Texaco	Getty	10.1	1984
Du Pont	Conoco	6.8	1981
U.S. Steel	Marathon Oil	6.2	1982
Connecticut General	INA	4.3	1982
Occidental Petroleum	Cities Service	4.2	1982
Norfolk & Western Railway	Southern Railway	2.9	1982
Elf Aquitaine	Texasgulf	2.7	1981
Freeport Minerals	McMoRan Oil & Gas	2.5	1981

Source: "The 100 Largest Transactions," *Mergers & Acquisitions Almanac & Index* (Philadelphia: Information for Industry), 1984, p. 23; 1983, p. 19; 1982, p. 8. *Mergers & Acquisitions*, Summer 1984, p. 67; Fall 1984, p. R3.

Profit or loss
What results when a business subtracts its costs from its revenue.

to determine whether the seller is earning a **profit or loss.** Thus, for a business firm:

$$\text{profit or loss} = \text{revenue} - \text{costs.}$$

If revenue is $1,000,000 and costs are $800,000, the firm is earning a profit of $200,000. If revenue is $1,000,000 but costs are $1,500,000, there is a loss of $500,000.

Profit goes to those persons who own a firm and bear the risk of its success or failure. Thus, in a partnership or proprietorship, profit goes to the individual owner or owners who organize and operate the business, and in a corporation it goes to the stockholders.

As with economic goals for an individual, profit maximization or loss minimization for a business is a balancing process. A firm must weigh or balance the expected revenue and expected costs of each of the operating strategies from which it can choose, and then pick the one strategy that contributes most to its profitability. This balancing of revenues and costs is covered in detail in the next chapter.

Questions about Profit Maximization The goal of profit maximization or loss minimization is more controversial than the household goal of maximizing economic well-being. One point of controversy is the question of what exactly is meant by profit maximization. Does maximizing mean that a firm seeks the largest profit or smallest loss consistent with maintaining the quality of its product and meeting the needs of its work force? Or does maximizing imply producing a product with minimum regard for quality, working conditions, and wages for the sake of a larger profit? While the questions of what is implied by profit maximization and the desirability of the goal go beyond the scope of this book, they are nonetheless interesting and important.

While economists most often identify profit maximization as the fundamental goal of a firm, it is recognized that a seller might seek some alternative objective. For example, for some reason, such as a desire to hold large reserves of cash due to uncertainty about the future, a business might wish to make its inflow of revenues as large as possible, even if this can be accomplished only at the expense of some profit. Or a company's main goal might be to make the greatest possible impact on the market with a new product. Here, rather than maximizing current profit, the firm's goal would be to maximize its share of the market. Other objectives are also possible.

It is easy to see how profit maximization might be the most important goal in the operation of sole proprietorships or partnerships, where the owners tend to be involved in the making of business decisions. If an individual has enough interest in profit to form a business firm, and if he or she places a relatively high value on profit, profit maximization may be the best explanation of what motivates that person. It is more difficult to understand profit maximization in a large corporation where the owners who hold stock in the company are typically not directly involved in the decision-making process, and where managers who receive fixed salaries and not profits run the firm. Management, however, may be motivated by a concern for obtaining maximum profit for several different reasons.[11]

First, it is presumed that the directors and management of a corporation are to act in the best interest of its stockholders. Failure to do so may lead to a deterioration in the relationship between those groups. If the profit performance of a corporation is unsatisfactory in the eyes of its stockholders, they may attempt to replace the current directors and management.

Second, as pointed out earlier, much corporate stock is held by large institutional investors such as mutual funds, other corporations, and banks managing their clients' portfolios. Since these investors, who are well informed on market conditions and business practices, are likely to recognize (and react appropriately) when a corporation's management is failing to maintain acceptable profit levels, their presence may make management more conscious of the profit-maximizing objective.

Finally, the management of a corporation might be motivated to maximize profit by fear of a takeover by another corporation. Not all takeovers are friendly: one corporation may be captured by another against the wishes of the directors and management of the acquired firm. A decline in the profitability of a corporation may lead to a drop in the price of its stock; and as the corporation's stock price falls, it becomes cheaper and thus easier for another firm to acquire shares in an effort to gain control. Obviously, one defense against a takeover is to keep stock prices high by keeping profit high. Other tactics for avoiding unfriendly takeovers are explained in Application 10.3, "Deft Defenses."

---

[11]The following is based on: W. L. Baldwin, "The Motives of Managers, Environmental Restraints, and the Theory of Managerial Enterprise," *The Quarterly Journal of Economics* (May 1964), pp. 238–256, especially pp. 251–252.

Summary

A household is made up of an individual living alone or several persons living in a group. Although the number of households in the United States is increasing, the average number of persons per household is falling, and the percentage of households with one person is increasing. The majority of household income comes from the sale of resources, particularly labor. However, unearned income from government transfer payments has become increasingly important over the years. Of the different types of cash benefit transfer payments, social security is the largest.

The average income of all household heads taken as a group differs from the average income of various subgroups of household heads. This difference may be related to factors such as the sex, education, or age of the household head.

Household income can be saved, used for paying taxes, or spent, with the vast majority going to purchase goods and services. Purchases of goods can be divided between expenditures on durable and nondurable goods.

It is assumed that the main economic objective of an individual's spending and earning decisions is to maximize his or her economic well-being. Realizing this objective requires weighing alternatives and choosing the course of action that contributes most to economic satisfaction.

The satisfaction from consuming a good or service is called utility. To maximize the total utility from consuming several different goods and services, a purchaser must weigh the additional satisfaction received from consuming a unit of an item against that item's price and compare that with the additional satisfaction and price of other goods and services. If one good

Application 10.3
DEFT DEFENSES

Embattled managers who hope to avoid corporate takeovers can draw upon a wide array of defenses. Many have acquired exotic names: Pac-Man, shark repellent, white knight. Some are more effective than others, and none, alas, work all the time.

The first step is to hire outside advisers, including an investment bank and a law firm that specializes in mergers and acquisitions. Among law firms, New York City's Skadden, Arps, Slate, Meagher & Flom, for example, is well known for keeping unwanted suitors away. So feared is the firm's takeover specialist, Joseph Flom, 60, that 200 corporations pay fat retainers just to guarantee that Flom will work for them, and not against them, should they become takeover targets. . . .

Flom represented Allied Corp., which came to Bendix's defense after former Chairman William Agee's attempt to take over Martin Marietta failed and Martin Marietta counterattacked by buying Bendix stock. Allied bought Bendix stock so Martin Marietta could not buy enough to gain control. That made Allied a white knight.

Martin Marietta's tactic was a prime example of the Pac-Man defense, whereby a threatened costs twice as much as another but adds less than twice as much to total utility (satisfaction), the buyer should limit purchase of the first good in favor of the second.

Earning decisions also involve weighing and balancing. In this case, the added satisfaction from more income is weighed against the added dissatisfaction from forgoing alternatives such as leisure time in order to earn that income.

A business is an organization established for the purpose of producing and selling goods and services. A firm may be legally organized as a proprietorship, partnership, or corporation. Each of these legal forms of organization has certain advantages and disadvantages, such as the nature of the owner's liability. Numerically, there are more proprietorships in the U.S. economy than there are partnerships or corporations, but the largest volume of receipts goes to corporations.

Many corporations have a controlling amount of their stock owned by other corporations. When a corporation buys the controlling shares of stock in another corporation, a merger, or acquisition, has taken place. Because two firms are related through ownership is no reason to assume that the goods and services they produce are related in any functional way.

It is most often assumed in economics that the basic objective of a business firm is to maximize profit or minimize loss. Profit or loss equals revenue minus costs. As is the case with a household, business maximizing requires balancing: in this case, the expected revenues and costs from different operating strategies are considered.

Some controversy surrounds the profit-maximizing objective. Part of the controversy centers on what is meant by profit maximization as an objective,

---

company responds to a takeover bid by trying to buy up its attacker's stock. Another defense is the self-tender. A company threatened by takeover offers to buy its own shares at prices higher than the attacker's.

Still another tactic involves creating new shares, thereby diluting the voting power of current stock. When those new shares are distributed to shareholders of record, the effect is to strengthen their control greatly. . . .

Then there are other ploys called shark repellents. One of those involves revising corporate bylaws to stagger the terms of directors so that only a few come up for election in any one year. To get a majority, a raider would have to wait at least two years.

Another maneuver is to adopt a bylaw requiring a super-majority of outstanding voting shares, say 70 percent or 80 percent, for approval of a tender offer. Reincorporating in a state with rules that favor existing management is another defense. In Delaware, certain defensive tactics. . . can be approved by directors alone, without a vote by shareholders. . . . Many experts question the legality of shark repellents. Dissident shareholders challenge them, charging that they amount to changing the rules in the middle of the game.

Source: "Deft Defenses," *Time*, February 6, 1984, p. 47.

and part centers on whether firms actually seek profit maximization as their main objective. We would expect profit maximizing to be important to a sole proprietorship or partnership, but there are also reasons for it being important to a corporation.

Key Terms and Concepts

Household
Personal income
Durable good
Nondurable good
Utility
Utility maximization
Business
Proprietorship
Partnership
Corporation
Unlimited liability
General partner
Preferred stock
Common stock
Bond
Holding company
Merger or acquisition
Revenue
Profit and loss
Profit maximization

Discussion and Review Questions

1. Students who rent apartments close to campuses often say that they have to pay a lot for what they get. How could this fact make it difficult for a student to maximize the satisfaction from consuming goods and services with a limited income? Explain, in terms of the material in this chapter, why students will continue to rent at these high prices.
2. In his book *The Affluent Society,*[12] John Kenneth Galbraith suggests that the wants we have for some goods may be subject to a "dependence effect." This means that the wants are caused by the goods themselves: if the goods did not exist, the wants would not exist. Do you agree or disagree with the idea that wants are subject to a dependence effect? On what do you base your reasoning?
3. Suppose that you are a business organization consultant, and three people come to you, each wanting to start a business. The first person wants to start an engineering firm with her brother, the second a music store, and the third a barge line for moving coal on rivers. Each is seeking your advice on whether to organize as a sole proprietorship, partnership, or corporation. How would you advise each of them? As a practical matter, does it make any difference which form of organization each person chooses?

---

[12]John Kenneth Galbraith, "Ch. XI: The Dependence Effect," *The Affluent Society* (Boston: Houghton Mifflin Co., 1958), pp. 152–160.

4. "Trying to maximize its revenues from sales or its share of the market does not mean that a firm is giving up the objective of maximizing profit. Instead, it means that the firm is taking steps now to ensure that it will be able to maximize profit in the future." Do you agree or disagree with this statement?
5. Can you explain in economic terms why someone with a so-called sweet tooth might be more than willing to buy an expensive iced fudge cake but would not consider buying a high-quality steak?
6. What are the main sources of household income and the different uses to which household income can be put? How is household income affected by the head of household's age, sex, education, and other factors?
7. In a sole proprietorship the owner is often the manager, but in a corporation the owners are often different from the managers. What advantages and disadvantages might there be in having a separation of ownership and management?

Suggested Readings

Stanley E. Boyle, "Ch. 1, Appendix: Major Sources of Company and Industry Data," ***Industrial Organization: An Empirical Approach*** **(New York: Holt, Rinehart and Winston, Inc., 1972), pp. 19–23.** A survey of sources of financial and other data on business firms and on industries.

James S. Coleman, ***Power and the Structure of Society*** **(New York: W. W. Norton & Co., Inc., 1974).** A critical look at the relationship in society between individuals and corporate actors and how that relationship has changed over time.

John Kenneth Galbraith, "The Uses and Excuses for Affluence," ***The New York Times Magazine,*** **May 31, 1981, pp. 38–44, 50–52.** Discusses the enjoyment of wealth and spending and the excuses used to promote and defend the position of the wealthy.

George Katona, "Ch. 4: Psychological Economics," ***The Mass Consumption Society*** **(New York: McGraw-Hill, Inc., 1964), pp. 27–38.** Introduces the importance of considering psychological factors such as motives and attitudes in studying the economic behavior of households and businesses.

Wesley C. Mitchell, "The Backward Art of Spending Money," ***American Economic Review*** **(June 1912), pp. 269–281. Reprinted in Wesley C. Mitchell,** ***The Backward Art of Spending Money and Other Essays*** **(New York: Augustus M. Kelley, Inc., 1950), pp. 3–19.** A classic and entertaining article on the problems of consumer decision making.

Harry M. Trebing, ed., ***The Corporation in the American Economy*** **(Chicago: Quadrangle Books, Inc., 1970).** Readings by A. A. Berle, Emanuel Celler, Sumner Slichter, Robert Lekachman, and others on topics such as corporate management, ownership and control, mergers, and the size of corporations.

11 BENEFITS, COSTS, AND MAXIMIZATION

Chapter Objectives

1. To explain the basic process of balancing costs and benefits in economic decision making.
2. To define the manner in which individuals and businesses measure the costs and benefits of actions they take.
3. To identify the rules associated with the maximization of satisfaction by individuals and the maximization of profit by businesses.
4. To explain the measurement of business costs, revenues, and profit; and to differentiate between normal and economic profit.
5. To introduce the concepts of externalities and social costs and benefits.
6. To examine how individual costs and benefits form the basis of collective, or public, choices.

Chapter Ten showed that decision makers in households and businesses try to maximize their economic well-being or profit by balancing the benefits and costs of different courses of action in order to choose the one that contributes most to the attainment of their particular goals. In this chapter, the mechanics involved in balancing costs against benefits in order to decide which strategy to follow will be explained, and general rules for maximizing, which can be applied to both businesses and individuals, will be introduced. The mechanics will be illustrated through two examples: the first concerns a decision by an individual on how best to use an evening's time; the second concerns a business trying to maximize its profit. After the weighing of costs and benefits by individuals and businesses has been explored, the chapter will deal with costs and benefits as seen by society as a whole. Finally, the balancing of costs and benefits in making collective, or public, choices will be discussed.

The formal study of the process of balancing costs and benefits, referred to as cost-benefit analysis, is helpful in evaluating business investment and production decisions, government decisions concerning the construction of airports and hospitals, individual decisions concerning major purchases, and other such decisions. However, the principles of cost-benefit analysis are not limited in their usefulness to evaluating major economic and financial decisions by governments, businesses, or households. The principles can be applied to many more areas of human experience than those dealt with in modern economics. The story of Adam and Eve, and the choice to eat the apple in the Garden of Eden, is a lesson in balancing costs and benefits, as is an expression such as:

'T is better to have loved and lost
Than never to have loved at all.[1]

All rational decision making, be it economic or noneconomic, is based on the balancing of costs and benefits in order to, in the view of the decision maker, maximize something. This is true for the worker trying to maximize well-being by balancing the costs and benefits of forgoing more income for the sake of leisure, for the child weighing the costs and benefits of lying to a parent, or for the painter deciding whether to move the ladder or stretch to reach the last few inches on a wall.

BALANCING BENEFITS AND COSTS: THE INDIVIDUAL

Defining Benefits and Costs

The goal of decision making is to maximize, or to get the most from, a decision. In so doing, an individual, usually subconsciously, uses a type of mathematical process, or applies certain types of mathematical rules, to weigh the costs and benefits of different courses of action. This process and these rules will be thoroughly discussed shortly. However, before these mechanics are introduced, it is important to understand how an individual measures benefits and costs.

The benefit to a person from any good or service purchased is the amount of satisfaction received from the purchase. This satisfaction was discussed in Chapter Ten and is referred to as utility. In order to understand the behavior of utility, assume that each person has a small register in his or her mind called a "Util-O-Meter." This meter measures total utility by clicking off points according to the amount of satisfaction received from the purchase of each additional good or service. Satisfaction can also be received from actions as well as purchases. Taking this course in economics or visiting with a sick friend, for example, may add points to your meter.

[1]Alfred Tennyson, "In Memoriam," *The Poetic and Dramatic Works of Alfred Lord Tennyson*, W. J. Rolfe, ed. (Boston: Houghton Mifflin Co., 1898), p. 170.

Any measurement of satisfaction is highly subjective, as are the numbers registered on a Util-O-Meter for the benefits received from any purchase or action. Because of this, it is extremely difficult for two people to compare the degree of satisfaction received by each from taking the same action, such as eating a pizza. However, an individual can compare the satisfaction from different actions or purchases from which he or she can choose. You, for example, know whether you enjoy a popular recording more, much more, or not as much as Mahler's Seventh Symphony.

An individual usually measures the cost of an item by the dollars paid for it. As discussed in Chapter One, however, costs can also be measured in terms of the alternatives or opportunities forgone to acquire an item or take an action.[2] That is, the cost of something can be seen as the value of the alternative item or action which has been given up, or it can be measured in terms of its **opportunity cost.** For example, the cost of a $30 textbook could be measured by the dollars to obtain it or by the shirt, date, football tickets, or anything else that could have otherwise been purchased.

Opportunity cost
The cost of acquiring a good or service or taking an action measured in terms of the value of the opportunities or alternatives forgone.

An opportunity cost is associated with everything one does. The cost of attending a class could be lunch with a friend, finishing a game of bridge, watching a television program, or working an extra hour at a job. What is your opportunity cost of reading this chapter now?

We can relate opportunity costs to utility, or satisfaction, by measuring the points that would have been added to a Util-O-Meter had another course of action been chosen. For example, if by registering for next semester you gave up one hour of jogging, which would have added 125 points to your total utility, then the cost of registration was 125 points.

Measuring Benefits and Costs

The following example illustrates how individuals measure the benefits and costs of actions and how they apply maximizing rules to their decision making. This example deals with a student who is planning to spend an evening at a concert on campus. The concert features a number of performers and is lengthy and informal, with people allowed to come and go as they please. The concert is also free in the sense that there are no dollar costs, but the individual has an opportunity cost in terms of time.

In taking any action, a person attempts to maximize satisfaction. In this case, the individual going to the concert is attempting to maximize the satisfaction from the time spent during the course of the evening. This means that our concertgoer may spend the entire evening at the concert, or may at some point have something else preferable to do and leave the concert. In this example, we will determine whether satisfaction is maximized by attending the entire concert, which lasts for five hours, or by leaving after the first or second or third or fourth hour.

---

[2]See page 4.

Table 11.1
Utility Points from Attending a Concert

Marginal benefit, or utility, is the change in total benefit, or utility, from consuming an additional unit of a good, service, or activity.

Number of Hours Attended	Total Benefit (Utility)	Marginal Benefit (Utility)
0	0 points	
		400 points
1	400 points	
		300 points
2	700 points	
		200 points
3	900 points	
		100 points
4	1,000 points	
		0 points
5	1,000 points	

Marginal benefit (marginal utility)
The amount of satisfaction added to total satisfaction by consuming each additional unit of a good, service, or activity.

Total benefit (total utility)
The total amount of satisfaction received from consuming a specified number of units of a good, service, or activity.

Measuring Benefits By attending the concert, our student receives satisfaction, or utility—the concert adds points to the individual's Util-O-Meter. Each additional hour spent at the concert adds a certain number of points to total satisfaction. The amount added to total satisfaction by each additional hour is called **marginal benefit** or **marginal utility.** The total satisfaction received by attending the concert for a specified number of hours is called **total benefit** or **total utility.**

Let us assume that our student's Util-O-Meter registers zero before the concert. Let us further assume that by the end of the first hour 400 points of utility have clicked onto the meter. This means that the total benefit, or utility, from spending one hour at the concert is 400 points. At the end of the second hour 700 points are registered on the meter; or we can say that the total benefit from spending two hours at the concert is 700 points. At the end of three hours 900 points are registered; at the end of four hours the total utility received is 1,000 points; and after five hours the meter still registers 1,000 points. This information is given in Table 11.1 in the column labeled "Total Benefit (Utility)."

The marginal benefit, or utility, is the *addition* to total benefit received from attending the concert for each *additional* hour. Since the Util-O-Meter registered zero before the concert and 400 points at the end of one hour, the marginal benefit from the first hour is 400 points. During the first hour 400 points are added to the student's total utility. At the end of the second hour 700 points of total benefit are registered, which means that 300 additional points of utility are added during the second hour (700 points in total utility at the end of the second hour minus 400 points at the end of the first). Thus, the marginal utility or benefit of the second hour is 300 points. During the third hour 200 points of marginal benefit are added (total benefit increases from 700 to 900 points). The marginal benefit of the fourth hour is 100 points; and the marginal benefit of the fifth hour is zero points, since total benefit does not increase from the end of the fourth to the end of the fifth hour. These measures are given in Table 11.1 in the column labeled "Marginal Benefit (Utility)."

You may have noticed that the marginal benefit points given in Table 11.1 are listed midway between the hours. This is done because marginal values refer to changes in total values, and total values can either increase or decrease. That is, we can refer to the increase in total benefit by going from one to two, or two to three hours at the concert, or we can refer to the decrease in total benefit by going from three to two hours, or two to one. Because the numbers in the table can be read up or down, we list marginal values at midpoints between the hours.

Observe also that the marginal benefit points decrease with each additional hour. In this example, the individual really enjoys the first hour of the concert, finds the second hour slightly less satisfactory, and finds each successive hour less enjoyable than the previous one. By the fifth hour no additional satisfaction is received. This result is consistent with a principle in economics called the **Law of Diminishing Marginal Utility,** which states that, as additional units of an item are consumed, *beyond some point* each successive unit of the item consumed will add less to total utility than was added by the unit consumed just before it. In other words, as an individual consumes a good or service, there is some point beyond which he or she enjoys each additional unit of the item less.[3] Food is an excellent example of this principle. If you are eating pizza or tacos or donuts or anything else, there is some point at which each additional piece of pizza or taco or donut gives you less satisfaction than the one before it. Do you generally enjoy the fourth donut as much as the first? Would you enjoy a second bike or stereo as much as the first, and do you find the third hour of a three-hour lecture class as satisfying and stimulating as the second or first hour?

Law of Diminishing Marginal Utility
As additional units of an item are consumed, beyond some point each successive unit of the item consumed will add less to total utility than was added by the unit consumed just before it.

Measuring Costs In our example of the concertgoer, the student faces costs as well as receiving benefits from attending the concert. These costs are opportunity costs based on forgone activities, such as studying or watching television, that would have also given the student satisfaction, or would have added points to the student's Util-O-Meter. Thus, the costs of the concert can be measured by the number of forgone utility points from alternative opportunities.

Table 11.2 gives the total cost and marginal cost, measured in forgone satisfaction points, for spending the evening at the concert. **Total cost** is the cost of spending a specified number of hours at the concert. **Marginal cost** is the addition to total cost from each additional hour spent at the concert. As before, the marginal measurement is given at the midpoints between the hours.

Total cost
The cost of a specified number of units of a good, service, or activity produced or consumed.

Marginal cost
The addition to total cost from each additional unit of a good, service, or activity produced or consumed.

Our student has many alternatives to attending the concert. Assume that one alternative to attending the concert for one hour is loafing around. Assume also that this action would give our concertgoer 25 Util-O-Meter

---

[3]We are not suggesting that the second unit consumed of an item *will* add less satisfaction than the first, or that the third unit *will* add less satisfaction than the second. Rather, as successive units of an item are consumed, *eventually* a point will be reached where each additional unit consumed will add less to total satisfaction than was added by the previous unit. This point may arrive early on, as in the case of our concertgoer, or after the consumption of a large amount of an item.

Table 11.2
Total Cost and Marginal Cost of Attending a Concert

Both the total and marginal costs of an activity, such as attending a concert, can be measured in terms of the utility points that are given up by forgoing an alternative activity.

Hours Attended	Total Cost	Marginal Cost
0	0 points	
		25 points
1	25 points	
		50 points
2	75 points	
		100 points
3	175 points	
		200 points
4	375 points	
		625 points
5	1,000 points	

points, thereby making the marginal opportunity cost of the first hour at the concert 25 points. These 25 marginal cost points equal the total cost for attending the concert for one hour, since we are assuming that no previous total cost points have been accumulated.

To attend the second hour of the concert, assume that the student in our example gives up watching a television program that would have yielded 50 additional points of satisfaction, thereby making the marginal cost of the second hour 50 points. When these 50 marginal points are added to the total cost of 25 points for the first hour, the total cost of two hours at the concert becomes 75 points. The marginal cost of the third hour is 100 points of satisfaction which our student would have received from socializing with a friend. When these 100 marginal points are added to the 75 total cost points for two hours spent at the concert, the total cost of three hours at the concert becomes 175 points.

The alternative to the fourth hour at the concert is studying for an economics quiz that must be taken the following morning. The marginal cost of this hour is the 200 points that would be added to total satisfaction by understanding the material for the quiz. These points, when added to the 175 points for three hours, make the total cost of four hours at the concert 375 points. The marginal cost of the fifth hour is 625 points, which is the satisfaction that would be received by completing some math problems necessary to pass a course. These 625 marginal cost points bring the total cost of attending the entire five-hour concert to 1,000 points.

Observe that the marginal cost of attending each additional hour of the concert rises with the number of hours attended. The individual first gives up those alternatives which cost the least, and as the evening goes on, the alternatives become more and more expensive.

Maximizing Satisfaction

Thus far we have measured the benefits and costs for a student spending an evening at a concert. Remembering that the goal of any action is to maximize satisfaction, we will now evaluate these benefits and costs to determine the number of hours that the student should spend at the concert to accomplish this maximization objective.

Table 11.3
Benefits and Costs of Attending a Concert

Net benefit is maximized at the point where total benefit exceeds total cost by the greatest amount. Net benefit increases as long as marginal benefit is greater than marginal cost, and decreases when marginal cost is greater than marginal benefit.

Number of Hours Attended	Net Benefit	Total Benefit	Total Cost	Marginal Benefit	Marginal Cost
0	0	0	0		
				400	25
1	375	400	25		
				300	50
2	625	700	75		
				200	100
3	725	900	175		
				100	200
4	625	1,000	375		
				0	625
5	0	1,000	1,000		

Table 11.3 lists the concertgoer's total and marginal benefits, and total and marginal costs that were given in Tables 11.1. and 11.2. Table 11.3 also includes a measure of the net benefit received from spending a specified number of hours at the concert. Net benefit is what the concertgoer is trying to maximize. Table 11.3 indicates that the net benefit of one hour at the concert is 375 points, the net benefit of two hours is 625 points, and so on.

The net benefit points given in Table 11.3 show that satisfaction from the concert is maximized by attending for three hours. At the end of three hours, 725 net benefit points, the maximum that can be attained, have been realized. Attending the concert for just two hours or staying for four hours will yield less satisfaction than 725 points. To maximize the satisfaction that can be received that evening, the student should attend the concert for three hours.

Net benefit
That which results when total cost is subtracted from total benefit.

How is net benefit calculated? The **net benefit** for a specified number of hours at the concert is simply the difference between the total benefit and total cost of those hours. For example, as shown in Table 11.3, the total benefit from attending the concert for one hour is 400 points and the total cost is 25 points, leaving a net benefit of 375 points (400 − 25); the total benefit from attending for two hours is 700 points and the total cost is 75 points, leaving a net benefit of 625 points; for three hours the total benefit is 900 and the total cost 175, yielding a net benefit of 725 points; and so on.

Given total cost and total benefit, one can establish a maximizing rule. This rule states that *maximization of net benefit occurs where the positive difference between total benefit and total cost (total benefit minus total cost) is the greatest.* That is, maximization occurs where total benefit exceeds total cost by the greatest amount.

A second rule for determining the action that will yield the highest net benefit deals with marginal cost and marginal benefit. It states that *maximization of net benefit occurs where marginal cost equals marginal benefit.* Why is this so? The answer is found by comparing the marginal benefit and marginal cost figures in Table 11.3.

For the first hour of the concert, the marginal benefit is 400 points and the marginal cost is 25 points. If you think of marginal benefit as adding points to a Util-O-Meter, and marginal cost as subtracting points, then 400 points are added and 25 are subtracted during the first hour, leaving a gain in satisfaction, or net benefit, of 375 points. During the second hour, 300 more points, the marginal benefit, are added and 50 points, the marginal cost, are subtracted. The result is a gain of 250 points to be added to the gain from the first hour. Thus, the net benefit after two hours is 625 points (375 points from the first hour plus 250 points from the second hour). During the third hour, 200 marginal benefit points are added and only 100 marginal cost points are subtracted, again adding to the net registered on the Util-O-Meter.

Notice that for each of these three hours, marginal benefit is greater than marginal cost, causing net benefit to increase. But also notice that marginal benefit is shrinking and marginal cost is growing. At some point they will be equal.

During the fourth hour, the marginal benefit is only 100 points, but the marginal cost is 200 points, causing more to be subtracted from total satisfaction than is added. Because of this, net benefit falls. If our individual stayed at the concert for a fourth hour, that fourth hour would cost more satisfaction than it would give. During the fifth hour no points are added, but 625 are subtracted, causing net benefit again to fall.

It can once more be seen that net benefit is maximized by attending the concert for three hours. During the third hour more marginal benefit points are added than marginal cost points are subtracted, but during the fourth hour more marginal cost points are subtracted than marginal benefit points are added. The concertgoer should leave at the end of three hours because at this point marginal cost equals marginal benefit. This equality will be easy to see when this relationship is graphed later in this chapter.

From this we can conclude that as long as marginal benefit is greater than marginal cost, no matter how small the difference, an action should continue because net benefit keeps increasing. Once marginal cost becomes greater than marginal benefit, net benefit declines because more is subtracted than is added to satisfaction. Maximization occurs at the point where marginal cost equals marginal benefit.

In this example, our individual is increasing satisfaction, or net benefit, by attending the concert as long as more additional utility points are received from the concert than would be received from the alternatives. Once the alternatives become more attractive, it is to the individual's advantage to switch from the concert to something else.

In summary, this example indicates that there are two rules for maximization, both yielding the same result. Maximization occurs where the positive difference between total benefit and total cost is the greatest or where marginal cost equals marginal benefit.

Would you act as the student in our example did? Yes! Have you ever returned early from a date or concert or movie because an important test or assignment was due the next morning? You have applied the maximizing rules in countless situations where you, perhaps subconsciously, weighed the marginal cost and marginal benefit of an action. For example, the decision of whether to eat an extra piece of chocolate cake for dessert involves balancing the additional cost of the extra calories against the additional enjoyment from the cake. Other decisions, such as the determination of which route to take to work on a snowy day, or whether to buy the study guide accompanying a textbook, or whether to purchase an expensive or cheap pair of jeans, all involve an application of the maximizing rules. What are some of the marginal costs and marginal benefits that might be considered in deciding whether to break the speed limit to attend a class on time? Application 11.1, "Anything Worth Doing Is Not Necessarily Worth Doing Well," gives some additional examples of the application of cost-benefit principles. The reading "Surgeons Find Heart Repair Pays For Itself" listed at the end of this chapter, contains information about a cost-benefit study done to determine whether a type of heart operation is economically worth it.

Application 11.1
ANYTHING WORTH DOING IS NOT NECESSARILY WORTH DOING WELL

From early childhood most of us have been taught that "anything worth doing is worth doing well." If we were asked today if we still agree with the statement, many of us would say that we do. It is only natural for a person to prefer a job that has been done well to one that has been done not so well; indeed, such a preference is fully consistent with the basic assumption in economics that more (quality) is preferred to less (quality). It is also easy to see why a person may not like to re-do something that has already been done, particularly if the combined time involved is greater than the time that would have been required to do it right in the first place.

Obviously, people do not behave the way they profess they should. There is probably not a minister around who has not written what he considered at the time to be a poor sermon, and one of the authors recently built a bookcase that was more-or-less thrown together. Wives and husbands have cooked dinners they knew in their hearts were seriously deficient in one respect or another. Students regularly choose to work for a grade of a C (or a GPA far less than 4.0) instead of going all out for an A. This is true even though the A is the preferred grade. How many, do you suppose, of the students who are reading this have written a paper that by their own standards fell far short of a "well done" paper? In fact, can you say at this point that you have read the last few pages "well?"

Admittedly, people do some things well, but the point we wish to emphasize is that they frequently do things less than well, not because they do not want to do better, but because of the *additional* (or *marginal*) cost involved in improving the quality of whatever they are doing. Given the student's ability — which, as a matter of fact, is limited at any point in time — writing a "good" A paper generally requires more effort and time than writing a C paper. If the student spends additional time on the paper, he or she has less time for doing other things — less time to study the subject matter in other courses, in which case he or she may do less well or even fail. He or she cannot use the time for physical exercise, cannot spend the time in bed, or out on dates. To reiterate, there is usually an additional cost that must

Graphing Costs, Benefits, and Net Benefit

Our student's total cost and total benefit from attending the concert are shown in the upper graph of Figure 11.1, and the net benefit is shown in the lower graph of Figure 11.1. These figures are plotted from the information in Table 11.3. As long as total cost is less than total benefit, there is a positive net benefit. Graphically, as can be seen in Figure 11.1, net benefit is equal to the vertical distance between total benefit and total cost for any given number of hours spent attending the concert. Thus, maximization of net benefit occurs in the upper graph where the vertical distance between total benefit and total cost is the greatest, or at the highest point on the net benefit curve in the lower graph. This occurs at three hours.

Figure 11.2 plots, from Table 11.3, the marginal cost and marginal benefit

---

be borne for a higher quality paper, and it is because of this cost that he or she may rationally choose to turn in a paper that may "just get by." (Even so, the student may still hope for an A. Can you explain why?)

If the cost is not greater for higher quality work, then one must wonder why the job may be done poorly. The student will be able to have a higher quality paper without giving up anything. The problem of the poorly done work may be one of perception; that is, the student may perceive the additional cost to be greater than what it actually is, in which case he or she should respond appropriately if provided with accurate information. He or she may, in addition, inaccurately assess the benefits of a better performance.

Quite often one person will admonish another to do a good job. For example, professors may be distressed at the quality of the papers they receive, and may honestly feel that if their students are going to write a paper, they should write a good one. The professors may be even more upset if they find out that their students spent the last few days doing very little or having a "good time."

The values the professors and students place on different activities obviously differ. Professors may view the paper as being of greater value than do the students; they may view the "other activities" as being of less value. Consequently, they believe it is in the students' best interests to do better papers. However, since students view the value of the other activities as being higher, they, in effect, view the cost of doing the better paper as being higher. Of course, it is clearly rational for professors to want the students to turn in better papers, but if they had to bear the costs, they might change their minds.

The same line of argument can be used to explain why the preacher's sermon is of low quality even though he or she may have the ability to do better. By writing a better sermon, he or she may have to bear the cost of not seeing the parishioners at the hospital or of giving up something else that is considered valuable. In order to cook a better meal, the homemaker may have to forgo writing letters, discussions with neighbors, or hauling Little Leaguers to practice.

Source: Richard B. McKenzie and Gordon Tullock, *The New World of Economics* (Homewood, Ill.: Richard D. Irwin, Inc., 1978), pp. 27–29. Reprinted by permission of Richard D. Irwin, Inc.

Figure 11.1
Total Cost, Total Benefit, and Net Benefit

Graphically, net benefit is equal to the vertical distance between total benefit and total cost. Net benefit is at its maximum where total benefit exceeds total cost by the greatest amount.

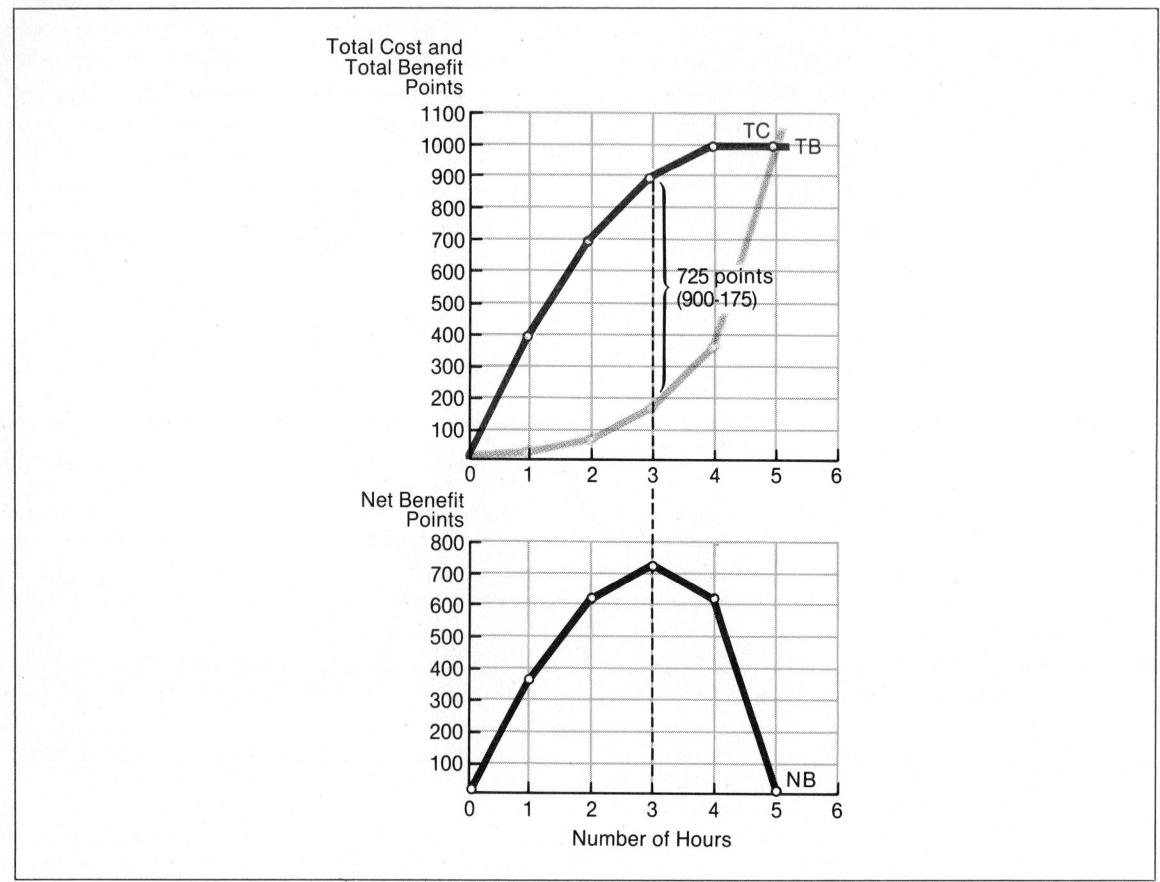

from attending the concert in the upper graph and the net benefit in the lower graph. Notice from this figure that as long as marginal benefit is greater than marginal cost, net benefit increases, and when marginal cost is greater than marginal benefit, net benefit falls. Net benefit reaches its maximum where marginal cost equals marginal benefit. This again occurs at three hours. You might also notice that marginal cost and marginal benefit are plotted at the midpoints, just as they were given at the midpoints in the tables.

Figure 11.2
Marginal Cost, Marginal Benefit, and Net Benefit

Net benefit is increasing when marginal benefit is greater than marginal cost; it is at its maximum when marginal benefit equals marginal cost; and it is decreasing when marginal benefit is less than marginal cost.

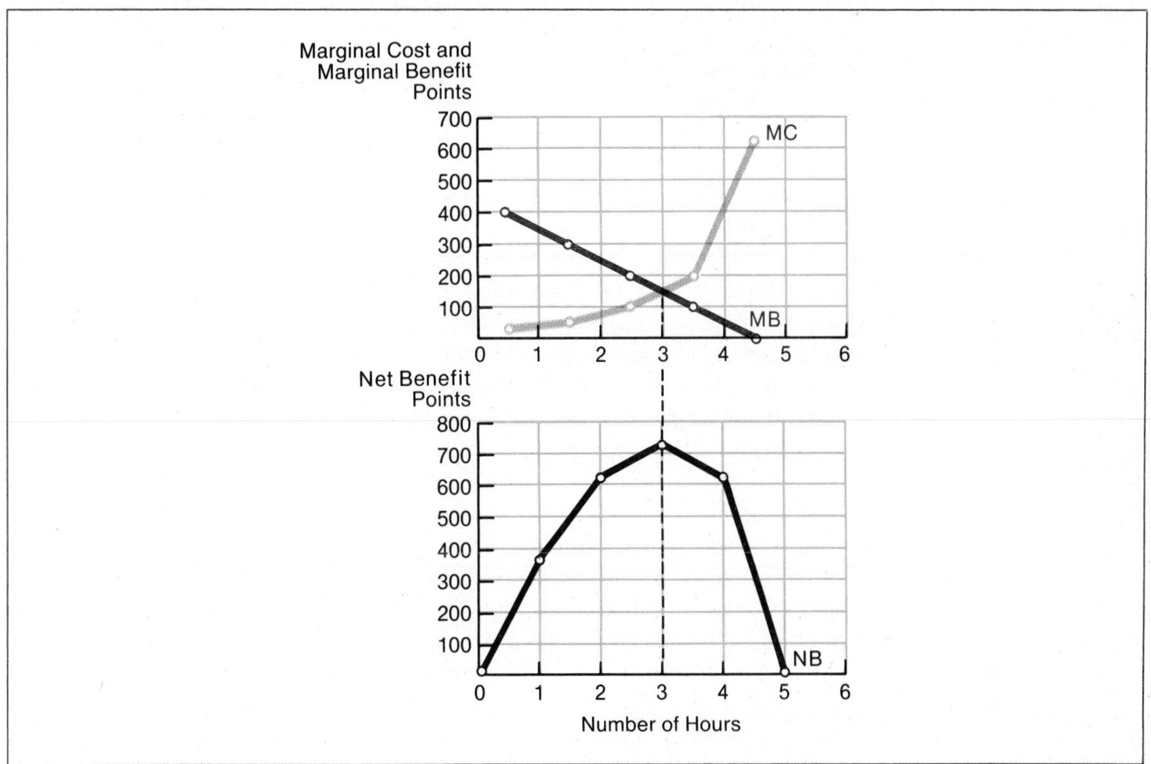

BALANCING BENEFITS AND COSTS: THE BUSINESS

Defining Benefits and Costs

It was seen in Chapter Ten that businesses are similar to individuals in two important ways. First, like individuals, they too try to maximize their economic well-being. And second, as with individuals, maximizing by a business requires balancing the costs and benefits of different courses of action to find the one most in its interest.

But a business differs from an individual in that its economic well-being is generally measured in terms of profit rather than utility, or satisfaction.

Thus, a business is maximizing its economic well-being when it balances the costs and benefits of operating at different levels of output and chooses the one that maximizes its profit. Since profit is equal to revenue minus costs, the benefits and costs to be balanced are measured in terms of the revenue earned from selling the firm's good or service, and the costs of producing the good or service.

The costs of producing a firm's good or service fall into two categories. The first category is payments made by the business to acquire its work force, raw materials, machinery, equipment, and so forth. These payments are actual dollar outlays that the firm must provide to outsiders from whom it buys factors of production. Costs from this first category are sometimes called **explicit costs.**

Explicit costs
Payments that a business makes to acquire factors of production such as labor, raw materials, and machinery.

The second cost category is the profit required by the owner(s) or entrepreneur(s) to keep a business in operation. An owner or entrepreneur must get something in return for the time, effort, and other resources that he or she invests in a business in order to continue its operation. Thus, the cost of operating a business includes not only wages, rent, interest, and other payments to outsiders, but also a certain amount of profit that must be paid to the owner(s) or entrepreneur(s). This profit is called **normal profit** and is equal to what an owner could earn in his or her next best alternative. In other words, it is equal to the opportunity cost of owning a business. For example, if an owner could use his or her talent and money in an alternative that could earn $20,000 a year, the opportunity cost of continuing with the current business would be $20,000 per year. If the owner earned less than $20,000 in the current business, he or she might eventually disband the current business and pursue the alternative. Thus, unless normal profit is earned, production will soon cease.

Normal profit
Profit necessary to keep a business in operation; considered to be a cost of production.

Any profit beyond normal profit is called **excess profit**, or **economic profit.** For example, if an entrepreneur were to require $20,000 per year to remain in business, and if actual profit were $32,000, $20,000 of that actual profit would be normal profit and the remaining $12,000 would be economic, or excess, profit. Economic, or excess, profit is not a cost, since the entrepreneur would remain with the business even if it were not earned.

Excess profit (economic profit)
Profit received beyond normal profit; not considered a cost of production.

The main difference between normal profit and the costs from the first category (explicit costs) is that the wage, rent, interest, and other payments from the first category are payments that the business must make to other persons, but normal profit is a payment that the business makes to the owner(s) or entrepreneur(s). Since normal profit does not involve the direct passing of money from the firm to an outside group, it is sometimes referred to as an **implicit cost.** Thus, the costs of operating a business are equal to its explicit costs (wage, rent, interest, and other payments) plus its implicit cost (normal profit). The **economic cost of production** always includes both of these.[4]

Implicit cost
A payment that a business must make to its owner(s) if it is to remain in operation; normal profit.

Economic cost of production
Includes all explicit and implicit costs from producing a good or service.

[4]This is different from the method for calculating costs in accounting, where only explicit costs are figured into the calculation.

Table 11.4
Revenues from Selling Pocket Watch Cases

The total revenue from selling an item, such as pocket watch cases, is calculated by multiplying the price of the item times the quantity demanded at that price. Marginal revenue is the change in total revenue from selling one more unit of an item.

Price	Quantity Demanded	Total Revenue	Marginal Revenue
$45,000	0	$ 0	
			$40,000
40,000	1	40,000	
			30,000
35,000	2	70,000	
			20,000
30,000	3	90,000	
			10,000
25,000	4	100,000	

Measuring Revenues and Costs

The fundamental mechanics of profit maximization by a firm are exactly the same as those set out in the example of the student maximizing satisfaction at a concert. The only difference is *what* is being balanced and *what* is being maximized: in this case, revenues and costs from operations are being balanced to maximize profit. Thus, the example we are about to work through introduces no new principles. Rather, it shows how the principles already learned for an individual can be applied to a business.

Measuring Revenues Suppose a jeweler designs and produces a solid gold, diamond-encrusted pocket watch case. Although this is an exclusive, high-priced item that would sell to very few people, the jeweler knows that the way to sell more is to lower the price. That is, the watch case is subject to the Law of Demand.

The jeweler's problem is to determine how many pocket watch cases to produce and sell in order to maximize profit. The solution to the problem is found by balancing the costs from producing different quantities of the watch case against the benefits, which in this example are the revenues, from different levels of sales. The revenues that the jeweler could earn from selling different quantities of the watch case at different prices are shown in Table 11.4.

The first two columns of the table show different watch case prices and the quantity of watch cases demanded at each of those prices. At a price of $45,000, no watch cases would be demanded. But if the price were lowered to $40,000, one watch case would be demanded; and if the price were $35,000, two watch cases would be demanded; and so on. Thus, the first two columns of Table 11.4 show how the Law of Demand operates with the jeweler's potential buyers.

Total revenue
Revenue received from selling a certain quantity of an item; calculated by multiplying the price of an item by the quantity demanded at that price.

The total revenue column in Table 11.4 shows how much revenue would be earned by the jeweler at each level of demand. **Total revenue** is calculated by multiplying the price of an item by the quantity demanded at that price. For example, two pocket watch cases demanded at $35,000 each would generate $70,000 in total revenue.

Marginal revenue
The change in total revenue when one more (or additional) unit of an item is demanded.

Marginal revenue measures how much total revenue changes as one more (or additional) unit of output is demanded. In Table 11.4 the marginal revenue column gives the change in total revenue with each additional pocket watch case demanded. For example, when the number of watch cases demanded goes from zero to one, total revenue changes from $0 to $40,000, making the marginal revenue from the first case equal to $40,000; when the number of watch cases demanded goes from one to two, total revenue increases from $40,000 to $70,000, making the marginal revenue from the second case equal to $30,000; and so on. As was done with marginal benefits and marginal costs in the previous example, the marginal revenues in Table 11.4 are listed at the midpoints between the quantities demanded.[5]

Measuring Costs The jeweler's costs are shown in Table 11.5. To keep matters simple, let us say that these costs, including normal profit, come to $25,000 for each pocket watch case.

Total cost
Cost of producing a specified number of units of a good, service, or activity.

Marginal cost
The change in total cost when one more (or additional) unit of a good, service, or activity is produced.

Table 11.5 shows the jeweler's **total cost,** which is the cost per case times the quantity of cases produced. At a cost of $25,000 per case, the jeweler's total cost would be zero if no cases were produced ($25,000 × 0), $25,000 if one case were produced ($25,000 × 1), $50,000 if two were produced, and so on. **Marginal cost** measures how much total cost changes as each additional unit of an item is produced. In this case, the marginal cost column of Table 11.5 shows the additional cost of producing one more watch case. For example, when the quantity goes from zero to one, total cost goes from $0 to $25,000, making the marginal cost of the first case equal to $25,000. When the quantity changes from one to two, total cost goes from $25,000 to $50,000, and the marginal cost of the second case is again $25,000. As was done with the previous marginal values, the marginal costs in Table 11.5 are listed between the quantities produced.

---

[5]You might have noticed that when the quantity demanded is two, three, or four watch cases, marginal revenue is less than the price of the case. For example, when two cases are demanded at a price of $35,000, only $30,000 is added to total revenue by selling the second case. Why is this so?

If the jeweler only sells one watch case, he or she will earn $40,000 in revenue. However, in order to sell the second case, the jeweler must lower the price to $35,000. But with the second buyer paying only $35,000, the jeweler is going to have to charge $35,000 to the first buyer as well. This means that rather than receiving $40,000 from the first buyer, the jeweler will have to give the buyer a $5,000 discount. Because of this, what is added to total revenue from the sale of the second watch case is not its price. Rather, what is added to total revenue, or the marginal revenue, from the second unit sold is the price of the second unit minus the discount given to the first buyer, or $35,000 − $5,000 = $30,000. Likewise, if the jeweler wishes to sell a third case, the price must be lowered to $30,000. But if the third buyer pays only $30,000, $30,000 must also be charged to each of the first two buyers who would have otherwise paid $35,000. Thus, the marginal revenue from the third unit sold is not equal to the $30,000 price. Instead, the marginal revenue from the third unit sold equals the $30,000 price minus the two $5,000 discounts that were given to the first and second buyers, or $30,000 − $10,000 = $20,000. To test your understanding of this principle, see if you can explain why the marginal revenue from the fourth unit is $10,000, while its price is $25,000.

Table 11.5
Costs from Producing Pocket Watch Cases

Total cost is the cost of producing a specified number of units of output, and marginal cost measures the change in total cost from producing each additional unit of output.

Quantity	Total Cost	Marginal Cost
0	$ 0	
		$25,000
1	25,000	
		25,000
2	50,000	
		25,000
3	75,000	
		25,000
4	100,000	

Maximizing Profit

The number of pocket watch cases that the jeweler should produce and sell to maximize profit can be shown by combining the information from Tables 11.4 and 11.5. This is done in Table 11.6. But before analyzing the numbers in the table, let us review what we should expect to find.

Remember that both the individual at the concert and the jeweler are trying to maximize their net benefit by weighing costs and benefits. The rules for doing so are the same for the concertgoer and the jeweler; the only difference between the two is the actual benefits and costs to be measured and what is being maximized. For the jeweler, benefits are measured in terms of dollar revenues, costs are the costs of production, and net benefit is the profit from selling pocket watch cases. Applying the maximizing rules, we should expect the jeweler's profit to be at a maximum where his or her total revenue exceeds total cost by the greatest amount. We should also expect marginal revenue to equal marginal cost at the output level where profit is at a maximum. Table 11.6 lets us determine whether these expectations are borne out for the jeweler.

Profit or loss
What results when a business subtracts its total cost from its total revenue.

The profit column in Table 11.6 shows that a maximum profit of $20,000 occurs at two units of output. How does this relate to total revenue and total cost? **Profit** is derived by subtracting total cost from total revenue at each level of output. For example, if the jeweler were to produce and sell three

Table 11.6
Revenues, Costs, and Profit on Pocket Watch Cases

The maximum profit that can be obtained from producing and selling pocket watch cases occurs at two units. At this output level, total revenue exceeds total cost by the greatest amount and marginal revenue equals marginal cost.

Price	Quantity	Profit	Total Revenue	Total Cost	Marginal Revenue	Marginal Cost
$45,000	0	$ 0	$ 0	$ 0		
					$40,000	$25,000
40,000	1	15,000	40,000	25,000		
					30,000	25,000
35,000	2	20,000	70,000	50,000		
					20,000	25,000
30,000	3	15,000	90,000	75,000		
					10,000	25,000
25,000	4	0	100,000	100,000		

pocket watch cases, total revenue minus total cost would be $90,000 − $75,000, or $15,000. The largest, or maximum, profit for a business occurs where total revenue exceeds total cost by the greatest amount. This is as expected.

What about the relationship between marginal revenue and marginal cost where profit is maximized? Reading down the last two columns in Table 11.6, it can be seen that from zero to one, and from one to two units of output, marginal revenue is greater than marginal cost: each pocket watch case adds more to total revenue than to total cost, causing profit to increase. This can be verified by noticing that the numbers in the profit column increase as output and sales go from zero to two units.

On the other hand, in Table 11.6 marginal cost is greater than marginal revenue as output goes from two to three, and from three to four units. In this case, the third and fourth units are adding more to total cost than to total revenue, causing profit to fall. This too is confirmed by the figures in the profit column.

Since marginal revenue is greater than marginal cost up to two units of output, and since marginal revenue is less than marginal cost beyond two units of output, marginal revenue and marginal cost must be equal at two units. Thus, the two rules for maximizing are satisfied. At an output level of two units, total revenue exceeds total cost by the greatest amount, and marginal revenue equals marginal cost.

Graphing Costs, Revenues, and Profit

The relationships between marginal revenue, marginal cost, and profit, and between total revenue, total cost, and profit which were set out in Table 11.6 are illustrated in Figure 11.3. The bottom graph of Figure 11.3a shows that net benefit, or profit, is at its maximum where two watch cases are produced and sold. The upper graph in Figure 11.3a shows that marginal revenue and marginal cost are equal at exactly two units of output. For smaller output levels, marginal revenue is greater than marginal cost, which causes profit in the lower graph to increase. For output levels larger than two units, marginal revenue is less than marginal cost, causing profit to fall. Finally, in Figure 11.3b the vertical distance by which total revenue exceeds total cost in the upper graph is at its maximum at two units of output, which, of course, is the output level where profit is maximized in the lower graph.

In summary, regardless of whether an individual, business, or government unit is being considered, the net benefit to the decision-making unit from an activity will be maximized if it operates where total benefit exceeds total cost by the greatest amount. This is also where marginal benefit and marginal cost are equal. The main difference between the decision-making units is not that they follow different rules. Rather, the difference is what is being maximized and how costs and benefits are measured. You can test your understanding of the maximizing rules by working through the example in Application 11.2, "Test Yourself: Maximizing Profit."

Figure 11.3
Marginal Revenue–Marginal Cost, Total Revenue–Total Cost, and Profit

Graphically, profit is maximized at the output level where the marginal revenue curve crosses the marginal cost curve, or where the total revenue curve exceeds the total cost curve by the greatest amount.

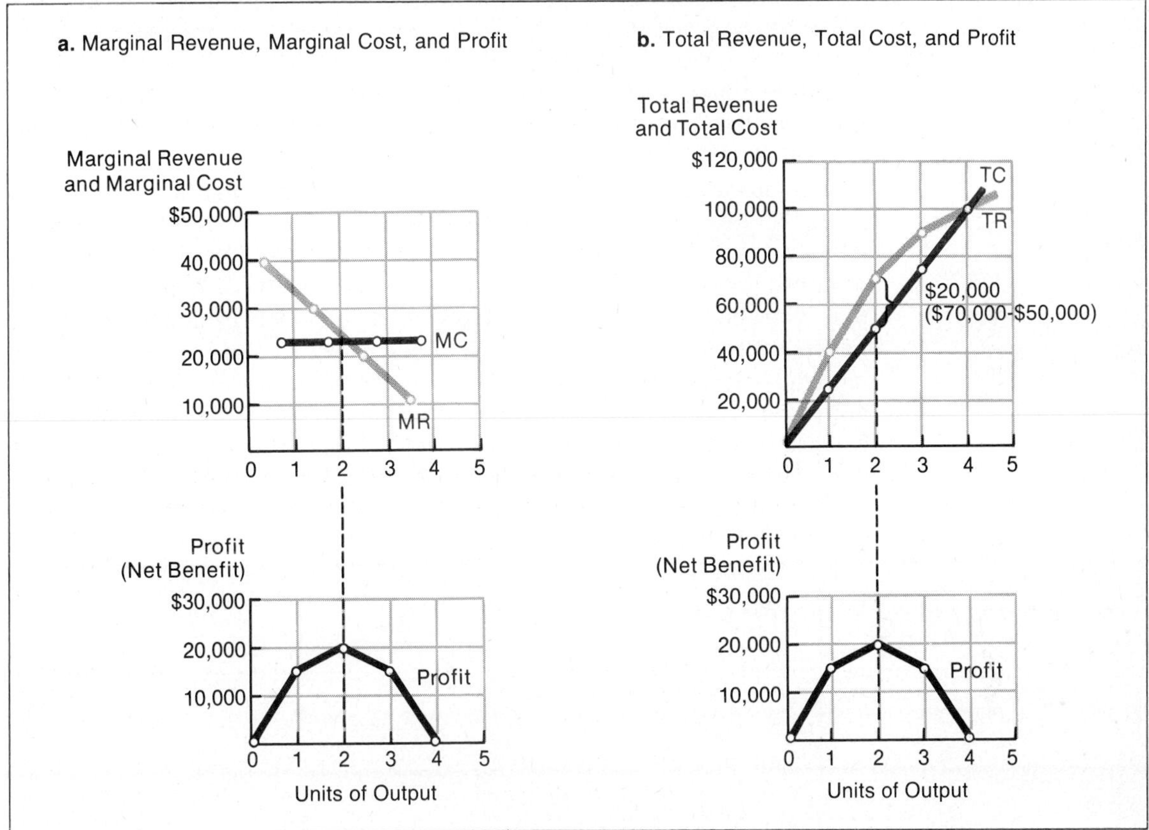

PRIVATE VS. SOCIAL BENEFITS AND COSTS

In the cases just discussed, any concern over whether, how, or to what extent others might be affected by the individual's or business's decisions was absent. People often choose courses of action after considering only factors that affect them directly, even though sometimes what they do will benefit or impose a cost on others. Because of this, individuals' perceptions of the costs and benefits of their actions may differ from society's perception of the costs and benefits of those same actions.

The level of activity that maximizes a particular business's or individual's net benefit may be greater or less than the level that would maximize society's net benefit. This can be illustrated by returning to the first example discussed earlier, where the individual's net benefit from an evening out was maximized by spending three hours at a concert. Instead of dealing with a concert, assume that the same numbers apply to our student filling sandbags to hold back water from a flooding river in a nearby town. As with attending the concert, the student's net benefit from sandbagging would be maximized if the student quit at the end of three hours. But if the effect on society is considered, the net benefit of the townspeople would probably be higher if the student stayed and bagged for four or five hours. Or suppose that the example applied to an evening of drinking and driving by our student. In this case, society's net benefit would probably be maximized if our individual spent less than three hours drinking and driving or even, perhaps, no time at all.

Externality
The effect of an action that falls on a person or thing that was not one of the primary parties to the action. The effect may benefit (create a positive externality) or cost (create a negative externality) the affected person or thing.

The effects that actions have on persons or things that are not primary parties to the actions are called **externalities.** These externalities may be either positive and beneficial to others, or negative and costly to others. For example, getting a vaccination against a contagious disease may benefit not only you, but also those around you who might have otherwise become infected. Keeping your car well maintained benefits you and also all the people who might have been delayed if you broke down on the highway. In both cases your actions have worked to the advantage of others and have created positive externalities. On the other hand, a production facility that pollutes the air or water, or individuals who abandon cars or leave litter by roadsides may be contributing to the detriment of others and creating negative externalities. Because of pollution, for example, residents of a community might be paying more to clean the environment or on medical care

Application 11.2
TEST YOURSELF: MAXIMIZING PROFIT[a]

Pete Casso has been invited to exhibit two of his works in the annual student art show and sale. Although those who are invited to participate in the show receive a great deal of personal satisfaction or "psychic income" from having been selected, the show also presents an opportunity for the exhibitors to earn some money. Pete is concerned about making as much money as he can from this sale to help defray tuition costs for next semester. Since he studied economics last year, he realizes the importance of pricing his works of art correctly in order to maximize profit.

Pete has chosen to include a pen-and-ink drawing of a house and a colorful lithograph in the show because both of these items can bring multiple sales. The house drawing will serve as a sample of Pete's custom work in this area. That is, he produces pen-and-ink drawings of individual homes from photographs and, based on the sample, can take orders for these custom drawings. The lithograph that he has chosen can be easily reproduced many times without losing its design and color, so he can sell multiples of this work.

Table 1 gives the demand schedule that Pete thinks to be true for custom house drawings. He calculates his cost for each house drawing at $12, which includes his time and materials. If Pete intends to maximize his profit from these drawings, what price will he charge and how many drawings will he produce? Is his roommate correct in advising him to go for volume and charge $18 per drawing? Why or why not?

Table 2 gives the demand schedule for Pete's

than they would have otherwise. Application 11.3, "Forests Declining Throughout Eastern United States," deals with a recently discovered externality that is generating great interest and concern.

These positive and negative effects must be added to the private, or individual, benefit-cost calculations to determine how society is affected by different actions. The total effect on society of the private benefits and costs plus the externalities of an action are the action's **social benefits** and **social costs.** Thus, we can say:

Social benefits and costs
The total effect on society that results from the private benefits, private costs, and externalities of actions.

private benefits + any positive external effects = social benefits;
private costs + any negative external effects = social costs; and
social benefits − social costs = net benefits to society.

The method by which net benefit is calculated for society is exactly the same as that used for businesses and individuals. The only difference is that now we are concerned with social rather than private benefits and costs. Thus, the net benefit to society from an activity is maximized where the total social benefit from the activity exceeds its total social cost by the greatest amount, or where marginal social benefit equals marginal social cost.

How do externalities affect the relationship between private and social net benefits? If the action of an individual or business has no effect on others, there will be no externalities, and the level of activity that maximizes the individual's or business's net benefit will also maximize the net benefit of

---

Table 1
Demand for Custom-Drawn Houses

Price per Drawing	Number of Drawings Demanded
$66	1
60	2
54	3
48	4
42	5
36	6
30	7
24	8
18	9

Table 2
Demand for Lithographs

Price per Lithograph	Number of Lithographs Demanded
$170	1
160	2
150	3
140	4
130	5
120	6
110	7
100	8
90	9
80	10

lithograph. The cost of producing the first lithograph is high—$200—but the marginal cost for each additional print is only $5. What price should Pete charge for his lithograph? What is the maximum profit that he can expect to make from the sale of his lithograph?

[a]Answers can be found on page 327.

society. But where individual actions impose costs on others and cause negative externalities, the level of activity that maximizes society's net benefit will be *less* than the level where individual net benefit is maximized. For example, if the profit-maximizing output for a business is accompanied by a large amount of air pollution, the cost of which is borne by society, society would be better off if the firm produced a lower level of output and less pollution.

Where individual actions benefit others and cause positive externalities, the level of activity that maximizes society's net benefit will be *greater* than the level that maximizes individual net benefit. For example, a person might maximize private net benefit by purchasing storm windows for only half of his or her home to save on energy costs. But because of a fuel shortage, society might be best off if the homeowner were to purchase storm windows for the entire house to conserve energy.[6]

---

[6]The relationship between private and social net benefits can be shown with graphs such as those given in Figures 11.4 and 11.5. Suppose that the private marginal costs and benefits to an individual from performing an activity are represented by MC and MB in Figure 11.4. Here private net benefit would be maximized where MB = MC, which occurs at the level of activity shown by point Y on the horizontal axis of Figure 11.4.

But also suppose that this activity imposes costs or negative externalities with no offsetting benefits to other people. From society's point of view these negative externalities must be added to the private costs of the individual performing the act to determine social costs, and from that, the best activity level for society. When the negative externalities are added to the private costs, marginal social cost can be calculated and is represented by MC_s in Figure 11.4. From society's perspective, the best level of activity is shown by point X on the horizontal axis of Figure 11.4. At that point, the marginal benefit to society, MB (which is the same as private marginal benefit

Application 11.3
FORESTS DECLINING THROUGHOUT EASTERN UNITED STATES

Rapidly accumulating evidence indicates that forests throughout the Eastern United States, not just in isolated spots in the Northeast, are in decline, perhaps seriously. . . .

New research has shown that some species of softwood trees are losing their foliage, dying and failing to reproduce at high elevations in the Southeastern part of the Appalachians. Until recently, observations of forests throughout the nation had found such problems only in the Northeast.

As disturbing, in the view of some scientists and foresters, are data from a number of studies and a survey by the U.S. Forest Service showing a large-scale, rapid and simultaneous drop in the growth rates of at least a half-dozen species of coniferous trees in the East. . . .

The forest decline is most pronounced at higher altitudes, but is found at all elevations. Scientists say tree core samples and other evidence show that the slowdown in tree growth is without precedent, as far as they can determine.

Scientists, federal officials, forestry experts and industry spokesmen interviewed in the last two weeks said more research was needed to determine the causes and implications of the forest decline. They said they could not rule out natural causes.

since the act provides no positive externalities) equals marginal social cost, MC_s. In this case, it would be in the interest of society to persuade the individual to cut back his or her level of activity from point Y to point X.

The situation with a positive externality is shown in Figure 11.5. The individual performing the activity in question would maximize personal net benefit where private marginal benefit, MB, and marginal cost, MC, were equal, or at point Y on the horizontal axis of Figure 11.5. But suppose that this activity benefits society with no offsetting addition to cost, or negative externality. The additional benefit, or positive externality, must be added to the private benefit to determine the activity level which would best serve society. These benefits are added together with the resulting marginal social benefit shown by MB_s in Figure 11.5. In this case, where there are benefits but no costs imposed on society, the best position for society would be at activity level Z in Figure 11.5, where $MB_s = MC$. In this situation it would be in society's interest to induce the person to increase the level of activity from point Y to point Z.

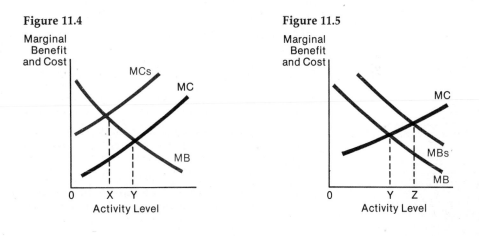

Figure 11.4

Marginal Benefit and Cost
MCs
MC
MB
0
X
Y
Activity Level

Figure 11.5

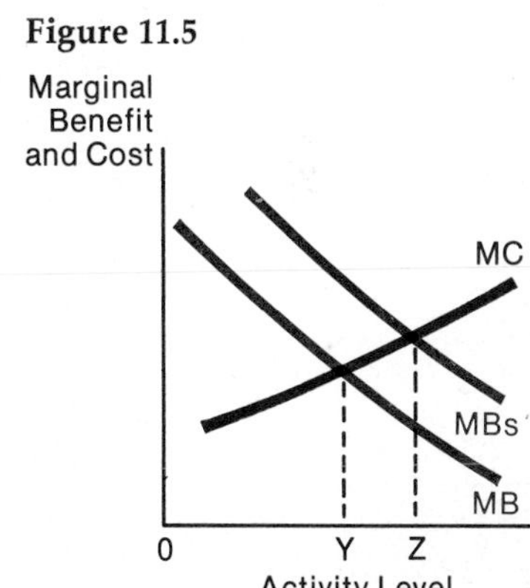

But most of them said the evidence so far strongly suggested that air pollution from power plants, factories, motor vehicles and other human activity, either by itself or in combination with natural stresses, was responsible for the declining state of the trees. . . .

"Something very dramatic is happening very quickly to the forests of the Eastern United States," said Robert I. Bruck, a plant pathologist at North Carolina State University. . . .

Bruck has recently discovered that red spruces and, apparently, Fraser firs are deteriorating and dying at the top of Mount Mitchell near Asheville, N.C., the highest peak on the Eastern Seaboard. His studies have found that virtually no plant life is reproducing there, leaving the once lush mountaintop increasingly barren. He described it as scary.

No consensus has been reached on what role, if any, is played by acid rain in damaging or slowing the growth of the forests. Acid rain occurs when air pollutants, chiefly sulfur dioxide and nitrogen oxides, change chemically in the atmosphere and fall to earth as acidic rain, snow, fog or dry particles.

Acid rain is now generally conceded to be destroying life in some lakes and ponds in the Northeast. But several of the experts interviewed said the potential threat to forests, because of their commercial, ecological and esthetic importance, was a much greater cause for concern than the sterilization of several hundred lakes. . . .

Source: Philip Shabecoff, "Forests Declining Throughout Eastern U.S.," *St. Louis Post - Dispatch*, O. 17A, February 29, 1984.

How can society induce individuals and businesses to increase desirable and decrease undesirable activities? The example of an individual winterizing a home suggests one effective method: financial incentives. In this case, society, acting through the government, might give the homeowner an incentive such as a tax break to induce more purchases than would otherwise occur. In addition to a tax reduction, people may also be induced to carry out activities that benefit society through direct grants of money, or subsidies, where part of the cost of the action is absorbed by the government. Activities that work to the detriment of society might be reduced through fines, taxation, or outright prohibition.

PUBLIC CHOICE

The goal of maximizing economic well-being and the principles of cost-benefit analysis are easily understood in the context of individual and business decision making. In our economic system, however, many important decisions are also made collectively, that is, made as a group. Collective decision making occurs primarily at the government level. As a group we make choices on questions such as how many missiles to purchase, whether to fund space projects, how much money to allocate to the needy, and whether to permit budget deficits.

How do individuals participate in collective decision making? In the United States, the voting mechanism is the root of collective choice. Individuals elect officials at the federal, state, and local government levels who receive the power and authority to act in behalf of the group. Thus, voting provides the link that transforms individual decision making into collective choice.

Public choice
The study of the economic motives and attitudes of voters and public officials in collective decision making.

Public choice is the term used to describe the set of economic theories that explains the motives and attitudes of voters and public officials in collective decision making. The basic idea behind public choice is that people try to maximize their own well-being, or operate in their own self-interest, in making collective choices. Thus, the fundamental rules of decision making do not change when a group is involved. An examination of the voting process helps to illustrate the basics of public choice.

Participation in an election involves three considerations for the individual: (1) whether to vote, (2) how much information to seek about candidates and issues, and (3) for whom to vote. Each of these considerations carries costs and benefits with it.

The act of voting gives individuals varying degrees of satisfaction: if people believe that their votes are important, voting gives them more satisfaction than if they feel that their votes are insignificant. Voting also imposes costs on individuals, especially the opportunity cost of time. Thus, a person's decision about whether or not to vote in an election depends upon his or her marginal benefit and marginal cost of voting. If marginal benefit is greater than marginal cost, a person will vote in an election; if marginal cost is greater than marginal benefit, he or she will not vote. Since voter turnout for a particular election is the result of all of the individual decisions of voters, and since a relatively small percentage of the electorate generally votes, we can conclude that most people believe that it is not in their best interest to participate in collective decision making.

A second consideration in voting involves the amount of information about candidates and issues that a voter possesses when making a decision at the polls. Generally, when individuals make private decisions about spending large sums of money, they attempt to gather as much information as possible. Do you, for example, know someone who is about to purchase a car? That person is probably reading magazines that rate automobiles, taking test drives, and asking current car owners about the advantages and problems of particular models. Many persons will pay the government as much in taxes this year as the cost of a new auto. Are those persons investing as much time and energy in gathering information about the elected representatives to whom they are entrusting their tax dollars as they would if they were using an equivalent sum of money to buy a car? Probably they are not.

Information seeking about candidates and issues takes time. As a result, the opportunity cost of becoming an informed voter can be high. A rational voter may perceive the marginal benefit from becoming better acquainted with a candidate's record and position to be far less than the marginal cost of enlightenment. Because of this, voters often make choices based on scanty information that comes from brief advertisements to quickly sell a candidate.

Which candidate does a voter choose? Again, the principles of cost-benefit analysis apply. A voter will select the candidate perceived to bring him or her the greatest net benefit. This decision could be based on the candidate's record, the position of the candidate on an issue important to the voter, or any other consideration.

Special interest group People who share a common position on a particular issue and actively promote that position.

Public choice theory, with its emphasis on self-interest, helps to explain many of the problems that result from collective decision making. For example, in the collective process, **special interest groups** often cause the will of a minority to be imposed on the majority. Public choice theory explains that members of special interest groups actively seek their positions through letters, ads, campaign contributions, and other means because of the benefits they expect to receive. The response to these issues from the rest of the population is weak because of lack of interest or because the opportunity cost of responding is too high. Elected officials are sensitive to the pleas of special interest group members because it is in the officials' best interest.

SUMMARY

There are general rules for maximizing economic well-being that can be applied to any decision-making unit, be it an individual, business, or society. These rules involve the balancing of costs and benefits from different courses of action in order to select the one that contributes most to economic well-being. Formal study of these rules and the balancing of costs and benefits is called cost-benefit analysis. These rules can be applied to many more areas of human endeavor than those traditionally studied in economics courses.

For an individual, the benefits of an activity can be measured in terms of the satisfaction, or utility, received from the action. Costs can be measured by the opportunities forgone in accomplishing that action.

For a business, benefits are measured by the total revenue received, which is calculated by multiplying the price of an item times the quantity of the item sold. Business costs include explicit costs, which are direct payments for factors of production, and implicit costs, which are payments required by the owner(s) to keep the business in operation. Implicit cost is called normal profit and is equal to what the owner(s) could earn in the next best alternative. Economic profit is not a cost of production; it is that profit in excess of normal profit.

Marginal benefit or revenue is the additional benefit received from each additional unit of an activity performed or unit of output sold. Marginal cost is the additional cost of producing or adding one more unit of activity or output. Total benefits and total costs are, respectively, the benefits received and the costs incurred from producing a particular amount of activity or output.

The rules for maximizing economic well-being, or net benefit, are that an activity should be carried out to the point where total benefit exceeds total cost by the greatest amount, or where marginal benefit equals marginal cost. Both rules are satisfied at exactly the same level of activity. The main difference in how these rules are applied to various decision-making units is in what is maximized and how benefits and costs are measured. The individual tries to maximize net satisfaction, and profit is typically the net benefit to be maximized when the rules are applied by a business.

Activities by individuals or businesses may favorably or adversely affect others in addition to themselves. These effects are called externalities, and because of externalities, an individual's or business's net benefits from its actions may differ from society's net benefits from those same actions.

Net benefits are calculated for society in exactly the same way they are calculated for individuals and businesses. The only difference is that while the individual or business may measure its net benefits in terms of its own private costs and benefits, society must measure its net benefits in terms of social costs and social benefits. Social costs are private costs plus any negative external effects. Social benefits are private benefits plus any positive external effects. When negative externalities are present, society's net benefit is maximized at a level of activity lower than that which will maximize private net benefit. When positive externalities are present, society's net benefit is maximized at a level of activity greater than that which will maximize private net benefit.

Public choice deals with the economic theory behind collective decision making, which is carried out through the voting process. How the voting mechanism is used by each individual depends upon that individual's costs and benefits from the acts of voting, information seeking, and candidate selection. Problems that arise from collective decision making, such as the impact of special interest groups, can be explained through the use of cost-benefit analysis.

Key Terms and Concepts

Cost-benefit analysis
Opportunity cost
Marginal benefit or utility
Total benefit or utility
Law of Diminishing Marginal Utility
Marginal cost
Total cost
Net benefit
Maximization rules
Explicit costs
Normal profit
Excess, or economic, profit
Implicit cost
Economic cost of production
Total revenue
Marginal revenue
Profit
Externality
Social benefits and costs
Public choice
Special interest group

Discussion and Review Questions

1. In each of the following situations, determine what the decision maker might be seeking to maximize and indicate (1) some factors that should be included in the calculation of costs, and (2) some factors that should be included in the calculation of benefits.
   a. The decision to get a college education
   b. The decision by a shoplifter to steal a coat
   c. The decision by voters to increase property taxes
   d. The decision by a business to market a new product
   e. The decision to adopt a child
   f. The decision to lie
2. Explain why (1) net benefit is at a maximum when marginal benefit equals marginal cost; (2) net benefit increases when marginal benefit exceeds marginal cost; and (3) net benefit falls when marginal benefit is less than marginal cost.
3. Identify some of the negative externalities associated with living in a city that has a high crime rate.
4. Air pollution is a well-known example of a negative externality. What are some of the costs imposed on society by air pollution? In answering this question be sure to consider possible effects from pollution on health, property values, the maintenance of buildings and other property, and taxes.

5. Suppose that you are on a special task force to develop methods for reducing air pollution.
   a. What methods would you propose to reduce air pollution if it were caused mainly by the production of output by businesses?
   b. Would you recommend the same methods for reducing air pollution that you did in question a if the pollution were caused primarily by a large volume of auto traffic? If not, what methods would you recommend?
   c. What are some costs and benefits that would accompany each of the methods you proposed in questions a and b?
   d. Since air pollution causes a negative externality, would you back a proposal to curb air pollution completely? Why?
6. In what respects are the following four maximizing decisions similar to each other and in what respects do they differ?
   a. The decision by an individual as to how much of an item to consume
   b. The decision by a society as to how many resources to devote to law enforcement
   c. The decision by a business as to how much of a product to produce and sell
   d. The decision by an individual as to how many hours to work
7. Suppose that you have a friend who has decided to start a business. This decision is based largely on her calculation that at the end of one year there would be $22,000 in profit after all explicit costs were met. If your friend could perform the same type of work for a firm and earn $24,000 per year, would you recommend that she start the business? Why? What would be her normal profit?

do

8. Answer the questions following the cost and revenue information given below.

Units of Output	Total Revenue	Total Cost
0	$ 0	$ 0
1	50	25
2	90	35
3	120	40
4	140	50
5	150	70
6	150	100
7	140	140
8	120	200

   a. What are the marginal revenue and marginal cost of each unit of output?
   b. At what levels of output is marginal cost greater than marginal revenue, and at what levels is marginal revenue greater than marginal cost?

c. What is the profit-maximizing level of output?
d. What is total profit at the profit-maximizing level of output?

9. Use public choice theory to explain:
   a. Low voter turnout for the election of a few candidates for minor offices
   b. Voting along party lines instead of judging each candidate's individual merits
   c. A change before an election in an incumbent's position on an issue
   d. Voting according to the recommendations given in a local newspaper
10. Based on public choice theory, is it realistic to assume that government policies to control U.S. forest destruction such as that described in Application 11.3 will be forthcoming?

Suggested Readings

Jerry E. Bishop, "Surgeons Find Heart Repair Pays For Itself," *The Wall Street Journal,* August 29, 1980, p. 13. Discusses a study by a group of surgeons on the costs and benefits of a particular type of heart operation.

James M. Buchanan, "From Private Preferences to Public Philosophy: The Development of Public Choice," *The Economics of Politics* (London: The Institute of Economic Affairs, 1978), pp. 3–20. A discussion of the development of public choice theory.

Marshall Jevons, *Murder at the Margin* (Glen Ridge, N.J.: Thomas Horton and Daughters, 1978). A murder mystery that is solved using economic principles.

Heinz Kohler, "Ch. 4: The Optimization Principle," *Scarcity and Freedom* (Lexington, Mass.: D. C. Heath and Co., 1977), pp. 30–40. An additional explanation of how marginal costs and benefits are compared in determining the most desirable level for carrying out an activity.

Allen V. Kneese and Charles L. Schultze, "Ch. 2: Some Technical Background," *Pollution, Prices, and Public Policy* (Washington, D.C.: The Brookings Institution, 1975), pp. 11–29. Deals with the externalities of air and water pollution in terms of their types, costs of control, and the effects of control on different groups in society.

Roland N. McKean, "The Nature of Cost-Benefit Analysis," *Microeconomics: Selected Readings,* Edwin Mansfield, ed. (New York: W. W. Norton & Co., Inc., 1979), pp. 509–518. Sets out and discusses common elements of cost-benefit studies.

G. Tullock and R. B. McKenzie, *The New World of Economics,* 4th ed. (Homewood, Ill.: R. D. Irwin, Inc., 1985). A cost-benefit approach to marriage, divorce, crime, learning, and other topics.

Test Yourself Answers (Application 11.2)

To maximize profit from the custom house drawings, Pete should charge $42 and produce 5 drawings. In going for volume, as suggested by his roommate, he would earn less total profit than by producing and selling 5. As to lithographs, Pete should charge $90 each and sell 9, earning a total profit of $570.

12 PRODUCTION AND THE COSTS OF PRODUCTION

Chapter Objectives

1. To identify some methods for categorizing productive activity in the U.S. economy.
2. To explain the nature and importance of production methods.
3. To explore the relationship between production methods and technology.
4. To differentiate between production in the short run and production in the long run.
5. To define various types of costs associated with production: fixed, variable, total, average total, and marginal.
6. To explain the behavior of costs as the level of production changes in both the short run and the long run.

This chapter concerns production, which is the process of transforming inputs into outputs of goods and services. It also concerns the costs of production, which are the costs of bringing these goods and services into being. Technically, production is carried out in all sectors of the economy: in businesses, households, and governments. Steel is produced by a business firm; a homemaker produces meals; and the local government's fire department provides fire protection. But while each of these areas of the economy produces goods and services, the vast majority of measured production is by businesses. Consequently, this chapter focuses on the production and the costs of production of business firms.

The first section of the chapter provides an overview of production in the U.S. economy. The second section deals with methods of production and the relationship between those methods and technology. The third section is devoted to the approach most commonly used in economics for classifying and evaluating production and the costs of production: viewing them in terms of short-run and long-run time frames.

Before embarking on the chapter it should be noted that there is an important connection between a firm's production, its costs of production, and its ability to realize the objective of maximum profit. As was introduced in Chapter Ten, and emphasized in the example of the jeweler in Chapter Eleven, profit is what remains after costs are subtracted from revenue. All other things remaining unchanged, the lower the cost of producing a product, the greater the firm's profit from selling that product.

OVERVIEW OF PRODUCTION IN THE U.S. ECONOMY

In 1975 U.S. business firms produced an output of goods and services valued at over $1.5 trillion. By 1984 the value of output had grown to $3.7 trillion.[1] Much of this output, especially that from corporations, is generated by firms that each produce several different types of products. For example, in addition to its beer operations, Anheuser-Busch, through its divisions and subsidiaries, produces bakery goods, other foods, and yeast; operates transportation services and parks for family entertainment; fields a major league baseball team; and is in real estate development.[2]

With so many businesses producing so many different types of goods and services, gaining an overview of production in the U.S. economy can be formidable. To help simplify this task, a classification system has been developed to group similar types of goods and services together. For example, there are obvious differences between automobiles and cheese, and between cheese and corn. But cheese and corn have something in common that they do not share with automobiles — they are agricultural products. Thus, cheese, corn, and related products can be classified into one group (agricultural products), while automobiles can be classified into another group (manufactured products) along with items such as locomotives, machinery, and gutters and downspouts.

Sectors
A broad classification system for grouping the production of goods and services.

These broad categories for output bring order to an overview of production in the economy and allow us to think of the economy as a collection of separate major producing areas. These major producing areas are called **sectors.**

Producing Sectors

Table 12.1 identifies the major producing sectors of the economy, along with examples of the productive activities included in each sector and each sector's contribution to private domestic output in 1983.

[1] U.S., *Economic Report of the President* (Washington, D.C.: U.S. Government Printing Office, 1985), p. 232. 1984 figures are preliminary.

[2] Anheuser-Busch, Inc., *1983 Annual Report* (St. Louis: Anheuser-Busch, Inc., 1984), pp. 19–26.

Table 12.1
Major Producing Sectors of the Economy

Any good or service produced by a business can be categorized into one of the producing sectors of the economy. Over the years, manufacturing has consistently been the largest producing sector.

Sector	Examples of Productive Activities	Percent of Private Domestic Output in 1983
Agriculture, forestry, and fishing	Crop and livestock production, agricultural services, forestry, fishing, hunting and trapping	2.5%
Mining	Metal, coal and lignite mining, oil and gas extraction	3.9
Construction	Building, highway and heavy construction, general contracting and special contracting	4.6
Manufacturing	Production of apparel, food products, fabricated metal products, electrical machinery, transportation equipment and chemical products, petroleum refining, printing and publishing	23.9
Transportation	Railroad, water, pipeline and air transportation, trucking and warehousing	4.0
Communications	Radio and television broadcasting, telephone and telegraph	3.2
Electric, gas, and sanitary services	Natural gas transmission and distribution, sewer systems, electric services	3.5
Wholesale trade	Wholesale auto supplies, electrical appliances, sporting goods	8.0
Retail trade	Food and general merchandise stores, restaurants, building supply and garden stores, auto dealers, gasoline stations	10.7
Finance, insurance, and real estate	Banking, commodity and security brokerage, insurance, real estate	18.9
Services	Personal and business services, health, legal and educational services	16.7

Source: Executive Office of the President, Office of Management and Budget, *Standard Industrial Classification Manual,* 1972 (Washington, D.C.: U.S. Government Printing Office), pp. 5–7, 49–50, 235, 237–238, 242, 244–245; United States Department of Commerce, *Survey of Current Business* (July 1984), p. 69.

A few points should be noted about Table 12.1. First, in analyzing the table it must be remembered that although we can distinguish different sectors of the economy, those sectors are closely knit together in the production and distribution of goods and services. The natural gas extracted by the mining sector is made available to households through the electric, gas, and sanitary services sector. The crops and livestock produced in the agricultural sector become food products in the manufacturing sector. These food products then move from the manufacturers' to households' shelves through the wholesale and retail sectors, with the assistance of services from the transportation sector.

Second, as the economy grows, the relative importance of some of the different sectors may change. From 1930 through the present, the position of manufacturing as the dominant producing sector of the economy has remained unchallenged. But changes have occurred in the relative importance of other sectors. From 1930 to the mid-1950s, the agriculture, forestry, and fishing sector contributed more to total output than did either the construction or transportation sectors. But in the late 1950s the relationship reversed, and contributions to total output by the construction and transportation sectors each surpassed that of the agricultural sector. Also, in more recent years, the finance, insurance, and real estate sector and the services sector have grown in importance.[3]

Finally, dividing productive activity into sectors helps order our thinking about production in the economy, but the sectors are broadly defined and include activities that, while related, are not always closely related. For example, frog farming and landscape planning are both included in the agriculture, forestry, and fishing sector.[4] For this reason, it is helpful to classify production into narrower categories than those shown in Table 12.1. One such classification method that is widely used divides productive activities into groups called industries.

Industries

Industry
A group of firms producing similar products.

An **industry** is a group of firms producing similar products. This similarity may be in the processes and factors used by the firms to produce the products, or it may be caused by buyers viewing the firms' products as interchangeable or as substitutes for one other. Examples of industries are the cigarette, greeting card, aircraft, sporting goods, and automobile industries.

How do industry classifications compare with the sector classifications in Table 12.1? The finance, insurance, and real estate sector provides an illustration. Insurance is one type of activity listed for this sector in Table 12.1. Although the provision of insurance services is a narrower category than the sector classification, it does not fit the definition of an industry, because not all insurance is similar: having one's home insured for theft protection is not a substitute for a hospitalization plan. Thus, within the insurance services category are several more narrowly defined groups, or industries. These insurances industries, along with examples of the types of protection offered by each, are listed in Table 12.2.

---

[3]U.S. Bureau of the Census, *Historical Statistics of the United States, Colonial Times to 1970, Bicentennial Edition, Part 1,* Washington, D.C., 1975, p. 239; U.S. Bureau of the Census, *Statistical Abstract of the United States: 1984* (104th ed.), Washington, D.C., 1983, p. 454.

[4]Executive Office of the President, Office of Management and Budget, *Standard Industrial Classification Manual,* 1972 (Washington, D.C.: U.S. Government Printing Office), pp. 24, 27.

Table 12.2
Industries Providing Insurance Services

Firms producing similar products are grouped into the same industry. There are a number of industries that provide different types of insurance services.

Industry	Examples of Services Provided by Firms in the Industry
Life insurance	Life insurance, including insurance through fraternal and cooperative organizations; funeral and burial insurance
Accident and health insurance	Accident and health insurance, hospitalization insurance
Hospital and medical service plans	Hospital and medical service plans, dental insurance, group hospitalization plans
Fire, marine, and casualty insurance	Property damage, automobile, theft, and worker's compensation insurance
Surety insurance	Liability insurance, employee bonding, job completion bonding
Title insurance	Title insurance, mortgage insurance
Pension, health, and welfare funds	Management of pension, retirement, and welfare funds

Source: Executive Office of the President, Office of Management and Budget, *Standard Industrial Classification Manual,* 1972 (Washington, D.C.: U.S. Government Printing Office) pp. 286–287. Insurance of deposits in financial institutions is excluded from the table since it is undertaken by a government agency.

The services provided in any one of the seven insurance related industries listed in Table 12.2 are easily distinguishable from the services provided in any of the other industries listed in the table. A clear separation exists between life and health insurance, or between any other types of insurance.

Notice that many of the services listed in the different industries in Table 12.2 could be offered by the same firm. That is, a single insurance company might provide several different types of coverage, such as life, health, and casualty. When this occurs, the firm is simultaneously operating in several industries. In the insurance example the industries are closely related. But they need not be. Recall that Anheuser-Busch operates in several unrelated areas, some of which are beer, real estate, and professional sports.

More specific classifications than industries can be developed for grouping businesses. For example, suppose you are interested in securing data about firms producing dental insurance. In this case, the hospital and medical service plans industry grouping, in which dental insurance is listed, would be too broad. You would be better served with something narrower than this industry classification. Thus, depending on one's needs, there are many different levels from which production in the economy can be viewed. The focus can be on major producing sectors, industries, narrower parts of industries, or individual firms.

METHODS OF PRODUCTION

Production, or the transforming of inputs into outputs, does not occur haphazardly. Rather, it is systematic and occurs according to a plan called a production function.

The Production Function

Production function
Shows the type and amount of output that can be attained from a particular group of inputs when those inputs are combined in a certain way.

A **production function** shows the type and amount of output that can be attained from a particular group of inputs when those inputs are combined in a certain way. Production functions exist for virtually every good and service: for agricultural products, machinery, magazines, chemicals, hamburgers and fries, and everything else that can be produced. For some types of goods and services, production functions can be clearly defined. For other productive activities, such as learning or child rearing, the functions are not as well understood. But in each case, we can think of an output as that which is produced by a set of inputs combined in a particular way.

One common form of a production function, which can be used to illustrate the basic features of all production functions, is a recipe such as that shown in Table 12.3. In this production function the output is 32 toffee bars. The inputs include the ingredients listed at the top of the recipe—butter, flour, chocolate, and so forth—as well as kitchen equipment and the labor provided by the person preparing the toffee bars. The method for combining those inputs is explained in the text of the recipe and involves such operations as heating, mixing, and spreading. All production functions are concerned with exactly the same types of considerations that this recipe deals with: the type and amount of output, the numbers and types of inputs, and how the inputs are combined.

At any given time there can be more than one method available to a business for producing a particular good or service. A painting contractor might paint the exterior of a house using brushes or spraying equipment. A business document might be edited by someone sitting at a desk with a pencil or by the same person sitting in front of a word processing machine. Because a business often can choose among several methods to produce an output, it is helpful to differentiate between those methods. One way of doing this is to distinguish between labor-intensive production and capital-intensive production.

Table 12.3
Toffee Bars

A production function indicates the number and types of inputs and how those inputs are combined to produce a particular type and amount of output. A recipe is a simple example of a production function.

1 cup packed brown sugar
1 cup margarine or butter, softened
1 egg yolk
1 teaspoon vanilla
2 cups all-purpose* or whole wheat flour
¼ teaspoon salt
1 bar (4 ounces) milk chocolate candy
½ cup chopped nuts

Heat oven to 350°. Mix brown sugar, margarine, egg yolk and vanilla. Stir in flour and salt. Press in greased oblong pan, 13 × 9 × 2 inches. Bake until very light brown, 25 to 30 minutes (crust will be soft). Remove from oven; immediately place separated pieces of chocolate candy on crust. Let stand until soft; spread evenly. Sprinkle with nuts. Cut into bars, about 2 × 1½ inches, while warm. 32 cookies.

*If using self-rising flour, omit salt.

Spicy Bars: Stir in 1 teaspoon ground ginger with the salt. Omit chocolate and substitute ¼ cup chopped salted nuts and ¼ cup flaked coconut for the nuts.

Source: General Mills, Inc., *Betty Crocker's Cookbook* (New York: Golden Press, 1980), p. 272.

Labor-intensive production
Production that is strongly dependent on labor inputs.

Capital-intensive production
Production that emphasizes capital inputs.

Labor-intensive production involves production techniques exhibiting a strong dependence on labor as compared to machinery, equipment, and other types of inputs. The greater the dependence on labor, the more labor-intensive is the production. **Capital-intensive production** involves production techniques that emphasize the use of capital: the greater the emphasis on capital, the more capital-intensive is the production. A painter using brushes or an editor working by hand would be examples of labor-intensive production, while a painter spraying a house or an editor using a word processing machine would represent more capital-intensive production.

The way in which labor and capital are combined and the extent to which production tends to be more labor-intensive or capital-intensive differ in the various sectors of an economy. For example, distribution of electricity and natural gas depends extensively on capital inputs such as power lines, pipelines, generating stations, and storage facilities. Per-worker expenditures on capital equipment by firms in this sector are very high. The construction of a building, on the other hand, requires a great deal of labor, and firms in this sector spend much less on capital inputs per worker. Expressed differently, the distribution of electricity and natural gas is more capital-intensive, while construction is more labor-intensive.

Choosing a Method of Production

Differences in the way capital and labor are combined to produce goods and services are not limited to different sectors of the economy; they are also found in the production techniques used by different firms in the same industry. For example, the management of one retail store might try to control theft by using security personnel, while the management of another store might depend on cameras and other electronic surveillance devices. Or one farmer might use an irrigation system for crop production while another does not.

What causes different firms in the same industry to choose different production techniques? Recall that the objective of a firm is to maximize profit, and that profit is what remains after costs are subtracted from revenue. Each method of production has a cost associated with it, and the cost of using one production method will usually differ from the cost of using another method. In light of this, a firm will try to maximize profit by selecting the production method that gives it the desired output at the lowest cost. When a firm produces a good or service in the least-cost manner, **efficient production** and the efficient use of resources occurs.

Efficient method of production
The least-cost method of production.

It is important to understand that the least-cost method of production differs from seller to seller, depending upon the particular circumstances faced by each seller. It might be less costly, and therefore more profitable, for a large retail organization to protect itself from theft by using electronic surveillance devices rather than by paying a large staff of security personnel. On the other hand, a smaller, lower traffic retailer may attain a comparable level of protection at the lowest cost by hiring a guard or by simply advising the sales personnel to be on the lookout for shoplifters. A farmer who has poor quality soil may be able to produce average per-acre yields only by incurring the cost of an irrigation system.

The quest for profit also explains why some sellers in an industry continue to use old, outdated production techniques when newer, more efficient techniques are available. Even if a new method of production is more efficient than an existing method, the cost of transferring from the current to the new sytem could be so high that it would cancel out any cost saving that the new system would offer. That is, once the costs of purchasing and installing new equipment, removing the old, and perhaps taking a loss on its sale are added up and compared with what could be gained by converting, the seller might deem the change not justifiable on a profitability basis.

Production and Technological Change

In the production of most goods and services, new and presumably better approaches to production commonly compete with existing methods. For example, new procedures are continually being developed and adopted for the provision of health care services; more advanced types of communication and information systems are being designed and produced; and more fuel-efficient buildings continue to be constructed. The list of such developments that compete with older sytems goes on and on.

Technology
The body of knowledge that exists about production and its processes.

Examples such as these illustrate an important relationship between the methods of production used by businesses and technology. **Technology** is simply the state of knowledge that society possesses about production at a particular time: the more that is known about the production of a good or service, the greater is the technology relating to that item. Technology refers not only to our knowledge of the design of machinery and equipment, but also to our understanding of such things as the scheduling of production, packaging, personnel relations, and transportation.

The relationship between production and technology is important for two reasons. First, technology restricts the range of production methods from which a business can choose: the choice of methods is limited by what is known at the time about the production of an item. Second, what is known about production at a particular time becomes embodied in the equipment and methods used for production. A machine developed in 1986 embodies the state of knowledge about that type of machinery as of 1986. Therefore, when a business selects equipment for production, it is committing itself to operating on the basis of what was known when the equipment was designed.

This last point is important, because over a period of time as technology grows, new ideas are developed and appear in more advanced production methods and equipment. Thus, technological change causes existing methods and equipment to become obsolete unless they can somehow be adapted to incorporate newly developed knowledge. Because of this, technology causes continual change in production methods as businesses abandon older ways for newer, more efficient production methods in an effort to achieve the goal of maximum profit.

Creative destruction
New technologically advanced machinery and processes cause the disuse and ultimate disappearance of old machinery and methods.

The economist Joseph Schumpeter referred to this process as **creative destruction.** Simply put, creative destruction means that new machinery, production methods, and other fruits of technological change frequently do not exist alongside the old. Rather, the new often replaces the old, causing one area of the economy to grow and prosper, and another to shrink and perhaps ultimately disappear. For example, the introduction of robotics into assembly lines has affected not only the demand for labor, but has also caused some of the formerly used machinery and equipment to become obsolete; the availability of sophisticated computerized word processing equipment is causing the conventional office typewriter to disappear. Application 12.1, "Technology and the Steam Locomotive," gives an account of the destruction of the steam locomotive industry caused by technological change.

ECONOMIC TIME, PRODUCTION, AND THE COST OF PRODUCTION

The production technique that a firm chooses is influenced by the time frame in which it views or plans its operations. Generally, a business's production may be regarded as taking place in a short-run or in a long-run period of time. These time periods are not defined in terms of hours, months, or years (the usual manner of measuring time). Rather, they are defined in a more abstract way.

Short run
A production time frame in which some factors of production are fixed and some are variable.

The **short run** is the time frame in which production takes place using some factors that can be varied in amount and some that cannot. Those fac-

Application 12.1
TECHNOLOGY AND THE STEAM LOCOMOTIVE

In 1825 there was one steam locomotive in the United States, operated as an experiment by Col. John Stevens on a circle of track in Hoboken. Ninety-nine years later the steam locomotive census reached its peak with over 65,000 owned by Class One railroads, plus the uncounted thousands operating on short lines and industrial, terminal and logging roads. The next year, 1925, began the decline, and by some strange coincidence the first diesel was listed by the Association of American Railroads that same year.

Many studies have been made and much has been written about the disappearance of the steam locomotive, but the hard facts of economics, highway competition and improved steam locomotive technology brought the decline to 40,041 locomotives in 1940. The spectacular ability of the railroads to move freight and passengers was tested during World War II and the statistics show fantastic records of achievements made with 40 percent fewer engines than in 1924, but of far greater efficiency. Since there

Fixed factors
Factors of production that do not change in amount as the level of production increases or decreases.

tors of production that cannot be changed are termed **fixed factors.** Because the amounts of fixed factors cannot be altered as the level of production increases or decreases, their costs do not change, and they must be paid for regardless of whether the firm produces anything or not. Examples of fixed factors might include a building or other production facility, some machinery, and insurance. In essence, the short run is the time period in which fixed factors of production form a boundary within which production takes place.

Long run
A production time frame in which all factors of production are variable.

The **long run** is the time frame in which all factors are regarded as changeable, or variable: there are no fixed factors to limit production. In the long run, a much wider range of production choices is open, since all resources, including buildings and other production facilities, can be altered.

Suppose that the owners of a restaurant are trying to evaluate the methods and costs of producing meals. If they can alter the number of waiters, tables, and menu selection but not the size of the dining or kitchen area, they are planning in the short run. Those same owners are planning in the long run when they analyze the methods and costs of producing meals as their facilities are expanded, or as they add new restaurants or, more generally, when they regard their fixed facilities as alterable.

This concept of planning in different time frames can be applied to a student's production of a college education. The long run would be a period in which general plans for attaining a degree are formulated and evaluated. In this long-run period all factors can be altered: the selection of a college, the course of study to be followed, the number of hours to be taken each semester, and the commitment to a part-time job. Once some of these decisions are made and a student is enrolled in particular courses, producing a college education can be viewed in the short run. Each semester could represent a short-run time frame because a student is producing an education within

---

were less than 4,000 diesels and electrics on the rails during the war, this was chiefly an accomplishment of steam power.

With the peace in 1945 the decline of steam was resumed. General Motors, ALCO, Baldwin-Lima-Hamilton, General Electric, Fairbanks-Morse and others began mass-producing diesel locomotives like automobiles, and the fate of the steam locomotive was inevitable. In 1952, with more diesels and ever fewer steam locomotives, the lines on the graph crossed and ten years later, in 1962, there were less than one hundred surviving steam engines in the Association of American Railroads listing of Class One roads. Few of these can operate and most are museum pieces or are awaiting the scrapper's torch.

boundaries set by the school attended, the selected course of study, and other factors to which the student is obligated.

In order to make production decisions in either the short run or the long run, a business needs to determine the costs associated with producing various amounts of its output. Because production is planned differently in each time frame, we will examine costs in the short run and long run separately.

Short-Run Costs

In the short run, all factors used in the production of a good or service can be classified as either fixed or variable. Fixed factors, as stated earlier, are those that do not change with a change in the level of production. When a business employs a fixed factor, the cost of that resource is called a **fixed cost.** Thus, the rent or mortgage on a building could be regarded as a fixed cost. Fixed costs must be paid whether the business produces anything or not.

Fixed cost
The short-run cost of a fixed factor of production.

Variable factors are those that increase or decrease in usage as the amount produced increases or decreases. Raw materials, labor, and energy could be regarded as variable factors. **Variable costs** are those costs associated with the use of variable factors. All costs in the short run can be classified as fixed costs or variable costs depending upon whether they refer to the costs of fixed or variable factors.

Variable factors and costs
Factors of production that change in usage as production levels change; variable costs are the costs of using variable factors.

A hypothetical example follows in which the short-run costs of operating a swimming pool servicing company are calculated and analyzed. The costs given in this example are those for the daily cleaning and maintaining of average size swimming pools for one month.

Total Costs Calculation of the costs of this pool service can begin by adding together all bills that must be paid regardless of the number of pools serviced: that is, by determining the fixed costs. The fixed costs might include monthly payments on loans for the purchase of equipment and a truck, and payments for a storage facility, insurance, advertising, and an office or answering service. Assume that these fixed costs for the pool service are calculated to be $800 per month.

Table 12.4, which illustrates the costs to the company of servicing from zero through nine pools, gives the **total fixed cost** (TFC) for the firm's operations in the second column. Notice that the $800 fixed cost does not change as more or fewer pools are maintained. Notice also that the $800 per month must be paid even if no pools are serviced. This is because, regardless of how many pools are cleaned, the fixed factors, and thus the costs of the fixed factors, remain unchanged.

Total fixed cost
The cost of all fixed factors; total fixed cost does not change as the level of output changes.

Next, the variable costs that the firm must pay must be calculated. Since these are costs that change as the number of pools serviced changes, variable costs might include expenditures for items such as labor, gasoline, chemicals, and repair of the truck and machinery. The third column of Table 12.4 gives

Table 12.4
Monthly Costs of Cleaning and Maintaining Swimming Pools

Total fixed cost does not change as output levels change and must be paid even if nothing is produced. Total variable cost is zero when nothing is produced, and both total variable cost and total cost increase as output increases.

Number of Pools Maintained	Total Fixed Cost (TFC)	Total Variable Cost (TVC)	Total Cost (TC)
0	$800	$ 0	$ 800
1	800	400	1,200
2	800	450	1,250
3	800	550	1,350
4	800	700	1,500
5	800	950	1,750
6	800	1,300	2,100
7	800	1,790	2,590
8	800	2,440	3,240
9	800	3,295	4,095

Total variable cost
The cost of all variable factors of production; total variable cost increases as the level of output increases.

the company's **total variable cost** (TVC) for servicing from zero through nine pools. For example, if this firm were to clean and maintain four pools a month, it would face variable costs of $700. Notice that the variable costs are zero if the firm cleans no pools, that they continually increase as more pools are serviced, and that they increase significantly when a large number of pools are cleaned. The pattern of this variable cost increase will be explained shortly.

Total cost
The cost of acquiring and using all factors of production; total cost is total fixed cost plus total variable cost.

The total cost of servicing from zero through nine pools is given in the last column of Table 12.4. The **total cost** (TC) for a particular level of output is all fixed costs plus all variable costs at that level of production. For example, the total cost of maintaining five pools is $1,750: $800 in fixed costs plus $950 in variable costs.

Average total cost
The cost per unit of output produced.

Unit Costs In addition to determining its total costs, a business usually finds it essential to ascertain per unit costs at each level of output. The per unit cost when producing a particular level of output is termed **average total cost** (ATC). Average total cost is found by dividing total cost by the number of units produced.

Table 12.5 gives the total cost of servicing swimming pools from Table 12.4 and the average total cost of servicing each individual pool when a specified number of pools are maintained. For example, the average total cost of servicing each pool when three pools are maintained is $450: on the average each pool costs $450 to service. The average total cost of $450 is found by dividing the total cost of $1,350 by three. The average total cost of $370 when seven pools are maintained is found by dividing the total cost of $2,590 by seven.

Marginal cost
The addition to total cost when one more (additional) unit of output is produced.

Table 12.5 also gives the marginal cost of servicing swimming pools. As stated in the previous chapter, **marginal cost** (MC) is the additional cost of producing one more unit of output, or, in this case, servicing one more pool. Marginal cost is calculated by determining the change in total cost when an additional unit is produced. For example, if no pools are serviced, the total

Table 12.5
Total, Average Total, and Marginal Costs of Maintaining Swimming Pools

Average total cost measures the per unit cost at a specific production level, and marginal cost measures the change in total cost from producing an additional unit of output.

Number of Pools Maintained	Total Cost (TC)	Average Total Cost (ATC)	Marginal Cost (MC)
0	$ 800	—	
			$400
1	1,200	$1,200	
			50
2	1,250	625	
			100
3	1,350	450	
			150
4	1,500	375	
			250
5	1,750	350	
			350
6	2,100	350	
			490
7	2,590	370	
			650
8	3,240	405	
			855
9	4,095	455	

cost given in Table 12.5 is $800; if one pool is serviced, total cost increases to $1,200. Thus, the marginal cost of the first pool is $400 ($1,200 − $800). As in the previous chapter, marginal cost is listed midway between the units of output. Table 12.6 summarizes how total cost, average total cost, and marginal cost are calculated and computes these costs for the servicing of three pools.

A business could analyze its unit costs even further. It could, for example, determine its fixed costs per unit (average fixed costs) and variable costs per unit (average variable costs). Although these will not be calculated in this text, can you at this point make these computations?

The Pattern of Short-Run Costs

There are patterns to the way total cost, average total cost, and marginal cost behave as production increases in the short run. These patterns can be seen by examining tabular cost figures such as those listed in Tables 12.4 and

Table 12.6
Determining Costs for Servicing Three Pools a Month

Total cost gives the cost of producing a specified amount of output; average total cost gives the per unit cost; and marginal cost gives the cost of producing one more unit of output.

Total Cost:
TFC + TVC = TC or $800 + $550 = $1350 (TC)

Average Total Cost:
TC / Number of units of output produced = ATC or $1350 / 3 = $450 (ATC)

Marginal Cost:
Change in TC per additional unit of output = MC or $1350 − $1250 = $100 (MC)

12.5. But they can be more easily observed when the short-run costs are graphed.

Total Cost Pattern Figure 12.1 plots the total cost, given in Table 12.5, of servicing from zero through nine swimming pools per month. Notice, either from the numbers in Table 12.5 or from the graph in Figure 12.1, that the total cost of servicing swimming pools continually increases as more pools are serviced. Since the fixed cost of servicing these pools never changes, this increase is due solely to the change in variable costs.

A closer analysis of total cost shows that in the early stage of production, when few pools are maintained, total cost increases slowly. In the latter

Figure 12.1
Total Cost of Servicing Swimming Pools

Total cost increases slowly when just a few pools are serviced because few variable factors are needed with the fixed factors. At larger levels of output, total cost increases quickly as more variable factors are needed to compensate for the limitations imposed by the fixed factors.

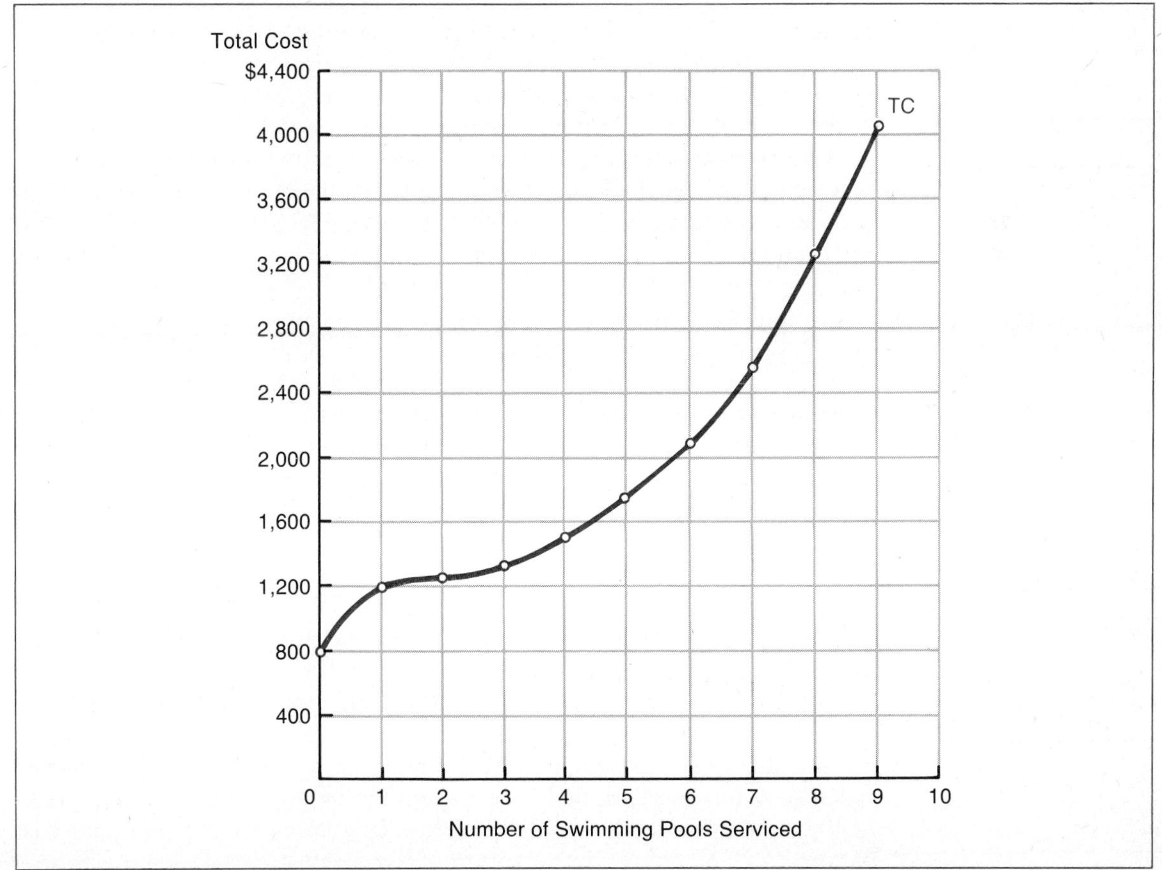

stage of production, when many pools are maintained, total cost increases quickly. Why does total cost follow this pattern?

If this company plans to service just a few pools, it might manage by hiring one employee to use the truck and equipment. For each pool maintained, the company would also need to provide other variable factors such as chemicals for the pool and gasoline for the truck. However, once labor was hired, the company would not encounter significant increases in the other variable costs to clean each additional pool if just a few were serviced. Thus, the total cost of servicing a few pools increases slowly at first because the increase in variable factors needed to accompany the fixed factors is small.

After a while, maintaining more pools necessitates more than just an increase in chemicals and gasoline. Labor costs increase as more workers are needed or as the existing help is paid overtime. As the truck, machinery, and equipment are used more often, breakdowns occur, causing the cost of repairs to increase. Also, the owner of the firm may expect a higher normal profit in return for the effort and responsibility of increasing production. At some point, these increases in variable costs cause total cost to begin to increase more quickly as production grows.

As production increases to even higher levels, the number of pools serviced will begin to seriously strain the capabilities of the fixed factors, and variable costs will increase substantially as the firm tries to compensate for the limits of the fixed factors. Perhaps, with the existing machinery and truck, the company might reasonably expect to maintain only six or seven pools. If it tries to service eight or nine pools, many variable factors will be needed to fill in for the limitations of the fixed factors. At this point the company may encounter considerably higher variable costs as it rents another truck and more machinery, leases additional storage space, and hires a manager.

In short, total cost increases slowly at first because, with a given amount of fixed factors, few variable factors can increase production significantly. As output levels become larger, total cost increases more rapidly because more variable factors are needed with the fixed factors to increase production. At high levels of production, costs increase very quickly because the fixed factors are approaching the limits of their productivity, and many variable factors are needed to compensate for the fixed factor boundary.

Marginal Cost and Average Total Cost Patterns Let us next examine the patterns of marginal cost (MC) and average total cost (ATC) as production increases. The marginal cost and average total cost data given in Table 12.5 are graphed in Figure 12.2.

Notice that marginal cost, or the additional cost of servicing one more pool, decreases at first and then increases. As with total cost, this drop and rise are due to the behavior of the variable factors as reflected in variable costs. With this in mind, the same reasoning that applies to the explanation of the total cost pattern applies to the explanation of the marginal cost pattern.

Figure 12.2
Marginal Cost and Average Total Cost of Servicing Swimming Pools

Both marginal cost and average total cost fall and then rise as production increases. When marginal cost is less than average total cost, it pulls average total cost down; when marginal cost is greater than average total cost, it pulls average total cost up.

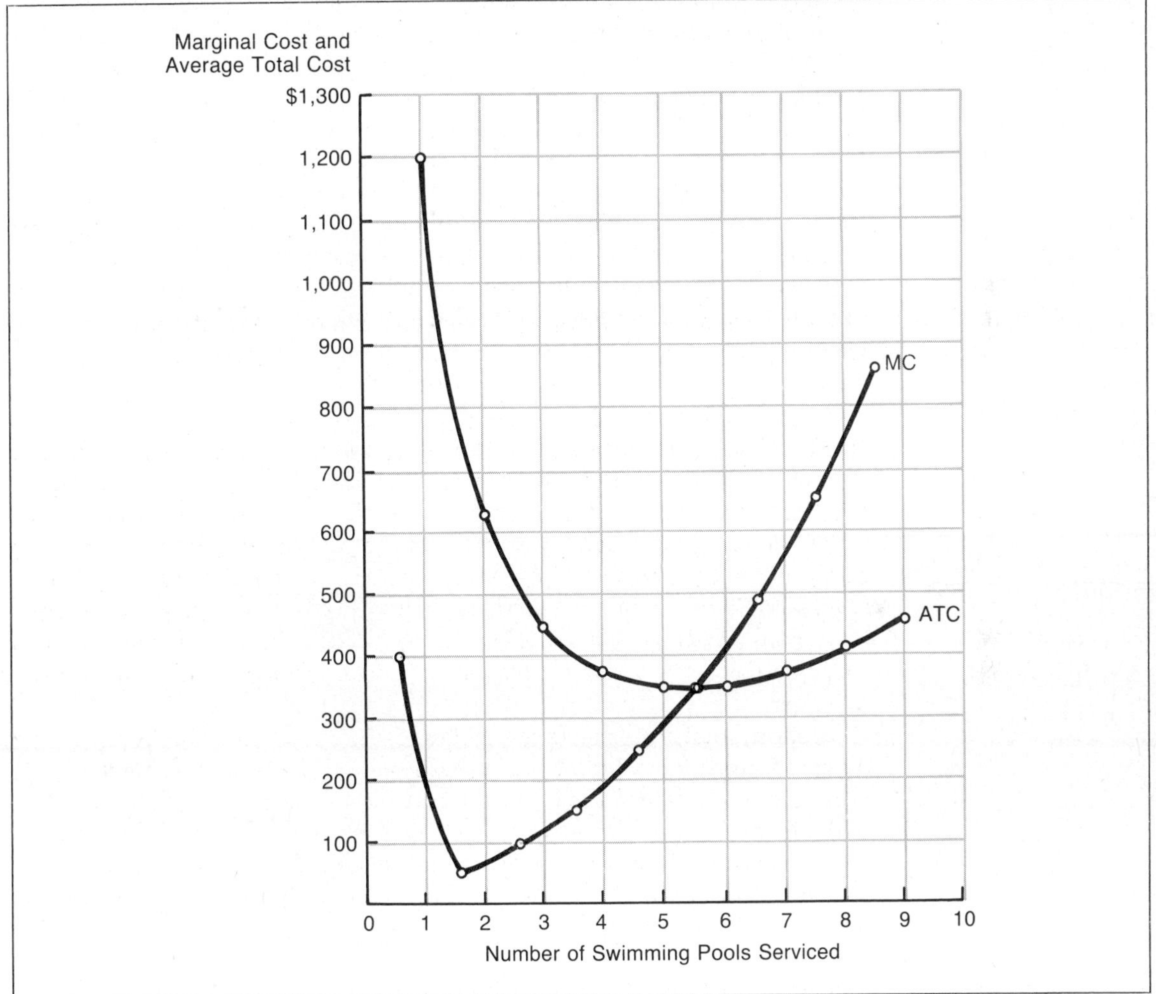

To service the first pool, the marginal cost is $400. If you refer to Table 12.4 you will discover that this equals the change in variable cost associated with servicing one pool rather than no pools. Much of this $400 increase is probably due to the hiring of labor. To service a second pool, the marginal cost is only $50. This decrease in marginal cost occurs because the additional variable factors needed to service the second pool cost the firm only $50. As stated earlier, at this point there will be only a slight increase in the use of some variable inputs such as chemicals.

When a third pool is maintained, marginal cost begins to rise because of the increases in variable factors needed to increase production. As more and more pools are serviced, marginal cost increases more rapidly. This is due to the limits placed on production by the fixed factors and the large amounts of variable factors that are required to compensate for these limits.

Return to Figure 12.2 and observe the average total cost curve. Average total cost decreases and then increases with more production. Why is this so?

The cost per unit falls initially because marginal cost is lower than average total cost. When marginal cost is less than average total cost, it pulls average total cost down. When marginal cost becomes greater than average total cost, it pulls average total cost up.[5] Thus, average total cost behaves the way it does because of the behavior of marginal cost. You encounter this relationship between marginal and average values in determining your average in a course as you take additional exams. If you make a grade on an exam (remember: each additional exam that you take is a marginal exam) that is lower than your average, the marginal exam will pull your average down. If

[5]If average total cost falls when marginal cost is less than average total cost and rises when marginal cost is greater than average total cost, then, as Figure 12.2 shows, marginal cost must cross average total cost at minimum average total cost.

Application 12.2
TEST YOURSELF: CALCULATING COSTS AND AVERAGES[a]

1. A student's grade in a Civil War history class at a state university is determined by averaging the percentage scores of four examinations. Answer the following questions for a student who earns a grade of 92 percent on the first examination, 84 percent on the second, 85 percent on the third, and 91 percent on the fourth.

   a. The student's average after the first examination is ____.

   b. The student's average in the course after the second examination will ____ (rise or fall) because the marginal score from the second examination is ____ (higher or lower) than the average after the first exam. The average after the second examination is ____.

   c. The student's average in the course after the third examination will ____ (rise or fall) because the marginal score from the third exam is ____ (higher or lower) than the average after the second examination. The average after the third examination is ____.

   d. The student's average in the course after the fourth examination will ____ (rise or fall) because the marginal score from the fourth examination is ____ (higher or lower) than the average from three exams. The average after the fourth examination, or for the course, is ____.

2. The manager of a college food service has determined that the daily fixed cost of operation is $855. She has also calculated that the total variable cost for preparing 900 meals is $1,170; for preparing 1,800 meals, it is

you make a grade higher than your average on a marginal exam, your average will increase. For example, if you have an average of 93 percent in your economics course, and you earn a grade of 70 percent on your next exam, your average will fall. On the other hand, if you earn a grade of 98 percent on your next exam, your average will rise. Application 12.2, "Test Yourself: Calculating Costs and Averages," provides an opportunity for you to further understand the average-marginal relationship and to determine the short-run costs discussed earlier.

The Law of Diminishing Returns

Law of Diminishing Returns
As additional units of a variable factor are added to a fixed factor, beyond some point the additional product from each additional unit of the variable factor decreases.

Underlying all of these short-run cost patterns is a basic principle termed the **Law of Diminishing Returns.** This law states that as additional units of a variable factor are added to a fixed factor, beyond some point the additional product from each additional unit of the variable factor decreases. This is easily illustrated with an example.

Assume that you own a small restaurant and plan to begin hiring people to prepare and serve meals. The fixed factors in this example are the dining room outfitted with tables and other restaurant furniture, and a fully equipped kitchen. The labor used to work in the restaurant is a variable factor.

$2,565; and when 2,700 meals are prepared, total variable cost equals $5,328. Given this information, the average total cost per meal when 900 meals are prepared is ____, average total cost when 1,800 are prepared is ____, and when 2,700 meals are prepared each costs ____ on the average.

3. Fill in the following table.

Output	Total Fixed Cost	Total Variable Cost	Total Cost	Average Total Cost	Marginal Cost
0	$85	$ 0	____	—	
1	____	145	____	____	____
2	____	165	____	____	____
3	____	185	____	____	____
4	____	315	____	____	____
5	____	465	____	____	____
6	____	665	____	____	____
7	____	895	____	____	____
8	____	1,195	____	____	

[a]Answers can be found on page 354.

If one person is hired to work in the restaurant, that person working alone will be able to prepare and serve a certain number of meals per day. If a second person is hired to work, the two persons together can interact, specialize, and work more efficiently. One person can prepare meals and the other can serve them. Together the two will probably more than double the number of meals that can be prepared and served by one person alone. If you hire a third person, work can be further divided, and the number of meals may again significantly increase.

At some point, perhaps after the fourth person is hired, the number of meals that can be prepared and served per day will no longer proportionately increase with additional workers. That is, the number of *additional* meals prepared and served after hiring a fourth worker will not be as great as the number of *additional* meals prepared and served after hiring the third worker. Four workers cannot operate as efficiently as three because the fixed facility is becoming crowded. In other words, the boundary imposed by the fixed factors begins to limit the productivity of the variable factor. When this occurs, and the additional output from hiring an additional worker begins to fall, diminishing returns have set in.

Beyond this point, as more (five, six, seven) people are hired, the additional work accomplished by each will further diminish. They will become less efficient, and the fixed factors will more severely limit their full utilization. It would, incidentally, be possible to hire so many restaurant workers that they would get in each other's way, causing the additional output to become negative.[6]

The Law of Diminishing Returns governs all production in the short run. For example, when a student tries to produce sufficient knowledge to pass an exam by studying for an extended and uninterrupted period of time, the Law of Diminishing Returns takes effect. During the first few hours of reading and reviewing, each hour will produce more additional knowledge than the hour before as the material is comprehended. After a while, however, as the student becomes tired and the fixed factor of the mind approaches its limit, diminishing returns takes effect as each additional hour of study is less productive than the one before it. Can you use the Law of Diminishing Returns to explain why it is better to study on a consistent basis for shorter periods of time than it is to cram the night before an exam?

The Law of Diminishing Returns and the resulting pattern of costs given here are common to all production in the short-run time frame. Cost figures in the real world, and their graphs, may not be as smooth and clear-cut as our examples, but they may be explained in terms of these patterns. The limitation of the fixed factors, which gives the short run its definition, causes diminishing returns to occur and thus causes marginal, average total, and total costs to rise in the latter stages of production increases.

---

[6]This means that a point can be reached where more would be produced if some of the workers would quit.

Long-Run Costs

The long run has been defined as the time frame in which a business regards all of its factors of production as variable and none as fixed. Thus, calculating the cost of production in the long run means determining the cost of a given level of output if a business can alter any and all of its resources. In the long run, production costs are not divided between fixed costs and variable costs because all costs are variable.

In analyzing its costs in the long run, a firm can calculate its long-run total cost of production (LRTC), long-run average total cost (LRATC), and long-run marginal cost (LRMC). Table 12.7 gives the long-run costs of producing from zero through 100,000 units of an item by a hypothetical company. For the sake of simplicity, assume that the product is produced in blocks of 10,000 at a time. The second column of Table 12.7 gives the **long-run total cost** of producing from zero through ten blocks of 10,000 each. Notice that long-run total cost increases as more is produced.

Long-run total cost, average total cost, and marginal cost
Total cost, per unit cost, and cost per additional unit of output, respectively, calculated for production in the long run.

Long-run total cost can be used to calculate **long-run average total cost,** which is determined in the same manner as short-run average total cost: total cost is divided by the quantity of output produced. In this case, long-run average total cost refers to the cost per block of 10,000. **Long-run marginal cost** can also be calculated from long-run total cost. It is found by

Table 12.7
Long-Run Total Cost, Average Total Cost, and Marginal Cost

Long-run total cost is the total expenditure for each level of output in the long run. Long-run average total cost measures the per unit cost; and long-run marginal cost measures the cost of producing an additional unit of output in the long run.

Output (Blocks of 10,000)	Long-Run Total Cost (LRTC) (Blocks of 10,000)	Long-Run Average Total Cost (LRATC) (Per Block of 10,000)	Long-Run Marginal Cost (LRMC) (Per Block of 10,000)
0	$ 0	—	
			$400,000
1	400,000	$400,000	
			100,000
2	500,000	250,000	
			100,000
3	600,000	200,000	
			100,000
4	700,000	175,000	
			175,000
5	875,000	175,000	
			175,000
6	1,050,000	175,000	
			350,000
7	1,400,000	200,000	
			600,000
8	2,000,000	250,000	
			700,000
9	2,700,000	300,000	
			800,000
10	3,500,000	350,000	

determining the change in long-run total cost as one more unit is produced. In this case, where the relevant "unit" is a block of output, long-run marginal cost is the marginal cost of increasing production by 10,000.

Economists typically focus on long-run average total cost in analyzing the pattern of long-run costs. Figure 12.3 plots the long-run average total cost from Table 12.7. In Figure 12.3, long-run average total cost at first decreases as a larger output is produced. With an ability to vary production facilities that were fixed in the short run, the company finds that, initially, the cost per unit drops. At some point long-run average total cost reaches a minimum, and, in this example, stays at that level as output grows. But after a while, as production continues to grow, the cost per unit of output increases. This decreasing, constant, and increasing cost pattern is typical of long-run average total cost.

Economies of Scale, Diseconomies of Scale, and Constant Returns to Scale When long-run average total cost decreases in the initial stages of production, a firm is experiencing **economies of scale.** This means that the larger size (scale) of the operation permits a business to produce each unit of output more cheaply than it could at a smaller size of operation. What causes economies of scale to occur?

Economies of scale
Occur when the increasing size of production in the long run permits the per unit cost of production to fall.

As a firm becomes larger it is feasible for it to use specialized inputs that are more efficient and, consequently, capable of producing output at a lower

Figure 12.3
Long-Run Average Total Cost

A typical long-run average total cost curve follows a pattern of decreasing, constant, and increasing per unit costs.

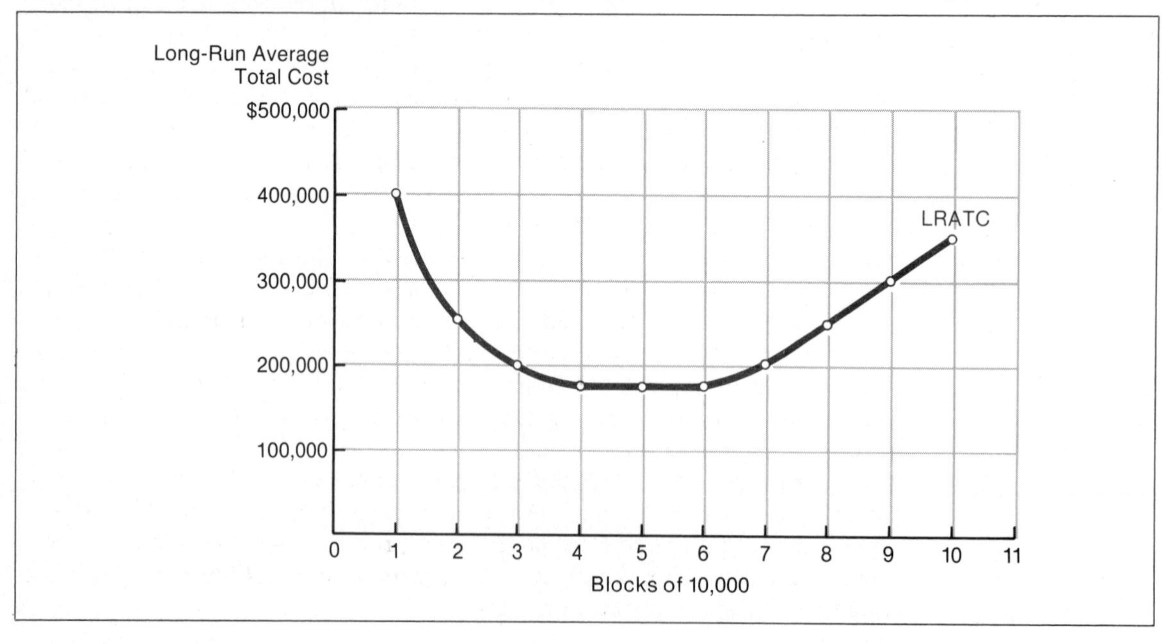

per unit cost. A large company can employ more assembly-line techniques, more equipment especially suited for performing a narrow range of tasks, more computer hardware, and more specialized personnel. For example, restaurants that are part of a chain are able to utilize a number of these efficient or cost-saving opportunities. Food can be prepared in assembly-line fashion at a central processing plant under the supervision of one highly skilled chef, sent frozen to each restaurant, and heated by unskilled labor for the customer.

Economies of scale also permit individual managers to focus all of their attention on specific subparts of a company's operation. In a smaller business, any one of these subparts might not be important enough to warrant full-time consideration and would compete with other aspects of the operation for a manager's attention. With more attention directed to a particular task in a business, the person performing that job may become more efficient, thereby lowering per unit costs for the company. Finally, as a business becomes larger, it may receive quantity discounts on some resources that it buys and may be able to negotiate lower interest rates on money that it borrows.

Diseconomies of scale
Occur when the increasing size of production in the long run causes the per unit cost of production to rise.

When per unit costs increase in the latter stage of long-run production, a firm is said to be experiencing **diseconomies of scale.** In this case, the size or scale of the operation has become so large that the cost per unit increases.

Diseconomies of scale generally arise because a company has become so large that control over its operation is difficult. As the organization grows and the chain of command lengthens and becomes more complex, it might be necessary to hire more managers at all levels, thereby increasing the cost of output. With a longer chain of command, authority and responsibility may become overly decentralized and disjointed. Factors of production may be wasted due to a lack of accountability or poor control. Costs may be affected by the amount of time required to pass information and commands through such a large organization. Perhaps it is diseconomies of scale that account for inefficiencies in the federal government.

Constant returns to scale
Occur in the range of production levels in which long-run average total cost neither increases nor decreases but is constant.

Between the outputs where economies of scale end and diseconomies of scale begin is a range of production where long-run average total cost neither increases nor decreases. Throughout this range the firm is said to be experiencing **constant returns to scale,** which means that the operation has become so large that it has exhausted all available economies of scale, but has not become large enough to encounter diseconomies of scale.

Many real-life examples attest to the existence of decreasing, constant, and increasing long-run average total costs. This does not mean, however, that every company faces a long-run average total cost curve that looks exactly like that in Figure 12.3. Instead, the long-run average total cost of each firm's product differs in the length and strength of its decreasing, constant, and increasing ranges. A company producing automobiles, for example, will have a different shape to its long-run average total cost curve than will a fast food chain producing hamburgers. Figure 12.4 illustrates the three stages of long-run production costs.

Figure 12.4
The Three Phases of the Long-Run Average Total Cost Curve

The long-run average total cost curve goes through three phases: a decreasing per unit cost phase caused by economies of scale; a phase of constant returns to scale where per unit costs neither increase nor decrease; and a phase where per unit costs increase due to diseconomies of scale.

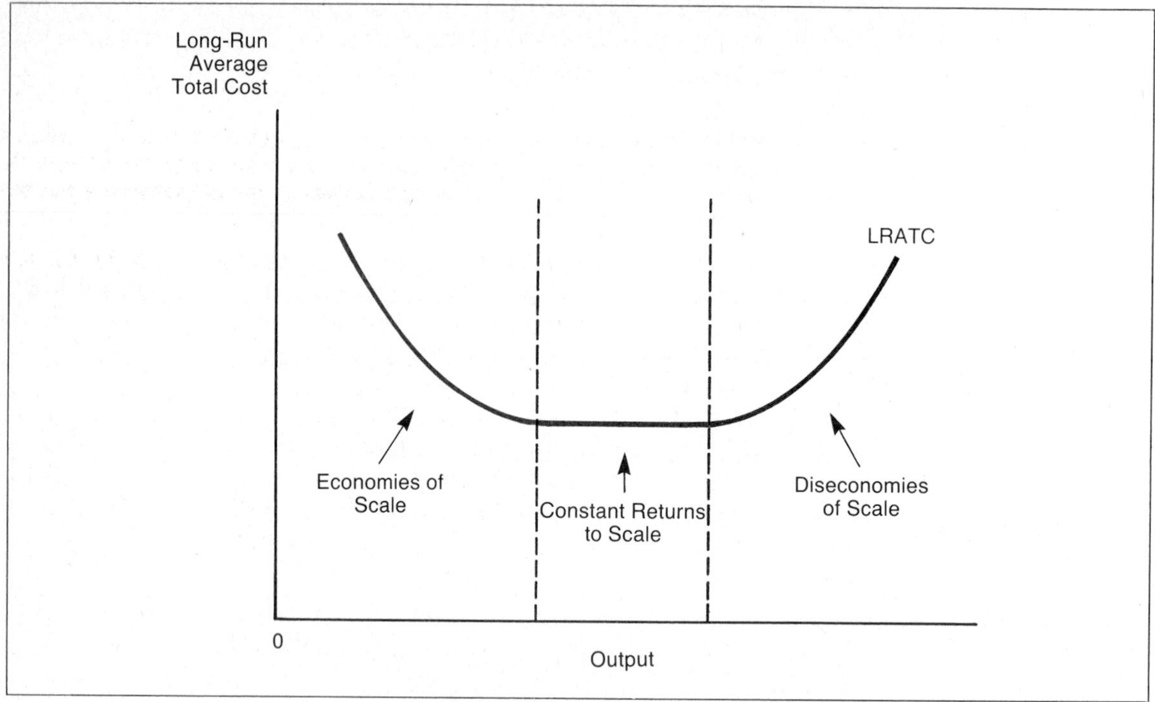

SUMMARY

Goods and services are produced by households and government units as well as by businesses, but the majority of measured output comes from business firms. Since there are so many different firms producing different types of goods and services, categories have been developed for classifying those goods and services. One categorization is according to major producing sectors, such as the construction sector, manufacturing sector, and communications sector. These sectors are interrelated, and as the economy grows and changes over time their relative importance also changes.

A second method for classifying outputs is according to industries. An industry is a group of firms producing similar products. The similarity is in the processes used or because buyers view the products as substitutes for one another. Industrial classifications are narrower than sectoral classifications. A single firm might operate simultaneously in several industries.

A production function shows the output that results when a group of inputs are combined in a certain way. At any time, a firm might be able to choose from several different methods to produce its good or service. Some of these different techniques can be characterized as labor-intensive or capital-intensive. The greater the dependence on labor, the more labor-intensive is the production; the greater the dependence on capital, the more capital-intensive is the production.

The production method actually chosen by a firm seeking to maximize its profit will be the one that gives the desired quantity of output at the lowest cost. The least-cost method for a particular seller depends on the specific circumstances faced by that seller.

The development of new productive machinery and techniques is the result of technological change. Technology limits the choice of methods for producing a good or service. As time passes and technology changes, existing production methods become increasingly obsolete. Technological change is said to lead to creative destruction: as new machines and methods are found to replace the old, some areas of the economy grow and prosper while others decline.

The choice of a method of production is influenced by the time frame in which a business plans its operations. The short run is a time period in which some factors of production are variable and some are fixed. The capabilities of the fixed factors, because they cannot be changed, serve as a boundary within which production takes place. The long run is a time period in which all factors are regarded as variable.

In the short run, the total cost of producing a certain level of output is found by adding total fixed cost and total variable cost. Total fixed cost is the same regardless of how much is produced; total variable cost increases as production increases. Average total cost is the cost per unit of output at some level of production and is found by dividing total cost by the number of units of output produced. Marginal cost is the change in total cost resulting from the production of an additional unit of output.

In the short run, total cost increases slowly at low levels of production and rapidly at high levels of production. Average total cost decreases and then increases, as does marginal cost. These patterns are the result of the way in which variable factors increase as production increases. At high levels of production, large amounts of variable factors are needed to compensate for the limits imposed by the fixed factors. Underlying these patterns of short-run costs is the Law of Diminishing Returns.

Long-run average total cost illustrates the pattern of costs in the long run. Its shape is the result of economies of scale, constant returns to scale, and diseconomies of scale.

Key Terms and Concepts

Production
Sectors
Industry
Production function
Labor-intensive production
Capital-intensive production

Technology
Creative destruction
Short run
Long run
Fixed factors and costs
Variable factors and costs
Total cost
Average total cost
Marginal cost
Law of Diminishing Returns
Patterns of short-run and long-run costs
Long-run average total cost
Economies and diseconomies of scale
Constant returns to scale

Discussion and Review Questions

1. Can you construct a production function for earning an "A" in this course?
   a. What are the necessary inputs?
   b. How much of each input is required?
   c. How are the inputs combined?
2. Suppose that a particular product is produced in Country A using labor-intensive techniques and in Country B using capital-intensive techniques. What are some possible explanations for the difference in the techniques used in the two countries?
3. Technological change causes creative destruction. Because of new technology, one area of the economy may expand while another contracts and perhaps disappears. Give some examples of the process of creative destruction. How is the process carried out in each of your examples?
4. The short-run average total cost curve and the long-run average total cost curve are similarly shaped. What causes the short-run average total cost curve to assume its shape? What causes the long-run average total cost curve to assume its shape?
5. A friend has just explained that, as far as the costs of operating a business are concerned, short-run costs are the costs which are incurred within the current year and long-run costs are all costs which are incurred for more than one year. As a student of economics, do you agree with your friend's opinion? Why?
6. Indicate whether each of the following is most probably a fixed factor or a variable factor in the short run.
   a. Raw materials going into a production process
   b. The steam heat required to keep the pipes in a factory from freezing
   c. Electricity used to run machinery and equipment
   d. The only person in a company who knows the formula to a highly profitable product

7. When marginal cost is less than average total cost, average total cost decreases. When marginal cost is greater than average total cost, average total cost increases. Why is this so?

8. If the total cost of producing 24 units of output is $168, and the total cost of producing 25 units of output is $187.50, what is the marginal cost of the twenty-fifth unit, the average total cost when 24 units are produced, and the average total cost when 25 units are produced?

Suggested Readings

Leslie Cookenboo, Jr., "Production and Cost Functions for Oil Pipe Lines," *Price Theory in Action,* eds. Donald S. Watson and Malcolm Getz (Boston: Houghton Mifflin Co., 1981), pp. 110–117. Reprinted from Leslie Cookenboo, Jr., *Crude Oil Pipe-Lines and Competition in the Oil Industry* (Cambridge, Mass.: Harvard University Press, 1955), pp. 13–24, 27–32. Explains production functions, the behavior of short-run and long-run costs, economies of scale, and other topics relating to oil pipe lines.

Edwin Mansfield, "Ch. 2: Technological Change and Productivity Growth," *Technological Change* (New York: W. W. Norton and Co., 1971), pp. 9–38. Explores the relationship between technological change and production functions, factors influencing the rate of technological change, changes in productivity, measures of technological change, and other subjects.

David F. Noble, "The Wedding of Science to the Useful Arts — I: The Rise of Science-Based Industry," *America By Design* (Oxford: Oxford University Press, 1977), pp. 3–19. Examines the early growth of science-based industries and the role of technology in the development of industries.

Roger W. Schmenner, "Before You Build a *Big* Factory," *Harvard Business Review* (July-August 1976), pp. 100–104. Points out that economies of scale can be specified more narrowly to refer to economies of volume and/or capacity and/or process technology.

E. F. Schumacher, "Part III, Ch. 2: Social and Economic Problems Calling for the Development of Intermediate Technology," *Small Is Beautiful* (New York: Harper and Row, 1973), pp. 161–179. An argument that the needs of a less developed economy might be best met by not using the most sophisticated, advanced technology available for production.

Harry Townsend, *Scale, Innovation, Merger and Monopoly* (Oxford: Pergamon Press, 1968), Chs. 1–4. Chapters cover several aspects of production such as economies and diseconomies of scale, research and development, and automation, with examples primarily from industries in the United States and United Kingdom.

Test Yourself Answers (Application 12.2)

1a. 92%; **1b.** fall, lower, 88%; **1c.** fall, lower, 87%; **1d.** rise, higher, 88%.

2. $2.25; $1.90; $2.29.

3.

Output	TFC	TVC	TC	ATC	MC
0	$85	$ 0	$ 85	$—	
					$145
1	85	145	230	230	
					20
2	85	165	250	125	
					20
3	85	185	270	90	
					130
4	85	315	400	100	
					150
5	85	465	550	110	
					200
6	85	665	750	125	
					230
7	85	895	980	140	
					300
8	85	1,195	1,280	160	

13 COMPETITION AND MARKET STRUCTURES

Chapter Objectives

1. To introduce the concept that a firm's pricing and profit behavior are related to the amount of competition it faces in the market.
2. To define what is meant by a market and explain how its boundaries are determined.
3. To give the basic characteristics of the four market structures: pure competition, monopolistic competition, oligopoly, and monopoly.
4. To show how an individual firm's demand curve, pricing behavior, and nonprice competition differ according to the market structure in which it operates.
5. To explain how a firm's long-run pricing and profit behavior are affected by the amount of competition in a market.
6. To develop, in an appendix, the explanation of how a firm determines its profit-maximizing price and output level.

There are over 16 million business firms in the U.S. economy, each behaving differently with respect to the control it has over the prices it charges, the types of nonprice decisions it makes, and its ability to continually earn economic profit (profit beyond what is required to stay in business). Some firms have great control over the prices their products command, while others have little or no control. Some firms spend millions of dollars on advertising, public relations, and other methods of bringing attention to their products; other firms spend nothing. Some firms have the ability to earn economic profit on a regular basis, while other firms, no matter how well they are managed, have no such prospect.

These differences in pricing and nonprice behavior and in ability to earn economic profit over the long run are influenced by the type and severity of competition that individual firms face from other sellers in a market. All other things being equal, the greater the competition in a market, the less control a firm in that market has over the price its product commands, and the less likely the firm is to earn economic profit on an ongoing basis. The less the competition in a market, the greater the control an individual firm has over the price it receives for its product, and the more likely the firm is to earn economic profit over the long run.

The degree of competition and the exact form it assumes differ from market to market. However, patterns can be identified that allow us to group sellers into different classes of markets, or **market structures.** On the basis of these patterns, economists have adopted four market structures to classify different competitive situations: pure competition, monopolistic competition, oligopoly, and monopoly. These four structures encompass a spectrum of competitive conditions. At one end of the spectrum is pure competition, where the competitive pressure is the strongest, and at the other end is monopoly, where there is no direct competition. In between are monopolistic competition, which is closer to pure competition, and oligopoly, which is closer to monopoly.

Market structures
A classification system for grouping markets according to the degree of competition among sellers.

In this chapter we will analyze each of the four market structures. Particular attention will be paid to the major characteristics that distinguish each type of market from the others, and to how those characteristics affect firms' behavior and profit expectations. But before discussing the market structures, it is necessary to distinguish between a market and an industry.

MARKETS VS. INDUSTRIES

We know from Chapter Twelve that an **industry** is composed of a group of firms that produce similar products. A **market,** where buyers and sellers come together, is also composed of firms producing similar products. Since sellers in an industry and in a market both offer similar products, can we equate the two? The answer is no. For a group of sellers to be included in the same industry, they need only produce similar products; but to be included in the same market, they also must compete for the same group of buyers.

Industry
A group of firms producing similar products.

Market
Firms are in the same market when they produce similar products and compete for the same buyers.

Two auto repair shops, one in Milwaukee and the other in San Diego, may produce nearly identical services, thereby placing them in the same industry. But since the repair shops do not compete for the same buyers (a person from Milwaukee would not ordinarily consider going to San Diego for a tune-up), they are not in the same market. A motion picture theater in downtown Chicago and one in Manhattan are in the same industry since their services are similar, but because they do not compete for the same buyers they are not in the same market.

The boundaries of a market are determined by geographic and substitution considerations. The geographic boundary of a market depends upon the size of the area from which buyers are drawn. In this regard, markets may be local, regional, national, or international. An ice cream shop that draws its customers from a particular neighborhood or town competes in a local market, whereas an automobile manufacturer is in an international market because the competition for buyers extends across national borders.

The boundary of a market is also defined by substitutability; that is, sellers are in the same market if buyers in that market view their products as substitutes. If a stereo phonograph produced by one seller is seen as substitutable for that produced by a second seller, then the phonographs of those two sellers compete in the same market. If a stereo phonograph is seen as substitutable for a tape recorder, a stereo radio, or a radio-television combination, then all of those items are in the same market.

In reality, defining the exact boundaries of a market can be difficult. For example, what are the geographic boundaries of the market for beer, given that some beers are sold regionally and others are sold nationally? Should each region be considered separately, or is there a national market? Where do you draw the line when it comes to substitutability? For example, a stereo phonograph may be substitutable for a tape recorder, but technically it may also be substitutable for a video cassette recorder or a bicycle if you are trying to decide whether to spend your leisure time listening to music, seeing movies, or going for rides in the country. Do we really want to go so far as to say that stereo phonographs and bicycles are in the same market?

Because of the uncertainty about the boundaries of a market, the question of which firms and products are included in a particular market can be controversial. One place where this controversy becomes important is in courts of law hearing cases on alleged violations of the antitrust laws.

The antitrust laws, which are designed to protect competition in markets, will be more fully discussed in Chapter Fifteen. For now, however, we can

Application 13.1
DEFINING THE BOUNDARIES OF A MARKET: *UNITED STATES* V. *DU PONT*

During the period that is relevant to this action, Du Pont produced almost 75% of the cellophane sold in the United States, and cellophane constituted less than 20% of all "flexible packaging material" sales. . . .

Note: There are two possible market definitions here. The first considers cellophane as a separate market. According to this definition, Du Pont produced nearly 75% of the entire output sold in the market. The second definition considers flexible packaging material (cellophane, foils, paper products, etc.) as the relevant market. According to this definition, Du Pont controlled less than 15% (75% × 20%) of the market.

The court accepted the second (broader) definition of the market and found in favor of Du Pont. Some of the reasoning in arriving at that opinion is given below.

The Government asserts that cellophane and other wrapping materials are neither substantially fungible [substitutable] nor like priced. For these reasons, it argues that the market for other wrappings is distinct from the market for cellophane and that the competition afforded cello-

note that one type of antitrust case heard by the courts involves a firm accused of taking over, or monopolizing, a market. In cases such as this, the definition of the boundaries of the market is of critical importance. The more broadly the market is defined, the smaller will be a firm's control, and the easier it will be for the defense to argue that the company has not monopolized the market.

One problem that the court faces is that the accused firm might present one definition of its market's boundaries, and the accuser might present another. The court must then determine which definition is correct and, partly on that basis, decide on the guilt or innocence of the firm. An example of the type of market definition problem a court faces is given in Application 13.1, "Defining the Boundaries of a Market: *United States* v. *Du Pont*." The excerpt deals with two possible market definitions the Supreme Court had to weigh in deciding whether Du Pont had monopolized a market with its production of cellophane.

THE MARKET STRUCTURES

It was noted earlier that the degree of competition that exists in a market influences a business's behavior — the prices it charges, the profit it makes, and the amount of nonprice competition in which it engages. It was also noted that, in order to analyze the effects of competition, economists have created four market models, called market structures, each representative of a different degree of competition: pure competition, monopolistic competition, oligopoly, and monopoly.

phane by other wrappings is not strong enough to be considered in determining whether Du Pont has monopoly powers. . . .

It may be admitted that cellophane combines the desirable elements of transparency, strength and cheapness more definitely than any of the others. . . .

But, despite cellophane's advantages, it has to meet competition from other materials in every one of its uses. . . .

"The record establishes [that] plain cellophane and moistureproof cellophane are each flexible packaging materials which are functionally interchangeable with other flexible packaging materials and sold at same time to same customers for same purpose at competitive prices; there is no cellophane market distinct and separate from the the market for flexible packaging materials; the market for flexible packaging materials is the relevant market for determining nature and extent of Du Pont's market control; and Du Pont has at all times competed with other cellophane producers and manufacturers of other flexible packaging materials in all aspects of its cellophane business."[1]

[1]The Supreme Court is quoting the lower court.
Source: *United States v. E. I. du Pont de Nemours & Co.*, 351 U.S. 377 (1956), pp. 379, 380, 398, 399, 403.

Each of these market models has a set of characteristics that differentiates it from the other market models. For example, certain features are associated with a monopoly structure and others with oligopoly. The distinguishing characteristics of each of the four market models center around three basic areas. The first area concerns the number of sellers in the market. A market may have one seller, thousands of sellers, or some number in between. The second area concerns whether the product sold in the market is identical from seller to seller, or whether each seller offers a differentiated product. If a firm can distinguish its product from that of its competitors through size, color, or any other attribute, then nonprice competition can arise. The third area concerns the ease or difficulty with which firms can enter or leave the market. It may be extremely easy for new firms to begin selling in the market, or it may be virtually impossible. The characteristics that emerge in each of these three areas are important for defining the amount of competition that exists in a market.

The remainder of this chapter is devoted to defining each of the four market structures and analyzing the behavior of firms in each of the market structures. For each structure we will evaluate the control that a business has over the price it charges, the influence and effect of nonprice competition, and whether or not firms in that market structure tend to make an economic profit in the long run.

PURE COMPETITION

Characteristics of Pure Competition

Purely competitive markets
Those markets with large numbers of independent sellers producing identical products, and with easy entry for new firms into the market.

Barriers to entry
Factors that keep firms from entering a market; can be a financial, legal, technical, or other barrier.

Purely competitive markets are those that have a very large number of sellers, each acting independently of the other. The outputs produced by these sellers are virtually identical: buyers cannot distinguish the product of one seller from that of another. Entry by business firms into purely competitive markets is easy. There are no legal restrictions, fees, impossibly high capital requirements, patents, or other **barriers to entry.**

Although it is difficult to find many cases of pure competition, the markets for individual agricultural crops such as corn, oats, and wheat have traditionally provided the classic examples of purely competitive markets. In each of these markets there are thousands of independent suppliers, and the output of any one supplier is indistinguishable from the output of any other. Entry into these markets is easy because little is required to grow a crop on a small scale.

The market in which a corporation's common stock is traded may also provide an example of pure competition. With companies such as General Motors, Exxon, and AT&T, millions of shares of stock are held by thousands of owners. Each share of a company's stock is identical to each other share, and it is easy to enter the market to buy and sell.

Figure 13.1
Market Demand and Supply for a Grain Crop

In a purely competitive market, market demand and supply determine the equilibrium price and quantity of a product.

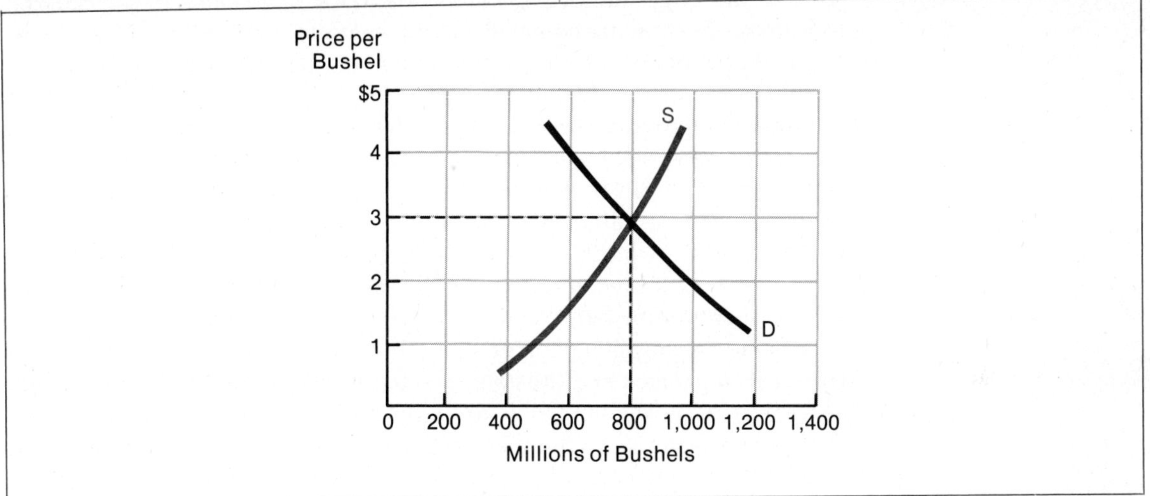

Behavior of a Firm in Pure Competition

Pure competition is the ideal market structure and that to which other markets are compared. As will be shown, it is particularly ideal from the buyer's point of view because of the pricing, cost, and profit behavior that results from the competition.

Control over Price One of the most important aspects of the behavior of purely competitive sellers is that no individual firm has any control over the price it receives for its product. Price is determined solely through the market's competitive forces; that is, price is determined by the interaction of *market* supply and *market* demand. The price that a firm charges is a result of the decisions of *all* buyers and *all* sellers in the market taken together.

Figure 13.1 illustrates the market for a grain crop and allows us to review the price-setting process first introduced in Chapter Three. D is the market demand curve showing the different amounts of grain that all buyers together plan to purchase at each price. As expected, the curve is downward sloping, indicating that the lower the price, the greater is the quantity demanded in the market. S is the upward sloping market supply curve, showing that all sellers (grain farmers) together offer more of the product for sale at a higher price. The actual price that emerges in this market is $3 per bushel. This is the equilibrium price that equates market demand and supply.

In this example, an individual purely competitive firm can sell as much or as little as it wishes at the price of $3 per bushel. It cannot charge more than $3 and will not charge less than $3. Why is this so?

Due to the large number of independently acting sellers in the market, the entire production of any one firm represents a "drop in the bucket" compared with the total available output. A firm that would charge a price higher than that in the market would sell nothing, because buyers can choose from thousands of alternative sellers. Also, since one seller's product is identical to that of all other sellers, it makes no difference with whom a buyer deals. The same product can be purchased from thousands of other sources.

It would also be pointless for a single seller to offer output at less than the market price. A grain farmer would not sell grain at $2, $2.50, or even $2.99 per bushel, knowing that the entire production can be sold at the market price of $3 per bushel.

The same pricing behavior exists with regard to common stock. If you own a particular stock and the going price per share is $9.50, you cannot sell your shares for more than $9.50 and have no reason to sell them for less.

Thus, because of large numbers of independent sellers producing identical products, purely competitive suppliers have neither the willingness nor the ability to deviate from the price set in the market.

Market demand curve The demand curve that results when all buyers in the market are considered together.

Individual firm's demand curve Shows the amounts of an individual firm's product that buyers are willing to purchase at particular prices.

Demand for an Individual Firm's Product For any product sold, there is a **market demand curve** such as that shown in Figure 13.1. In addition to the market demand curve, however, each individual firm or seller also has its own demand curve for its product. This represents the amounts of the *firm's* product that buyers are willing to purchase at certain prices. Thus, the **individual firm's demand curve** dictates the price a firm will receive when it chooses an output to sell.

As just stated, in pure competition the price an individual firm receives for its product is set by the forces of supply and demand in the market, and each firm supplies a minute fraction of the market. Since the firm's output is negligible when compared to the total, it can offer as much or as little as it chooses at the market price. Thus, the demand curve for any single purely competitive seller's product is graphed as a straight, horizontal line at the equilibrium market price.

The grain example in Figure 13.1 can be used to illustrate this concept. At an equilibrium price of $3 in the market, the demand curve for a single grain farmer's output would be like that shown in Figure 13.2. At $3 per bushel, buyers are willing to purchase 1,000 bushels, 5,000 bushels, or whatever output the farmer wants to offer. If the farmer were to charge more, say even $3.01, sales would drop to zero. There would also be no incentive to sell for less than $3 per bushel, since that is the price buyers are prepared to pay.

There is thus a relationship between the equilibrium market price and the individual firm's demand curve. If the equilibrium price in the market increases or decreases, the individual firm's demand curve will also increase (shift upward) or decrease (shift downward). If, for example, a large number

Figure 13.2
Demand Curve for the Output of a Purely Competitive Seller

A firm in a purely competitive market can sell as much as it wants at the market price.

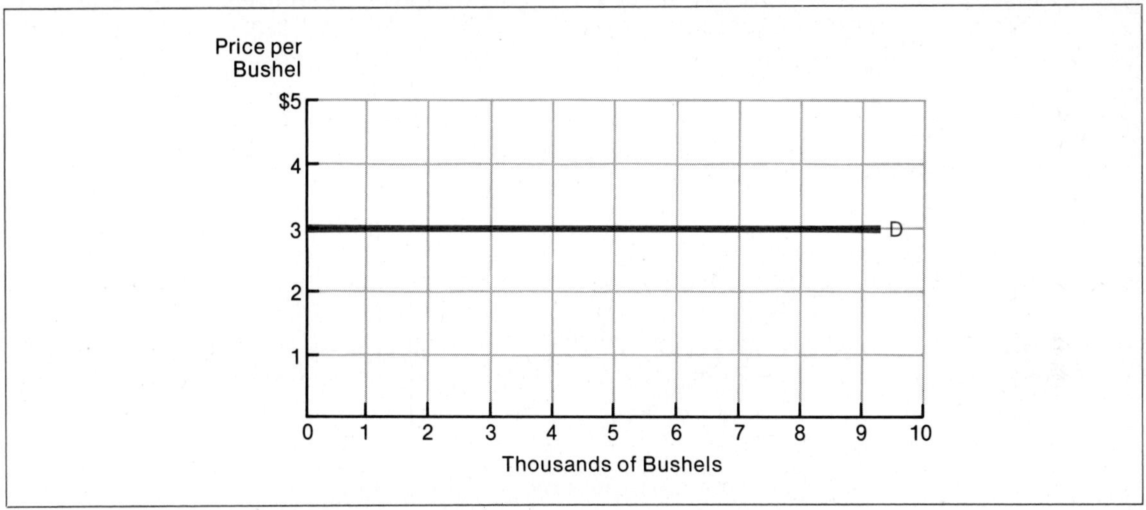

of new buyers enters the market for grain, the market demand curve will shift to the right. As a consequence, the equilibrium price in the market rises, and the individual farmer's demand curve shifts upward. This is shown in Figure 13.3 where the price increases from $3 to $4 after market demand increases from D1 (old) to D2 (new). What would be the effect on an individual firm's demand curve from an increase in market supply?

Pricing, Profit, and Loss The price that a firm in pure competition receives for its product determines whether that firm operates with a profit or a loss. In the short run, the price could be causing the firm to operate at a loss, to break even, or to make an economic profit. In the long run, a firm that continually receives prices so low that it cannot cover its costs will eventually go out of business. (Remember that normal profit is the profit necessary to stay in business and is included in the cost of production. Economic profit is that profit earned beyond normal profit.)

It is easy to see the profit or loss position of a firm by graphically comparing the firm's demand curve and its average total cost curve. The firm's demand curve gives the price it will receive for each unit of output sold, and the average total cost (ATC) curve gives the cost for producing each unit of output. If price is greater than average total cost, an **economic profit** is earned; if price is less than average total cost, a **loss** occurs; and if price equals average total cost, the firm is **breaking even.** Figure 13.4 illustrates these three possible conditions.

Economic profit, loss, breaking even
Occurs when price is greater than average total cost, less than average total cost, or equal to average total cost, respectively.

Figure 13.4a shows a firm in pure competition that is operating with an economic profit regardless of the output level chosen by the firm. Profit

Figure 13.3
Effect on the Individual Firm of an Increase in Market Demand

An increase in the market demand for a product will increase its equilibrium price and cause the individual firm's demand curve to shift upward.

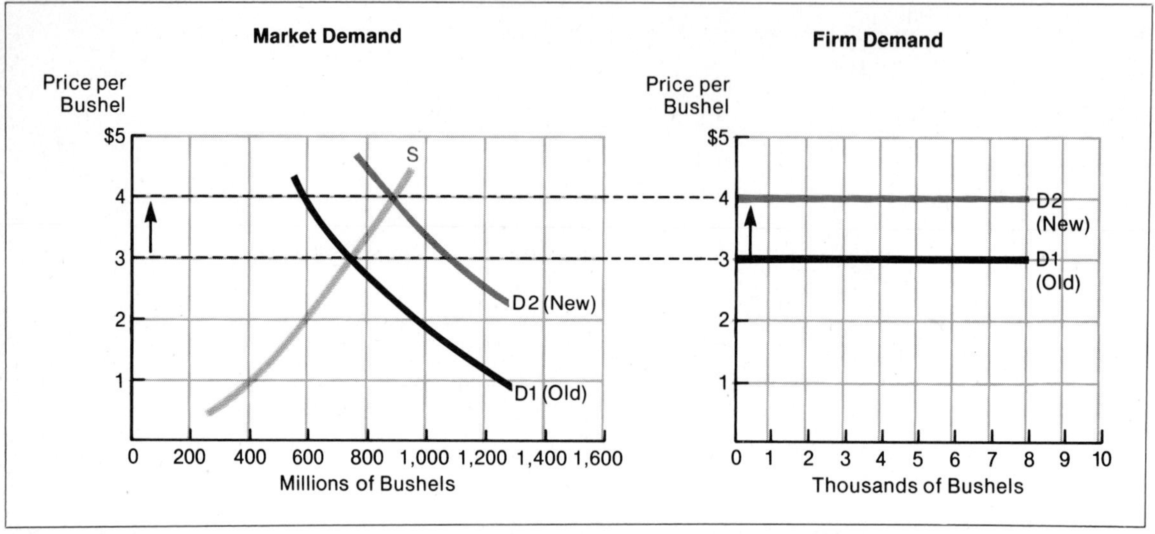

results at all output levels because the firm's demand curve is above the average total cost curve, or price is higher than average total cost.

Figure 13.4b illustrates a firm in pure competition operating with a loss. This loss occurs because the average total cost curve is above, or higher than, the demand curve regardless of the level of output produced. In Figure 13.4c a firm is just breaking even if it produces and sells Q_X units of output because average total cost is equal to price at that level of output.[1]

The appendix at the end of this chapter deals in greater detail with the profit maximizing or loss minimizing decisions that a firm in pure competition makes.

Nonprice competition
Occurs when firms focus on some feature other than price (for example, quality or a guarantee) in an attempt to attract buyers for their products.

Nonprice Competition A significant behavioral aspect of firms producing in purely competitive markets is the lack of **nonprice competition.** Purely competitive sellers make no expenditures on advertising, public relations, or other efforts to bring their firm or product to a buyer's attention. The reason for this should be obvious. With so many sellers producing identical products, the output of any one producer is indistinguishable from the outputs of all others, and efforts at creating buyer awareness of a particular firm's product would be an exercise in futility.

[1]A firm that is breaking even is making a normal profit, since normal profit is included in the cost of production. As long as a business breaks even, it will continue to operate.

Figure 13.4
Purely Competitive Seller Operating with an Economic Profit, with a Loss, or Breaking Even

A seller will operate with an economic profit, with a loss, or will break even, depending upon whether price is greater than, less than, or equal to average total cost, respectively.

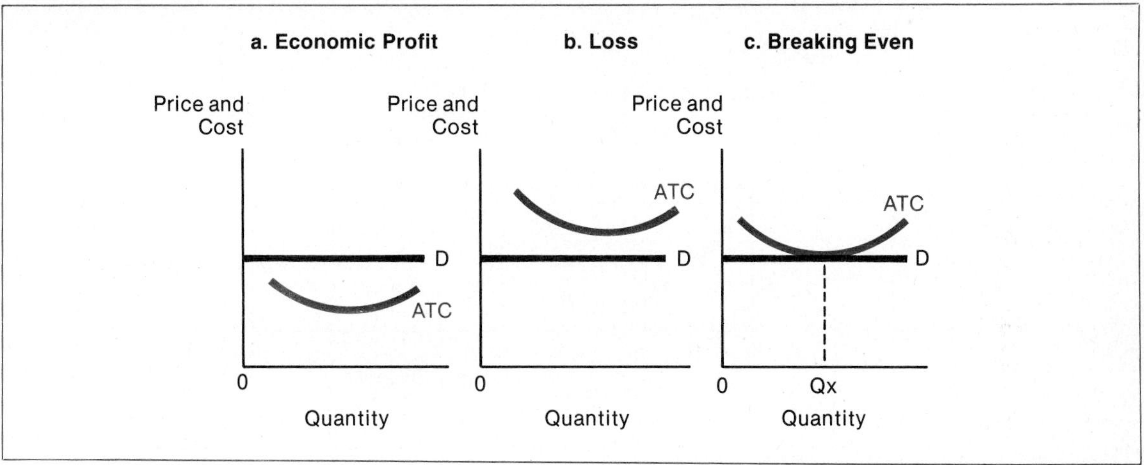

The benefit to consumers from this lack of nonprice competition is that with no promotional expenditures, firms' costs are lower than they would otherwise be. This in turn means that over the long run, buyers pay less for products than they would if firms engaged in nonprice competition.

Long-Run Costs and Profit One of the most important aspects of pure competition is the long-run behavior of firms in this market structure. In the long run, firms operate at the lowest possible cost, charge the lowest price that they can without going out of business, and earn no economic profit. All of these conditions are ideal from the consumer's point of view and result from competition among the sellers.

The long-run position of a purely competitive seller is illustrated in Figure 13.5. This figure shows a simple long-run average total cost (LRATC) curve exhibiting economies and diseconomies of scale, and the firm's demand curve. In the long run, an individual seller's position is such that its demand curve just brushes the bottom of its long-run average total cost curve.

A firm operating under the conditions given in Figure 13.5 would sell 4,000 units of output at $3 per unit, or would operate at point A, because any other output level would result in a loss. Notice that A is the lowest point on the firm's long-run average total cost curve, which means that the firm is producing at the lowest possible cost per unit. Notice also that at point A price equals average total cost, causing the entrepreneur to earn only normal and no excess profit. Thus, in the long run in pure competition the cost of production and the price of the product are as low as they can pos-

Figure 13.5
Long-Run Position of a Purely Competitive Seller

In the long run, a purely competitive seller operates where price equals lowest average total cost, which just allows a normal profit.

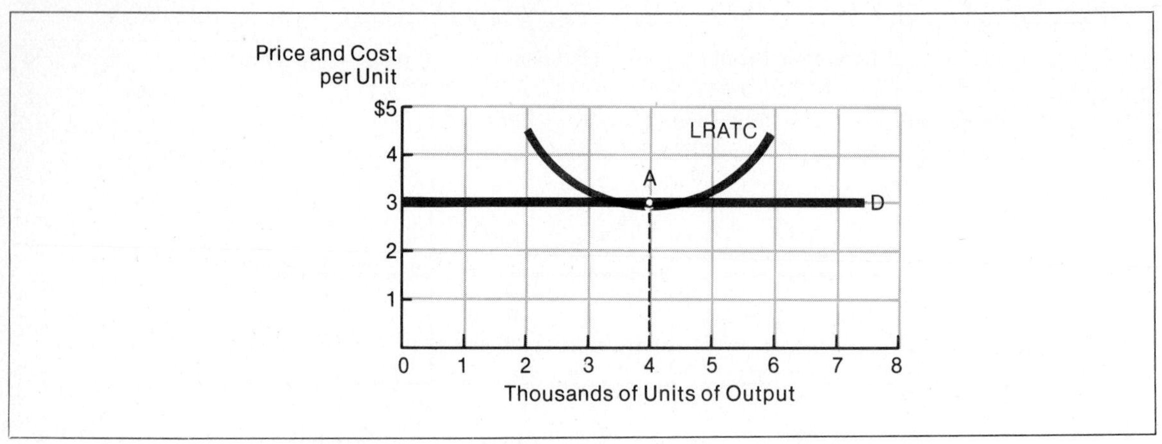

sibly be, and the consumer pays no economic profit. Why does this long-run condition occur?

Easy entry into and exit from the market are the basis for the position of the purely competitive firm in the long run. When firms in a purely competitive market earn excess profits, other sellers recognize the opportunity to also earn such profits and, because of easy entry, come into the market. As additional sellers enter the market, the market supply increases, causing the equilibrium market price to fall. As the equilibrium price falls, each individual seller's excess profit begins to disappear. This process of entry and reduction in both the market price and excess profit continues until each seller operates where price equals average total cost, or with just a normal profit.

The mechanics of this process are illustrated in Figure 13.6. With market price P_1 and the individual firm's demand curve D1 (right-hand graph), the firm is making an economic profit because the long-run average total cost curve lies below D1. As other firms, attracted by this economic profit, enter the market, the market supply curve (left-hand graph) increases from S1 to S2, market price falls to P_2, and the individual seller's demand curve falls to D2, which allows no economic profit.

If firms are losing money and experiencing less than normal profits, some sellers will close their operations and leave the market. As sellers leave, the market supply falls, causing the equilibrium price to increase. As the price increases, the losses to remaining sellers disappear. This process continues until, again, price equals average total cost.

Figure 13.7 illustrates the effect on an individual firm of an exodus of other firms from the market. At market price P_1, the individual firm is operating at a loss because the cost of producing each unit is greater than the

Figure 13.6
Effect of Entry on an Individual Firm's Demand and Profit

When individual firms in pure competition make an economic profit, new firms are attracted to the market, causing market supply to increase and equilibrium price to fall. Eventually, the price that each firm receives is equal to the firm's lowest average total cost.

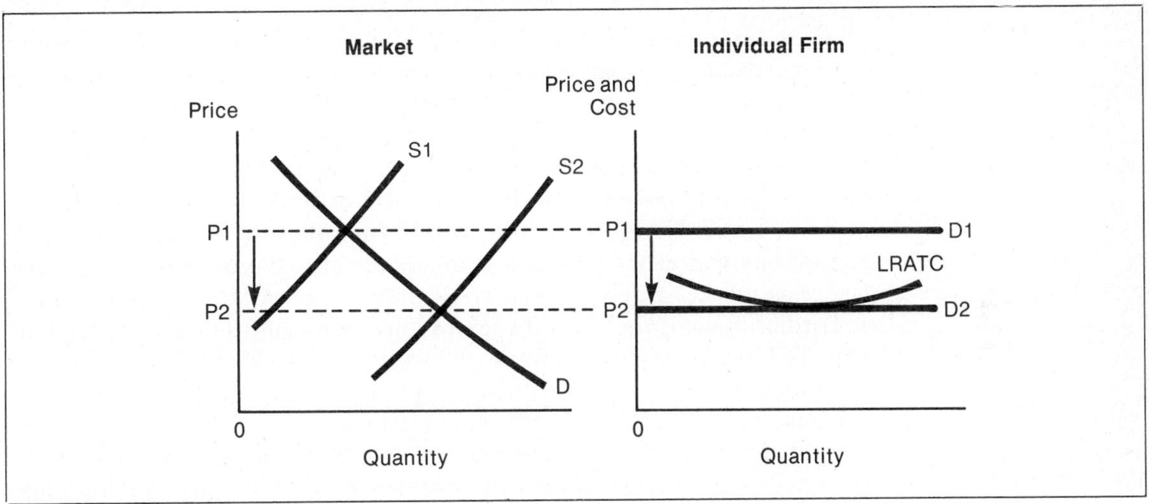

Figure 13.7
Effect of Exit on an Individual Firm's Demand and Profit

When individual firms in pure competition operate with a loss, some drop out of the market in the long run, causing market supply to decrease and equilibrium price to rise. Price will increase until it equals the lowest average total cost of the remaining firms.

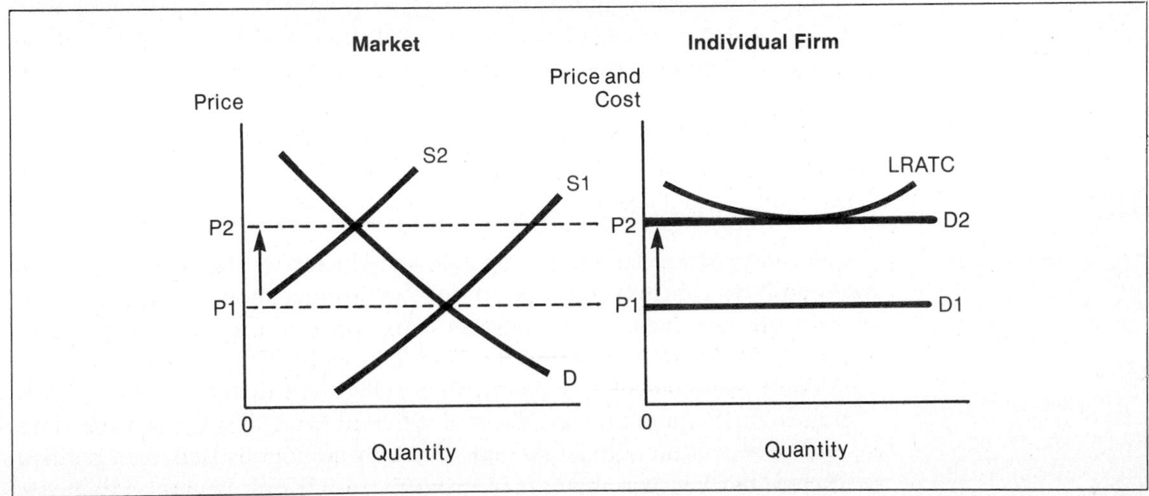

price. As firms leave the market, the market supply curve shifts to the left, from S1 to S2, causing market price and the individual firm's demand curve to rise. When the price rises to P_2 the firm is operating without a loss.

Is There Pure Competition?

There is a question about the extent to which pure competition is found in the real world. Consider agriculture, which has provided the classic examples of purely competitive markets because of the large number of economically independent agricultural sellers. From time to time farmers have organized into groups to present their grievances about prices, costs, and other problems to the government. Does political activity such as this influence market prices? There is also the U.S. Department of Agriculture, which administers various government loan and assistance programs, to consider. Is a grain market purely competitive if these programs affect market price?

Further, there is the question of entry into and exit from agricultural markets. To farm on anything other than a very small scale can require substantial outlays for land, equipment, and other inputs such as seed and fertilizer. It is possible that the costs of starting a farm could act as a barrier to entry into the market. Also, exit from the market may not be easy. A farmer wishing to use land and equipment for something other than agriculture might discover that it is not well suited for anything else. Or a farming couple wishing to leave production completely by selling their land and equipment or by passing it on to their children might have to alter their plans after considering the effects of tax laws on the disposal of their property.

With problems such as these, of what value is the study of pure competition? Despite issues such as those just raised, the purely competitive model does help us better understand the behavior of firms in certain markets. It also provides an ideal against which real-world markets can be judged. In this regard, pure competition is like human health. There may be no perfectly healthy person, just as there may be no purely competitive market. But we cannot understand the meaning of illness or good health without having the ideal of perfect health for comparison.

MONOPOLISTIC COMPETITION

Characteristics of Monopolistic Competition

Monopolistic competition
The market structure characterized by a large number of sellers with differentiated outputs and fairly easy entry into and exit from the market.

Differentiated outputs
The products of competing firms are different and can be recognized as such by buyers.

The second market structure, and the one closest to pure competition, is **monopolistic competition.** Like pure competition, monopolistically competitive markets have large numbers of sellers—not as many as in pure competition, but large numbers nonetheless. Unlike pure competition, the outputs of monopolistically competitive sellers are **differentiated:** buyers can distinguish among the products of different firms. Finally, as is the case in pure competition, entry into and exit from monopolistically competitive markets is fairly easy.

Examples of monopolistically competitive markets may be found where a large number of small retailing establishments such as drug stores, shoe stores, restaurants, or record shops compete with each other. In these examples each seller's product is somewhat different: location, service, style, guarantees, and such vary from seller to seller. It is also relatively easy to open a small store or restaurant: a building can be rented; there is no need for highly trained or technical personnel; and the requirements for capital equipment are not too great.

Another slightly different example of a monopolistically competitive market is the labor market for college graduates in a particular discipline such as accounting. Each year a large number of accounting majors is graduated from colleges and universities. Each of these graduates is unique from the rest in terms of grades, background, experience, selection of courses, and initiative. Entry into this market is relatively easy: the only necessary major expenditure is the cost of a college degree.

Behavior of a Firm in Monopolistic Competition

Because of differences in the characteristics of monopolistically competitive and purely competitive markets, there are differences in the behavior of firms in these structures. Notably, unlike pure competitors, monopolistic competitors have some control over the prices they receive for their products, and they engage in nonprice competition.

Control over Price With a large number of firms selling identical products, the individual purely competitive firm has no control over the price it receives for its output. In monopolistic competition there is also a large number of sellers, but because the sellers' products are differentiated, buyers do not view the product of one seller as a perfect substitute for the product of another. For this reason, when a monopolistically competitive firm raises its price, it will lose some, but not all, of its sales. Some buyers will continue with the firm because they see its product as different from those of its competitors. Thus, product differentiation allows a firm to carve out a little market of its own within the larger market. Within each individual firm's smaller market are buyers who are willing to stay with the seller if its product's price is raised.

However, even with product differentiation there are limits to the amount of control a monopolistically competitive seller has over price. Since many other firms produce similar products, a firm that raises its price too much risks losing a large share of the market. Some buyers may be willing to pay a little extra for better service or a distinctive style, but if they have to pay a great deal extra, the alternatives become more attractive.

In short, a firm selling in a monopolistically competitive market has some control over price because of its ability to differentiate its product, but that control is limited by the presence of many other firms producing similar products.

Figure 13.8
Demand Curve for the Output of a Monopolistically Competitive Seller

Because of product differentiation, a seller in monopolistic competition will lose some, but not all, of its buyers if it raises its price. This causes the demand curve for the seller's product to slope downward.

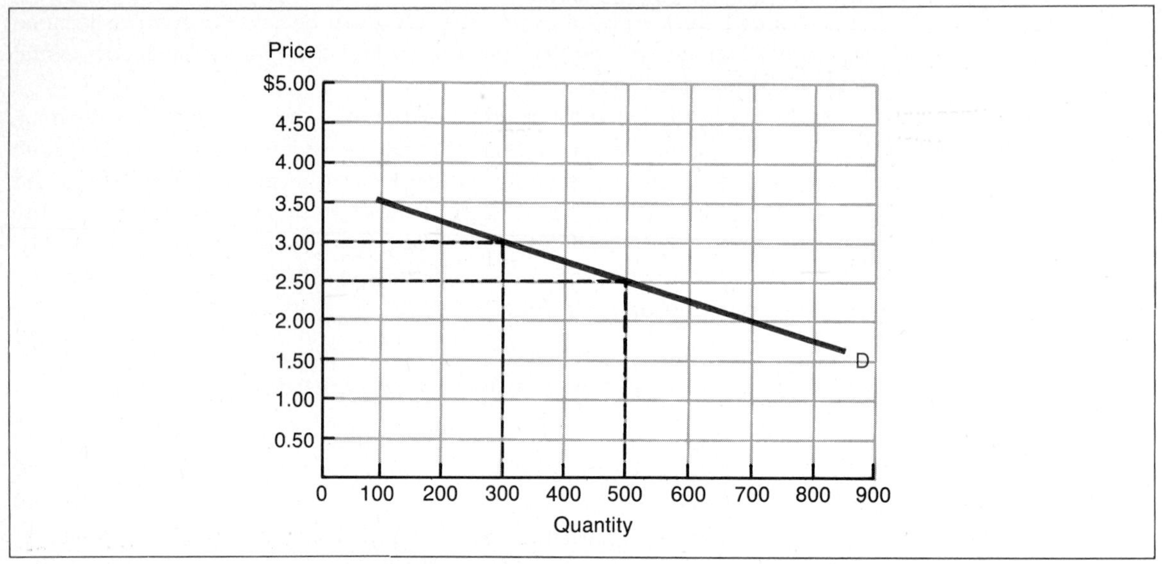

Demand for an Individual Firm's Product Because of product differentiation, the demand curve faced by an individual monopolistic competitor is downward sloping, like that in Figure 13.8. This demand curve indicates that if the firm raises its price, it will lose some, but not all, of its sales. For example, in Figure 13.8, when the price is raised from $2.50 to $3 per unit, the quantity demanded falls from 500 to 300 units, not from 500 units to zero as would happen if the seller were a pure competitor.

Pricing, Profit, and Loss As was the case with a firm operating in a purely competitive market, the profit or loss position of a firm operating in a monopolistically competitive market can be determined by comparing the demand curve and average total cost curve for its product. If the average total cost curve lies below the demand curve, or the cost per unit of output is less than the price, an economic profit is earned. This is shown in Figure 13.9a. If the average total cost curve is above the demand curve, or the cost per unit of output is greater than the price, a loss occurs. This is shown in Figure 13.9b.

Nonprice Competition Obviously, sellers in monopolistically competitive markets can compete with one another for buyers by lowering prices. But because their products are differentiated, rivalry through nonprice competition also becomes important.

Figure 13.9
Monopolistically Competitive Seller Operating with an Economic Profit or a Loss

A seller in monopolistic competition earns economic profit when the price of its product is greater than average total cost (the demand curve is above the average total cost curve). It operates with a loss when price is less than average total cost (the demand curve is below the average total cost curve).

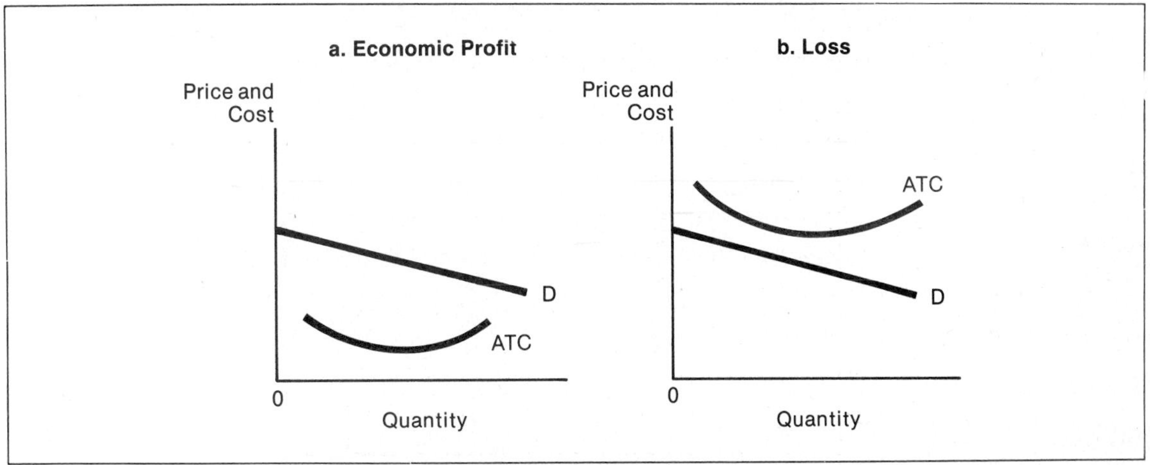

Nonprice competition includes all forms of rivalry not involving price. A firm competes for customers through its packaging, distribution, service, location, quality, selection, and guarantees. An ice cream parlor, for example, can attract customers because of a varied and high quality selection of flavors, the hours it is open, and access to parking. The importance of nonprice competition can be seen by the amount of advertising and sales promotion directed to that end. Notice how infrequently advertisements in magazines or on television stress price as the selling feature.

Business firms are attracted to nonprice competition for two reasons. First, nonprice competition provides a way for a firm to increase the demand for its product. By increasing buyer acceptance through advertising, packaging, and other devices, a firm can shift the demand curve for its product to the right—thereby selling more at each price. Second, by highlighting differences and playing down similarities, nonprice competition helps an individual firm make its product appear unique. As this occurs, the seller becomes less sensitive to the presence of rivals. Uniqueness allows a seller to raise prices without losing as many sales as would otherwise be the case.

Controversy exists over the desirability of nonprice competition—especially through advertising. In most instances, nonprice competition increases the cost of doing business, and higher costs can lead to higher prices for buyers. Some people argue that buyers' interests would be better served if rivalry were limited to price competition or if nonprice competition were at least reduced. Others think that nonprice competition can benefit consumers and that it should be encouraged. After years of buying goods and services, what is your position on this question?

Product differentiation and nonprice competition are important characteristics of many snack food markets. Application 13.2, "The Public Doesn't Get a Better Potato Chip Without a Bit of Pain," illustrates some of the nonprice factors that one company considers in developing new chips for the market. Can you identify some of the costs created for this company because of its product differentiation focus?

Long-Run Costs and Profit Over the long run, sellers in monopolistically competitive markets earn only normal profits, an attribute shared by firms in purely competitive markets. The reason for this is that, like purely competitive markets, monopolistically competitive markets are easy to enter and exit. If firms are earning economic, or excess, profit (like the firm shown in Figure 13.9a), new sellers enter the market and take some of the demand away from the existing sellers. This causes the demand curves of these sell-

Application 13.2
THE PUBLIC DOESN'T GET A BETTER POTATO CHIP WITHOUT A BIT OF PAIN

Coming up with new products is essential to keeping [its lead in the snack food business], and Frito-Lay is good at it. Company managers consider hundreds of suggestions each year, but their screening process is so tough that only five or six get much past the idea stage. To go from being a gleam in the eye to a bag on the shelf, a new chip has to make it through the test kitchen, consumer taste testing, naming, package design, ad planning, manufacturing and test-marketing. A poor grade on one of the tests—or a poor decision about the name or ad theme—can kill a new product.

A successful one, though, can be worth $100 million or more a year in added revenue. So, although Frito-Lay develops certain products to meet specific competitive threats, its researchers are constantly trying to dream up new ideas simply in hopes of selling more snacks. . . .

Inspiring these searchers for the perfect snack is the success of products like Doritos, Tostitos and Ruffles. Frito-Lay brought out Ruffles potato chips in 1960, giving them an unusual ridged texture. Twenty-three years later, the company still sells Ruffles and flourishes; it markets $425 million (retail) of them every year. Doubtless there will be rewards for the product manager who can duplicate that success. . . .

These days, Frito-Lay has several up-and-coming new chips, chief among them Ta-Tos and O'Gradys. These are both made of potatoes, but they are not to be confused. Around Frito-Lay, Ta-Tos are known as "super-crispy wavy." O'Gradys aren't like that. They are "extra-thick and crunchy." . . .

[O'Gradys] needed a name, so product managers set about finding one that would give the right impression. Mr. Todd [marketing director for new products] explains the thinking: "This product was of the earth, it was thicker, a natural-tasting product." It also would have local competitors. So Frito began screening hearty names that would make the chips sound locally made.

Among the candidates was O'Gradys. Consumers were asked what a person named O'Grady might be like. They replied, variously, that O'Grady would be fun, jovial, male, happy-ers to shift to the left until economic profit is competed away and only normal profit remains. If firms are sustaining losses (like the firm shown in Figure 13.9b), sellers leave the market, causing the demand curves of the remaining sellers to shift to the right until the remaining firms operate at a normal profit.

Due to easy entry and exit, the long-run position of a monopolistically competitive seller is like that shown in Figure 13.10. The firm in Figure 13.10 can earn a normal profit by selling 300,000 units of output at $3 each. At any smaller or larger output the long-run average total cost curve is above the demand curve, causing the firm to produce at a loss.

While purely competitive and monopolistically competitive sellers both earn only a normal profit over the long run, the two types of sellers differ in

an important way. A firm in a purely competitive market operates at the minimum possible cost in the long run, and a firm in a monopolistically com-

go-lucky, hearty and big. It was just the image Frito wanted. . . .

A wrong name can hold back a worthy chip. Tiffles "light corn chips" failed in two test markets, until a different product manager got hold of them and called them Sunchips, the "corn chips for potato-chip lovers." They are in a third test market now, and are selling almost twice as well as before.

Even so, manufacturing needs have to be considered. Sunchips are made of ground corn using a special extrusion process, so if Frito-Lay goes national with them, it probably will have to build new production lines. Similarly, the cutting machines used to make O'Gradys during the current test marketing won't accept potatoes longer than four inches. To make O'Gradys on a large scale, the company would have to either buy bigger cutters or sort its potatoes. . . .

Getting the right package means more decisions. How should it be sealed? What color should it be? Should it say "potato chips" or "potato crisps"? Should the chips show through a window on the package? Frito figures that for a chip sold nationally, a window costs $1 million to $2 million extra a year.

Then, of course, there is the advertising theme, one of the toughest but most important of decisions. Frito-Lay managers spare no effort to get this one right. . . .

If advertisements can't get people to buy potato chips, maybe the deliverymen can. Frito-Lay's 9,500 truck drivers get only a small weekly salary but a 10% commission on all the chips they sell. They can earn $40,000 a year if they really deliver.

So the drivers stop to talk with supermarket managers, angling for an extra foot of shelf space. In a small drive-in grocery, where the direction of the flow of shoppers can be gauged, deliverymen may tilt the bags on the shelf to face the oncoming consumer.

And they know a bit about psychology. Some shoppers pass over a half-empty shelf, perhaps thinking the potato chips on it have been there awhile and are getting stale. A smart deliveryman will "fluff" the shelf, laying the rear bags on their sides to fill space so the others reach the front. . . .

Source: Janet Guyon, "The Public Doesn't Get a Better Potato Chip Without a Bit of Pain," *The Wall Street Journal*, March 25, 1983, pp. 1, 10. Reprinted by permission of *The Wall Street Journal*,

Figure 13.10
Long-Run Position of a Monopolistically Competitive Seller

Like a purely competitive seller, a monopolistically competitive seller earns no excess profit over the long run; but unlike a purely competitive seller, it operates at a long-run average total cost that is greater than the minimum.

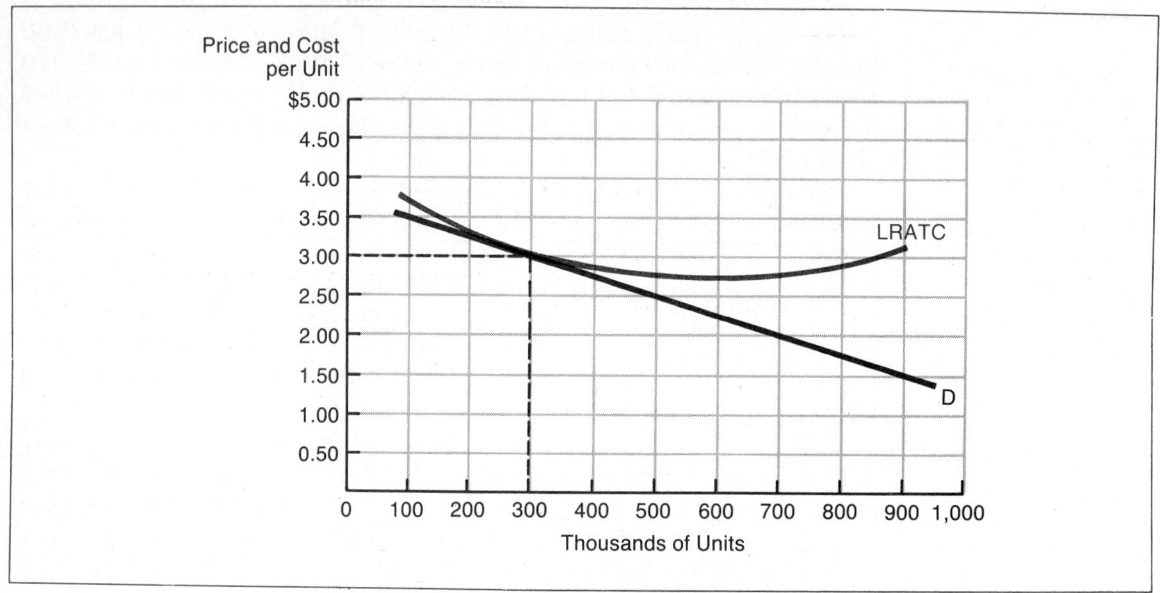

petitive market does not. The firm in Figure 13.10 is operating at a price and per unit cost of $3. If it were a pure competitor, its price and per unit cost would be $2.75—the minimum point on the long-run average total cost curve. It is impossible for a monopolistic competitor to operate in the long run with price equal to minimum long-run average total cost because of product differentiation and the downward sloping demand curve. This difference gives rise to an important criticism of monopolistic competition: even though price equals long-run average total cost, the cost and price are higher than they would be in pure competition.

OLIGOPOLY

Oligopoly is further removed from pure competition than is monopolistic competition. In fact, it is so far removed that it makes more sense to discuss how oligopoly and pure competition differ than to discuss what they have in common. While pure competition may be the ideal market structure, oligopoly is the dominant market structure in the U.S. economy. More business is transacted in oligopolistic markets than in any of the three other market structures.

Characteristics of Oligopoly

Oligopolistic markets
Those markets dominated by a few large sellers with either differentiated or identical products and where entry by new firms into the market is difficult.

Oligopolistic markets are those dominated by a few large sellers. In some cases the products of oligopolists are differentiated, and in others they are identical. Entry of firms into oligopolistic markets is quite difficult, much more so than entry into purely or monopolistically competitive markets. Barriers to entry include the sheer size of the capital requirement necessary to allow a potential rival to compete equally with established sellers, and the difficulty of taking enough sales away from existing firms to make operating worthwhile.

The automobile market is a good example of an oliogopoly with differentiated products. There are a few large domestic sellers and a handful of foreign competitors; products are differentiated in terms of style, size, mileage, luxury, and other factors; and entry into the market by a new firm is extremely difficult. The market for aluminum ingot provides an example of an undifferentiated oligopoly. There are a few large aluminum firms; ingot is an undifferentiated product; and the cost of entering the market is substantial.

Examples of oligopoly are everywhere. The next time you are in a grocery store notice how few firms produce all of the highly differentiated breakfast cereals. Then go to the sugar section and notice how few firms produce white granulated sugar, an undifferentiated product. Examples of oligopolies are found in the markets for baseball gloves, stereo equipment, gasoline, light bulbs, and cigarettes. Table 13.1 gives some other markets that are dominated by a few large firms. This table lists the percentage of shipments in various U.S. industries that are accounted for by the largest four firms in that industry. Notice, for example, that the largest four firms in the aircraft industry accounted for 59 percent of the total aircraft shipped.

Table 13.1
Percent of Total Shipments by the Four Largest Manufacturing Companies in Selected U.S. Industries: 1977

Oligopolistic markets, where a few large firms account for a significant percentage of shipments, are the most common type of market structure in the U.S. economy.

Industry	Percent of Shipments
Motor vehicles and car bodies	93%
Organic fibers, noncellulosic	78
Photographic equipment and supplies	72
Tires and inner tubes	70
Automotive stampings	65
Guided missiles and space vehicles	64
Aircraft	59
Soap and other detergents	59
Construction machinery	47
Farm machinery and equipment	46
Blast furnaces and steel mills	45

Source: U.S. Bureau of the Census, *Statistical Abstract of the United States: 1982–83* (103d ed.), Washington, D.C., 1982, p. 784.

Behavior of a Firm in an Oligopolistic Market

Control over Price Because of the small number of sellers, each oligopolist's output comprises a large share of the market. This share allows the firm some control over its price—quite unlike the pure competitor whose output is so small that the firm is at the mercy of the market.

But the existence of few competing sellers introduces an interesting twist to oligopoly. While to a certain degree it frees firms from control by the market, it also presents a complicating factor that significantly affects behavior. With so few sellers, the price, output, advertising, and other policy actions of one firm affect the other firms in its market and may cause these other firms to react. For example, if one automobile company offers a rebate on its cars, it may affect the sales of the other firms in the market. These firms may in turn offer rebates of their own or follow other policies that would be detrimental to the sales of the first company. If one cereal company includes a desirable toy in its cereal boxes, this may reduce the sales of a competing company, which could respond with a promotional program of its own. As a result, in the oligopolistic market structure, sellers are constantly watching and weighing the actions and reactions of their competitors.

Mutual interdependence
Occurs when there are so few sellers in the market that each seller must weigh the actions and reactions of rival sellers in any decision making.

This phenomenon is called **mutual interdependence.** Because of mutual interdependence, sellers must consider not only the effects of their pricing and other policies on buyers, but the effects on their rivals and their rivals' reactions as well. This is the really unique aspect of oligopolistic markets.

Price of an Individual Firm's Product Because mutual interdependence manifests itself in different ways, there is no single explanation for oligopoly pricing. Rather, several theories have been developed to accommodate different types of interdependence. Two of the best known theories are leadership pricing and the kinked demand curve model.

Leadership pricing
One firm in a market sets a price that the other firms in the market then adopt.

With **leadership pricing** one firm in a market sets a price that is then adopted by other sellers. The firm that sets the price is called the price leader, and the firms that respond are the followers. Leadership pricing is not uncommon. Often firms in industries such as aluminum, steel, and banking follow suit when a price increase is announced by one of their competitors. The price increases by the followers often come within a few days of the leader's announcement.

A seller may emerge as price leader for several reasons. For one, it may be the largest firm in its market, causing rivals to choose to adopt its price rather than attack it head-on and face a possible price war. Or, it may become price leader because it is more sensitive to changing market conditions than are its rivals. In this case, the rivals respond to the leader's price announcements because that firm acts as a barometer of changing market conditions that will eventually affect other sellers. Banks, for example, experience the same changes in money market conditions, causing a price leadership pattern to emerge with regard to interest rates.

Kinked demand curve
Based on the assumption that rivals will not follow price increases but will follow price decreases; it illustrates that as a seller's price rises, the amount of its product demanded decreases substantially, but as its price falls, the amount demanded increases only slightly.

The second theory, the **kinked demand curve** model, is based on the assumption that rivals do not follow a seller's price increases but do follow price decreases. The theory gets its name from the unusual shape of the individual oligopolist's demand curve under this assumption. A kinked demand curve is illustrated in Figure 13.11.

The price currently charged and the corresponding output sold by the firm are shown at the kink, or bend, in the demand curve. For the firm in Figure 13.11, the current price is $3 and sales are 400,000 units. If the firm raises its price above $3, and its rivals do not follow, it stands to lose a large number of buyers to those other sellers. For example, when it increases its price from $3 to $4, its sales fall by 200,000 units, from 400,000 to 200,000. But notice that when the firm lowers its price from $3 to $2, its sales increase by only 50,000 units, to 450,000. This is because, when a seller's price is lowered, the seller's rivals also cut their prices to avoid losing buyers. With everyone's price lower, fewer buyers are willing to switch to the seller that initiated the price cut.

Thus, the relatively flat portion of the kinked demand curve above the current price shows that a firm increasing its price stands to lose a large number of sales if its rivals do not follow its lead. The steep portion of the curve below the current price illustrates that, with rivals following price cuts, sales increase only slightly. The conclusion to be drawn from this model is that prices are relatively stable in oligopoly markets where there is no incentive to either raise or lower price. In other words, there is not much price com-

Figure 13.11
Kinked Demand Curve for the Output of an Oligopolist

The kinked demand curve of an oligopolist is based on the assumption that the firm's rivals will follow a price decrease but not a price increase.

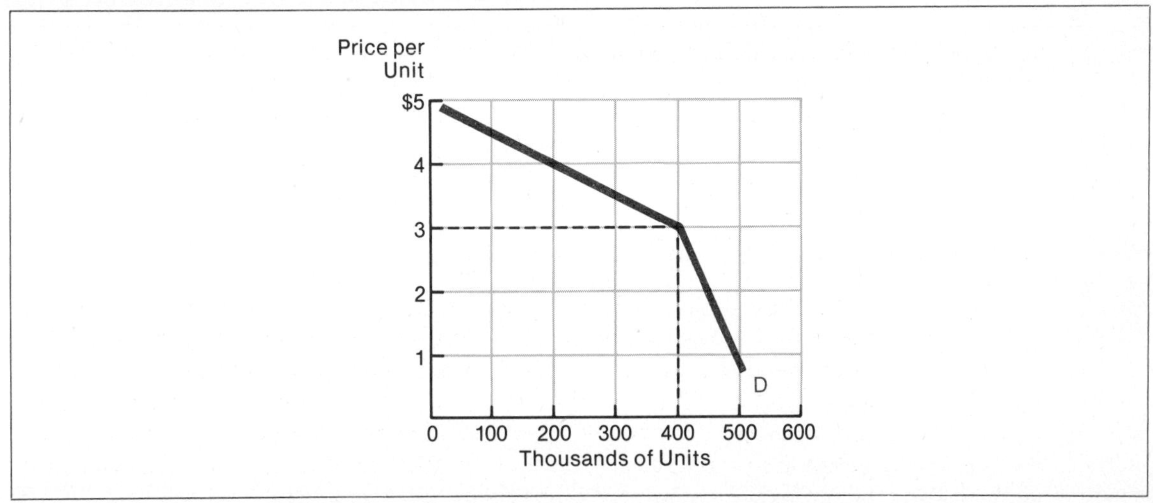

petition. The kinked demand curve model has been attacked because some economists believe that the assumption of rivals not following price increases is unrealistic. The model, however, does illustrate one way in which mutual interdependence might affect the demand for a seller's product.

Nonprice Competition Nonprice competition in oligopolistic markets differs according to whether the products sold in the market are differentiated or not. Where rivals produce physically identical products, advertising campaigns that stress the product itself would be inappropriate. On the other hand, a strong advertising campaign emphasizing the product itself makes sense where sellers' outputs are clearly differentiable on the basis of quality, style, size, or some other characteristic. Automobile ads, for example, often stress the differentiable characteristics of the product itself.

Nonprice competition is important if a seller faces a situation where price cuts do not lead to large increases in sales. In this case, nonprice competition provides an alternative to price competition. However, sellers must recognize that mutual interdependence also exists with regard to nonprice competition. Application 13.3 illustrates the speed with which one airline's attempt to attract passengers via a win-a-ticket game was met by similar games by its competitors.

Long-Run Costs and Profit Over the long run, purely competitive and monopolistically competitive sellers earn only normal profit: easy entry allows new firms to come into the market and compete economic profit away. But with oligopoly, entry is not easy. Therefore, oligopolists can con-

Application 13.3
AIRLINES PLAY GAMES FOR CUSTOMERS

Three airlines are hoping that win-a-ticket games will help them lure new customers.

The airlines — Trans World, United and American — hope the games will bring them a larger part of the U.S. travel dollar in today's tight economy.

United Airlines ... was the first airline to plunge into this promotional territory by announcing its "Takeoff Game" on March 24 [1980]. During April, United travelers will be given a game card on which three spots are scratched off to reveal symbols underneath. Anyone coming up with three airplane symbols wins a ticket to any U.S. city served by United.

American announced its "Great American Game of Baseball" in full-page newspaper advertisements Thursday [April 3, 1980]. The game, which runs between April 10 and May 9, offers 50,000 prizes, including 10 free monthlong travel passes and 10,000 free round trips to cities served by American.

Trans World Airlines decided Wednesday

tinue to earn economic profit over the long run because new sellers cannot readily enter the market.

The ability to earn economic profit over the long run affects the price buyers pay for a product. With pure competition, easy entry ensures that price is equal to cost and is as low as possible. But the ability of an oligopolist to earn economic profit means that the firm's price can be greater than its cost. Thus, over the long run, restricted entry may result in economic profit for the firm and in higher prices for the buyer.

MONOPOLY

Characteristics of Monopoly

Monopoly market
A market with one seller who maintains that position because entry by new sellers is impossible.

Of the four market structures, none is further removed from pure competition than is monopoly. In a **monopolized market** there is only one seller — the monopolist. Since the firm faces no direct competition from other sellers' products, the question of whether or not its product is differentiated is meaningless. The monopolist enjoys its position as sole seller in the market because entry by new sellers is virtually impossible.

Entry into a monopolized market can be forestalled for several reasons. First, it may be more efficient to have one rather than several sellers in a market. This happens when production is accompanied by significant economies of scale that cause long-run average total cost to fall as the seller becomes larger and output expands. In this case, buyers stand to pay less with one large firm producing all of the output at a lower average total cost

---

[April 2, 1980] to announce a game called "Win the World." According to airline spokesman Kevin M. Byrne, 10,000 tickets will be given away between April 10 and May 10 for flights anywhere in the world served by TWA. In addition, a drawing will be held among the 10,000 winners for a grand prize — a free trip a year for life.

"We couldn't ignore what United did, because they would just take customers away," Byrne said. "This is a good indication of how competitive deregulation has made the airline industry." . . .

Byrne traced this latest round in the airlines' promotional war to January [1980], when American announced family discounts. So, TWA went one better by offering free flights for children, he said.

The latest game "is a new type of marketing for us," Byrne said. "There are people who will compare us to fast-food restaurants, but fast-food places have been successful in attracting customers with games like this."

Source: Marjorie Mandel, "Airlines Play Games For Customers," *St. Louis Post-Dispatch*, April 4, 1980, p. 1-C.

than they would if several firms each produced part of the total supply at a higher average total cost. Thus, if a firm, by servicing the entire market, can take advantage of the cost and price lowering effects of economies of scale, it can keep potential rivals out of the market. Such a situation is called a **natural monopoly** and will be further discussed in Chapter Fifteen.

Natural monopoly
A market situation where it is more efficient (less costly) to have the entire output of a product come from one large seller rather than several smaller sellers.

If a monopoly is a public utility—the only firm providing natural gas, electricity, or some other essential service to a community—entry of new rivals may be blocked by their inability to receive permission to operate from a regulatory authority. Or a monopolist may owe its market power to the ownership of a patent on a product or a process. Any potential rival trying to use the product or process without the monopolist's permission can be sued. A company could also be a monopolist because it is the sole owner of a factor necessary for production, such as the franchise for operation of a professional sports team. Finally, a firm may be a monopolist because it has engaged in illegal practices involving prices and contracts that keep potential rivals out of the market.

Examples of monopolies include a company that owns the only pipeline carrying natural gas into a city, a company that is the sole distributor of gas to business and residential users, an electric power company, the only newspaper in a city, a professional sports team, and a holder of a patent.

Related to monopoly is the situation where several sellers formally join together with the intention of acting as if they were a single firm monopoly. The organization they form is called a **cartel,** and its purpose is to obtain more profit and other benefits for its members than they would receive if they competed with one another. The best known example of a cartel is the Organization of Petroleum Exporting Countries (OPEC). Cartels are illegal in the United States.

Cartel
An arrangement whereby sellers formally join together in a market to make decisions as a group on matters such as pricing; the behavior of a cartel is like that of a monopoly.

Behavior of a Monopolist

Control over Price Two important facts about a monopolist's pricing result because it is the only seller in its market. First, all other things being equal, a monopolist has more control over its price than does a firm in any other market structure. There are no direct competitors to take buyers away when a monopolist raises its price. Second, because a monopolist is the only seller in a market, its demand curve *is* the market demand curve: all buyers demanding the product demand it from the monopolist.

Demand for a Monopolist's Product Since market demand curves are downward sloping, and since the monopolist's demand is identical to the market demand, the monopolist's demand curve is also downward sloping.

Unlike the pure competitor, whose price is determined by the forces of market supply and demand and who must accept the price dictated by the market, a monopolist will search its downward sloping demand curve to find the particular price and output combination that will maximize the firm's profit. That is, a monopolist will assess the costs and revenues from oper-

Figure 13.12
Demand Curve for the Output of a Monopolist

A monopolist will search its demand curve and choose the one price and output combination that will maximize its profit.

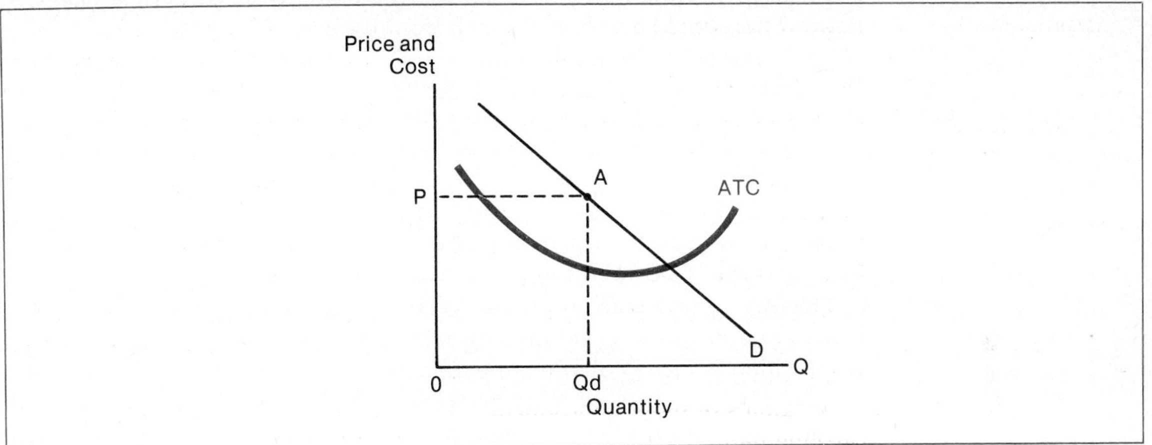

ating at various levels of output or various points on the demand curve and select the one price and output combination that maximizes profit. Let us say that point A in Figure 13.12 represents such a profit-maximizing price and output combination.[2]

One of the significant features about pricing in a monopoly market structure is that since the monopolist's demand and the market demand are the same, the monopolist is establishing the price and output level for the whole market. In other words, one firm makes all of the supply decisions. In addition, once the monopolist chooses a price, there are no competitive forces to lower it. The monopolist has no fear of entry by new firms.

Nonprice Competition Because monopolists face no direct competitors, the nonprice competition in which they engage is slightly different from that typically used by oligopolists or monopolistic competitors. In those market structures nonprice competition is designed primarily to attract buyers to a particular brand of a product. For example, in the passenger car market, nonprice competition encourages buyers toward a Ford, General Motors, Chrysler, American Motors, or foreign automobile. But with monopoly there are no competing brands; there is simply the product. In this situation, a monopolist's advertising and other nonprice competition may be designed to make people aware of the good or service itself, not the seller. For example, many

[2]Notice in Figure 13.12 that profit maximization does not occur at the output level where the distance between price (or the demand curve) and average total cost is the greatest. This is because the objective is to maximize total profit and not profit per unit. See the appendix at the end of this chapter for a further explanation.

people are probably more aware of the advertising slogan "A diamond is forever" than they are of De Beers Consolidated Mines, Ltd., the company with which the slogan is associated. While not a total monopolist, De Beers supplies the vast majority of the world's diamonds. If you buy a new diamond, it is very likely to have come from De Beers.

Long-Run Costs and Profit The monopolist enjoys its position as sole seller in its market because of impassable entry barriers that keep potential rivals out. Those same barriers allow the monopolist to enjoy economic profit over the long run. Due to barriers to entry, no new rivals can come into the market, force the monopolistic firm to lower its price, and compete economic profit away. The monopolist can protect its economic profit as long as its monopoly position can be maintained.

However, even with the monopolist's exclusive position in the market, some restraints on its profit making ability may exist. While it faces no direct competition in its own market, the monopolist must be concerned with competition from products in other markets. A natural gas distributor may have no direct competition from other gas distributors, but in some respects, it faces competition from suppliers of other types of energy. For example, a home builder may have the choice of installing gas, electric, oil, or solar heat, and a home owner always has the option of converting from one type of heat to another. Thus, if the gas company's price becomes too far out of line, over the long run it could lose business, not to other gas distributors, but to companies supplying alternative forms of energy.

The monopolist is also restrained in its profit making ability where it is a public utility. In this case, the price it charges is overseen by a public authority or a regulatory commission. Here price is set in such a way that the utility's ability to earn excess profit is limited.

MARKET STRUCTURES AND THE CONSUMER

The effects on consumers of buying from sellers in each of the four market structures should be reviewed. Buyers fare best when facing purely competitive sellers. Not only is price equal to average total cost over the long run, but average total cost is also as low as possible. In pure competition, over the long run no economic profit goes to the sellers, and consumers get the good or service at the lowest possible price.

In monopolistic competition, price is again equal to average total cost in the long run, so that sellers receive no economic profit. But since the demand curve for an individual seller's product is downward sloping, the long-run average total cost of what is offered for sale is not at its lowest possible level. Thus, buyers do not get the good or service at the minimum possible cost, but they pay no economic profit to the seller.

In oligopoly and monopoly the price of a product can remain above its average total cost over the long run. That is, in these market structures, the prices buyers pay may include an economic profit to the seller. Because of this and other manifestations of the market power of oligopolists and

Table 13.2
Conditions Faced by Consumers in Each of the Four Market Structures

Consumers fare best when buying in purely competitive markets: sellers have no control over price, and over the long run, average total cost and price are at their minimum attainable levels and sellers earn no economic profit.

Market Structure	Do Sellers Control Price?	Must Sellers Produce at Minimum Average Total Cost Over the Long Run?	Is Price Necessarily Equal to Minimum Average Total Cost Over the Long Run?	Can Sellers Earn Excess Profit Over the Long Run?
Pure Competition	No	Yes	Yes	No
Monopolistic Competition	Yes: limited control	No	No	No
Oligopoly	Yes: more control than in monopolistic competition	No	No	Yes
Monopoly	Yes: most control	No	No	Yes

monopolists, the government has taken steps from time to time to modify their behavior. Some of those measures are taken up in Chapter Fifteen.[3] Table 13.2 summarizes the conditions faced by consumers buying from firms in each of the four market structures.

SUMMARY

A market is composed of firms selling similar products to the same group of buyers. The boundaries of a market are determined by product substitutability and geographic considerations. The degree of competition in a market influences a firm's pricing and nonprice policies as well as its ability to continually earn economic profit. To analyze competition and its effects, markets can be classified into one of four structures: pure competition, monopolistic competition, oligopoly, and monopoly.

Pure competition is characterized by a large number of independent firms producing identical products in a market that is easy to enter and exit. Individual purely competitive firms have no control over price, which is set by the forces of supply and demand in the market. An individual firm's demand curve is a straight, horizontal line at the market price, indicating that it can sell as much as it wishes at that price but nothing at a higher price. Nonprice competition is nonexistent in purely competitive markets since sellers' products are identical.

Due to easy entry and exit, in the long run a purely competitive seller's price is equal to minimum long-run average total cost, resulting in the lowest possible price that can be charged in the market and no economic profit for

[3]The order of Chapters Fourteen and Fifteen can be reversed for those who wish to immediately take up the question of government influence on market forces.

the firm. From the buyer's point of view this makes pure competition the ideal market structure. In the real world, actual purely competitive markets are difficult to find.

Monopolistic competition is characterized by a large number of sellers producing differentiated products in a market that is fairly easy to enter and exit. Due to product differentiation, individual sellers exercise some control over their prices, resulting in a downward sloping demand curve for each firm's product. This control, however, is limited by the large number of sellers offering buyers similar products. Nonprice competition through advertising, packaging, location, and other methods is important in these markets.

Since entry into and exit from the market is fairly easy, over the long run monopolistic competitors operate where price equals long-run average total cost, resulting in no economic profits. However, these firms do not produce at the lowest point on their long-run average total cost curves, so their prices and costs are higher than they would be if the firms were pure competitors.

Oligopoly is characterized by a few sellers producing identical or differentiated products in a market that is difficult to enter. By virtue of their relatively large size in the market, oligopolists have some control over their prices. But large size also causes the competitive decisions of one firm to affect other firms in its market, giving rise to mutual interdependence among the sellers.

Since mutual interdependence can assume different forms, there are several explanations for oligopoly pricing. Two popular explanations are leadership pricing, which occurs when one firm changes its price and others follow, and the kinked demand curve model, which is based on the assumption that rivals follow price decreases but not price increases. With the entry of potential rivals into the market impeded, oligopolists may be able to charge prices greater than average total cost and earn economic profits over the long run.

Monopoly is characterized by a single seller facing no direct competition in a market that is impossible to enter. All other things being equal, a monopolist has more control over its price than does a firm in any other market structure. Since it is the only seller in its market, the monopolist's demand curve is the market demand curve, and the monopolist chooses the price and output combination on the demand curve that maximizes its profit. With the entry of new rivals blocked, the monopolist can charge a price greater than its average total cost and earn economic profit over the long run.

Key Terms and Concepts

Market structures
Market vs. industry
Pure competition
Barriers to entry
Market demand
Individual firm's demand
Economic profit or loss
Breaking even
Nonprice competition
Long-run profit behavior

Monopolistic competition
Identical vs. differentiated outputs
Oligopoly
Mutual interdependence
Leadership pricing
Kinked demand curve
Monopoly
Natural monopoly
Cartel

Discussion and Review Questions

1. Pure competition is said to be the most competitive of all the market structures. If this is true, why is there no mutual interdependence in pure competition: why is it that no one firm is concerned with what any other firm does?
2. The desirability of advertising is often debated. What arguments can be made that advertising helps the consumer, and what arguments can be made that advertising hurts the consumer? To what extent are these arguments valid or invalid, and why?
3. You have a friend who believes that the automobile industry should be made monopolistically competitive by breaking it into a large number of small firms. Do you agree or disagree with your friend's proposal? Why?
4. Into which of the four market structures would you place each of the following? Why would you make this classification?
   a. A small grain farmer producing wheat on 50 acres
   b. A large grain farmer producing wheat on 2,500 acres
   c. A major airline
   d. A college or university
   e. A local water company that faces no direct competition
   f. A small retail shoe store in a large city
   g. A shoe department in a department store in a large city
5. A market is defined according to geographic considerations and the extent to which buyers view sellers' products as substitutes. What, in your opinion, would be the substitutes and relevant geographic market for each of the following? Be able to defend your answers.
   a. Beer from a small brewery
   b. A four-door automobile made by a large U.S. manufacturer
   c. A ski resort in the Rocky Mountains
   d. A major state university
6. How do firms in each of the four market structures differ in terms of their number of rivals, control over price, product differentiation, and ability to continually earn economic profit?
7. What does it mean for a firm to operate at a profit, a loss, or to break even? What is the relationship between a pure competitor's demand curve and average total cost curve in each of these situations?

8. In the United States, people are increasing their purchases from catalogues and through mail orders. Does this growth in catalogue and mail order businesses increase competition for retail stores, or are these firms in a different market? Explain your reasoning.

Suggested Readings

Walter Adams, ed., *The Structure of American Industry,* 5th ed. (New York: The Macmillan Publishing Co., Inc., 1977). A survey of the operation, structure, history, and other aspects of the auto, computer, beer, physicians' services, and other American industries. The book also includes chapters on conglomerate firms and public policy.

John R. Emshwiller and Neil Behrmann, "How De Beers Revived World Diamond Cartel After Zaire's Pullout," *The Wall Street Journal,* July 7, 1983, pp. 1, 12. A look at the operation of De Beers and the international market for diamonds.

Michael E. Porter, "Ch. 1: The Structural Analysis of Industries," *Competitive Strategy: Techniques for Analyzing Industries and Competitors* (New York: The Free Press, 1980), pp. 3–33. Discusses factors such as barriers to entry and bargaining power of buyers and suppliers that affect competition in an industry.

Roger Sherman, *Antitrust Policies and Issues* (Reading, Mass.: Addison-Wesley Publishing Co., 1978), Ch. 1–2. Explores the growth of corporations, the benefits of competition, the effects of monopoly, and other topics.

Leonard W. Weiss, *Case Studies in American Industry,* 3d ed. (New York: John Wiley and Sons, 1980). Provides an analysis of the operation of purely competitive, oligopolistic, and monopolistically competitive industries, and regulated monopolies, using specific examples. Also included are chapters on introductory material, input markets, and the performance of industries in the economy.

Appendix to Chapter 13
DETERMINING THE PROFIT MAXIMIZING PRICE AND OUTPUT FOR A FIRM

PROFIT MAXIMIZING BEHAVIOR OF A FIRM IN PURE COMPETITION

Given that a firm in pure competition can sell any output it chooses at the market price, how does it determine what quantity it actually will produce and sell? The objective of decision making by a purely competitive firm is to choose the output level that will maximize profit.

In Chapter Eleven it was noted that a firm will maximize its profit by operating where the additional cost and the additional revenue from the last unit produced and sold are equal. That is, the firm will maximize profit by operating where marginal cost equals marginal revenue. Consider how this rule applies to a purely competitive firm.

Table 13A.1 gives some price, quantity, and revenue information for a purely competitive grain farmer operating in a market where the equilibrium

Table 13A.1
Price, Quantity, and Revenue Information for a Purely Competitive Seller

Because a seller in pure competition receives the same price for its product regardless of the quantity demanded, the seller's marginal revenue is always equal to market price.

Price	Quantity Demanded	Total Revenue	Marginal Revenue
$3.00	0	$ 0	
			$3.00
3.00	1	3.00	
			3.00
3.00	2	6.00	
			3.00
3.00	3	9.00	
.	.	.	.
.	.	.	.
.	.	.	.
$3.00	1,001	$3,003.00	.
			$3.00
3.00	1,002	3,006.00	
			3.00
3.00	1,003	3,009.00	
.	.	.	.
.	.	.	.
.	.	.	.
$3.00	8,001	$24,003.00	.
			$3.00
3.00	8,002	24,006.00	
			3.00
3.00	8,003	24,009.00	

price is $3 per bushel. The first two columns of the table list the demand schedule for the farmer's grain which shows that regardless of how much is demanded — be it 3, 1,003, or 8,003 bushels — the farmer receives a price of $3 per bushel. Total revenue, given in the third column, is calculated by multiplying price times quantity demanded at each level of output. Total revenue with a demand of three bushels is $9; with 1,003 bushels it is $3 × 1,003 = $3,009; and so on.

Marginal revenue is determined by calculating the change in total revenue as one more unit of a product is demanded. The marginal revenue figures in Table 13A.1 indicate that each time one more bushel of grain is demanded, marginal revenue is $3. No matter how much or how little is produced, the next unit demanded always adds $3 to the farmer's total revenue. Recalling that $3 is the price at which the farmer can sell each bushel of grain, it can be concluded that in pure competition the firm's marginal revenue is equal to its price.

When graphed, marginal revenue becomes a straight, horizontal line at the equilibrium market price of $3 per bushel. In other words, in pure competition the individual seller's marginal revenue curve is identical to its demand curve.

The marginal cost for a purely competitive seller behaves like the marginal cost discussed in Chapter Twelve. Graphically, it is "fishhook" shaped: as output increases it decreases to a minimum and then increases.

The profit maximizing output for a firm can be found by superimposing its marginal cost curve over its marginal revenue curve. This is done, using the grain farmer as an example, in Figure 13A.1. Notice that the marginal revenue curve is labeled MR = D to indicate that the marginal revenue and demand curves are identical.

To maximize its profit, the firm should produce where its marginal cost curve intersects its marginal revenue curve. This occurs in Figure 13A.1 at point A. Reading down from point A to the horizontal axis, one can see that the profit maximizing output is 6,000 bushels of grain. Reading over to the vertical axis from point A, one can see that the profit maximizing price is $3.

An additional note about profit maximizing behavior is necessary. Up to this point, the marginal cost equals marginal revenue rule has been presented as a guide to lead the firm to maximum profit. But what if a firm is operating at a loss? What if, at every level of output, its costs are greater than its revenues? Here again the marginal cost equals marginal revenue rule leads to the "best" (where best means least bad) output level.

When a firm is producing at the point where marginal cost equals marginal revenue, it is operating at the strongest net revenue position it can reach. Where revenue is greater than costs, this leads to maximum profit, but where revenue falls short of costs, this leads to minimum loss. Thus, whether the firm is trying to maximize its profit or minimize its loss, the decision-making rule is the same: operate where marginal cost equals marginal revenue.

We can determine whether a firm is operating at a profit or loss by measuring whether the cost of producing each unit of output is less or more than

Figure 13A.1
Profit Maximizing Output for a Purely Competitive Seller

Graphically, the purely competitive seller's marginal revenue is identical to its demand, and profit is maximized by operating at the output level where marginal revenue equals marginal cost.

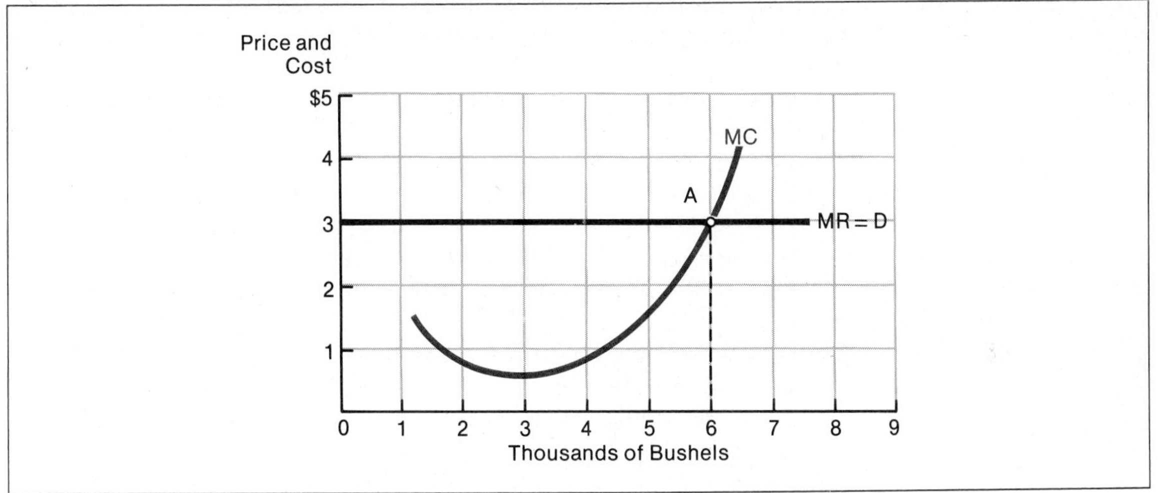

its price. Graphically, this is indicated by whether the average total cost curve lies below or above the demand curve at the output level where marginal cost equals marginal revenue.

Figure 13A.2 shows a grain farmer operating with an economic profit where marginal cost equals marginal revenue. At the maximizing output of 6,000 bushels, the price is \$3 per bushel, and the average total cost is only \$2 per bushel. In this case the farmer is earning an economic profit of \$1 per bushel, or \$6,000 in total economic profit (\$1 × 6,000 bushels).

Figure 13A.3 shows a grain farmer operating at a loss where marginal cost equals marginal revenue. At the loss minimizing output of 6,000 bushels, the cost per bushel is \$4 and the price received only \$3. The farmer is taking a loss of \$1 per bushel, or a total loss of \$6,000.

Thus, economic profit is maximized if price is greater than cost per unit, or if the average total cost curve lies below the demand curve at the output where marginal cost equals marginal revenue. A minimum loss is incurred if cost per unit is greater than price, or if the average total cost curve is above the demand curve at the output where marginal cost equals marginal revenue.

PROFIT MAXIMIZING BEHAVIOR OF A FIRM WITH A DOWNWARD SLOPING DEMAND CURVE

If a firm faces a downward sloping demand curve, at what price-output combination, or point on its demand curve, will it choose to operate? If the firm is maximizing profit (or minimizing a loss), it will produce the output at

Figure 13A.2
Purely Competitive Seller Maximizing Profit

If a purely competitive seller's demand curve is above its average total cost curve, it will maximize profit by operating at the output level where marginal revenue equals marginal cost.

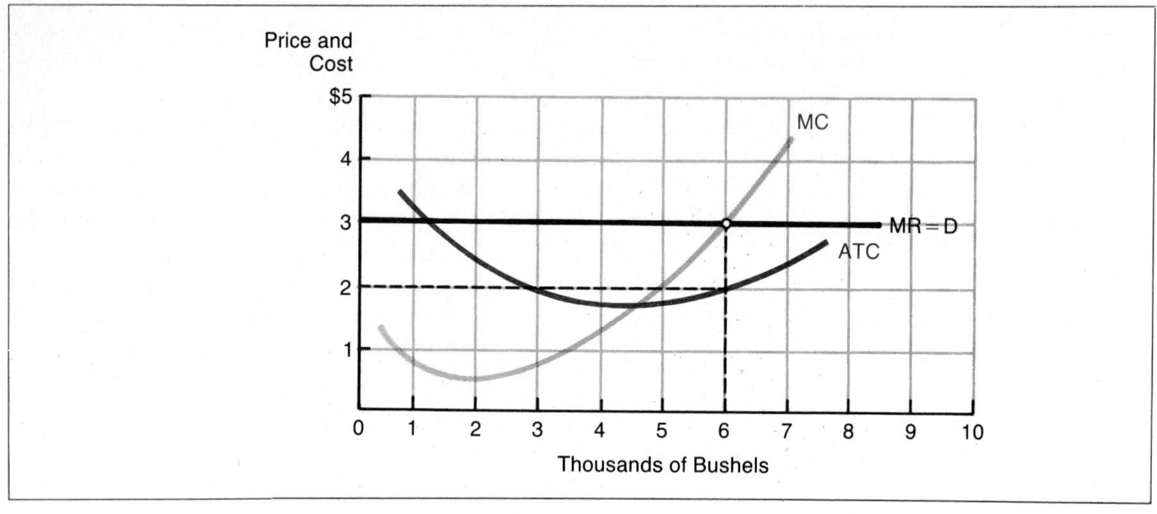

Figure 13A.3
Purely Competitive Seller Minimizing a Loss

If a purely competitive seller's demand curve is below its average total cost curve, it will minimize its loss by operating at the output level where marginal revenue equals marginal cost.

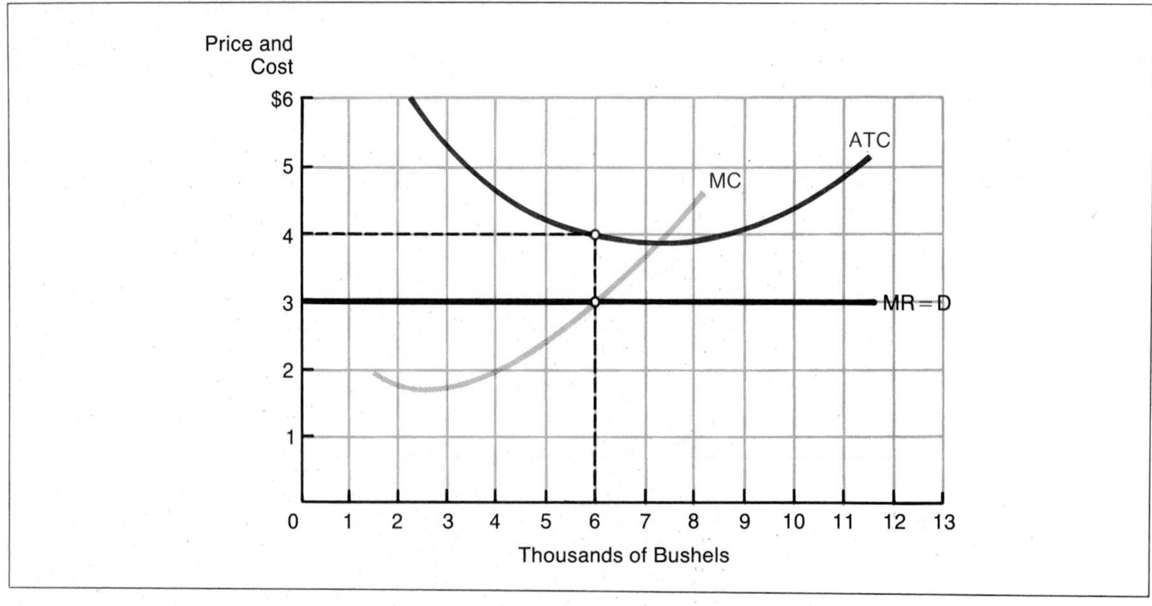

which marginal cost equals marginal revenue, and charge the price given by the demand curve at that output.

A firm with a downward sloping demand curve, where more can be sold only by lowering price, faces demand conditions identical to those given in the example in Chapter Eleven of the jeweler selling pocket watch cases. Table 11.4 showed that with demand behaving in this way, the jeweler's marginal revenue from each unit sold was less than its price. Since price is shown on the demand curve, and since marginal revenue is less than price, the jeweler's marginal revenue curve for pocket watch cases must be below its demand curve. Similarly, any firm with a downward sloping demand curve has its marginal revenue curve lying below its demand curve. To illustrate this principle, Table 11.4 is reproduced in footnote 1, along with the demand and marginal revenue curves associated with that table.[1]

The marginal cost curve for a seller with a downward sloping demand curve is like that for any type of firm: it decreases to a minimum and then

---

[1]Jeweler's Revenues from Selling Pocket Watch Cases

P	Q Demanded	TR	MR
$45,000	0	$ 0	
			$40,000
40,000	1	40,000	
			30,000
35,000	2	70,000	
			20,000
30,000	3	90,000	
			10,000
25,000	4	100,000	

The downward sloping demand curve, shown below, is found by plotting price and quantity demanded from the table. The marginal revenue curve below is found by plotting the numbers in the marginal revenue column. Remember, marginal revenue is plotted midway between the quantities. For example, the marginal revenue of $40,000 for the first unit is plotted at one-half unit.

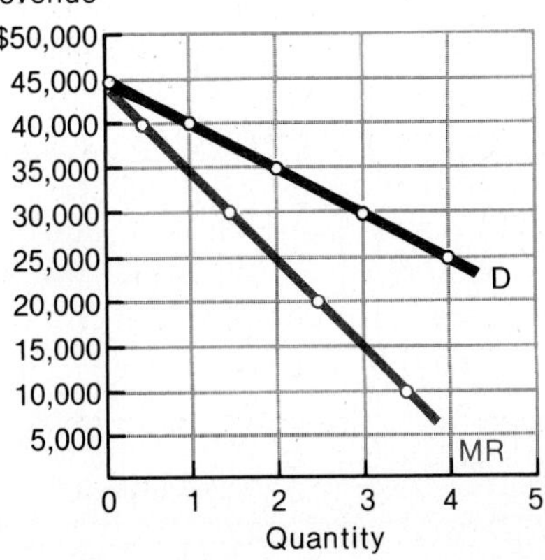

Figure 13A.4
Profit Maximizing Output for a Firm with a Downward Sloping Demand Curve

The rule for maximizing profit is the same for a firm with a downward sloping demand curve as it is for a firm in pure competition: operate at the output level where marginal revenue equals marginal cost.

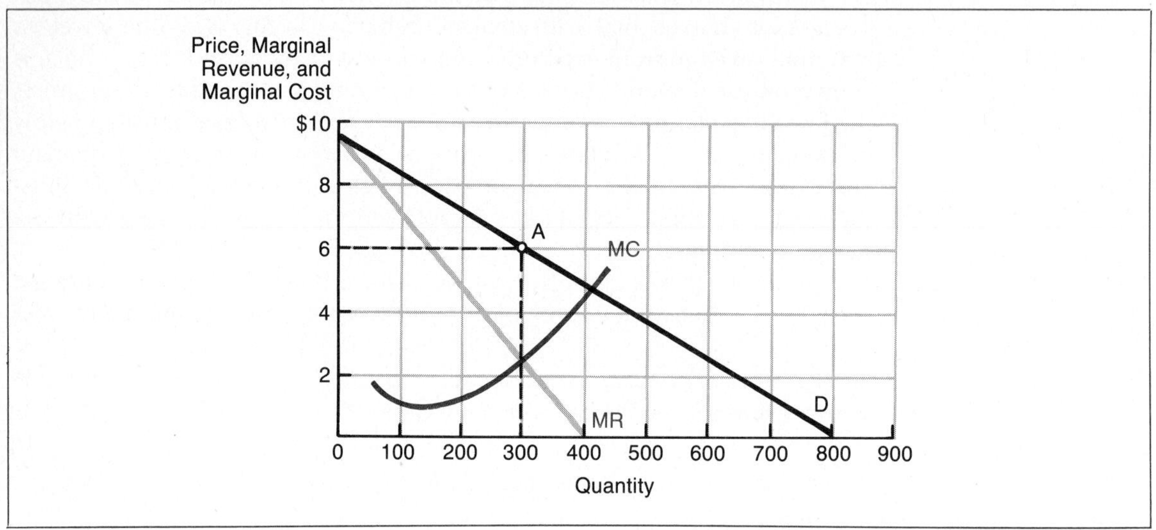

increases. The demand, marginal revenue, and marginal cost curves illustrated in Figure 13A.4 are representative of those for a firm with a downward sloping demand curve.

To determine the profit maximizing position for the seller in Figure 13A.4, the intersection of its marginal cost and marginal revenue curves must be located. To find the profit maximizing output, one reads from the point where marginal cost equals marginal revenue to the quantity axis. The profit maximizing output is 300 units. The profit maximizing price is found by reading up from the intersection where marginal cost equals marginal revenue to the demand curve, and from the demand curve to the vertical axis. For this seller, the profit maximizing price is $6 per unit. Thus, point A on the demand curve shows the profit maximizing position for this seller.

As is the case with a purely competitive firm, whether a firm with a downward sloping demand curve is operating with an economic profit or a loss depends upon the relationship between price and average total cost at the output level where marginal cost and marginal revenue are equal. If the average total cost curve lies below the demand curve, economic profit is maximized, and if the average total cost curve lies above the demand curve, the firm is incurring a minimum loss.

14 LABOR MARKETS, UNIONS, AND THE DISTRIBUTION OF INCOME

Chapter Objectives

1. To understand the reasons for the downward slope of a labor demand curve.
2. To explain, using a basic supply and demand model, how wage rates are determined, and to explain the real world considerations that modify the model.
3. To discuss the types and structure of unions, the process of collective bargaining, and major legislation affecting labor.
4. To examine the distribution of income in the United States and discuss some explanations for that distribution.
5. To define poverty, and to identify the poverty population in the United States and some government programs for alleviating poverty.

In Chapter Thirteen we learned how the prices of goods and services are determined in different types of output, or product, markets. In these markets businesses supply their goods and services to buyers, who may be households, governments, or other businesses.

In order to produce the outputs they intend to sell, firms need land, labor, capital, and entrepreneurship. These factors of production are acquired in resource, or input, markets. In these markets, as in output markets, prices are determined basically by the forces of supply and demand. But unlike output markets, in input markets businesses are the primary buyers.

While there are input markets for land, labor, capital, and entrepreneurship, this chapter focuses on the operation of labor markets. One reason for concentrating on labor markets is that wages, salaries, and other labor income constitute the vast majority of income generated in the U.S. economy. Over the last 25 years, labor income has accounted for about 70 percent of all income.[1] Labor markets also merit special attention because they are affected by important institutional forces such as unions and laws regulating wages and working conditions.

The first section of this chapter introduces a simple demand and supply model of a labor market, an explanation of the factors determining the demand for and supply of labor, and some complications that modify the simple model. Unions, union membership, and collective bargaining are discussed in the second section. The last section of the chapter presents a survey of the distribution of income, some explanations of why individuals' earnings differ, and an examination of poverty in the United States.

LABOR MARKETS

In a market system, as just noted, labor is bought and sold in the same manner as are goods and services: through the interaction of demand and supply. In the case of labor, however, businesses are the primary buyers and individuals in households are the sellers.

Wage
The price of labor.

The price of labor is called its **wage.** If someone works for a wage rate of $6.72 an hour, this is the price at which that person is willing to sell his or her labor, and the price at which a buyer is willing to acquire that labor.

Figure 14.1 gives a basic supply and demand model for wage determination, using as an example a competitive market for workers who produce an item we will call good B. The vertical axis of the figure is labeled wage rate (price), and the horizontal axis gives the quantity of labor demanded and supplied. In this particular market, the equilibrium wage rate is $4.75 an hour, and the number of workers employed is 600.

According to Figure 14.1, the demand curve for labor is downward sloping, and the supply curve of labor is upward sloping; buyers are willing to hire more labor as the wage rate falls, and more labor is offered in the market as the wage rate increases. Why is this so?

The Demand for Labor

Derived demand
The demand for a factor of production depends upon the demand for the good or service the factor produces.

The demand for labor, or for any other factor of production, is a **derived demand,** meaning that it is derived from, or depends on, the demand for the good or service the factor produces. Auto workers have jobs because automobiles are demanded; grocery clerks are employed because families buy groceries; and the professors who teach your courses do so only because students enroll in them.

---

[1]See Table 10.2, page 279.

Figure 14.1
Market for Good B Workers

In a competitive market for labor, there is a downward sloping demand curve and an upward sloping supply curve for workers.

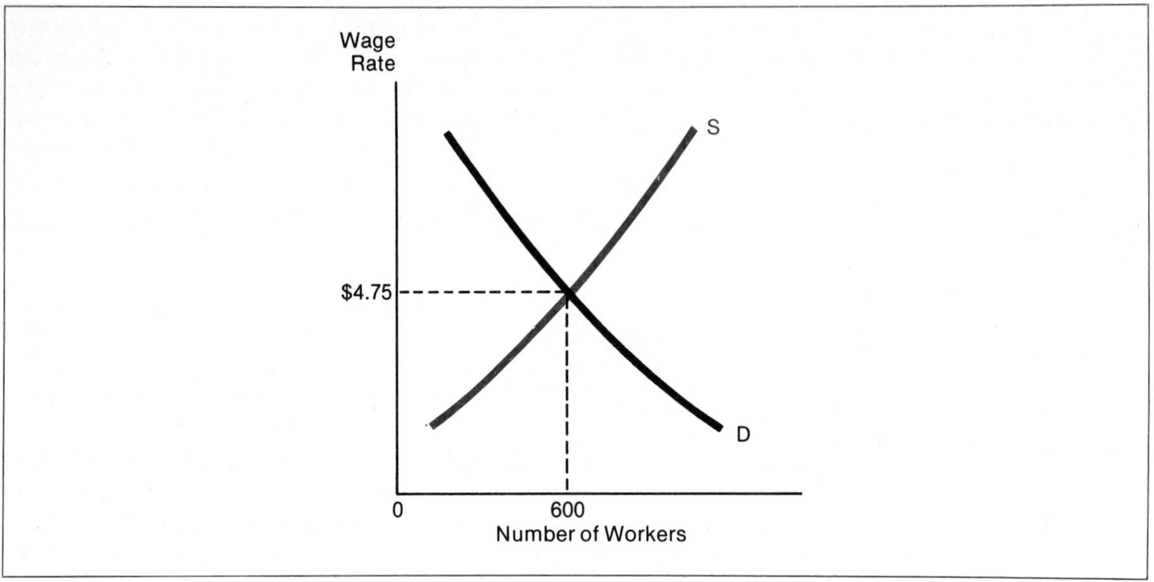

From the point of view of an individual firm, the wage rate that the firm is willing to pay for a unit of labor is based on the dollar value of the labor's productivity—that is, what the worker's product is worth in dollars to the company. An employee whose daily product is valued at $50 will not be paid $75 per day. In fact, the company will not be willing to pay the employee over $50 a day. No firm can afford to hire at a wage rate greater than the employee's dollar contribution to the company. A restaurant that is willing to pay $4 an hour to each of the six waiters it employs, determines this rate based on the value of the waiters' productivity. Baseball players offered in excess of $500,000 annually command that amount largely because of their expected financial contributions to their teams. Outstanding players attract fans who purchase tickets to ball games and increase revenues for the clubs.

As seen in Figure 14.1, the typical market demand curve for labor is downward sloping. This demand curve behaves as it does because each individual firm's demand curve for labor is downward sloping: a firm is willing to hire more labor when the wage rate falls and less labor when the wage rate increases.[2] If the amount a firm is willing to pay for labor is based upon the dollar value of workers' productivity, then the slope of the demand curve

[2]Recall from Chapter Three that market demand curves are found by adding together individual demand curves.

Table 14.1
Total Product and Marginal Physical Product of Labor for a Producer of Good X

As more workers are hired, after some point the Law of Diminishing Returns causes each additional worker's marginal physical product to decline.

Number of Workers	Total Product	Marginal Physical Product
0	0	
		100
1	100	
		80
2	180	
		60
3	240	
		40
4	280	
		20
5	300	
		0
6	300	

indicates that the dollar value of labor's productivity falls as more labor is hired. Why is this so?

The declining value of productivity and the resulting downward sloping demand curve for labor occur for two reasons: (1) decreasing marginal productivity as more labor is hired; and (2) the need to lower product price in order to increase the quantity of a good or service demanded.

Law of Diminishing Returns
As additional units of a variable factor are added to a fixed factor, beyond some point the additional product from each additional unit of the variable factor decreases.

Marginal physical product
The change in total product that results when an additional unit of labor or other variable resource is utilized.

Labor Demand and Productivity In discussing the pattern of short-run production costs in Chapter Twelve, the **Law of Diminishing Returns** was introduced. This law says that the extra (marginal) product from adding successive units of a variable resource to a fixed resource diminishes beyond some point. In other words, as more of a variable resource is used, at some point that resource's marginal product falls. This concept applies to labor.

Table 14.1 provides an example of a hypothetical company varying the amount of labor it utilizes to produce good X. The second column of the table shows the total product (TP) that results when a specific number of workers is employed: for example, four workers together produce 280 units of good X. The third column gives the **marginal physical product** (MPP) of each additional unit of labor. The marginal physical product is the additional physical output produced when one more worker is hired; or, put differently, marginal physical product is the change in total product resulting from the utilization of an additional unit of labor. In Table 14.1 the second worker has a marginal physical product of 80 units of good X (total product of 180 − 100), and the fifth worker has a marginal physical product of 20 units (total product of 300 − 280).

The most important observation from Table 14.1 is that marginal physical product declines as more workers are used.[3] This decline is significant to the

[3]In this example it is assumed that diminishing returns set in after the first worker. This is not always the case.

company employing the labor because it shows that, due to the Law of Diminishing Returns, each additional unit of labor utilized produces less and is therefore worth less to the firm.

Declining marginal productivity can be found in almost all work situations. Imagine the limited productivity of a baseball team's third, fourth, or fifth catcher! A restaurant will find that at some point the marginal productivity of its waiters declines as more and more are employed. And a high school that hires several assistant principals may find each successive one adding less to total product.

Labor Demand and Product Price The second reason for the declining value of labor's productivity and the resulting downward sloping labor demand curve is the price–quantity demanded relationship for the good or service the factor is producing.

In all market situations, except pure competition, firms face downward sloping demand curves for their products: consumers will increase their purchases of a company's product only if the price falls. This downward sloping demand curve for the good or service labor produces causes the value of labor's productivity to decrease, since the increased output resulting from hiring more workers can be sold only at lower prices. Thus, additional units of labor are worth less to the company because the product they produce is sold for less.

To illustrate this point, Table 14.2 gives the total product information presented in Table 14.1 for the producer of good X. It also includes a third column listing the prices at which good X can be sold. The price and total product columns reflect the inverse relationship between price and quantity demanded: if the company intends to sell more and more of its product, it must lower the price. And by lowering price, it decreases the value of what labor produces.

In short, the demand curve for labor is downward sloping because the marginal productivity of each additional unit of labor decreases, and because the value of additional production is diminished by the decline in price necessary to sell the product. In other words, the Law of Diminishing Returns and the Law of Demand combine to determine the value of labor.

Table 14.2
A Good X Producer's Total Product and Price per Unit of Good X

A firm facing a downward sloping demand curve for its product can sell the increased total product that results from hiring more workers only if it lowers the price.

Number of Workers	Total Product	Price per Unit
0	0	$6.25
1	100	6.00
2	180	5.75
3	240	5.50
4	280	5.25
5	300	5.00
6	300	5.00

Table 14.3
A Good X Producer's Total Product, Price, and Revenue

Marginal revenue product is the change in total revenue that results when one more unit of a variable factor such as labor is utilized.

Number of Workers	Total Product	Price per Unit	Total Revenue	Marginal Revenue Product
0	0	$6.25	$ 0	
				$600
1	100	6.00	600	
				435
2	180	5.75	1,035	
				285
3	240	5.50	1,320	
				150
4	280	5.25	1,470	
				30
5	300	5.00	1,500	
				0
6	300	5.00	1,500	

Combining Declining Marginal Productivity and Declining Product Price It is possible to combine the effects of declining marginal productivity and decreasing product price to determine what each unit of labor is worth to a company, or the wage rate a firm is actually willing to pay. This is done in Table 14.3, which returns to the good X example and adds two columns to those given in Table 14.2.

The fourth column of Table 14.3 gives the total revenue (TR) received when various amounts of good X are sold. (Remember: total revenue is price times quantity.) For example, with a total production of 240 units that can be sold for $5.50 each, a total revenue of $1,320 (240 × $5.50) is received.

Marginal revenue product
The change in total revenue that results when one more unit of labor or other variable resource is utilized.

The last column of Table 14.3 is labeled **marginal revenue product** (MRP). Marginal revenue product is the change in total revenue that results when one more unit of labor (or other variable resource) is utilized.[4] When one worker is hired, 100 units of good X are produced and sold for $6 each, bringing in $600 for the company. Since the total revenue with no workers is $0, the marginal revenue product of the first worker is $600. When a second unit of labor is employed, 180 units of output are produced and sold for $5.75 each, creating a total revenue of $1,035. Thus, when the second worker is utilized, the company's total revenue increases from $600 to $1,035, or the second unit of labor brings in an additional $435 in total revenue. $435 is the marginal revenue product of the second worker. For the third unit of labor, the marginal revenue product is $285 because total revenue increases from $1,035 to $1,320. The marginal revenue product of the fourth worker is $150, and of the fifth worker is $30.

Marginal revenue product is important because it determines the firm's demand curve for labor. In the example in Table 14.3, this firm would not

[4]Be careful to distinguish this from marginal revenue, which is the change in total revenue when one more unit of *output* is sold.

be willing to hire any labor if the wage rate were above $600, say, $700. In this case, the wage paid would be greater than the extra revenue created by the production of any worker. The producer would, however, be willing to hire one worker at a wage rate of $600. At $600 the first worker's contribution (marginal revenue product) equals his or her wage rate.

When would the producer of good X consider hiring two units of labor? The wage rate would need to fall to $435, the marginal revenue product of the second worker, before the producer would hire two units of labor. At any wage higher than $435, the second worker's contribution to the firm's revenue (marginal revenue product) would be less than the wage. For three units of labor to be employed, the wage rate must fall to $285, the marginal revenue product of the third worker. At any higher wage, the third worker would not contribute enough to the firm's revenue to cover his or her wage. Four workers would be demanded at a wage of $150, and five at $30.

When the wage rates and the amounts of labor the good X producer is willing to hire at each of those rates are plotted in a graph, the firm's demand curve for labor results. This is given in Figure 14.2. Notice that the demand curve is equal to the marginal revenue product of labor.

Application 14.1, "Computer Games," concerns a study to determine whether the high salaries paid to some baseball players are justified. The author of the study used such factors as attendance at home games and hot dog sales to determine a player's marginal revenue product.

Changes in the Demand for Labor

In any labor market, certain changes can occur that will cause the demand for labor to increase or decrease and the demand curve for labor to shift to the right or left. When these changes in demand take place, the equilibrium wage rate and amount of labor hired are affected. An increase in the demand for labor, for example, causes the demand curve to shift to the right, resulting

Application 14.1
COMPUTER GAMES

Critics say that economists know the price of everything and the value of nothing. But Paul M. Sommers, an economist at Vermont's Middlebury College who seems to know both, is arguing that baseball owners who have paid huge prices for free agents have got value for their money. Assistant Professor Sommers concluded this after studying the original 25 free agents of 1976. Included were Outfielder Reggie Jackson, Relief Pitcher Rollie Fingers and several stars hampered by injuries in the ensuing year. Sommers' key finding: the free agents more than earned their keep during the season that followed their signing. Jackson, for example, was easily worth the $400,000 salary that the New York Yankees paid him.

Figure 14.2
A Firm's Demand for Good X Workers

A firm's demand for labor is based on the marginal revenue product of labor, which declines as additional workers are hired.

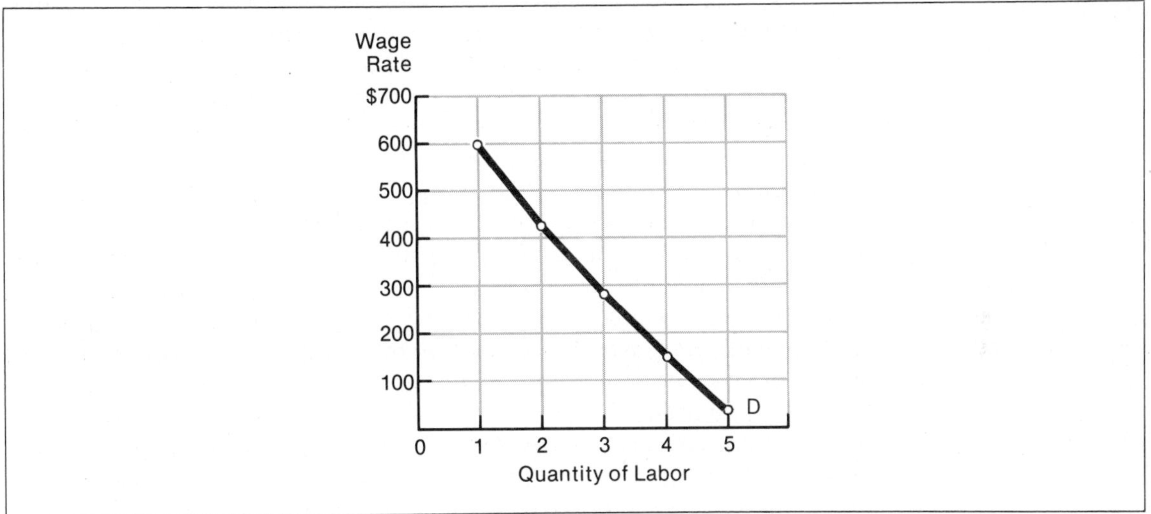

in an increase in both the equilibrium wage rate and the number of workers employed. (Work this through graphically to satisfy yourself that it is correct.)

Several factors cause the demand curve for labor to shift. Notable among these are changes in the prices of substitute inputs, technology, and changes in the demand for the good or service the labor is producing. Let us consider each of these.

Sommers used an econometric model to measure the "marginal revenue product" of the players. He fed such facts as the players' on-field performance plus the attendance at home games and the number of hot dogs sold at the ballpark into a computer that measured costs against income. The study . . . showed that five of the top 14 players brought in nearly triple their annual salary in extra earnings for the owners. Yogi Berra probably never talked to Casey Stengel about his "marginal revenue product," but Yankee Owner George Steinbrenner undoubtedly understands. Says he: "You measure a ballplayer's value by how many fannies he puts in the seats."

Source: "Computer Games," *Time*, November 30, 1981, p. 69.

Because of the profit motive, businesses seek the least-cost method of production and are continually assessing the cost and utilization of their inputs. If a good or service can be produced with either labor or machinery, a firm will obviously choose the cheaper alternative. This means that if one type of input that can be substituted for another becomes less expensive, the demand for the more expensive input will be lessened.

Take restaurant dishwashing—a task that can be accomplished by a machine or by hand—as an example. If restaurants are primarily using labor, and if automatic dishwashers begin to fall in price, the demand curve for labor to perform this task will shift to the left as restaurants make the switch to machinery. There are many other examples: cheaper assembly-line robots will decrease the demand for assembly-line workers, less expensive toll booths with self coin-deposit machines will decrease the demand for persons to collect tolls, and an increase in day care center fees will increase the demand for nannies.

Technology increases the demand for some types of labor while decreasing the demand for others. The advent of the computer age has created and increased a demand for different types of data processing personnel such as programmers and systems analysts. At the same time, computers have altered the inventory process for many retailers, bringing with it a decrease in the demand for workers to determine the stock on hand. Also, checkout by computer in many grocery stores has eliminated the need for persons to hand stamp each grocery item.

Finally, a change in the demand for the good or service a type of labor is producing may change the demand for that labor. When the demand for automobiles is down and sales are falling, companies cut back on their production, causing the demand curve for auto workers to shift to the left. As the school age population drops, the demand for primary and secondary education falls, and with it, the demand for teachers. When the fast food industry entered its growth stage and the public wanted more burgers, fries, and tacos, the demand for fast food employees increased.

Changes in Demand and Changes in Quantity Demanded The distinction made in Chapter Three between a change in demand and a change in quantity demanded applies to the demand for labor. We have seen that a **change in the demand for labor** refers to a shift of the entire demand curve to the right or left as a result of changes in such factors as the prices of substitute inputs, technology, and product demand. A **change in the quantity of labor demanded** occurs only as a result of a change in the wage rate (price) of labor. With a change in quantity demanded, the firm moves from one wage rate–quantity combination on its demand curve to another. For example, if the wage rate increased from $435 to $600 on the demand curve in Figure 14.2, the quantity of labor demanded would fall from two workers to one.

Change in the demand for labor
A shift in the demand curve for labor caused by changes in factors other than the wage rate.

Change in the quantity of labor demanded
A change in the amount of labor demanded that occurs when the wage rate changes.

Figure 14.3
Supply Curve for Labor

A typical labor market supply curve indicates that a direct relationship exists between wage rates and the quantity of labor supplied.

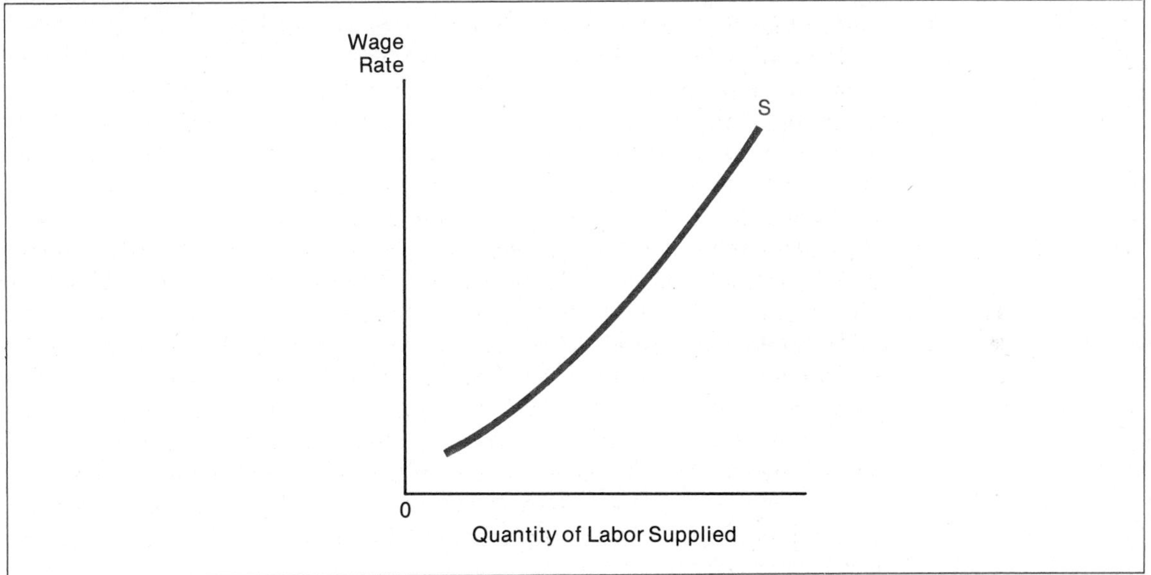

The Supply of Labor

In a typical labor market there is a direct relationship between the wage rate and the quantity of labor supplied, causing the labor supply curve to slope upward like that given in Figure 14.3. This relationship says that less labor will be attracted to a market at a lower wage rate than at a higher wage rate. In short, more people are willing to work for a higher wage.

In a labor market, many important factors other than wage or salary influence the supply curve, or the amount of labor available for a job; money may be only part of the consideration in seeking a particular type of employment. These nonwage factors include psychological rewards, locational preferences, long-term work objectives, overall economic conditions, and other considerations.

Many people seek a position that gives them a "psychic" income; that is, they seek a job that is psychologically rewarding in some way. The psychological reward could be in the form of prestige, self-fulfillment, a sense of accomplishment, or freedom from authoritative direction. Such a reward can induce people to work for a lower wage than would otherwise be the case. A scientist, for example, might prefer to receive a smaller salary from a prestigious university in order to teach and do independent research than to take employment at a higher wage in a corporate laboratory. A free-lance writer might sell material for a paltry sum because he or she receives a psychic reward from having an article in print.

Location affects the supply of labor in some markets. In a small town with a few major employers, workers face limited choices among labor markets. When earning a higher salary means leaving home, family, and friends, many people are willing to work at a lower wage. Likewise, when there are many job opportunities in an area, workers can be more selective and sensitive to wage rates.

The possibility of long-term gains can influence the availability of labor. A college graduate may take a position with an employer at a lower salary than that offered by other employers because the potential for future advancement is great or because the job will look good on a résumé.

Economic conditions also affect the supply of labor. A recession, for example, may force members of a household who are not its primary income earners into labor markets as they attempt to fill in the income lost by the unemployed head of their household. Other factors affecting supply include: the safety, cleanliness, and working conditions on a job; the degree of skill or formal training required; the need to obtain a license to work; and the fulfillment of certain jobs by sex role models (such as male plumbers and female secretaries).

Application 14.2
WORKING

The book Working *by Studs Terkel contains individual interviews about jobs and working that the author had with over 125 people in many different occupations. Each of the following excerpts focuses on some nonwage aspect of a person's job and comes from a different interview in this book.*

From Carl Murray Bates, Stonemason:
I get a lot of phone calls when I get home: how about showin' me how and I'll do it myself? I always wind up doin' it for 'em. (Laughs.) So I take a lot of pride in it and I do get, oh, I'd say, a lot of praise or whatever you want to call it. I don't suppose anybody, however much he's recognized, wouldn't like to be recognized a little more. I think I'm pretty well recognized. . . .

Stone's my life. I daydream all the time, most times it's on stone. Oh, I'm gonna build me a stone cabin down on the Green River. I'm gonna build stone cabinets in the kitchen. That stone door's gonna be awful heavy and I don't know how to attach the hinges. I've got to figure out how to make a stone roof. That's the kind of thing. All my dreams, it seems like it's got to have a piece of rock mixed in it.

From Beryl Simpson,
Employment Counselor and former Airlines Reservationist:
I had much more status when I was working for the airlines than I have now. I was always introduced as Beryl Simpson, who works for the airlines. Now I'm reduced to plain old Beryl Simpson. I found this with boyfriends. I knew one who never dates a girl with a name. He never dates Judy, he never dates Joan. He dates a stewardess or a model. He picks girls for the glamor

Application 14.2 gives excerpts from the book *Working*, by Studs Terkel. These excerpts focus on some of the nonwage factors that people interviewed for the book mentioned about their jobs and working.

Modifications of the Labor Supply and Demand Model

The labor market model introduced in Figure 14.1 at the beginning of the chapter is a useful starting point for analyzing how wages are determined through the forces of supply and demand. But just as there are imperfections in output markets, there are certain factors at work in real world labor markets that go beyond what is explained in the simple supply and demand model, and have an impact on the determination of wages and the amount of labor employed. Three of these factors — wage rigidities, legal considerations, and unequal bargaining power—merit special consideration.

Wage Rigidities In a labor market such as that shown in Figure 14.1, a decrease in the demand for labor would shift the demand curve to the left, causing fewer workers to be hired and the equilibrium wage rate to fall. In reality, a decrease in the demand for labor will most likely cause employment to drop, but not wages. Firms whose sales have fallen usually respond

of their jobs. He never tells you their names. When I was with the airlines, I was introduced by my company's name. Now I'm just plain old everyday me, thank God.

From Vincent Maher, Policeman:
Each child has a dream. I had two. One was to be a marine and the other was to be a policeman. I tried other endeavors but I was just not cut out for it. I am a policeman. It is one of the most gratifying jobs in the world. . . .

When I worked as a bartender, I felt like a nonperson. I was actually nothing. I was a nobody going nowhere. I was in a state of limbo. I had no hopes, no dreams, no ups, no downs, nothing. Being a policeman gives me the challenge in life that I want. Some day I'll be promoted. Somebody's gonna say, "Maher has had it for a long time. Let's give him something." Some sort of recognition. I've proven myself. I don't think it's necessary for a man to prove himself over and over and over again. I'm a policeman, win, lose, or draw.

From Eugene Russell, Piano Tuner:
I don't think I'll ever retire. I'm like the window washer who was asked, "Do you enjoy washing windows?" He said, "No, I don't." They said, "Why don't you quit your job?" He said, "What else is there to do?" (Laughs.) I love that.

(Quickly.) Of course, I enjoy my work. And I know others in the field have a high opinion of me.

Source: *Working: People Talk About What They Do All Day And How They Feel About What They Do*, by Studs Terkel.

by laying workers off rather than by lowering their wages. On the supply side, contrary to the operation of the simple model, an increase in the number of workers in a market (a shift of the supply curve to the right) may not lower the wage rate. Thus, money wages tend to adjust upward but not downward to changing labor market conditions.

There are several reasons why wages tend not to fall. First, some workers are earning the minimum wage, and by law their employers can pay them no less. Second, an employer may be bound by a labor agreement to pay workers a certain wage below which the employer cannot go. Third, it may be in a worker's best interest to be laid off rather than to take a cut in pay. When laid off, a worker may become eligible for unemployment compensation, can use the idle time to secure an alternative source of income, and will not be acknowledging to an employer that he or she is willing to work for less.

Minimum wage law
Legislation that specifies the lowest hourly earnings that an employer may pay an employee.

Legal Considerations Labor markets are affected by legislation that influences wages and the demand for and supply of labor. The most obvious example of legislation affecting wages is the **minimum wage law.** By specifying the minimum hourly earnings a worker can receive, this law can override the operation of a free market by not allowing the wage rate to fall to its equilibrium level.

Figure 14.4 shows the influence of the minimum wage law on a market. The equilibrium wage rate in Figure 14.4 is $3 per hour, and the equilibrium employment is 220 workers. If the government establishes a minimum wage above the equilibrium rate, say, $4 per hour, employers will want to hire fewer than 220 workers—in this case, 180 workers. On the supply side, at the minimum wage of $4, more than 220 workers, in fact, 240 workers, will be available. As a result, a surplus of labor will develop in the market; in this case the surplus will be 60 workers (240 − 180). Many critics of minimum wage legislation point out that it causes unemployment in some labor markets. The graphics in Figure 14.4 suggest this is so.

Some legislation can change the demand for labor. For example, the minimum wage law may reduce the demand for a certain type of labor if it makes the employment of those workers more costly than the purchase and use of a piece of machinery that performs the same task. Rules, such as those of the Occupational Safety and Health Administration (OSHA) that specify safety and working conditions, may affect employers' costs of using labor and in turn their demand for labor. There are also laws relating to the hiring of special groups in the labor force, such as women and minorities, that influence labor demand.

The supply of labor is also affected by various laws. Licensing and certification requirements for physicians, beauticians, and others performing personal services have an impact on the supply of labor. Laws limiting the amount persons can earn while on social security, laws pertaining to unem-

Figure 14.4
Effect of a Minimum Wage on a Labor Market

When the equilibrium wage rate in a labor market is lower than the minimum wage, the minimum wage prevails, and a surplus of workers results in that market.

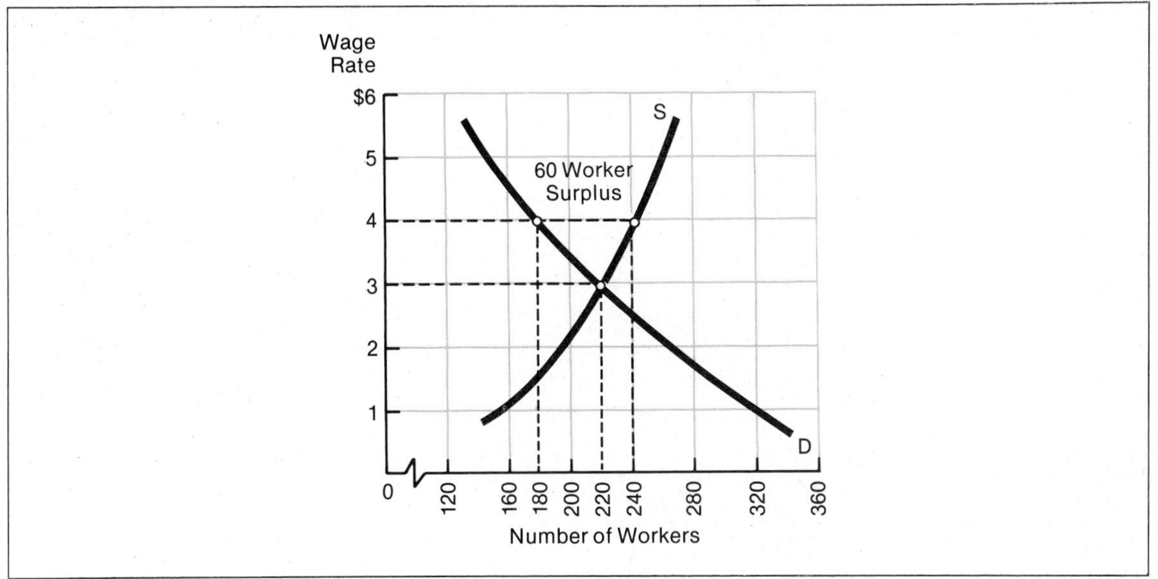

ployment compensation, and legislation such as child labor laws also affect the supply of labor.

Unequal Bargaining Power The equilibrium wage rate of $4.75 in the labor market in Figure 14.1 was determined by employers and employees who had equal bargaining power. In many markets this is not the case. In some instances the employer has greater strength than the employees in determining wages, and in others the employees exert more power.

If the bargaining power is on the side of the buyer (the firm), the wage will likely be below that set when both parties are of equal strength. For example, workers living in a town with one major employer may be paid a lower wage rate than they would be paid if there were several firms competing for their services. In general, the fewer the alternative employers from which workers can choose, the weaker the workers' bargaining power.

If the bargaining strength is on the side of labor suppliers, the wage will likely be above that set when buyers and sellers have equal power. In general, the greater their control over the labor available to a particular employer, the greater the suppliers' ability to raise wages above the competitive level. The primary method used by workers to marshal their strength to raise wages is unionization.

UNIONS

Union
An organization of workers that bargains in its members' behalf with management on wages, working conditions, fringe benefits, and other work-related issues.

A **union** is an organization of workers that bargains in its members' behalf with management. The main areas of concern for unions in representing their members are wages, working conditions, fringe benefits such as health insurance and pensions, rules relating to seniority, layoffs and firings, and the clarification of tasks to be performed. Unions in the United States are primarily economic in their focus. There is some political activity such as endorsing candidates and presenting a point of view to the government, but by and large, the main emphasis is on bargaining with employers in behalf of a union's membership.

Types of Unions and Union Membership

The fraction of the nonagricultural labor force belonging to unions has not been stable over the years. Union membership as a percentage of nonagricultural employment grew in importance through the 1930s and 1940s, accounted for over 30 percent of nonagricultural employment through much of the 1940s and 1950s, and has fallen in importance since the 1950s. By 1978, only 23.6 percent of nonagricultural employees belonged to a union.[5]

Craft union
A union that represents workers with a specific skill or craft.

Labor unions fall into two categories: craft unions and industrial unions. **Craft unions** restrict their membership to workers who possess specific skills, such as bricklayers or plumbers. Thus, for example, bricklayers on a particular construction job would be represented by one union and plumbers on the same job by another.

A craft union may require that its members complete an apprenticeship program or meet some other entrance requirement. By setting such conditions on the practice of the occupation it represents, the union has some control over the supply of workers, and may thus be better able to keep its members' wages and fringe benefits above what they would be if there were open competition for jobs. This can be seen in a simple supply and demand model for wage determination. Any action that restricts supply (shifts the supply curve to the left) results in a higher wage rate. This result is shown in Figure 14.5, where a decrease in the supply of labor from S1 to S2 leads to an increase in the wage rate from W_1 to W_2. Notice also that this action lessens employment, in this case reducing it from Q_1 to Q_2.

Industrial union
A union that represents all workers in a specific industry regardless of the type of job performed.

An **industrial union,** rather than limiting itself to workers with a single skill, seeks to represent all of the workers in a specific industry. For example, workers performing different jobs in the automobile industry may be represented by the United Auto Workers, communications workers performing different tasks may be represented by a single union, and so may steel workers. Thus, when it comes to membership, craft unions are narrow in their focus while industrial unions are not.

---

[5]Source: For 1930–1945: U.S. Bureau of the Census, *Historical Statistics of the United States, Colonial Times to 1957,* Washington, D.C., 1960, p. 98. For 1950–1978: U.S. Bureau of the Census, *Statistical Abstract of the United States: 1984* (104th ed.), Washington, D.C., 1983, p. 439.

Figure 14.5
Restriction of Supply in a Labor Market

By limiting the supply of labor, which is shown by a shift of the supply curve to the left from S1 to S2, a craft union can obtain higher wages for its members than they would earn if entrance into the occupation were not restricted.

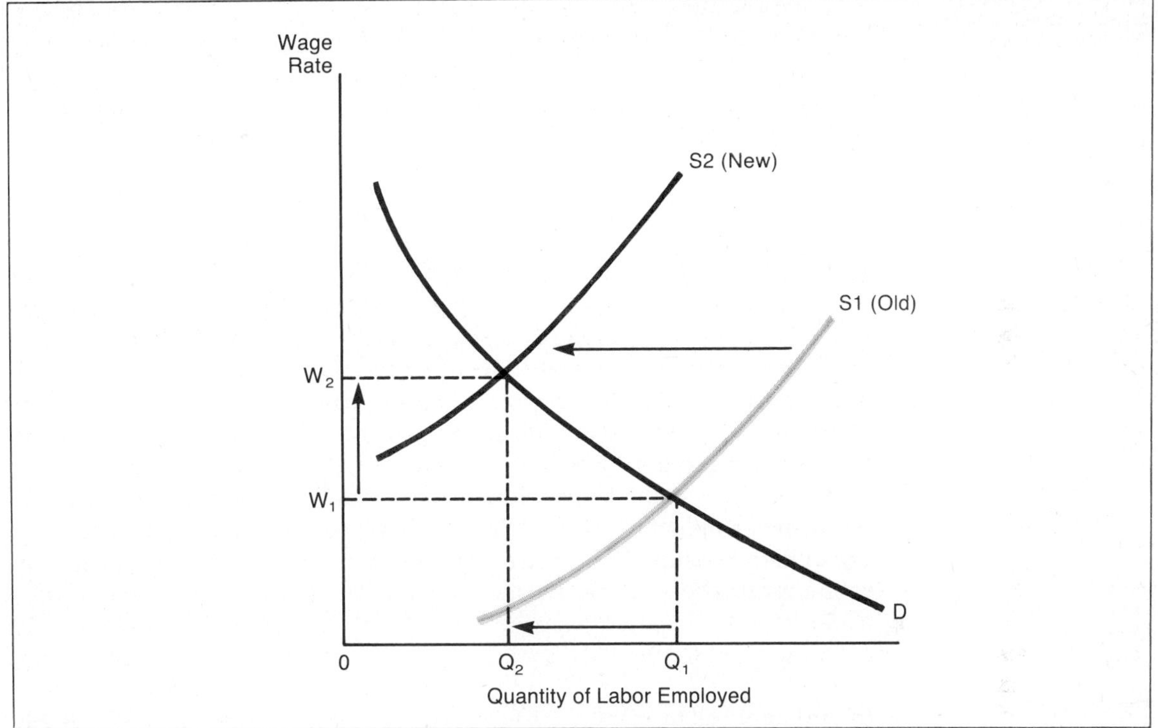

A union, whether craft or industrial, is typically headed by a national or international organization that operates in behalf of all of the members. Below this headquarters organization are individual locals to which the members belong. In some cases, such as musicians, members who work for different employers in a particular area belong to the same local. In other cases, such as auto workers, a local represents members working for a single employer or in a single plant.

Although each union faces its own unique problems in bargaining for wages and working conditions, there are several interests, such as developing educational programs on unionism and supporting or opposing worker-related legislation, that unions have in common. In an effort to further their common interests, labor unions have formed umbrella organizations to which they can belong. The best known of these is the **American Federation of Labor-Congress of Industrial Organizations: the AFL-CIO.** The AFL-CIO is actually two organizations that have merged. The American Federation of Labor dates back to 1886 and was formed with a craft union

AFL-CIO
An organization for furthering the common interests of labor unions; does not engage in bargaining with management.

Table 14.4
The Ten Largest Unions According to Membership

Some unions in the United States have a sizable membership: over 1 million workers.

Union	Membership in 1980
Teamsters	1,891,000
National Education Association	1,684,000
Automobile Workers	1,357,000
Food and Commercial Workers	1,300,000
Steel Workers	1,238,000
State, County and Municipal Employees	1,098,000
Electrical (International Brotherhood of Electrical Workers)	1,041,000
Carpenters	784,000
Machinists	754,000
Service Employees	650,000

Source: U.S. Bureau of the Census, *Statistical Abstract of the United States: 1984* (104th ed.), Washington, D.C., 1983, p. 440.

orientation. The Congress of Industrial Organizations was formed with an industrial union orientation after several unions split from the AFL in the 1930s. In 1955 the two organizations joined to form the AFL-CIO. Not all unions belong to the AFL-CIO.

Some unions in the United States have a sizable membership; several represent over a million workers. Table 14.4 ranks the ten largest unions according to membership. The largest two, the Teamsters and the National Education Association, are "independent" and do not belong to the AFL-CIO.

Collective Bargaining and Strikes

In the simple labor market model, wages are set by the interaction of supply and demand. With unions, the process of wage determination is more complicated. Wages are still established by supply and demand in the sense that a union represents the suppliers of labor, and management represents a business demanding labor. But now the impersonal forces of the market are replaced by negotiations between union and management representatives seeking to reach an agreement on wages, fringe benefits, and other aspects of a labor contract. This process in which a union negotiates a contract in behalf of its members is referred to as **collective bargaining.**

Collective bargaining
The process through which a union and management negotiate a labor contract.

The objectives bargained for by a union and management in a negotiation are primarily economic: wages, retirement income, payments for health care, and such. But the actual bargaining process itself is largely political. That is, negotiation involves a give-and-take process where each side tries to gain the most of what it seeks while giving up the least. Union representatives go into a negotiation with a list of objectives they want to attain. Management does the same. As the contracting develops, each side may give way on some of its objectives in return for the other side's acceptance of other objectives that are of greater importance. Thus, the terms of a negotiated contract depend in large part on the relative bargaining ability and strength of the participating parties. The greater the ability or strength of one side to withstand the other's demands, the more likely it is that the contract will go in its favor.

If the parties to a negotiation fail to agree on the terms of a contract within a certain amount of time, the union may go on strike against the employer. With a **strike,** union members stop working and ordinarily set up a picket line that other workers may refuse to cross. The purpose of the strike is to bring economic pressure on the employer to return to the bargaining table and draft an agreement more acceptable to the union than the one discussed when the workers walked out.

Strike
Work stoppage by union members.

A strike is not a riskless strategy for a union to follow, and its effect on the outcome of the bargaining depends largely on which side is able to endure the strike the longest. For rank-and-file union members, this is determined by their ability to manage without a paycheck from the struck employer. Such factors as the union's strike fund, alternative employment, accumulated personal savings, and the income of other family members affect this capability.

For the employer, the capacity to withstand a strike depends upon management's ability to minimize its effect on the company's operations and profit. Management might respond to a strike by assuming the tasks performed by union workers or by "living off" accumulated production inventories. Also, lower operating costs from not having to pay the striking workers help offset the effect of any lost revenue resulting from the work stoppage.

If a strike becomes more costly than a business is prepared to absorb, its management may agree to contract terms that previously would have been unacceptable. If the union finds that the strike is not having the desired effect, its representatives may do the same.

Collective Bargaining and the Law

Over the years a large body of laws has developed concerning the rights and responsibilities of labor unions in collective bargaining and related matters. Two such laws that have been especially important in establishing and defining these rights and responsibilities are the National Labor Relations Act of 1935 and the Labor Management Relations Act, better known as the Taft-Hartley Act, of 1947.

National Labor Relations Act (Wagner Act)
Legislation supportive of unionization; strengthens collective bargaining.

Passed in the depths of the depression, the **National Labor Relations Act** (also called the **Wagner Act**) strongly supports organized labor. It contributes to unionization in three ways. First, the law specifically gives workers the right to organize and bargain collectively, to choose who will represent them in their collective bargaining, and to carry out "concerted activities" for collective bargaining or other purposes that would advance their interests. Second, the law defines certain actions by employers that are considered to be unfair labor practices. For example, it would be unfair for an employer to interfere in the organizing or operation of a labor union, to discriminate against employees on the basis of their membership in a union, or to refuse to enter into contract negotiations with a representative chosen by a majority of the employees. Third, the act created the **National Labor Relations Board (NLRB),** which hears complaints on unfair labor practices, and can order that those practices cease and be remedied where they are found to exist.[6]

National Labor Relations Board (NLRB)
Hears complaints on unfair labor practices and orders remedies where appropriate.

Taft-Hartley Act
The 1947 legislation that contains several provisions limiting union activities.

The **Taft-Hartley Act** of 1947 became law in a much different environment than that in which the National Labor Relations Act was passed. The year 1946 was particularly troublesome for work stoppages. While the total number of stoppages was not exceptionally large, the number of idle worker-days as a result of those stoppages — 116 million days — was much greater than at other times.[7] It was in this setting that the Taft-Hartley Act was passed. The law in part amends the National Labor Relations Act and is generally less supportive of organized labor than the 1935 legislation.

The Taft-Hartley Act limits union activities in several ways. First, while the National Labor Relations Act gives workers the right to organize or join a union and to bargain collectively, under certain circumstances the Taft-Hartley Act gives workers the right to not join a union or otherwise engage in organized labor activities. One aspect of this right is spelled out in Section 14(b) of the law, which says that union membership cannot be a condition of employment in states that have passed laws to that effect. With membership not required as a condition of work, a union's ability to control the supply of labor is diminished, and the union's bargaining strength is weakened. This is better known as the "right to work" issue, and the state laws prohibiting union membership as a condition of employment are called **right to work laws.**

Right to work laws
State laws prohibiting union membership as a condition of employment.

Second, while the National Labor Relations Act defines unfair labor practices for employers, the Taft-Hartley Act defines similar practices for labor organizations. For example, unions cannot induce employers to discriminate against certain employees, nor can they refuse to negotiate with employers, charge excessive or discriminatory fees to new members, or require employers to pay for services that have not been rendered.

Third, the Taft-Hartley Act allows the president of the United States to impose an 80-day "cooling-off period" during which a particular strike or lockout (when an employer prevents laborers from entering a work site) cannot occur if, in the president's opinion, the work stoppage is a threat to the national interest. If, after 80 days, the situation leading to the strike or lockout is not corrected, the ban is lifted, and the work stoppage can continue.[8]

---

[6] *United States Statutes at Large,* Vol. 49, Pt 1, *Public Acts and Resolutions* (Washington, D.C.: U.S. Government Printing Office, 1936), pp. 452–454.

[7] U.S. Bureau of the Census, *Historical Statistics of the United States, Colonial Times to 1957,* Washington, D.C., 1960, p. 99.

[8] *United States Statutes at Large,* Vol. 61, Pt 1, *Public Laws Reorganization Plans Proposed Amendment to the Constitution* (Washington, D.C.: U.S. Government Printing Office, 1948), pp. 136, 140–142, 151, 155–156.

Table 14.5
Division of Total Income Among Families

Income is not distributed evenly among families in the U.S. In 1983 the poorest one-fifth of U.S. families earned 4.7 percent of total income while the richest one-fifth earned 42.7 percent of the total.

	Percent of Total Income		
Percent of Families	**1963**	**1973**	**1983**
Lowest 20%	5.0%	5.5%	4.7%
Second 20%	12.1	11.9	11.1
Middle 20%	17.7	17.5	17.1
Fourth 20%	24.0	24.0	24.4
Highest 20%	41.2	41.1	42.7
Total	100.0	100.0	100.0

Source: 1963 from U.S. Bureau of the Census, *Historical Statistics of the United States, Colonial Times to 1970, Bicentennial Edition, Part 2,* Washington, D.C., 1975, p. 293. 1973 from U.S. Bureau of the Census, *Statistical Abstract of the United States: 1978* (99th ed.), Washington, D.C., 1978, p. 455. 1983 from *Statistical Abstract of the United States: 1985,* p. 448.

THE DISTRIBUTION OF INCOME

Distribution of income
The way in which income is divided among the members of a society.

The **distribution of income** is the way income is divided among the members of society. It reflects the extent to which individuals share in the rewards from the production of goods and services.

One of the main questions in evaluating the distribution of income centers on equality. Were the distribution of income to individuals perfectly equal, everyone would receive the same amount: no one would earn more or less than anyone else. But income is obviously not divided equally among the members of society. Some persons or families are better or worse off than others; and at the extremes, some are very rich and others are very poor.

One method for analyzing the distribution of income in the United States is illustrated in Table 14.5. In the first column of this table, families are divided into five groups according to the amount of income they received. Each group represents 20 percent of all families. The lowest group represents the 20 percent of all families that received the lowest incomes, and the highest group is the 20 percent of all families that received the largest incomes. The remaining columns of the table give the percent of total income that went to each of the five groups in 1963, 1973, and 1983.

With an equal distribution of income among families, each of the five groups would have received 20 percent of the total income. However, in each of the years shown in Table 14.5, the lowest 20 percent received less than 6 percent of the total income, while the highest 20 percent of the families had claim to over 40 percent.[9]

Obviously, not all members of society fare equally well in the distribution of income: some are more likely to be at the lower or higher ends than oth-

[9]Over the past 25 years the distribution of income has varied little as measured according to the quintile method in Table 14.5. Data for sample years since 1960 indicate that the poorest 20 percent of all families received between 4.7 percent and 5.6 percent of total income, while the richest 20 percent received between 40.4 percent and 42.7 percent. See: data sources for Table 14.5.

Table 14.6
Average Family Income by Characteristics of Family Heads in 1983

The average income going to families differs according to the education, occupation, and other characteristics of the family head.

Characteristics	Average Family Income[a]
Education of family head	
0–8 grades	$ 8,870
High school diploma	20,000
College degree	35,000
Occupation of family head	
Manager	35,000
Craftsman or foreman	22,075
Operative, labor, or service worker	14,000
Race of family head	
Caucasian	21,000
Nonwhite and Hispanic	12,722
Stage of life of family head	
Under 45 years of age, unmarried with no children	15,000
Under 45 years of age, married with children	25,800

[a]Average family income is median income.

Source: Robert G. Avery et al., "Survey of Consumer Finances: 1983," *Federal Reserve Bulletin* (September 1984), p. 682.

ers. In Chapter Ten it was noted that, on the average, household heads with certain characteristics tend to earn more than household heads with other characteristics.[10] For example, male household heads typically earn more than female household heads. Evaluating the status of these various groups provides a second method for analyzing the distribution of income. The average family income in 1983 according to selected characteristics of family heads is summarized in Table 14.6.

In comparing occupations, one sees that families headed by a manager received more income than families headed by a person in another occupation. The data also show that, overall, households headed by white persons fared better than those headed by nonwhite persons, and households headed by a college graduate fared better than those headed by an individual with less education.

Explanations for the Distribution of Income

Why is income distributed as it is? Why do some households enjoy a large annual income while others do not? There is no single answer to these questions. Some explanations for the distribution of income focus on differences in the income-earning abilities of individuals, while others focus on factors separate from the individuals themselves. In this section we will look at five of the many explanations for the variations in income: differences in pro-

[10]See page 278 and Table 10.4 on page 280.

ductive resources, human capital investments, discrimination, bargaining power, and inheritance.

Differences in Productive Resources One explanation for the distribution of income—differences in productive resources—is based on the simple premise that income depends upon the quality and quantity of the productive resources that individuals possess, and the uses to which those resources are put. When factors of production differ in quality, the outputs from those factors may differ. Because of this, the owners of superior resources stand to earn more money. For example, an outstanding athlete may be more highly paid than teammates with less impressive performances; a highly productive salesperson will probably earn more on commission than less productive fellow workers; and an acre of farmland in the heart of Illinois should generate more income from the production of soybeans than an acre in the hills of Pennsylvania.

Variations in income may also be traced to differences in the quantity of resources that individuals possess. All other things being equal, you would expect a person owning many productive factors to earn a greater income than one possessing few resources. A family that has a highly skilled household head, owns farmland, an apartment complex, and blue-chip stocks will have a higher income than a family that receives its only income from the labor of a highly skilled household head.

Differences in the income from productive resources may also be due to the ways in which individuals choose to use their resources. Consider two people equally skilled at gardening. If one goes to work for an exclusive landscaping contractor while the other chooses to become a grounds keeper for the city, differences in their incomes may appear because of the different choices they made about using their talents.

Human Capital Investments The concept of investment for productivity gains is usually associated with expenditures on machinery, equipment, factories, and technological advances that increase production. In certain respects, people are like machines: their productive capabilities are influenced by what is invested in maintaining and improving themselves. The notion of **human capital investment** refers to the concept that people can affect their productivity, and therefore their income, through money spent for education, training, health care, and other means of self-improvement.

Human capital investment
An expenditure made to improve the productivity of a person.

The impact on income from investing in oneself is suggested by the figures shown at the top of Table 14.6, where the average incomes of families are listed according to the years of education of the family head.[11] Not surprisingly, there is a direct relationship between education and income:

[11]In reading the figures at the top of Table 14.6, remember that all things other than formal education were not held constant. That is, there may be factors other than education that were important in determining income.

greater investments in education are associated with larger average incomes. Families headed by an individual with no more than an eighth grade education on the average earned only $8,870 in 1983, roughly 25 percent of the $35,000 average income for families headed by a person with a college degree.

Human capital expenditures take several different forms. The most obvious is formal education, but training acquired at trade schools and on the job is important, too. Human capital investments also involve less obvious expenditures, such as those for health care. The healthier a worker, the greater his or her ability is to perform tasks effectively and maintain a low absence rate, both of which contribute to higher productivity. In this vein, some companies are encouraging exercise and paying employees to quit smoking or to lose weight. Health care expenditures as a human capital investment are not limited to those incurred while working. The type of health care an individual receives in his or her youth affects productivity and income-earning ability in later years.

Discrimination
Unequal treatment in a labor market because of an employer's perception of a worker.

Discrimination Workers experience **discrimination** when they are treated unequally in the labor market because they are placed in different categories and judged on the basis of the employer's perception of the category to which they belong, rather than on the basis of their skills or productive capabilities. In the United States, concern over discrimination centers mainly on the labor market experiences of nonwhite as compared to white workers, female as compared to male workers, and older as compared to prime-age workers. But discrimination can be based on any type of categorical distinction between workers, such as religious or political preference, or ethnic origin.

Discrimination shows itself in several different ways. It occurs where a worker, because of race, age, sex, or such, receives less pay than others for equal work. It also occurs where a worker, because of race, age, sex, or such, has a smaller or otherwise less desirable selection of employment opportunities from which to choose.

The effects of discrimination on income can also be indirect. For example, unequal access to good housing, medical care, or educational opportunities might lead to smaller or less productive human capital investments, which in turn can result in lower incomes. Affirmative action programs and the Equal Employment Opportunity Commission have been created in the United States in an effort to reduce discrimination and its effects.

Bargaining Power Income can be raised by bargaining power, which is the ability of a labor supplier to withhold resources from the buyer if the supplier does not receive a satisfactory income. Control over the supply of labor may be exercised by a union bargaining for an entire group of workers or by a single individual who has a unique talent that is in strong demand. Part of this explanation for the distribution of income was covered in the discussion of collective bargaining earlier in this chapter.

Inheritance According to another explanation for the distribution of income—inheritance—a person can receive income not from his or her own labor but as the beneficiary of someone else's effort. Typically, this income is from the ownership of inherited capital, real estate, natural resources, or securities.

A Word of Caution A word of caution is in order regarding these various explanations for the distribution of income. Several of the factors just discussed may simultaneously affect the income pattern for an individual or group of persons in society. For example, the income of a prime-age male worker might be greater than that of a prime-age female worker because of sex discrimination. But the variation could also be due to differences in the amount of time spent by men and women in the labor force or the kinds of human capital investments each makes. On the other hand, the types of human capital investments men and women make may be influenced by the existence of sex discrimination in the labor market. In short, any one explanation for the distribution of income does not rule out the remaining explanations and, what is more, the different explanations may be related.

Poverty

In Table 14.5 it was shown that, in 1983, income was distributed in such a way that the lowest 20 percent of all families received only 4.7 percent of the total income, and the next lowest 20 percent received only 11.1 percent. Are these families considered to be the "poor" in our society?

What is meant by "poor"? In general, poverty is based on a person's level of material well-being: the type of housing, clothing, and food that can be afforded, and the ability to acquire medical care, recreation, reading materials, and other goods and services. However, to label a person or household as poor is a value judgment. Each of us has a different concept of poverty. What constitutes being poor to someone living a comfortable existence may be different from the definition of poverty given by an average income earner. One who drives a late-model, expensive automobile may view as poor a person who drives an old, obviously used car. One who drives an old, used auto may view as poor a person who can afford no car at all.

Government Measures of Poverty In order to calculate an "official" measure of poverty in the United States, the federal government has created a series of income measures called poverty levels. These **poverty levels** are based primarily on family size and indicate the amounts of annual money income that must be received to be considered *not* poor. Any individual or family receiving an income below its designated level is classified as poor and is included in government poverty statistics.

Poverty levels
Government designated levels of income that must be received to be considered *not* poor.

Table 14.7 gives the average annual poverty levels for families and individuals in 1970 and 1983. The table shows that the poverty levels increase

Table 14.7
Poverty Levels for Families and Individuals

Poverty levels vary according to family size and age of the householder, and indicate the annual money income that must be received to be considered *not* poor.

Size of Unit	Income Level[a] 1970	1983
1 person	$1,954	$ 5,061
under 65 years	2,010	5,180
65 years and over	1,861	4,775
2 persons	2,525	6,483
householder under 65 years	2,604	6,697
householder 65 years and over	2,348	6,023
3 persons	3,099	7,938
4 persons	3,968	10,178
5 persons	4,680	12,049
6 persons	5,260	13,630

[a]1970 and 1983 data are not strictly comparable because of revised procedures; figures are a weighted average.

Source: U.S. Bureau of the Census, *Statistical Abstract of the United States:* 1985 (105th ed.), Washington, D.C., 1984, p. 429.

as the number of persons in a family increases, and that the measures vary according to whether or not the head is under 65 years of age.

In 1983, 35.3 million persons, or 15.2 percent of the total population, lived in poverty—that is, in households where the money income fell below the poverty levels. Table 14.8 on page 420 gives some characteristics of this 1983 poverty population. Notice, for example, that many of these 35.3 million persons were aged and children, and that many lived in families in central cities. Also, not shown in the table, in poverty-level families headed by a male or by a female with a husband present, the head worked full-time in

Application 14.3
NEW DATA CHANGE IMAGE OF POVERTY

[N]ew long-term studies question the prevailing belief that the poor form a permanent underclass in the United States that is perpetuated by welfare and a "culture of poverty."

A survey by the University of Michigan's Institute for Social Research in Ann Arbor shows that one in four people in this country lived in a family that required at least some welfare income between 1969 and 1978. Many of those who accepted government aid returned to self-sufficiency within a year or two, the researchers found. Only about 2 percent of the population depended heavily on welfare for more than seven of 10 years.

Many people on all rungs of the economic ladder experience "tremendous changes" in family composition, income and employment, says survey director Greg J. Duncan. As a result, welfare touches many lives.

About half of those who required welfare during the 1970s had a short-term need. "Many families receiving welfare . . . were in the early stages of recovery from an economic crisis caused by the death, departure or disability of the fami-

39.7 percent of the cases in 1982. And, over 50 percent of those who did not work were ill, disabled, or unable to find a job.[12] These facts, combined with the information in Table 14.8, should dispel the belief that the poor are poor simply because they choose not to work. There is a large number of working poor and a large number of poor who are unable to work because of age or disability. Application 14.3, "New Data Change Image of Poverty," gives further evidence against the beliefs that people continually remain in poverty and that poor children grow to be poor adults.

There has been some disagreement over the definitions of the official poverty levels. Many argue that the levels are too low and do not represent a true measure of poverty. For example, according to Table 14.7, in 1983 the poverty level for a family of four was $10,178 — far below the median family income of $24,580.[13] Also, according to the poverty levels in Table 14.7, a family of three persons earning $7,939 in 1983 would not have been "poor" because their income was $1 above the poverty line.

Some argue that the poverty income levels overstate the plight of the poor because they do not account for in-kind transfers (the receipt of noncash benefits such as food stamps or medical care) that improve one's material standard of living. For example, using the money income poverty level approach in Table 14.7, 15.2 percent of the population was below the pov-

[12]U.S. Bureau of the Census, *Statistical Abstract of the United States: 1985* (105th ed.), Washington, D.C., 1984, p. 458.

[13]U.S. Bureau of the Census, *Statistical Abstract of the United States: 1985* (105th ed.), Washington, D.C., 1984, p. 446.

---

ly's major wage earner," notes Duncan. Government assistance helped these people over a temporary rough spot.

In their annual interviews with individuals from a representative national sample of 5,000 families, Duncan and colleagues Richard D. Coe and Martha S. Hill also found that most of the children raised in families receiving welfare do not themselves go on welfare after leaving home.

. . . One-third of the welfare-dependent population is old (over 65) or lives in families headed by the old; about 40 percent live in households headed by single women with children at home; two-thirds live in the South, mostly in rural areas.

In a book based on the survey, *Years of Poverty, Years of Plenty,* Duncan says that traditional one-time surveys of national poverty cannot track patterns of family economic change. The U.S. Census Bureau, for example, has found that the size of the richest, middle-income and poorest segments of the population remains fairly stable, but the Michigan study shows that membership in these segments changes significantly from year to year. . . .

Source: B. Bower, "New data change image of poverty," *Science News,* March 17, 1984, p. 169. Reprinted with permission from SCIENCE NEWS, the weekly newsmagazine of science, copyright 1984 by Science Service, Inc.

Table 14.8
Some Characteristics of Persons Living Below the Poverty Levels

Many of the poor are children, elderly, and persons living in central cities. Many are unable to work because of age or disability.

Characteristics	Numbers in 1983
Number of persons living below poverty levels	35.3 million
Percent of the total population	15.2%
Number of below poverty-level families inside central cities	2.7 million
Percent of families inside central cities	16.3%
Number of children under 16 years of age below the poverty levels	12.5 million
Percent of children under 16 years of age	22.7%
Number of persons 65 years and older below the poverty levels	3.7 million
Percent of persons 65 years and older	14.1%
Number of below poverty-level families where the head completed less than 8 years of education	1.3 million
Percent of families where the head completed less than 8 years of education	27.6%
Number of below poverty-level families where the head completed one or more years of college	1.0 million
Percent of families where the head completed one or more years of college	4.7%

Source: U.S. Bureau of the Census, *Statistical Abstract of the United States: 1985* (105th ed.), Washington, D.C., 1984, pp. 456, 458.

erty levels in 1983. However, if government noncash transfer payments for food and housing (such as food stamps and subsidized rental housing) were added to people's money incomes, then 13.8 percent of the population would have fallen below the poverty levels. And, if to that were added government noncash transfers for medical care, then 10.5 percent of the population would have been below the poverty levels.[14]

Government Programs and Poverty Government outlays to individuals and households in the form of cash transfer payments and in-kind benefits are substantial. These payments and benefits include social security, unemployment compensation, food stamps, medical care, vocational rehabilitation, public assistance, job training, and others. Among these, there is no single program aimed specifically at persons living below the poverty levels. Rather, each federal and state program has its own eligibility requirements for which a poor person may qualify. For example, a poverty-level retired couple could be eligible for social security if they made payments into the system, or a low income could entitle a household to food stamps. One problem with government programs is that some, such as social security or unemployment compensation, are closed to the poor who have no regular

[14]U.S. Bureau of the Census, *Statistical Abstract of the United States: 1985* (105th ed.), Washington, D.C., 1984, p. 459. The values of noncash transfers are based on the purchase prices of the goods in the private market.

Table 14.9
Average Monthly Payments from Various Government Programs

There are many government cash and in-kind benefit programs. Each program has its own eligibility requirements, and the actual amount of the benefit from some programs can differ significantly from state to state.

Government Program	Average Monthly Payment in 1983
Aid to Families with Dependent Children	
Per family	$320
Per recipient	109
Food Stamps (average monthly value per recipient)	43[a]
Supplemental Security Income	
For the disabled	245
For the aged	158
For the blind	256
Social Security	
Retired workers	441[a]
Disabled workers	456[a]
Children of disabled workers	136
Federal Civil Service Retirement	
Age and service	1,150
Disability	851
Black Lung Benefit	
Miner's family	441
Widow's family	315
Unemployment Compensation	516[b]

[a]Preliminary value.
[b]Figure is for 1982.

Source: U.S. Bureau of the Census, *Statistical Abstract of the United States: 1985* (105th ed.), Washington, D.C., 1984, pp. 123, 365, 366, 370, 374, 376, 379.

employment. As a result, some government benefits may not be received by poverty-level families.

For those living under the poverty levels, the most likely source of government cash transfers is public aid, which includes such programs as old-age assistance, general assistance, and aid to families with dependent children (AFDC). Table 14.9 lists the average monthly payments for various government programs in 1983. The first few listed are those most likely to be received by someone living in poverty. Notice that the average monthly payment for a family with dependent children was $320, or $109 per recipient. In practice this payment varies from state to state, causing considerable deviation from the average. For example, in Mississippi the average family monthly payment in 1982 was $89, while in Alaska it was $516.[15]

SUMMARY

The prices of land, labor, capital, and entrepreneurship are determined basically by the forces of supply and demand, with businesses as the primary buyers. The demand for labor and all other inputs is derived from the demand for the goods or services that the inputs produce.

[15]U.S. Bureau of the Census, *Statistical Abstract of the United States: 1985* (105th ed.), Washington, D.C., 1984, p. 381.

The demand curve for labor is downward sloping because of diminishing marginal productivity, and because of the need to lower output prices to increase sales in all but purely competitive markets. The labor demand curve for an individual firm is equal to the marginal revenue product of its labor.

A change in the demand for labor is shown by a shift of the demand curve to the right or left, and results from changes in such factors as the prices of substitute inputs, technology, and product demand. A change in the quantity of labor demanded results from a change in the wage rate.

The market supply curve of labor is upward sloping, indicating a direct relationship between the wage rate and the amount of labor offered in the market. The supply of labor is affected not only by the wage rate, but also by other factors such as psychic income and locational preference.

The simple supply and demand approach to the market for labor can be modified to account for certain real world considerations. Wage rigidities, legislation, and unequal bargaining power influence the determination of wages.

A union is a workers' organization that bargains in its members' behalf with management on such matters as wages, fringe benefits, and working conditions. The number of workers represented by unions has been changing over the years. A craft union represents workers who possess a particular skill, while an industrial union represents workers who perform different jobs in a particular industry. Unions are structured around a headquarters organization with locals to which the members belong.

The process through which union contracts are negotiated is called collective bargaining. A strike may occur if the parties to a negotiation fail to reach an agreement on a contract. A strike, designed to bring economic pressure on a business firm, is not without risk to a union, and its effect depends largely on whether the union members or the employer can survive the work stoppage the longest.

Two important laws affect collective bargaining: the National Labor Relations Act (Wagner Act) of 1935, and the Labor Management Relations Act (Taft-Hartley Act) of 1947. The National Labor Relations Act is basically supportive of unionism, while the Taft-Hartley Act serves in several ways as a limiting force on unionism.

Income distribution refers to how income is divided among the members of society. In the United States, families with the lowest incomes receive less than a proportional share of the total, while those with the highest incomes receive more than a proportional share. There are many explanations as to why income is distributed as it is. Some of these include: differences in productive resources, human capital investments, discrimination, bargaining power, and inheritance.

The U.S. government has created an official measure of poverty in the United States. The basis for defining poverty is an annual money income level, which varies according to the size of the family. Many of the poor in the United States are old, children, or in a household headed by a person who is employed. Of the government programs providing cash transfers to families, the most likely to be received by a poverty-level household is public aid.

Key Terms and Concepts

Wage
Derived demand
Marginal physical product
Diminishing marginal productivity
Marginal revenue product
Changes in the demand and the quantity demanded of labor
Nonwage influences on supply
Wage determination
Minimum wage law
Union
Craft union
Industrial union
AFL-CIO
Collective bargaining
National Labor Relations Act
Taft-Hartley Act
Right to work laws
Distribution of income
Human capital investment
Discrimination
Poverty levels

Discussion and Review Questions

1. What would be the effect of each of the following on Company X's demand for labor? (Remember the distinction between a change in demand and a change in quantity demanded.)
   a. An increase in the price of Company X's major competitor's product
   b. A decrease in the price of an input that can be substituted for Company X's work force
   c. A decrease in the number of buyers in Company X's product market
   d. A decrease in the price of Company X's product
   e. An increase in the wage paid to Company X's workers
2. The history of organized labor shows that at certain times the laws and courts have supported unions, while at other times they have not. How might this shifting back and forth in the government's position on unions be explained?
3. Sometimes a business makes investments in machinery and equipment and those investments do not pay off—the business does not recover its costs plus something more. Is it possible for an individual to make a human capital investment that does not pay off? In making an informed human capital decision on, say, a college education, what sorts of information would you want to know, and why?
4. You have a friend who argues that poverty is really not a problem in this country because the poor are better off than millions of people in other parts of the world. Evaluate this position.
5. Give some examples of how the simple supply and demand model can be modified to account for real world considerations in determining wages.

6. Explain fully why the demand curve for labor is downward sloping. Given the following information, determine this producer's demand for labor.

Units of Labor	Total Product	Price per Unit
1	100	$12
2	170	11
3	230	10
4	280	9
5	320	8
6	350	7

7. What is meant by the expression "income distribution"? Explain why, in your opinion, incomes are unequally distributed.
8. What are some major provisions of the National Labor Relations Act and the Taft-Hartley Act and, generally, what is the impact of each act on organized labor in the U.S.?
9. What are the eligibility requirements in your state for a family to receive AFDC (Aid to Families with Dependent Children)? What are the requirements to receive food stamps? What is the monthly AFDC payment? What is the monthly allotment of food stamps? If the qualifications for these two programs are different, explain how and why.

Suggested Readings

Barry R. Chiswick and June A. O'Neill, eds., *Human Resources and Income Distribution* (New York: W. W. Norton & Co., 1977). Readings on income distribution, unemployment, women and the aged, and health and education, based on chapters from various editions of the *Economic Report of the President.*

Beth B. Hess, "New Faces of Poverty," *American Demographics* (May 1983), pp. 26–31. Focuses on changes in the characteristics of the poverty population since 1960, and stresses the greater susceptibility of women who head households to fall below the poverty line.

Juanita Kreps and Robert Clark, *Sex, Age, and Work* (Baltimore: Johns Hopkins University Press, 1975). An analysis of the changing labor market behavior of women and men, and the effects of those changes on mobility, human capital investments, and the distribution of income.

Lawrence D. Maloney et al., "The Desperate World of America's Underclass," *U.S. News & World Report,* March 26, 1984, pp. 54–56. A description of what it is like to be poor, and the various programs to aid the poor.

Bradley R. Schiller, *The Economics of Poverty and Discrimination,* 3d ed. (Englewood Cliffs, N.J.: Prentice-Hall, 1980). Explores the scope and causes of poverty, and public programs for dealing with poverty.

Adam Smith, "Ch. X; Part I: Inequalities arising from the Nature of the Employments themselves," *The Wealth of Nations* (New York: Random House, Modern Library, 1937), pp. 100–110. A charming explanation of five factors leading to inequalities in wages among various occupations.

15 QUESTIONS AND ISSUES IN THE MICROECONOMY: GOVERNMENT AND THE MARKETS

Chapter Objectives

1. To introduce antitrust activity and regulation as the two main forms of government intervention into the operation of markets, and to indicate some reasons why government intervention might be sought.
2. To identify the major federal antitrust statutes, the business practices toward which they are directed, and the penalties they carry.
3. To distinguish among horizontal, vertical, and conglomerate mergers, and to indicate the relative importance of each.
4. To discuss government regulation, identify its forms and organization, and distinguish between industry regulation and special purpose regulation.
5. To explain some reasons for industry regulation and to study price regulation as an important aspect of industry regulation.
6. To introduce deregulation and the controversy over the effectiveness and desirability of regulation.

This chapter completes the section of the book dealing with microeconomics. Throughout this section, the role of markets and competition in economic decision making and in determining the well-being of businesses and households has been of great importance. A seller's price, output, promotional, and other related decisions are influenced by the type of market and degree of competition the seller faces. The amount of profit a firm can earn is affected by the market in which it sells. And the wages workers earn depend upon the forces of supply and demand and the impact of factors such as unequal bargaining power in the market.

Economies where decisions are made primarily by individual businesses and households are built on the philosophy that free markets and competition should be at the foundation of economic activity. Although the U.S. economy is based on this philosophy, historically the U.S. government has intervened in the operation of markets in several important ways. For this reason, a view of the microeconomy is not complete without an understanding of how government influences market forces.

Basically, there are two main forms of government intervention in the operation of market forces in the United States: antitrust activity and regulation. Accordingly, this chapter is divided into two sections, the first on antitrust and the second on regulation.

A spectrum of views exists on the appropriate types and amounts of government intervention. Some observers feel that current intervention is too extensive; others feel that it is too little. Some hold that government involvement is not achieving its intended results or that it creates an unjustified administrative or financial burden on firms in the private sector; others are satisfied with its effects and comfortable with the requirements it imposes.

Why would people who basically favor the principle of free markets seek government intervention in the operation of those markets? One reason is a concern that the amount of competition in a particular market is inappropriate. For example, government intervention might be sought in cases where the number of firms in a market is very small or where a firm's size is so great as to significantly weaken competitive forces. Second, as is the case with many gas and electric companies, the argument for government intervention is that the public interest may be better served by a single large, efficient seller, answerable in its operations to a public body, than by several less efficient, smaller sellers competing with one another.

A third reason for seeking government intervention is security. As the economist John Maurice Clark wrote:

> . . . competition has two opposites: which we may call monopoly and security. . . . Nearly everyone favors competition as against monopoly, and nearly everyone wants it limited in the interest of security. And hardly anyone pays much attention to the question where one leaves off and the other begins.[1]

Competition introduces certain risks into private decision making in markets. The desire to reduce these risks may inspire support for some form of government intervention. For example, laws specifying the ground rules as to what types of rivalry are and are not allowed may reduce the risk of failure for smaller or weaker sellers in a market. Laws that create regulated monopoly sellers, such as gas or electric suppliers, increase security for buyers; such legislation ensures a continuous supply of output by these firms at prices that are supervised by a public authority.

---

[1]John Maurice Clark, *Alternative to Serfdom* (New York: Alfred A. Knopf, 1948), p. 61.

ANTITRUST

Antitrust laws
Laws designed to promote the operation of market forces by prohibiting certain practices that reduce competition.

Monopolization and attempts to monopolize
A firm acquires or attempts to acquire a monopoly share of its market through unreasonable means.

Combinations and conspiracies in restraint of trade
Practices carried out jointly by two or more firms that unreasonably restrict competition.

Antitrust activity centers on a series of laws designed to promote the operation of market forces by limiting certain practices that reduce competition. Specifically, **antitrust laws** are aimed at two broad categories of practices.

The first is **monopolization and attempts to monopolize,** which occurs when a firm, through unreasonable means, acquires or attempts to acquire such a large share of its market that it does not feel strong competitive pressure from its rivals. To appreciate the effect that a firm with a great deal of market power can have on competition, consider the comparison made by economist Walter Adams between rivalry among firms and a poker game where one player has many more funds than the others.

> . . . in a poker game with unlimited stakes, the player who commands disproportionately large funds is likely to emerge victorious. If I have $100 while my opponents have no more than $5 each, I am likely to win regardless of my ability, my virtue, or my luck.[2]

The second type of activity toward which antitrust laws are directed is that of **combinations and conspiracies in restraint of trade,** which includes practices carried out jointly by two or more firms that unreasonably limit competition, such as price fixing and the division of sales territories. These two categories of practices, monopolization and attempts to monopolize, and combinations and conspiracies in restraint of trade, will be explained more fully as we review the major antitrust statutes.

Antitrust enforcement is carried out by both the federal and state governments, with the main responsibility falling on the Department of Justice and the Federal Trade Commission at the federal level. In addition to federal and state enforcement, private parties such as business firms can bring charges that companies have violated the laws.

Administration of the laws depends heavily on the courts and is carried out on a case-by-case basis. That is, each violation is treated separately. In some instances a pretrial agreement can be reached where the accused firm promises to discontinue a practice or settles in some other way. In other instances a trial is required before the issue is resolved. Antitrust cases can become very long, costly, and complicated before they are settled.

In summary, antitrust is concerned with the relationships between firms, especially rival firms. When a problem arises, the government does not respond by becoming a participant in the market and overseeing the behavior of sellers on an ongoing basis. Rather, monopoly and conspiracy questions are dealt with on a case-by-case basis through the courts.

---

[2]Estes Kefauver, *In a Few Hands* (New York: Pantheon Books, 1965), p. 196. In this illustration Professor Adams was referring to a problem that may arise with conglomerate mergers, which are described later in this section.

The Antitrust Laws

Combinations and conspiracies between two or more firms and monopolization by a single firm can occur in several different ways, and the antitrust laws are designed to deal with these problems in their various forms. At the federal level, where we will focus our attention, the antitrust statutes range from laws that are broadly worded to those that are specific about the practices at which they are aimed. There are five main federal antitrust laws: the Sherman Act (1890), the Federal Trade Commission Act (1914), the Clayton Act (1914), the Robinson-Patman Act (1936), and the Celler-Kefauver Act (1950). The 1936 and 1950 acts both amend the Clayton Act.

Sherman Act (1890)
Original and most broadly worded federal antitrust statute; condemns combinations and conspiracies in restraint of trade, and monopolization and attempts to monopolize.

The Sherman Act (1890) The original and most broadly worded federal antitrust statute is the **Sherman Act.** Its first section condemns combinations and conspiracies in restraint of trade without defining what types of policies fall within that category, and reads in part:

> Every contract, combination in the form of trust or otherwise, or conspiracy, in restraint of trade or commerce among the several States, or with foreign nations, is hereby declared to be illegal.[3]

The second section attacks monopolization and attempts to monopolize, again without specifying what types of activities are involved. Section Two reads in part:

> Every person who shall monopolize, or attempt to monopolize, or combine or conspire with any other person or persons, to monopolize any part of the trade or commerce among the several States, or with foreign nations, shall be deemed guilty. . . .[4]

Per se violations
Anticompetitive agreements between firms where proof of the agreement is sufficient to establish guilt; include agreements to jointly fix prices and divide sales territories.

Combinations and conspiracies condemned by Section One of the Sherman Act are either per se or Rule of Reason violations. **Per se violations** are agreements between firms where proof of the agreement is sufficient to establish guilt: there is no defense for a per se violation. Price fixing and division of sales territories among firms are included in this category. One explanation for the per se rule is that the court's time is a scarce resource, and the likelihood of society benefiting from acts such as price fixing or territorial division is so remote that it would be a waste of time to require a court to listen to a defense for these acts.

Price fixing
Joint action by sellers to influence their product prices; considered to be highly anticompetitive.

Price fixing occurs where sellers take joint action to influence the market pricing mechanism. For example, an understanding between competing sellers as to the prices they will charge their buyers or the prices below which

---

[3]*United States Statutes at Large,* Vol. 26 (1889–1891), p. 209.

[4]*United States Statutes at Large,* Vol. 26 (1889–1891), p. 209.

they will not sell would be price fixing, as would an agreement on a system for determining who will submit the lowest offer when pricing is done with sealed bids. With price fixing, competition is diminished and sellers act more like monopolists.

Territorial division
Joint action by sellers to divide sales territories among themselves; considered to be highly anticompetitive.

Territorial division exists when firms divide a sales area among themselves: one firm concentrating on one geographic location, and other firms concentrating on other locations. For example, territorial division would occur where two national firms agreed that one would sell exclusively east of the Mississippi River if the other would sell only west of the river. As with price fixing, territorial division diminishes competition.

Rule of Reason violations
Violations of the antitrust laws involving actions that are not necessarily anticompetitive; the challenged restraint on competition must be shown to be unreasonable.

Rule of Reason violations occur where firms come together in a way which may or may not unreasonably restrain trade. With the Rule of Reason, there is no blanket condemnation of business practices as there is with price fixing and territorial division. Rather, each challenged practice must be examined to see whether *in this particular instance* the restraint is reasonable or unreasonable.

Trade association
An organization representing firms in a particular industry that performs certain functions that benefit those firms.

Activities of industry trade associations fall under the Rule of Reason umbrella. A **trade association** is an organization of firms in a particular industry, such as construction or furniture manufacturing, that performs certain functions that benefit its members. One function that these associations may perform is the collection and distribution of information on the state of the industry. If the reporting includes data on overall industry trends, or general information on supply conditions or buyer behavior, and if it is equally available to all interested parties, the trade association activity may enhance competition by improving the general state of knowledge in the industry. But if the information gives specific details on the terms of each firm's sales and the names of its buyers, or if the information is not equally available to all interested parties, the trade association's information gathering might help to foster a price fixing agreement or division of buyers among sellers, and would therefore be subject to condemnation under the Sherman Act.

Cases involving the Sherman Act Section Two violations of monopolization and attempts to monopolize rest largely on two issues: the specific actions taken by a firm indicating its intent to monopolize its market, and the firm's share of its market. Where the seller's market share is small and it is clearly not a monopolist, an attempt to monopolize may be inferred from actions such as pricing below cost in an attempt to drive rivals out of the market, or from contracts with critical suppliers and distributors that would foreclose their services to the firm's rivals.

As the firm's share of its market grows, monopolization may be inferred less from what it does and more from its relative size in comparison to its rivals. For example, in *United States* v. *Aluminum Company of America,* a leading monopolization case, the court enunciated what has come to be known as the "30-60-90 Rule," which is a rough guide for analyzing Sherman Act monopolization questions: "[a greater than ninety per cent share of the market] is enough to constitute a monopoly; it is doubtful whether sixty or sixty-four per cent would be enough; and certainly thirty-three per cent is not."[5]

An extremely important aspect of monopolization cases is the definition of the relevant market, which was discussed in Chapter Thirteen. The more broadly a market is defined in terms of its geographic boundaries and/or the number of substitute products, the smaller will be the share of that market taken by any one firm. The more narrowly a market is defined, the larger will be the share taken by the firm. Thus, it is to the advantage of a firm accused of monopolizing a market to define that market as broadly as possible.

For example, in the Aluminum Company of America case, in which Alcoa was accused of monopolizing the aluminum market, there were several possible components to the relevant market: primary domestic ingot, secondary aluminum, imported ingot, and aluminum fabricated by Alcoa. By including or excluding one or more of these components, different definitions of the relevant market could be developed, and each definition resulted in a different market share for Alcoa. As stated by the Supreme Court:

> There are various ways of computing "Alcoa's" control of the aluminum market — as distinct from its production — depending upon what one regards as competing in that market. The judge figured its share — during the years 1929–1938, inclusive — as only about thirty-three percent; to do so he included "secondary," and excluded that part of "Alcoa's" own production which it fabricated and did not therefore sell as ingot. If, on the other hand, "Alcoa's" total production, fabricated and sold, be included, and balanced against the sum of imported "virgin" and "secondary," its share of the market was in the neighborhood of sixty-four per cent for that period. The percentage we have already mentioned — over ninety — results only if we both include all "Alcoa's " production and exclude "secondary."[6]

The actual boundaries of a market are not always obvious. For example, how would you define the relevant market for the firm in Application 15.1? Is it the publishing and licensing of all music? Of gospel music? Of something else?

Federal Trade Commission Act (1914) Created the Federal Trade Commission and empowered it to prevent unfair methods of competition, which include antitrust violations.

The Federal Trade Commission Act (1914) The Federal Trade Commission (FTC) was created by the **Federal Trade Commission Act** and granted power to " . . . prevent persons, partnerships, or corporations, . . . from using unfair methods of competition in commerce."[7] Included among unfair methods of competition are antitrust violations.

---

[5]*United States* v. *Aluminum Company of America,* 148 F. 2d 416 (1945), p. 424.

[6]*United States* v. *Aluminum Company of America,* 148 F. 2d 416 (1945), p. 424.

[7]*United States Statutes at Large,* Vol. 38, Part 1 (1915), p. 719.

When the FTC feels that a business is engaged in unfair competition, it can issue a complaint and arrange a hearing to determine whether the practice should be prohibited. If it is found that the practice is unfair competition, the FTC can issue a "cease and desist order" requiring the firm to stop the activity. If a seller fails to follow the order, or if it feels the order is incorrect, either the FTC or the accused firm can have the order brought before a court for a ruling.[8]

Clayton Act (1914)
Federal antitrust statute prohibiting specific activities, such as exclusionary practices, that substantially reduce competition or create a monopoly.

The Clayton Act (1914) Practices that " . . . substantially lessen competition or tend to create a monopoly in any line of commerce . . ."[9] are the concern of the **Clayton Act**. Unlike the Sherman Act and the Federal Trade Commission Act, which are not specific as to the practices they disallow, the Clayton Act is directed toward several particular activities: exclusionary practices, interlocking directorates, price discrimination, and the acquisition of one firm by another.

Exclusionary practices
Practices through which a seller attempts to prevent its suppliers or buyers from dealing with a competitor.

Exclusionary practices occur when a seller of a product forecloses its rivals from the market by following policies that make it impossible for the rivals to compete. For example, Company X could agree to sell its product to a buyer only on the condition that it would supply all of the buyer's needs for that type of item. Such an agreement would effectively give the seller a monopoly over the buyer's demand for that product.

Another example of an exclusionary practice is a "tying contract." This could occur when a buyer requires two goods that are used together. Suppose that many firms, including Company X, produce good A, but that Company X is the only seller of good B. If Company X "ties" the sale of good A to good B—that is, if it will sell good B only as long as the buyer also purchases good A from Company X—it engages in a tying contract. In

[8]*United States Statutes at Large,* Vol. 38, Part 1 (1915), pp. 719, 720.

[9]*United States Statutes at Large,* Vol. 38, Part 1 (1915), p. 730.

Application 15.1
DEFINING THE RELEVANT MARKET

The Hill Music Company publishes sheet music and also licenses performances and recordings of its music. By any absolute measure, Hill is very small. But Hill accounts for more than 95 percent of the revenues arising from the publication and licensing of "gospel music," which is characterized by lyrics dealing with spiritual and religious subjects in a personal and homely vein sung to distinctly secular rhythms and tunes. There is nothing else that will equally satisfy its devotees. If this were the only evidence, would you hold Hill to be a monopolist under §2 [of the Sherman Act]?

Source: Phillip Areeda, *Antitrust Analysis,* 2d ed. (Boston: Little, Brown & Co., Inc., 1974), p. 218.

this way, Company X is using its monopoly of good B to gain a monopoly on good A.

Interlocking directorate
The same person sits on the boards of directors of different corporations.

An **interlocking directorate** occurs where the same person sits on the boards of directors of different corporations. For example, an interlock would exist between a manufacturing corporation and a shipping corporation if the same individual served on the boards of directors of both firms. Interlocking directorates are not necessarily anticompetitive, but problems could occur. For instance, how might competition be lessened if the same person sat on the boards of directors of two firms producing similar products for the same market? Or how might competition be reduced if an individual sat on the board of a large manufacturing corporation and also on the board of one of several firms competing to sell machinery to that manufacturer?

In each of the activities addressed by the Clayton Act, as well as those included under its amendments, the practices themselves do not automatically constitute violations of the antitrust laws. They become violations only when the activities tend to significantly reduce competition or create a monopoly.

Robinson-Patman Act (1936)
Federal antitrust statute concerned with anticompetitive price discrimination; amends Section Two of the Clayton Act.

Price discrimination
Different buyers acquire the same product from the same seller with the same treatment and service but pay different prices.

The Robinson-Patman Act (1936) Section Two of the Clayton Act is amended by the **Robinson-Patman Act**, which deals with price discrimination. **Price discrimination** occurs when a seller charges different buyers different prices for the same product. For example, if a firm sells you an item at one price, and then sells exactly the same item with exactly the same treatment and service to someone else at a lower price, you are discriminated against in terms of price. The Clayton Act condemns price discrimination when it weakens competition or leads to a monopoly, and the Robinson-Patman Act elaborates further on that condemnation.

Price discrimination can injure competition between a seller and its rivals. Through price discrimination, a seller can lower its price where there is intense competition for potential buyers, while keeping the price unchanged, or even raising it, for remaining customers. If a rival is unable to meet these price cuts, it may lose sales and perhaps be driven from the market.

A buyer's market position can also be injured when, because of discrimination, it must pay a higher price for what it purchases than the price its rival pays. Because of the difference in price, the discriminated against firm's costs are higher than its rival's costs. This in turn could force the firm to raise its price, or keep its price unchanged but absorb the higher cost through forgone profit, either of which is damaging to its competitive position.

The Robinson-Patman Act attacks outright price discrimination as well as several types of "indirect" price discrimination. The latter includes practices such as granting quantity discounts on terms that only a few large buyers can meet, paying purchasers for services that have not been rendered, and treating buyers unequally in the provision of sales facilities.[10]

---

[10]*United States Statutes at Large*, Vol. 49, Part 1 (1936), pp. 1526–1527.

Celler-Kefauver Act (1950)
Federal antitrust statute concerned with anticompetitive mergers and acquisitions of firms; amends Section Seven of the Clayton Act.

The Celler-Kefauver Act (1950) Section Seven of the Clayton Act is amended by the **Celler-Kefauver Act**, which deals with anticompetitive mergers and acquisitions of firms.

A business can be acquired or merged with another in two ways: by the purchase of a controlling number of shares of stock, or by the outright purchase of assets. Interestingly, the original Clayton Act had a loophole in that it condemned anticompetitive acquisitions through stock purchases but said nothing about the purchase of assets. This loophole was closed by the Celler-Kefauver Act, which attacks anticompetitive acquisitions either by stock or asset purchase.[11]

Horizontal merger
Two or more sellers competing in the same market join together.

There are three main types of mergers or acquisitions, each with its own potentially anticompetitive effects: horizontal, vertical, and conglomerate mergers. A **horizontal merger** occurs where two or more sellers competing in the same market join together. A plumbing contractor who buys out a competitor in the same town, or competing manufacturers serving a national market who combine to form one corporation are examples of horizontal mergers.

If a market contains many firms, and two extremely small sellers merge, the consequence may be unnoticeable: a small grain farmer buying a second farm will have no effect on the grain market. But where the acquiring and/or acquired firm has a substantial market share, their joining may have an anticompetitive effect by creating a larger organization with an even greater share of the market. For example, suppose a local area is served by four dairies: one receives 40 percent of the total sales, another 30 percent, another 20 percent, and another 10 percent. If the second and third largest sellers were to merge, it would create a single entity controlling 50 percent of the total sales, and would result in a market made up of only two large sellers and one much smaller seller. Because of its effect on the market, this merger could constitute a Celler-Kefauver Act violation.

Vertical merger
A firm joins with a supplier or distributor.

A **vertical merger** involves the joining of a firm with a supplier or a distributor. A meat packing company that buys a cattle ranch or a furniture manufacturer that purchases retail stores through which to sell its merchandise are examples of vertical acquisitions or mergers.

A vertical merger may be anticompetitive if it forecloses a firm's rivals from key suppliers or distributors. For example, suppose three lumber yards provide building materials to contractors in a particular area. If one of the contractors were to acquire all of the lumber yards, he or she could shut off the local supply of building materials to all rivals and possibly force them out of business. Or a manufacturer of a specialized type of machinery could put its rivals at a competitive disadvantage by acquiring the only firm in an area that distributes and services that type of machinery. If competition is injured, a vertical merger can result in a Celler-Kefauver Act violation.

---

[11]*United States Statutes at Large,* Vol. 38, Part 1 (1915), pp. 731–732; *United States Statutes at Large,* Vol. 64, Part 1 (1952), pp. 1125–1126.

Conglomerate merger Two or more sellers who are not related as competitors, suppliers, or distributors join together.

Conglomerate mergers are those between firms that are not related as competitors, suppliers, or distributors. The joining of a steel wire manufacturer and a telephone answering service would be a conglomerate merger, as would be the combining of a chemical company and a chain of retail clothing outlets.

Conglomerate mergers can have anticompetitive effects because of what is known as the "deep pocket." For example, a large, profitable manufacturer of musical instruments might acquire one of several small competing candy companies. As a result of the acquisition, the candy firm could receive financial allocations from the manufacturer's "deep pocket" full of money for expenditures on such things as advertising, expansion of facilities, and a larger sales staff. On the basis of these funds, the candy company could increase its sales and share of the market at the expense of its rivals who do not have comparable financial resources with which to compete.

The frequency of the different types of mergers is suggested in Table 15.1, which categorizes the number and percentage of large acquisitions in mining and manufacturing from 1948 through 1979 into horizontal, vertical, or conglomerate mergers. A large acquisition is one where the acquired firm had assets of at least $10 million at the time of the merger.

Far and away, the greatest amount of merger activity involved conglomeration. Over the 1948–1979 period there were 1,491 large conglomerate acquisitions in mining and manufacturing, which accounted for 73.7 percent of all mergers in that group. Horizontal mergers were a distant second, followed by vertical mergers.

Historically, mergers have tended to occur in waves: at times there have been relatively few mergers, and at other times there have been many. Table 15.2 lists the number of mining and manufacturing concerns acquired from 1925 through 1979. Notice the period of relative inactivity from 1935 through 1944. In contrast, compare this with the large number of acquisitions in the last half of the 1960s. How might you explain this uneven pattern of acquisition activity?

In 1982 the Department of Justice issued a set of merger guidelines to assist companies in determining whether an acquisition would violate the antitrust laws. The guidelines, which were updated in 1984, are based on an

Table 15.1
Large Acquisitions in Mining and Manufacturing: 1948–1979

From 1948 through 1979, the greatest amount of merger activity in mining and manufacturing has involved conglomeration, followed by horizontal and vertical mergers, respectively.

Type of Acquisition	Number of Acquisitions	Percent of Acquisitions
Horizontal	331	16.4%
Vertical	201	9.9
Conglomerate	1,491	73.7
Total	2,023	100.0

Source: Federal Trade Commission, *Statistical Report on Mergers and Acquisitions 1979* (Washington, D.C.: U.S. Government Printing Office, 1981), pp. 98, 99, 109. Only acquisitions for which data were publicly available are listed in the table.

Table 15.2
Number of Mining and Manufacturing Concerns Acquired: 1925–1979

There is no consistent pattern for the amount of merger activity from year to year. During some periods, such as the late 1960s, there was a relatively large amount of merger activity, while the opposite took place in the late 1930s and early 1940s.

Years	Number of Acquired Business Concerns
1925–1929	4,583
1930–1934	1,687
1935–1939	577
1940–1944	906
1945–1949	1,505
1950–1954	1,424
1955–1959	3,365
1960–1964	4,366
1965–1969	8,213
1970–1974	4,749
1975–1979	2,717

Source: U.S. Bureau of the Census, *Statistical Abstract of the United States: 1982–83* (103d ed.), Washington, D.C., 1982, p. 531.

index (called the Herfindahl-Hirschman Index) which measures the extent to which a market would be dominated by a few large firms following a merger. In addition to the index, the guidelines give other factors, such as easy of entry into the market and whether the acquired firm would be able to survive on its own, that should be considered in determining whether a merger is injurious to competition.

Antitrust Penalties A business found guilty of violating the antitrust laws may face one or more of four types of penalties, depending on the offense committed and who is bringing the suit. The penalties include imprisonment and fines, both of which are self-explanatory, and structural remedies and treble damages.

Structural remedies involve preventing two or more firms from merging or dividing an offending firm into two or more unrelated units. Preventing firms from merging is appropriate where a proposed merger would violate the antitrust laws. In this situation, competition can be promoted by disallowing the merger and requiring the companies to remain unrelated. Dividing an offending firm might be used where a single firm has been found guilty of monopolizing a market. Here the monopoly could be broken by separating one or more of the company's divisions into independent units.

With treble damages, an injured party can, under certain conditions, collect three times its damages from the offending firm. For example, suppose it was proven in a court suit that over the last three years Company B lost $6 million in profit because of an antitrust violation committed by Company A. On the basis of this, the court could require Company A to pay Company B not $6 million to compensate for the lost profit, but three times $6 million, or $18 million, in damages.

GOVERNMENT REGULATION

Government regulation
Government participation, through various agencies and commissions, in business decision making; may be industry regulation or special purpose regulation.

The second major way in which government intervenes in the market process is through regulation. The expression **government regulation** refers to participation by the federal and state governments, through various agencies and commissions, in business decision making. Regulatory activities include the actions of the Securities and Exchange Commission (SEC), Federal Communications Commission (FCC), Interstate Commerce Commission (ICC), state utility commissions, and other such agencies.

In some cases, government regulation involves direct participation in specific aspects of a company's operations. Important decisions concerning such areas as the company's product price, its rate of profit, and the market it serves must be approved by a regulatory commission before they can be carried into practice. In other cases, government regulation involves indirect participation in business operations through setting standards for firms to follow. These standards pertain to matters such as safety, health, and the environment. The Food and Drug Administration (FDA), for example, sets purity and safety standards for food and drugs, and the Environmental Protection Agency (EPA) sets pollution standards.

While the antitrust laws are directed at the relationships between businesses and the degree of competition in specific markets, regulation is concerned with the interests of particular groups in the economy. For example, some regulation is aimed at protection of the consumer, some at labor, and some at the general public.

Government regulation can be divided into two basic types: industry regulation and special purpose regulation. The first type involves regulation of all businesses in a particular industry. In the United States, the railroad, public utility, communications, and some other industries are subject to this type of regulation. Generally, industry regulation is direct: the government plays an important role in determining price, profit, and other aspects of the firms' operations.

With special purpose regulation, a regulatory body is created to deal with a particular problem that is common to businesses in many different industries. The commissions with authority over job discrimination (Equal Employment Opportunity Commission), consumer product safety (Consumer Product Safety Commission), and unfair business practices (Federal Trade Commission) are examples of agencies that carry out this type of regulation. Much special purpose regulation is indirect and involves setting standards for businesses to follow.

At the federal level, more than 50 regulatory agencies have been established at one time or another. Table 15.3 lists these in chronological order. Notice that a large number of regulatory agencies was created in the early 1970s. Although historically we associate the Great Depression and the New Deal era with the growth of regulation, the number of federal agencies originated in the 1970s was more than double the number created during the 1930s.

Table 15.3
Chronology of Federal Regulatory Agencies

Regulatory agencies have been formed throughout the history of the economy, with a large number created in the 1930s and 1970s.

Year	Agency	Department Association[a]
1836	Patent and Trademark Office	Department of Commerce
1863	Comptroller of the Currency	Department of the Treasury
1870	Copyright Office	Library of Congress
1887	Interstate Commerce Commission	
1899	Army Corps of Engineers	Department of Defense
	[Regulatory duties from this date; established 1824]	
1903	Antitrust Division	Department of Justice
1913	Federal Reserve System (Board of Governors)	
1914	Federal Trade Commission	
1915	Coast Guard	Department of Transportation
1916	Tariff Commission	
	[Became International Trade Commission in 1975]	
1920	Federal Power Commission	
	[Became Federal Energy Regulatory Commission in 1975]	
1922	Commodity Exchange Authority	Department of Agriculture
	[Became Commodity Futures Trading Commission in 1974]	
1927	Bureau of Customs	Department of the Treasury
	[Became Customs Service in 1973]	
1931	Food and Drug Administration	Department of Health and Human Services
1932	Federal Home Loan Bank Board	
1933	Farm Credit Administration	
1933	Federal Deposit Insurance Corporation	
1934	Federal Communications Commission	
1934	Securities and Exchange Commission	
1935	National Labor Relations Board	
1936	Maritime Administration	Department of Commerce
	[Regulatory functions were transferred to the Federal Maritime Commission in 1961]	
1937	Agricultural Marketing Service and Other Agencies	Department of Agriculture
	[Duties were transferred to other services in 1972 and 1977]	
1938	Civil Aeronautics Authority	
	[Became Civil Aeronautics Board in 1940] *[Abolished in 1985]*	
1940	Fish and Wildlife Service	Department of Interior
	[First established as Bureau of Fisheries in 1871]	
1946	Atomic Energy Commission	
	[Functions were transferred to the Nuclear Regulatory Commission in 1975]	
1951	Renegotiation Board	
	[Abolished in 1979]	
1953	Foreign Agricultural Service	Department of Agriculture
1953	Small Business Administration	
1958	Federal Aviation Agency	Department of Transportation
	[Became Federal Aviation Administration in 1967]	
1961	Agricultural Stabilization and Conservation Service	Department of Agriculture
1963	Labor-Management Services Administration	Department of Labor

[a]Not all agencies are associated with a department.
Source: Ronald J. Penoyer, *Directory of Federal Regulatory Agencies — 1982 Update,* Center for the Study of American Business, Formal Publication Number 47 (St. Louis: Washington University, June 1982), pp. 43–48.

Year	Agency	Department Association[a]
1964	Equal Employment Opportunity Commission	
1966	Federal Highway Administration	Department of Transportation
1966	National Transportation Safety Board	Department of Transportation
	[Reestablished as independent agency in 1974]	
1966	Federal Railroad Administration	Department of Transportation
1969	Council on Environmental Quality	
1970	Cost Accounting Standards Board	
	[Abolished in 1980]	
1970	Environmental Protection Agency	
1970	National Credit Union Administration	
1970	National Highway Traffic Safety Administration	Department of Transportation
1970	Occupational Safety and Health Administration	Department of Labor
1971	Employment Standards Administration	Department of Labor
1971	Occupational Safety and Health Review Commission	
1972	Bureau of Alcohol, Tobacco and Firearms	Department of the Treasury
1972	Consumer Product Safety Commission	
1972	Domestic and International Business Administration	Department of Commerce
	[Became International Trade Administration in 1980]	
1973	Drug Enforcement Administration	Department of Justice
1973	Federal Energy Administration	
	[Became Economic Regulatory Administration in 1977, Department of Energy]	
1973	Mining Enforcement and Safety Administration	Department of the Interior
	[Became Mine Safety and Health Administration in 1977, Department of Labor]	
1974	Council on Wage and Price Stability	
	[Abolished in 1981]	
1975	Federal Election Commission	
1975	Materials Transportation Bureau	Department of Transportation
1976	Federal Grain Inspection Service	Department of Agriculture
1977	Office of Neighborhoods, Voluntary Associations and Consumer Protection	Department of Housing and Urban Development
	[Abolished in 1981 and functions transferred to Office of Assistant Secretary of HUD]	
1977	Office of Surface Mining Reclamation and Enforcement	Department of the Interior
1979	Office of the Federal Inspector of the Alaska Natural Gas Transportation System	
1982	Packers and Stockyards Administration	Department of Agriculture
	[Previously existed from 1967 to 1978]	

The Structure of Regulation

A particular industry or a specific problem is under federal or state regulation depending upon whether interstate or intrastate commerce is involved. Federal agencies have jurisdiction over interstate commerce. For example, rates on long-distance telephone calls, when they cross state lines, are overseen by the Federal Communications Commission. State commissions regulate where intrastate commerce is involved. The rates charged by utility companies that serve customers within a particular state are under the regulatory jurisdiction of a state public utility commission.

Federal regulatory agencies such as the Occupational Safety and Health Administration (OSHA), the Interstate Commerce Commission (ICC), and others are established by Congress. The legislation authorizing a regulatory agency usually includes the overall mandate for the regulatory body, the administrative structure of the agency, and other important information pertaining to its operation.

The authority given to a regulatory agency in its enabling legislation is usually stated in more general rather than specific terms. For example, the Nuclear Regulatory Commission (NRC), which was established in 1975 and took over the functions of the Atomic Energy Commission, was given the mandate to license and regulate: radioactive waste storage facilities; the construction, operation, and safety of nuclear reactors; the processing, transport, and handling of nuclear materials; and other related matters.[12]

When a regulatory agency is established, it is given the power to carry out the general mandates stated in the enabling legislation. In order to do so, the agency may make detailed rules and regulations that businesses under its jurisdiction must follow. For example, if an agency's mandate is airline safety, it may establish detailed rules regarding air personnel qualifications, airplane inspection, equipment, and such.

An agency also has the power to enforce its own rules and regulations and to punish those that do not comply. In many instances noncompliance results in a fine levied by the agency. Companies that choose to dispute their treatment by an agency may appeal their case to a court of law.

As Table 15.3 illustrates, some regulatory agencies are established as independent bodies governed by commissioners who are appointed to oversee the operations of the agency. Other agencies are created as part of an existing department (such as the Department of Commerce) and are headed by an administrator within that department. For example, the Nuclear Regulatory Commission is an independent body governed by five commissioners appointed by the president of the United States and confirmed by the Senate, whereas the Federal Aviation Administration (FAA) is within the Department of Transportation and is headed by one of its administrators.[13]

---

[12] *United States Statutes at Large,* Vol. 88, Part 1 (1974), pp. 1242–1248.

[13] *Directory of Federal Regulatory Agencies,* 2d ed. 1980, compiled by Ronald J. Penoyer, Center for the Study of American Business, Formal Publication Number 31 (St. Louis: Washington University, April 1980), pp. 43, 70.

State public utility commissions, the most important of state regulatory agencies, are usually headed by commissioners who are either elected or appointed by the governor.

Industry Regulation

Industry regulation
Regulation affecting several aspects (such as pricing, entry of new sellers, and conditions of service) of the operations of firms in a particular industry.

As noted earlier, **industry regulation** applies to firms in certain industries, such as the railroad, communications, and electric power industries. This type of regulation deals with such matters as pricing, entry of new sellers into the market, extension of service by existing sellers, and the quality and conditions of service. In other words, the private decision making ability of a business in a free market does not exist for this type of regulated firm.

In some regulated industries, the firm itself is not free to independently choose or alter the price it charges for its product. Instead, it must seek approval from its regulatory agency to raise or lower its price. For example, for years the airlines needed government approval to change air fares or to offer a special package or reduced fare plan. Also, in many regulated industries, new firms cannot begin operation unless they receive permission or a license from that industry's regulatory body. Sewage, water, electric, and other utility companies cannot be initiated at will.

Firms already in existence may be required to obtain permission to abandon service or to extend or alter current services. For years the railroads were not permitted to drop unprofitable passenger routes, and an electric company cannot simply cut off service to a university because the company disagrees with the political statements made by some students and professors. These firms may also be subject to a host of other regulations, such as on the quality of the product offered for sale (for example, chemicals permitted in the local water supply) and safety.

Reasons for Industry Regulation There are two frequently cited explanations as to why certain industries are subject to detailed regulation: the first is economic, and the second is related to the public interest.

The economic justification for regulation is based on efficiency. There are certain production situations where it is more efficient (less costly) to have the entire output in a market come from one large seller rather than from several smaller sellers. In these instances, a **natural monopoly** is said to exist. A good example of a natural monopoly is an electric power company. It would be quite inefficient and complicated to have several electric companies serving one area.

Natural monopoly
A market situation where it is more efficient (less costly) to have the entire output of a product come from one large seller rather than several smaller sellers.

Natural monopolies occur because of strong economies of scale in production and distribution. With economies of scale, which were introduced in Chapter Twelve, a seller's long-run unit or average total cost falls as it grows in size. Economies of scale can result from a firm's ability to spread its expenditures on machinery and equipment over more units of output, or when a firm becomes large enough to combine previously separate processes into one, or when a firm's size justifies installing highly specialized equipment.

The effect of economies of scale on average cost, and the logic of the natural monopoly, are illustrated in Figure 15.1. Economies of scale are shown by the downward sloping region on the long-run average total cost (LRATC) curve. This indicates that as the level of output increases, the unit or average cost of producing that output falls. This gives rise to the notion of the natural monopoly.

To illustrate, suppose we wanted to produce 100,000 units of the output given in Figure 15.1. One method would be to have one firm produce the entire amount at a cost per unit of $1, as indicated in the figure. Another method would be to divide the output between, say, two sellers, with each producing 50,000 units at an average cost of $2.25, also shown in Figure 15.1. Obviously, the total cost of production with one seller ($100,000) is considerably less than with two ($225,000). Thus, significant economies of scale can lead to a natural monopoly: it can be more efficient to have one seller rather than several in a market.

Figure 15.1
Economies of Scale and Long-Run Average Total Cost

If, because of economies of scale, the long-run average total cost of production and distribution is lower with one seller in a market than with several, the seller could be classified as a natural monopoly.

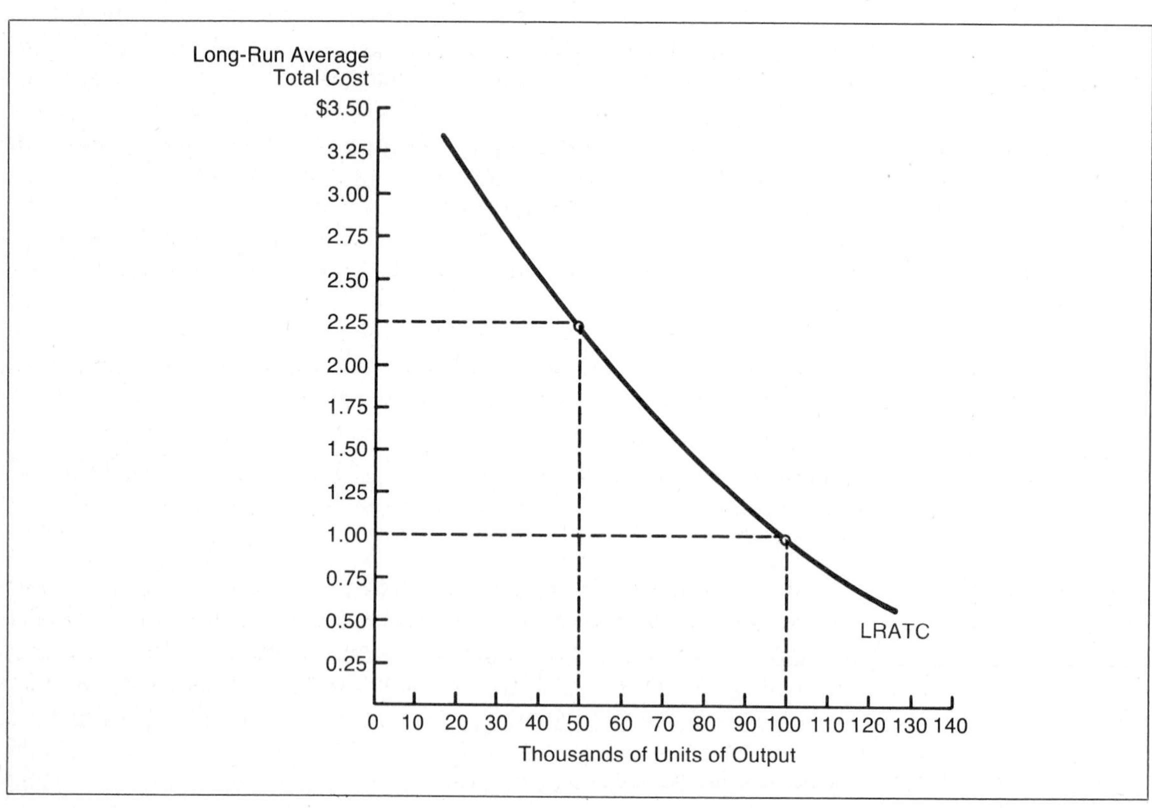

Significant economies of scale are experienced by organizations such as electric power companies. Because of the high cost of plants and equipment (generators, power lines, and so forth), it is extremely inefficient to have several small electric companies serve the same market. By having one large company and "spreading the overhead," the cost per kilowatt hour is considerably less. Can you understand how economies of scale also affect production costs for gas pipeline, telephone, and water companies?

Unfortunately, natural monopolies create a dilemma for the consumer. On the one hand, because of economies of scale, buyers benefit from lower unit costs when dealing with one seller. But on the other hand, as the only seller in the market, the firm may abuse its monopoly power. The solution to this dilemma is to resort to regulation that allows only one firm in the market, while at the same time placing the firm's operations under detailed scrutiny by a public authority so that it cannot unreasonably exploit its monopoly power.

Natural monopoly may explain regulation in certain areas of the economy where there are advantages to having only one seller in a market. But what about the operation of firms such as motor carriers, communications companies, railroads, and others which produce in industries where there is more than one seller in a market? These instances of regulation may be explained using the second justification: the public interest.

According to this justification, there are certain types of businesses that provide goods or perform services particularly important to the public well-being. Examples of such businesses include radio and television companies whose programming can influence public opinion, and transportation firms such as railroads, motor and water carriers, and airlines, without whose services the nation's commerce would come to a halt. The public interest argument is that businesses such as these are significant enough for the performance of the economy and the well-being of its citizens that the public has a right to be assured of their proper operation. This assurance comes through regulation.

One of the best known statements justifying regulation in the public interest is found in *Munn* v. *Illinois,* an 1877 case concerning the regulation of grain elevator operators. Here the court held that:

> When . . . one devotes his property to a use in which the public has an interest, he, in effect, grants to the public an interest in that use, and must submit to be controlled by the public for the common good. . . .[14]

Notice that the public interest justification is not as narrow as the natural monopoly argument in terms of the situations to which it can be applied. The natural monopoly rationale pertains only to markets where it is most efficient to have one seller. The public interest justification applies to any

[14]*Munn* v. *Illinois,* 94 U.S. 113 (1877), p. 126.

market where it can be argued that the welfare of the public can be so affected by the operation of a business that it is desirable to bring that business under regulation. The breadth of this justification was defined in 1934 in one of the most important court decisions on regulation, *Nebbia* v. *New York*. In this case, which dealt with the regulation of milk prices, the Supreme Court stated:

> It is clear that there is no closed class or category of businesses affected with a public interest. . . . [A] state is free to adopt whatever economic policy may reasonably be deemed to promote public welfare, and to enforce that policy by legislation adapted to its purpose. . . . If the laws passed are seen to have a reasonable relation to a proper legislative purpose, and are neither arbitrary nor discriminatory, the requirements of due process are satisfied. . . .[15]

Price Regulation One important aspect of industry regulation is the public authority's overseeing of the prices, or rates, charged by a regulated company. When a regulated firm, such as a gas or electric company, seeks to raise or lower its rates, the firm presents an argument supporting its request to the appropriate agency, which either approves or denies the request.

Cost-plus pricing
Prices are designed to generate enough revenues to cover operating costs plus a fair return to stockholders.

Regulated firms have two concerns in making rate requests: they must cover their costs and, being privately owned, they must earn enough profit to attract and retain stockholders. Because of this, pricing by regulated firms is commonly carried out on a "cost-plus" basis. That is, with **cost-plus pricing** the rates, or prices, buyers pay are designed to generate revenues sufficient to cover the costs of operation plus return a fair amount to those who invest in the business.

There is one major problem with cost-plus pricing: it does not promote economic efficiency. A regulated firm that is granted permission to collect revenues to cover its costs plus a fair return to its investors may not have as much incentive to keep its costs down as would an unregulated firm competing with other sellers.

Special Purpose Regulation

Special purpose regulation
Regulation aimed at correcting a problem, such as pollution or job discrimination, found in several industries; not limited to a specific industry.

Special purpose regulation is aimed at correcting a situation considered to be problematic, such as pollution, or at protecting a particular group in the economy, such as workers or consumers. Rather than focusing on a single industry, special purpose regulation applies to all firms in any industry that are affected by the mandate of the regulatory body.

Unlike industry regulation, this type of regulation does not involve direct intervention into a company's price, profit, and other related decisions. Instead, it is concerned with such matters as the manufacture and use of the product itself, employees' working conditions, and situations created by the

---

[15]*Nebbia* v. *New York*, 291 U.S. 502 (1934), pp. 536, 537.

firm that could be harmful to the general public. The Occupational Safety and Health Administration (OSHA), which is concerned with worker safety and working conditions, is a good example of an agency dealing with special purpose regulation.

Table 15.4 lists some of the federal agencies responsible for special purpose regulation, along with a brief description of each agency's function. The table is divided according to the main focal points of this type of regulation: protection of the general public, the consumer, the worker, and the environment. A section is also included in the table for special regulation dealing with international trade.

Notice that some of the agencies listed in the table affect a broader range of firms and industries than do others. For example, how many industries can you name that might be directly affected by a ruling of the National

Table 15.4
Some Special Purpose Regulatory Agencies

The efforts of agencies concerned with special purpose regulation are directed mainly at protecting the general public, consumers, workers, and the environment.

Agency	Function of Agency
Protection of the General Public and Consumer:	
Federal Trade Commission (FTC)	Ensure fair competition in the market
National Transportation Safety Board (NTSB)	Promote safe transportation on land and in air
Food and Drug Administration (FDA)	Protect against unsafe foods, drugs, cosmetics, medical devices and radiation
Drug Enforcement Administration (DEA)	Control narcotics and other dangerous drugs
National Highway Traffic Safety Administration (NHTSA)	Set standards for motor vehicle safety, fuel economy and state highway safety programs
Consumer Product Safety Commission (CPSC)	Protect against unreasonable injury risks with consumer products
Protection of the Worker:	
Equal Employment Opportunity Commission (EEOC)	Prevent discrimination in employment practices
National Labor Relations Board (NLRB)	Administer laws relating to collective bargaining
Occupational Safety and Health Administration (OSHA)	Set and enforce worker safety and health regulations
Employment Standards Administration (ESA)	Administer various employment standards
Labor-Management Services Administration (LMSA)	Regulate employee welfare and benefit plans
Protection of the Environment:	
Council on Environmental Quality (CEQ)	Administer environmental impact statements and develop and recommend policies to protect and improve environmental quality
Environmental Protection Agency (EPA)	Protect physical environment
Directed toward International Trade:	
International Trade Commission (ITC)	Eliminate unfair import practices
International Trade Administration (ITA)	Regulate some aspects of international trade

Source: *Directory of Federal Regulatory Agencies*, 3d ed. 1981, compiled by Ronald J. Penoyer, Center for the Study of American Business, Formal Publication Number 38 (St. Louis: Washington University, May 1981), pp. 33, 35, 37, 38, 47, 48, 51, 52, 65, 69, 74, 75, 76, 78, 84.

Highway Traffic Safety Administration? How does this compare with the number of industries where hiring practices could be influenced by a decision of the Equal Employment Opportunity Commission?

Deregulation

The spectacular growth of regulation in the early and mid-1970s did not carry into the 1980s. Rather, the trend changed as the Carter and Reagan administrations took steps to deregulate the economy. Since the late 1970s, the airline, trucking, natural gas, banking, telephone, and other industries have been deregulated. And, as shown in Table 15.5, the number of permanent full-time positions in federal regulatory agencies has fallen from a high of over 90,000 in 1980.

Interest in deregulation grew out of concern over the performance of regulation and its effects on business firms and the economy in general. This concern centers largely on the costs of regulation and the extent to which it benefits society. Unfortunately, the answer to the cost-benefit question is not clear. Some people argue that the costs are too high and/or the benefits are too low, while others hold that, on net, regulation benefits society. Application 15.2, "Mending the Rules," provides two examples of how the costs and benefits of regulation and deregulation can be viewed in different ways. Can you relate what you have learned in Chapter Eleven on the role of interest groups in the political process to this application and to the direction of deregulation in the economy?

SUMMARY

Despite the free market philosophy underlying the U.S. economy, government intervenes in the operation of markets in two important ways: through antitrust laws and through regulation. This intervention occurs for several

Application 15.2
MENDING THE RULES

One of the toughest regulatory decisions of 1981 involved open warfare between two important industries. In an extremely controversial decision, National Highway Traffic Safety Administration director Raymond Peck rescinded a regulation requiring automakers to install air bags or automatic seat belts to protect passengers in the case of a crash. The decision, which will save the ailing auto industry approximately $1 billion a year, brought cheers from the automakers—and a storm of protest from consumer advocates. But the real threat to deregulation came from the insurance industry, which had hoped that passive restraints would reduce the cost of accident claims. "You're talking very big dollars," says Washington attorney Michael Sohn, who is representing the State Farm Mutual Automobile Insurance Co. in a suit to restore the standard.

Table 15.5
Permanent Full-Time Positions in Federal Regulatory Agencies (Fiscal Year)

The number of full-time positions in federal regulatory agencies has decreased from the peak reached in 1980.

Year	Positions
1970	27,661
1975	74,006
1980	90,495
1981	86,666
1982	79,745
1983	76,918
1984[a]	77,005
1985[a]	77,507

[a]Estimated.

Source: Kenneth W. Chilton and Ronald J. Penoyer, "The Hazards of 'Purse String' Regulatory Reform: Regulatory Spending And Staffing Under The Reagan Administration, 1981–85," Center for the Study of American Business (St. Louis: Washington University, April 1984), p. 4.

reasons: a concern that the level of competition in particular markets is inappropriate, a desire to take advantage of efficiencies resulting from large-scale operations, or a search for security that is not provided by market forces.

Antitrust laws are concerned with the relationships between firms—especially rival firms—and with the level of competition in a market. They are designed to promote market forces by attacking monopolization and combinations and conspiracies in restraint of trade. This type of government intervention is carried out at the federal and state levels, and depends heavily on the judicial system.

There are five major federal antitrust laws: the Sherman, Federal Trade Commission, Clayton, Robinson-Patman, and Celler-Kefauver Acts. The Sherman Act condemns combinations and conspiracies in restraint of trade, and monopolization. Combinations and conspiracies in restraint of trade may be either per se or Rule of Reason violations. Monopolization cases depend largely on the actions and market share of the firm being challenged.

Deregulation can also raise some highly charged emotional issues, as when the White House attempted to pare down rules designed to ensure that handicapped people have full access to public transportation and buildings. Soon after entering office, the Administration proposed to abolish the Architectural and Transportation Barriers Compliance Board, which established the access standards in the first place. Both Congress and handicapped groups were aghast. Compliance board chairman Mason Rose angrily vowed that the disabled would not return to "using back doors and freight elevators." Ultimately the board and the Administration struck a compromise in which 95 percent of the guidelines would remain intact. Only the most costly would be eliminated or deferred.

Source: Harry Anderson, "Mending the Rules," *Newsweek*, January 11, 1982, p. 51.

The Federal Trade Commission Act created the Federal Trade Commission, which, along with the U.S. Department of Justice, carries the primary responsibility for initiating antitrust activity for the federal government. The Clayton Act condemns exclusionary practices, interlocking directorates, price discrimination, and horizontal, vertical, and conglomerate mergers, where the effects of these activities are anticompetitive. The price discrimination and merger provisions of the Clayton Act were amended by the Robinson-Patman and Celler-Kefauver Acts, respectively. The penalties facing those found guilty of violating the antitrust laws include imprisonment, fines, structural remedies, and treble damages.

Regulation refers to participation by federal and state governments, through agencies and commissions, in business decision making. Unlike antitrust, which is concerned with the relationships between sellers, regulation is aimed at controlling certain industries and problem areas, and at protecting certain groups in the economy. In some instances an agency directly participates in a company's decision making, while in others the regulation is indirect and carried out through methods such as setting standards.

The division of regulatory authority between federal and state agencies depends upon whether the activity overseen is in interstate or intrastate commerce. Federal agencies, some of which are independent and some of which are attached to departments such as the Department of Labor, are created by the laws of Congress. Over the decade of the 1970s there was considerable growth in the number of federal regulatory agencies.

Regulation can be divided into industry and special purpose regulation. Industry regulation is direct and involves government participation in pricing, output, profit, and other decisions of firms in certain industries such as the electric, gas, and telephone industries. Special purpose regulation tends to be indirect and is not limited to firms in any single industry.

Two frequently cited reasons for industry regulation are the existence of a natural monopoly due to economies of scale and effects on the public's welfare from the operation of certain businesses. An important aspect of industry regulation is the setting of prices. This is typically done on a cost-plus basis, where prices are designed to generate enough revenue to cover expected costs plus a fair return to investors.

Special purpose regulation focuses mainly on the protection of the general public, the consumer, workers, and the environment. In recent years interest in deregulation has grown due to concern over the costs and benefits of industry and special purpose regulation.

Key Terms and Concepts

Antitrust laws

Monopolization and attempts to monopolize

Combinations and conspiracies in restraint of trade

Sherman Act

Per se violations
Price fixing and territorial division
Rule of Reason violations
Trade association
Federal Trade Commission Act
Clayton Act
Exclusionary practices
Interlocking directorates
Robinson-Patman Act
Price discrimination
Celler-Kefauver Act
Horizontal, vertical, and conglomerate mergers
Government regulation
Industry regulation
Natural monopoly
Cost-plus pricing
Special purpose regulation
Deregulation

Discussion and Review Questions

1. Horizontal mergers, vertical mergers, conglomerate mergers, price discrimination, and interlocking directorates may or may not be anticompetitive. For each of these five activities describe a set of circumstances where you think the effect would be anticompetitive and a set of circumstances where it would not be anticompetitive.
2. The antitrust laws are designed to control the growth of monopoly power in specific markets. What are some economic reasons for concern over monopoly power? Are there any noneconomic reasons for wanting to control this power?
3. Two types of regulation, industry and special purpose, have been identified in this chapter. In what respects are these types of regulation similar and in what respects are they different?
4. Antitrust laws reenforce the operation of free markets, while regulation replaces free market forces with an authoritative body. How do you explain that certain economic problems are dealt with by strengthening market forces while others are dealt with by replacing the market mechanism with regulatory authority?
5. What activities are prohibited by the Sherman Act, the Clayton Act, the Robinson-Patman Act, and the Celler-Kefauver Act, respectively?
6. Suppose legislation were passed to repeal the major federal antitrust statutes. How do you think such a repeal would affect competition? Would competition between sellers continue to exist much the same as before the repeal? Would there be a blossoming of monopoly power? Would something else occur?
7. What is a natural monopoly, and how is it related to economies of scale? What sort of dilemma does the combination of efficiency and monopoly power create for the consumer and the policy maker?
8. What are some benefits and some costs of regulation? How might people's attitudes on the costs and benefits of regulation explain the dramatic growth of regulation in the 1970s and the move toward deregulation in the 1980s?

Suggested Readings

William Breit and Kenneth G. Elzinga, *The Antitrust Casebook: Milestones in Economic Regulation* (Hinsdale, Illinois: The Dryden Press, 1982). Selections from leading court cases on price fixing and market division, mergers, monopolization, and exclusionary practices.

Alfred E. Kahn, "Environmental Values are Economic," *Challenge* (May–June 1979), pp. 66–67. An argument that the costs and benefits of environmental and other regulation should be measured to account for externalities before arriving at conclusions about its desirability or undesirability.

Robert A. Katzmann, *Regulatory Bureaucracy: The Federal Trade Commission and Antitrust Policy* (Cambridge: The MIT Press, 1980). An analysis of the organization of the Federal Trade Commission and case selection within the commission.

Paul W. MacAvoy, *The Regulated Industries and the Economy* (New York: W. W. Norton & Co., 1979). An analysis of the extent and effect of regulation on the economy and of regulatory reform.

"The Regulatory Process," *Federal Regulatory Directory: 1983-84* (Washington, D.C.: Congressional Quarterly, Inc., 1983), pp. 1–78. A survey of the regulatory process covering reasons for regulation, the history of regulation, approaches to regulation, costs and benefits of regulation, and other topics.

U.S., "Chapter 5: The Burden of Economic Regulation," *Economic Report of the President* (Washington, D.C.: U.S. Government Printing Office, 1983), pp. 96–123. A case for deregulation of the economy and a description of deregulation in the energy, transportation, communications, and financial markets.

Suzanne Weaver, *Decision to Prosecute: Organization and Public Policy in the Antitrust Division* (Cambridge: The MIT Press, 1977). A description of the organization and operation of the Antitrust Division of the U.S. Department of Justice.

IV THE INTERNATIONAL ECONOMY

16 THE INTERNATIONAL ECONOMY: TRADE

Chapter Objectives

1. To present an overview of U.S. international trade by highlighting major U.S. exports and imports, and countries with which the United States trades.
2. To explain the principle of comparative advantage.
3. To define free trade and discuss some arguments given in its favor.
4. To explain each of the major tools for restricting trade: tariffs, quotas, and embargoes.
5. To define protectionism and discuss some arguments given in its favor.

An introduction to economics would be incomplete without an overview of international economics. As the name suggests, international economics concerns the economic relationships among nations, particularly the movement of goods and services, and financial transactions. Since trading and financial transactions among nations have many dimensions, several topics are included under the heading of international economics. For example, the import and export of goods such as steel, wine, grain, and automobiles, foreign aid, military and security-related activities, and overseas investments are all relevant to this area.

This chapter introduces some of the important topics in international economics that relate to trade. It begins with an overview of U.S. international trade. Next, the concept of comparative advantage, a basic theory underlying international trade, is presented. This is followed by a section on one of the great debates in international economics: free trade vs. protectionism. Chapter Seventeen will deal with the financial aspects of international economics.

Before beginning this chapter, remember that the economic relationships among nations are important for many reasons. Not only do these relationships affect the domestic economies of various countries, but they also have implications for national politics, international relations, and social understanding. For example, an administration facing reelection may have its chances of returning to office reduced by a poor performance of the nation's currency in international trade. Or the dependence on a foreign supplier for a critical resource may affect political relations between two countries. Or, if the value of a nation's money falls internationally, it becomes more expensive, and therefore more difficult, for people in that nation to travel and learn firsthand about life in other societies.

AN OVERVIEW OF U.S. INTERNATIONAL TRADE

International trade
The buying and selling of goods and services among different countries.

An important aspect of international economics is **international trade:** the buying and selling of goods and services among different countries. International trade is important because of its effect on the availability of various goods and services, and its impact on the levels of production, employment, and prices in the trading countries. For example, sales in overseas markets would make a particular item available to foreign buyers and could result in the employment of more workers and machinery than would be the case if only domestic demand were met. On the other hand, the presence of a strong foreign competitor in a domestic market could lead to a drop in a domestic firm's sales, which in turn could foster a reduction in production and employment. Also, the presence of foreign goods increases competition in a market, which in turn influences product prices. And for a country that is dependent on a foreign product, increases in the price of the foreign product can influence that country's inflation rate.

The Size and Composition of U.S. Trade

Export
A good or service sold abroad.

Import
A good or service purchased from abroad.

The importance of international trade to the U.S. economy is illustrated in Table 16.1, which lists data on the **export** and **import** of goods and services for selected years. In the middle columns, titled "Exports" and "Imports," it can be seen that in recent years U.S. export and import transactions have resulted in the movement of hundreds of billions of dollars in goods and services annually. For example, in 1984 exports and imports amounted to $363.7 billion and $429.6 billion, respectively. Not surprisingly, the data in the middle columns also show that the dollar values of exports and imports have grown over the years.

The last two columns of Table 16.1 list exports and imports of goods and services as percentages of gross national product (GNP) for each of the selected years. Notice that both export and import activities have grown in relative importance when compared to GNP. In 1950 an amount equal to 5.0 percent of GNP was exported, and 4.3 percent of GNP was imported. By 1980 exports had grown to 12.9 percent of GNP, and the value of imports to 12.0 percent. One can conclude from Table 16.1 that foreign trade has become an increasingly important part of the U.S. economy over the last 30 years.

Table 16.1
Exports and Imports of Goods and Services (Billions of Dollars)

Both the dollar amounts of exports and imports, and exports and imports as a percentage of GNP have increased over the last thirty years.

Year	Gross National Product	Exports	Imports	Exports as a Percent of GNP	Imports as a Percent of GNP
1950	$ 286.5	$ 14.4	$ 12.2	5.0%	4.3%
1955	400.0	21.0	18.0	5.2	4.5
1960	506.5	28.9	23.4	5.7	4.6
1965	691.1	41.1	32.3	5.9	4.7
1970	992.7	65.7	59.0	6.6	5.9
1975	1,549.2	154.9	128.1	10.0	8.3
1980	2,631.7	338.8	314.8	12.9	12.0
1981	2,957.8	369.9	341.9	12.5	11.6
1982	3,069.3	348.4	329.4	11.4	10.7
1983	3,304.8	336.2	344.4	10.2	10.4
1984[a]	3,661.3	363.7	429.6	9.9	11.7

[a]Preliminary figures.

Source: U.S., *Economic Report of the President* (Washington, D.C.: U.S. Government Printing Office, 1985), pp. 232, 233.

What types of goods and services does the United States export and import? Table 16.2 illustrates the distribution of U.S. exports and imports by commodity group for selected years. A commodity group is composed of several different, broadly related types of products. For example, the "food and live animals" group includes such items as meat, dairy products, grains, fruits, nuts, vegetables, and animal feed.[1]

In the upper half of the table, it can be seen that the most important class of U.S. exports, by far, has been "machinery and transportation equipment," followed by "other manufactured goods," and "food and live animals." The "machinery and transportation equipment" category encompasses products ranging from electronic computers and telecommunications equipment, to pipe valves, railway vehicles, textile machinery, automobiles, and civilian aircraft. "Other manufactured goods" includes such products as tires and tubes, paper and paperboard, iron and steelmill products, and clothing.[2]

Imports by commodity group are shown in the lower half of Table 16.2. The table indicates that in recent years the most important import groups were "machinery and transportation equipment," "other manufactured goods," and "mineral fuels and related materials." Included within these three groups are several products that are important imports to the United States: petroleum, automobiles and auto parts, telecommunications equipment, office machines, and clothing.[3] Notice that "machinery and transportation equipment" and "other manufactured goods" are important both as U.S. exports and imports. Why is this the case? Is it a coincidence? Does it suggest something about what is traded or with whom we trade?

---

[1]U.S. Bureau of the Census, *Statistical Abstract of the United States: 1985* (105th ed.), Washington, D.C., 1985, p. 820.

[2]*Statistical Abstract of the United States: 1985*, p. 821.

[3]*Statistical Abstract of the United States: 1985*, p. 822–823.

Table 16.2
Percentage Distribution of U.S. Exports and Imports by Broad Commodity Group

Machinery and transportation equipment has become the most important export and import commodity group.

Commodity Group	1960	1965	1970	1975	1980	1983
Exports						
Food and live animals	13.2%	14.7%	10.2%	14.6%	12.8%	12.1%
Beverages and tobacco	2.4	1.9	1.6	1.2	1.2	1.4
Inedible crude materials (except fuels)	13.7	10.5	10.8	9.2	11.0	9.3
Mineral fuels and related materials	4.1	3.5	3.7	4.2	3.7	4.7
Chemicals	8.7	8.8	9.0	8.2	9.6	9.8
Machinery and transportation equipment	34.3	37.3	42.0	43.0	39.1	41.2
Other manufactured goods	18.7	18.0	17.9	15.6	17.8	15.2
Others	4.9	5.3	4.8	4.0	4.8	6.3
Imports						
Food and live animals	19.9%	16.1%	13.5%	8.8%	6.4%	6.0%
Beverages and tobacco	2.6	2.6	2.1	1.5	1.1	1.3
Inedible crude materials (except fuels)	18.3	14.5	8.3	5.8	4.3	3.7
Mineral fuels and related materials	10.5	10.4	7.7	27.5	33.9	22.5
Chemicals	5.3	3.6	3.6	3.8	3.5	4.2
Machinery and transportation equipment	9.7	13.8	28.0	24.4	24.7	33.4
Other manufactured goods	30.3	35.1	33.3	24.9	22.9	31.7
Others	3.4	3.9	3.5	3.3	3.2	0.0

Source: U.S. Bureau of the Census, *Statistical Abstract of the United States: 1985* (105th ed.), Washington, D.C., 1984, p. 820.

One important fact that Table 16.2, especially the import section, conveys is that the distribution of goods and services in international trade changes over time. For example, in 1965 the dollar value of coffee imported to the United States was higher than the value of imported automobiles and auto parts! Also, while imports of food and live animals have fallen in importance over the years, imports of mineral fuels and related materials have grown. The growth in importance of fuels and related materials is due in large part to the increased price of imported oil. In 1970 the value of crude and partly refined petroleum imports was $1.4 billion. By 1975, after the initial round of oil price increases, the value had grown to $19.3 billion, and by 1980 it was $65.7 billion. Since 1980 the value has sharply dropped due to decreasing prices.[4]

The experience with oil provides a useful example of how changes in international economic and noneconomic conditions can affect the amounts, types, and prices of goods and services that nations import and export, and ultimately the nations' domestic economies.

The Geographic Distribution of U.S. Trade

The percentages of U.S. exports to and imports from the continents and selected countries with which the United States traded in 1983 are given in Table 16.3. The majority of U.S. exporting and importing occurred with

[4]U.S. Bureau of the Census, *Statistical Abstract of the United States: 1984* (104th ed.), Washington, D.C., 1983, p. 840.

Table 16.3
Geographic Distribution of U.S. Exports and Imports in 1983

The majority of U.S. trade occurs with developed nations in North America, Europe, and Asia. Canada is the United States' most important trading partner.

Trade Between the U.S. and:	Percent of U.S. Exports	Percent of U.S. Imports
North America	26.4%	30.2%
Canada	18.8	20.2
Mexico	4.5	6.5
South America	5.3	6.2
Brazil	1.3	1.9
Venezuela	1.4	1.9
Europe	29.3	21.4
Federal Republic of Germany	4.3	4.9
Poland	0.2	0.1
Spain	1.4	0.6
United Kingdom	5.2	4.8
USSR	1.0	0.1
Africa	4.5	5.6
Algeria	0.3	1.4
Egypt	1.4	0.1
Nigeria	0.4	1.4
Asia	32.1	35.4
China (Mainland)	1.1	0.9
China (Taiwan)	2.3	4.3
Israel	1.0	0.5
Japan	11.0	16.0
Saudi Arabia	4.0	1.4
Australia and Oceania	2.4	1.2

Source: U.S. Department of Commerce, Bureau of the Census, *FT 455/1983, December and Annual, Vol. I, U.S. Exports* (Washington, D.C.: U.S. Government Printing Office, May 1984), pp. 1–4; and *FT 155/1983, December and Annual, Vol. I, U.S. Imports* (Washington, D.C.: U.S. Government Printing Office, May 1984), pp. 1–4.

nations in North America, Europe, and Asia, with Asian trade accounting for about one-third of U.S. trade. In terms of specific countries, Canada is the most important trading partner of the United States. Other nations such as Japan, Mexico, England, Germany, and Saudi Arabia are also important exporters and/or importers. Notice from Table 16.3 the relatively small percentage of trade between the United States and the Soviet Union. Notice also that U.S. trade with Taiwan is greater than with Mainland China.

COMPARATIVE ADVANTAGE AND INTERNATIONAL TRADE

Scarcity and Specialization

In the discussion of the definition of economics in Chapter One, it was pointed out that a scarcity of the material things in life forms the basis of the economic problem; that is, there are limited resources to produce goods and services to satisfy unlimited material wants and needs.

Specialization
Resources used in production are concentrated on a narrow range of tasks or on the production of a limited variety of goods and services.

One way the scarcity problem can be lessened is through increases in production gained by specialization. **Specialization** occurs when productive resources concentrate on a narrow range of tasks or on the production of a limited variety of goods and services. The concept applies to all factors of production but is most often associated with individuals and locations. For example, a doctor may specialize in cardiovascular surgery; a student may select accounting as her major; and Gary, Indiana is known for its steel production.

Specialization permits greater levels of production than would be attained without it. By concentrating on one type of productive activity, rather than acting in a "jack-of-all-trades" manner, a factor of production can be used more efficiently — and greater efficiency results in greater output. Specialization, however, depends on the ability to sell what one produces and to buy what one needs from someone else, or on the ability to trade. Thus, the availability of appropriate markets and the ability to trade are necessary accompaniments to specialization.

Specialization occurs on an international level when countries concentrate their productive efforts on the goods and services they are best at producing, and trade for the goods and services that are more costly to produce. A country that has a relatively inexpensive labor force might specialize in producing items requiring substantial labor inputs; a country with good agricultural resources might concentrate on growing basic grain crops or on livestock; and a country possessing sophisticated technological equipment and production methods might use these to its benefit. When each country concentrates on what it does more efficiently than other countries, international specialization increases total production and permits a lessening of the scarcity problem on a worldwide level.

The Principle of Comparative Advantage

Comparative advantage
One country has a lower opportunity cost of producing a good or service than does another country.

The basic principle behind the proposition that international trade can lessen the scarcity problem by increasing production is called **comparative advantage.** The root of comparative advantage is the concept that if countries produce those goods and services in which they have an advantage in comparison to other countries, and trade for what they are less adept at producing, the world will have more goods and services than it otherwise would. In essence, the principle of comparative advantage is a restatement of the benefits of international specialization.

To have an advantage in comparison to another country means that fewer units of other goods or services are given up to produce one unit of a certain good or service in one country than are given up to produce one unit of the same item in the other country. Put briefly, it means the opportunity cost of production is lower in the country with the comparative advantage.

To illustrate how comparative advantage works, and how it results in overall gains in output, let us examine a hypothetical production and trade relationship between the United States and Japan.

Assume that with 1 *unit* of resources (where 1 unit is equal to some combination of land, labor, capital, and entrepreneurship) the United States can produce either 10 tons of corn or 1 television set. Assume further that with 1 *unit* of resources Japan can produce either 1 ton of corn or 10 television sets. Table 16.4 illustrates these production possibilities.

The comparative advantage of each country in this example is obvious: the United States has the advantage in corn, and Japan in television sets. How is this determined? Opportunity costs in each country are compared.

The opportunity cost of producing 10 tons of corn in the United States is just 1 television set, while the opportunity cost of producing 10 tons of corn in Japan is 100 television sets. That is, Japan would be required to give up 100 television sets to produce 10 tons of corn, but the United States would need to give up only 1 television set. Clearly, the opportunity cost (measured in forgone television sets) of producing corn in the United States is lower than it is in Japan, giving the United States the comparative advantage in corn. The opportunity cost of producing 1 television set in the United States is 10 tons of corn, whereas in Japan producing 1 television set would mean giving up only one-tenth of a ton of corn. Clearly, the opportunity cost of producing a television set is lower in Japan, giving Japan the comparative advantage in television sets.

Earlier it was stated that the world would be better off in terms of the amounts of goods and services produced if comparative advantage and trade were exercised. Let us continue the corn and television example to illustrate this point. Assume now that the United States has 2 *units* of resources to employ, and uses 1 unit for the production of corn and 1 unit for the production of television sets. In this case, the United States will produce 10 tons of corn *and* 1 television set. Assume further that Japan also has 2 *units* of resources to employ and also uses 1 unit for the production of corn and 1 unit for television sets. In this case Japan will produce 1 ton of corn *and* 10 television sets. With resources employed in this manner, total production of these items by these two countries is 11 tons of corn and 11 television sets. This is shown in Table 16.5.

Now assume that Japan and the United States each decides to devote their productive resources to the good in which they have the comparative advantage and to engage in international trade. The United States will rely on

Table 16.4
Production Possibilities from the Employment of One Unit of a Country's Resources

The United States and Japan have a choice of production possibilities between corn and television sets when employing one unit of resources.

Country	Production Possibilities
United States	10 tons of corn or 1 television set
Japan	1 ton of corn or 10 television sets

Table 16.5
Production of Corn and Television Sets by the United States and Japan with 2 Units of Resources per Country

When the United States and Japan both produce corn and television sets with 2 units of resources each, 11 tons of corn and 11 television sets can be produced.

Item	Amount of Production
Corn	10 tons (U.S.) + 1 ton (Japan) = 11 tons total production
Television Sets	1 TV (U.S.) + 10 TVs (Japan) = 11 TVs total production

Japan to provide one of its favorite sources of information and recreation, and Japan will defer to the United States for some necessary foodstuffs. The United States will now devote its 2 units of resources to the production of corn, creating 20 tons of corn instead of 10 tons of corn and 1 television set. With Japan's 2 units of resources, it will now produce 20 television sets instead of 10 television sets and 1 ton of corn. Table 16.6 summarizes the resulting production when each country exercises its comparative advantage.

The increased total production registered in Table 16.6 (as compared to the figures in Table 16.5) demonstrates the benefits of specialization and trade. Without international specialization, a total of 11 tons of corn and 11 television sets could be produced by both countries together. With production based on comparative advantage, Japan and the United States can together produce a total of 20 tons of corn and 20 television sets using the same amount of resources. Clearly, the scarcity problem can be lessened through the exercise of comparative advantage and trade.

Free trade
Goods and services can be exported and imported by anyone in any country with no restrictions.

Does the principle of comparative advantage work in the real world? How closely is it followed? In order to fully exercise comparative advantage and reap its benefits, an environment of free trade is necessary. **Free trade** exists when goods and services can be bought and sold by anyone in any country with no restrictions. Everyone is free to choose with whom he or she deals,

Table 16.6
Production of Corn and Television Sets Based on Comparative Advantage with 2 Units of Resources per Country

When countries devote their resources to the production of goods in which they have a comparative advantage, the total production of these goods increases.

Item	Amount of Production
Corn	20 tons (U.S.) + 0 tons (Japan) = 20 tons total production
Television Sets	0 TVs (U.S.) + 20 TVs (Japan) = 20 TVs total production

regardless of location, and there are no barriers to trade. Import taxes are not imposed to artificially raise prices and discourage purchases, and limits are not set on the amounts that can be bought and sold. This free flow of trade permits specialization to work to its fullest.

FREE TRADE VS. PROTECTIONISM

In practice, international trade is carried out in a restricted manner. Policies that impede the international flow of goods and services are often imposed by different trading nations. Such policies, despite the fact that they may reduce a country's ability to fully exploit its various comparative advantages, are generally justified on the grounds that they are in the best interest of the nation that is imposing them.

Protectionism
The philosophy that it is in the best interest of a country to restrict importing and/or exporting.

The philosophy that it is in a country's best interest to restrict free trade is known as **protectionism.** According to the protectionist viewpoint, unrestricted importing and/or exporting may lead to certain economic and non-economic consequences injurious to the economy as a whole, to certain subgroups within the economy such as workers in particular industries, and/or to national security. Because of these potentially adverse effects, protectionists argue that restrictions should be imposed on international trade.

Protectionist policies can be employed to varying degrees. One nation may have very detailed regulations as to what, how, and with whom trade is conducted, while the import and export activity of another nation may be

Application 16.1
SAVING THE WORLD ECONOMY

In theory free trade benefits everybody. Tariffs and other trade barriers, it is said, encourage inefficiency, restrict commerce and lower the general standard of living. But the theory of free trade is rooted in a world that no longer exists. Adam Smith first advanced it in 1776, when Great Britain had a near monopoly in industrialization. Competition benefited some British industries and not others, but it did not affect Britain's total employment. As other nations industrialized (almost invariably behind temporary tariff walls), free trade prospered because there were abundant world markets and only a few key nations — no more than four or five — representing homogeneous cultures with comparable living standards operating by the discipline of the gold standard.

Today's world economy, by contrast, contains at least 20 significant trading nations of widely different cultural backgrounds with great variations in labor costs and standards of living, each claiming sovereign control over its economic decisions. In such conditions, competition became more ruthless and its impact more drastic. No longer does one sector of industry within one country benefit at the expense of another; rather whole industries decline simultaneously or even move from one country to another. The problems of our steel and automobile industries require no elaboration; very few television sets are still subject to loose restrictions. Also, a nation may alter the degree to which it relies on protectionist policies as economic and noneconomic conditions change.

The merits of free trade versus the merits of protectionism have been a source of debate for literally hundreds of years. Application 16.1, "Saving the World Economy," gives the viewpoint of a noted specialist in international relations on this controversy. In light of this debate over free trade and protectionism, it is useful to know some arguments on both sides of the issue in order to better form your own opinions. But before introducing the cases for free trade and for protectionism, let us examine the different types of trade restricting policies that a country may employ.

Trade Restricting Policies

Tariff
A tax on an import.

Three basic policies can be used to restrict trade: tariffs, quotas, and embargoes. A **tariff** is a tax placed on an import. Tariffs have the effect of raising import prices to domestic buyers, thereby making foreign goods less attractive to them. This in turn limits the quantities of imports demanded and makes it easier for domestic producers to sell their own products.

Examples of tariffs on goods entering the United States are illustrated in Table 16.7. The columns at the right-hand side of the table classify nations into three categories for tariff purposes. The column headed "G.S.P. Countries" is for nations importing under what is termed the "generalized system of preferences." Most countries, including Canada, Mexico, Israel, and Bra-

made in the United States. Many European countries with high expenditures for social welfare and inflexible labor costs are in an even more difficult position.

All political pressures and incentives of the modern democratic state work against the acceptance of the bitter medicine of government-sponsored austerity and cutthroat foreign competition. The loss of jobs sets up fierce pressures for protectionism. Nearly all industrial democracies — even while they give lip service to the ideals of free trade — have sought to nudge the terms of trade in a nationalist direction. Subsidies of exports, nontariff barriers to imports, guaranteed credits, as well as the manipulation of exchange rates become the order of the day. While one or two nations can occasionally manipulate the free-trading system to their advantage, the attempt by all nations to do so will surely wreck it.

The hope for recovery of a cooperative world order depends on the preservation of the free trading system. The industrial democracies must either agree to adhere to the principles of free trade — or else they will live in a mercantilistic world of unilateral actions and bilateral deals. At the same time, the free-trading system will not survive in a world of chronic recession. There is no hope of resisting the tide of protectionism unless the world returns to a path of economic growth.

Source: Henry A. Kissinger, "Saving the World Economy," *Newsweek*, January 24, 1983, pp. 46–47.

Table 16.7
Tariffs for Selected Goods

Tariffs, which raise the prices of imported goods to domestic buyers, can be expressed as a dollar amount or as a percentage of the value of the imported good.

	Tariff in 1985		
Item	**G.S.P. Countries**	**L.D.D. Countries**	**Communist Countries**
Ginger ale, ginger beer, lemonade, and soda water	1¢ per gal.	1¢ per gal.	15¢ per gal.
Champagne and other sparkling wines	$1.17 per gal.	$1.17 per gal.	$6 per gal.
Cigarettes	$1.06 per lb. plus 5% of value	$1.06 per lb. plus 5% of value	$4.50 per lb. plus 25% of value
Ornamented men's and boys' textile neckties	16.9% of value	16.9% of value	90% of value
Guitars:			
Value not over $100.00	9.4% of value	6.8% of value	40% of value
Other	14.0% of value	13% of value	40% of value
Fountain pens including ballpoint pens, ballpoint pencils	1.1¢ each plus 7.4% of value	0.8¢ each plus 5.4% of value	6¢ each plus 40% of value
Works of art by American artists temporarily living abroad	Free	Free	Free

Source: United States International Trade Commission, *Tariff Schedules of the United States Annotated 1985* (Washington, D.C.: U.S. Government Printing Office, 1984), pp. 1-81, 1-82, 1-88, 3-101, 7-59, 7-101, 7-103.

zil, fall into this category. The column headed "L.D.D. Countries" is for "least developed developing countries." Included in this group are Bangladesh, Chad, Haiti, Nepal, and other nations that have not reached a high level of economic development. Finally, the column headed "Communist Countries" is for nations such as the USSR, Albania, Bulgaria, and the communist-dominated parts of Korea.[5]

Notice that tariffs differ according to the three country categories given in Table 16.7. The highest tariffs are paid by communist countries, while the lowest, where applicable, are paid by least developed developing countries.

Quota
A restriction on the quantity of an item that can be imported into a country.

Quotas are restrictions on the quantities of various goods that can be imported into a country. For example, a country may impose a quota allowing only 10 million bushels of wheat to be imported over a one-year period. Once that amount is reached, no more wheat can flow into the country for the remainder of the year. Thus, a quota, like a tariff, restricts the ability of foreign goods to compete with domestic production. Examples of quota restrictions are found in Table 16.8, which lists limits on the amounts of certain textile products that can be imported to the United States from Taiwan.

[5]United States International Trade Commission, *Tariff Schedules of the United States Annotated 1985* (Washington, D.C.: U.S. Government Printing Office, 1984), pp. 3, 5, 6.

Table 16.8
Limits on Textile Imports from Taiwan (Effective January 1, 1985)

Absolute quotas limit the amounts of specific goods that can be imported into the United States over a defined period of time, such as one year.

Commodity	Limit (in dozens)
Men's and boys' wool suit-type coats	12,465
Men's and boys' wool trousers, slacks, and shorts	5,387
Women's, girls', and infants' wool coats	19,812
Women's, girls', and infants' wool trousers, slacks, and shorts	11,792
Men's and boys' man-made fabric knit shirts	642,951
Man-made fabric dresses	309,934

Source: United States Customs Service, Department of the Treasury, January 29, 1985.

In practice, there are two types of quota restrictions importers to the United States might face — absolute quotas and tariff-rate quotas. Absolute quotas, such as those illustrated in Table 16.8, limit the amount of a good entering the country over a certain period of time. Tariff-rate quotas place no restrictions on how much of a good enters the country, but limit the amount that can be imported at a lowered tariff.[6]

Embargo
A ban on trade in a particular commodity with another country.

An **embargo** is an outright refusal to trade in a particular commodity with another nation. For example, when an arms embargo is imposed, producers from one country are not allowed to sell weapons to buyers in another country. In this example the trade restriction has probably occurred for noneconomic reasons.

Free Trade Arguments

Arguments favoring unrestricted international trade center on the ability of free trade to increase economic efficiency, to increase the availability of goods and services and decrease their prices, and to provide a source of competition.

Trade, Specialization, and Efficiency Free trade permits the markets in which goods and services are bought and sold to expand, and the possibility of additional sales from expanded markets makes it feasible for resources to specialize in narrower ranges of tasks. In turn, this specialization allows resources to be used more efficiently than would otherwise be the case.

By using resources more efficiently, more goods and services can be produced, lessening the scarcity problem. This was illustrated earlier in the principle of comparative advantage. Recall the corn and television set example given in Table 16.5 and Table 16.6.

Increased Availability of Goods and Lower Prices A second argument in favor of free trade is that, in the absence of trade restrictions, consumers will

[6]United States Customs Service, Department of the Treasury, *Import Quotas* (Washington, D.C.: Customs Publication No. 519, July 1980).

pay lower prices and have larger quantities of goods from which to choose. Tariffs have the effect of raising prices; thus, their absence benefits the consumer by making foreign goods available at lower prices. The removal of quotas has the obvious effect of increasing the amounts of goods available for sale.

Trade and Competition A third argument for free trade is that it increases competition in a market, with resulting benefits to consumers. Recall from Chapter Thirteen that consumers fare better when there are more, rather than fewer, sellers in a market. As the number of sellers increases, the ability of an individual firm to exercise monopoly power over price and output diminishes, and price moves more toward cost. Thus, with foreign producers in a market, domestic sellers are in less of a position to extract economic profits.

Notice that in each of the three arguments just presented for free trade, the major beneficiary is the consumer. In the protectionist arguments, this is not the case.

Protectionist Arguments

The main thrust of the protectionist arguments is that, for either economic or noneconomic reasons, it is in the best interest of a nation to place restrictions on the international flow of goods and services. The major protectionist arguments include protection of infant industries and domestic employment and output, diversification, and national security.

Infant industry
An industry in the early stages of its development.

Protection of Infant Industries As the name suggests, an **infant industry** is an industry in the early stages of its development. Technological breakthroughs in areas such as electronics or fuels, the availability of previously unknown or inaccessible resources, or the opening of new regions where production can take place, can spawn industries new to an economy. In the formative stages, or infancy, of an industry, the newly developing businesses may face strong competitive pressures from established foreign sellers of rival products that can inhibit or even destroy any prospect for growth. When this occurs, a government may impose trade restrictions to allow its newly forming domestic industry to establish itself and grow in a protected environment.

For example, due to the construction of a new dam that provides electric power and allows water navigation by large vessels, it may be feasible for a small nation to begin developing a domestic steel industry. A problem, however, is that there are many countries, such as the United States, Japan, and Germany, that also produce steel and whose products could compete in the developing industry's domestic markets. In such a situation, a proponent of protectionism for the sake of infant industries would likely suggest that tariffs or quotas be imposed on foreign steel to allow the young industry to develop a domestic market for its products.

Protection of Domestic Employment and Output According to this protectionist argument, both foreign and domestic goods compete for the same domestic consumers' dollars. When consumer demand is not strong enough to support both foreign and domestic producers, the sale of one more unit of an imported good may come at the expense of its domestically-produced counterpart. In other words, the availability of foreign goods may lead to lower domestic output and higher domestic unemployment than would otherwise be the case.

An obvious solution to the problem from the protectionist point of view is to impose trade restrictions that would make it more difficult, or impossible, for foreign goods to complete in domestic markets. Such a policy, it is argued, would help to increase employment and output at home. Support for this argument frequently comes from both manufacturers and unions in specific industries facing a great deal of foreign competition, such as the U.S. automobile and steel industries.

Diversification The protectionist argument for diversification is a variation on the theme of not putting all of your eggs in one basket. According to this position, there are risks inherent in developing a significant dependency on foreign-produced goods because changes in the prices and/or availabilities of those goods can lead to economic disruptions at home. A striking example of this problem is the domestic energy crisis that followed from changes in the price and availability of OPEC oil.

The protectionist argument is that situations like this could be averted, or at least their impacts reduced, by *not* specializing to the point where a country develops critical dependencies on foreign products. Rather, domestic production should be diversified so that there are feasible alternatives to foreign-produced goods. Such a strategy would reduce the potential for outside sources to disrupt the economy. Accordingly, the imposition of tariffs and quotas to stimulate domestic production for the sake of diversification would be justifiable.

National Security For a variety of reasons, arguments have been put forward to impose tariffs, quotas, and embargoes in the name of national security. These reasons include the need to develop strong domestic defense-related industries, and the need to diversify in anticipation of interruptions of foreign supplies resulting from military or economic aggression or some other type of international hostility. Application 16.2, "National Security and Shoes," reprints a letter to the chairman of the Armed Services Committee from the president of the Footwear Industries of America, a trade group lobbying for protection of the shoe industry. This letter uses the argument of national security to ask for protection for domestic footwear manufacturers. Do you agree with the letter writer's point of view?

Evaluating the Arguments

It is up to you to decide which of these arguments has more merit than the others and whether you lean more toward free trade or protectionism. Are there any positions which you think are incorrect? Are there counterarguments to any of the arguments listed here?

The Real World of International Trade

Most countries do not choose a strict free trade or protectionist philosophy and then adhere to only those policies aligned with that philosophy. Instead, these two philosophies are the extremes toward which a country may lean. A country may adopt a comprehensive trade policy based on the principles of free trade or protectionism, or it may adopt more liberal terms of trade with some of its favored trading partners and restrict trade with other countries.

A country's policies concerning international trade also tend to shift with changing political and economic conditions. Since the early 1800s there have been movements toward and movements away from free trade policies by the United States. During a recession or economic downswing, a country's mood tends to become protectionist, resulting in a greater tendency to raise

Application 16.2
NATIONAL SECURITY AND SHOES

From a letter of August 6, 1984, to Senator John Tower, chairman of the Armed Services Committee, from George Langstaff, president of the Footwear Industries of America, a trade group lobbying for legislation to protect the shoe industry from imports.

Dear Mr. Chairman:

The recent decision of the International Trade Commission to deny import relief to the domestic nonrubber footwear industry has many ramifications, but one of the most serious has been little discussed. This is the fact that, in the event of war or other national emergency, it is highly unlikely that the domestic footwear industry could provide sufficient footwear for the military and civilian populations.

It is true that the military is required by law to purchase only domestically made footwear. However, no law confers on workers the skills necessary to make a quality product for the military. And with each plant closing—thirty-two so far in 1984—we lose the skilled workers as well as the productive facilities needed to produce footwear.

In the event of a mass mobilization, the United States will not have time to train new tanners, cutters, or heelers. And we won't be able to wait for ships to deliver shoes from Taiwan or Korea or Brazil or Eastern Europe. Because imported shoes now make up more than 70 percent of the domestic market—and because the ITC has refused the footwear industry's request to reduce that flood of imports—our country today is extremely vulnerable.

In recent years both NATO and the United

tariff barriers than would be the case during a period of economic growth. The Smoot-Hawley Tariff, which was passed in 1930 at the beginning of the Great Depression, raised tariff rates to some of the highest levels established by the United States in the twentieth century.

Trade subsidy
A government subsidy to the domestic producer of a good that is exported.

Instead of restricting trade, a country will sometimes adopt policies to promote the export of a domestically-produced good. That is, it will not restrict imports but will encourage its own exports. One method for accomplishing this objective is for government to **subsidize** the production of the good the country wishes to export. For example, if the United States decided that it wanted to encourage foreign purchases of its domestically-produced pianos, it could offer domestic piano manufacturers a subsidy for each piano sold abroad. This policy, which might be considered unfair by foreign piano makers, would be useful if the United States wanted to corner the world piano market.

Dumping
Selling a product in a foreign market below cost or below the price of the product in its own domestic market.

On occasion a country has been accused of **dumping** its products. This occurs when a good is sold in a foreign market below its actual cost or below the price at which it is sold in its own domestic market. Countries pursue this policy to eliminate excess production or to gain a share of a foreign market.

Finally, in the interdependent world of foreign trade, a change in a country's trade philosophy, a change in a tariff, quota, embargo, or subsidy, or

---

States have moved to "lighten" infantry divisions by placing less emphasis on tanks and armor and more emphasis on foot soldiers. Central to this strategy is the dismounting of the foot soldier; he will walk or run rather than ride on a mechanized vehicle, allowing him the flexibility to outflank and infiltrate the enemy's position.

But this strategy will fail if the foot soldier is without shoes.

Recent history bears this out. In 1982, the inadequate footwear of the British troops almost cost them their victory in the Falklands. Because their combat boots were poorly designed and cheaply made, by the end of the war *half* of all British troops were suffering from trenchfoot, an excruciatingly painful disease that makes walking almost impossible. If the war had gone on much longer, the cases of trenchfoot would have so depleted the British forces that they would have been unable to carry their campaign to completion.

Our dependence on foreign shoes is greater than our dependence on foreign oil. The Department of Defense is greatly concerned about this problem, and its Defense Support Personnel Center has begun a study of the ability of the domestic footwear industry to provide shoes to the military in wartime (CT-86-8430-S-01, *Shrinkage of the U.S. Shoe Industry*).

We are sure that this report will make official what our industry has been saying for years: the United States cannot afford to be without a domestic shoe industry. We must act *now* to save it.

Sincerely,
George Langstaff
President

Source: "National Security and Shoes," *Harper's* (November 1984), p. 19. Reprinted by permission of Footwear Industries of America, Inc.

dumping may cause retaliation by a trading partner. And there is always the danger that changing policies and retaliations will result in a trade war. When a trade war breaks out, the benefits of specialization on an international scale are jeopardized. No one seems to benefit. Application 16.3, "Is World on Brink of Trade War?", examines some recent actions that could bring undesirable results.

SUMMARY

International economics treats a variety of topics dealing with the economic relationships among countries. International trade, one aspect of this broad area, is concerned with the exporting and importing of goods and services and is important because it affects production, employment, and prices in the trading countries. In the United States, the amount of international trading has grown over the years to the point where the value of exports, as well as the value of imports, has been over 10 percent of GNP. The largest class

Application 16.3
IS WORLD ON BRINK OF TRADE WAR?

Among rich nations and poor, new trade tensions are threatening to explode into open economic warfare that could wreak havoc on the United States and its allies.

One after another, nations are putting up barriers to foreign competition in order to provide jobs at home. . . .

New trade obstacles are appearing at every turn. European countries are waging a battle with the United States over farm exports. The United States is struggling to get Japan to buy its cigarettes, beef and baseball bats. France is trying to block Swiss cheese. China is retaliating against U.S. restrictions on textile imports.

In Washington, Congress is debating action to keep out foreign-made cars, and trade agencies are considering clamping down on imports of shoes, frozen orange juice, cement, bicycles and hundreds of other products. . . .

The impact of a 1930s-style trade war with one retaliatory step followed by another could be enormous. When countries stop buying from each other, exports dwindle further and even more jobs are lost, economists note. . . .

Behind trade pressures are the economic woes of a world groping with recession. Since 1979, the number of jobless in industrialized nations has gone from 16 million to 32 million, says Peter Shore, economic spokesman of Britain's out-of-power Labor Party. What's more, despite signs of recovery, the total is expected to remain high for months.

In the United States, "you can definitely pin protectionist sentiment on unemployment," says Gerard Adams, professor of economics at the Wharton School of the University of Pennsylvania. "The real issue in Congress is that here are the basic traditional industries — autos, steel and tires — doing miserably and at the same time we're buying cars from Japan." . . .

A look around the world shows an explosion of methods to block imports. Some nations simply limit the amount of goods that can enter the country. The United States, for instance, is presof U.S. exports and an important class of imports has been machinery and transportation equipment. Most U.S. trade is with developed countries, particularly those in Asia, Europe, and North America.

Specialization, which occurs when productive resources concentrate on a narrow range of tasks or on the production of a limited variety of goods and services, permits a more efficient use of resources and greater levels of output than would otherwise be the case. Specialization on an international scale can be based on the principle of comparative advantage. A country has a comparative advantage when the opportunity cost (measured in forgone items) of producing a good or service is less in that country than in another.

The utilization of comparative advantage and international trade can increase overall production levels and lessen the scarcity problem. For comparative advantage to be fully exercised, an environment of free trade is necessary.

Free trade occurs when there are no restrictions on the flow of international trade. The alternative to free trade is protectionism, which is based on the viewpoint that restricted trade may be in the best interest of a country.

suring Japan to remove the quotas that restrict the amount of foreign beef and fruit that the Japanese buy. The quotas are blamed for driving up the price of a steak in Tokyo to $35.

New tariffs that raise the price of foreign goods are being levied. Europe has imposed tariffs of 12 to 19 percent on fertilizer from the United States, alleging that the U.S. is dumping excess fertilizer in Europe. Washington is threatening to raise tariffs on heavy motorcycles from Japan and West Germany.

More subtle ways of keeping out imports are sprouting. Japan irritates U.S. cosmetics and pharmaceutical firms by insisting on lengthy tests in Tokyo. The U.S. requires that American-made goods alone be used for bridges and highways financed by the new 5-cent-a-gallon gasoline tax. . . .

To become competitive, many countries feed massive doses of cash to hardpressed industries. The biggest row between the United States and the European Economic Community right now is over 15 billion dollars in subsidies to European farmers—about half for exporting their crops. . . .

Subsidies allow European farmers to lower prices when they sell food abroad, undercutting their U.S. competitors who want to sell there, too. In retaliation, the United States is selling 1 million tons of subsidized wheat flour to Egypt for $155 per ton, pushing French competitors out of the picture. Europeans fear that the United States next will dump some of its huge dairy surplus on world markets.

Country after country is hurling charges of subsidy at its neighbors. Lumber firms in the United States are asking for tariffs on Canadian lumber on the ground that exports are subsidized. Aircraft manufacturers complain that Airbus, the European maker, is supported by the EEC. The United States claims that Canada and Europe offer unreasonably low interest rates on loans to importing countries. . . .

Source: Excerpted from "Is World on Brink of Trade War?," by Michael Doan, *U.S. News & World Report,* March 14, 1983, pp. 57–58.

Protectionist policies may include: tariffs, which are taxes on imports; quotas, which are quantity limits on imports; or embargoes, which are outright refusals to trade a product.

The arguments for free trade center on the production gains that can be obtained from comparative advantage, the increased availability and lower prices of goods and services for consumers, and the benefits received from more competition in the market.

The protectionist arguments for trade restrictions include the need to protect infant industries and domestic output and employment, to diversify in case of economic disruptions, and to protect national security.

Key Terms and Concepts

International trade
Export
Import
U.S. trading partners
Specialization
Comparative advantage
Free trade
Protectionism
Tariff
Quota
Embargo
Free trade arguments
Protectionist arguments
Infant industry
Trade subsidy
Dumping

Discussion and Review Questions

1. The state of tariffs and quotas on foreign cars is a source of continual debate in the United States. What is the current tariff and quota situation on automobiles imported from Japan, Germany, and Sweden? Would you favor increasing or decreasing these tariffs and/or quotas? Why?
2. Some people favor free trade while others favor protectionism. This suggests that some groups gain from free trade while others lose, and that some gain from protectionism while others lose. Who gains and who loses from free trade and from protectionism?
3. International trade must occur in free markets if countries' comparative advantages are to be fully exploited. Why is this so? If the United States produced according to its comparative advantage, in what goods and services do you think it would specialize?
4. Explain how international trade might affect a country's levels of production, employment, and prices.
5. "Comparative advantage is the application of specialization on an international level." What is meant by this statement? Define comparative advantage and explain how comparative advantage lessens the basic scarcity problem of economics.
6. Differentiate among a tariff, a quota, and an embargo, and show how each restricts trade. Determine the current tariff or quota on a foreign

product by locating it in a government publication or by contacting a seller of the foreign product.

7. Protectionists argue that putting a tariff on a good protects a domestic industry's output and employment; others argue that the country hurt by the tariff may retaliate by restricting trade from the country imposing the tariff. The end result could be a loss of output and employment in an exporting industry of the country that initiated the tariff action. Comment.
8. With 1 unit of resources, China could produce either 20 tons of wheat or 60 tons of rice, and Hungary could produce either 40 tons of wheat or 4 tons of rice. Which country has the comparative advantage in wheat? Which country has the advantage in rice? What is China's opportunity cost of 1 ton of wheat and of 1 ton of rice? What is Hungary's opportunity cost of 1 ton of wheat and 1 ton of rice?
9. Given the information in question 8, if each country had 2 units of resources and devoted 1 unit to the production of wheat and 1 unit to the production of rice, how much wheat and rice would be produced? If each country used both units to produce the item in which it has a comparative advantage, how much wheat and rice would be produced?

Suggested Readings

M. Frederic Bastiat, "Petition From the Manufacturers of Candles, Wax-lights, Lamps, Chandeliers, Reflectors, Snuffers, Extinguishers; and From the Producers of Tallow, Oil, Resin, Alcohol, and Generally of Everything Used for Lights," ***Sophisms of Protectionism*** **(New York: G. P. Putnam's Sons, 1893), pp. 73–80.** A satirical petition to government that a law be passed to protect candlemakers and others by banning sunlight.

Lester Brown, "The U.S.–Soviet Food Connection," ***Challenge*** **(January–February 1983), pp. 40–49.** Discusses the decline in production of basic agricultural commodities by the Soviet Union in recent years and the increasing dependence of the Soviet Union on the United States for food.

Irving B. Kravis, "The Current Case for Import Limitations," ***Changing Patterns in Foreign Trade and Payments,*** **ed. Bela Balassa, 3d ed. (New York: W. W. Norton & Co., Inc., 1978), pp. 1–26.** The author argues against import limitations by pointing out the weaknesses of many protectionist arguments and the costs of protectionism.

"Special Report: Japan's Strategy For the '80s," ***Business Week,*** **December 14, 1981.** A special issue containing 20 separate articles relating to Japan's future role in the area of high-technology production and exporting in industries such as semiconductors and information processing.

"The cost of protecting Detroit," ***Consumer Reports,*** **March 1985, pp. 149–150.** Discusses the costs to consumers, in specific dollar terms, of restricting the number of Japanese cars that can be imported to the United States.

17 THE INTERNATIONAL ECONOMY: FINANCE

Chapter Objectives

1. To understand the flow of payments that occurs with international financial transactions.
2. To identify the two major categories of financial movements: the current account and assets movements.
3. To define balance of trade and balance of trade surplus and deficit, and discuss the annual balance of trade for the United States for the past few decades.
4. To introduce the problems created for the international financial system by large-scale foreign borrowing and the inability of some borrowing nations to meet their obligations.
5. To define exchange rates and explain how they are determined under both fixed and flexible exchange rate systems.

Chapter Sixteen centered primarily on international trade, or the exporting and importing of goods and services. There are, however, many other types of international transactions that are important to an economy. These include military aid, foreign assistance, grants, loans and investments, and private gifts to foreigners. The first section of this chapter deals with international financial transactions, showing how different types affect payment flows between countries and how transactions are classified for analysis purposes. Discussions of the balance of trade, an important and often referred to transaction classification, and problems arising from foreign borrowing by some nations are also included in this section.

Since international financial transactions involve flows of payments between countries, some method for determining the values of foreign currencies and for exchanging domestic money for foreign money is necessary. This is important because the value of a country's currency in foreign money markets affects the prices of its exports, imports, and foreign investments. In that regard, the value of the dollar in relation to the yen, pound, and other foreign currencies is so important to U.S. international transactions that it is given in many daily news broadcasts and in most major newspapers. The second part of this chapter deals with exchanging currencies, exchange rates, and how those rates are determined.

INTERNATIONAL TRANSACTIONS AND BALANCES

International transactions are important because they involve flows of payments from one country to another. These flows in turn have an impact on the values of nations' monies in international trade. Because of the economic effects of the flows of payments between nations, it is necessary for a country to regularly assess the figures for its international transactions that cause payment outflows and inflows. This is done to determine whether more payments are flowing out of a country than are flowing in, or vice-versa, or whether these payments are in balance.

In the United States an outflow of dollars occurs when businesses, individuals, or government units buy foreign products, travel abroad, invest in foreign private or public securities, or take any other action in which U.S. dollars are expended for foreign items. Examples include U.S. purchases of French wine or Japanese automobiles, the buying of an electronics plant in Belgium by a U.S. firm, and the granting of a few million dollars in aid to an earthquake-ravaged South American country. Foreign payment inflows to the United States occur when foreigners purchase U.S. products and securities, or take some other action that results in the expenditure of foreign money for U.S. items. Money spent by a British tourist to visit Disney World, the buying of a U.S. farm by a Canadian, the tuition paid to a U.S. college by a Saudi Arabian student, and the purchase of Treasury securities by an Australian investor are all examples of transactions leading to foreign currency inflows to the United States.

In order to analyze the many and varied types of international transactions that occur, two major categories of financial movements have been developed. Each category consists of several components. Through the use of these categories the accounting process for international transactions is simplified and areas with payment imbalances can be readily identified. The first major category is the current account and the second is assets movements.

The Current Account

Current account
A category of international transactions that includes figures for imports and exports of merchandise, unilateral transfers, and other foreign dealings.

The **current account** category includes exports and imports of merchandise (goods), income from investments, and other components such as military transactions, foreign travel and transportation, and unilateral transfers (gifts). Table 17.1 lists the major components of the current account and their dollar values for 1983. In calculating these figures, dollar payment outflows are given as negative numbers and dollar payment inflows as positive num-

Table 17.1
Current Account Components and Balance

The current account lists net payment flows for various categories of international transactions and indicates whether an overall surplus or deficit in the current account resulted.

Component		Billions of Dollars in 1983
Exports of merchandise	$200.3	
Imports of merchandise	−261.3	
Net balance (balance of trade)		−$61.0
Net investment income		23.5
Net military transactions		0.5
Net travel and transportation receipts		− 4.6
Net, other services		8.7
Remittances, pensions, and other unilateral transfers		− 8.7
Balance on current account		−$41.6

Source: U.S., *Economic Report of the President* (Washington, D.C.: U.S. Government Printing Office, 1985), p. 344.

bers. For example, the value of U.S. exports of merchandise in 1983 is listed as $200.3 billion, a positive number because exports bring in payments. The value of imports of merchandise in 1983 is given as −$261.3 billion, a negative number since dollars flow out when foreign goods are purchased. When merchandise imports are subtracted from exports, a net figure called the **balance of trade** results. In 1983 the balance of trade was −$61.0 billion.[1]

Balance of trade
The figure that results when merchandise imports are subtracted from exports.

Notice the dollar figures in the various classifications in Table 17.1. Most are given as net figures; that is, the payment outflows have already been subtracted from the inflows and are not given separately as were merchandise exports and imports. For example, on net income from investments, more payment inflows than outflows occurred, resulting in a net figure of $23.5 billion; but for the travel and transportation component, payment outflows were greater than inflows, causing a −$4.6 billion figure.

All of these net figures are added together to arrive at the current account balance, which was −$41.6 billion in 1983. This figure means that transactions from the current account components caused 41.6 billion *more* U.S. dollars to flow out for payment than the value of money that flowed in. This is referred to as a **current account deficit.** Had the figure been a positive number, there would have been a **current account surplus.**

Current account deficit (surplus)
A negative (positive) figure results when all current account transactions are added together.

Balance of Trade As indicated in Table 17.1, the balance of trade is only one part of the current account balance. It is, however, significant because it involves the flow of a substantial amount of money, reflects the results of a nation's international trade activity, and is frequently cited in studies and discussions of international transactions. When the value of a country's

[1] Be careful to notice that the term balance of trade is different from the term net exports, which was discussed in Chapter Five. The balance of trade is calculated on the basis of exports and imports of goods, whereas net exports is calculated on the basis of exports and imports of both goods and services.

Balance of trade surplus
The value of a country's merchandise exports is greater than its imports.

Balance of trade deficit
The value of a country's merchandise imports is greater than its exports.

exports of goods is greater than the value of its imports, a **balance of trade surplus** occurs; when the value of a country's imports of goods is greater than the value of its exports, a **balance of trade deficit** arises.

Figure 17.1 charts the annual balance of trade for the United States for 1950 through 1983. Observe that prior to the 1970s, the United States primarily experienced trade surpluses. In the 1970s and especially the 1980s, however, sizable trade deficits occurred. These deficits can be explained in part by increases in the price of imported oil. Other factors, such as the popularity of foreign-built automobiles and home electronic equipment, strong foreign rivals in markets for U.S. export products, and the strength of the dollar in international trade, are also causes of the deficits.

Figure 17.1
U.S. Balance of Trade: 1950–1983

In the 1970s and 1980s, the United States began running significant balance of trade deficits as the value of merchandise imports exceeded the value of exports.

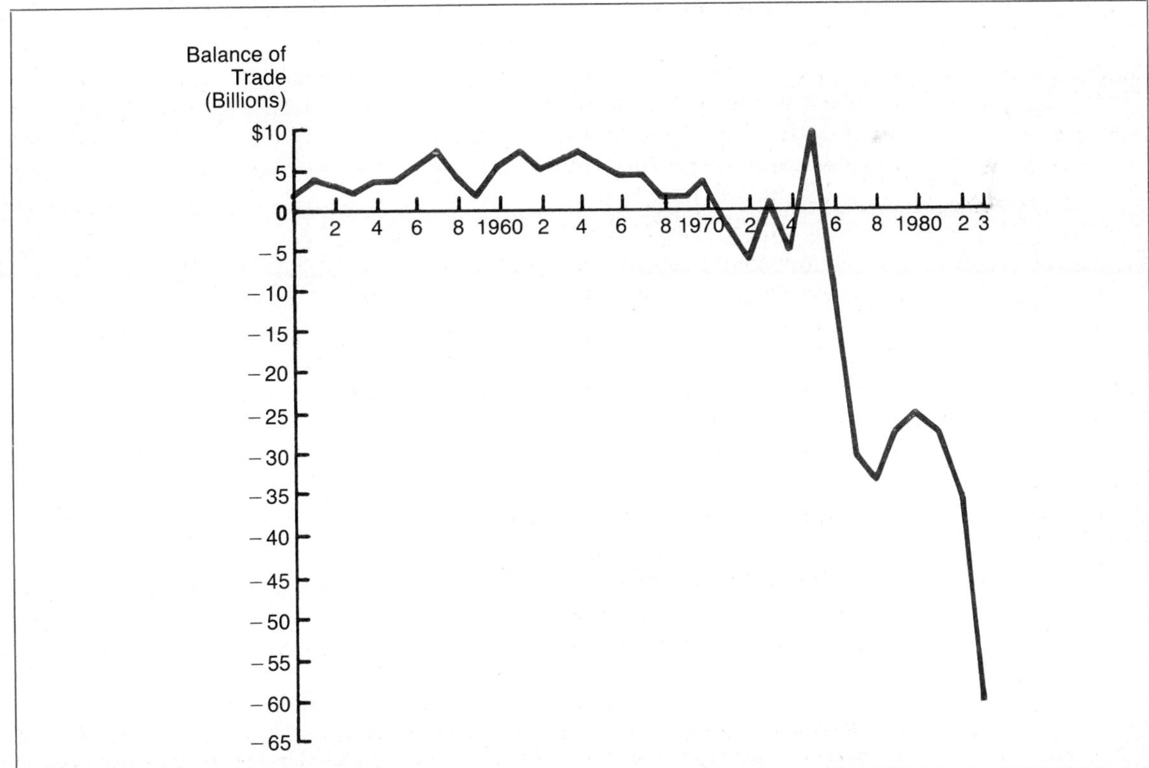

Source: U.S., *Economic Report of the President* (Washington, D.C.: U.S. Government Printing Office, 1985), p. 344.

Assets Movements

Assets movements The international transactions category that includes foreign investments, government loans, and other asset related movements.

The second category of international transactions involves assets—both U.S. assets abroad and foreign assets in the United States. Included in this category, titled **assets movements,** are such items as government loans, private investments and securities, and holdings that satisfy payment imbalances. The major components of the assets movements category are given in Table 17.2.

Loans made by the U.S. government, and U.S. private expenditures for foreign investments and securities are the basic components of the movement of U.S. assets abroad. These components, which totaled $887.5 billion in 1983 according to Table 17.2, cause payment outflows from the United States. (Table 17.2 does not report dollar outflows as negative numbers as does Table 17.1.)

Loans from foreign sources and foreign expenditures for U.S. investments and securities are the primary components of the movement of foreign assets to the United States. According to Table 17.2, these components, which cause payment inflows to the United States, totaled $781.5 billion in 1983. As shown at the bottom of Table 17.2, in 1983, assets movements between the United States and foreign countries resulted in more payments flowing

Table 17.2
U.S. International Assets Movements

U.S. assets abroad cause payments to flow from the United States to foreign countries, and foreign assets in the United States cause payments to flow to the United States. In 1983 the position of the United States with regard to assets movements was −$106.0 billion, indicating that U.S. asset movements abroad were greater than foreign asset movements to the United States.

Type of Transaction	Billions of Dollars in 1983	
U.S. Assets Abroad (cause outflows from the U.S.)		
U.S. official reserve assets		$ 33.7
U.S. government assets other than official reserve assets		79.3
U.S. loans and other long-term assets	$ 77.6	
U.S. foreign currency holdings and short-term assets	1.7	
U.S. private assets		$774.4
Direct investments abroad	$226.1	
Foreign securities	84.8	
Other	463.5	
Total U.S. assets abroad		$887.5
Foreign Assets in the U.S. (cause inflows to the U.S.)		
Foreign official assets in the U.S.		$193.9
Other foreign assets in the U.S.		587.6
Direct investments in the U.S.	$133.5	
U.S. Treasury securities	33.9	
Other	420.1	
Total foreign assets in the U.S.		$781.5
Net International Investment Position of the U.S.		−$106.0

Source: U.S., *Economic Report of the President* (Washington, D.C.: U.S. Government Printing Office, 1985), p. 349.

out of than flowing into the United States. To be exact, $106.0 billion more in U.S. assets moved abroad than foreign assets moved to the United States.

When the figure showing the net position on the assets movements account is combined with the figure showing the balance on the current account, it can be determined whether the combined effect of all payments transactions caused a net inflow or outflow, or resulted in a positive (surplus) or negative (deficit) figure for the year. If an overall payment deficit occurs, and more dollars flow out than foreign money flows in, is there a means for settling this deficit? If the opposite holds true, and more money flows in than out, must any special financial arrangements be made?

In the years prior to the late 1960s and early 1970s, payment deficits were often settled in gold. A country holding, say, $1 million worth of U.S. money because of a payment imbalance, could redeem these dollars for gold from the official U.S. gold reserves. It was due to persistent payment deficits and their redemption in gold that the U.S. gold supply dwindled in the 1950s and 1960s and was, as noted earlier, finally frozen.[2]

Because the United States no longer redeems its money in gold, its international payments imbalances primarily alter foreign dollar holdings. Overall, U.S. payment deficits increase foreign holdings of dollars, and surpluses reduce them. Deficits and surpluses may also alter holdings of various instruments created for international monetary transactions, such as SDRs —Special Drawing Rights.[3] Changes in the holdings of dollars and foreign monies and in other reserve assets are included in the figures in Table 17.2.

It must be noted at this point that persistent U.S. deficits result in accumulated foreign holdings of U.S. dollars that may, at some point, reduce the value of the dollar in international trade. This issue will be discussed shortly. One institution that has played an important role in the loan-making component of assets movements is the International Monetary Fund. Application 17.1, "What the I.M.F. Does," provides a brief history and description of the Fund's activities.

The External Debt Crisis

As indicated in the assets movements account in Table 17.2, one important class of international financial transactions involves loan making among countries. Many nations, especially those that are developing, borrow from lenders, such as banks, in other countries to help finance investments and other activities. This type of borrowing is termed **external debt** since it is owed to lenders outside of, or external to, the borrowing country. For some borrowing nations, the size of their external debt has become so large that

External debt
Money owed by a country to a lender in another country.

[2]See Chapter Seven.

[3]SDRs (Special Drawing Rights) are a type of international money created by the International Monetary Fund that can be used to obtain currency of other countries. From Colin D. Campbell and Rosemary Campbell, *An Introduction to Money and Banking*, 5th ed. (Hinsdale, Illinois: The Dryden Press, 1984), p. 205.

serious concerns have been raised over the ability of these nations to repay the interest on their loans, much less repay the loans themselves.

The magnitude of the external debt problem is illustrated in Table 17.3, which ranks several countries according to the amount each owes to foreign lenders as a percentage of that country's GNP. At one extreme, countries such as the United States, the USSR, and Japan owe relatively small amounts to outsiders when compared to the sizes of their GNPs. At the other extreme, countries such as Costa Rica and the Ivory Coast owe more in external debt than their entire economy produces in one year. In between are the less dramatic but still critical situations where nations' debts to outsiders represent a significant share of their GNPs.

If borrowing countries fail to pay their debts to foreign lenders, serious financial consequences result for individuals and institutions in the lending countries. But honoring these financial obligations may require the borrowing countries to submit to harsh and perhaps unacceptable measures. Application 17.2, "Postponement of Third World Debts Threatens Upheaval, Financial Collapse," explains what is at stake for lenders and borrowers in the external debt crisis and discusses some problems that stand in the way of solving the crisis.

EXCHANGE RATES

U.S. goods and services and U.S. investment opportunities such as stocks, bonds, and real estate, carry price tags that are expressed in dollars. You can buy a particular car for, say, $10,000, or invest in a piece of real estate for, say, $1,200 per acre. Regardless of who directly buys or invests in U.S. goods and services, be they from the United States, France, Saudi Arabia, or some

Application 17.1
WHAT THE I.M.F. DOES

The International Monetary Fund, created while World War II raged, was designed to help nations prevent the sort of economic chaos that followed World War I.

One of its major responsibilities has been to make loans to any of its 146 member countries that have trouble paying their bills. The I.M.F. has a pool of . . . [billions of dollars], as well as a special fund . . . to meet emergencies.

The fund's responsibilities were hammered out at a conference in Bretton Woods, N.H., in July 1944. It was agreed then that an organization should be formed to secure monetary cooperation among nations and expand liquidity to fuel a postwar recovery.

In its early history, the fund's major duty was to promote fixed rates for the exchange of foreign currencies. That responsibility faded in 1973, however, when most nations began to "float" their currencies without regard to fixed rates.

The fund, based in Washington, operates much like a commercial bank. It makes decisions

Table 17.3
External Debt as a Percentage of GNP

When external debt as a percentage of GNP is measured, some countries owe a small percentage while others have an external debt that is greater than their annual GNP.

Country	External Debt as a Percentage of GNP
USSR	2.1%
United States	9.8
Japan	10.3
Mexico	60.5
Jordan	65.8
Argentina	70.6
Panama	77.7
Uruguay	81.8
Chile	89.0
Jamaica	100.0
Costa Rica	108.6
Ivory Coast	116.1

Source: Based on "Per-Capita Picture" *The Wall Street Journal,* June 22, 1984, p. 29. Reprinted by permission of *The Wall Street Journal,* © Dow Jones & Company, Inc. (1984). All Rights Reserved.

other nation, payment for these items is usually made in dollars. Similarly, buyers and investors, regardless of their nationality, typically pay pounds to acquire British goods and yen to acquire Japanese items. Thus, importing from or investing in another country ordinarily involves converting one's money into the money of the nation with which one is dealing. An American auto importer who has borrowed dollars to buy Japanese cars will likely convert those dollars to yen to transact business with the Japanese auto manufacturer.

Importers and investors need to know how much foreign goods and services or investment opportunities cost in terms of their own money. For example, the U.S. importer of Japanese automobiles must know not only

on loans only after usually long negotiations on changes in economic policy that must be followed by a nation requesting funds. Those talks are supposed to be apolitical, but rarely are.

Because the United States provides 20 percent of the money for I.M.F. loans, Washington has 20 percent of the vote on loan decisions, and thus an effective veto. . . .

Two men were the prime movers behind the establishment of the fund: [Harry] Dexter White, assistant to then-Secretary of the Treasury Henry Morgenthau Jr., and John Maynard Keynes, the British economist who was an adviser to the British Treasury.

Forty-four governments signed the agreement at Bretton Woods, which also led to the establishment of the International Bank for Reconstruction and Development, or World Bank, a source of investment capital for its members.

Source: "What the I.M.F. Does," *The New York Times,* December 11, 1982, p. 42. Copyright © 1982 by The New York Times Company. Reprinted by permission.

how many yen each car will cost, but also, and perhaps more importantly, how many *dollars* that price represents. In order to determine the dollar cost of a car purchased from Japan, the U.S. importer will use the exchange rate between the U.S. dollar and the Japanese yen.

Exchange rate
The number of units of a nation's money that is equal to one unit of another nation's money.

The **exchange rate** between two nations' monies is the number of units of one nation's money that is equal to one unit of the other nation's money. For example, the exchange rate between the French franc and the dollar might be 10 francs to $1, or 1 franc to $0.10. At this exchange rate, an item selling for 400 francs in Paris could be purchased by a U.S. tourist for the equivalent of $40. If the exchange rate were 5 francs to the dollar, then each franc would be equal in value to $0.20, and the same 400 franc item could now be purchased by the tourist for the equivalent of $80.

Exchange rates between the U.S. dollar and several foreign monies are

Application 17.2
POSTPONEMENT OF THIRD WORLD DEBTS THREATENS UPHEAVAL, FINANCIAL COLLAPSE

On Aug. 19, 1982, Mexico's finance minister, Jesus Silva Herzog, visited Citibank executives in New York to alert them to what he would tell all bankers the following day: Mexico couldn't repay its foreign loans.

As news filtered into Citibank's ranks, one of the bank's lending officers in Mexico City gravely predicted: "We're going to be talking about developing-country debt problems for a long time. It'll probably be two years before we're out of the woods."

Two years may have seemed like a long time to that Citibank banker, but it hasn't been nearly long enough to solve the international debt crisis. Since August 1982, the debt problem has been largely pushed forward, day to day, week to week. Principal payments falling due over the next year are postponed, while new loans are made to help pay interest on the old ones. Belts are tightened a bit more. And the result is that it's all still there—looking bigger than ever. . . .

[Many] believe, the pattern of postponement is wearing thin under rising interest rates, growing protectionism, and continued Third World recessions. Each short-term push now isn't forward but is down, deeper into the debt hole. The internal economies of the developing countries are cracking under the weight of their debt burdens; some of their political structures are stretching to the breaking point. And the threat increases that countries, facing internal political upheavals, will walk away from their debts, disrupting the international financial system.

Little surprise, then, that the recent jitters in the financial markets stem partly from concern that the debt crisis hasn't been confronted, just papered over. Last month, Manufacturers Hanover Trust Co., the nation's fourth-largest bank, came under a siege of rumors concerning liquidity problems. Its stock plummeted, and it dragged down with it the shares of other money-center banks.

It was no coincidence, bankers believe, that Manufacturers Hanover tops the list of big U.S. banks in relative exposure to troubled Latin American borrowers. At the end of 1983, Hanover's $6.5 billion in loans to the four largest Latin American debtors amounted to 284% of its shareholders' equity. . . .

Yet any real solution has real costs; the major questions are how much and who pays. The cost for debtor countries is slower economic growth given in Table 17.4. Using the Austrian schilling as an example, Table 17.4 shows that on March 11, 1985, 1 schilling was worth \$0.04266, or 23.44 schillings could have been exchanged for 1 dollar (\$1/0.04266 = 23.44). Notice that the exchange rate quotations in the table are for one day only. This is because exchange rates between nations' monies are continually changing in response to economic and noneconomic factors. How and why these rates change is the subject of the next section.

How Exchange Rates Are Determined

Prior to late 1971 exchange rates between the dollar and many other monies were based primarily on gold. That is, the value of the dollar and other monies was expressed in terms of the amount of gold one unit of each country's

---

and more poverty. Industrial countries face more unemployment if their corporations can't sell to cash-strapped developing nations. Bank stockholders have lost much already and may lose a lot more. And if the U.S. government bails out debtor nations, the cost will be higher taxes for U.S. citizens; if the government bails out the banks, the result may be higher inflation.

And perhaps more than anything else, the distribution of costs will permeate the political affairs of the debtor countries and their relations with the U.S. Mexico's political and economic difficulties have spilled into the U.S. in the form of illegal immigration. In the Dominican Republic, about 50 people died in rioting after the government increased prices as part of an International Monetary Fund austerity package. And as Brazil and Argentina try to move toward democracy, their economic troubles raise a disturbing question: Can you have recessions and budding democracies without social disorder? . . .

According to the International Monetary Fund, during 1983 about 30 developing countries completed or were engaged in debt refinancings. The total debt of these countries came to about \$400 billion at the end of 1983, or more than half the total developing-country debt.

Most of these refinancings consisted of postponing principal payments due over the following year or so. . . .

The upshot: There is a big debt hump ahead, and countries won't be able to pay it. . . .

Yet the current emergency solutions don't provide the debtor countries with the means to get out of their debt hole by growing. Most of the countries are following contractionary IMF policies designed to put them in better shape for economic growth after a couple of years. But today, with lenders wary and foreign exchange eaten up by interest payments, growth isn't likely.

Moreover, IMF policies call for a cutback in imports and an expansion of exports. But if all these troubled countries cut back imports, who is left to buy the exports? . . .

Meanwhile, rising U.S. interest rates hasten the search for long-term answers to the global debt crisis. . . .

Each percentage-point increase in the interest rates translates into an annual increase in debt payments of about \$750 million in Brazil, \$350 million in Argentina, and \$900 million in Mexico. Mexico argues that the rise in the U.S. prime rate this year has wiped out the \$1 billion increase in nontraditional exports achieved last year. . . .

Source: Lawrence Rout, "Postponement of Third World Debts Threatens Upheaval, Financial Collapse," *The Wall Street Journal*, June 22, 1984, pp. 25, 28. Reprinted by permission of *The Wall Street Journal*,

Table 17.4
Exchange Rates Between the U.S. Dollar and Selected Foreign Monies (March 11, 1985)

Exchange rates show how much of one nation's money is equal to one unit of another nation's money.

Nation	Number of Dollars Required to Equal One Unit of Foreign Money	Amount of Foreign Money Equal to One Dollar
Austria	$0.04266 = 1 schilling	23.44 schillings = $1.00
Britain	1.09 = 1 pound	0.9174 pounds = 1.00
France	0.09814 = 1 franc	10.19 francs = 1.00
Israel	0.001317 = 1 shekel	759.45 shekels = 1.00
Japan	0.00386 = 1 yen	259.10 yen = 1.00
Mexico	0.004115 = 1 peso	243.00 pesos = 1.00
West Germany	0.2997 = 1 mark	3.3370 marks = 1.00

Source: "Foreign Exchange," *The Wall Street Journal,* March 12, 1985, p. 56. Reprinted by permission of *The Wall Street Journal,* © Dow Jones & Company, Inc. (1985). All Rights Reserved.

money would command. For example, if 1 dollar was worth ⅟₃₅ of an ounce of gold, and if 4 West German marks were worth ⅟₃₅ of an ounce of gold, then the exchange rate between the dollar and the mark would have been 1 dollar equals 4 marks, or 25 cents equals 1 mark.

By basing the values of different monies on gold, the exchange rates between those monies were generally fixed; they fluctuated through a very narrow range. The only way a major change could occur in exchange rates was if one nation redefined the value of its money in gold: for example, if the United States were to have declared that 1 dollar would be worth ⅟₄₀ rather than ⅟₃₅ of an ounce of gold.

Devaluation
When the amount of gold backing a nation's monetary unit is reduced.

When a country declared that its monetary unit had less gold backing it than previously, that country devalued its money. **Devaluation** of a nation's money constituted an important international economic policy tool because it changed all exchange rates between the devaluing nation's money and all other monies. This in turn had an effect on international trade, investments, and other transactions. For example, when the United States devalued the dollar prior to 1971, it made the U.S. dollar worth less and other countries' monies that were backed by gold worth more. It would then take more U.S. money to buy one unit of foreign currency and less foreign money to buy one U.S. dollar. The result was to encourage foreign purchases of U.S. items because U.S. items became cheaper to foreigners, and to discourage purchases of foreign items by those in the United States because they became more expensive.

Floating (flexible) exchange rates
Exchange rates that fluctuate because they are basically determined by the forces of demand and supply.

Today most economies are on a system of **floating, or flexible, exchange rates,** where the rates at which nations' monies exchange are determined by the forces of demand and supply. As demand and supply conditions change, exchange rates change. The process of determining exchange rates under this system can be illustrated with a hypothetical example involving the U.S. dollar and the French franc.

The Demand For Francs To show how the exchange rate between the dollar and the franc is established, let us look first at the demand for francs by those with U.S. dollars who wish to import French goods or take advantage of French investment opportunities. The demand curve of those importers and investors for French francs is illustrated in Figure 17.2. The horizontal axis indicates the quantity of francs demanded, while the vertical axis shows the price *in U.S. dollars* that must be paid per franc. As expected, the demand curve is downward sloping. At a price of $0.25 per franc in Figure 17.2, 100 million francs are demanded, while at a price of $0.05 per franc, 800 million are demanded.

The reason for the inverse relationship between the price and quantity demanded of French francs is that, as the dollar price of francs goes up, the prices of French goods and investment opportunities also increase for buyers wishing to convert their dollars to francs. With French goods and investment opportunities becoming more expensive to these buyers, they desire to purchase less of these items, causing the quantity of francs demanded to be lower.

For example, suppose that a particular French automobile has a price tag of 80,000 francs. At an exchange rate of $0.10 = 1 franc, the cost of the car to U.S. importers would be $8,000. If the price of francs to U.S. buyers were to rise to $0.20 each, the same 80,000 franc car would cost importers $16,000. This higher cost would be enough to cause some buyers to cancel their orders, which in turn would lower the quantity of francs demanded.

Figure 17.2
Demand Curve for French Francs

The demand curve for foreign money is downward sloping, indicating that less of the money is demanded as its price in U.S. dollars increases.

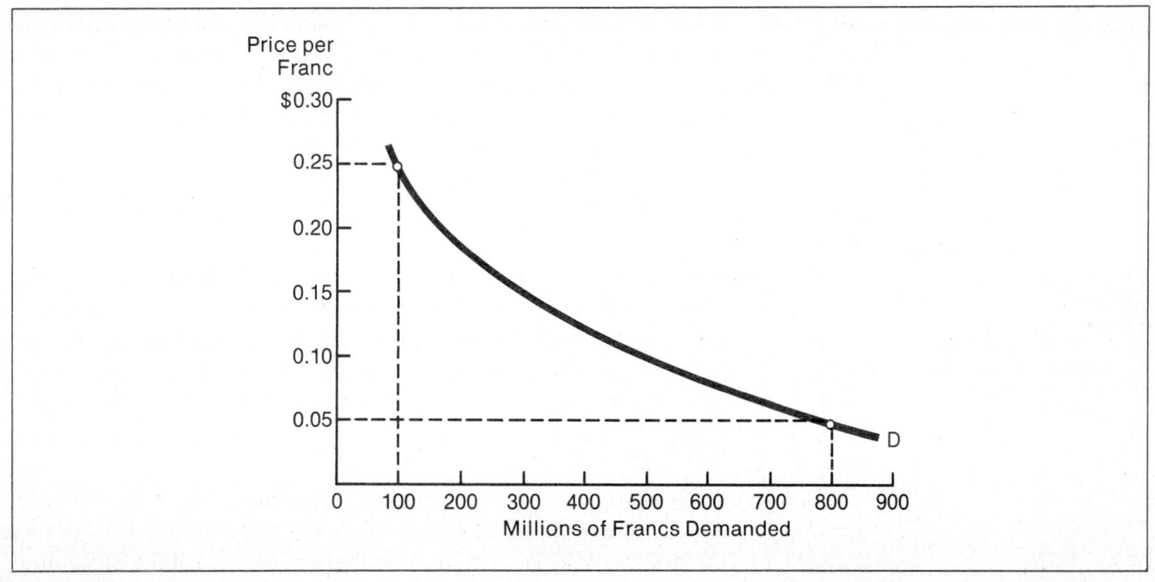

The Supply of Francs The supply curve showing the number of francs made available to those who wish to buy French goods and make French investments with U.S. dollars is shown in Figure 17.3. Notice that the supply curve is upward sloping. As suppliers receive higher prices (more dollars) for their francs, the quantity of francs made available increases. For example, in Figure 17.3, at a price of $0.10 per franc, 100 million francs would be supplied, and at a price of $0.25 per franc, 700 million francs would be supplied.

Determining the Rate of Exchange The rate of exchange between the U.S. dollar and the French franc can now be determined by combining the supply and demand curves just given. This is done in Figure 17.4. Given these supply and demand conditions, the exchange rate that emerges is $0.15 = 1 france, because this is the price per franc shown at the intersection of the two curves. At this rate, the number of francs supplied to and demanded by buyers who want to convert U.S. dollars to francs is 300 million.

As presented in Chapter Three, a shift in either the supply curve or demand curve leads to a change in the equilibrium quantity and price. In this instance, shifts in the demand for and/or supply of foreign money lead to changes in its exchange rate. For example, when demand increases (the curve shifts to the right), the price of the money will increase, as will the

Figure 17.3
Supply Curve for French Francs

The supply curve for foreign money is upward sloping, indicating that more of the money is made available as its price increases.

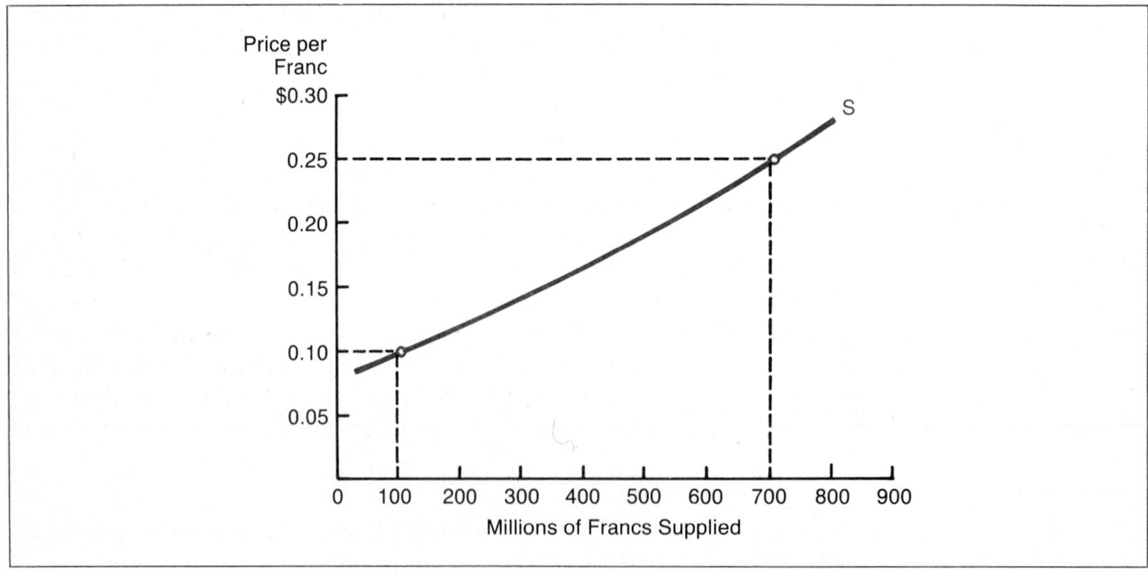

Figure 17.4
Supply and Demand for French Francs

The exchange rate for a nation's money is determined by the intersection of the supply and demand curves for that money.

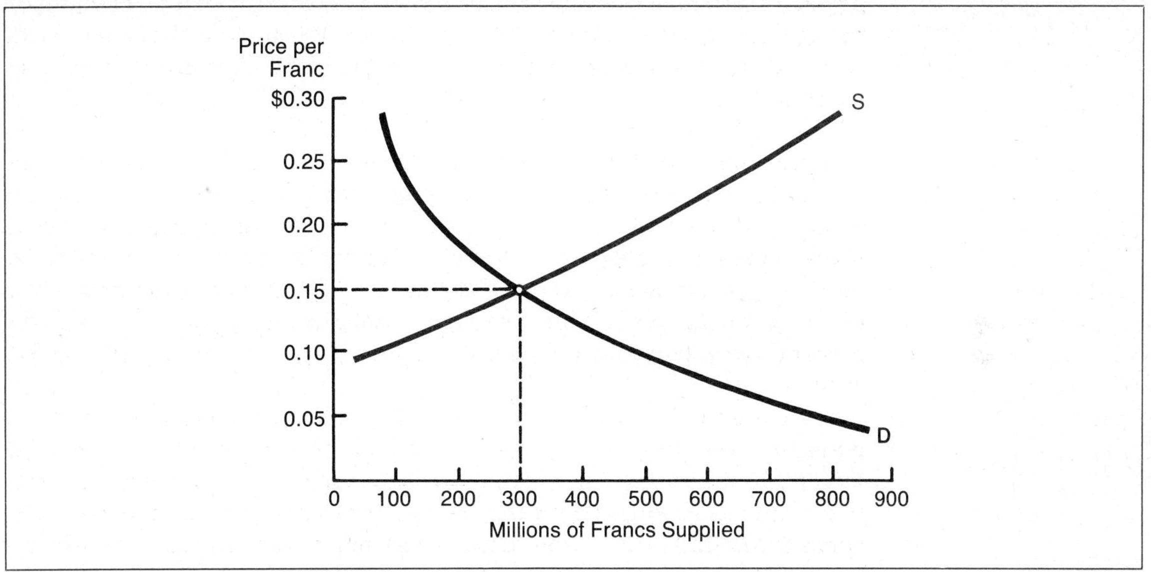

amount exchanged. Test your understanding of this concept by graphically determining the results of an increase in supply.[4]

Several factors can cause a change in the international supply of and/or demand for a nation's money. One factor is a change in the economic conditions of either the supplying or demanding country. For example, consider the effect of inflation on the demand for francs by U.S. importers and investors. If the inflation occurs in the United States, it will make the price tags on French goods relatively lower for U.S. importers and investors, thereby causing the U.S. demand curve for francs to increase, or shift to the right. As a result, the price of francs will rise, as will the number of francs exchanged. If the inflation occurs in France, it will make the cost of French goods relatively higher for U.S. investors and importers, and lead to a decrease, or leftward shift in the demand curve, for francs. As a result, the price of francs will fall and so will the amount exchanged.

Second, the demand for a nation's money can be affected by changes in the overall demand for one or several of its products. Consider U.S. grain production. A poor crop year in some areas of the world may lead to a significant increase in the international demand for U.S. grain. As the demand

[4]Graphically, the supply curve will shift to the right, causing the price of the money to fall and the amount exchanged to rise.

for grain increases, the demand for U.S. dollars to purchase that grain also increases, causing the demand curve for U.S. dollars to shift to the right. The price of the dollar in international exchange markets will then rise.

Third, the supply of a nation's money may be affected by payment imbalances. Persistent and cumulative payment outflows can lead to a buildup of the international supply of a nation's money. This buildup shifts the supply curve of the money to the right, causing its price, or its value, to drop. This point is of particular interest to the United States with its persistent payment outflows and deficit trade balances encountered in recent years.

Fourth, the supply and demand of a nation's money in international markets may be influenced by government policies. For example, in an effort to keep its exchange rates from falling, a government might pursue policies to keep the supply of its money from increasing or policies to stimulate its demand. Expectations about the value of a nation's money because of a political mood or policy can also cause demand or supply to shift and the exchange rate to change.

SUMMARY

All international transactions that cause payment outflows or inflows are of economic importance. For accounting and analysis purposes these payment transactions are categorized either into the current account or as assets movements.

The current account includes the merchandise export-import balance (the balance of trade), as well as figures for investment income, unilateral transfers, travel and transportation, and other transactions. When the current account balance is a negative number, more dollars have flowed out than foreign payments in and a current account deficit is said to exist. When the current account balance is a positive number, more foreign payments have flowed in than dollars out, resulting in a current account surplus. Prior to the 1970s, the U.S. balance of trade was primarily a surplus figure. Since that time, substantial deficits have occurred.

The assets movements category includes such items as investments, loans, and financial holdings resulting from payment imbalances. Since the late 1960s and early 1970s, U.S. payments deficits have been satisfied by increased foreign holdings of dollars and other designated instruments rather than by gold.

Several nations have accumulated large external debts that may be beyond their ability to readily repay. This debt crisis presents problems for both lending and borrowing countries, and there is no simple solution to the problem.

In order to translate the prices of foreign goods, services, and investments into a domestic money, an exchange rate is needed. An exchange rate is the number of units of one country's money that is equivalent to one unit of another country's money. In the past, exchange rates were often fixed because they were tied to the value of the gold backing a country's money. When the gold backing was lessened, devaluation occurred.

Today, most exchange rates are flexible and continually change because they are basically determined by supply and demand. The demand curve for a country's money by those holding another country's money is downward sloping, and the supply curve is upward sloping. A number of factors can cause this demand and supply — and, consequently, the exchange rate — to change. These include changes in economic conditions such as inflation, changes in the demand for products, payment imbalances, and government policies.

Key Terms and Concepts

Current account
Balance of trade
Current account deficit
Current account surplus
Balance of trade deficit
Balance of trade surplus
Assets movements
External debt
Exchange rate
Devaluation
Floating (or flexible) exchange rate
Exchange rate determination

Discussion and Review Questions

1. Suppose that Country A is currently suffering from a severe payments deficit. What effect would each of the following have on the deficit and why?
   - **a.** An increase in foreign investment in Country A
   - **b.** An improvement in Country A's balance of trade
   - **c.** A loan made by Country A to Country B so that Country B can buy machinery from Country A
   - **d.** Gifts to persons in Country B from their relatives in Country A
   - **e.** A growth in international popularity of a resort area in Country A
   - **f.** Purchases of stock of the businesses in Country B by investors in Country A
2. As discussed in this chapter, the United States has primarily experienced balance of trade deficits since the early 1970s. What could be the short-term and long-term effects if this condition persists throughout the 1980s? What policy actions would you recommend to reverse this trend?
3. Locate a recent listing of foreign exchange rates. (These are given in *The Wall Street Journal* and many other major newspapers.) Compare the recent rates with those given in Table 17.4. Are there any instances in which the rate has changed substantially? If so, give your opinion as to what factors might have caused such a change.

4. Explain why devaluation of a nation's currency could increase the demand for that nation's exports and decrease the demand by that nation for imports.
5. Illustrate graphically the supply and demand for a foreign money. Show how the exchange rate is determined, and show how the rate would be affected by an increase and decrease in demand, and by an increase and decrease in supply.
6. What are some major components of the current account category? Give some examples of international transactions that would cause a positive dollar amount to register in the current account and examples that would cause a negative dollar amount to register in the current account.
7. What problems would arise if a developing country defaulted on its external debt? Who would be hurt? What policies would you recommend to ease the external debt crisis, and what would be the effects of these policies in the borrowing country?

Suggested Readings

William R. Cline, Rudiger Dornbusch, Martin Feldstein, Gustav Ranis, "The International Debt Problem," ***Challenge*** **(July–August 1984), pp. 4–30.** Four articles evaluating the external debt crisis.

Readings in International Finance **(Chicago: Federal Reserve Bank of Chicago, 1983).** Readings from various sources on the balance of payments, international banking, foreign exchange markets, and other topics.

Daniel Rosen, ***The Basics of Foreign Trade and Exchange*** **(New York: Federal Reserve Bank of New York).** Discusses comparative advantage, foreign exchange trading, changes in exchange rates, and other topics in international trade and finance.

"World Debt in Crisis," ***The Wall Street Journal,*** **June 22, 1984, pp. 25–29.** A special report containing articles, figures, and summaries on the external debt problem.

GLOSSARY

Acquisition The acquiring of one company by another company; can be accomplished by buying a controlling amount of stock.

Actual legal reserves A financial depository institution's reserve account plus its vault cash.

AFL-CIO (American Federation of Labor-Congress of Industrial Organizations) An organization for furthering the common interests of labor unions; does not engage in bargaining with management.

Antitrust laws Laws designed to promote the operation of market forces by prohibiting certain practices that reduce competition.

Assets movements The international transactions category that includes foreign investments, government loans, and other asset related movements.

Assumption A condition held to be true, usually in a model.

Automatic stabilization Automatic changes in taxes and/or government expenditures that occur as the level of economic activity changes and that help to control unemployment or demand-pull inflation; important automatic stabilizers include the personal income tax and some transfer payments, especially unemployment compensation.

Average total cost The cost per unit of output produced; determined by dividing total cost by the number of units of output produced.

Balanced budget Occurs when a government's total outlays equal its total revenues.

Balance of trade The figure that results when the value of a country's merchandise imports is subtracted from its exports.

Balance of trade deficit The value of a country's merchandise inports is greater than its exports.

Balance of trade surplus The value of a country's merchandise exports is greater than its imports.

Barriers to entry Factors that keep firms from entering a market; can be a financial, legal, technical, or other barrier.

Barter system A system where goods and services are exchanged directly rather than for money; occurs where a medium of exchange does not exist and requires a coincidence of wants between the buyer and the seller.

Base year The year against which prices in other years are compared in a price index; assigned the number 100.0 in a price index.

Basic economic decisions Include: (1) what goods and services to produce and in what quantities; (2) how to produce these goods and services; and (3) who receives the production.

Black market An illegal market that sometimes emerges when price or quantity restrictions are imposed in a free market.

Board of Governors-Federal Reserve System Seven member board heading the Federal Reserve System; develops objectives pertaining to monetary policy and banking and other financial institutional practices, and determines the appropriate policies to be followed to meet those objectives.

Bond A financial instrument through which a corporation can borrow long-term funds; sold in $1,000 denominations with a specified interest rate and maturity date (date on which the bond is redeemed).

Business An organization established for the purpose of producing and selling goods and services; may be legally organized as a proprietorship, partnership, or corporation.

Business cycles Recurring periods of growth and decline (or expansion and contraction) in an economy's real output, or real GNP.

Capital All man-made items such as machinery and equipment used in the production of goods and services.

Capital-intensive production Production that emphasizes capital inputs.

Capitalism An economic system based on private property and free enterprise; economic decision making occurs in a market environment.

Cartel An arrangement whereby sellers formally join together in a market to make decisions as a group on pricing and such; the behavior of a cartel is like that of a monopoly.

Celler-Kefauver Act (1950) Federal antitrust statute concerned with anticompetitive mergers and acquisitions of firms; amends Section Seven of the Clayton Act.

Change in demand A change in the demand schedule for a product, or a shift in the product's demand curve; caused by a change in a nonprice influence on demand.

Change in quantity demanded A change in the amount of a product demanded that is caused by a change in its price; represented by a movement along a demand curve from one price-quantity point to another.

Change in quantity supplied A change in the amount of a product supplied that is caused by a change in its price; represented by a movement along a supply curve from one price-quantity point to another.

Change in supply A change in the supply schedule for a product, or a shift in the product's supply curve; caused by a change in a nonprice influence on supply.

Change in the demand for labor A shift in the demand curve for labor which is caused by changes in factors other than the wage rate.

Change in the quantity of labor demanded A change in the amount of labor demanded that occurs when the wage rate changes.

Charter The legal document that creates a corporation.

Circular flow model A diagram showing the real and money flows between households and businesses, and the relationships between households and businesses in output, or product, markets and input, or resource, markets.

Classical economic theory Popularly accepted theory prior to the Great Depression of the 1930s which says that the economy will automatically operate at full employment.

Classical school School of economic thought that holds that the economy will automatically operate at full employment.

Clayton Act (1914) Federal antitrust statute prohibiting specific activities, such as exclusionary practices, that substantially reduce competition or create a monopoly.

Collective bargaining The process through which a union and management negotiate a labor contract.

Combinations and conspiracies in restraint of trade Practices carried out jointly by two or more firms that unreasonably restrict competition.

Command economy A planned economy; decisions are made by "command" rather than by individual businesses and households.

Commercial bank An institution that holds and maintains checking accounts, or demand deposits, for its customers and performs other functions such as making loans.

Commodity monetary standard Exists when an economy's money is backed by something of tangible value such as gold or silver.

Common stock Stock that pays a dividend dependent upon the profit position of a firm after all other financial obligations have been met.

Comparative advantage One country has a lower opportunity cost of producing a good or service than does another country.

Conglomerate merger Two or more sellers who are not related as competitors, suppliers, or distributors join together.

Constant GNP Real GNP; GNP with inflation erased from the figures; measures real production.

Constant returns to scale A range of production levels in the long run through which long-run average total cost neither increases nor decreases but is constant.

Consumer price index (CPI) Measures changes in the prices of goods and services that consumers typically purchase, such as food, shelter, clothing, and medical care.

Corporation A legal entity owned by stockholders which can carry on in its own name the functions of business normally performed by individuals.

Correspondent banking An interbank relationship involving deposits and various services.

Cost-benefit analysis The formal study of the process of balancing costs and benefits.

Cost of living adjustment (COLA) An arrangement whereby an individual's wages automatically increase with inflation.

Cost-plus pricing Prices are designed to generate enough revenues to cover operating costs plus a fair return to stockholders.

Cost-push inflation Occurs when price increases are caused by pressure coming from the sellers' side of the market, particularly from increases in costs.

Craft union A union that represents workers with a specific skill or craft.

Creative destruction New technologically advanced machinery and processes cause the disuse and ultimate disappearance of old machinery and methods.

Crowding out Occurs when borrowing by the federal government reduces borrowing by households and businesses.

Currency Coins plus paper money.

Current account The category of international transactions that includes figures for imports and exports of merchandise, unilateral transfers, and other foreign dealings.

Current account deficit (surplus) A negative (positive) figure results when all current account transactions are added together.

Current GNP Money GNP; measures the value of production in terms of prices at the time of production.

Cyclical unemployment Involuntary unemployment that results from a downswing in the business cycle, or a recession.

Decrease in demand A change in a nonprice influence on demand causes less to be demanded at each price; the demand curve shifts to the left.

Decrease in supply A change in a nonprice influence on supply causes less to be supplied at each price; the supply curve shifts to the left.

Deficit budget A government's expenditures are greater than its revenues; a negative number results when total expenditures are subtracted from total revenues; has an expansionary or inflationary impact on the economy and is appropriate for controlling unemployment.

Demand A buyer's plan giving the amounts of a product that would be purchased at different prices in a defined time period.

Demand curve A line on a graph that illustrates a demand schedule; slopes downward because of the inverse relationship between price and quantity demanded.

Demand deposits Checking account balances kept primarily at commercial banks.

Demand-pull inflation Caused by pressure on prices coming from the buyers' side of the market; tends to occur when buyers' demands (or spending) are greater than the abilities of sellers to supply goods and services.

Demand schedule A list of the amounts of a product that a buyer would purchase at different prices in a defined time period.

Depository Institutions Deregulation and Monetary Control Act of 1980 Legislation that altered the traditional roles of many financial institutions by permitting different types of depository institutions to perform nearly identical functions; increased the control of the Federal Reserve System over nonmember depository institutions.

Derived demand The demand for a factor of production depends upon, or is derived from, the demand for the good or service the factor produces.

Devaluation When the amount of gold backing a nation's monetary unit is reduced.

Differentiated outputs The products of competing firms are different and can be recognized as such by buyers.

Direct relationship One that occurs when two variables move in the same direction: when one increases, so does the other; graphs as an upward sloping line.

Discount rate The interest rate that a Federal Reserve Bank charges a financial institution for borrowing reserves.

Discretionary fiscal policy Deliberate changes in taxes and/or government expenditures to control unemployment or demand-pull inflation.

Discrimination Unequal treatment in a labor market because of an employer's perception of a worker.

Diseconomies of scale Occur when the increasing size of production in the long run causes the per unit cost of production to rise.

Distribution of income The way in which income is divided among the members of a society.

Dual banking system The label given to the U.S. banking system because both the federal and the state governments have the right to charter banks.

Dumping Selling a product in a foreign market below cost or below the price of the product in its own domestic market.

Durable good A good that has a useful lifetime of over one year.

Easy money policy A policy by the Federal Reserve to increase excess reserves of depository institutions in an effort to increase spending and reduce unemployment; carried out primarily through Fed purchases of government securities in the open market and/or a reduction in the reserve requirement and/or a reduction in the discount rate.

Econometrics The use of statistical techniques to describe the relationship between economic variables.

Economic cost of production Includes all explicit and implicit costs from producing a good or service.

Economic growth An increase in an economy's full production output level over time.

Economic policy An action taken to change an economic condition.

Economic profit, loss, breaking even Occurs when price is greater than average total cost, less than average total cost, or equal to average total cost, respectively.

Economics The study of how scarce, or limited, resources are used to satisfy unlimited material wants and needs.

Economic system The way in which an economy is organized; defined by the method chosen to make the basic economic choices.

Economic theory A formal explanation of the relationship between economic variables.

Economies of scale Occur when the increasing size of production in the long run permits the per unit cost of production to fall, or each unit of output to be produced more cheaply.

Efficient method of production The least-cost method of production.

Embargo A ban on trade in a particular commodity with another country.

Employment Act of 1946 Legislation giving the federal government the right and responsibility to provide an environment for the achievement of full employment, full production, and stable prices.

Entrepreneurship The function of organizing resources for production and taking the risk of success or failure in a productive enterprise.

Equation of exchange $MV = PQ$; illustrates how changes in the supply of money (M) influence the level of prices (P) and/or the output of goods and services (Q).

Equilibrium (in the macroeconomy) Occurs when the amount of total planned spending on new goods and services equals total output in the economy.

Equilibrium price The price at which demand equals supply; shown by the intersection of the demand and supply curves in a graph; the price toward which the free market automatically moves. At the equilibrium price there are no shortages or surpluses.

Equilibrium quantity The quantity at which demand equals supply; shown by the intersection of the demand and supply curves in a graph; the quantity toward which the free market automatically moves.

Excess, or economic, profit Profit received beyond normal profit; not considered a cost of production.

Excess reserves Actual legal reserves of a financial depository institution over and above the amount it is required to maintain; actual legal reserves minus required reserves.

Exchange rate The number of units of a nation's money that is equal to one unit of another nation's money.

Exclusionary practices Practices whereby a seller attempts to prevent its suppliers or buyers from dealing with a competitor.

Expectations Anticipations of future economic activity; expectations of a recession can prompt households and businesses into taking actions that will cause a recession, and expectations of inflation can prompt actions causing inflation.

Explicit costs Payments that a business makes to acquire factors of production such as labor, raw materials, and machinery.

Exports Those goods and services that are produced in one country and sold to someone in another country.

External debt Money owed by a country to a lender in another country.

Externality The effect of an action that falls on a person or thing that was not one of the primary parties to the action; the effect may benefit (create a positive externality) or cost (create a negative externality) the affected person or thing.

Factors of production (resources) Persons and things used to produce goods and services; limited in nature; categorized as land, labor, capital, and entrepreneurship.

Federal Deposit Insurance Corporation (FDIC) A government agency established in 1933 to insure deposits in commercial banks up to a specified amount.

Federal Reserve Banks Twelve banks, located in different parts of the country, that deal with commercial banks and other financial institutions. Each bank supervises and examines Federal Reserve System member banks, maintains and services reserve accounts, puts coins and paper money into circulation, clears checks, and serves as a fiscal agent for the U.S. government. Each bank is an independent corporation with its own board of directors.

Federal Reserve Notes Paper money issued by the Federal Reserve Banks; includes almost all paper money in circulation.

Federal Reserve System Established in 1914; coordinates commercial banking operations, regulates some aspects of all depository institutions, and oversees the U.S. money supply; organized on both a geographic and functional basis.

Federal Trade Commission Act (1914) Created the Federal Trade Commission and empowered it to prevent unfair methods of competition, which include antitrust violations.

Financial institutions Organizations such as banks, savings and loans, and insurance companies, which provide a means for channeling savings into borrowing.

Fiscal policy The changing of taxes and/or government expenditures to control unemployment or demand-pull inflation; may be discretionary or automatic.

Fixed cost The short-run cost of a fixed factor of production.

Fixed factors Factors of production that do not change in amount as the level of production increases or decreases; as long as some factors of production are fixed, a business operates in a short-run time frame.

Floating (flexible) exchange rates Exchange rates that fluctuate because they are basically determined by the forces of demand and supply.

Free enterprise The right of a business to make its own decisions and to operate with a profit motive.

Free trade Goods and services can be exported and imported by anyone in any country with no restrictions.

Frictional unemployment Occurs when people are voluntarily out of work and in the process of obtaining a new job.

Full employment In an overall sense it refers to a condition where all available factors of production are employed. As pertains to the labor force, it occurs when only those voluntarily out of work are unemployed, or the unemployment rate drops to a level which includes only frictional unemployment; currently full employment occurs when approximately 94–95% of the labor force is employed.

Full production Occurs when an economy is producing at its maximum capacity, or when it is experiencing full employment.

General partner An owner of a partnership who is subject to unlimited liability; every partnership must have at least one general partner.

GNP deflator A composite price index that measures price changes for the entire economy, regardless of whether the goods and services measured go to households, businesses, or the government.

GNP gap The difference between actual GNP and the GNP that could be produced with full employment.

Government expenditures All dollar outlays by government units; includes purchases of goods and services, transfer payments, interest on money borrowed, expenses incurred in operating public enterprises, and intergovernmental grants.

Government purchases of goods and services Government spending for new goods and services.

Government regulation Government participation, through various agencies and commissions, in business decision making; may be industry regulation or special purpose regulation.

Graph An illustration showing the relationship between two variables that are measured on the vertical and horizontal axes.

Gross national product (GNP) A dollar figure that measures the value of all finished goods and services produced in an economy in one year.

Guidelines Voluntary wage-price controls; also called wage-price guideposts.

Holding company A corporation formed for the purpose of owning or holding stock in other corporations.

Horizontal merger Two or more sellers competing in the same market join together.

Household A person living alone or a group of related or unrelated persons who occupy a house, apartment, separate group of rooms, or other such housing unit; along with businesses and government, households are one of the basic decision-making units in the economy.

Human capital investment An expenditure made to improve the productivity of a person; examples include expenditures on education, training, and health care.

Humphrey-Hawkins Full Employment and Balanced Growth Act Passed by Congress in 1978, it requires that the government set annual numerical goals for such things as unemployment over a 5-year period.

Implicit costs Payments that a business must make to its owner(s) if it is to remain in operation; normal profit.

Imports Those goods and services sold in one country that are produced in another country.

Increase in demand A change in a nonprice influence on demand causes more to be demanded at each price; the demand curve shifts to the right.

Increase in supply A change in a nonprice influence on supply causes more to be supplied at each price; the supply curve shifts to the right.

Indexing Factor payments and/or transfer payments and such are automatically increased as prices rise.

Individual firm's demand curve Shows the amounts of an individual firm's product that buyers are prepared to purchase at particular prices.

Industrial Revolution A time period during which an economy becomes industrialized; characterized by social and technical changes such as the growth and development of factories.

Industrial union A union that represents all workers in a specific industry regardless of the type of job performed.

Industry A group of firms producing similar products.

Industry regulation Regulation affecting several aspects of the operations of firms in a particular industry; influences pricing, entry of new sellers, conditions of service, and so on.

Infant industry An industry in the early stages of its development.

Inflation An increase in the general level of prices.

Injections into the spending stream Spending that comes from a source other than household earned income; includes household spending from borrowing and transfer payments, business investment spending, government purchases of goods and services, and export expenditures.

Input markets Those markets in which the factors of production are bought and sold; households are sellers and businesses are buyers.

Interest Income return to the owners of capital.

Interest rate The price that is paid to borrow money; is a percentage of the amount borrowed.

Interlocking directorate The same person sits on the boards of directors of different corporations.

International trade The buying and selling of goods and services among different countries.

Inverse relationship Occurs when two variables move in opposite directions: when one increases, the other decreases; graphs as a downward sloping line.

Investment spending Business spending on new goods and services such as new machinery, equipment, and buildings; influenced by the expected rate of profit and other factors such as the interest rate. Because of its fluctuations, it is a primary cause of changes in economic activity.

Invisible hand doctrine Adam Smith's concept that producers acting in their own self-interest will provide buyers with what they want, and thus advance the interests of society.

Keynes, John Maynard (1883–1946) British economist who focused on the role of aggregate spending in determining economic activity; his most famous work was *The General Theory of Employment Interest and Money*, published in 1936.

Keynesian economics Based on the work of John Maynard Keynes, who focused on the role of aggregate spending in determining the level of macroeconomic activity; is the basis of much current macroeconomic theory; replaced classical economic theory as the dominant macroeconomic theory.

Keynesians Persons who advocate the work of John

Maynard Keynes; generally believe in stabilizing the economy through the use of fiscal policy.

Kinked demand curve An oligopoly pricing model based on the assumption that rivals will not follow price increases but will follow price decreases; illustrates that as a seller's price rises the amount of its product demanded decreases substantially, but as its price falls the amount demanded increases only slightly.

L The broadest definition of the money supply; includes M-3 plus commercial paper, savings bonds, liquid treasury obligations, and other items.

Labor All physical and mental human effort used to produce goods and services.

Labor force All persons 16 years of age and older who are working or actively seeking work.

Labor-intensive production Production that is strongly dependent on labor inputs.

Laissez-faire capitalism Capitalism with little or no government interference.

Land All productive inputs that originate in nature, such as coal and fertile soil.

Law of Demand There is an inverse relationship between the price of a product and the quantity demanded; when price increases, quantity demanded falls, and when price decreases, quantity demanded increases.

Law of Diminishing Marginal Utility As additional units of an item are consumed, beyond some point each successive unit of the item consumed will add less to total utility than was added by the unit consumed just before it.

Law of Diminishing Returns As additional units of a variable factor are added to a fixed factor, beyond some point the additional product from each additional unit of the variable factor decreases.

Law of Supply There is a direct relationship between the price of a product and the quantity supplied; when price increases or decreases, quantity supplied increases or decreases, respectively.

Leadership pricing One firm in a market charges a price that the other firms in the market then adopt.

Leakages from the spending stream Uses for earned income other than spending, such as taxes, saving, and import expenditures.

Lockout An employer prevents laborers from entering a work site.

Long run A production time frame in which all factors of production can be changed or are variable.

Long-run total cost, average total cost, and marginal cost Total cost, per unit cost, and cost per additional unit of output calculated for production in the long run.

Lower price limit A price floor; a government set minimum price that must be charged for a particular good or service; if the equilibrium price is below the lower price limit, a surplus will develop.

M-1 The narrowest definition of the U.S. money supply; includes coins and paper money in circulation, nonbank-issued traveler's checks, most demand deposits at commercial banks, and other checkable deposits.

M-2 Definition of the money supply which includes M-1 plus money market deposit accounts, savings deposits, time deposits of less than $100,000, money market mutual funds, and other items.

M-3 Definition of the money supply which includes M-2 plus time deposits of $100,000 and more, and other items.

Macroeconomics The study of the operation of the economy as a whole.

Marginal benefit The amount of satisfaction added to total satisfaction by consuming each additional unit of a good, service, or activity.

Marginal cost The change in total cost when one more, or additional, unit of a good, service, or activity is produced.

Marginal physical product The change in total product that results when an additional unit of labor or other variable resource is utilized.

Marginal revenue The change in total revenue when one more, or additional, unit of an item is demanded.

Marginal revenue product The change in total revenue that results when one more unit of labor or other variable resource is utilized.

Marginal utility The amount of satisfaction added to total satisfaction by consuming each additional unit of a good, service, or activity.

Market A place or situation in which the buyers and sellers of a product interact for the purpose of exchange; firms are in the same market when they produce similar products and compete for the same group of buyers.

Market clearing price The equilibrium price in a market; the price at which supply equals demand and there are no shortages or surpluses.

Market demand The demand in a market for a particular good or service; is composed of all of the individual demands for the product.

Market demand curve The demand curve that results when all buyers in the market are considered together.

Market economy One in which the basic economic decisions are made by the interaction of buyers and sellers in a market through the language of price.

Market failure Occurs when a market system generates a problem or cannot achieve a goal set by society.

Market socialism A socialistic economic system in which some goods and services are allocated through markets, and others are allocated by planners.

Market structures A classification system for grouping

markets according to the degree of competition among sellers; the four market structures are pure competition, monopolistic competition, oligopoly, and monopoly.

Market supply The supply of a particular good or service in a market; is found by adding together all individual supply curves or schedules.

Marxian economic theory Based on the work of Karl Marx (1818–1883), who argued that recessions are a symptom of a fundamental flaw in capitalism because the quest for profit by capitalists forces workers out of jobs as they are replaced by machines.

Measure of value A function of money; the value of every good, service, and resource can be expressed in terms of, or as a multiple of, an economy's basic unit of money.

Medium of exchange The general acceptability of something as payment for goods, services, and resources; the primary function of money.

Mercantilism An economic system or a philosophy in which the interests of the nation are of the greatest importance; individual interests are subservient to those of the nation.

Merger The acquiring of one company by another company; can be accomplished by buying a controlling amount of stock.

Method for storing wealth and delaying payments The function of money that allows for saving, or storing wealth for future use, and permits credit, or delayed payments.

Microeconomics The study of individual decision-making units and markets within the economy.

Minimum wage law Legislation that specifies the lowest hourly earnings that an employer may pay an employee.

Mixed capitalism An economic system with the basic features of capitalism but with some degree of government intervention in economic decision making.

Mixed economy One in which the basic economic decisions are made through a combination of market and centralized decision making.

Model The setting within which an economic theory is presented.

Monetarism The school of thought that favors stabilizing the economy through controlling the money supply.

Monetarists Persons who favor the economic policies of monetarism.

Monetary policy Influencing the levels of aggregate output and employment or prices through changes in the money supply; carried out by the Federal Reserve through open market operations and/or changes in the reserve requirement and/or changes in the discount rate.

Money Anything that is generally acceptable as a medium of exchange, or means of payment for goods, services, and resources.

Money GNP (current GNP) Measures the value of production in prices at the time of production.

Money multiplier The multiple by which an initial change in excess reserves in the banking and financial institutions system can change the money supply.

Monopolistic competition. The market structure characterized by a large number of sellers with differentiated outputs and fairly easy entry into and exit from the market.

Monopolization and attempts to monopolize A firm acquires or attempts to acquire a monopoly share of its market through unreasonable means.

Monopoly market A market with one seller who maintains that position because entry by new sellers is impossible.

Multiplier effect The change in total output and income generated by a change in nonincome-determined spending is larger than, or a multiple of, the spending change itself.

Mutual interdependence Occurs when there are so few sellers in the market that each seller must weigh the actions and reactions of rival sellers in any decision making.

National bank A commercial bank incorporated under a federal rather than a state charter; a national bank must belong to the Federal Reserve System.

National debt The total accumulated debt of the federal government due to deficit spending.

National Labor Relations Act (Wagner Act) Legislation, passed in 1935, supportive of unionization; strengthened collective bargaining, defined unfair labor practices, and set up the NLRB.

National Labor Relations Board (NLRB) Hears complaints on unfair labor practices and orders remedies when appropriate; created by the National Labor Relations Act in 1935.

Natural monopoly A market situation where economies of scale make it more efficient (less costly) to have the entire output of a product come from one large seller rather than several smaller sellers.

Net benefit That which results when total cost is subtracted from total benefit.

Net exports Exports minus imports; can be a positive or negative number.

New Deal A series of programs and legislative reforms instituted during the administration of Franklin D. Roosevelt in the Great Depression of the 1930s.

Nondurable good A good that has a short useful lifetime.

Nonincome-determined spending Spending that does not come from household earned income; includes household spending from transfer payments and borrowing, business investment spending, and government and net foreign purchases of goods and services.

Nonprice competition Occurs when firms focus on some feature other than price (for example, quality or a guarantee) in an attempt to attract buyers for their products.

Nonprice factors influencing demand Factors such as income, taste, and expectations that help to formulate the demand for a product.

Nonprice factors influencing supply Factors such as the cost of production and the number of sellers that help to formulate the supply of a product.

Normal profit The profit necessary to keep a business in operation; considered to be a cost of production; is equal to the opportunity cost of the next best alternative.

Oligopolistic markets Those markets dominated by a few large sellers with either differentiated or identical products and where entry by new firms into the market is difficult.

Open Market Committee Determines general policy on the buying and selling of securities by the Federal Reserve System on the open market.

Open market operations The buying and selling of securities, primarily U.S. government securities, on the open market by the Federal Reserve; method most often used by the Federal Reserve to change financial depository institutions' excess reserves.

Opportunity cost The cost of acquiring a good or service or taking an action measured in terms of the value of the opportunities or alternatives forgone.

Other checkable deposits Interest-bearing accounts such as NOW and ATS accounts and credit union share drafts that are similar to demand deposits and are offered by banks, savings and loans, and other financial institutions.

Output markets Those markets in which businesses are sellers and households are buyers; consumer goods and services are exchanged.

Paper money standard Exists when money is not backed by anything of tangible value such as gold or silver; is backed by confidence in the money and a willingness to accept the money in exchange for goods, services, and resources.

Participation rate The percentage of some specified group that is in the labor force.

Partnership The legal organization of a business that is similar to a proprietorship but has two or more owners.

Peak The phase of the business cycle during which real GNP or output reaches its maximum.

Per se violations Anticompetitive agreements between firms where proof of the agreement is sufficient to establish guilt; include agreements to jointly fix prices and divide sales territories.

Personal consumption expenditures Household spending on new goods and services.

Personal income Household gross, or pretax, income; income households use to pay taxes, spend, and save.

Personal taxes Taxes paid by households.

Phases of a business cycle The four stages through which every business cycle goes: recovery, peak, recession, and trough; accordingly, real GNP expands, reaches a maximum, declines, and reaches a minimum.

Phillips curve A curve showing the relationship between an economy's unemployment and inflation rates.

Planned economy One in which the basic economic decisions are made by planners rather than by private individuals and businesses.

Poverty levels Government designated levels of income that must be received to be considered *not* poor.

Preferred stock Stock that pays a stated dividend to its holders.

Price ceiling A government set maximum price that can be charged for a particular good or service; if the equilibrium price is above the price ceiling, a shortage will develop.

Price discrimination Different buyers acquire the same product from the same seller with the same treatment and service, but pay different prices.

Price elastic A strong response to a price change; occurs when the percentage change in the quantity demanded or supplied is greater than the percentage change in price.

Price elasticity A measurement of the strength of a buyer's or seller's response to a price change; a weak response is termed inelastic and a strong response is elastic.

Price fixing Joint action by sellers to influence their product prices; considered to be highly anticompetitive.

Price floor A government set minimum price that can be charged for a particular good or service; if the equilibrium price is below the price floor, a surplus will develop.

Price index Measures changes in the prices of an item or a group of items using a percentage scale; all figures are compared to a base year which is designated by a value of 100.0 on the price index.

Price inelastic A weak response to a price change; occurs when the percentage change in the quantity demanded or supplied is less than the percentage change in price.

Price system A market system; one in which buyers and sellers communicate their intentions through prices in a market.

Producer price index (PPI) Measures changes in the prices of goods that businesses buy either for further processing or for sale to consumers; formerly termed the wholesale price index.

Production The process of creating goods and services that satisfy wants and needs.

Production function Shows the type and amount of output that can be produced from certain types and amounts of inputs and a particular production process.

Production possibilities table or graph An illustration of the various amounts of two goods that an economy can produce with full employment and fixed resources and technology.

Productivity Concept of assessing the amount of output produced by an economy's resources; often measured in terms of output per worker.

Product markets (output markets) Those markets in which businesses are sellers and households are buyers; consumer goods and services are exchanged.

Profit or loss What results when a business subtracts its total costs from its total revenue; the income return for performing the entrepreneurial function.

Progressive tax One where the percentage of income taxed increases as income increases, and decreases as income decreases; there is a direct relationship between the percentage of income taxed and the size of the income. The federal personal income tax is a progressive tax.

Proportional tax One which taxes the same percentage from any income regardless of size.

Proprietorship A one-owner business; owner is subject to unlimited liability.

Protectionism The philosophy that it is in the best interest of a country to restrict importing and/or exporting.

Public choice The study of the economic motives and attitudes of voters and public officials, and their effects on collective or government decision making.

Public good A good (or service) available to all of society; no one is excluded from use of a public good.

Purely competitive markets Those markets with large numbers of independent sellers producing identical products, and with easy entry for new firms into the market.

Quota A restriction on the quantity of an item that can be imported into a country.

Rational expectations The proposition that the effects of macroeconomic policies might be distorted by the adjustment of business and household behavior in anticipation of policy makers' strategies.

Real GNP (constant GNP) GNP with inflation erased from the figures; measures real production.

Real income The amount of goods and services that can be purchased with a particular amount of money income.

Recession The phase of the business cycle during which real output falls; in general terms it is a period in which an economy's production is falling and unemployment is rising; sometimes used to refer to the condition of an economy when real GNP has fallen for two successive quarters.

Recovery The phase of the business cycle during which real GNP or output is increasing.

Regressive tax One where the percentage of income taxed increases as income decreases, or decreases as income increases; there is an inverse relationship between the percentage of income taxed and the size of the income. A sales tax is a regressive tax.

Rent Income return to the owners of land resources.

Required reserves The amount of actual legal reserves that a financial depository institution must keep to back its deposits.

Reserve account A deposit in the name of a financial institution that is held at a Federal Reserve Bank or other designated place.

Reserve requirement A specified percentage of deposits that a financial depository institution must keep as actual legal reserves.

Resource markets Those markets in which factors of production are bought and sold; households are sellers and businesses are buyers.

Resources (factors of production) Persons and things used to produce goods and services; limited in availability; categorized as land, labor, capital, and entrepreneurship.

Retained earnings Business savings; the portion of a business's profit that has been retained for investment or other purposes.

Revenue Money that a company receives from selling its product.

Right to work laws State laws prohibiting union membership as a condition of employment.

Robinson-Patman Act (1936) Federal antitrust statute concerned with anticompetitive price discrimination; amends Section Two of the Clayton Act.

Rule of Reason violations Violations of the antitrust laws involving types of agreements between firms that are not necessarily anticompetitive; the challenged restraint on competition must be shown to be unreasonable.

Saving-investment relationship The relationship between the amount saved by households and businesses and the amount returned to the spending stream through investment and household borrowing.

Scarcity The condition of not having enough material goods and services to satisfy the wants and needs of all individuals, households, and societies.

Sectors A broad classification system for grouping similar types of goods and services produced.

Sherman Act (1890) Original and most broadly worded federal antitrust statute; condemns combinations and conspiracies in restraint of trade, and monopolization and attempts to monopolize.

Shortage Occurs in a market when the quantity demanded is greater than the quantity supplied, or at a price below the product's equilibrium price.

Short run A production time frame in which some factors of production are fixed and some can be varied.

Smith, Adam (1723–1790) A Scottish philosopher who wrote *The Wealth of Nations,* 1776, which extolled the benefits of an economic system based on individual decision making;

considered to be the most important early spokesman for capitalism.

Social benefits and costs The total effects on society that result from the private benefits, private costs, and externalities of actions.

Socialism An economic system in which many of the factors of production are collectively owned and there is an attempt to equalize the distribution of income.

Special interest group People who share a common position on a particular issue and actively promote that position.

Specialization Resources used in production are concentrated on a narrow range of tasks or on the production of a limited variety of goods and services.

Special purpose regulation Regulation aimed at correcting a problem found in several industries, such as pollution or job discrimination; not limited to a specific industry.

Stagflation Occurs when an economy is experiencing high rates of both inflation and unemployment.

Strike Work stoppage by union members.

Structural unemployment Involuntary unemployment that results when a worker's job is no longer part of the production structure of the economy; may be caused by technological change, such as worker replacement by a machine, or by changes in the pattern of demand.

Supply A seller's plan giving the amounts of a product that would be offered for sale at different prices in a defined time period.

Supply curve A line on a graph that illustrates a supply schedule; slopes upward because of the direct relationship between price and quantity supplied.

Supply schedule A list of the amounts of a product that a seller would offer for sale at different prices in a defined time period.

Supply-side economics Policies to stimulate the supply side of the market; proposals center on the use of tax policy and regulatory reform to stimulate business investment activity and productivity.

Surplus Occurs in a market when the quantity demanded is less than the quantity supplied, or when the product's price is above the equilibrium price.

Surplus budget A government's revenues are greater than its expenditures; has a contractionary effect on economic activity and is appropriate for controlling demand-pull inflation.

Taft-Hartley Act The 1947 legislation that contains several provisions that limit union activities.

Tariff A tax on an import.

Technology The body of knowledge that exists about production and its processes.

Territorial division Joint action by sellers to divide sales territories among themselves; considered to be highly anticompetitive.

Tight money policy A policy by the Federal Reserve to reduce excess reserves of depository institutions in an effort to reduce spending and inflationary pressure; carried out primarily through the sale of government securities in the open market by the Fed and/or an increase in the reserve requirement and/or an increase in the discount rate.

Token money Money with a face value greater than the value of the commodity from which it is made.

Total benefit or total utility The total amount of satisfaction received from consuming a specified number of units of a good, service, or activity.

Total cost Cost of producing a specified number of units of a good, service, or activity.

Total fixed cost The cost of all fixed factors of production; total fixed cost does not change as the level of output changes.

Total revenue Revenue received from selling a certain quantity of an item; is calculated by multiplying the price of an item times the quantity demanded at that price.

Total, or aggregate, spending The total combined spending of all units in the economy (households plus businesses plus government plus foreign) for new goods and services; changes in aggregate spending cause changes in aggregate output, employment, and income, and sometimes in the price level.

Total variable cost The cost of all variable factors of production; total variable cost increases as the level of output increases.

Trade association An organization representing firms in a particular industry that performs certain functions that benefit those firms.

Trade subsidy A government subsidy to the domestic producer of a good that is exported.

Transfer payment Money from the government for which no work is performed in return; examples include social security and unemployment compensation.

Trough The phase of the business cycle in which real GNP which has been falling during a recession reaches its minimum.

Underground economy Productive activities that are not reported for tax purposes and are not included in GNP.

Unemployment A resource available for production is not being used.

Unemployment rate The percentage of the labor force that is unemployed; can also refer to the percentage of a group in the labor force that is unemployed.

Union An organization of workers that bargains in its members' behalf with management on wages, working conditions, fringe benefits, and such.

Unlimited liability A business owner's personal assets are subject to use as payment for business debts.

Upper price limit A ceiling price; a government set maximum price that can be charged for a particular good or service; if the equilibrium price is above the upper price limit, a shortage will develop.

U.S. Treasury bill A U.S. Treasury security that matures in 13, 26, or 52 weeks.

U.S. Treasury bond A U.S. Treasury security that matures in 10 years or longer.

U.S. Treasury note A U.S. Treasury security that matures in 2 to 10 years.

U.S. Treasury security A financial instrument issued by the federal government when it borrows money; states the federal government's promise to make specified interest payments and to repay the loaned funds on a particular date.

Usury law Establishes the maximum rate of interest (an interest ceiling) that can be charged on a particular type of loan.

Utility Satisfaction realized from consuming a good or service; the goal of individual economic decision making is to maximize total utility.

Value judgment The relative values one assigns to alternatives in making a decision or analyzing a situation.

Value of money Measured by the goods, services, and resources that money can purchase.

Variable factors (and costs) Factors of production that increases and decreases; variable costs are the costs of using variable factors.

Vertical merger A firm joins with a supplier or distributor.

Wage Income return to labor; price of labor.

Wage-price controls Mandatory government-imposed restrictions on increases in prices, wages, and other incomes.

Wage-price guideposts Voluntary wage-price controls sought by the government; also called guidelines.

Wealth A measure of the value of economic assets; includes items such as real estate and corporate securities.

INDEX

Definitions of terms appear on page numbers in italics.

Acquisition, *293*. *See also* Merger
Actual legal reserves, *227–28*
AFL–CIO, *409–10*
Aggregate spending. *See* Total (aggregate) spending
American Federation of Labor–Congress of Industrial Organizations. *See* AFL–CIO
Antitrust legislation, *428*
  Celler-Kefauver Act, 434
  Clayton Act, 432–33
  Federal Trade Commission Act, 431–32
  purposes of, 428
  Robinson-Patman Act, 433
  Sherman Act, 429–31
Antitrust penalties, 436
Assets movements, *476–77*
Assumption (in modeling), *15–16*
Automatic stabilization (fiscal policy), *183*
Average total cost,
  in long run, *347–48*, 350
  in short run, *339*, 342–45

Baker, Russell, 176–77
Balance of trade, *474–75*
Balanced budget, *184*
Banks. *See also* Federal Reserve Bank(s)
  chartering of, 212
  commercial, *210*–12
  national, *212*
  regulation of, 211–12
Bargaining. *See* Collective bargaining
Bargaining power,
  and income distribution, 416
  unequal, 407
Barriers to entry, *360*
Barter system, *201*–2
Baseball players, salaries of, 400–401
Base year (for price indexes), *114*
Benefit. *See also* Benefits and costs
  marginal, *303*–4, 305–11
  net, *306*–11
  total, *303*–4, 305–11
Benefits and costs,
  for businesses,
    defining, 311–12
    maximizing profit, 315–16, 318–19
    measuring, 313–14
  for individuals,
    balancing, 300–1
    defining, 301–2
    maximizing satisfaction from, 305–8
    measuring, 302–5
  private versus social, 317–22
    social, 319–20
Board of Governors of the Federal Reserve System, *213*–14
Bond, *289*
Borrowing,
  government, effects of, 193–94, 244–45
  household, 137–38
Budget, government. *See* Government budget
Business cycles, *133*, 129–34
Businesses, *285*. *See also* Corporation(s)
  business ownership of, 291–93
  goals and decisions of, 293–95
  legal forms of, 286–90
  numbers and sizes of, 290–91
Business sector,
  in aggregate spending, 139–44
  and circular flow of economic activity, 141

Capital, *6*
Capital-intensive production, *334*
Capitalism, *43*
  British foundations of U.S., 45–47
  laissez-faire, *46*
  mixed, *43*
  in U.S., history of, 48–53
  versus socialism, 43–45
Cartel, *380*
Celler-Kefauver Act, *434*
Change in demand, *68–70*, 73
  for labor, *402*
Change in quantity demanded, *66–67*, 73
  of labor, *402*
Change in quantity supplied, *66–67*, 73
Change in supply, *70–72*, 73
Checkable deposits, *206*–7
Circular flow of economic activity
  and business sector, 141, 142, 143
  and foreign sector, 150–51
  and government sector, 146–48
  and household sector, 135–37
Circular flow model, *35*. *See also* Circular flow of economic activity
  for market economy, 35–37
  for mixed economy, 41
Classical economic theory, *265*
Clayton Act, 49, *432–33*

COLA. *See* Cost of living adjustment
Collective bargaining, *410*
  laws concerning, 411–12
  and strikes, 410–11
Combinations and conspiracies in restraint of trade, *428*–29
Command economy. *See* Planned economy
Commercial banks. *See* Banks
Commodity monetary standard, *208*–9
Common stock, *288*–89
Comparative advantage, *456*–60
Conglomerate merger, *435*–36
Constant (real) gross national product, *119*–21
  changes in, 129–34
Constant returns to scale, *349*
Consumer price index, *113*–14, 115–16
  table, 1952–84, 115
Consumption, maximizing satisfaction from, 282–84
Corporate raiders, 296–97
Corporation(s), *287*
  holding company as, 292–93
  mergers of, 293
  structure of, 290
  takeover bids for, 296–97
Correspondent banks, *218*, 228
Cost. *See also* Benefits and costs
  defining,
    for business, 311–12
    for individuals, 300–1
  explicit, *312*
  fixed, *338*
  implicit, *312*
  long-run. *See* Long-run cost
  marginal, *304*–11, *314*
  of production, economic, 312, 336–50
  short-run, 338–45
  total. *See* Total cost
  variable, 338
Cost-benefit analysis, 300–323. *See also* Benefits and costs
Cost-benefit balancing
  for business, 311–17
  for individuals, 300–11
Cost of living adjustment, *110*
  and indexing, *264*
Cost-plus pricing, *444*
Cost-push inflation, *112*–13, 257. *See also* Inflation
Craft union, *408*–9. *See also* Unions
Creative destruction, 335–*36*
Crowding out, *194*
Currency, 203–5
  disposal of, 216–17
Current account, *473*–75
Current (money) gross national product, *119*–21
Cyclical unemployment, *100*–1

Debt, external. *See* External debt
Decrease in demand, *70*
Decrease in supply, *71*–*72*
Deficit
  in balance of trade, 475
  in budget, *184*
  in current account, 474
Demand, *59*–60
  changes in, 67–70, 73
  decrease in, 70, 74–75
  derived, *395*
  increase in, 68, 73–74
  for labor, 395–402
  law of, *60*
    and interest rates, 234
  nonprice influences on, 67, 73
  price elasticity of, 84–85
Demand curve, *60*
  kinked, 377–78
  for labor, 396–97
  in monopolistic competition, 370
  in monopoly, 380–81
  in oligopoly, 377–78
  in purely competitive markets, 362–63
  shortages and surpluses on, 67
Demand deposits, *206*, 207
Demand-pull inflation, *112*, 155–56. *See also* Inflation
Depository Institutions Deregulation and Monetary Control Act, 210, *218*–19
Deregulation, 446–47
Derived demand, *395*
Devaluation, *482*
Direct relationship (in graphing), *16*
Discount rate, *241*
  as monetary policy tool, 240–41
Discretionary fiscal policy, *182*–83
Discrimination,
  and income distribution, *416*
  price, *433*
Diseconomies of scale, *349*
Distribution of income, *413*–14
  and bargaining power, 416
  and differences in productive resources, 415
  and discrimination, 416
  explanations for, 414–17
  and human capital investment, 415–16
  and inheritance, 417
  and poverty, 417–21
Dual banking system, *212*
Dumping (in international trade), *467*
Durable goods, *280*–81

Easy money policy, *239*
Econometrics, *11*
Economic activity. *See also* Circular flow of economic activity
  and business sector, 139–44
  changes in level of, 129–34
  and expectations, 156–60
  and foreign sector, 148–51

Economic activity. *(Continued)*
 and government sector, 144–48
 and household sector, 135–38
 and inflation, 155–56
 total spending and, 134–60
Economic choices,
 in classification of economies, 44–45
 and economic systems, 30
 in a market economy, 37–40
 and scarcity, 28–29
Economic cost of production, *312*
Economic growth, *118*
 and full production, 117–18
Economic models. *See* Models, economic
Economic policy, *12*
 and theory, 10, 12–13
Economic profit, *312, 363*
Economic Recovery Tax Act, 176, 182
Economic systems, *30*
 and basic economic choices, 30
 types of
  capitalism, 43
  market economy, 33–40
  mixed capitalism, 43
  mixed economy, 40–43
  mixed socialism, 44
  planned economy, 31–33, 34–35
  socialism, 44
 in U.S., history of, 45–53
Economic theory, *10*–12
 classical, *265*
 Keynesian, *265*–67
 monetarism, *267*–68
 and policy, 10, 12–13
 rational expectations, *270*
 supply-side, *123, 268*–69
Economics, *2*–4
Economies of scale, *348*
 in long-run production, 348–49
 in natural monopolies, 441–44
Economy, underground, *122*
Efficient (least-cost) method of production, *38*–39, *334*–35
Elasticity. *See* Price elasticity
Embargo, *463*
Employment. *See also* Unemployment and full employment
 discrimination in, 416
 and protectionism, 465
 statistics on, 101–5
Employment Act of 1946, 52–*53*, 95, 124, 181
Entrepreneurship, *6*
Equation of exchange, *226*–27
Equilibrium, macroeconomic, *165*–68
Equilibrium price, *65*
 changes in, 73–77
 and wage-price controls, 262–63
Equilibrium quantity, *65*
 changes in, 73–77
Excess profit, *312*
Excess reserves, *228*–30
 and the Federal Reserve, 238–39
 and interest rates, 233–38
 and loans, 231
Exchange rates, *480*
 determination of, 481–86
 flexible (floating), 482
 and international transactions, 478–81
 table of, 482
Exclusionary practices, *432*–33
Expectations
 and economic activity, 156–60
 of profit, in business sector, 139
Expenditures, household, 280–81
Explicit cost, *312*
Exports, *148*–49, *453*
 by commodity group, 454–55
 and current account, 473–74
 and dumping, 467
 embargoes on, 463
 geographic distribution of, 455–56
 of goods and services, 454
 net, 150–51, 474
 as percentage of GNP, 453–54
 subsidies for, 467
External debt, *477*–*78*
 as percentage of GNP, 479
 of third-world countries, 480–81
Externality, *318*–21

Factors of production, *5*–9
 fixed, *337*
 and income, 6–7
 variable, *338*
Federal Deposit Insurance Corporation (FDIC), 212
Federal regulatory agencies, 437–440, 445
 chronology chart of, 438–39
Federal Reserve Bank(s), *214*
 functions of, 216–18
 organization of, 214–15
Federal Reserve Notes, *205*
Federal Reserve System, *213*
 and bank regulation, 212
 Board of Governors of, 213–14
 and Monetary Control Act, 218–19
 and monetary policy, 238–43
 Open Market Committee of, 214, 241
 organization of, 213–15
Federal Trade Commission,
 establishment of, 49
 powers of, 431–32
Federal Trade Commission Act, *431*–32
Financial institutions, *137. See also* Banks
 types and purposes of, 209–13
Fireside chat (Franklin D. Roosevelt speech), 158–59
Fiscal policy, *160*–61, *181*–89
 automatic stabilization, 183
 and budgetary realities, 187–89
 discretionary, *182*–83

and government budget, 185–87
mechanics of, 181–82
public choice role in, 188–89
Fixed cost, *338*
Fixed factors of production, 336–*337*
Floating (flexible) exchange rate, *482*
Foreign exchange. *See* Exchange rates
Foreign sector
in aggregate spending, 148–51
and circular flow of economic activity, 150–51
Forests, decline of, 320–21
Free enterprise, *43*
Free trade, *459*
arguments for, 463–64
and comparative advantage, 459–60
versus protectionism, 460–61
in the real world, 466–68
Frictional unemployment, 99–*100*
Friedman, Milton,
biographical sketch of, 268–69
on monetarism, 267–68
Full employment, *100*
goal of, 105–7
tradeoff with inflation, 253
Full production, *117*
and economic growth, 117–18

General partner, *287*
GNP. *See* Gross national product
GNP deflator. *See* Gross national product deflator
Gold reserves
at Federal Reserve Bank of New York, 210–11
and monetary standards, 208–9
and payment deficits, 477
Gold standard, 208–9
Government budget, 184–89. *See also* National debt
balanced, *184*
proposed constitutional amendment for, 190–91
deficit, *184*
and monetary policy, 244–245
and fiscal policy, 185–89
surplus, *184*
types of, 184–85
Government expenditures, *178*–80
Government intervention. *See also* Antitrust legislation; Government regulation
via antitrust laws, 428–36
in markets, 426–27
in a mixed economy, 40–43
in pricing, 77–82
via regulation, 437–46
Government purchases of goods and services, *144*–46
Government regulation, *437*
versus deregulation, 446
federal agencies for, 438–39
of industry, 441–44
special purpose, *444*–46
structure of, 440–41
and U.S. capitalism, 53
wage-price controls as, 258–63
Government revenues, 171–76
Government sector
in aggregate spending, 144–48
and circular flow of economic activity, 146–48
role in macroeconomy, 170–97
Government transfer payments. *See* Transfer graph payments
graph, *13*
as economists' tool, 13–14
interpreting, 16–17
Graphing, 24–27
Great Depression, 96, 97–98
Gross national product (GNP), *118*
as measure of production, 118–22
money (current), *119*–21
real (constant), *119*–21, 129–34
Gross national product deflator, *114*, 116

Herfindahl-Hirschman index, 436
Holding company, 292–*293*
Horizontal merger, *434*
Households, *277*
characteristics of, 277
expenditures of, 280–81
income of, 277–80
Household sector
in aggregate spending, 134–38
and circular flow of economic activity, 135–37
Human capital investment, *415*
and income distribution, 415–16
Humphrey-Hawkins Full Employment and Balanced Growth Act, *106*–107, 124

Implicit cost, *312*
Imports, *148*–49, *453*
by commodity group, 454–55
and current account, 473–74
geographic distribution of, 455–56
as percentage of GNP, 453–54
quotas on, 462–63
taxes (tariffs) on, 461–62
Income,
distribution of. *See* Distribution of income
household, 277–80
and inflation, 108–10
maximizing satisfaction from, 284–85
personal, 278–80
real, 108
types of, 7
Increase in demand, *68*
Increase in supply, *71*

Indexes. *See* Price indexes; Consumer price index; Producer price index; Gross national product deflator; Herfindahl-Hirschman index
Indexing, *264*
Industrial Revolution, British, *47*
Industrial union, *408*–9. *See also* Unions
Industry, *331, 357*
  classifications, 331–32
  government regulation of, *441*–44
  infant, *464*–65
  trade associations, 428
Infant industry, *464*–65
Inflation, *107*–17
  and aggregate spending, 155–56
  causes of, 111–13
  consequences of, 108–11
  cost-push, 112–13, 257
  demand-pull, 112
  and income, 108–10
  and indexing, 264
  and the interest rate, 110–11
  measures of,
    consumer price index, *113*–14, 115–16
    GNP deflator, *114*, 116
    producer price index, *114*, 116, 117
  social and political consequences of, 111
  table, 1950–84, 255
  tradeoff with unemployment, 253
    Phillips curve showing, 253–58
  and wage-price controls, 258–63
  and wealth, 111
Inheritance and income distribution, 417
Injections into spending stream, *138*
  from business sector, 141–44
  from government sector, 146–48
  from household sector, 138
  and macroeconomic equilibrium, 165–68
  summary of, 151–53
Input markets, 35–*36*
Interest, *7*
  as income, 7
  on national debt, 193
Interest rate, *234*
  determination of, 235–38
  effect on spending, 234–35
  and government borrowing, 244–45
  inflation and, 110–11
  and investment spending, 139–40, 142–43, 234–35
  prime, 231
Interlocking directorate, *433*
International Monetary Fund, 478–79
International trade, *453*
  and comparative advantage, 456–60
  dumping in, 467
  Kissinger on, 460–61
  protectionism in, 460–63, 464–65
  in the real world, 466–68
  restrictions on. *See also* Trade restrictions
    embargoes, *463*
    quotas, *462*–63
    tariffs, *461*–62
  subsidies for, 467
  trade wars in, 463–64
  of United States,
    geographic distribution of, 455–56
    overview of, 453–56
    size and composition of, 453–55
  unrestricted, arguments for, 463–64
International financial transactions,
  assets movements as, 476–77
  and balance of trade, 474–75
  current account in, 473–74
  exchange rates and, 479–86
  external debt and, 477–78
Inverse relationship (in graphing), 16–*17*
Investment spending, *139*
  and economic activity level, 141–44
  and interest rate, 139–40, 142–43, 234–35
Invisible hand doctrine, *46*

Keynes, John Maynard,
  biographical sketch of, 266–67
  economic theories of, 265–66
  on fiscal policy, 181
  on inflation, 111
  on role of spending, 161
Keynesian economics, *265*–*67*
Keynesians, *266*
Kinked demand curve, *377*–*78*
Kissinger, Henry A., 460–61
Korean War, wage-price controls during, 260

Labor, *6*. *See also* Labor demand
Labor demand, 395–402
  changes in, 400–*402*
  and marginal revenue product, 399–400
  and productivity, 397–98
  and product price, 398–99
Labor force, *101*–2
  participation rates, 102–3
  statistics on, 101–5
Labor-intensive production, 334
Labor market models, 396, 405–7
Labor supply, 403–5
  factors affecting, 403–5
  restriction of, 408–9
Labor supply and demand model, 395, 405–7
  legislation affecting, 406–7
  modifications of, 405–7
  and unequal bargaining power, 407
  wage rigidities affecting, 405
Labor unions. *See* Unions
Laissez-faire capitalism, *46*
Land, *6*
Law of demand, *60*
  and interest rates, 234
Law of diminishing marginal utility, *304*
Law of diminishing returns, *345*–46, *397*

Law of supply, *62*
Layoffs, ripple effect of, 156–57
Leadership pricing (in oligopoly), *376*
Leakages from spending stream, *138*
from business sector, 141–44
from government sector, 146–48
from household sector, 138
and macroeconomic equilibrium, 165–68
summary of, 151–53
Least-cost method of production. *See* Efficient (least-cost) method of production
Loans,
interest on, and spending level, 233–35
and reserves, 231
Long run, *337*–38
costs in, 347–50
economies of scale in, 348–49
Long-run costs,
average, *347*
marginal, *347*
and profit,
in monopolistic competition, 372–74
in monopoly market, 382
in oligopolistic market, 378-79
in purely competitive market, 365–68
total, *347*
Lower price limit, 81–82

M1, *203*, 204
Macroeconomic policy,
alternative approaches to,
classical theory, *265*
Keynesian theory, *265*–67
monetarism, *267*–68
rational expectations, *270*
supply-side, *123, 268*–69
evaluating, 270–71
goals of, 253
and total spending, 160–61
wage-price controls as, 258–63
Macroeconomics, *85*–86
Macroeconomy, 128–29. *See also* Macroeconomics; Macroeconomic policy
aggregate spending in, 134–60
changes in activity level, 129–34
equilibrium in, *165*–68
goals of, 94–124
Marginal benefit, *303*–4, 305–11
Marginal cost
for business, *314*
for individuals, *304*–11
in long run, *347*–48
in short run, *339*–40, 342–45
Marginal physical product, *397*–98
Marginal productivity, 399–400
Marginal revenue, *314*
Marginal revenue product, *399*
of baseball players, 400–401
Marginal utility, *303*–4, 305–11
Market(s), *33, 63–64, 357*
boundaries of, 357–59
versus industries, 357–59
input (resource) type, 35–36
output (product) type, 35, 36
price setting in, 64–65
structures of, 359–60, 382–83. *See also* Market structures
Market clearing price, *65*
Market demand, *64*
Market economy, *33*
circular flow model for, 35–37
economic decisions in, 37–40
government intervention in, 40–43
input markets in, 35–36
least-cost production in, 38–39
operation of, 35–38
output markets in, 35, 36
strengths and weaknesses of, 39–40
Market failure, *43*
Market socialism, *44*
Market structures, *357*, 359–60. *See also* Monopoly; Monopolistic competition; Oligopoly; Pure competition
and the consumer, 382–83
monopolistic competition, 368–74
monopoly, 379–82
oligopoly, 374–79
pure competition, 360–68
Market supply, *64*
Maximizing
benefits, 303–4
costs, 304–5
economic well-being, 281–82
public choice in, 322–23
profits, 294–95, 315–16, 318–19
satisfaction from consuming, 282–84, 305–8
satisfaction from earning, 284–85
utility, 282–84, 301–5
Measure of value, money as, *202*
Medium of exchange, *201*
Mercantilism, *45*–46
Merger, 42, *293*
conglomerate, *435*–36
horizontal, *434*
vertical, *434*
Method for storing wealth and delaying payments, money as, *202*
Microeconomics, *87*
Mill, James, 265
Minimum wage law, *406*–7
Mixed capitalism, *43*
Mixed economy, *40*
government's role in, 40–43
market failure in, 43
Models, economic, *15*–20
Monetarism, *267*–68
Monetarist, *267*

Monetary Control Act of 1980, 218–19
Monetary policy, *160*–61, *239*
  advantages and disadvantages of, 245–47
  discount rate and, 240–41
  easy money, 239
  and Federal Reserve, 238–39
  and government deficits, 244–45
  open market operations and, 241–43
  reserve requirements and, 239–40
  tight money, 239
Monetary standards, 208–9
Money, *201*
  creation of, 227–33
  devaluation of, 482
  foreign. *See* Exchange rates
  forms of, 202
  functions of, 201–3
  as measure of value, 201–2
  as medium of exchange, 201
  multiple expansion of, 230–33
  for storing wealth and delaying payments, 202–3
  supply of. *See* Money supply
  token, *203*–5
Money (current) gross national product, *119*–21
Money multiplier, *232*–33
Money supply, 203–8
  components of, 203–8
  and economic activity level, 225–27
  and equation of exchange, 226–27
  and government deficits, 244–45
  increases and decreases in, 227–30, 233
  and interest rates, 234–35
  and loans, 225
  measures, 203, 207–8
  M1, *203*, 204, 207
  and total spending, 225–27
Monopolistic competition, *368*
  characteristics of, 368–69
  demand curve in, 370
  long-run costs and profit in, 372–74
  pricing, profit, and loss in, 370
Monopolization and attempts to monopolize, *428*
  and Sherman Act, 429
Monopoly, *379*
  and cartels, 380
  characteristics of, 379–80
  demand curve in, 380–81
  long-run cost and profit in, 382
  natural monopoly, *380, 441*
    and industry regulation, 441–44
  price control in, 380
Muckrakers, 51
Multiplier effect, *154*, 153–55
Munn v. *Illinois*, 443
Mutual interdependence (in oligopoly), *376*

National banks, *212*
National debt, *189. See also* Government budget
  assessing, 193–96
  financing, 189–91
  interest on, 193
  and interest rates, 194–95
  size of, 191–93
  statistics, table on, 1900–84, 192
National Labor Relations Act (Wagner Act), *411*–12
National Labor Relations Board, *412*
Natural monopoly, *380, 441*
  and industry regulation, 441–44
Nebbia v. *New York*, 444
Net benefit, *306*–11
  private versus social, 317–22
Net exports, *150*
  versus balance of trade, 474
  and total spending, 150–51
New Deal, *52*
Nondurable goods, *280*–81
Nonincome-determined spending, *153*–55
Nonprice competition, *364*
  in monopolistic competition, 370–72
  in monopoly, 381–82
  in oligopoly, 378
  in pure competition, 364–65
Nonprice factors
  influencing demand, *67*
  influencing supply, *68*
Normal profit, *312*

Oligopoly, 374, *375*
  characteristics of, 375
  kinked demand curve in, 377–78
  leadership pricing in, 376
  long-run costs and profit in, 378–79
  price control in, 376
Open Market Committee of Federal Reserve System, *214, 241*
Open market operations, *241–3*
Opportunity cost, *4–5*, *302*
Output markets, *35*, 36

Paper monetary standard, *209*
Participation rate, *102*–3
  for selected subgroups, 103
  statistics on, 102
Partnership, *287*, 290
Per se violations, *429*
Personal consumption expenditures, *135*, 136
Personal income, *278*–80
Phases of business cycle, *133*
Phillips curve, *253*–57
  analyzing behavior of, 257–58
Planned economy, *31*–33
  strengths and weaknesses of, 33

Poverty,
  government programs for, 420–21
  levels, *417*–20
Preferred stock, *288*
Price(s)
  limiting movement of, 77–82
  setting of, and markets, 64–65
Price ceiling, *79*–81
Price discrimination, *433*
Price elastic, *84*
Price elasticity, *83*–85
Price fixing, *429*–30
Price floor, *81*–82
Price indexes, *114*
  base year for, 114
  consumer price index, *113*–14, 115–16
  GNP deflator, *114*, 116
  producer price index, *114*, 116, 117
Price inelastic, *84*
Price limits, 79–82
Price regulation, 444
Price system, *33*–34
Pricing, profit, and loss,
  in monopolistic competition, 370–72
  in monopoly, 380–82
  in oligopoly, 376–79
  in purely competitive markets, 363–64
Prime rate, 231
Producer price index, *114*, 116
  table, 1952–83, 117
Product markets. *See* Output markets
Production, *117*
  basic economic decisions regarding, 28–29
  capital-intensive, *334*
  economic cost of, 312
  efficient method of, 38–39, *334*–35
  fixed factors of, *337*
  full, and economic growth, *117*–18
  labor-intensive, *334*
  and law of diminishing returns, 345–46
  long-run cost of, 347–50
  measures of, 118–22
  methods of, 332–36
  short-run cost of, 336–45
  and technological change, 335–36
  in U.S., overview of, 328–32
Production function, *333*–34
Production possibilities, *17*–20
Productivity, *122*–23
Profit, *7*
  economic, *312*
  excess, *312*
  or loss, of businesses, 293–*294*, *315*–16
  normal, 312
Profit maximization
  of businesses, 294–95, 315–16, 318–19
  with downward-sloping demand curve, 389–92
  and output level, 387–89
  in pure competition, 387–89
Progressive tax, *175*
Proportional tax, *175*–76
Proprietorship, *286*–87, 290
Protectionism, *460*
  arguments for, 464–65
  versus free trade, 460–61. *See also* Trade restrictions
Public choice, *188, 322*
  and fiscal policy, 188–89
  in maximizing economic well-being, 322–23
Public goods, *178*
Pure competition, *360*
  characteristics of, 360
  demand curve in, 362–63
  long-run costs and profit in, 365–68
  price control in, 361–62
  pricing, profit, and loss in, 363–64
  profit maximization in, 387–92
Purely competitive markets. *See* Pure competition

Quotas, trade, *462*–63

Rational expectations (economic theory), *270*
Real (constant) gross national product, *119*–21
  changes in, 129–34
Real income, *108*
Recession, *133*
Recovery, *133*
Regressive tax, *176*
Regulation. *See* Government regulation
Regulatory agencies. *See* Federal regulatory agencies
Rent, as income, *7*
Required reserves, *228*
Reserve account, *216*
Reserve banks. *See* Federal Reserve Bank(s)
Reserve requirement, *228*, 231
  as monetary policy tool, 239–40
Reserves,
  actual legal, *227*–28
  excess. *See* Excess reserves
  and loans, 230–31
  required, 228
Resource markets. *See* Input markets
Resources, *5*–9
Retained earnings, *141*
Returns, diminishing. *See* Law of diminishing returns
Revenue, *293*
  of businesses, 293–94
  and costs, balancing. *See* Benefits and costs
  marginal, *314*
  measuring, 313–14
  total, 313
Right-to-work laws, *412*
Robinson-Patman Act, *433*
Roosevelt, Franklin D., 158–59

Rule of Reason violations, *430*
Russia, planned economy in, 34–35

Satisfaction, maximizing,
  from consuming, 282–84, 305–8
  from earning, 284–85
Saving
  and business spending, 141–44
  and household spending, 137–38
Saving-investment relationship, *141*–44
Scarcity, *3*–4
  and economic decisions, 28–29
  and international trade, 456–57
  modeling, 15–17
  reasons for, 4–6
Schumpeter, Joseph, 336
Sherman Antitrust Act, 49, 429–31
Shoe industry, protection of, 466–67
Short run, *336, 429*
  cost patterns in, 340–45
  costs in, 338–40. *See also* Short-run costs
  and law of diminishing returns, 345–46
Short-run costs,
  average total, 339, 342–45
  marginal, 339–40, 342–45
  pattern of, 341–42
  total, 339, 341–42
  total variable, 338–39
Shortages, *64*–65
  measuring, on demand and supply curves, 67
  and wage-price controls, 262–63
Smith, Adam,
  classical economic theory of, 265
  on laissez-faire capitalism, 46
Social benefits and costs, *319*–22
Social Security System, 176–77
Socialism, *44*
  versus capitalism, 43–45
Special drawing rights (SDRs), *477*
Special interest groups, *323*
Special purpose regulation, *444*–46
Specialization (in international trade), *456–457*
  and free trade, 463
Spending,
  nonincome-determined, 153–55
  total. *See* Total (aggregate) spending
Spending stream,
  injections into, 138, 141–44, 146–48, 151–53, 165–68
  leakages from, 138, 141–44, 146–48, 151–53, 165–68
Stagflation, *187*
Stock,
  common, 288–89
  preferred, 288
Strike (labor), *411*
  and collective bargaining, 410–11
Structural unemployment, *101*
Subsidies (trade), *467*
Supply, *60–61*
  changes in, 67, 68, 70–73
  decreases in, 71–72, 76–77
  increases in, 71, 75–76, 77
  of labor, 403–5
  law of, *62*
  nonprice influences on, 68, 73
  price elasticity of, 85
Supply curve, *62*–63
  for labor, 403, 408–9
Supply-side economics, *123, 268*–69
Surplus, *65*
  in balance of trade, 474–75
  in current account, *474*
  measuring, on demand and supply curves, 67
Surplus budget, *184*

Taft-Hartley Act, *412*
Takeover bids, corporate, 296–97
Tariff, *461*–62
Tax(es)
  business, as leakage, 144
  as government revenue, 171–76
  and household spending, 137–38
  progressive, proportional, and regressive, 175–76
  reforms in, 176–77
Tax Equity and Fiscal Responsibility Act, 183
Technology, *335*
  and production, 335–56
Territorial division, *430*
Third-world debts, 480–81
Tight money policy, *239*
Token money, *203*–5
Total (aggregate) spending, *134*
  in business sector, 139–44
  and economic activity level, 134–60
  expectations and, 156–60
  in foreign sector, 148–51
  in government sector, 144–48
  in household sector, 135–38
  inflation and, 155–56
  and macroeconomic policy, 160–61
  and money supply, 225–27
  summary of, 151–53
Total benefit, *303*–4, 305–11
Total cost, *339*
  for business, *314*
  for individuals, *304*–11
  in long run, *347*–48
    average, *347*–48
  in short run, *339*, 342–45
    average, *339*, 342–45
Total fixed cost, *338*
Total revenue, *313*
Total utility, *303*–4, 305–11
Total variable cost, *339*

Trade. *See* Free trade; International trade
Trade associations, *430*
Trade restrictions
  arguments for, 464–65
  versus free trade, 460–61
  in the real world, 466–68
  types of, 461–63
Trade war, international, 468–69
Transfer payments, *138*
  as government expenditures, 178
  and household spending, 137–38
Traveler's checks, 205–6, 207
Treasury security, *189*
  bill, *189*
  bond, *189*
  note, *189*

Underground economy, *122*
Unemployment, *95*
  consequences of, 96–98
  cyclical, *100*–101
  frictional, 99–*100*
  and full employment, 95–107
  losses from, 96–98
  psychological costs of, 98–99
  relation to inflation, 253
    Phillips curve showing, 253–58
  statistics on, 101–5
  structural, *101*
  table, 1950–84, 255
  types of, 99–101
Unemployment rate, *103*–5
  determining, 104–5
  under full employment, 106–7
  for selected subgroups, 104
  statistics on, 102
Unions, *408*
  collective bargaining by,
    laws concerning, 411–12
    and strikes, 410–11
  craft, *408*–9
  industrial, *408*–9
  ten largest, 410
  types of and membership in, 408–10
United States v. *Aluminum Company of America*, 430–31
United States v. *E. I. du Pont de Nemours*, 358–59
Unlimited liability, *287*
Upper price limit, *79*–81
Utility, *282*
  defining, 301–2
  marginal, 303–4, 305–11
  maximizing, 282–84
  and measuring benefits, 303–4
  and measuring costs, 304–5
  total, 303–4, 305–11

Value of money, *201*
Value judgment, *3*–4
Variable cost, *338*
  total, 338–39
Variable factors, *338*
Vertical merger, *434*

Wage-price controls, *258*–59
  advantages and disadvantages of, 262–63
  in early 1970s, 261
  during Korean War, 260
  during World War II, 259–60
Wage-price guideposts/guidelines, *259*
Wages, *7, 395*
  and bargaining, 407
  determination of, 395, 405–407
  minimum, 406–7
  rigid, 405–6
Wagner Act, 411–12
Wealth, *111*
  and inflation, 111
  money as method for storing, 202
Wholesale price index. *See* Producer price index
World War II, wage-price controls during, 259–60